ENCYCLOPEDIA OF
NATURE

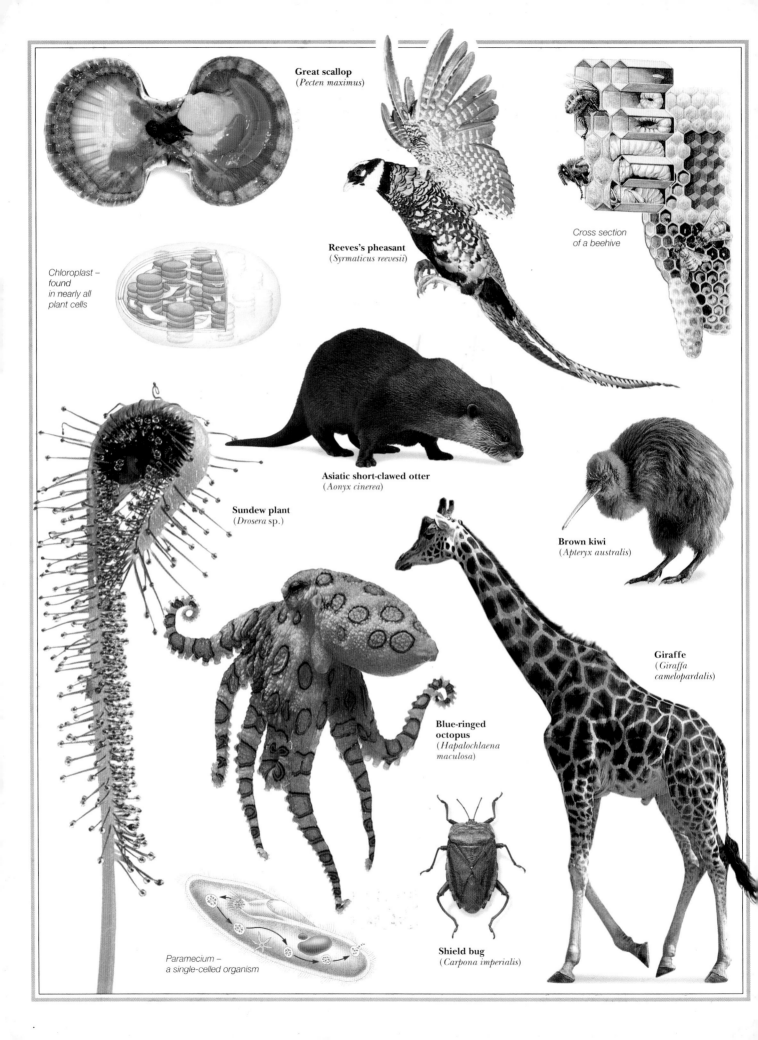

Great scallop
(*Pecten maximus*)

*Cross section
of a beehive*

Reeves's pheasant
(*Syrmaticus reevesii*)

*Chloroplast –
found
in nearly all
plant cells*

Asiatic short-clawed otter
(*Aonyx cinerea*)

Sundew plant
(*Drosera* sp.)

Brown kiwi
(*Apteryx australis*)

Giraffe
(*Giraffa
camelopardalis*)

**Blue-ringed
octopus**
(*Hapalochlaena
maculosa*)

*Paramecium –
a single-celled organism*

Shield bug
(*Carpona imperialis*)

ENCYCLOPEDIA OF
NATURE

DK

LONDON, NEW YORK, MUNICH,
MELBOURNE, and DELHI

Senior Editors Hazel Egerton, Fran Jones
Senior Art Editors Rachael Foster, Marcus James
Editors Gill Cooling, Maggie Crowley, Ben Morgan,
Veronica Pennycook, Amanda Rayner, Selina Wood
Art Editors Tina Borg, Ann Cannings, Tory Gordon-Harris,
Neville Graham, Jane Tetzlaff, Martin Wilson
US Editor Jill Hamilton **US Associate Editor** William Lach
DTP designer Andrew O'Brien
Picture research Mollie Gillard, Melanie Simmonds
Special photography Frank Greenaway, Harry Taylor
Production Josie Alabaster

Editorial Consultant David Burnie
US Editorial Consultants Joseph DiConstanzo, Ray Rogers
Authors David Burnie, Jonathan Elphick, Theresa Greenaway,
Barbara Taylor, Marek Walisiewicz, Richard Walker

2007 Edition
Editor Jenny Finch
Managing Editor Linda Esposito
Managing Art Editor Diane Thistlethwaite
Production Controller Seyhan Esen-Yagmurlu
DTP Designer Siu Chan
Jacket Designer Sheila Collins
Jacket Editor Mariza O'Keeffe
US Editor Margaret Parrish

Giant lacewing
(*Osmylus fulvicephalus*)

Ostrich
(*Struthio camelus*)

First published in the United States in 1998
This revised edition published in 2007
by DK Publishing
375 Hudson Street
New York, New York 10014

07 08 09 10 11 10 9 8 7 6 5 4 3 2 1
KE373 – 03/07

DK books are available at special discounts when purchased in bulk
for sales promotions, premiums, fund-raising, or educational use.
For details, contact: DK Publishing Special Markets,
375 Hudson Street, New York, New York 10014
SpecialSales@dk.com

A catalog record for this book is available from the Library of Congress.

ISBN: 978-0-7566-3111-6

Color reproduction by Colourscan, Singapore
Printed and bound by Toppan, China

**Discover more at
www.dk.com**

CONTENTS

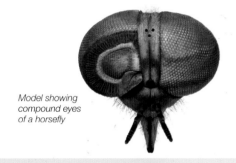

*Evolution of
the Asian
elephant*

THE NATURAL WORLD 10

*Model showing
compound eyes
of a horsefly*

HOW LIVING THINGS WORK 18

Rose periwinkle
(*Catharanthus roseus*)

ECOLOGY 62

Common tufted mycena
(*Mycena galericulata*)

HOW LIVING THINGS ARE CLASSIFIED 108

Male fern
(*Dryopteris filix-mas*)

PLANTS 116

Common starfish
(*Asterias rubens*)

ANIMALS 140

Honeybee
(*Apis mellifera*)

Worker

Queen

Verreaux's eagle
(*Aquila verreauxii*)

Hippopotamus
(*Hippopotamus amphibius*)

Zebra moray eel
(*Gymnomuraena zebra*)

REFERENCE SECTION

HOW TO USE THIS BOOK

THIS ILLUSTRATED ENCYCLOPEDIA of nature provides detailed information on every major plant and animal group, arranged in an easy-to-follow order. The book begins with a section on how life evolved, and looks at how living things work and fit into their individual habitats. It then describes the five kingdoms of the living world, investigating the characteristics of many species. Each animal or plant entry opens with an introduction to the subject, then goes into more detail, using photographs and artworks to illustrate the facts. There is a glossary of scientific terms and a comprehensive index to guide you directly to the subject you want.

Abbreviations used in this book

sp.	species
spp.	species (plural)
Imperial	
ft	feet
in	inches
yd	yards
sq miles	square miles
mph	miles per hour
°F	degrees Fahrenheit
oz	ounces
lb	pounds
Metric	
m	meters
mm	millimeters
cm	centimeters
km	kilometers
sq km	square kilometers
kmh	kilometers per hour
°C	degrees Celsius
g	grams
kg	kilograms

ANIMAL AND PLANT PAGES

Most of the pages in this book look at specific groups of animals and plants. The pages illustrated on the right, for example, look at different types of cats – from pumas to tigers. The pages usually have a description of typical animal anatomy or plant structure. They also provide further detail, such as how they move, feed, reproduce, or hunt for food. There may also be information on individual species within these groups.

ECOLOGY PAGES

The section on ecology provides information on different habitats, such as coral reefs, deciduous forests, wetlands, and deserts. These pages give a description of the habitat and explain how living things are influenced by their surroundings as well as by the other species that live there. In this section there are also pages on the relationship between people and nature. These describe how people need plants and animals to survive, but how some living things are endangered through human interference.

COLOR BORDERS

Each section of the book has a different color border to help you locate the section easily. This page on cats has the color used for all the animal pages.

ANNOTATIONS

Many photographs and artworks have explanatory text in *italic* letters. This points out features that are described more fully in the text.

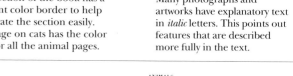

[Cats page illustration]

CATS

CATS ARE NATURE'S MOST efficient hunters. These carnivorous (meat-eating) animals feed almost entirely on vertebrates, and use cunning and stealth to stalk their victims silently before attacking...

256

[Coral reefs page illustration]

LOCATOR MAPS

Maps on the habitat pages show the worldwide distribution of that particular habitat. The equator, tropic lines, and Arctic and Antarctic circles give an indication of the climate in these areas. This map shows the warm, tropical areas where coral reefs are located.

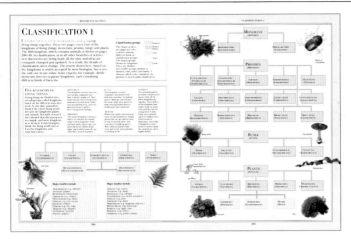

CLASSIFICATION CHARTS

Scientists usually divide the living world into five kingdoms – monerans, protists, fungi, plants, and animals. In the reference section of the book there are two classification charts that show you how this division works. The charts, which are color-coded for easy use, show where living things fit into the natural world and how they are related to other species.

SCIENTIFIC NAMES

Most animal and plant species in this book are labeled with their common name in **bold** letters and their scientific name in *italics*.

PROFILE BOXES

Many pages have a special profile box that highlights a particular species of animal or plant from the group shown on those pages. There are six key facts (five in the case of plants) that provide extra information on animals or plants that are often unusual or special in some way.

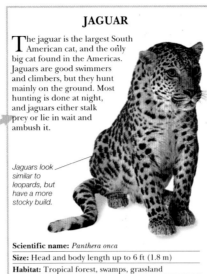

JAGUAR

The jaguar is the largest South American cat, and the only big cat found in the Americas. Jaguars are good swimmers and climbers, but they hunt mainly on the ground. Most hunting is done at night, and jaguars either stalk prey or lie in wait and ambush it.

Jaguars look similar to leopards, but have a more stocky build.

Scientific name: *Panthera onca*
Size: Head and body length up to 6 ft (1.8 m)
Habitat: Tropical forest, swamps, grassland
Distribution: From Belize to northern Argentina
Reproduction: Females have 1–4 offspring per litter
Diet: Peccaries, capybaras, agoutis, deer, sloths, birds, turtles, fish

SPECIFICATIONS

Quick-reference information at the bottom of each profile box gives you specific facts about the animal or plant including its scientific name, size, and habitat.

HOW LIVING THINGS WORK

There are 44 pages in the book that take a close look at how living things work. In addition to describing basic processes, such as feeding, movement, and respiration, they also explain patterns of behavior, including migration and communication. This section provides background information for the animal and plant pages.

FIND OUT MORE BOXES

In the bottom right corner of the plant and animal pages is a Find Out More box. This directs you to other pages in the book where you can discover more about a particular subject. For example, this page on cats explains how they stalk their prey. You can find out more about how other animals hunt on page 52.

Find out more

ANIMALS IN DANGER: *100*
HUNTING: *52*
MOVEMENT ON LAND: *34*
SOCIAL ANIMALS: *54*

PHOTOGRAPHS

Dramatic color photography reveals special features. For example, this close-up of a male tau emperor moth shows the feathery antennae that it uses to pick up the scent of a female.

ARTWORKS

Specially commissioned artworks, such as this illustration of an anglerfish, accompany the text. There are also cross-sections that reveal the inside workings of a plant or an animal.

THE NATURAL WORLD

Wherever you live on Earth, you are likely to be surrounded by an extraordinary range of living things. They exist in a variety of shapes and sizes. Trees, for example, may grow to incredible heights and live for hundreds of years, whereas some microscopic organisms survive for just a few days. Some living things, such as plants, live and die in one place. Others, including most animals, are free to move about – sometimes alone, or often in large, social groups. This encyclopedia explores the diversity of the natural world and explains how living things have evolved, where they are found, and why they behave as they do.

CRADLE OF LIFE
Water is essential to life because it dissolves chemicals that living things need to survive. No other planet has oceans that rival those on Earth, although one of Jupiter's moons – Europa – probably has liquid water beneath a thick surface covering of ice. Ice has also been found on Mars.

Water covers 70 percent of the Earth's surface.

A WORLD OF OPPORTUNITIES
Living things are able to survive in a wide range of habitats. They are found in the air, on land, in lakes, on coasts, on the seabed, or even in rock several miles below ground. Together, the world's habitats make up the biosphere – a word used to describe every region of the Earth where living things exist. Within the biosphere, energy and nutrients are constantly on the move.

Grazing mammals feed together at the Ngorongoro Crater, Tanzania.

Sunshine provides energy for most life on Earth.

LIVING PLANET
The Earth is home to millions of different kinds of living things, which are all linked in many ways. Together, they make up the complex world of nature. Some are rivals or enemies, while others depend on each other for survival. In parts of Africa, for example, some animals eat grass. These herbivores are attacked and eaten by carnivorous animals. The remains are broken down by bacteria and fungi, releasing nutrients into the soil.

Birds of prey such as the tawny eagle (Aquila rapax) travel huge distances in search of food, soaring high over open countryside.

Coniferous forests grow in places where they can survive cold winters.

Freshwater animals live in lakes and rivers.

Woodlands   *Grasslands*

Cave animals live on bacteria or on food swept underground by water.

Some microorganisms, such as bacteria, live deep beneath the ground.

Shallow seabed

The greater kudu (Tragelaphus strepsiceros) lives in bushlands and woodlands, feeding on leaves from bushes and trees.

Coasts provide a habitat for many different kinds of animal and plant life, including seabirds, seaweed, and lichens.

Coral reefs are made up of living things. Dead coral may accumulate to form coral islands.

PROTISTS

MONERANS

ENERGY FOR LIFE
Most life on Earth is powered by energy from the Sun. Plants capture energy from sunlight and use it to grow. When plants are eaten, they pass on their energy to other living things. However, some forms of life, principally bacteria, do not depend on sunlight. They live in caves or around deep-sea volcanic vents, and obtain their energy from dissolved minerals that seep out of the Earth's crust.

The Sun provides energy for many forms of life.

KINGDOMS OF LIFE
Biologists divide the living world into overall groups called kingdoms. In one system of classification, which is used in this book, there are five kingdoms. Three of them – animals, plants, and fungi – contain organisms that have many cells, while monerans and protists are single-celled. Although convenient, this system does have flaws. For example, the protist kingdom contains many organisms that are not closely related.

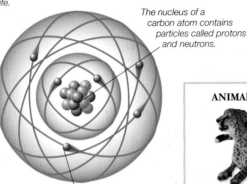

The nucleus of a carbon atom contains particles called protons and neutrons.

CARBON
The key chemical to life is carbon. It combines with other elements to make an amazing number of very different substances. Inside living things, these substances are continually built up and broken down in an endless series of chemical reactions. These reactions allow living things to grow, to repair themselves, and to survive within their local environment.

Six particles called electrons circle the nucleus.

ANIMALS

PLANTS

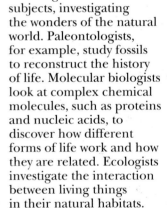
FUNGI

CHEMICALS OF LIFE
Carbon-based substances work in many different ways that enable living things to function and survive. For example, deoxyribonucleic acid (DNA) is a carbon-containing substance that stores coded instructions. Called genes, these instructions make living things work. Hemoglobin is also a carbon-containing substance that enables animals to carry oxygen in their blood. It collects oxygen in an animal's gills or lungs, and then takes it to other parts of the body.

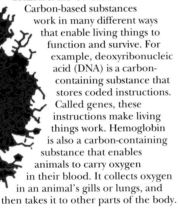

Closeup of a hemoglobin molecule carrying oxygen molecules (blue).

STUDYING NATURE
Scientists specialize in a range of different subjects, investigating the wonders of the natural world. Paleontologists, for example, study fossils to reconstruct the history of life. Molecular biologists look at complex chemical molecules, such as proteins and nucleic acids, to discover how different forms of life work and how they are related. Ecologists investigate the interaction between living things in their natural habitats.

An ecologist at work in the rainforest canopy, Costa Rica.

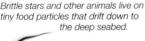

Brittle stars and other animals live on tiny food particles that drift down to the deep seabed.

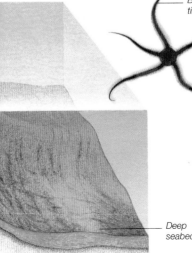

Deep seabed

Some bacteria survive below ground by getting their energy from minerals in the rocks.

Marella fossil in Burgess Shale in Canadian Rocky Mountains indicates life during Cambrian period.

UNANSWERED QUESTIONS
Despite continuing research and discoveries, the natural world is still full of mysteries and unsolved puzzles. Scientists are still unsure why animal life suddenly flourished about 550 million years ago, more than 3 billion years after life itself first appeared. This relatively short period, called the "Cambrian explosion," produced a vast range of new species in the world's seas, including *Marella*, which is related to arthropods.

Find out more

CLASSIFICATION 1: *286*
CLASSIFICATION 2: *288*
FOOD CHAINS AND WEBS: *66*
NUTRIENT CYCLES: *64*

HOW LIFE BEGAN

THE PLANET EARTH probably formed about 4.5 billion years ago. Originally, its surface was made of molten rock, which was stirred up by intense heat and pounded by meteorites falling from space. There was no liquid water and the atmosphere was very poisonous. By about 4 billion years ago, the Earth had changed. It had become cooler, allowing liquid water to form. Some parts of its surface were solid and were ripped apart by volcanic explosions. Other parts were covered by warm, salty seas, where conditions were much more stable.

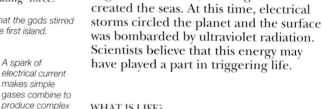

CREATION MYTHS
Many traditional stories teach that the world was created suddenly, together with all living things. This system of belief is called creationism. Although evolutionists believe life developed slowly over a very long period of time, some people believe that life may have been started off by a sudden "creating" force.

Japanese myth says that the gods stirred the ocean to create the first island.

EARLY EARTH
When the Earth first formed, the intense heat of its interior made it a very unstable place. Its atmosphere contained carbon dioxide, nitrogen, and steam, but little oxygen. As the planet cooled, the steam began to condense, forming rain that created the seas. At this time, electrical storms circled the planet and the surface was bombarded by ultraviolet radiation. Scientists believe that this energy may have played a part in triggering life.

Volcanoes produce steam that cools to form the world's oceans.

FIRST STEPS TO LIFE
Although people were not around to witness how the first living cells arose millions of years ago, scientists have devised experiments to imitate the conditions that probably existed at that time. These experiments show that some of life's chemicals can form by chance. Once these chemical building blocks appeared, they may have combined to form the first living things.

A spark of electrical current makes simple gases combine to produce complex molecules.

Gases such as methane and hydrogen simulate ancient Earth's atmosphere.

WHAT IS LIFE?
A flame, or fire, releases stored energy, it produces waste, and it also "reproduces" – three characteristics of a living thing. So, is a flame alive? The answer is no, because living things have other important characteristics. They react to their surroundings and they maintain a steady state, despite changes around them. Also, all life is able to change or evolve as one generation succeeds another.

Flame may show characteristics of life, but is not a living organism.

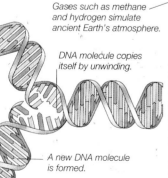

DNA molecule copies itself by unwinding.

A new DNA molecule is formed.

REPLICATING CHEMICALS
Life on Earth is based on chemicals that contain carbon. Once simple substances containing carbon appeared, some joined together to form chemicals that could copy themselves. Deoxyribonucleic acid (DNA) is one such chemical, and it lies at the heart of all living things. It controls the function of cells and copies itself when cells divide.

Deep-sea vents are found on ocean floors

WHERE LIFE BEGAN
Life began in water, but exactly where is not known. One theory, first proposed over a century ago, is that it might have started in shallow, seashore pools. Today, most scientists think that it is more likely to have begun in warm, mineral-rich water, like the water that gushes out of deep-sea vents. Dissolved minerals in the water could have supplied the energy needed for early life.

FIRST CELLS

Cells are the smallest units of living matter. They are surrounded by a protective membrane that allows essential chemicals to pass in and out of them. Although cells appear to be essential for life, scientists are unsure how they came into existence. However, biologists can guess what the first cells may have looked like. They were probably very similar to the most primitive kinds of bacteria, which have existed for more than 3 billion years.

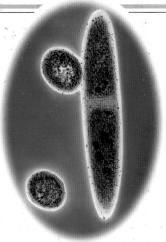

Light micrograph of archaebacteria

BREATHABLE AIR

The first organisms to exist using photosynthesis were cyanobacteria (blue-green algae), some of which made rocky mounds, called stromatolites. Photosynthesis releases oxygen as waste, so from the time they appeared, cyanobacteria have helped produce oxygen to provide breathable air.

Stromatolites off the coast of Western Australia

Lightning and ultraviolet light provided the energy needed to make carbon-containing chemicals.

A bubbling hot pool of sulfurous water contains mineral-rich mud, produced from the first weathering of rocks.

Steam rises and condenses to make clouds.

Slime molds join to form a sluglike organism.

TEAMING UP

Many forms of life are complex and consist of thousands, or even millions, of cells living and working together. Multicellular life probably began when some cells began to live together after dividing, instead of splitting up. Today, some living things can switch between a single-celled and multicellular existence. Microscopic slime molds spend most of their lives as separate cells. When they reproduce, they join to form a sluglike blob that travels across the ground.

Ropelike coils are found today in a type of lava called "pahoehoe."

LIFE BEYOND EARTH?

A growing number of scientists suspect that life may exist on other planets, in or beyond our own solar system. In 1996, NASA scientists thought they had found fossils in a meteorite from Mars, but research later showed that the "fossils" probably came from Earth. However, since then, complex carbon compounds have been found in other meteorites – a possible sign that life evolved elsewhere.

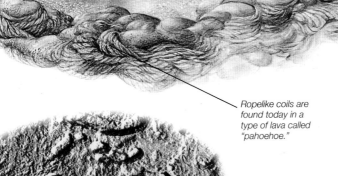

Meteorite from Mars showing fossil-like features

Find out more
CELLS: *20*
EVOLUTION: *14*
PREHISTORIC LIFE: *16*
SINGLE-CELLED ORGANISMS: *112*

EVOLUTION

EVER SINCE PEOPLE began to study nature, they have been aware that living things are superbly designed to fit the ways they live. Birds' bills, for example, seem to be just the right shape for collecting particular types of food, while cats' claws are perfect weapons for catching their prey. But why should this be so? Some people believe it is because each different species has been specially created. Other people – including most scientists – believe it is because living species gradually change, or adapt, to particular ways of life. This process of change is called evolution. Evidence for evolution can be seen in plants and animals that lived in the past – and in everything that is alive today.

DARWIN'S FINCHES

A British naturalist, Charles Darwin, was the first person to assemble evidence for evolution and to suggest how it occurs. In 1831, Darwin set off on a five-year voyage on a ship called the *Beagle*. He visited the Galápagos Islands in the Pacific Ocean, where he realized that different finches on the islands were probably descended from a single species that had flown there from South America. Each species of finch had evolved a unique beak to feed on a certain type of food.

Warbler finch
(*Certhidea olivacea*)

Medium ground-finch
(*Geospiza fortis*)

Woodpecker finch
(*Camarhynchus pallidus*)

Vegetarian finch
(*Camarhynchus crassirostris*)

NATURAL SELECTION

Land crabs produce millions of eggs when they breed, but only a tiny proportion of the eggs become adults. Charles Darwin realized that this kind of thinning out is a powerful force. He called the force natural selection. Nature selects individuals with the most useful characteristics, which slowly become more widespread. As a result, the species gradually changes, or evolves.

Land crab (Gecarcoidea natalis) surrounded by thousands of young

EVIDENCE FROM THE PAST

Fossils are like a record book of life on Earth. They show that living things can change, because the species that existed in the distant past are not the same as the ones that are alive today. Fossils also show the path that evolution has taken. For example, fossils of an extinct species called *Archaeopteryx* show that birds evolved from reptiles. *Archaeopteryx* has some features found in reptiles, such as teeth, and some features seen in birds, such as feathers.

Fossil of Archaeopteryx showing outlines of feathers and a long, bony tail

Archaeopteryx

USEFUL CHARACTERISTICS

Living things do not evolve during a single lifetime. Instead, adaptations gradually build up as one generation follows another. In giraffes, for example, natural selection favored individuals with long necks, because they can reach more food than animals with shorter necks. In the past, giraffes with extra-long necks probably produced more young that survived into adulthood, so extra-long necks have slowly become a feature of the species as a whole.

Giraffe (Giraffa camelopardalis) reaching for leaves

EVOLUTION OF ELEPHANTS

Scientists can often trace the evolution of a complete group of species by looking at fossils. Elephants, for example, belong to a group of animals called proboscideans, which includes more than 150 species that are now extinct. The earliest proboscideans were small animals with short tusks and trunks. As time went by, their tusks, trunks, and bodies became larger.

This species is alive today.

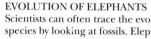
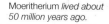

Moeritherium *lived about 50 million years ago.*

Phiomia *lived about 35 million years ago.*

Gomphotherium *lived about 20 million years ago.*

Deinotherium *lived until 2 million years ago.*

Asian elephant
(*Elephas maximus*)

EVIDENCE FROM THE PRESENT

Evolution never starts from scratch. Instead, it works by adapting features that already exist, turning them to new uses. This means that all living things contain built-in clues that show how they have evolved. A dolphin and a chimpanzee, for example, look nothing like each other, and live in different ways. However, underneath, their skeletons share the same pattern of bones. This shared pattern shows that they have evolved in different ways from the same distant ancestor.

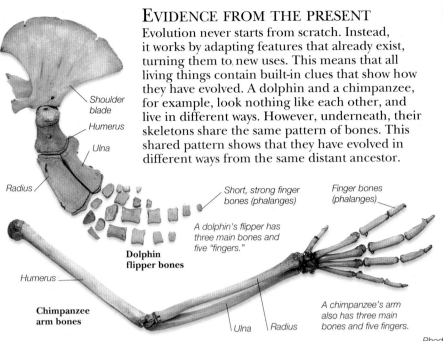

Shoulder blade

Humerus

Ulna

Radius

Short, strong finger bones (phalanges)

A dolphin's flipper has three main bones and five "fingers."

Dolphin flipper bones

Finger bones (phalanges)

Humerus

Chimpanzee arm bones

Ulna *Radius*

A chimpanzee's arm also has three main bones and five fingers.

HORSESHOE CRAB

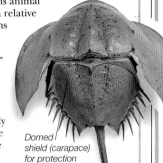

Despite its name, this animal is not a crab, but a relative of spiders and scorpions that lives in shallow seawater. Horseshoe crabs are "living fossils" – members of a group that has changed little in millions of years. They are thought to have evolved very slowly because they eat a wide range of foods and live in a stable habitat.

Domed shield (carapace) for protection

Scientific name: *Tachypleus tridentatus*

Size: Approximately 2 ft (60 cm) long

Habitat: Sandy and muddy shores

Distribution: Indian and Pacific Oceans

Reproduction: Female lays thousands of eggs. They develop into swimming larvae.

Diet: Mollusks, worms, and small seabed animals

ARTIFICIAL SELECTION

Natural selection is not the only reason why animals and plants change. In artificial selection, humans control the way living things reproduce. Many different breeds or varieties can be produced from a single original species. Dogs, for example, are all descendants of the gray wolf, which was domesticated about 12,000 years ago. Some breeds of dog were used for hunting, and others for rounding up animals or pulling sleighs.

Gray wolf
(*Canis lupus*)

Rhodesian ridgeback

Kerry blue terrier

Alaskan malamute

CONVERGENT EVOLUTION

During the course of evolution, things that live in similar conditions often adapt in the same ways. Sometimes they become so alike that they are difficult to tell apart. This process is called convergent evolution. It explains why some spurges resemble cacti. Many spurges have evolved spines and water-holding stems to help them survive in dry places.

Sharp spines protect the plant from grazing animals.

Spurge
(*Euphorbia tescorum*)

Cactus
(*Corryocactus melanotrichus*)

CHANGING TRACK

Evolution does not always make animals and plants more complicated. Some living things adapt by losing features they once had. Whales, for example, evolved from four-legged ancestors that lived on land. When they took up life in the water, their hind limbs slowly disappeared and were replaced by tail paddles called flukes. In most whales, all that remains of the hind limbs is a collection of tiny bones.

Remnants of hind limb bones

Pygmy right whale
(*Caperea marginata*)

SPECIATION

New species can evolve in several different ways. Through the most common method, an original species spreads across a wide area and scattered groups are kept separate. These groups breed in isolation, and each one develops features that make it distinct. That is what has happened with the butterflies shown here. If the butterflies continue to evolve separately, they will become so different that they will be unable to interbreed. At this stage, each type becomes a new species.

The wing colors of this butterfly species vary from place to place.

Amazonian Agrias butterfly
(*Agrias claudina*)

Find out more

BUTTERFLIES AND MOTHS: *176*
DOGS: *252*
ELEPHANTS AND HYRAXES: *266*
PREHISTORIC LIFE: *16*

PREHISTORIC LIFE

SINCE LIFE BEGAN, more than 3.5 billion years ago, evolution has produced an enormous variety of living things. Some have been preserved as fossils that tell us about how they lived. They show that animal life underwent an explosive burst of evolution about 545 million years ago. The first plants moved from water onto land about 440 million years ago, and by about 325 million years ago, the first flying insects had taken to the air. However, there have also been setbacks – on at least five occasions, mass extinctions have wiped out huge numbers of species.

A BRIEF HISTORY OF LIFE

Until about a billion years ago, most living things were microscopic, single-celled organisms, such as bacteria. By about 545 million years ago, animals with hard shells and body cases had appeared. They were all invertebrates – the first vertebrates did not appear until 45 million years later. The first multicellular life-forms to move onto land were probably plants. The first land animals were arthropods, such as scorpions and centipedes.

Dinosaurs become common on land (170 million years ago).

Small mammals become more diverse (80 million years ago).

Dinosaurs die out (65 million years ago).

Birds evolve from reptiles (147 million years ago).

Invertebrates with hard cases, such as trilobites, appear in the seas (545 million years ago).

Plants spread onto land (440 million years ago).

Modern humans appear (300,000 years ago).

The first bacteria appear (3.8 billion years ago).

Earth forms (4.6 billion years ago).

Fish (the first vertebrates) are now the dominant form of life in the seas (400 million years ago).

Amphibians evolve from fish and spread onto land (360 million years ago).

THE FIRST ANIMALS

Although animal life evolved about one billion years ago, the first animals to leave clear, fossilized remains are more recent. Fossil animals from the Ediacara Hills in Australia are about 680 million years old; those in Canada's Burgess Shale – a famous, fossil-rich area in the Rocky Mountains – date back about 530 million years. Some of these animals had strange body forms that have not been seen since. Many zoologists think that they were evolutionary "experiments" that lost the struggle for survival.

Bony tail club

The powerful, swinging tail made a formidable weapon.

Fossil and artwork reconstruction of Anomalocaris – one of the strange animals found in the Burgess Shale.

LIFE IN THE SEA

For more than 3 billion years, living things existed only in water. The first marine animals were all invertebrates, but by 500 million years ago they had been joined by the first vertebrates – the jawless fish. Some of these fish, such as *Cephalaspis*, had heavily armored heads. They spent most of their lives on seabeds or riverbeds, sucking up food through their mouths.

Fossil of the fish Cephalaspis, one of the first vertebrates

Model of Ichthyostega, one of the first vertebrates to walk on land.

FOREST SWAMPS

Around 310 million years ago, humid conditions allowed vast forests to form on swampy ground. The trees in these forests were all relatives of today's club mosses and horsetails. The forests were also home to giant millipedes, cockroaches, scorpions, and dragonflies, the longest with a 28 in (70 cm) wingspan. There were no birds or mammals because these had not yet evolved. Over millions of years, the remains of these forests formed huge deposits of coal.

FIRST FOUR LEGS

The first vertebrates to spend part of their lives on land were species such as *Ichthyostega*, which were the forerunners of today's amphibians. These animals evolved from fish, and their bodies still had long tails and fishlike scales. They crawled out of the water on widely splayed legs that had evolved from lobe-shaped fins. Like modern amphibians, these early ancestors laid their eggs in water.

THE AGE OF REPTILES

Reptiles evolved from amphibians, and the first species appeared about 340 million years ago. Unlike amphibians, early reptiles were well adapted to life in dry places and they spread to many new habitats. For nearly 200 million years, reptiles dominated life on land and certain types grew to a phenomenal size. They also spread to water, while some – the pterosaurs – evolved leathery wings and could fly or glide.

A herd of hadrosaurs – plant-eating dinosaurs that lived around 70 million years ago.

DINOSAURS

The dinosaurs were the largest, most varied group of prehistoric reptiles. They ranged from animals about the size of a chicken to giants such as the plant-eating *Brachiosaurus*, which weighed up to 50 tons. Unlike today's reptiles, some dinosaurs may have been warm-blooded, allowing them to be more active and alert. Some may also have incubated their eggs and perhaps guarded their young.

Euoplocephalus, *a plant-eating dinosaur from western North America.*

Armored skin protected this dinosaur from predators.

Strong legs made Euoplocephalus *a nimble runner.*

GIANT SCORPION

This extinct scorpion lived around 320–290 million years ago. It was nearly 10 times as big as the largest scorpion alive today and had a huge sting at the end of its tail. Its fossilized remains were found in Scotland – a part of the world where lush forests existed when the scorpion was alive.

Fragment of jointed leg

Scientific name: *Gigantoscorpio*

Size: Up to 3 ft (90 cm) long

Habitat: Forest floor

Distribution: Warm regions worldwide

Reproduction: Female probably gave birth to live young and may have carried them on her back

Diet: Insects and other animals

PRESERVED IN AMBER

Most fossils are preserved in rock, but prehistoric remains can be preserved in other ways. Millions of years ago, the spider, gnat, and conifer twig below became trapped in sticky tree resin. The resin then set solid, and changed into a hard substance called amber. Animals trapped in amber are sometimes so well preserved that they look as if they have just died. Under a microscope, every structure in their bodies can be clearly seen.

Spider (40 million years old)

Fungus gnat (40 million years old)

Conifer twig (40 million years old)

MASS EXTINCTION

Throughout life's history, millions of species have slowly become extinct. On some occasions, however, mass extinctions of vast numbers of species have occurred in a relatively short period – perhaps because of environmental catastrophes. The last mass extinction, 65 million years ago, may have been caused by a meteorite striking the Earth. The extinction swept away the dinosaurs and many other reptiles.

This crater in Arizona was formed by a meteorite that struck the Earth about 50,000 years ago.

THE RISE OF MAMMALS

Mammals first appeared while reptiles dominated the land and for a long time they remained small and unobtrusive. But when dinosaurs and other reptiles died out, mammals took their place. Over the past 65 million years, mammals have developed a huge range of shapes and sizes and have spread to most habitats. However, in recent times, prehistoric humans may have helped drive many species to extinction – including mammoths, which died out about 8,000 years ago.

Long hair helped woolly mammoths survive in the Ice Age.

Many mammoths had colossal tusks.

Woolly mammoth (*Mammuthus primigenius*)

Find out more

MAMMALS: *232*
REPTILES: *198*
SINGLE-CELLED ORGANISMS: *112*
VERTEBRATES: *182*

HOW LIVING THINGS WORK

LIVING THINGS DIFFER enormously in shape and size and in the lives they lead. Some are highly active and always on the move, while others seem to do very little and hardly look alive. Despite these differences, living things all share a set of basic characteristics that make life work. One of the most fundamental of these is respiration, or the release of energy from food. Another is the uptake of nutrients, which in turn requires the disposal of waste substances. Living things also grow and develop as they age, and they respond to their surroundings, often by moving around. Finally – and most importantly – all living things reproduce.

THE ESSENTIALS OF LIFE

This tiny crustacean, known as *Cyclops*, lives in freshwater habitats. Although only about 0.08 in (2 mm) long, it is a complex piece of living engineering. It gets energy by catching food, it grows by shedding its skin, and it reproduces by scattering eggs. Like most animals, *Cyclops* is very sensitive to its surroundings and responds very quickly. Plants can also sense certain things in their surroundings, such as sunlight and touch, but they respond more slowly than animals.

Cyclops model
(*Cyclops* sp.)

NUTRITION

Nutrients provide living things with the raw materials that they need. In many living things – including all animals – they also provide the energy that is needed to make cells work. However, not all living things get their energy from nutrients. Plants and some bacteria get their energy directly from sunlight in a process called photosynthesis.

Nutrition
Cyclops *uses a pair of small antennae to touch and smell food.*

Toad
(*Bufo* sp.)

This mouse will provide the energy needed to power the toad's body.

RESPONSE SYSTEMS

For animals, rapid responses are essential for survival. In all but the simplest species, they are co-ordinated by nerves – cells that are specially adapted to carry signals from one part of the body to another. A quick-acting nervous system allows a chameleon to spot a fly, judge exactly how far away it is, and hit it with its sticky tongue.

Response systems
Cyclops *has a single central eye that guides it toward light.*

Waste disposal
Cyclops *releases waste substances into the surrounding water.*

Movement
Cyclops *swims by moving its legs.*

Jackson's chameleon
(*Chamaeleo jacksonii*)

WASTE DISPOSAL

All the chemical processes in living things produce waste products. If these are allowed to build up, they can poison living cells. To prevent this from happening, waste has to be expelled. Important kinds of waste include carbon dioxide gas, which many animals expel through their gills or lungs, and substances containing nitrogen, which are often carried away as urine.

Elephant droppings contain waste left over after food has been digested.

Powerful muscles help a springbok (Antidorcas marsupialis) escape.

MOVEMENT

All living things can move in some way, even though it may only happen on a tiny scale. Plants can move their leaves and flowers, and many micro-organisms can travel from place to place. However, the best movers by far are animals. Animals are the only living things that have evolved muscles – groups of special cells that can contract rapidly to make parts of the body move.

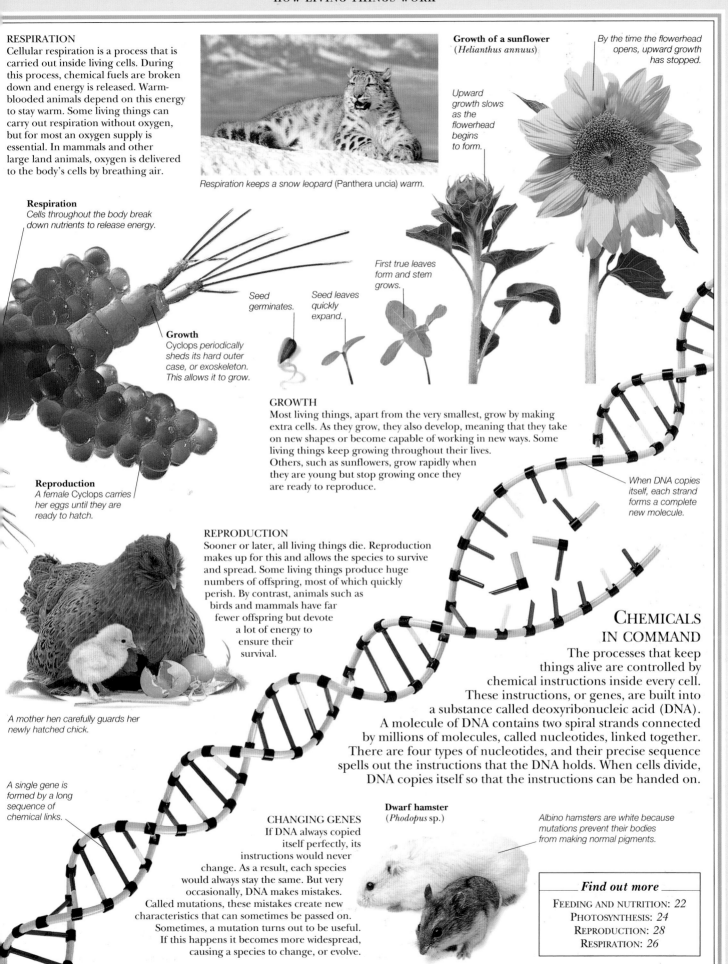

RESPIRATION

Cellular respiration is a process that is carried out inside living cells. During this process, chemical fuels are broken down and energy is released. Warm-blooded animals depend on this energy to stay warm. Some living things can carry out respiration without oxygen, but for most an oxygen supply is essential. In mammals and other large land animals, oxygen is delivered to the body's cells by breathing air.

Growth of a sunflower
(*Helianthus annuus*)

By the time the flowerhead opens, upward growth has stopped.

Respiration keeps a snow leopard (Panthera uncia) warm.

Upward growth slows as the flowerhead begins to form.

Respiration
Cells throughout the body break down nutrients to release energy.

First true leaves form and stem grows.

Seed germinates.

Seed leaves quickly expand.

Growth
Cyclops periodically sheds its hard outer case, or exoskeleton. This allows it to grow.

GROWTH

Most living things, apart from the very smallest, grow by making extra cells. As they grow, they also develop, meaning that they take on new shapes or become capable of working in new ways. Some living things keep growing throughout their lives. Others, such as sunflowers, grow rapidly when they are young but stop growing once they are ready to reproduce.

Reproduction
A female Cyclops carries her eggs until they are ready to hatch.

REPRODUCTION

Sooner or later, all living things die. Reproduction makes up for this and allows the species to survive and spread. Some living things produce huge numbers of offspring, most of which quickly perish. By contrast, animals such as birds and mammals have far fewer offspring but devote a lot of energy to ensure their survival.

When DNA copies itself, each strand forms a complete new molecule.

A mother hen carefully guards her newly hatched chick.

CHEMICALS IN COMMAND

The processes that keep things alive are controlled by chemical instructions inside every cell. These instructions, or genes, are built into a substance called deoxyribonucleic acid (DNA). A molecule of DNA contains two spiral strands connected by millions of molecules, called nucleotides, linked together. There are four types of nucleotides, and their precise sequence spells out the instructions that the DNA holds. When cells divide, DNA copies itself so that the instructions can be handed on.

A single gene is formed by a long sequence of chemical links.

CHANGING GENES

If DNA always copied itself perfectly, its instructions would never change. As a result, each species would always stay the same. But very occasionally, DNA makes mistakes. Called mutations, these mistakes create new characteristics that can sometimes be passed on. Sometimes, a mutation turns out to be useful. If this happens it becomes more widespread, causing a species to change, or evolve.

Dwarf hamster
(*Phodopus* sp.)

Albino hamsters are white because mutations prevent their bodies from making normal pigments.

Find out more

FEEDING AND NUTRITION: *22*
PHOTOSYNTHESIS: *24*
REPRODUCTION: *28*
RESPIRATION: *26*

CELLS

CELLS ARE THE building blocks that make up most living things. They are usually far too small to see without a microscope, but despite their tiny size, they are remarkably complicated. Each cell is controlled by genes, which are usually held in the cell nucleus in the form of a chemical called DNA (deoxyribonucleic acid). The smallest living things consist of just a single cell. Larger forms of life, such as animals and plants, have millions or even billions of cells, many of which are specialized to carry out specific tasks. All these cells work together to keep the organism alive.

Microvilli absorb dissolved substances from outside the cell.

Vesicles carry large particles into the cell.

Cytoplasm

Membrane

An organelle where many proteins are made.

Lysosomes contain enzymes that break things down.

Mitochondria obtain energy from food.

ANIMAL CELL

A typical animal cell is just 0.0008 in (0.02 mm) across. It is surrounded by a thin outer layer called a membrane, which acts as a barrier between the cell and its surroundings. Inside the cell, structures called organelles are set in a jellylike fluid called cytoplasm. The organelles carry out processes such as controlling energy flow or making proteins. Most animal cells are soft and flexible. To survive, they must absorb food from their surroundings.

Centrioles help cells divide to make new cells.

The nucleus holds most of the cell's genes.

Magnified view of an Acinetobacter bacterium

SIMPLE CELLS

Bacteria have much smaller cells than other forms of life. Although they have cell walls and membranes, they lack nuclei and mitochondria and have no organelles. Cells like these are called "prokaryotic" in contrast with the "eukaryotic" cells of most other living things. Prokaryotic cells were the first to evolve after life appeared on Earth.

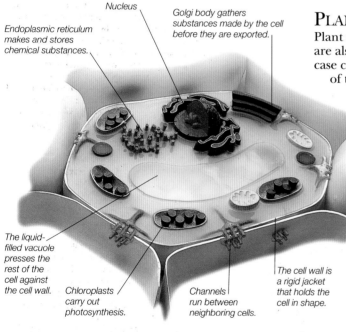

Nucleus

Endoplasmic reticulum makes and stores chemical substances.

Golgi body gathers substances made by the cell before they are exported.

The liquid-filled vacuole presses the rest of the cell against the cell wall.

Chloroplasts carry out photosynthesis.

Channels run between neighboring cells.

The cell wall is a rigid jacket that holds the cell in shape.

PLANT CELL

Plant cells have membranes but are also enclosed by a tough outer case called a cell wall. The interior of the cell is under pressure and presses outward against the wall to keep the whole cell rigid. Unlike animal cells, plant cells contain bright green organelles called chloroplasts. Chloroplasts harness the energy in sunlight and use it to make food and building materials for the cell. This process is called photosynthesis.

Muscle cells contain long molecules that slide together when a muscle contracts.

Types of cell

Nerve cells carry electrical signals around an animal's body at high speed.

Red blood cells carry oxygen around many animals' bodies.

Pore

Guard cells open and close pores in leaves.

Mermaid's wine glass
(Acetabularia)

GIANT CELLS

Although most cells are microscopic, some are visible to the naked eye. For example, a marine alga called mermaid's wine glass (*Acetabularia*) has a single mushroom-shaped cell that grows up to 3 in (8 cm) long. However, the largest cells of all belong to animals. In giraffes, some nerve cells can reach more than 13 ft (4 m) in length. An unfertilized ostrich egg consists of a single cell that can weigh more than 3 lb 5 oz (1.5 kg).

SPECIALIZED CELLS

In single-celled organisms, one cell carries out all the activities needed to sustain life. Multicellular organisms, such as animals and plants, have many kinds of cells, and each is specially shaped for the work it carries out. As well as looking different, the cells have varied life spans. In animals, for example, red blood cells last for only a few weeks before they are replaced, but nerve cells last for life.

Creeping buttercup
(*Ranunculus repens*)

Leaves contain cells specialized for carrying out photosynthesis.

Creeping stems form cells that can develop into new plants.

Roots contain cells specialized for carrying water and nutrients.

EUGLENA

This tiny single-celled organism is common in fresh water throughout the world. It is very adaptable because it can harness energy from the Sun (like a plant) or switch to eating food (like an animal). *Euglena* propels itself by its whiplike flagellum, which beats to make the cell spin through the water.

Flagellum

Scientific name:	*Euglena viridis*
Size:	About 0.002 in (0.05 mm) long
Habitat:	Ponds and ditches
Distribution:	Worldwide
Reproduction:	Divides in two
Diet:	Bacteria and small food particles

WORKING TOGETHER

In multicellular organisms, different types of cells are not mixed up randomly. Instead, they are organized in ways that allow them to work together. Groups of identical cells are arranged into sheets called tissues. Separate tissues are then arranged to form organs, such as leaves, roots, lungs, or eyes. Different organs often work together – such as in the root system of a plant or in the nervous system of an animal.

Buttercup root

Vascular cells carry water and dissolved nutrients up the plant.

Storage cells store food made by the plant's leaves.

Root hairs absorb water and dissolved nutrients from the soil.

Each root hair is formed by an individual cell.

MAKING THINGS MOVE

Some cells are able to move themselves, while others can move things around them. They do this by changing shape or by waving microscopic hairs called flagella and cilia. Human sperm cells, for example, swim toward an egg cell by beating their long flagella. At the same time, the egg cell is carried toward the sperm by cilia that line the inside of the fallopian tube. When a sperm cell meets an egg cell, the two join together to form an embryo.

HOW MANY CELLS?

Most animals and plants have a large number of cells, but the exact total varies from one individual to another. In a few species, every individual has exactly the same number of cells once they are fully grown. One example is the tiny nematode worm *Caenorhabditis elegans*, which has been studied intensively by biologists. When they are mature, these worms always have exactly 959 cells. Nearly a third of the cells are involved in the nervous system.

Caenorhabditis elegans lives in soil and feeds on bacteria.

Magnified view of sperm (yellow) and cilia (green and mauve) inside a uterus

Animal cell dividing

Cell constricts in center.

The nucleus divides before the main part of the cell.

This cell has just undergone mitosis, producing two identical cells.

The cell cytoplasm divides after the nucleus.

CELLS THAT SELF-DESTRUCT

Living things often change shape as they grow. During this process, cells sometimes "commit suicide" by digesting themselves from within. This happens when a tadpole changes into a frog and when a caterpillar changes into a butterfly. The dead cells are not wasted. When they have been broken down, their raw materials are absorbed by other cells and reused.

Cells in a tadpole's tail self-destruct as it changes into a frog.

CELL DIVISION

In order to grow and reproduce, living things have to make new cells. They do this by cell division. In the most common form, the cell copies its genes, its nucleus divides, and two identical cells are produced. This is called mitosis. In another type of division, the original cell divides, and the new cells divide again. The four new cells each have a unique mixture of genes and half the usual number of chromosomes. Called meiosis, this is only used in sexual reproduction.

Find out more

ANIMALS: *140*
BACTERIA AND VIRUSES: *110*
PHOTOSYNTHESIS: *24*
SINGLE-CELLED ORGANISMS: *112*

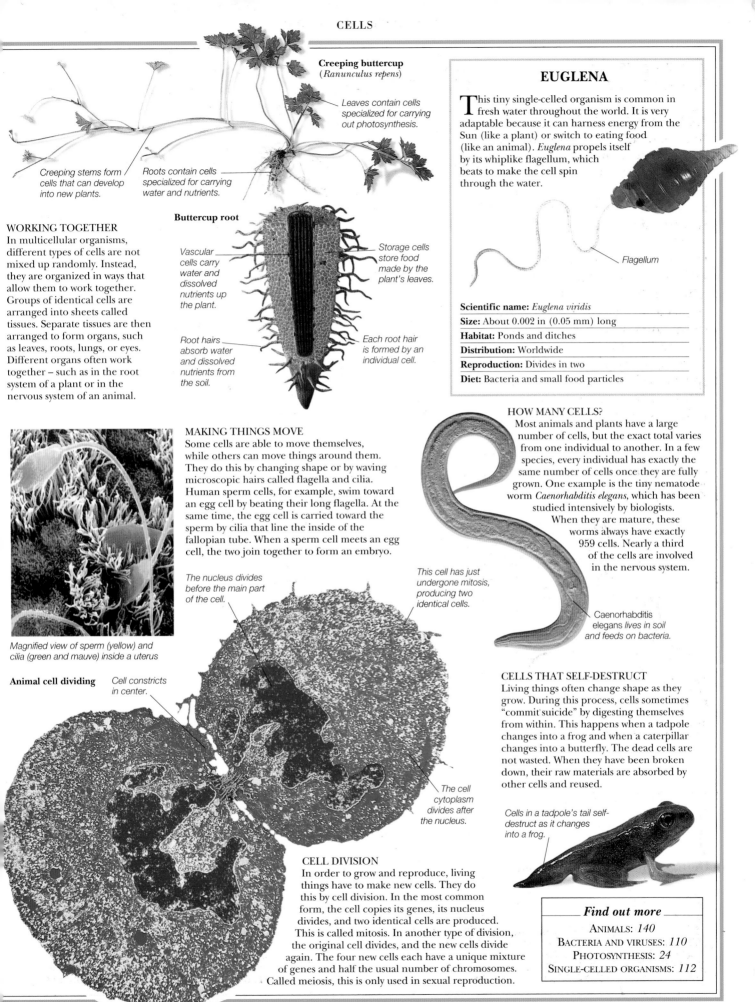

FEEDING AND NUTRITION

FOOD IS THE FUEL THAT enables animals to survive. It provides the raw materials for growth, and fuels muscles and body processes. Animals eat a huge range of different foods, including plants, other animals, and dead remains. Each species has its own techniques for getting the food that it needs. Hunters and grazers may wander long distances in search of a meal, but some animals stay in one place and collect food that comes within reach. Once food has been eaten, it must be digested so that the animal can absorb the nutrients. Foods are often broken down with the help of microorganisms that live inside animals' bodies.

Zebras are herbivores that graze on grass.

Plants capture the energy in sunlight and use it to grow.

A plant absorbs simple nutrients from the soil.

Plants contain a store of nutrients that animals can eat.

A caterpillar digests plant food to obtain the energy that it needs.

PLANT-EATERS

Plant-eating animals are known as herbivores. Plant food is often easy to find, but it is sometimes low in nutrients. Seeds can be packed with energy-rich food, but other parts of plants – particularly stems and leaves – contain fewer nutrients that animals can use. To survive, grazing and browsing animals have to spend a large amount of each day eating, and have specialized digestive systems to get the maximum nutrition from their food.

DIGESTING PLANT FOOD

To extract nutrients from cellulose – the tough substance found in leaves and stems – many animals get help from microorganisms. In ruminant mammals, such as sheep, antelope, and cattle, microorganisms live in a large stomach chamber called the rumen. After the microorganisms have broken down the cellulose, the food passes into other stomach chambers to be digested.

Ruminant digestive system

After eating, a ruminant re-chews its food to help digestion.

Microorganisms break down food in the rumen.

Reticulum collects some food for re-chewing.

Absorption of water and small molecules takes place in the omasum.

Remaining particles proceed through the abomasum.

Further digestion takes place in the cecum.

STAYING ALIVE

Living things can be divided into two different groups according to the kinds of nutrients that they need. Autotrophs, which include plants, need simple nutrients, such as minerals from the soil. They do not need to eat food because they can get energy directly from sources such as sunlight. Heterotrophs, which include fungi and animals, cannot do this. Instead, they get energy from nutrients in food. Without autotrophs to make food in the first place, heterotrophs could not exist.

A boa constrictor can swallow an animal half its own weight.

Boa constrictor
(*Boa constrictor*)

The snake's digestive system breaks down almost everything except the prey's fur.

Rat prey

MEAT-EATERS

Animals that eat meat are known as carnivores. Compared to plants, animal food contains lots of useful nutrients. However, unlike plants, animals have many more ways of avoiding attack, so predators often have to work hard to get a meal. Small, warm-blooded predators, such as shrews, need a constant supply of food and have to hunt much of the day. By contrast, a large, cold-blooded hunter, such as a python or crocodile, uses relatively little energy for its size. Predators like these can often survive for many weeks between meals.

OMNIVORES

Instead of specializing in plant or animal food, omnivores eat almost anything edible that they come across. Omnivores include mammals such as bears, raccoons, and foxes, and also many birds. Compared to other animals, most omnivores are good at adapting to changes to their habitat. Many have learned to live alongside humans, where they can eat leftover food and animals that have been hit by cars.

A pied crow (Corvus albus) feeding on a roadside casualty.

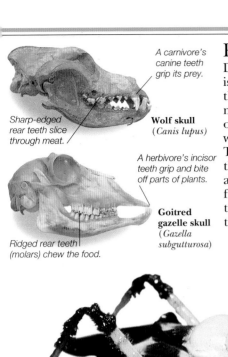

A carnivore's canine teeth grip its prey.

Sharp-edged rear teeth slice through meat.

Wolf skull
(*Canis lupus*)

A herbivore's incisor teeth grip and bite off parts of plants.

Goitred gazelle skull
(*Gazella subgutturosa*)

Ridged rear teeth (molars) chew the food.

PROCESSING FOOD

Digestion works fastest when food is cut up into small pieces. To do this, mammals use their teeth. A mammal's upper and lower teeth occlude (they fit together precisely when the animal closes its jaws). This allows the teeth to chew or slice through food. The teeth of other animals – such as many reptiles and fish – do not work like this. Instead, they often simply grip the food so that it can be caught and swallowed.

GREATER FLAMINGO

Flamingos are the only birds that live entirely by filter feeding. Holding the tips of their bills upside-down, they wade through the shallows, pumping water with their tongues and straining it through comblike devices called bill lamellae. Flamingos, like pigeons, are unusual in feeding their young on a milklike fluid that they produce in their crops.

Scientific name:	*Phoenicopterus ruber*
Size:	Up to 5 ft (1.5 m) long
Habitat:	Salty lakes and lagoons
Distribution:	Southern Europe, North and tropical Africa, Caribbean islands, and Central America
Reproduction:	Female lays single egg each year
Diet:	Crustaceans and other small animals (filtered)

The bug uses its bill-like mouth to stab other insects.

Assassin bug
(*Velinus malayus*)

LIQUID LUNCH

Not all predators swallow their prey. Instead, some have special mouthparts that they use to inject digestive juices into their victims. Once these juices have done their work, the hunter sucks up the nutritious fluid that is produced. Animals that feed in this way include spiders and scorpions, and also predatory bugs. Once one of these hunters has finished eating, all that is left of the prey is a dry, lifeless husk.

The victim's tissues are liquefied by the bug's digestive juices.

Water is sucked in through the sea squirt's oral siphon.

Water is pumped out through the atrial siphon.

The pharynx filters out particles of food that pass to the stomach.

Sea squirt filter system

FILTER FEEDERS

Filter feeders include some of the world's smallest animals, as well as some of the largest. They filter food particles from water, using special body parts that work like sieves. In sea squirts, the sieve is a basket-shaped structure called a pharynx. In other filter feeders, different body parts carry out the same work. These include modified gills in the case of mollusks, special bills in birds, and baleen plates in whales.

Scarlet macaws (Ara macao) pecking at a cliff that is rich in mineral nutrients.

ESSENTIAL MINERALS

All living things need mineral nutrients. Plants usually get them from the soil, and although they use some in tiny quantities, they cannot grow normally if any of them are in short supply. Animals get their mineral nutrients from their food, and sometimes from the fluids that they drink. In some places – particularly in the tropics – animals gather at places where vital nutrients are easy to obtain.

NATURE'S RECYCLERS

Some living things specialize in feeding on the dead remains of other forms of life. Known as saprotrophs, they break down organic remains so that their nutrients can be recycled. Saprotrophs include animals such as earthworms, but the most abundant species by far are bacteria and fungi. Vast numbers live in soil, turning dead remains into a substance called humus.

Lemon fairy cup
(*Bisporella citrina*)

Yellow fruiting bodies formed by fungus growing on rotting wood.

Find out more	
CARNIVOROUS PLANTS:	*138*
FUNGI:	*114*
HUNTING:	*52*
PARTNERS AND PARASITES:	*56*

PHOTOSYNTHESIS

PLANTS, LIKE OTHER LIVING THINGS, need energy to survive. But instead of getting their energy from food, they get it directly from sunlight. This process is called photosynthesis, which means "putting together through light." During photosynthesis, a plant traps light energy with its leaves and uses it to make a sugar called glucose from water and carbon dioxide. Glucose can be used as a fuel or as a building block to make the substances needed for growth. Photosynthesis is one of the most important processes in nature. Without it, plants could not grow, and without plants, few animals would exist.

HOW PHOTOSYNTHESIS WORKS

During photosynthesis, leaves absorb sunlight. They also take up water through their roots, and carbon dioxide from the air. They use the sun's energy to convert water and carbon dioxide into glucose. Oxygen is produced as a waste product. The glucose may leave the leaf and be carried around the plant. At the same time, waste oxygen escapes into the air.

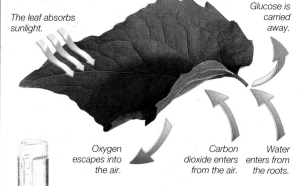

The leaf absorbs sunlight.

Glucose is carried away.

Oxygen escapes into the air.

Carbon dioxide enters from the air.

Water enters from the roots.

LEAF MOSAIC

In most plants, photosynthesis takes place in the leaves. Leaves usually face the sun, and are often arranged so as not to overlap and shade one another. Some trees have more than half a million leaves. Together, they have a huge surface for catching the light.

Seen from above, Mahonia leaves fan out to catch the light.

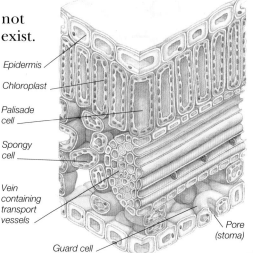

Waterproof top surface of leaf

Epidermis

Chloroplast

Palisade cell

Spongy cell

Vein containing transport vessels

Guard cell

Pore (stoma)

STRUCTURE OF A LEAF

Leaves are made up of several different types of cell. At the top is a protective layer of transparent cells called the epidermis. Below this is a layer of tall palisade cells packed with green chloroplasts, which carry out photosynthesis. Beneath the palisade cells are loosely arranged spongy cells, surrounded by air spaces connected to pores on the underside of the leaf. Transport vessels in the veins take water to the leaf's cells and carry away glucose.

Membrane

CHLOROPLASTS

Photosynthesis takes place in tiny structures called chloroplasts. These contain stacks of membranes that work like solar panels. Chlorophyll is stored on the surface of the membranes, and as sunlight shines through the leaf, the chlorophyll captures its energy.

CHLOROPHYLL

Plants contain a green pigment (colored chemical) called chlorophyll. This pigment is essential in photosynthesis. It absorbs the energy in sunlight and converts it into chemical energy. Not all the light energy is absorbed, however. Although sunlight consists of a mixture of different colors, chlorophyll mostly absorbs red and blue light. Green light is reflected, which is why our eyes see plants as green.

Purified chlorophyll

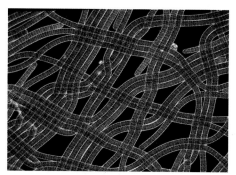

Strands of the cyanobacterium Oscillatoria

PHOTOSYNTHETIC BACTERIA

Plants are not the only living things that carry out photosynthesis. Many bacteria make their food this way, and have done so for much longer than plants. The most important of these simple life forms are called cyanobacteria. The chloroplasts in plants evolved from bacteria-like organisms millions of years ago.

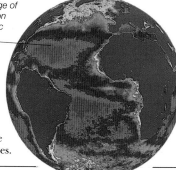

Satellite image of phytoplankton in the Atlantic Ocean

PHOTOSYNTHESIS IN THE SEAS

Cyanobacteria and microscopic algae in the sea make up a mass of drifting life, called phytoplankton, which provides food for nearly all sea animals. This satellite image shows vast quantities of phytoplankton in the Atlantic Ocean. The areas with the most phytoplankton are red or yellow, while those with the least are pink. Phytoplankton grow best in the nutrient-rich waters near coasts and the Poles.

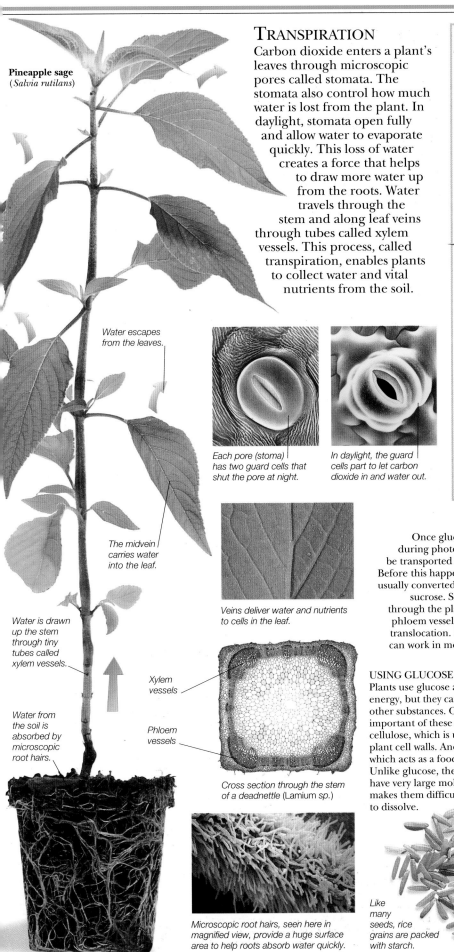

Pineapple sage
(*Salvia rutilans*)

TRANSPIRATION

Carbon dioxide enters a plant's leaves through microscopic pores called stomata. The stomata also control how much water is lost from the plant. In daylight, stomata open fully and allow water to evaporate quickly. This loss of water creates a force that helps to draw more water up from the roots. Water travels through the stem and along leaf veins through tubes called xylem vessels. This process, called transpiration, enables plants to collect water and vital nutrients from the soil.

Water escapes from the leaves.

Each pore (stoma) has two guard cells that shut the pore at night.

In daylight, the guard cells part to let carbon dioxide in and water out.

The midvein carries water into the leaf.

Veins deliver water and nutrients to cells in the leaf.

Water is drawn up the stem through tiny tubes called xylem vessels.

Xylem vessels

Phloem vessels

Water from the soil is absorbed by microscopic root hairs.

Cross section through the stem of a deadnettle (Lamium sp.)

Microscopic root hairs, seen here in magnified view, provide a huge surface area to help roots absorb water quickly.

FEROCACTUS

Like most cacti, this plant has spines instead of leaves, and carries out photosynthesis in its barrel-shaped stem. It opens its pores (stomata) only at night when the air is cooler, and stores carbon dioxide for use during the day. This helps to reduce the amount of water it loses through transpiration during the heat of the day.

Scientific name: *Ferocactus wislizenii*

Size: Grows into a column up to 7 ft (2 m) tall

Habitat: Desert

Distribution: North and Central America

Reproduction: Red or yellow flowers appear on the crown, eventually producing sticky yellow berries

TRANSLOCATION

Once glucose has been made during photosynthesis, it has to be transported around the plant. Before this happens, the glucose is usually converted into a sugar called sucrose. Sucrose is then moved through the plant in cells arranged in phloem vessels. This process is called translocation. Unlike transpiration, it can work in more than one direction.

USING GLUCOSE

Plants use glucose as a source of energy, but they can also turn it into other substances. One of the most important of these substances is cellulose, which is used to build plant cell walls. Another is starch, which acts as a food store in seeds. Unlike glucose, these substances have very large molecules, which makes them difficult to dissolve.

Like many seeds, rice grains are packed with starch.

Sucrose is carried to the main root of a carrot plant to be stored.

In spring, sucrose is carried back up to help new leaves grow.

Find out more

CARNIVOROUS PLANTS: *138*
FEEDING AND NUTRITION: *22*
FOOD CHAINS AND WEBS: *66*
PLANTS: *116*

RESPIRATION

MOST LIVING THINGS NEED a supply of oxygen to stay alive. Land animals generally breathe in oxygen from the surrounding air and, like all animals, use it to release energy inside their cells. As they do this, they produce a gas called carbon dioxide, which they have to get rid of. This whole process – including the part that happens inside cells – is called respiration. For very small organisms, such as flatworms, getting enough oxygen is not a problem. It simply flows through their outer surface and then spreads to where it is needed. Bigger organisms, including mammals, use special respiratory organs, such as lungs, to obtain the oxygen they need.

Thick-walled arteries carry blood away from the heart.

The heart pumps blood throughout the body.

Thin-walled veins carry blood back to the heart.

CIRCULATION

Blood is a liquid delivery system. It circulates around the body, carrying oxygen to where it is needed and taking away carbon dioxide waste. Blood also carries out other tasks, such as delivering food to cells, spreading heat, and fending off attacking micro-organisms. In simple animals, blood travels through open spaces in the body, but in vertebrates, such as horses, it travels in tubes called blood vessels. The beating of a vertebrate's heart pumps the blood through its blood vessels.

BREATHING

On land, most large animals get oxygen from the air with the help of lungs. In chimpanzees and other mammals, each lung contains thousands of branching air tubes that lead to tiny air sacs called alveoli. The alveoli are surrounded by blood vessels and have very thin linings so that oxygen can flow through them and into the blood. After most of the oxygen has been absorbed, the chimp exhales the stale air and breathes in again.

Air flows in through the mouth and nostrils.

The air flows down smaller and smaller airways until it reaches tiny air sacs.

Oxygen flows through the lining of the air sacs and into the blood.

Each lung consists of several overlapping segments called lobes.

Red blood cells seen through an electron microscope.

BLOOD AND OXYGEN

Blood gets its color from chemicals called pigments. A blood pigment collects oxygen in lungs or gills and then carries it around the body to where it is in short supply. In invertebrates, such as crustaceans, blood pigments are often dissolved in the blood itself, but in vertebrates they are concentrated in coin-shaped red blood cells. These contain a bright red pigment called hemoglobin.

BREATHING UNDERWATER

Water does not contain as much oxygen as air, but there is still enough for animals to use. Some aquatic animals such as fish get their oxygen through stacks of thin flaps called gills. Instead of breathing in and out, fish pump water over the gills in a one-way flow. Fish gills do not work in air because the flaps collapse and stick together.

Gills contain thousands of flaps that absorb oxygen from water.

Air flows around a locust's body in tubes called tracheae.

Flexible air sacs help pump the air along.

Air enters through holes called spiracles.

HOW INSECTS BREATHE

Insects are small but often highly active, so they need a lot of oxygen. Instead of using lungs, they collect air through a network of microscopic air pipes called tracheae. An insect's tracheae lead into its body through openings called spiracles. The tracheae divide many times, forming branches that reach individual cells. Some insects also have air sacs that help to control air flow.

Comet goldfish
(*Carassius auratus*)

Water escapes from behind gill cover.

Water flows in through the fish's mouth.

Muscles in the mouth and gills pump water through the gill chamber.

ENERGY FROM FOOD

Food contains energy that is locked up in chemical form. To release this energy, animals use oxygen to break up the food's chemical bonds. This is part of respiration. This process works somewhat like burning, because burning something also uses oxygen. However, burning is very rapid, and it releases a dangerous amount of heat. Respiration works more gradually and releases energy in a form that can be used.

Burning releases energy in a sudden and uncontrolled way.

During respiration, food energy is released gradually.

MOTTLED FLATWORM

This brightly colored marine flatworm can swim as well as crawl, so it needs a good supply of oxygen to power its muscles. However, because it is flat and thin it has no need for special respiratory organs – it simply absorbs all the oxygen it needs directly through its skin.

Marine flatworms swim by rippling their sides.

Scientific name: *Pseudoceros reticulatus*

Size: Average 1.4 in (3.5 cm) long, 0.8 in (2 cm) wide

Habitat: The seabed in tropical oceans

Distribution: Indian and Pacific Oceans

Reproduction: Hermaphrodite; lays eggs after mating

Diet: Smaller animals and dead bodies on sea floor

POWER FOR LIFE

For a young puma cub, taking a breath is only the first step in respiration. A much more important step takes place inside its body cells, once oxygen has been delivered. Each of the puma's cells contains mitochondria – microscopic power stations that use oxygen to break down glucose, a chemical fuel obtained from food. Once glucose has been broken down, the energy that is released enables the puma's young body to work.

Energy is released in muscles when a puma moves.

Respiration provides the energy needed to run.

Puma
(Felis concolor)

Day   **Night**

Leaves take in carbon dioxide from the air and use it to make glucose during photosynthesis.

Leaves give off carbon dioxide, a waste product of respiration.

Leaves give off oxygen, a waste product of photosynthesis.

Leaves take in oxygen and use it for respiration.

RESPIRATION IN PLANTS

Although plants cannot breathe, they still have to take in gases from their surroundings. In daylight, a plant uses the Sun's energy to make glucose by a process called photosynthesis. During photosynthesis, the plant's leaves absorb carbon dioxide from the air and give off oxygen as a waste product. At night, photosynthesis stops but respiration (which takes place all the time) continues. During respiration, the plant absorbs oxygen from the air and gives off carbon dioxide.

SURVIVING WITHOUT OXYGEN

Most living things need oxygen for respiration, although they can manage without for short periods. But some forms of life, including yeast and bacteria, are able to respire without using oxygen at all. This is called anaerobic respiration, which means respiration without air. Anaerobic respiration does not release much energy, but it is enough to keep these small organisms alive.

Wine is made by yeasts that live by anaerobic respiration.

Find out more		
BIRDS: *208*		
FISH: *184*		
PHOTOSYNTHESIS: *24*		
WORMS: *144*		

REPRODUCTION

REPRODUCTION IS THE MOST important process in nature – without it, life on Earth would soon grind to a halt. Every animal, plant, and microbe struggles throughout its life to produce offspring, and to give its young the best possible chance of survival. Many parents die as soon as they have achieved this goal. The rate at which living things reproduce varies enormously. A whale may have less than a dozen calves during its lifetime, while a cod may produce millions of offspring. However, animals or plants that reproduce in great numbers face an intense struggle for survival. Only a tiny proportion of their young live long enough to have offspring of their own.

THE NEXT GENERATION
For these newly hatched spiders, life is full of danger – very few will live long enough to have young of their own. The constant struggle for survival actually helps organisms adapt to the world around them. Although many perish, the ones that do survive pass on their successful genes to future generations. This allows species to change, or evolve, over a period of time.

Ball of eggs held in mother's jaws

Young spiderlings hatching from eggs

Daddy-long-legs spider (*Pholcus* sp.)

Strawberry plant growing from a runner

Strawberry (*Fragaria* sp.)

Runner

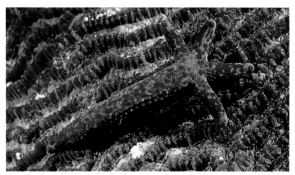
A new starfish growing from a broken arm

ASEXUAL REPRODUCTION
Asexual reproduction is the simplest form of reproduction because only one parent is needed. The parent may split into two, or a part of its body may break off and take up life on its own. With no need for courtship or mating, asexual reproduction is quick and efficient. However, it has a major drawback – the offspring are nearly always identical to the parent, so all share the same weaknesses.

VEGETATIVE REPRODUCTION
Plants often reproduce asexually using a process called vegetative reproduction – new roots and shoots grow from special extensions of the parent plant. Strawberries, for example, send out horizontal stems called runners, which take root at a distance to produce small plantlets. Quaking aspen trees (*Populus tremuloides*) can produce new trees from their roots – in some places, whole forests have grown from a single plant.

Prickly pear (*Opuntia ficus-indica*)

New cactus stems grow upward from broken fragments on the ground.

DIVIDING IN TWO
The simplest form of asexual reproduction is known as fission. The "mother" splits in half to form two "daughters." Fission is very common in single-celled organisms, such as bacteria and amoebas, but it is rarer in more complicated forms of life. Animals that can reproduce in this way include flatworms and sea anemones.

A sea anemone (Anemonia viridis) dividing into two "daughters"

SPROUTING STEMS
Some cacti, such as prickly pears, have flattened stems that snap off easily if they are touched. When part of a stem falls to the ground, it grows roots and develops into a new plant. Cacti are able to do this because their stems hold a large amount of water. This store of water keeps the stem alive until its new roots can absorb water from the ground.

SEXUAL REPRODUCTION

Sexual reproduction involves a male and a female parent. Each makes special sex cells – the father makes sperm cells and the mother makes egg cells. A sperm cell must fertilize (fuse with) an egg cell in order to produce a new individual. Sexual reproduction is more complicated than asexual reproduction, but the offspring are unique and have different strengths. This enables the population to adapt to the ever-changing world.

All the kittens in this litter are slightly different.

INTERNAL FERTILIZATION

Fertilization is more difficult on land than in water because sex cells quickly dry out and die in the open air. Like most land animals, these shield bugs get around the problem by using internal fertilization. The male injects his sperm cells directly into the female's body, and fertilization takes place inside her. Animals that use internal fertilization have to find a partner and mate.

A female giant clam releasing egg cells

EXTERNAL FERTILIZATION

Most aquatic animals reproduce by external fertilization – they release sperm and egg cells into the water around them and allow the sex cells to fuse outside the parents' bodies. Female giant clams (*Tridacna gigas*) blow spectacular clouds of egg cells into the open sea. The males have to release sperm cells at exactly the same time as the females release eggs so that fertilization can occur.

The male injects sperm into the female to fertilize her eggs.

Female shield bug

Both partners keep still to avoid being seen by predators.

Male shield bug

Green shield bug (*Palomena prasina*)

Female aphids produce identical daughters from unfertilized eggs.

Rose aphid (*Macrosiphum rosae*)

MEXICAN HAT PLANT

This common houseplant has an unusual way of reproducing. In addition to producing flowers and seeds, it develops tiny buds, or plantlets, along its leaf edges. Each bud is a miniature plant with rootlets. Eventually, the plantlets fall off and start to grow as soon as they reach the ground.

Plantlets fall to the ground.

Roots and leaves grow.

Scientific name: *Kalanchoe daigremontiana*

Size: Up to 3 ft 3 in (1 m) high

Habitat: Dry, rocky places

Distribution: Madagascar

Reproduction: By seeds and by plantlets dropped from leaves

FERTILIZATION IN PLANTS

Most plants reproduce by producing sex cells that can spread far and wide. In flowering plants, the male cells are packaged up in tiny pollen grains. These are transferred from one plant to another by animals such as bees, or by wind or water. This process is known as pollination. When the pollen grain reaches the right species of flower, it fertilizes a female egg cell to produce a seed.

Pollen grains

Meadow cranesbill (*Geranium pratense*)

Monkey plant (*Ruellia grandiflora*)

Thesium (*Thesium alpinum*)

BEST OF BOTH WORLDS

Some organisms use both asexual and sexual reproduction. Aphids multiply rapidly because they can reproduce without mating. During spring and summer, when there is plenty of food, unmated females give birth several times a day to identical daughters. In fall, when the food begins to run out, aphids give birth to males and egg-laying females. After mating, the females lay eggs that survive the winter.

Find out more

AMPHIBIANS: *192*

EVOLUTION: *14*

FLOWERS AND SEEDS: *128*

GROWTH AND DEVELOPMENT: *32*

COURTSHIP, MATING, AND PARENTAL CARE

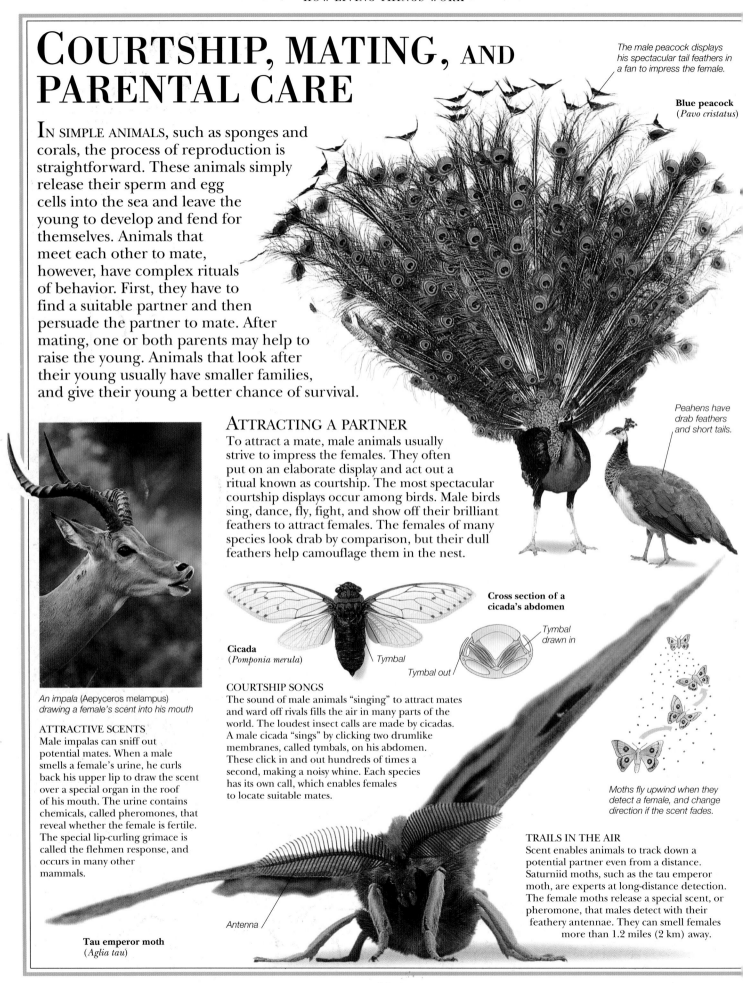

The male peacock displays his spectacular tail feathers in a fan to impress the female.

Blue peacock
(*Pavo cristatus*)

IN SIMPLE ANIMALS, such as sponges and corals, the process of reproduction is straightforward. These animals simply release their sperm and egg cells into the sea and leave the young to develop and fend for themselves. Animals that meet each other to mate, however, have complex rituals of behavior. First, they have to find a suitable partner and then persuade the partner to mate. After mating, one or both parents may help to raise the young. Animals that look after their young usually have smaller families, and give their young a better chance of survival.

Peahens have drab feathers and short tails.

ATTRACTING A PARTNER

To attract a mate, male animals usually strive to impress the females. They often put on an elaborate display and act out a ritual known as courtship. The most spectacular courtship displays occur among birds. Male birds sing, dance, fly, fight, and show off their brilliant feathers to attract females. The females of many species look drab by comparison, but their dull feathers help camouflage them in the nest.

An impala (*Aepyceros melampus*) drawing a female's scent into his mouth

ATTRACTIVE SCENTS

Male impalas can sniff out potential mates. When a male smells a female's urine, he curls back his upper lip to draw the scent over a special organ in the roof of his mouth. The urine contains chemicals, called pheromones, that reveal whether the female is fertile. The special lip-curling grimace is called the flehmen response, and occurs in many other mammals.

Cicada
(*Pomponia merula*)

Tymbal

Cross section of a cicada's abdomen

Tymbal drawn in

Tymbal out

COURTSHIP SONGS

The sound of male animals "singing" to attract mates and ward off rivals fills the air in many parts of the world. The loudest insect calls are made by cicadas. A male cicada "sings" by clicking two drumlike membranes, called tymbals, on his abdomen. These click in and out hundreds of times a second, making a noisy whine. Each species has its own call, which enables females to locate suitable mates.

Moths fly upwind when they detect a female, and change direction if the scent fades.

TRAILS IN THE AIR

Scent enables animals to track down a potential partner even from a distance. Saturniid moths, such as the tau emperor moth, are experts at long-distance detection. The female moths release a special scent, or pheromone, that males detect with their feathery antennae. They can smell females more than 1.2 miles (2 km) away.

Antenna

Tau emperor moth
(*Aglia tau*)

MATING

Female animals are often wary of males and may fight off any suitors that come too close. But when a female has chosen her partner and is ready to breed, her behavior changes. She signals that she is ready to mate and the male quickly responds. Female baboons show they are ready to mate by displaying bright red patches of skin on their behinds. These last about three weeks but fade at the end of the breeding season.

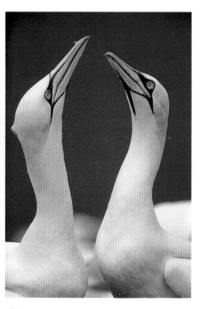

Hamadryas baboons (Papio hamadryas) mating

SUSPENDED SLUGS

Great gray slugs mate by twisting around each other and hanging upside down on a rope of slime. Unlike most animals, slugs are hermaphrodites – each has both male and female reproductive organs. During mating, their reproductive organs entwine and exchange sperm. Afterward, the slugs climb back up the rope of slime (which one of them eats) and crawl away. Both slugs will later lay eggs.

Rope of slime

Great gray slug (Limax maximus)

Mating slugs secrete large amounts of slime.

The slugs' reproductive organs entwine and exchange sperm.

Courting gannets (Sula bassana) raising their beaks to greet each other

STAYING TOGETHER

Many animals part company after mating, but some stay together for a long time – even for life. Gannets form lifelong partnerships and use special ceremonies to strengthen the bond between them. When a pair meet, they greet each other by stretching upward and rubbing their beaks together. Gannets nest in crowded colonies by the sea. Males and females work together to raise their young.

The tiny male angler fish lives permanently attached to his mate's body. The female's skin grows over him.

Deep-sea anglerfish (*Edriolychnus schmidti*)

BLUE-FOOTED BOOBY

This fish-eating seabird has drab plumage but bright blue feet. During his courtship display, the male raises his tail and parades in front of the female, lifting his feet as high as he can with each step. This march persuades the female to mate.

Boobies also use their large feet to keep their eggs warm.

Scientific name: *Sula nebouxii*

Size: 31 in (80 cm)

Habitat: Coasts

Distribution: Western coast of American Tropics

Reproduction: Females lay a pair of eggs each year

Diet: Boobies dive into shallow seas for fish

PARENTAL CARE

Animals that produce thousands of offspring usually take no part in looking after them. Those that have fewer babies often help them through the dangerous early days of life. These parents protect and feed their young, and teach them the skills needed to survive. Some parents use their bodies as a living home – marsupials carry babies in special pouches, and mouth-brooding cichlid fish shelter young in their mouths.

Orangutan (*Pongo pygmaeus*)

Young orangutans stay with their mothers for at least three years.

PERMANENT PARTNERS

In the blackness of the deep sea, males and females have difficulty finding each other. Anglerfish have a remarkable solution to this problem. The male is much smaller than the female, and when he locates a partner, he locks his jaws onto her skin. A female may collect several males, which live permanently attached to her body.

Find out more

BUTTERFLIES AND MOTHS: *176*

FROGS AND TOADS: *196*

MARSUPIALS: *236*

REPRODUCTION: *28*

GROWTH AND DEVELOPMENT

MOST LIVING THINGS begin life as a single cell no bigger than a period. The cell soon divides to become two cells, then four, eight, and so on, until a tiny body (an embryo) starts to take shape. As time passes, the embryo grows. At the same time, it changes shape and becomes more complicated (develops). In this way, the original cell can grow and develop into a giraffe, a lobster, or a tree. Some living things, such as trees and crocodiles, grow throughout their lives. Others, including humans and butterflies, stop growing when they become adults.

Newborn foal

TAKING SHAPE

Most baby mammals develop while floating in a bag of liquid inside the mother's body. The baby obtains food through a tube called the umbilical cord. At first, the baby is called an embryo, and later it is called a fetus. A baby horse takes about 11 months to develop inside its mother. When the foal is born, it is big enough to walk and follow its mother, but it continues to grow and develop for another five years.

Development of a horse fetus
(*Equus caballus*)

Umbilical cord Fluid-filled bag Hooves form Mane grows Full coat grows Fetus changes position ready for birth.

2 months **4 months** **8 months** **10 months** **11 months**

GERMINATION

A plant seed contains a tiny embryo with its own supply of food. When conditions outside are right, the embryo suddenly starts to grow, and the seed germinates. At first, the young plant grows using its food supply and water from the soil. Once its leaves have opened, it makes food from sunlight by photosynthesis. A beechnut takes just a day or so to germinate, but years to grow into a mature tree.

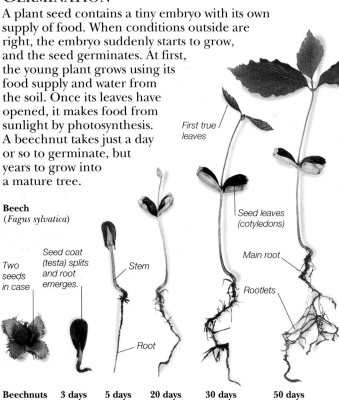

First true leaves

Beech
(*Fagus sylvatica*)

Two seeds in case

Seed coat (testa) splits and root emerges.

Stem

Root

Seed leaves (cotyledons)

Main root

Rootlets

Beechnuts **3 days** **5 days** **20 days** **30 days** **50 days**

GROWING UP

Mammals not only get larger as they grow up, they also change shape. A fox cub starts life with a large head, small ears, and short legs. At first it cannot see, hear, or walk. It has a short snout to make it easier to suck milk from its mother's teats, and rolls of puppy fat keep it warm and provide a store of nutrients. As it grows, its ears and legs get proportionally longer, its snout lengthens, and the puppy fat gets used up.

Newborn fox cub **2 weeks** **4 weeks**

SHAPED BY ITS SURROUNDINGS

Plants grow in a different way from animals, and their shape is affected much more by their surroundings. This hawthorn tree (*Crataegus monogyna*) has grown by the sea, and has developed a lopsided shape because of the wind. The wind and salt spray kill buds facing the sea, so most growth occurs in the opposite direction.

Hawthorn tree shaped by the wind

GROWING OLD

Apart from single-celled organisms, all living things eventually grow old and die. Mayflies survive as adults for only a day or so, while giant tortoises may live for over a century. But compared to some plants, even giant tortoises have short lifespans – the world's oldest tree, a bristlecone pine, is approximately 4,900 years old.

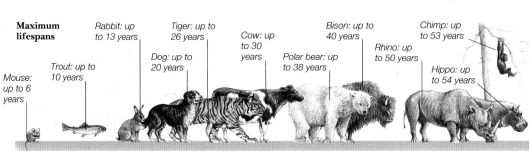

Maximum lifespans

Mouse: up to 6 years

Trout: up to 10 years

Rabbit: up to 13 years

Dog: up to 20 years

Tiger: up to 26 years

Cow: up to 30 years

Polar bear: up to 38 years

Bison: up to 40 years

Rhino: up to 50 years

Chimp: up to 53 years

Hippo: up to 54 years

METAMORPHOSIS

Some animals – such as frogs, crabs, and many insects – do not become adults simply by growing larger. Instead, their bodies are transformed by a process called metamorphosis. A newly hatched mealworm beetle, for example, has a wormlike body with no wings, and is called a larva. The larva eats voraciously, shedding its skin as it grows. Eventually, it stops eating, turns into a hard-cased pupa, and lies dormant while its body is broken down and rebuilt. After several weeks, the pupa splits and an adult emerges.

Mealworm beetle
(*Tenebrio molitor*)

The larva has a wormlike body.

The larva stops moving and turns into a pupa.

Several weeks later, an adult beetle crawls out of the pupal case. It looks very different from the larva.

CHAMBERED NAUTILUS

This unusual sea-dwelling mollusk uses its shell to control its buoyancy. As it grows, it adds a new chamber to its shell. The new chamber is filled with fluid that is gradually absorbed and replaced by gas. An opening in each chamber allows the animal to control the amount of gas inside.

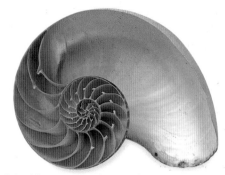

Scientific name: *Nautilus pompilius*

Size: About 8 in (20 cm) across

Habitat: Seas down to about 1,640 ft (500 m)

Distribution: Indian and Pacific Oceans

Reproduction: Females fasten egg capsules onto rocks

Diet: Fish and crabs

Growth of a red fox
(*Vulpes vulpes*)

Ears grow longer and more pointed.

At six weeks old, the fox cub is alert and inquisitive.

6 weeks   **8 weeks**   **10 weeks**

SKELETONS AND CASES

When an animal grows, its skeleton must grow as well. Animals such as insects and crabs have rigid outer body cases called exoskeletons, which cannot expand. In order to grow, these animals periodically shed their body cases. The soft skin underneath then quickly expands and hardens to form a new, larger exoskeleton in place of the old one.

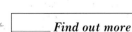

A locust wriggles out of its old body case.

REGROWING LOST PARTS

If a crab loses its claw, a new claw slowly grows in its place. This is an example of regeneration – a special kind of growth that is triggered by an injury. The animal with the most remarkable powers of regeneration is the sponge. A sponge can be broken into hundreds of tiny fragments, each of which will survive and grow into a new sponge.

A new claw grows in place of the old one.

Shore crab
(*Carcinus maenas*)

Giant sequoia: up to 4,000 years

Bristlecone pine: up to 5,000 years

Indian elephant: up to 77 years

Olive tree: 3,000 years or more

Eagle owl: up to 68 years

Dolphin: up to 65 years

Giant tortoise: up to 150 years

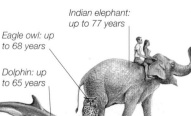

Find out more
AMPHIBIANS: *192*
CRUSTACEANS: *158*
INSECTS: *162*
REPRODUCTION: *28*

MOVEMENT ON LAND

ALMOST ALL LIVING THINGS can move some part of themselves. Plants turn their leaves and flowers to face the sun, and most animals can move their entire body, which allows them to travel from place to place. The way an animal moves depends on its shape, surroundings, and size. The slowest land animals move by creeping or crawling, and keep a large part of their body in contact with the surface. The fastest move on long legs which propel them farther forward with each stride.

Domestic horse
(*Equus caballus*)

MUSCLES

Muscles provide the power that allows animals to move. Each muscle consists of bundles of cells that contain microscopic chemical filaments (threads). When a nerve triggers a muscle into action, the filaments slide past each other, making the muscle contract. In order to work, muscles must have something to pull against. In vertebrates, such as the horse, the muscles pull against bones. The area where different bones meet is called a joint. Bones in the joints are covered by smooth cartilage so that they can move against each other easily.

When a muscle contracts, its filaments slide past each other like interlocking fingers.

Muscles are attached to bones by tough cords called tendons.

Joints allow the leg to bend.

Muscles inside exoskeleton of leg

Cross section of an insect's leg joint

Flexible area allows segments of leg to hinge against each other.

EXOSKELETONS
Unlike vertebrates, spiders and other arthropods have a hard skeleton on the outside of their bodies. Their legs are like rows of tubes with muscles hidden inside. For their size, arthropods are often fast runners. Although their bodies are encased in a rigid exoskeleton, flexible leg joints allow them to move freely.

FUELED BY FOOD

Horses travel using four main patterns of leg movements – the walk, trot, canter, and gallop. About 60 percent of a horse's weight is made up of muscle. Like all animals, it needs two substances to make its muscles work. One is a chemical fuel – usually glucose – which it gets from food, the other is oxygen, which it gets from the air. The horse's muscle cells use oxygen to break down the fuel. This releases energy, which makes the muscle cells contract.

Cheetah
(*Acinonyx jubatus*)

Hairy-nosed wombat
(*Lasiorhinus latifrons*)

The legs of fast-running animals are light for fast movement.

ANIMAL LEVERS
Legs work like levers – when the legs push backward, the animal moves forward. In fast-moving animals such as cheetahs, long legs produce a large amount of leverage, which propels the animal across the ground. In slow-moving, burrowing animals, such as the hairy-nosed wombat, the legs do not move as far with each stride, but they are more stocky and powerful.

CREEPING AND CRAWLING

Slugs and snails creep over the ground on a flat, singular foot that works like a sucker. The foot is made of muscle that contracts in waves, running from the rear to the front. The foot always remains in contact with the ground – this keeps the animal stable but also limits its speed. Slugs and snails secrete a slimy mucus that helps them slide over rough surfaces.

Slimy mucus smooths the path of the Roman snail (Helix pomatia) over the ground.

LOOPING AHEAD

"Looping" is a method of movement used by some caterpillars and leeches. Caterpillars of the Geometridae family are often called looping caterpillars or inchworms because they loop their bodies as they inch forward. A looping caterpillar firmly anchors its rear end with its claspers and then reaches forward as far as it can. Next it anchors its front end and pulls its rear end up to form a loop.

Looping caterpillars have no legs in the middle part of the body.

Clasper

Legs

A long, flexible backbone helps give the horse a big stride.

Horse galloping

All four legs off the ground

A millipede has two pairs of legs on each body segment.

Each leg is slightly out of step with the ones in front and back.

LOTS OF LEGS

The largest land animals have four legs, while the smallest can have six, eight, or in the case of a millipede, more than a hundred. All animals need to be carefully coordinated when they walk or run. A millipede moves its legs in waves, which prevents each one from colliding with those in front or behind. It uses large numbers of short legs to force its way through soil.

Western gray kangaroo
(*Macropus fuliginosus*)

Kangaroo pushes off the ground with large back feet.

JUMPING

Animals that jump use their legs to catapult themselves into the air. The most successful jumpers, such as kangaroos, store energy in their elastic tendons every time they hit the ground. This energy helps the animal make its next leap. Fleas store energy in pads of an elastic substance called resilin. When the resilin is allowed to expand, it suddenly flicks the flea's back legs. The result is a giant jump.

STANDING UPRIGHT

Apart from humans and flightless birds, few animals walk on two legs regularly. Some animals, such as the basilisk lizard (*Basilicus plumifrons*), run on their back legs when they need to make a quick escape. Verreaux's sifaka, a type of lemur, spends most of its life in the trees, but descends to the ground to feed, where it moves on two legs by hopping and leaping.

Verreaux's sifaka
(*Propithecus verreauxi*)

Diagonally opposite feet move together.

Cockroach
(*Periplaneta americana*)
3.3 mph (5.3 kmh)

Spiny-tailed iguana
(*Ctenosaura* sp.)
21.7 mph (35 kmh)

Ostrich
(*Struthio camelus*)
45 mph (72 kmh)

Pronghorn antelope
(*Antilocapra americana*)
55 mph (88 kmh)

Cheetah
(*Acinonyx jubatus*)
62 mph (100 kmh)

AMPHIBIANS

Amphibians are adapted for moving both on land and in water. The powerful back legs of frogs and toads enable them to hop or crawl on land and propel themselves forward when swimming. Salamanders walk by moving diagonally opposite feet forward at the same time. The other two feet remain in the same position on the ground, pushing the body forward, ready for the next step.

Tail helps salamander to balance.

TOP SPEEDS

An animal's top speed is affected by its body size, the shape of its legs, and the way its muscles work. Small animals, such as cockroaches and crabs, can accelerate quickly from a standing start. Larger animals take longer to get up speed, but can move much faster. The cheetah is the fastest animal on land over short distances. The pronghorn antelope can maintain a high speed over longer distances.

With its front legs firmly locked in place, it pulls its rear end up.

The caterpillar's body stretches out again.

Find out more
ARTHROPODS: *156*
FLIGHTLESS BIRDS: *210*
HORSES, ASSES, AND ZEBRAS: *268*
RESPIRATION: *26*

MOVEMENT IN AIR

ALTHOUGH A THOUSAND TIMES lighter than water, air can help support living things as they move. The smallest living objects, such as bacteria and plant spores, are so light that they can be blown long distances before gravity pulls them down to Earth. Larger organisms fall more quickly and need special adaptations to stay aloft. Some animals can glide for short distances on fins or flaps of skin, but animals with wings (such as birds, bats, and insects) can remain airborne for long periods. These animals often use flight to hunt in midair, escape from predators, or migrate to other habitats.

A buteo's flight feathers splay out like fingers at the tips of its wings.

POWERED FLIGHT

Of all animals capable of powered flight, birds fly the fastest and farthest. Their wings are powered by large chest muscles attached to a projection of the breastbone, called a "keel." Small birds, such as finches, fly almost entirely by flapping their wings. Large birds, such as eagles or buteos, often save energy by gliding. Various species of swift and swallow are such good fliers they can stay airborne for up to two years.

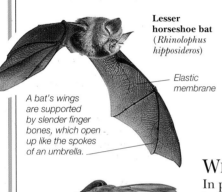

Lesser horseshoe bat
(*Rhinolophus hipposideros*)

Elastic membrane

A bat's wings are supported by slender finger bones, which open up like the spokes of an umbrella.

WINGS

In prehistoric times, huge flying reptiles dominated the skies, but today, insects, birds, and bats are the only animals capable of powered flight. The wings of flying animals are very varied. Birds' wings consist of forelimbs hidden by their feathers, whereas bats have modified, elongated hands covered with an elastic membrane of skin. Insects have one or two pairs of wings formed from their hard body covering. Their wing muscles are inside the middle part of the body (the thorax).

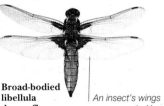

Rock dove
(*Columba livia*)

Birds adjust the shape of their wings to alter their speed and direction.

Broad-bodied libellula dragonfly
(*Libellula depressa*)

An insect's wings are supported by a network of thickened veins.

The power comes from the breast muscles.

Red-tailed hawk
(*Buteo jamaicensis*)

1. Air flowing above the wing travels farther than air flowing beneath it.

2. This difference in air flow produces an upward force called lift.

3. Lift helps to counteract the downward force of gravity, keeping the bird in the air.

SLICING THROUGH THE AIR

Birds' wings work partly by pushing air downward and backward when they flap, and partly by generating a force called lift. A wing produces lift because it has a curved cross section called an airfoil. As the bird flies, the air pressure above the wing drops. As a result, lift sucks the wing upward, helping counteract the downward force of gravity.

INSECT FLIGHT

Insects' wings are very flexible. They work like propellers, pushing air downward and backward, in a figure eight, to speed the insect along. Most insects have two pairs of wings, which either beat together or in opposite directions. In beetles, such as the cockchafer, the rigid forewings provide lift but do not beat.

Forewings are raised during flight, providing lift.

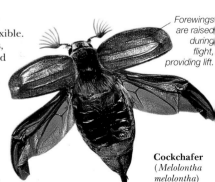

Cockchafer
(*Melolontha melolontha*)

HOVERING

Hovering fliers include kestrels, hummingbirds, pollen-eating bats, and many insects. Kestrels often need a headwind to help them stay in one place. Hovering in midair uses up a large amount of energy because the wing muscles have to beat very quickly. In order to produce this energy, the diet of hovering animals is often high in carbohydrates.

Long-tongued bat (*Leptonycteris curasoae*)

A soaring bird flies in a spiral, and is carried upward by the rising air.

Sugar glider
(*Petaurus breviceps*)

GLIDING AND SOARING

Gliding animals rarely flap their wings, but stretch them out to slow their fall. Most of them cannot travel far, and land a few seconds after takeoff. Soaring birds, such as eagles, float upward on thermals (columns of warm rising air). When they reach the top of one thermal, they descend to the next. They often repeat this cycle several times before they land.

A streamlined shape minimizes drag, or friction, with the air.

When the wing pushes down, the buteo's body is lifted up.

As the bird flaps its wings, the inner part of the wing provides most of the lift, and the outer part provides most of the power.

GLIDERS

Most of the world's gliding mammals live in forests, and glide from tree to tree on flaps of elastic skin. This sugar glider lives in the forests of Australia. It can glide up to 165 ft (50 m) in a single jump. Although they cannot flap their "wings," many gliders can steer, which helps them to make a safe landing.

Large bird 16,400 ft (5,000 m)	
Small bird 6,560 ft (2,000 m)	
Small insect 500 ft (150 m)	
Bat 165 ft (50 m)	
Butterfly 82 ft (25 m)	

HIGH FLIERS

This chart shows the average altitudes reached by different animals. Some birds, such as geese and swifts, fly high when they migrate, but otherwise stay nearer to the ground. Insects usually stay close to the ground, but may be swept up high by strong winds. Aphids are sometimes swept several miles high during thunderstorms, but often perish in the process.

A lacewing can twist and turn in midair as it comes in to land.

Lacewings can take off vertically.

Fluffy coverings on milk thistle

Spiderling suspended on its thread

AIRBORNE DRIFTERS

The smallest airborne animals are so tiny that they cannot steer a course of their own. Instead they drift with the wind. These animals include thrips, aphids, and young spiders. Spiderlings (baby spiders) drift through the air by letting out a long loop of silk, which acts like a sail. The wind catches the silk, and the spiderling is whisked away.

SEED DISPERSAL

Bacteria, spores, and pollen grains can also travel through the air. They ride on the gentlest air currents. Spores are much lighter than seeds and can travel much farther. Seeds that are spread by the wind often have special "sails" or "parachutes" to help them stay airborne. Others, such as the milk thistle (*Silybum marianum*), have fluffy coverings to help them float.

Giant lacewing
(*Osmylus fulvicephalus*)

MANEUVERING

Small flying animals are usually more agile than large ones because they have a greater muscle power in relation to their weight. Houseflies, for instance, can land upsidedown, whereas swans need a long run-up to get airborne, and then land by splashing down in water. Insects such as lacewings can take off vertically and land on the narrow tips of plant stems.

Find out more

BIRDS: *208*
INSECTS: *162*
MIGRATION AND NAVIGATION: *46*
SWIFTS AND SWALLOWS: *226*

MOVEMENT IN WATER

LIFE FIRST APPEARED IN WATER millions of years ago. Today it is the natural habitat for a remarkable range of living things – from tiny single-celled amoebae to giant whales. Living things move through water in two main ways. Fish and other large animals use their muscles to propel themselves through water, but smaller forms of life often drift along, pushed either by the water or wind. Water is much more dense than air, which helps support an animal's weight, but also slows it down. Many aquatic creatures have a slippery surface and a streamlined shape, which make it easier to swim.

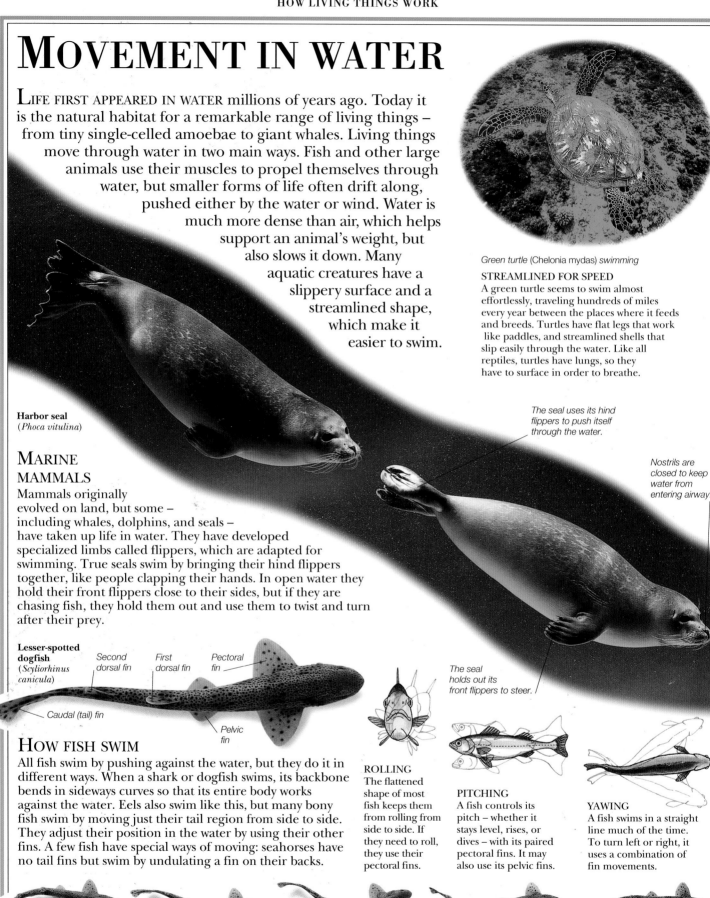

Green turtle (Chelonia mydas) swimming

STREAMLINED FOR SPEED
A green turtle seems to swim almost effortlessly, traveling hundreds of miles every year between the places where it feeds and breeds. Turtles have flat legs that work like paddles, and streamlined shells that slip easily through the water. Like all reptiles, turtles have lungs, so they have to surface in order to breathe.

Harbor seal
(*Phoca vitulina*)

The seal uses its hind flippers to push itself through the water.

Nostrils are closed to keep water from entering airway.

MARINE MAMMALS
Mammals originally evolved on land, but some – including whales, dolphins, and seals – have taken up life in water. They have developed specialized limbs called flippers, which are adapted for swimming. True seals swim by bringing their hind flippers together, like people clapping their hands. In open water they hold their front flippers close to their sides, but if they are chasing fish, they hold them out and use them to twist and turn after their prey.

The seal holds out its front flippers to steer.

Lesser-spotted dogfish
(*Scyliorhinus canicula*)

Second dorsal fin

First dorsal fin

Pectoral fin

Caudal (tail) fin

Pelvic fin

HOW FISH SWIM
All fish swim by pushing against the water, but they do it in different ways. When a shark or dogfish swims, its backbone bends in sideways curves so that its entire body works against the water. Eels also swim like this, but many bony fish swim by moving just their tail region from side to side. They adjust their position in the water by using their other fins. A few fish have special ways of moving: seahorses have no tail fins but swim by undulating a fin on their backs.

ROLLING
The flattened shape of most fish keeps them from rolling from side to side. If they need to roll, they use their pectoral fins.

PITCHING
A fish controls its pitch – whether it stays level, rises, or dives – with its paired pectoral fins. It may also use its pelvic fins.

YAWING
A fish swims in a straight line much of the time. To turn left or right, it uses a combination of fin movements.

A new curve begins as the dogfish swings its head slightly to the right.

The peak of the curve has passed along the body to between the pectoral and pelvic fins.

The curve has traveled to the region of the pelvic and first dorsal fins.

As the curve reaches the area between the two dorsal fins, the tail begins its right thrust.

This curve's peak reaches the tail. Meanwhile the head has begun another curve.

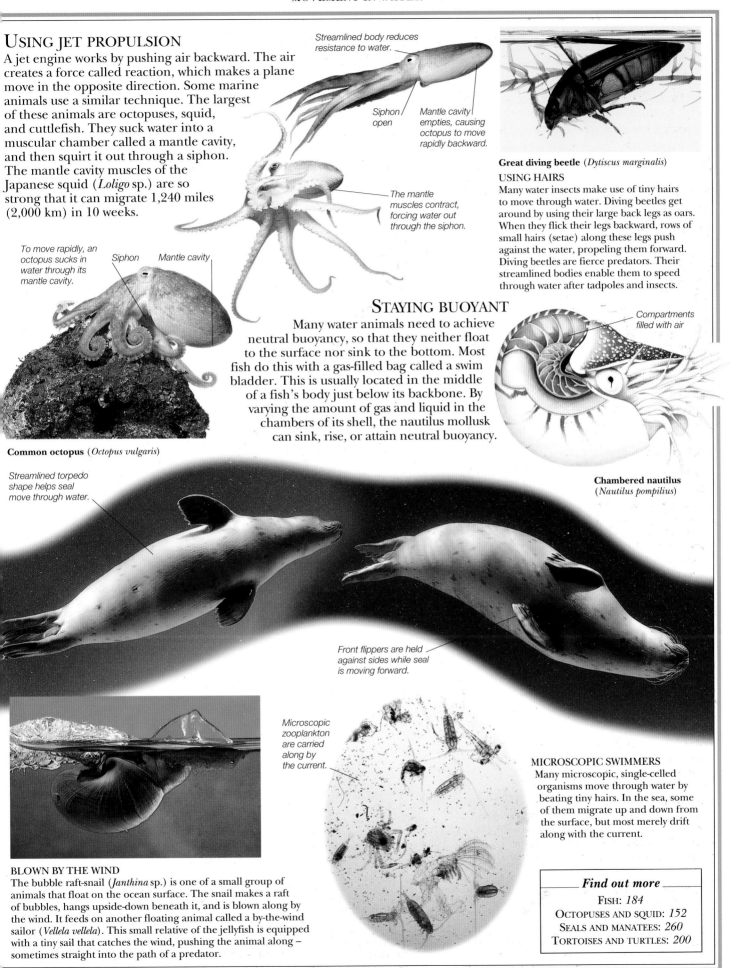

USING JET PROPULSION

A jet engine works by pushing air backward. The air creates a force called reaction, which makes a plane move in the opposite direction. Some marine animals use a similar technique. The largest of these animals are octopuses, squid, and cuttlefish. They suck water into a muscular chamber called a mantle cavity, and then squirt it out through a siphon. The mantle cavity muscles of the Japanese squid (*Loligo* sp.) are so strong that it can migrate 1,240 miles (2,000 km) in 10 weeks.

Streamlined body reduces resistance to water.

Siphon open

Mantle cavity empties, causing octopus to move rapidly backward.

The mantle muscles contract, forcing water out through the siphon.

To move rapidly, an octopus sucks in water through its mantle cavity.

Siphon

Mantle cavity

Common octopus (*Octopus vulgaris*)

Great diving beetle (*Dytiscus marginalis*)

USING HAIRS

Many water insects make use of tiny hairs to move through water. Diving beetles get around by using their large back legs as oars. When they flick their legs backward, rows of small hairs (setae) along these legs push against the water, propeling them forward. Diving beetles are fierce predators. Their streamlined bodies enable them to speed through water after tadpoles and insects.

STAYING BUOYANT

Many water animals need to achieve neutral buoyancy, so that they neither float to the surface nor sink to the bottom. Most fish do this with a gas-filled bag called a swim bladder. This is usually located in the middle of a fish's body just below its backbone. By varying the amount of gas and liquid in the chambers of its shell, the nautilus mollusk can sink, rise, or attain neutral buoyancy.

Compartments filled with air

Chambered nautilus (*Nautilus pompilius*)

Streamlined torpedo shape helps seal move through water.

Front flippers are held against sides while seal is moving forward.

Microscopic zooplankton are carried along by the current.

MICROSCOPIC SWIMMERS

Many microscopic, single-celled organisms move through water by beating tiny hairs. In the sea, some of them migrate up and down from the surface, but most merely drift along with the current.

BLOWN BY THE WIND

The bubble raft-snail (*Janthina* sp.) is one of a small group of animals that float on the ocean surface. The snail makes a raft of bubbles, hangs upside-down beneath it, and is blown along by the wind. It feeds on another floating animal called a by-the-wind sailor (*Vellela vellela*). This small relative of the jellyfish is equipped with a tiny sail that catches the wind, pushing the animal along – sometimes straight into the path of a predator.

> ### Find out more
> FISH: *184*
> OCTOPUSES AND SQUID: *152*
> SEALS AND MANATEES: *260*
> TORTOISES AND TURTLES: *200*

RHYTHMS OF LIFE

THE NATURAL WORLD IS FULL of rhythmic changes. The Sun rises and sets, the tides ebb and flow, and the seasons follow each other throughout the year. Living things have to fit in with these changes so that they can grow, feed, or reproduce when conditions are best. In the animal world, most species have a daily cycle of behavior. Some also have monthly cycles based on the Moon, and most have a yearly cycle as well. Plants also have daily and yearly cycles, helping them to grow, flower, and set seed at just the right time.

March:
Spring in the
Northern Hemisphere

December:
Summer in
the Southern
Hemisphere

Sun

June:
Summer in the
Northern Hemisphere

September:
Spring in the
Southern
Hemisphere

DAILY RHYTHMS

For many animals, the daily rising and setting of the Sun is the most important rhythm of all. Diurnal animals, such as the eyed lizard, are active during the day. Like all lizards, this European species is cold-blooded and cannot hunt effectively until it has warmed up. To warm itself, it emerges shortly after dawn and basks in the early morning sunshine. It rests in the heat of early afternoon, and then hides away at dusk as the air starts to cool.

NATURAL RHYTHMS OF LIFE

Rhythms of nature operate on many timespans, from hours to centuries. Most rhythms are caused by the rotation of the Earth, and by the Earth's movement around the Sun. Earth is slightly tilted on its axis, so the amount of sunlight reaching each part of the Earth varies throughout the year, creating seasons.

Eurasian long-eared bat
(*Plecotus auritus*)

Small eyes are typical of lizards that are active during the daytime.

Eyed (ocellated) lizard
(*Lacerta lepida*)

Huge ears enable bat to pinpoint insects.

Lizard activity clock

Midnight

Dusk — — Dawn

Midday

Bat activity clock

Midnight

Dusk — — Dawn

Midday

The eyed lizard and long-eared bat divide up their time awake in different ways. The lizard is active for most of the day, but the bat rarely flies for more than an hour at a time.

- Awake and active
- Awake but inactive
- Asleep

Skin absorbs heat when lizard basks in early morning sunshine.

NOCTURNAL ANIMALS

The Eurasian long-eared bat is a typical nocturnal animal. It is active at night, when most predators are asleep. Some nocturnal animals use touch or smell to find food, but the long-eared bat relies on echolocation – it "sees" by making high-pitched sounds and listening to the echoes. Instead of feeding throughout the night, the bat hunts in short bursts separated by long rests. Food, rather than sunshine, keeps the bat warm.

Common dandelion
(*Taraxacum officinale*)

PLANT RHYTHMS

Although plants do not move around, they still respond to day and night. Dandelions, for example, open their flowers at dawn and close them again at dusk. Some plants work the opposite way. Their flowers open at night, usually so they can be pollinated by night-flying insects or bats. A small number of plants – especially members of the pea family – fold up their leaves at night and open them again as the sun rises.

Bracts

At night, protective scales (bracts) keep the flowerhead shut.

Sunlight triggers the flowerhead to open just after dawn.

The yellow florets are revealed as the bracts fold back.

In bright sunshine, the flowerhead is fully open.

Fiddler crabs (Uca sp.) at low tide

TRIGGERED BY THE TIDE

The rise and fall of the tide shapes the behavior of many of the animals that live on seashores. Most of these animals become active at high tide, but fiddler crabs work the other way around. When the tide falls, they leave their burrows to scavenge for food on the exposed mud. Most animals that follow the tides have an inbuilt "clock" that tells them when to become active. The clock works even when the animals are moved away from the sea.

PERIODICAL CICADA

These insects have unusual life cycles. The young, or nymphs, live underground and take 17 years to become adults. In any one area, all the periodical cicadas breed at the same time, so for 17 years, no adults can be seen. In the 17th year, millions of nymphs emerge from the soil and climb up trees to shed their skins. After mating and laying eggs, the cicadas vanish for another 17 years. Other cicadas have a 5- or 13-year life cycle.

Scientific name: *Magicicada septemdecim*

Size: Adult body length 1.2 in (3 cm)

Habitat: Forests, grasslands, fields, and gardens

Distribution: Eastern North America

Reproduction: Females lay eggs in branches; nymphs burrow underground to reach tree roots

Diet: Nymphs feed on sap from roots, adults feed on sap above ground

YEARLY CYCLES

Near the Equator, the climate changes little during the year. In other parts of the world, conditions vary from one season to another. Seasonal changes have a major effect on living things, particularly in places where summer is warm but winter is very cold. Animals often migrate to avoid the winter, but plants cannot. Instead, many shed their leaves before the cold sets in.

In spring, lengthening days trigger a tree to produce new leaves.

In fall, shorter days trigger the tree to shed all its leaves.

BREEDING CYCLES

Many sea animals use the changing phases of the Moon as a signal to breed. In the tropics, reef-building corals release huge clouds of eggs and sperm into the water on several nights each year, around the time of a full Moon. By using the Moon as a clock, the corals ensure that their eggs and sperms get the best chance of meeting as they drift into the vastness of the ocean.

Staghorn coral (Acropora sp.) releasing eggs

The common dormouse (Muscardinus avellanarius) often hibernates in a nest of leaves and moss just underground.

HIBERNATION

Hibernation is a way of avoiding the hardships of winter. During hibernation, an animal's temperature drops, it becomes inactive, and it survives on food stored in its own body. Some animals hibernate for just a few weeks, but others hibernate for two-thirds of the year. Hibernation is common in mammals, reptiles, and amphibians, but rare in birds. The only bird known to hibernate is the common poorwill (*Phalaenoptilus nuttallii*) of North America, which hides away in rocky crevices.

The dormouse conserves heat energy by curling up.

The dormouse's temperature can drop to less than one degree above freezing.

Water level falls

The lungfish curls into a ball in its burrow.

A porous plug of mud allows air to pass through.

A mucous cocoon protects the lungfish while it waits for rain.

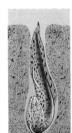

When the lake or river begins to dry up, the lungfish digs a burrow in the mud.

African lungfish digs a summer home

ESTIVATION

To avoid hot summers or droughts, some animals enter a special state called estivation. When its watery habitat dries out in the dry season, the African lungfish (*Protopterus* sp.) seals itself in a mucous cocoon buried deep in mud. It can stay in the cocoon for more than a year until rain wakes it up again. Unlike most fish, it has lungs and can breathe while out of water.

SENSES

Potentilla flower
(*Potentilla* sp.)

MOST ANIMALS LIVE in ever-changing surroundings, where just one badly judged move can make the difference between life and death. To find food and avoid danger, they rely on information gathered by their senses. An animal's senses provide it with information about its surroundings. They also supply information about its own body – for example, whether it is too hot or too cold, and whether it is stationary or moving. Senses work with the help of special nerve-endings, called receptors, that send signals to the brain. Touch receptors are scattered over the body, while receptors for vision, for example, are located in an animal's eyes.

*Flower as
seen by human*

*Flower as
seen by
honeybee*

Nectar guides

VISION

Nearly all animals are able to sense the difference between light and dark, and most can do much more than this. Using their sight, they build up a complete picture of their surroundings. Eyes work by gathering light and focusing it onto special receptors. These send signals to the brain, which combines the signals to form a complete image. Different animals may see different colors. For example, bees can detect ultraviolet light and see flower markings that are invisible to us.

Compound eye

COMPOUND EYES

A compound eye is divided into many identical facets, each a mini-eye with one or more lenses. Each facet detects light from a small part of the animal's surroundings. The animal's brain combines the separate signals to see a single image. Crustaceans, insects, and some other arthropods have compound eyes, which can vary greatly in size – a horsefly's eyes contain several thousand facets, while an ant may have fewer than 150 facets.

*Simple eyes
in center
of head*

Iris

*Pupil
(hole in iris)*

**Cross
section
through
simple eye**

Lens

Iris

*Light-
sensitive
retina*

**Model
showing
compound
eyes of a
horsefly**

*Optic nerve carries
signals to brain.*

*Six-sided facets
packed together*

Bat-eared fox
(*Otocyon
megalotis*)

SIMPLE EYES

A simple eye has only one lens. Simple eyes are found in vertebrates (animals with backbones), and also in a few invertebrates, such as octopuses. Light enters the eye through the iris, which has an opening called the pupil. The pupil adjusts in size in response to different levels of brightness. The light is focused by the lens onto a curved screen, called the retina. Receptors in the retina send signals along the optic nerve, which leads directly to the brain.

HEARING

Sound is made up of vibrations that travel through air, water, or solid objects. Some animals detect these vibrations with their ears. The ear converts the vibrations into nerve impulses that can be interpreted by the animal's brain. Animals rely on their hearing to detect predators or prey, allowing them to pinpoint things that cannot be seen.

SMELL

Animals use their sense of smell to detect chemicals that are dissolved in the air. These chemicals are recognized by special receptors that are found either in an animal's nose, or in other parts of its body, such as the antennae. Animals use their sense of smell to help them find food and to communicate with other members of their species.

*A male cheetah marks its territory with a
jet of strong-smelling urine.*

**Cross section of
mammal's ear**

*Ear flap
(pinna)*

*Inner
ear*

*Middle
ear*

Eardrum

*Air-filled
chamber*

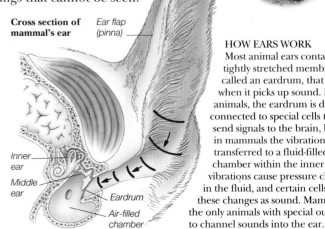

HOW EARS WORK

Most animal ears contain a tightly stretched membrane, called an eardrum, that vibrates when it picks up sound. In some animals, the eardrum is directly connected to special cells that send signals to the brain, but in mammals the vibrations are transferred to a fluid-filled chamber within the inner ear. The vibrations cause pressure changes in the fluid, and certain cells sense these changes as sound. Mammals are the only animals with special outer flaps to channel sounds into the ear.

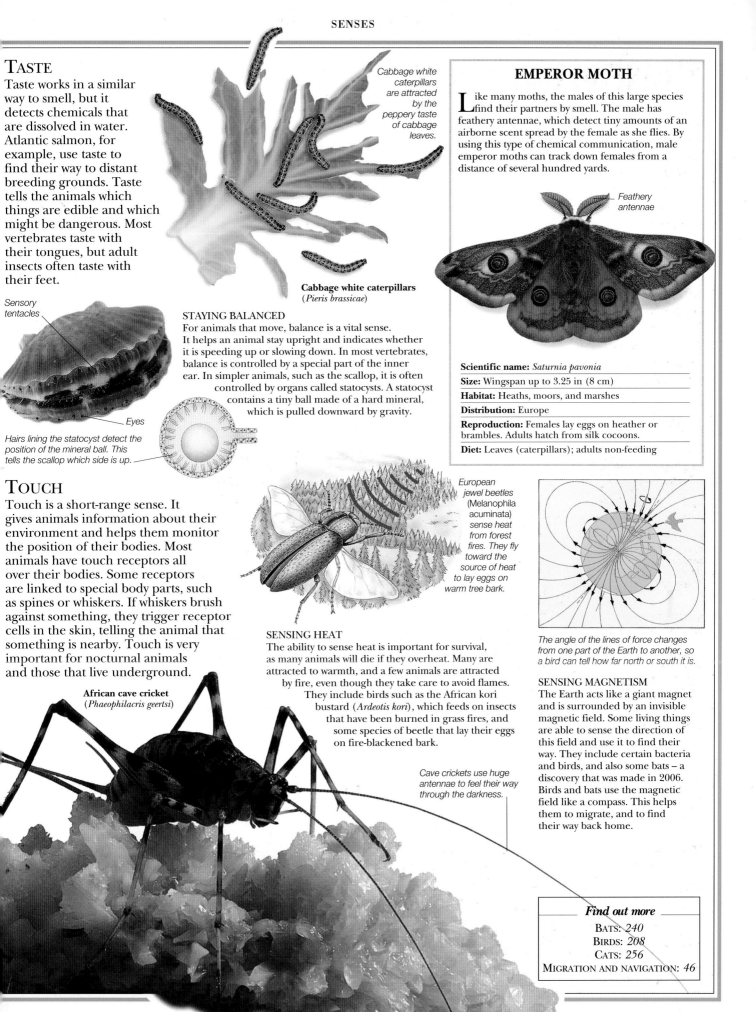

TASTE

Taste works in a similar way to smell, but it detects chemicals that are dissolved in water. Atlantic salmon, for example, use taste to find their way to distant breeding grounds. Taste tells the animals which things are edible and which might be dangerous. Most vertebrates taste with their tongues, but adult insects often taste with their feet.

Sensory tentacles

Eyes

Hairs lining the statocyst detect the position of the mineral ball. This tells the scallop which side is up.

Cabbage white caterpillars are attracted by the peppery taste of cabbage leaves.

Cabbage white caterpillars
(*Pieris brassicae*)

STAYING BALANCED
For animals that move, balance is a vital sense. It helps an animal stay upright and indicates whether it is speeding up or slowing down. In most vertebrates, balance is controlled by a special part of the inner ear. In simpler animals, such as the scallop, it is often controlled by organs called statocysts. A statocyst contains a tiny ball made of a hard mineral, which is pulled downward by gravity.

EMPEROR MOTH

Like many moths, the males of this large species find their partners by smell. The male has feathery antennae, which detect tiny amounts of an airborne scent spread by the female as she flies. By using this type of chemical communication, male emperor moths can track down females from a distance of several hundred yards.

Feathery antennae

Scientific name: *Saturnia pavonia*

Size: Wingspan up to 3.25 in (8 cm)

Habitat: Heaths, moors, and marshes

Distribution: Europe

Reproduction: Females lay eggs on heather or brambles. Adults hatch from silk cocoons.

Diet: Leaves (caterpillars); adults non-feeding

TOUCH

Touch is a short-range sense. It gives animals information about their environment and helps them monitor the position of their bodies. Most animals have touch receptors all over their bodies. Some receptors are linked to special body parts, such as spines or whiskers. If whiskers brush against something, they trigger receptor cells in the skin, telling the animal that something is nearby. Touch is very important for nocturnal animals and those that live underground.

African cave cricket
(*Phaeophilacris geertsi*)

European jewel beetles (Melanophila acuminata) sense heat from forest fires. They fly toward the source of heat to lay eggs on warm tree bark.

SENSING HEAT
The ability to sense heat is important for survival, as many animals will die if they overheat. Many are attracted to warmth, and a few animals are attracted by fire, even though they take care to avoid flames. They include birds such as the African kori bustard (*Ardeotis kori*), which feeds on insects that have been burned in grass fires, and some species of beetle that lay their eggs on fire-blackened bark.

Cave crickets use huge antennae to feel their way through the darkness.

The angle of the lines of force changes from one part of the Earth to another, so a bird can tell how far north or south it is.

SENSING MAGNETISM
The Earth acts like a giant magnet and is surrounded by an invisible magnetic field. Some living things are able to sense the direction of this field and use it to find their way. They include certain bacteria and birds, and also some bats – a discovery that was made in 2006. Birds and bats use the magnetic field like a compass. This helps them to migrate, and to find their way back home.

Find out more

BATS: *240*
BIRDS: *208*
CATS: *256*
MIGRATION AND NAVIGATION: *46*

COMMUNICATION

ALTHOUGH ANIMALS CANNOT talk, they can communicate in many other ways. Spiders, for example, send signals to each other by plucking the strands of their webs; bees "dance" to tell each other where to find food; and electric fish send pulses of electricity to each other through the water. In most cases the message is very simple – a warning of approaching danger, a call to find a lost baby, or an expression of anger. Animals usually communicate with members of their own species using a code that only they can understand. Sometimes, however, eavesdroppers are listening too. When tropical tree frogs call to their mates, for example, they risk being snatched by frog-eating bats.

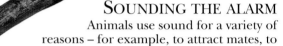

Grivets use special calls to warn each other of danger.

Grivet
(*Cercopithecus aethiops*)

SOUNDING THE ALARM
Animals use sound for a variety of reasons – for example, to attract mates, to startle enemies, and to locate relatives. The grivets of African grasslands call to other members of their group to warn them of approaching predators, such as snakes, eagles, or leopards. They use a different call to identify each type of predator, so that the group can select the most appropriate place to hide.

BIRDSONG
Birds usually sing to proclaim ownership of a territory and to advertise their presence to mates. Often, it is only the males that sing, although in some species males and females sing duets. While some songbirds repeat the same songs throughout their lives, others continually invent new songs by copying any sound they hear. Birds that live in flocks, such as laughingthrushes, babble noisily to keep in touch with the rest of the flock.

*Cape fur seal colony
(Arctocephalus pusillus), Namibia, in Africa*

Yellow-throated laughingthrush
(*Garrulax galbanus*)

Laughingthrushes sing to keep in touch with the rest of the flock.

FINDING OFFSPRING
Fur seals live in large breeding colonies, called rookeries, where offspring can be left in safety while their mothers swim out to sea to feed. When a mother returns, she has to find her pup among the crowds. At first, she bellows and listens out for the pup's distinctive reply. When she has moved in close, she confirms her pup's identity by its smell.

BODY LANGUAGE
When animals live close together, body language is often the best way to communicate – unlike sound, visual signals are less likely to attract the attention of predators. White storks nest high in trees or on roofs, and the parents work together to look after their young. When one returns to its partner after a period away, it must identify itself to avoid a hostile reception. It does this by swinging its head over its back and clapping its beak.

LONG-DISTANCE CALLS
Whales and dolphins produce complex underwater sounds to communicate with one another, but scientists have yet to unravel their meanings. The haunting "songs" of humpback whales can last up to 30 minutes, and change continually. They are usually made by solitary males, perhaps to attract mates. Sound travels farther in water than air, and humpbacks may be able to hear each other when they are hundreds of miles apart. Humpbacks also sometimes leap out of the water to make a noisy crash as they fall back in.

Humpback whales (Megaptera novaeangliae) communicate underwater with complex songs.

Male rhinoceroses can spray urine backward in a powerful jet.

A black rhinoceros (Diceros bicornis) spreads urine over the ground to mark his territory.

CHEMICAL SIGNPOSTS

Although humans do not use smells to communicate, many other mammals do. Odorous substances take a long time to fade, and can be left as signposts to mark out an animal's territory. Scents contain a lot of information – they tell visitors the sex of the animal, its age, and may even identify the individual. Male rhinoceroses often mark their territory by spraying urine on the ground. This warns visiting males to keep out.

TALKING ANTENNAE

Ants communicate by tapping their antennae together to pass on chemical signals – the antennae can "smell" whatever they touch. When a worker ant finds food, it returns to the nest to tell the other workers. Sometimes, the returning ant will regurgitate food into another ant's mouth after tapping its antennae. Good communication is vital for ants because they live in highly organized societies and need to work together to survive.

Ants tap their antennae together to pass on chemical signals.

FLASHLIGHT FISH

Experts think that flashlight fish use their flashing lights to keep in touch with the rest of the school at night. The light is created by bacteria in a pouch under the eye, and can be switched off by a flap of skin that covers the pouch. The fish may also use its lights to lure prey and confuse predators.

Flashlight fish emit the brightest light made by any living creature.

Scientific name: *Photoblepharon palpebrates*

Size: Up to 4 in (9 cm) long

Habitat: Crevices in coral reefs

Distribution: Tropical west Pacific Ocean

Reproduction: Females lay eggs; males fertilize them

Diet: Small marine animals in surface waters

RIPPLE DETECTORS

Pond skaters and water striders live on the surface of ponds and use their feet to feel for ripples made by flies that fall into the water. They also make ripples to communicate with each other. Males warn off rivals by tapping the water with their feet to produce 90 ripples per second. During courtship they make 22 ripples per second to attract females.

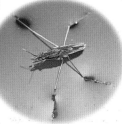

Pond skater
(*Gerris* sp.)

Male pond skaters tap the water to make tiny ripples.

Other pond skaters pick up the message with their feet.

After landing on the nest, the stork throws its head back to greet its partner.

FACE TO FACE

Encounters between animals often take place face to face, so facial expressions are an important way of signaling a mood. Staring eyes and bared teeth, for example, often show aggression. Chimpanzees use a variety of subtle facial expressions (as well as body postures and sounds) to communicate with other members of their social group. Their expressions convey a wealth of information, including social rank, anger, and happiness.

Begging for food   *Playful*   *Angry*   *Frightened*

White stork
(*Ciconia ciconia*)

The parents take turns to incubate their eggs.

The nest is a large platform of sticks with a central hollow.

Find out more
APES: *284*
BEES AND WASPS: *180*
SONGBIRDS: *228*
WHALES: *262*

MIGRATION AND NAVIGATION

UNLIKE PLANTS, MOST ANIMALS can move from place to place. Many animals spend their adult lives in one place, while others set off on special journeys at particular times of the year to breed or to avoid cold or drought. These journeys are called migrations. Animals migrate overland, in water, and in the air. The greatest travelers include birds and whales, which cover thousands of miles each year. During their migrations, animals often have to steer their way across unfamiliar terrain. Some find their way by following their parents or a herd of their own species, while others navigate using a variety of techniques, such as following the stars.

Spiny lobsters follow one another across the seabed.

MARCH OF THE LOBSTERS
In the Caribbean, the arrival of fall is the signal for spiny lobsters (*Panulirus argus*) to begin their long march into deep water. They migrate by forming lines of up to 50 animals, and then they move at a brisk pace across the seabed. During their stay in cold, deep water, they need less food and are able to avoid winter storms.

MYSTERIOUS EELS
Eels live and feed in the rivers of North America and Europe, but they do not breed there. Instead, they travel up to 3,000 miles (5,000 km) to lay their eggs in the depths of the Sargasso Sea, which lies on the western side of the North Atlantic. Their eggs hatch into leaf-shaped larvae, which are less than 2 in (5 cm) long. It takes the growing eels about three years to swim back to the rivers to feed.

The hooves of thousands of animals create crisscrossing paths across the grassland.

GREAT JOURNEYS
Some of the most spectacular overland migrations are carried out by huge numbers of herding mammals that live in the African savanna. Some, such as wildebeest and zebras, migrate to find fresh grass and water following monsoon rains. Animal movements are timed to fit in with the seasons and to make the most of changing food supplies, thereby reducing the competition for food and space.

Adult eels can slither over damp ground to reach lakes and ponds.

European eel
(*Anguilla anguilla*)

Migrating wildebeest in the Serengeti National Park, Tanzania

Migration of gray whale

ASIA

NORTH AMERICA

PACIFIC OCEAN

→ *Main migration routes*
■ *Winter range*
■ *Summer range*

Gray whale
(*Eschrichtius robustus*)

HEAVYWEIGHT MIGRANTS
During their lifetime, whales travel greater distances than any other mammal. The gray whale, for example, makes a migration of 11,200 miles (18,000 km) each year between its feeding grounds in the Arctic and its warmer breeding grounds off the coast of California in the eastern Pacific or Korea in the western Pacific. Gray whales migrate in groups of two or three and the journey takes them up to three months.

Grazing limpets on their daily feeding migrations

MINIATURE MIGRANTS
Some migrations can be short. Many small shore animals, such as limpets, travel less than a few feet a day. They move in step with the tides in search of food. Each limpet moves when the tide is high, but returns to its starting point as the tide falls. It feeds by scraping algae from submerged rocks. Once back at its resting place, the limpet clamps its shell securely against a slight hollow in the rock.

Migration of monarch butterfly

→ Migration routes across North America

Monarch butterfly
(*Danaus plexippus*)

Monarchs pack together tightly in their winter roosts.

MIGRATING MONARCHS

Despite their small size and light build, some butterflies migrate huge distances. One of the greatest travelers is the monarch butterfly, which lives throughout the Americas. Millions of monarchs spend their winters in the southern US and Mexico clustered on trees, away from the severe winter weather. When spring arrives, they fly north, laying eggs as they go. Their offspring may travel as far north as Canada before summer ends and their southward migration begins.

Snow goose
(*Chen caerulescens*)

FEATHERED MIGRANTS

Some birds have the longest, single migrations of all animals. During spring in the Northern Hemisphere, some birds fly north in huge flocks to take advantage of a growing supply of food. Many, such as the snow goose, end their journeys in the Arctic tundra, where lengthening days bring ideal conditions for breeding. To fuel their long flights, birds depend on their reserves of body fat. Some birds save energy by flying in a "V" formation. Disturbed air created by the flapping wings of the bird in front provides extra lift for the bird behind.

BLUE WILDEBEEST

Cowlike in appearance, the blue wildebeest (or gnu) belongs to a group of grazing mammals that includes cattle and antelope. During the dry season food and water are scarce, so these antelope migrate into woodland areas. When the wet season begins, they form huge herds and migrate across the plains in search of fresh grass. When the herd is not on the move, females and their young gather in groups of 10–1,000, and the males compete to breed with them.

Scientific name:	*Connochaetes taurinus*
Size:	Male up to 8 ft (2.4 m) long
Habitat:	Open grasslands
Distribution:	Southern Kenya and Angola to northern parts of South Africa
Reproduction:	Female produces one offspring, which is able to run within 15 minutes; gestation period 34 weeks
Diet:	Grasses and leaves

HOW BIRDS NAVIGATE

Migrating birds use several different methods to find their way. One of the simplest involves following landmarks, such as rivers and coastlines. This is why land birds often converge in particular places to cross the sea. Some birds also use a built in "compass" that works by following the Sun and stars. While flying its course, the bird's brain allows for the movement of the Sun and stars across the sky.

Navigation by the Sun in Northern Hemisphere

At midday, a bird traveling south can set its course by aiming toward the horizon beneath the Sun.

As the day continues, the Sun travels westward, but the bird's brain allows for this movement to stay on course.

Common toads (*Bufo bufo*) crossing a road at night

KNOWING WHEN TO GO

For all migrating animals, knowing when to set off is an important part of survival. Common toads become active as the days lengthen in early spring, but they only head for their breeding ponds when the air temperature reaches about 45°F (7°C). This ensures that they lay their eggs at the right time, so that their tadpoles have a chance of completing their development.

Siberian lemming
(*Lemmus sibiricus*)

SEARCHING FOR FOOD

Most animals migrate in a predictable way, and follow the same route every year. However, some species, such as lemmings, are much more erratic. If they become hungry or overcrowded, they set off on journeys that have no particular destination. These unpredictable migrations are called "irruptions." They are most common in species that live in the far north.

Find out more
CATTLE AND ANTELOPE: *278*
GRASSLANDS: *84*
MOVEMENT ON LAND: *34*
SEABIRDS: *212*

DEFENSE 1

FOR MOST LIVING THINGS, danger is all around. Often it strikes suddenly when a predator launches a surprise attack. In other cases it develops slowly – the onset of disease or threat of starvation, for example. Living things defend themselves from danger in countless ways. Many animals have sharp senses and take emergency action at the first sign of trouble. Most try to escape, but some have special protection that allows them to withstand an attack. Plants also need defenses, particularly against hungry animals. However, they are rooted to the ground and cannot run away as animals can. Instead, they use spines, thorns, and special chemicals to make themselves unpleasant or dangerous to eat.

A jackrabbit (Lepus sp.) bolts from a pursuing gray wolf (Canis lupus).

MAKING AN ESCAPE

When faced with danger, many animals react the same way – they make a sudden dash for safety. To be successful, this defense method relies on two things: the animal must be fast and it must have sharp senses so that it can detect an attacker before it is too late. In many mammals, a chemical called epinephrine is released into the bloodstream at times of danger. Epinephrine prepares the body for "fight or flight" – the heart beats faster, the eyes widen, and hairs stand on end.

Lying still on its back with its mouth agape, a grass snake pretends to be dead.

European grass snake
(*Natrix natrix*)

SAFETY IN NUMBERS
Keeping together is an important defense in the animal world. Animals that live in large groups stand a better chance of spotting approaching danger, and each one has less chance of being singled out for attack. Many fish protect themselves from predators by swimming in large schools. For a shark, a school is a difficult and confusing target. Most of the fish will escape when it attacks.

A school of jack mackerel (Trachurus symmetricus) scatters as a blue shark (Prionace glauca) searches for a victim.

PLAYING DEAD

When escape is impossible, some animals use special techniques to survive. One of the strangest methods is to play dead. This works because most predators hunt moving prey. If their prey stops moving, their hunting behavior may automatically stop as well. Many snakes play dead, as does the Virginia opossum (*Didelphis virginiana*) of North America. When the danger has passed, these animals suddenly "come back to life."

1. A stump is left where this lizard's tail was broken off.

Tree skink
(*Dasia sp.*)

2. Two months later, the tail has started to grow back.

3. After eight months, the new tail has almost grown to its original length.

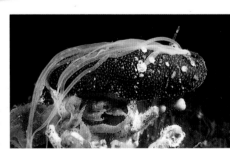

Sea cucumber (Holothuria sp.) squirting out its insides

SHEDDING BODY PARTS
If a lizard is caught by its tail, the tip of the tail may break off and wriggle around on the ground. This distracts the attacker, giving the lizard time to escape. Over the following weeks, the tail grows back until it is almost the same length as before. Many other animals use a similar technique to escape. Instead of shedding tails, insects and spiders often shed their legs.

ALL-OUT RESPONSE
Sea cucumbers have perhaps the most bizarre form of self-defense of all – when attacked, many squirt out their insides. Some species squirt out most of their digestive system. Others, such as the cotton spinner (*Holothuria forskali*), squirt out a mass of slender tubes that may be sticky or poisonous. Once a sea cucumber has used its remarkable defense, it slowly replaces the lost organs.

SPINES AND SCALES

One of the best ways to survive an attack is to be very difficult to eat. Hedgehogs and porcupines manage this with the help of spines, a technique shared by many plants. Other mammals, including armadillos and pangolins, rely on armor plating. In armadillos the armor consists of hardened skin, but in pangolins it is made of overlapping scales. The pangolin can roll up tightly into a ball to protect its head and feet. The sharp edges of the scales make it very difficult to attack.

Pangolin
(*Manis* sp.)

Armor plating made of overlapping scales

Scales have sharp edges.

When curled into a ball, the pangolin is safe from all but the largest predators.

MALAYAN PORCUPINE

This tropical rodent feeds mainly on the ground and fends off enemies with sharp, hollow quills, which are specially modified hairs. If threatened, the porcupine turns its back on its enemy, rattles its quills, and stamps its feet. If this fails to deter the enemy, the porcupine backs into the attacker, driving quills into its body. The quills break off easily and stay lodged in the enemy's skin.

Scientific name: *Hystrix brachyura*

Size: Up to 31 in (80 cm) long including tail

Habitat: Forests

Distribution: Southern and Southeast Asia

Reproduction: Female gives birth to one or two young in an underground burrow

Diet: Bark, roots, and fruit, also some insects and other small animals

The prickly ash has sharp spines when young but sheds them and becomes leathery when mature.

Alluaudia
(*Alluaudia* sp.)

Prickly ash
(*Zanthoxylum paniculatum*)

Long spines protect the short leaves from animals.

Leaflets open

Sensitive plant
(*Mimosa* sp.)

Leaflets closed

The leaves of the sensitive plant move suddenly when animals touch them.

PLANT WEAPONS

Plants use thorns and spines to protect their leaves from hungry animals. Thorns are often curved so that they tear into an animal's skin as it brushes against the plant. Spines can pierce an animal's mouth and then break off, leaving deep splinters that cause lasting pain. These defenses are most important for young plants that are small and easy to reach. When plants grow taller, their soft stems become tough and woody and their spines or thorns may disappear.

CLOSING UP

If an animal touches the sensitive plant, something remarkable happens. The plant's leaflets quickly fold up and the stalk collapses. With luck, the plant will merge into the undergrowth and the animal will not see it. This defense relies on special water-filled "hinges" at the base of each leaflet. If a leaflet is touched, water flows out of the hinge and the hinge shuts. The leaflets slowly open out again later.

INSECT REPELLENTS

Many plant-eating insects are so small that they can walk between spines and thorns. To keep them at bay, plants use microscopic hairs. The leaves of the sage plant (*Salvia officinalis*) are covered with thousands of tiny hairs that keep insects from reaching the leaf surface. Some of the hairs have sticky tips that make it difficult for the insects to move around.

Magnified view of insect-repelling hairs on a sage leaf

Find out more

ARMADILLOS AND ANTEATERS: *242*
HUNTING: *52*
LIZARDS: *202*
SNAKES: *204*

DEFENSE 2

HIDING FROM ENEMIES is often the best form of defense. Many animals use a special type of disguise, called camouflage, that helps them blend in with their surroundings. Other animals use the opposite strategy – their bodies are brightly colored to make them stand out from their surroundings. Bright colors are often a warning to would-be predators that an animal is poisonous, but sometimes the warning is deceptive. Certain animals are disguised to look like poisonous animals, but are actually harmless.

INSECT CAMOUFLAGE

Insects are the champions of camouflage. They disguise themselves in countless ways and imitate all sorts of objects, from thorns, twigs, and leaves to pebbles and even bird droppings. The Indian leaf butterfly (*Kallima inachus*) looks just like a dead leaf when its wings are closed. The undersides of the wings are brown and mottled and have lines that look like a leaf's veins.

An Indian leaf butterfly among dead leaves

The undersides of the wings look like leaves.

The upper sides are brightly colored.

From above, the fish looks dark to match deep water.

From below, the fish looks pale to match the lighter surface water.

HIDING IN WATER

Many fish have a type of camouflage called countershading. Their backs are dark to match deep water when seen from above, and their bellies are pale to match the lighter surface water when seen from below. Countershading helps fish hide from both diving seabirds and deep-swimming predators.

INVISIBLE LIZARD

Geckos often hunt during the night and use camouflage to hide during the day. This Australian leaf-tailed gecko (*Phyllurus cornutus*) rests on tree trunks, but its camouflage makes it almost impossible to spot. Since most geckos are unable to shut their eyelids, their eyes are often camouflaged as well.

A camouflaged leaf-tailed gecko resting on a tree

1. This chameleon is normally pale green with yellow stripes.

Yemeni veiled chameleon
(*Chamaeleo calyptratus*)

CHANGING COLOR

Some animals can change color to match different backgrounds. The change can take hours or even days. In chameleons, it usually takes several minutes, but in squid it can happen in less than a second. The precise color depends on the size of tiny packets of pigment in the skin, which the chameleon can expand or shrink accordingly.

2. When the chameleon is threatened, its skin begins to darken.

LIVING STONES

Camouflage is rare among plants, but some species do use it to avoid being spotted and eaten. Among the best camouflaged species are the living stones (*Lithops karasmontana*) of southern Africa. These plants live in dry places and are just a few inches high. Their small, rounded leaves store water and food, and look like stones scattered over the ground.

3. Eventually, the chameleon's skin turns dark brown.

MIMICRY

Animals mimic other creatures in order to trick their enemies. Some mimics imitate nonliving things, but many imitate animals that are dangerous. To complete the disguise, the impostor may even imitate the way a dangerous animal moves or smells. The caterpillar of a Costa Rican hawkmoth mimics a poisonous viper. When disturbed, it swings around its back end to display a false "face" with startling eyespots.

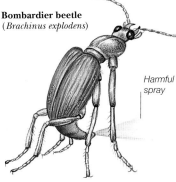

A Costa Rican hawkmoth caterpillar (Leucorhampha ornatus) mimicking a poisonous viper

Coral snake
(*Micrurus nigrocinctus*)

HOVERFLY

Many hoverflies are colored yellow and black, which makes them look like wasps or bees, so they scare off hungry birds. However, they are actually harmless mimics and do not have stings. The disguise is quite easy to see through – hoverflies have only one pair of wings, while wasps have two.

Hoverflies lack the distinctive narrow waists of wasps.

Scientific name:	*Syrphus ribesii*
Size:	0.5 in (1.3 cm) long
Habitat:	Fields and gardens
Distribution:	Europe and North America
Reproduction:	Lays eggs on plants
Diet:	Adults eat nectar, the larvae (grubs) eat aphids

COPYCAT SNAKE
These two American snakes look similar, but only the coral snake can inflict a lethal bite. The milk snake is a harmless mimic, imitating the coral snake's colors to ward off predators. Milk snakes have stripes of the same color as coral snakes, but in a different order.

Milk snake
(*Lampropeltis triangulum*)

Bombardier beetle
(*Brachinus explodens*)

Harmful spray

CHEMICAL WEAPONS

Many animals and plants use poisonous or foul-smelling chemicals to defend themselves. Some caterpillars, for example, store poisons from food in their bodies to make themselves inedible. Other animals can squirt or spit chemicals at an attacker. The bombardier beetle sprays its enemies with a jet of harmful chemicals that bursts out of its abdomen with an audible "pop."

Magnified view of a nettle's stinging hair

TOXIC STING
Stinging nettles are covered with needlelike hairs that pierce the skin of animals that touch them. At the base of each hair is a chamber containing poison. When the hair's tip breaks, the poison is injected into the wound, causing sudden pain.

Stinging nettle
(*Urtica dioica*)

Stinging hairs cover the leaves and stem.

Poison-dart frog
(*Dendrobates* sp.)

COLOR WARNING
Poison-dart frogs from Central and South America contain some of the most powerful poisons in the world. The poisons, made by special glands in the skin, can kill animals that try to eat the frogs. Like many poisonous animals, they are brightly colored to warn predators that they are dangerous.

Fiery sap oozes from a cut spurge stem.

FIERY SAP
Like animals, many plants use chemicals to make themselves unpleasant or dangerous to eat. Some have powerful-smelling oils in their leaves, while others have poisonous sap. Spurge plants produce a thick, milky sap called latex, which has a powerful burning taste. Latex persuades most animals to leave the plants alone.

Spurge
(*Euphorbia* sp.)

Find out more
ANTEATERS AND ARMADILLOS: *242*
BUTTERFLIES AND MOTHS: *176*
DEFENSE 1: *48*
HUNTING: *52*

HUNTING

A HUNTER IS A CARNIVORE – an animal that eats other animals for food. Although animal food is very nutritious, hunting is a demanding way of life. Prey animals are always on the alert for a hunter's approach and will often escape at the first sign of danger. To succeed, the hunter needs lightning reactions, cunning, and enough strength to overpower its victim. Hunters use many strategies to catch their prey. Some use stealth – they sneak up silently until they are close enough to make a sudden dash. Others construct traps, or simply lie in wait until the prey comes within striking distance. Most hunters are bigger than their prey, but some – such as army ants and wolves – hunt in groups and can kill animals much larger than themselves.

HIGH-SPEED RACER
The cheetah (*Acinonyx jubatus*) relies on an explosive burst of speed to catch fast-running antelope. It is the fastest animal on land, with a top speed of about 62 mph (100 kmh). When closing in for the kill, it strikes the prey's hind legs to bring the animal down, and then inflicts a suffocating bite to the throat. The sprint is so exhausting that the cheetah must give up if it has not caught its prey within about 20 seconds.

A cheetah closes in on a young gazelle. Only about half of a cheetah's chases are successful.

Hunting technique of lions

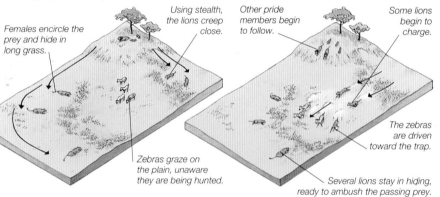

Females encircle the prey and hide in long grass.

Using stealth, the lions creep close.

Zebras graze on the plain, unaware they are being hunted.

Other pride members begin to follow.

Some lions begin to charge.

The zebras are driven toward the trap.

Several lions stay in hiding, ready to ambush the passing prey.

TEAMWORK
Working as a team enables hunters to catch their prey more easily. By hunting together, lions can herd zebras across open grassland and drive them into traps. A typical hunt starts when a group of female lions begins to move toward their prey, leaving the rest of the pride behind. Moving stealthily through the grass, the lions spread out to circle the prey without being seen. When the attack begins, some lions keep still, ready to burst out of hiding as the animals flee past.

ANT ATTACK
Tropical army ants form the largest hunting teams in the world. At dawn, thousands of ants pour across the forest floor, probing crevices, dead leaves, and fallen wood for signs of life. The ants quickly overpower any small animals that do not manage to escape. Army ants spend the night in temporary structures called "bivouacs" made of living ants with their legs locked together.

Army ants begin to dismantle the body of a grasshopper.

European common frog
(*Rana temporaria*)

DEATH TRAP
Web-making spiders trap flying insects in a tangle of sticky silk threads. Many spiders have poor vision but can feel the vibrations of a victim struggling to escape. When a fly is caught, the spider rushes into action. It paralyzes the prey with a venomous bite and then wraps it in silk. The spider's digestive juices turn the victim's insides into a nutritious liquid that the spider can suck out later.

AMBUSH
Some animals lie quiet and still until their prey comes close and then snatch the victim with a sudden, accurate movement. Frogs use this strategy to catch insects. They have sharp eyesight and are good at spotting small, fast-moving objects, such as flies. When a fly is near, a frog will watch it patiently until it comes into range. Then, in a split second, it leaps toward the fly and catches it on the sticky tip of its tongue.

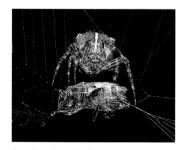

An orb-web spider (Araneus diadematus) with its paralyzed prey

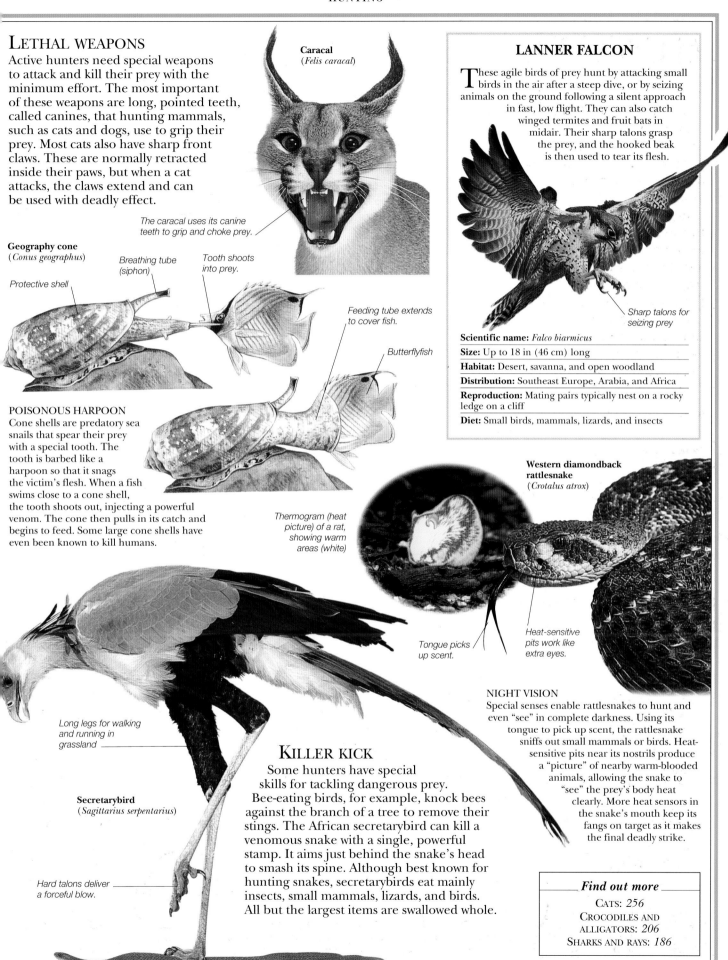

LETHAL WEAPONS

Active hunters need special weapons to attack and kill their prey with the minimum effort. The most important of these weapons are long, pointed teeth, called canines, that hunting mammals, such as cats and dogs, use to grip their prey. Most cats also have sharp front claws. These are normally retracted inside their paws, but when a cat attacks, the claws extend and can be used with deadly effect.

Caracal
(*Felis caracal*)

The caracal uses its canine teeth to grip and choke prey.

Geography cone
(*Conus geographus*)

*Breathing tube
(siphon)*

*Tooth shoots
into prey.*

Protective shell

*Feeding tube extends
to cover fish.*

Butterflyfish

POISONOUS HARPOON

Cone shells are predatory sea snails that spear their prey with a special tooth. The tooth is barbed like a harpoon so that it snags the victim's flesh. When a fish swims close to a cone shell, the tooth shoots out, injecting a powerful venom. The cone then pulls in its catch and begins to feed. Some large cone shells have even been known to kill humans.

LANNER FALCON

These agile birds of prey hunt by attacking small birds in the air after a steep dive, or by seizing animals on the ground following a silent approach in fast, low flight. They can also catch winged termites and fruit bats in midair. Their sharp talons grasp the prey, and the hooked beak is then used to tear its flesh.

*Sharp talons for
seizing prey*

Scientific name: *Falco biarmicus*

Size: Up to 18 in (46 cm) long

Habitat: Desert, savanna, and open woodland

Distribution: Southeast Europe, Arabia, and Africa

Reproduction: Mating pairs typically nest on a rocky ledge on a cliff

Diet: Small birds, mammals, lizards, and insects

**Western diamondback
rattlesnake**
(*Crotalus atrox*)

*Thermogram (heat
picture) of a rat,
showing warm
areas (white)*

*Tongue picks
up scent.*

*Heat-sensitive
pits work like
extra eyes.*

NIGHT VISION

Special senses enable rattlesnakes to hunt and even "see" in complete darkness. Using its tongue to pick up scent, the rattlesnake sniffs out small mammals or birds. Heat-sensitive pits near its nostrils produce a "picture" of nearby warm-blooded animals, allowing the snake to "see" the prey's body heat clearly. More heat sensors in the snake's mouth keep its fangs on target as it makes the final deadly strike.

*Long legs for walking
and running in
grassland*

Secretarybird
(*Sagittarius serpentarius*)

*Hard talons deliver
a forceful blow.*

KILLER KICK

Some hunters have special skills for tackling dangerous prey. Bee-eating birds, for example, knock bees against the branch of a tree to remove their stings. The African secretarybird can kill a venomous snake with a single, powerful stamp. It aims just behind the snake's head to smash its spine. Although best known for hunting snakes, secretarybirds eat mainly insects, small mammals, lizards, and birds. All but the largest items are swallowed whole.

Find out more
CATS: *256*
CROCODILES AND
ALLIGATORS: *206*
SHARKS AND RAYS: *186*

SOCIAL ANIMALS

SOME ANIMALS LEAD solitary lives, but social animals stay close to others of their own kind. Life in a group has several advantages. Predators are detected sooner because there are so many pairs of eyes and ears on the alert. It is also easier to find food and raise young when the task is shared. Animal groups may be quite loosely formed, with members joining and leaving all the time. Some species live in very close-knit groups, where all the members belong to a single family and depend on each other to survive. Animals that form groups like these are called "eusocial," and most of them are insects.

ON THE LOOKOUT

Giraffes can live on their own, but they often gather into loosely organized herds. This is an advantage for mothers because the other herd members watch out for danger and protect the young from attack. Males tend to live in bachelor herds as they approach adulthood, but become solitary later. Adult male giraffes are able to fend for themselves.

Giraffe
(*Giraffa camelopardalis*)

Giraffe herds contain up to ten animals. By taking turns to drink and to act as lookout, they avoid danger.

**Ringtailed coati
(coatimundi)**
(*Nasua nasua*)

FEMALES IN CHARGE

Coatis are long-tailed relatives of raccoons and live in the forests of North, Central, and South America. The adult females and their young form groups of up to 20 animals, but for most of the year the adult males live alone. During the breeding season, the females allow a single male to join their group, but soon after mating they drive him away.

TROOPING TOGETHER

Social living is particularly common in primates, such as chimps and baboons. Baboons live in Africa and Arabia, and spend their lives in troops that may contain as many as 750 members. The troop is divided into many smaller groups, each consisting of a dominant male who guards a "harem" of females and their young. Young males face fierce competition when looking for females of their own because the dominant males are always on the watch for rivals.

Hamadryas baboon
(*Papio hamadryas*)

— *Adult female*

Dominant males are usually much larger than females.

Lions (Panthera leo) live in social groups called prides.

COOPERATIVE CATS

Lions are the only cats that live in large social groups, or prides. A pride consists of several related lionesses, their cubs, and one or more adult males. The males protect the pride from rival lions, while the females do most of the hunting. Lionesses feed each other's young, but the males are less tolerant. They chase off growing males, and if they take over a new pride, they may kill the cubs.

Young baboons explore and search for food.

SCHOOL ON PATROL

Dolphins are very sociable animals. They live in schools that can contain hundreds of individuals, sometimes of more than one species. When they hunt, dolphins work together to surround and trap schools of fish, allowing them to catch more than they could alone. They use bursts of sound to detect their prey and to communicate with each other. Experiments have shown that dolphins recognize each other by sound alone – just as humans recognize other humans by the sound of their voices.

A school of Atlantic spotted dolphins (Stenella frontalis)

LAUGHING KOOKABURRA

The laughing kookaburra is the largest member of the kingfisher family, and is famous for its loud, laughing cry. Instead of diving into water for fish like many kingfishers, it swoops toward the forest floor to catch small animals. Unlike most birds, kookaburras live in family groups. Young birds stay with their parents for several years and help them rear more offspring.

Small feet for perching

Scientific name: *Dacelo novaeguineae*

Size: 18 in (46 cm)

Habitat: Open forest

Distribution: Eastern Australia

Reproduction: Female lays eggs in a treehole nest

Diet: Lizards, snakes, small mammals, and insects

INSECT CITIES

Ants live in giant family groups that build elaborate nests. Each nest is founded by a single female, or queen. She alone lays eggs, and her offspring become worker ants that forage for food, and raise further generations of young. This highly social lifestyle has also evolved in many species of bee and wasp, and in termites. It has enabled these insects to become immensely successful. In many places, ants outnumber all other forms of insect life.

Nest of the European black garden ant *(Lasius niger)*

Soil is piled into a mound.

Entrance hole

Eggs and larvae are carried around the nest to keep them at the optimum temperature.

In the heart of the nest is the queen's chamber, where she lays her eggs.

Eggs develop into larvae.

ROYAL RATS

Naked mole-rats, or sand puppies, are remarkable African mammals that have a eusocial lifestyle, similar to that of ants or termites. They spend all their lives underground, and live in groups of about 30 animals. In each group only one female – the queen – produces young. The other members of the group are workers. They tunnel through the ground in search of nutritious roots, and bring back food for the queen and her offspring.

The queen weighs about one and a half times as much as the workers.

Naked mole-rat
Heterocephalus glaber

Workers may be male or female but do not breed.

FAIRWEATHER FRIENDS

A cloud of midges is a typical example of a short-lived animal group. It consists almost entirely of males that dance a short distance above the ground, often in the shelter of a tree or bush. Females are attracted by the swarm and, as they fly toward it, they are quickly grasped by the males. These swarms usually form on calm evenings and rarely last for more than two or three hours.

A cloud of tiny male midges dancing in the still air above a country path.

IN PECKING ORDER

Birds that live in groups, such as farmyard chickens, develop a strict order of seniority. If a junior bird helps itself to food before an older one has begun to eat, it risks getting a sharp peck. The strongest bird can peck any of the others, but the weakest gets pecked by all the other members of the group.

Chicks learn their place in the pecking order from an early age.

Domestic chicken
(Gallus gallus)

Find out more

ANTS AND TERMITES: *178*
APES: *284*
BEES AND WASPS: *180*
DOGS: *252*

PARTNERS AND PARASITES

IN THE NATURAL WORLD, every species faces a constant struggle to survive. Some animals improve their chances of survival by forming special partnerships with other living things. In one common form of partnership, called mutualism or symbiosis, both partners benefit from the relationship. Commensalism is a relationship in which one partner benefits, but the other neither gains nor loses. In parasitic partnerships, the benefits are completely one-sided. A parasitic animal gets help from its partner, but gives nothing in return and may even harm or kill its host.

Suckerlike pad

Sharksucker
(*Echeneis naucrates*)

Sucker is a specially adapted dorsal fin.

TEAMING UP

African yellow white-eyes (*Zosterops senegalensis*) feed on the sugary nectar of flowering plants, such as bird of paradise flowers. In return, the birds spread the flowers' pollen, which they pick up on their bills and feet. This partnership between the bird and plant is an example of mutualism. Huge numbers of other animals, including hummingbirds, bats, bees, and butterflies, depend on partnerships with flowering plants.

Bird of paradise flowers
(Strelitzia reginae)

African yellow white-eye feeding

HITCHING A LIFT

Remoras such as the sharksucker are tropical fish that have a suckerlike pad on the top of their heads. They use this pad to fasten themselves to larger fish such as sharks, and also to the shells of turtles. It was thought that remoras shared their host's food, but most experts now think that they use larger animals just for transportation.

A clownfish in its sea anemone home

LIVING REFUGE

The brightly colored clownfish (*Amphiprion biaculeatus*) lives among the stinging tentacles of sea anemones. It feeds on the anemone's leftover food, and has a special slimy coat that prevents it from being stung. This partnership appears to be an example of commensalism, because the anemone seems to get nothing in return. However, the clownfish may lure other animals toward the stinging tentacles, helping the anemone get food.

The monkey has to eat large quantities of leaves to get enough nutrients.

Proboscis monkey
(*Nasalis larvatus*)

MICROSCOPIC PARTNERS

Many different animals, from termites to monkeys, feed on the leaves and stems of plants. This kind of food contains a lot of cellulose – a tough substance that most animals cannot digest. Animals rely on microorganisms living in their digestive systems to break down the cellulose into a food that can be absorbed. The proboscis monkey has a stomach adapted for extracting as many nutrients as possible from its diet of leaves.

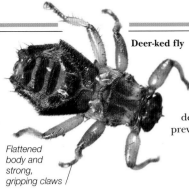

Deer-ked fly

Flattened body and strong, gripping claws

EXTERNAL PARASITES

The deer-ked fly (*Lipoptena cervi*) is an example of an ectoparasite (a parasite that lives on the outside of its host). It starts its adult life with wings, but when it finds a deer, its wings fall off and it lives by sucking the deer's blood. The deer-ked fly has specially strengthened claws to prevent it from falling off its host.

INTERNAL PARASITES

Parasites that live inside animals (endoparasites) are sheltered from the outside world and cannot be dislodged. Because they do not need to search for food, they can put all their energy into growth and reproduction. These parasites include many types of worms. Tapeworms normally live in the host's digestive system, but flukes and roundworms (nematodes) attack other parts of the body. Some species infect humans and domestic animals.

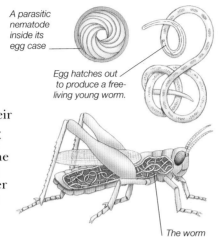

A parasitic nematode inside its egg case

Egg hatches out to produce a free-living young worm.

The worm infects a grasshopper and grows inside it.

BLUE GIANT CLAM

The brightly colored "lips" of this clam contain millions of microscopic algae, which can produce food by capturing the energy in sunlight (photosynthesis). The clam gives the algae somewhere safe to live, and in return it shares the food that the algae produce. Giant clams also collect food by filtering it from the water around them.

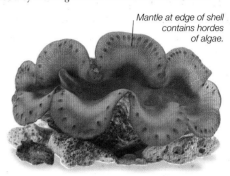

Mantle at edge of shell contains hordes of algae.

Scientific name: *Tridacna maxima*

Size: Width up to 1 ft (30 cm)

Habitat: Coral reefs

Distribution: Indian and western Pacific Ocean

Reproduction: Sperm and eggs are released into water; larvae drift in plankton before settling on reef and turning into adults.

Diet: Small particles of food filtered from water

Life cycle of a liver fluke

Cysts form in infected fish.

Eggs carried away in sewage

Eggs hatch into larvae.

Larvae infect water snails.

Tadpolelike stage (cercaria) infects fish.

Adult flukes develop when infected fish is eaten.

FROM HOST TO HOST

Many internal parasites have life cycles that involve more than one host. The Chinese liver fluke (*Opisthorchis sinensis*) enters the human body through infected raw fish. Inside the body, the fluke produces eggs that are released in human feces. The eggs then pass from sewage to fresh water and hatch into larvae that infect water snails. The tadpolelike larvae leave the snail and are eaten by fish. If an infected fish is caught and eaten, the parasite is passed on to humans once more. Cooking the fish, however, kills the parasite.

BROOD PARASITES

A brood parasite is an animal that tricks another species into raising its own young. In this way, the parasite avoids the hard work involved in finding food for a growing family. About one percent of bird species, including honeyguides, cowbirds, and cuckoos, are brood parasites. As soon as they hatch, young cuckoos push their foster parents' eggs out of the nest. Consequently, they get all the food for themselves.

EATEN ALIVE

This cabbage white caterpillar (*Pieris rapae*) has been attacked by a tiny braconid fly (*Cotesia glomeratus*) that laid its eggs in the caterpillar's body. The eggs hatched into grubs that have eaten the caterpillar from inside. The braconid fly is a parasitoid. Unlike most true parasites, parasitoids nearly always kill their hosts. They can be useful because they help to control insect pests.

Meadow pipit (*Anthus pratensis*)

Common cuckoo (*Cuculus canorus*)

The cuckoo is well fed and grows to a large size.

The foster parent does not realize that the huge cuckoo chick is not its own.

Find out more

FEEDING AND NUTRITION: *22*
INSECTS: *162*
PARASITIC AND EPIPHYTIC PLANTS: *136*

ANIMAL HOMES

ALTHOUGH SOME ANIMALS BUILD permanent homes,
many spend all their time on the move and never have
a true home. Others, such as birds, need homes for only
part of the year, usually during the breeding season.
Animals build shelters to protect themselves and their
young from predators or the weather. They also use homes
as lairs in which they can catch or store food. Animals make
amazing homes using a range of natural materials such as
sticks, grass, and mud. Some creatures even construct
homes out of saliva and silk, which they produce
from inside their own bodies.

If attacked, the hermit crab pulls its body inside the shell.

Reef hermit
(*Dardanus megistos*)

MOBILE HOMES

Small animals are in danger of being eaten by
predators when they search for food. To protect
themselves, some build mobile homes that make
it harder for predators to swallow them.
The larvae of insects called caddisflies live
in water and feed on small water creatures.
They construct tubular cases that they carry
around their bodies. Depending
on the type of species, these
cases are made from sand, tiny
sticks, or small shells, and are
fastened together with silk
from the larva's mouth.

Two caddisfly larvae protected by portable cases

Caddisfly
(*Limnephilidae* sp.)

A BORROWED HOME

The hermit crab has an unusual kind of mobile
home – it lives in a shell made by a mollusk. Because
these crabs have soft abdomens, they need to protect
themselves from attack by living in an empty shell. As
the hermit crab grows bigger, it has to change its home
for a larger model. Once it has found a suitable shell,
it feels inside with its claws to check whether the
shell is large enough before entering its new home.

BIRDS' NESTS

A bird's nest helps to keep eggs
warm while they are being incubated,
and also conceals eggs and young birds
from predators. A blue tit's nest is only
about the size of a teacup, while the largest
nests, made by birds of prey, can weigh
more than one ton. The nest of the
Rufous hornero (*Furnarius rufus*)
is very distinctive. Built of mud,
it dries as hard as stone, and
has a curved entrance that
makes it difficult for
predators to get inside.

Mud is baked hard by the sun.

Nest holds between 4 and 12 nestlings.

Nest sliced in half to show curved entrance

SHROUDED IN SILK

Each cocoon is made of a single thread of silk.

The pupae (chrysalises) of moths
are often surrounded by cocoons
of silk, which protect them as they
develop into adult moths. Silk
is used as a building material by
many insects and spiders. It starts
as a liquid inside an animal's body,
then turns into fibers when it
is squeezed out through special
nozzles called spinnerets. Silk
is very strong, and can stretch
a long way without breaking.

Blue tits (Parus caeruleus) build nests from twigs, moss, and spiders' silk.

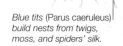

Horneros often build their nests on fence posts.

HOMES MADE OF PAPER

Many wasps build nests from chewed-up wood fibers mixed with their saliva. When spread out in a thin sheet, this mixture dries to form a substance like paper. Tropical wasps use paper to make cells for their eggs and grubs. A single female wasp starts the nest once she has mated, making a cluster of cells attached to the branch of a tree. In cooler climates, wasps add a layer of paper around the cells, which helps keep them warm.

The cells are fastened to a low branch.

Sealed cells containing developing eggs or grubs

Paper wasps (*Polistes* sp.)

A harvest mouse on its nest made of woven grass

MAMMAL NESTS

Compared to birds and insects, mammals are not noted for being accomplished builders. Many mammals dig burrows, but only a few build homes above ground. One of the most skillful builders is the tiny Old World harvest mouse (*Micromys minutus*) from Europe and Asia, which weighs just 0.25 oz (6 g). It makes a nest slung between the stems of grasses. The nest is about the size of a tennis ball, and is made of shredded blades of grass.

VILLAGE WEAVER

Weaver birds gather up strips of leaves, and use their legs and beaks to weave them into a nest. The nest is usually made by the male, and when it is finished, he hangs beneath it to persuade a female to move in. There are more than 100 species of weavers. The village weaver makes rounded nests with an entrance chamber on one side.

Scientific name: *Ploceus cucullatus*

Size: 7 in (18 cm) long

Habitat: Woodland and fields

Distribution: Most of Africa south of the Sahara Desert

Reproduction: Female lays 2–4 eggs per year

Diet: Mainly seeds

OVERNIGHT HOMES

When dusk begins to fall, baboons climb trees or cliffs where it is safer to sleep than on the ground. Baboons do not make overnight shelters, but some apes – including chimpanzees and orangutans – construct leafy nest platforms among tree branches. Each platform takes a few minutes to build and is normally used just once. Gorillas also make nest platforms in trees, although they often sleep on the ground. (Larger gorillas are too heavy to climb trees.)

By sleeping in trees, baboons reduce the chance of being preyed upon during the night.

Chacma baboon (*Papio ursinus*)

Silk-lined tunnel of the trapdoor spider

The trapdoor is slightly open.

The spider waits for food at the top of the tunnel.

Emergency hideout

Hinged door made of silk and soil

If danger threatens, the spider hides at the bottom of the tunnel.

The spider pulls the door shut behind it.

TRAPDOOR TUNNELS

For trapdoor spiders, home is more than a place to live – it is also a lair where they hide ready to ambush their prey. Trapdoor spiders build silk-lined tunnels in the ground. The top of each tunnel has a hinged lid made of silk, and the owner of the tunnel hides underneath the lid, rushing out if anything edible walks by. Some trapdoor-spider tunnels have a special chamber where they can hide if threatened with attack.

HOMES UNDERGROUND

Like many small mammals, jerboas construct homes underground. Jerboas are nocturnal creatures that live in dry places where it can be very hot by day, but cool at night. During the daytime, they often seal their burrows by plugging them with loose earth. This keeps moisture in and heat out. Some jerboa burrows have an emergency exit for making a sudden escape.

Main entrance is sealed during the day.

Emergency exit often ends just below ground.

Desert jerboa (*Jaculus* sp.)

The jerboa is sheltered from the heat of the day.

Find out more

BIRDS: *208*

COPING WITH EXTREMES: *60*

DESERTS: *86*

INSECTS: *162*

COPING WITH EXTREMES

IN MANY PARTS OF THE WORLD, where there is warmth and plenty of water, a wide variety of plants and animals are able to thrive. But in deserts, mountainous areas, and freezing tundra, conditions are much more extreme. Here, only the hardiest species can survive. These survival specialists cope with extremes in different ways. Some animals have dense fur to keep themselves warm, or special chemicals that stop their blood from freezing. Others have adapted so they can withstand intense heat, pounding waves, or biting winds. A few living things can survive without water for months or even years, then suddenly come back to life when it rains.

A volcanically heated spring in Yellowstone National Park, USA

LIFE IN HOT WATER

Most living things would die within seconds if they fell into a hot-water spring. But amazingly, some types of bacteria are quite at home in these surroundings. These bacteria use dissolved minerals as a source of energy, and they can survive and grow in temperatures above 158° F (70° C). On deep seabeds, some bacteria survive in superheated water from volcanic vents, which can be as hot as 239° F (115° C).

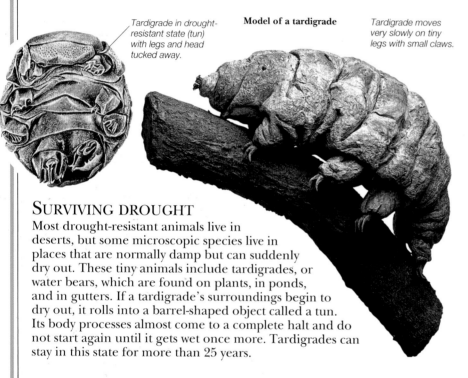

Tardigrade in drought-resistant state (tun) with legs and head tucked away.

Model of a tardigrade

Tardigrade moves very slowly on tiny legs with small claws.

SURVIVING DROUGHT

Most drought-resistant animals live in deserts, but some microscopic species live in places that are normally damp but can suddenly dry out. These tiny animals include tardigrades, or water bears, which are found on plants, in ponds, and in gutters. If a tardigrade's surroundings begin to dry out, it rolls into a barrel-shaped object called a tun. Its body processes almost come to a complete halt and do not start again until it gets wet once more. Tardigrades can stay in this state for more than 25 years.

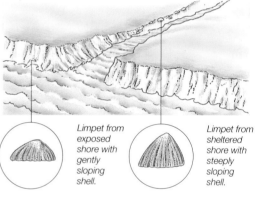

Limpet from exposed shore with gently sloping shell.

Limpet from sheltered shore with steeply sloping shell.

COPING WITH THE WAVES

Waves are so powerful that they can erode cliffs, and can even smash open blocks of concrete. Limpets survive seashore battering because they have a strong suckerlike foot, and an extremely tough conical shell. Limpets that live on sheltered rocks have tall shells, but ones that live in exposed places have flatter shells that are harder for waves to dislodge.

BRIEF LIVES

In deserts, many plants have tough leaves and deep roots, but others – called ephemerals – have a different way of surviving. These plants have very short life cycles. Their seeds can lie dormant in the ground for years, but germinate within hours if it rains. The young plants quickly grow and flower, shedding their own seeds before drought sets in once more. With their work done, the plants then wither and die.

Plants flower in the desert of Namaqualand, southwest Africa.

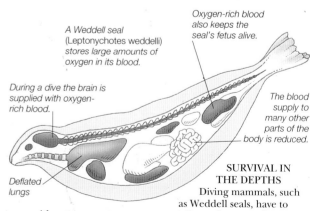

A Weddell seal (Leptonychotes weddelli) stores large amounts of oxygen in its blood.

Oxygen-rich blood also keeps the seal's fetus alive.

During a dive the brain is supplied with oxygen-rich blood.

The blood supply to many other parts of the body is reduced.

Deflated lungs

SURVIVAL IN THE DEPTHS

Diving mammals, such as Weddell seals, have to cope with extreme water pressure as well as a shortage of oxygen. The Weddell seal cannot dive with its lungs full of air, because the water pressure could make them burst. Instead, it breathes deeply on the surface, and then breathes out just before it dives. With its lungs almost empty, it can reach depths of 2,000 ft (600 m), and can stay underwater for more than an hour.

COPING WITH COLD

Wolves often live in cold places. They survive the winter because they have thick fur that provides good insulation. On particularly cold nights, they protect themselves by curling up in banks of snow. Although snow is cold, the air above it is often colder still. By sheltering in snow banks, wolves keep out of the wind, and they also conserve precious warmth. In the far north, many other animals – from polar bears to birds – also use snow as a natural blanket.

Antarctic icefish
(*Chaenocephalus aceratus*)

NATURAL ANTIFREEZE

Near the poles, the sea's temperature hovers near freezing point. Fish survive these low temperatures because they have chemicals in their blood that work like antifreeze. These chemicals prevent ice crystals from forming in the blood – which would quickly prove fatal. On land, some insects and other small animals also use antifreeze to survive in very cold habitats.

A gray wolf (Canis lupus) makes a shelter out of snow to cope with freezing temperatures.

TADPOLE SHRIMP

Tadpole shrimp live in puddles created by rare desert storms. These puddles soon dry out and, although the adult shrimp die, their eggs live on. The eggs can survive complete drought for more than 15 years, as well as temperatures up to 176°F (80°C). They hatch as soon as it rains.

Scientific name: *Triops* sp.

Size: About 1 in (2.5 cm) long

Habitat: Deserts and semideserts

Distribution: Worldwide

Reproduction: May be male, female, or hermaphrodite; eggs are scattered in drying mud

Diet: Eggs and larvae of insects; also tadpoles

SURVIVING HIGH UP

Mountain plants have to cope with strong sunshine, penetrating frost, and bitterly cold winds. Most of them avoid frost and wind by growing in sheltered crevices, or by having a cushionlike shape, which makes them less exposed. The leaves of mountain plants are often small and tough – which dry out less in the wind than larger leaves. Mountain soil is usually very thin, so mountain plants have deep roots that keep them firmly in place.

Cushion-shaped plant

How mountain plants adapt to the wind

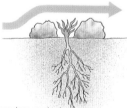

Rock crevices protect soft-stemmed mountain plants from the wind.

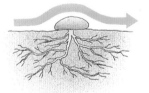

Wind blows over cushion-shaped mountain plant without causing any damage.

Vicuña
(*Vicugna vicugna*)

WHERE OXYGEN IS SHORT

On high mountains, the air is much thinner than it is at ground level, so it is harder for animals to get the oxygen that they need to breathe. Some mammals, such as the South American vicuña, overcome this problem by having a special form of the red blood pigment hemoglobin. This hemoglobin is unusually good at absorbing oxygen, and it allows vicuñas to survive at heights of more than 16,400 ft (5,000 m).

SURVIVAL IN THE SUN

Plants need sunlight to live, but sometimes the Sun's rays are too strong. This is particularly true in high tropical mountains, where the air is thin and the midday Sun is almost overhead. In this habitat, many plants, such as *Espeletia schultzii* from Venezuela, have silky hairs that cover their leaves. These hairs help screen out some of the sunlight during the day, and they also protect the plant from frost at night. Some of these plants grow as tall as trees and can live for more than a hundred years.

Find out more
DESERTS: *86*
MOUNTAINS AND CAVES: *88*
OCEANS: *68*
SEASHORES AND TIDEPOOLS: *70*

ECOLOGY

IN NATURE, NOTHING LIVES entirely on its own. Instead, living things are influenced by their surroundings as well as by the other species around them. The study of these relationships is called ecology. In ecological research, biologists try to find out how individual species fit into the world around them, and how different species interact. Ecology is a relatively new science, but it has become very important because it helps explain how species normally live in the wild. It also explains how changes made by people, such as farming and deforestation, can upset their way of life. By investigating ecology, biologists can often find ways of minimizing human impact on the natural world.

A deer's niche includes the way it feeds.

Deer and grass share the same habitat.

Deer form part of an ecosystem.

A biome is an ecosystem spread over a large area.

Biomes make up the biosphere – the parts of Earth in which life can be found.

ECOLOGICAL SCALE

The study of ecology covers the entire living world. To make this easy to study, ecologists divide it into small units. The smallest unit is a niche, a living thing's position in its environment, including small details such as diet and behavior. The next step is a habitat, which is the natural environment of several species. Together, separate habitats and their wildlife make up ecosystems. These form the biomes that make up the biosphere as a whole.

BIOMES

Biologists divide the living world into regions that share the same characteristic types of vegetation and wildlife. These are called biomes. Biomes are shaped mainly by climate, because this determines where different types of plants can grow. The areas shown on the map are based on the natural distribution of the world's biomes. They do not take into account changes made by people.

Alpine tundra in Denali National Park, Alaska

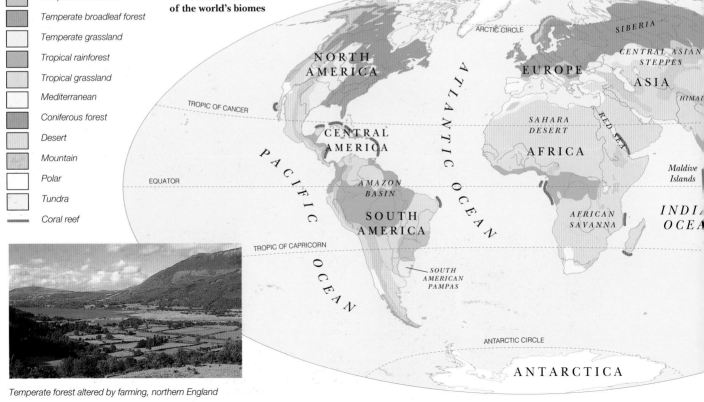

- Temperate rainforest
- Temperate broadleaf forest
- Temperate grassland
- Tropical rainforest
- Tropical grassland
- Mediterranean
- Coniferous forest
- Desert
- Mountain
- Polar
- Tundra
- Coral reef

Natural distribution of the world's biomes

ARCTIC OCEAN

ARCTIC CIRCLE

SIBERIA

CENTRAL ASIAN STEPPES

NORTH AMERICA

EUROPE

ASIA

ATLANTIC OCEAN

TROPIC OF CANCER

SAHARA DESERT

RED SEA

HIMA

CENTRAL AMERICA

AFRICA

PACIFIC OCEAN

AMAZON BASIN

EQUATOR

Maldive Islands

SOUTH AMERICA

AFRICAN SAVANNA

INDIA OCEA

TROPIC OF CAPRICORN

SOUTH AMERICAN PAMPAS

ANTARCTIC CIRCLE

ANTARCTICA

Temperate forest altered by farming, northern England

ECOSYSTEMS

An ecosystem is a complete community of living things, together with their surroundings. In each ecosystem, all the species are linked by a collection of different food chains. Ecosystems have no set size and can range from a single tree to a complete coral reef. Ecosystems are often treated as if they were separate units because this makes them easier to study. However, in reality, food and energy often flow from one ecosystem to another – for example, when fish migrate from rivers into the sea.

A solitary oak tree forms a complete ecosystem and supports a variety of wildlife.

Purple emperor butterflies drink honeydew – the sticky fluid that aphids scatter on leaves.

Oak
(*Quercus* sp.)

Blue tits feed on caterpillars and spiders.

Stag beetles feed on rotting wood.

Gray squirrels feed on acorns, buds, and the sap-rich wood underneath bark.

Marsupial mole
(*Notoryctes typhlops*)

Female has a backward-opening pouch.

Spadelike front feet with large claws

European mole
(*Talpa europaea*)

Velvety upright fur

Spadelike front feet with short claws

HABITATS AND NICHES

In a single ecosystem, there may be hundreds or thousands of species. Despite living closely together, each one occupies its own niche, or particular home and way of life. In the entire living world, no two species ever share exactly the same niche, but some have evolved remarkable similarities. For example, the marsupial mole of Australia lives in a very similar way to the European mole, even though the two animals are not closely related.

ECOLOGICAL SUCCESSION

Even without human interference, ecosystems are always changing. Some of these changes happen very slowly – for example, when glaciers advance and retreat during ice ages. Others, such as hurricanes and forest fires, happen much more quickly. When an ecosystem is suddenly swept clean by a disaster, nature slowly returns. During a process called ecological succession, different species move in until a stable mixture of species develops.

Larger plants gradually smother the original plants, providing more shelter for animals.

In this ecosystem, trees eventually become the dominant vegetation.

Insects and spiders arrive to feed among the plants.

Windblown seeds settle on open ground and germinate.

During the "pioneer" stage, short-lived plants flourish because they do not face any competition.

PACIFIC OCEAN

STRALIA

Great Basin desert, US

Great Barrier Reef

Soft and hard corals, Fiji, South Pacific

Find out more

DESERTS: *86*

FOOD CHAINS AND WEBS: *66*

HABITATS IN DANGER: *104*

NUTRIENT CYCLES: *64*

NUTRIENT CYCLES

THE EARTH CONTAINS about 90 natural elements, or pure substances. Of these elements, about 20 are essential to living things. Some, including carbon, oxygen, and nitrogen, are used by living things in large quantities. These are called macronutrients. Others, called micronutrients, are needed only in minute quantities. Living things obtain chemical nutrients from their food or their surroundings. They release these nutrients when they use energy, and when they die. As a result, chemical nutrients constantly pass between living and nonliving things. Some parts of these cycles take place in a matter of seconds, but others can take thousands of years.

Carbon from plant and animal remains may be stored in coal or oil.

Carbon dioxide is released when coal or oil are burned.

CARBON STORES
When living things die, they are normally broken down by microorganisms, and most of their carbon returns to the air. However, the microorganisms cannot fully break down carbon remains in places where there is little oxygen. Instead, the carbon stays locked up underground, and eventually turns into coal, oil, or natural gas. When these fossil fuels are burned, carbon is released.

THE CARBON CYCLE
All living things contain the element carbon. During photosynthesis plants absorb carbon from the air in the form of carbon dioxide gas. They convert the carbon dioxide into substances such as carbohydrates, which provide a store of energy. Animals take in carbon when they eat plants or other animals. Carbon dioxide is released back into the atmosphere when living things breathe out and when their remains are broken down.

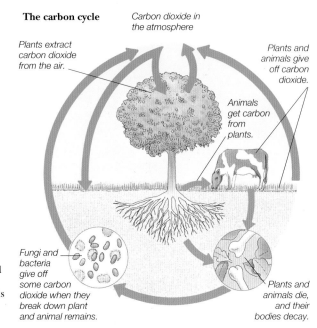

The carbon cycle

Carbon dioxide in the atmosphere

Plants extract carbon dioxide from the air.

Plants and animals give off carbon dioxide.

Animals get carbon from plants.

Fungi and bacteria give off some carbon dioxide when they break down plant and animal remains.

Plants and animals die, and their bodies decay.

THE NITROGEN CYCLE
Nitrogen is an important part of substances called proteins, which all cells need to survive. Nearly four-fifths of the atmosphere is nitrogen gas, but only bacteria can use this directly. All other living things rely on nitrogen that has been combined with other elements by nitrogen-fixing bacteria. Some of these bacteria live in soil, but others live in swellings on the roots of plants. When living things die, their nitrogen compounds are released by other bacteria.

The nitrogen cycle

Nitrogen gas in the atmosphere

Animals get nitrogen from plants.

Denitrifying bacteria take in nitrates and release nitrogen into the atmosphere.

Dead plants and animals release nitrogen compounds into soil.

Nitrifying bacteria in the soil convert nitrogen compounds from animals to nitrates.

Lightning combines nitrogen and oxygen. They fall in rain as weak nitric acid.

Nitrifying bacteria convert nitrogen compounds in the soil to nitrates.

Plants absorb nitrates through their roots.

Nitrates in the soil

The energy in lightning makes nitrogen and oxygen combine.

FIXED IN A FLASH
Bacteria are not the only things that can combine nitrogen gas into nitrogen compounds. When lightning flashes through the air, it produces nitrogen compounds that are washed into the soil by rain. Nitrogen is also fixed in chemical factories to make fertilizer that boosts the growth of crops. Every year, about 50 million tons of nitrogen are fixed in this way.

Fungus breaking down a dead locust

DECOMPOSITION
This locust has been dead for just a few hours, but it is already covered with the fluffy feeding threads of a fungus. During the next few days the locust's body will break down, and most of its chemical nutrients will be released. Fungi and bacteria that break down dead remains are called decomposers. They play a key part in nutrient cycles by recycling nutrients so that they can be used again.

THE PHOSPHORUS CYCLE

Unlike carbon and nitrogen, phosphorus is not found in the air. Instead, it comes from particles of rock mixed up in soil. Plants absorb phosphorus through their roots, and animals take it in when they eat plants or other animals. When living things die, their phosphorus is returned to the soil. Phosphorus dissolves easily, and it is constantly washed out of the soil and into the sea. After millions of years, it becomes phosphorus-bearing rock once more.

The phosphorus cycle

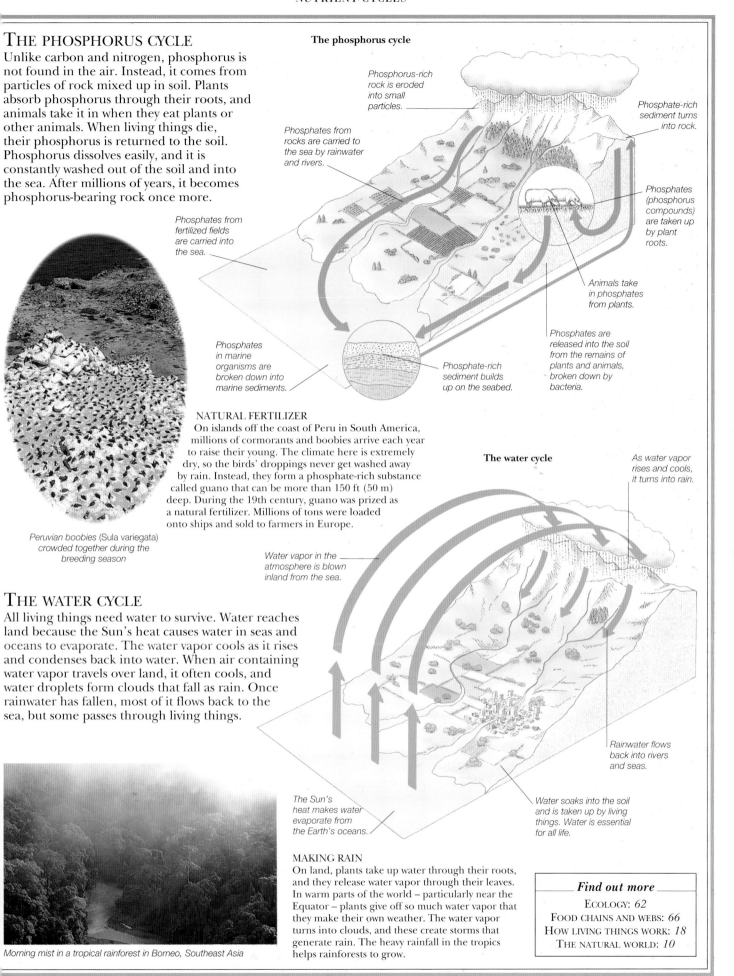

Phosphorus-rich rock is eroded into small particles.

Phosphate-rich sediment turns into rock.

Phosphates from rocks are carried to the sea by rainwater and rivers.

Phosphates (phosphorus compounds) are taken up by plant roots.

Phosphates from fertilized fields are carried into the sea.

Animals take in phosphates from plants.

Phosphates in marine organisms are broken down into marine sediments.

Phosphate-rich sediment builds up on the seabed.

Phosphates are released into the soil from the remains of plants and animals, broken down by bacteria.

Peruvian boobies (Sula variegata) crowded together during the breeding season

NATURAL FERTILIZER

On islands off the coast of Peru in South America, millions of cormorants and boobies arrive each year to raise their young. The climate here is extremely dry, so the birds' droppings never get washed away by rain. Instead, they form a phosphate-rich substance called guano that can be more than 150 ft (50 m) deep. During the 19th century, guano was prized as a natural fertilizer. Millions of tons were loaded onto ships and sold to farmers in Europe.

The water cycle

As water vapor rises and cools, it turns into rain.

Water vapor in the atmosphere is blown inland from the sea.

THE WATER CYCLE

All living things need water to survive. Water reaches land because the Sun's heat causes water in seas and oceans to evaporate. The water vapor cools as it rises and condenses back into water. When air containing water vapor travels over land, it often cools, and water droplets form clouds that fall as rain. Once rainwater has fallen, most of it flows back to the sea, but some passes through living things.

Rainwater flows back into rivers and seas.

The Sun's heat makes water evaporate from the Earth's oceans.

Water soaks into the soil and is taken up by living things. Water is essential for all life.

Morning mist in a tropical rainforest in Borneo, Southeast Asia

MAKING RAIN

On land, plants take up water through their roots, and they release water vapor through their leaves. In warm parts of the world – particularly near the Equator – plants give off so much water vapor that they make their own weather. The water vapor turns into clouds, and these create storms that generate rain. The heavy rainfall in the tropics helps rainforests to grow.

Find out more

ECOLOGY: *62*
FOOD CHAINS AND WEBS: *66*
HOW LIVING THINGS WORK: *18*
THE NATURAL WORLD: *10*

FOOD CHAINS AND WEBS

IN THE LIVING WORLD, ALL PLANTS and animals are potential food. Animals eat plants, animals eat each other, and even when living things die their remains are broken down to provide food matter for fungi and bacteria. The route that food follows is known as a food chain. It connects different species in an ecosystem, and links each species with the things that it eats. Most species eat several kinds of food, so they actually fit into several different food chains. Together, all the food chains in an ecosystem form a food web. A food chain usually contains less than six species, but a food web may contain thousands.

Cats eat birds such as blue tits and thrushes.

Spiders feed on aphids and are eaten by birds.

ENERGY FROM THE SUN

All living things need a constant supply of energy. For the vast majority, this energy comes from the Sun. The energy in sunlight is captured by plants or microorganisms, through a process called photosynthesis. This process turns solar energy into chemical energy, which other living things can use. Chemical energy is passed on when plants are eaten by animals, or when animals are eaten by each other.

All the plants and animals in this forest get their energy from sunlight.

Plants are food for many animals and for decomposers such as fungi.

Grass

Rabbits eat grass.

Foxes eat rabbits.

Thrushes eat snails.

FOOD CHAIN
This diagram shows a single food chain. Like all food chains, it begins with a producer (a living thing that uses energy to make its own food). In this case, the producer is grass, which, like all plants, makes its food using sunlight. The other species in the chain are called consumers. They cannot make their own food. Instead, they survive by eating producers, or each other.

Fungi and bacteria feed on plant matter.

Garden snails feed on plants.

Worms feed on dead plant and animal matter.

PYRAMID OF ENERGY

At each step in a food chain, energy is lost as well as passed on. This means that much more energy is available at the bottom of a food chain than at the top. The energy pyramid shown here arranges the different species according to their position (trophic level) in food chains. At the lowest trophic level are large numbers of producers, containing lots of energy. At the highest trophic level, there are relatively few large consumers, containing a small amount of energy.

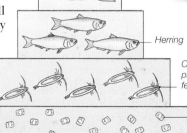

Gray seal

Herring

Copepods are small planktonic crustaceans that feed on marine phytoplankton.

Marine phytoplankton are single-celled, plantlike organisms that harness energy from sunlight.

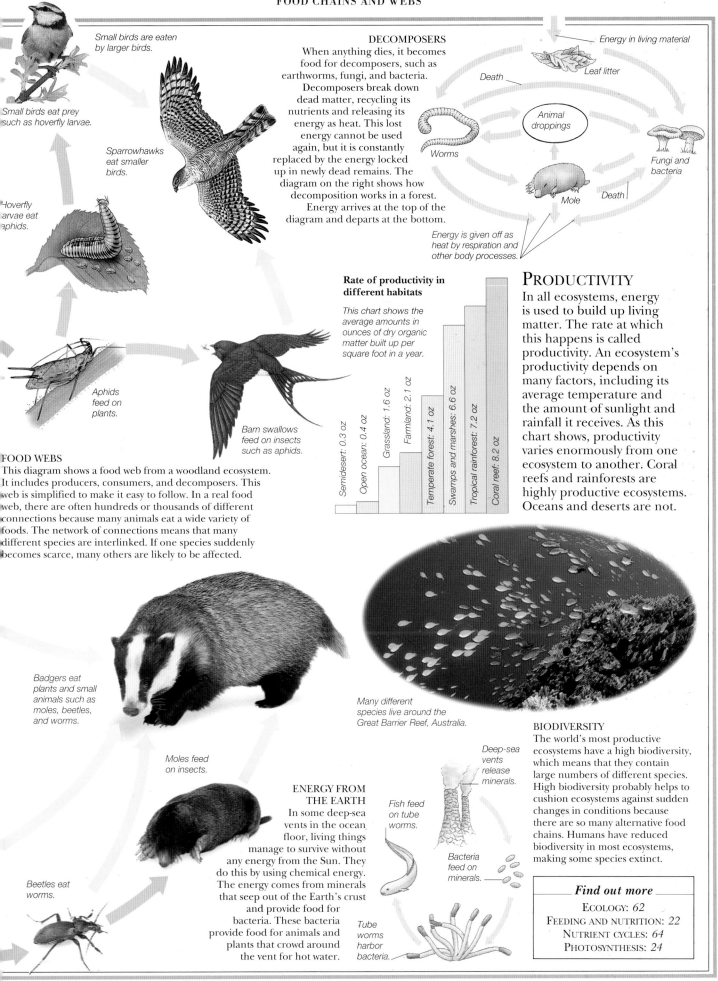

Small birds are eaten by larger birds.

Small birds eat prey such as hoverfly larvae.

Sparrowhawks eat smaller birds.

Hoverfly larvae eat aphids.

Aphids feed on plants.

DECOMPOSERS

When anything dies, it becomes food for decomposers, such as earthworms, fungi, and bacteria. Decomposers break down dead matter, recycling its nutrients and releasing its energy as heat. This lost energy cannot be used again, but it is constantly replaced by the energy locked up in newly dead remains. The diagram on the right shows how decomposition works in a forest. Energy arrives at the top of the diagram and departs at the bottom.

Energy in living material

Death

Leaf litter

Animal droppings

Worms

Fungi and bacteria

Mole

Death

Energy is given off as heat by respiration and other body processes.

Rate of productivity in different habitats

This chart shows the average amounts in ounces of dry organic matter built up per square foot in a year.

Semidesert: 0.3 oz
Open ocean: 0.4 oz
Grassland: 1.6 oz
Farmland: 2.1 oz
Temperate forest: 4.1 oz
Swamps and marshes: 6.6 oz
Tropical rainforest: 7.2 oz
Coral reef: 8.2 oz

PRODUCTIVITY

In all ecosystems, energy is used to build up living matter. The rate at which this happens is called productivity. An ecosystem's productivity depends on many factors, including its average temperature and the amount of sunlight and rainfall it receives. As this chart shows, productivity varies enormously from one ecosystem to another. Coral reefs and rainforests are highly productive ecosystems. Oceans and deserts are not.

Barn swallows feed on insects such as aphids.

FOOD WEBS

This diagram shows a food web from a woodland ecosystem. It includes producers, consumers, and decomposers. This web is simplified to make it easy to follow. In a real food web, there are often hundreds or thousands of different connections because many animals eat a wide variety of foods. The network of connections means that many different species are interlinked. If one species suddenly becomes scarce, many others are likely to be affected.

Badgers eat plants and small animals such as moles, beetles, and worms.

Many different species live around the Great Barrier Reef, Australia.

Moles feed on insects.

ENERGY FROM THE EARTH

In some deep-sea vents in the ocean floor, living things manage to survive without any energy from the Sun. They do this by using chemical energy. The energy comes from minerals that seep out of the Earth's crust and provide food for bacteria. These bacteria provide food for animals and plants that crowd around the vent for hot water.

Deep-sea vents release minerals.

Fish feed on tube worms.

Bacteria feed on minerals.

Tube worms harbor bacteria.

BIODIVERSITY

The world's most productive ecosystems have a high biodiversity, which means that they contain large numbers of different species. High biodiversity probably helps to cushion ecosystems against sudden changes in conditions because there are so many alternative food chains. Humans have reduced biodiversity in most ecosystems, making some species extinct.

Beetles eat worms.

Find out more
ECOLOGY: *62*
FEEDING AND NUTRITION: *22*
NUTRIENT CYCLES: *64*
PHOTOSYNTHESIS: *24*

OCEANS

THE EARTH IS A WATERY PLANET – almost three-quarters of its surface is covered by oceans. Below the surface, the sea becomes increasingly cold and very little light penetrates the water. Yet this apparently inhospitable environment is home to a wide variety of plants and animals, from microscopic plankton to giant whales. There are creatures at every depth of the ocean – some jellyfish and turtles float or swim near the surface, whales and squid live in the ocean's mid-depths, and a whole host of strange-looking creatures swim or crawl around the dark ocean depths.

Distribution of world's major oceans

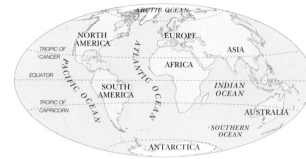

Multibar pipefish (Syngnathus sp.) hiding among sea grasses

Life in the ocean zones

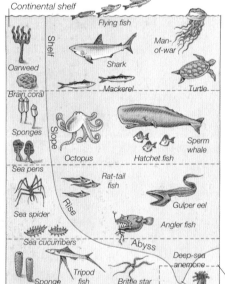

Continental shelf
Flying fish
Shelf
Man-of-war
Oarweed
Shark
Mackerel
Turtle
Brain coral
Slope
Sponges
Sperm whale
Octopus
Hatchet fish
Sea pens
Rat-tail fish
Rise
Gulper eel
Sea spider
Angler fish
Sea cucumbers
Abyss
Deep-sea anemone
Sponge
Tripod fish
Brittle star

Sunlit zone
Seasonal changes in water temperature

660 ft (200 m)

Twilight zone
Water temperature drops

3,300 ft (1,000 m)

Dark zone
Water very cold and pitch black

13,120 ft (4,000 m)

Abyss
Dark and cold

19,700 ft (6,000 m)

Deep-sea trench
There is still life below this depth.

SEA GRASSES

Beds of sea grasses – the only flowering plants to grow in the ocean – provide food, shelter, and breeding sites for turtles, eels, and other sea creatures. Sea grasses grow in shallow areas of warm and temperate seas. When they die, their remains provide a rich supply of nutrients for other organisms.

VERTICAL ZONES

Scientists divide the oceans into several distinct zones, according to the depth of the water. Each zone is home to a different community of living things, adapted to survive at that depth. In deep water, animals must cope with darkness, very cold temperatures, and pressures that would crush a human. Some twilight-zone animals swim up to the surface each night to feed on the rich supply of plankton and other food there, and then descend to rest in the day.

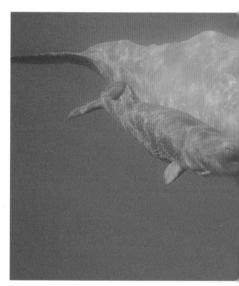

A sperm whale (Physeter catodon) with its calf

The tripod fish rests on its three long fin rays. This is a good position from which to ambush prey drifting by in the water.

Sea spiders feed by sucking the juices out of soft-bodied invertebrates.

DARK ZONE

Although the ocean depths are cold and dark, they are home to a surprising variety of creatures. Sponges, sea cucumbers, and sea spiders are just some of the unusual animals that live on the deep seafloor. They survive mostly on the remains of tiny plants and animals that slowly rain down from the layers above. Many deep-sea creatures also gather to feed on the remains of dead whales, turtles, and other animals that have sunk to the bottom.

The Venus' flower basket is a type of sponge. Its skeleton is made of silica.

Sea pens trap food particles in their palmlike fronds.

Sea cucumbers feed on food particles buried in the soft ocean bed.

Glassy strands keep these sponges anchored in the seabed.

Brittlestars collect food particles with their snakelike arms.

SUNLIT ZONE

Marine mammals, squid, fish, and other creatures that live in the sunlit zone have to be strong swimmers to move around in the surface currents. They also need camouflage to protect themselves because the water near the surface is well lit and there is nowhere to hide from predators. Fish, such as rays, often have dark backs that are hard to see from above against the darkness of the sea. From below, their light undersides are camouflaged against the brightly lit surface.

The spotted eagle ray (Aetobatus narinari) has a light underside that helps conceal it when it swims near the surface.

Adult sperm whales dive to depths of more than 6,560 ft (2,000 m).

Diatom
(*Campylodiscus hibernicus.*)

Diatom
(*Cymbella* sp.)

PLANKTON

All life in the oceans depends on millions of tiny floating organisms called plankton. Phytoplankton (plant plankton), such as diatoms, are the first stage in the ocean food chain. They provide food for zooplankton (animal plankton). Some planktonic animals, such as krill, spend all their lives in the open water. Others, such as barnacle larvae, eventually take up a settled way of life.

FLOATING AND SWIMMING

Some highly specialized creatures float at the ocean's surface. The by-the-wind-sailor (*Velella velella*) is a distant relative of the jellyfish that uses a gas-filled sail to float along. Water striders (*Halobates* sp.) are the only insects to live on the ocean. They skate across the surface, held up by the water's surface tension. Other creatures, like the lion's mane jellyfish, are active swimmers.

Lion's mane jellyfish
(*Cyanea capillata*)

TWILIGHT ZONE

Many twilight-zone creatures have large eyes to help them see in the dim light. They are well camouflaged – transparent in the upper layers, where there is more light, silvery farther down, and black or red in the deepest layers. Red appears black in the deep ocean because red wavelengths of light do not penetrate the water. Sperm whales need to surface to breathe air, but can remain submerged in the twilight zone for more than two hours, hunting giant squid and other prey.

HATCHET FISH

Many mid-depth fish, such as little hatchet fish, are very thin. This reduces the size of their outline when they are viewed by predators or prey swimming above or below them. Also, their silvery, scaleless bodies and the light organs along their undersides camouflage them against the light penetrating from the surface waters.

Hatchet fish
(*Sternoptyx* sp.)

BIOLUMINESCENCE

To survive in dim light or darkness, many fish have developed super-efficient senses. Some have lights on their bodies, produced by special organs called photophores that give off a greenish glow. This process is called bioluminescence. Fish use these lights to recognize members of their own species, or in lures to attract prey. Twilight-zone fish use the light as camouflage, as it blends in with light filtering down from the surface.

Black snaggletooth fish (Astronesthes sp.)

HYDROTHERMAL VENTS

In some places, hot, mineral-rich water gushes into the sea through cracks in the deep ocean floor, called hydrothermal vents. Some bacteria can live on the chemicals in this water, forming the basis of food chains that do not depend on sunlight and plants. Giant tube worms, clams, and blind white crabs all live around these vents.

Deep-sea crab near a hydrothermal vent

SEASHORES AND TIDEPOOLS

THE NARROW STRIP WHERE THE SEA meets the land is home to a rich variety of living things. Twice a day, the animals and plants that live along the seashore and in tidepools face dramatic changes in conditions as the sea level rises and falls. As the tide comes in, many plants and animals are plunged underwater; when it recedes, they are exposed to the sun or the cold night air. Many creatures have adaptations to help them cope with the constant barrage of wind and waves. Mollusks and barnacles have watertight shells that prevent them from drying out, while seaweeds anchor themselves to rocks with rootlike structures called holdfasts.

Eurasian curlew (Numenius arquata) feeding on burrowing invertebrates hidden in the sand

WADERS AND OTHER BIRDS
Coastal birds such as waders, wildfowl, and gulls are a familiar sight along the shoreline. Some species probe deep into wet sand for worms and other burrowing invertebrates; others use their strong bills to hammer open shells. Their movements are governed by the flow of the tides, as they can feed only when the tide is out.

Shoreline at Kearvaig Bay, Scotland, UK

TYPES OF SHORES
Seashores are usually divided into four main types: sandy, rocky, muddy, and gravel (shingle). Rocky shores provide shelter for a great variety of marine plants and animals. Sandy and muddy shores are generally inhabited by burrowing animals that live a few inches below the surface. Gravel beaches are the least hospitable habitats, since most living things find it impossible to survive under or between the constantly moving pebbles.

Below the surface of a rocky shore

Bivalve mollusks suck in food through a tube.

A second tube is used to expel waste.

Cockle

Baltic tellin

Sand star eating a sand gaper

Peppery furrow shell

Sand gaper

Lugworm

Lugworms live in U-shaped burrows. They suck water in, filter out food, then pump out waste behind them.

THE BURROWERS
When the tide is out, sandy and muddy shores appear almost deserted because most of their inhabitants stay buried in the sand or mud. In fact, beneath the surface, these habitats teem with life, ranging from microscopic bacteria to a whole variety of larger invertebrate animals, such as mollusks, crustaceans, worms, and sea urchins.

LIFE IN A TIDEPOOL
Tidepools form as the sea washes over the shore twice a day. They range from small puddles high on the shore to deep holes near the sea. These miniature seas are home to dozens of different plants and animals, many of which spend their whole lives in one pool, while others swim in and out with the tides. During the course of each day, tidepool inhabitants have to cope with huge variations in salt levels, temperature, and oxygen supply.

Painted top shell (Calliostoma zizyphinum)

The piddock grinds its way into the rock.

ROCK BORERS
On rocky shores, a group of mollusks called piddocks take refuge from predators and waves by boring a hole into solid rock. The piddock drills its way downward by twisting and rocking the two parts of its shell. Unlike shipworms, which bore into wood and cause serious damage to boats, piddocks cannot detect one another's presence in the rock, and sometimes will bore right through one another.

TIDAL ZONES

Various plants and animals live on different vertical levels, or zones, on the shore. These zones are particularly obvious on rocky shores where plants and animals live on the surface. At the top of the shore is the splash zone – an area that gets sprayed by waves, but not covered by the tide. The upper zone is washed by waves only at high tide, while most of the middle zone is covered by the tides twice a day. The lower zone is exposed only at low tides.

Rocky shore showing tidal zones

LIVING ON A CLIFF

Plants need to be hardy to survive life on a sea cliff. Thrift grows in round clumps that hug the ground, preventing the sparse surrounding soil and the plants' roots from drying out. The roots extend well into the soil, searching for water and nutrients. To reduce the amount of moisture lost through the leaf surface, the thrift plant has narrow, needlelike leaves.

Thrift
(*Armeria maritima*)

The toothed wrack (Fucus serratus) grips the rock with strong holdfasts.

The common limpet (Patella vulgata) clings to rock with its muscular foot.

The velvet swimming crab (Liocarcinus puber) sorts through debris to find food.

Beadlet anemones (Actinia equina) extend their tentacles in the water to catch prey.

The cushion star (Porania pulvillus) preys on anemones, tubeworms, and small sea urchins.

The snakelocks anemone (Anemonia viridis) has stinging tentacles to paralyze prey.

Harbor seals (Phoca vitulina) on a breeding beach

Scarlet serpent brittle star
(*Ophioderma* sp.)

TIDAL HUNTERS

Many animals hide when the tide is out, then hunt for food when the tide comes back in again. Crabs roam the shore, scavenging for almost anything edible, while brittle stars and starfish glide across the rocks in search of prey. Sea urchins graze on seaweed, and worms extend their heads and wave their tentacles in the water to trap tiny food particles.

SEAL-BREEDING BEACHES

Many species of seal migrate long distances from the open sea to gather and breed on the shore. They usually choose remote bays, headlands, and islands that are difficult for humans and other predators to reach. The amount of time each species spends ashore varies. A high-ranking male elephant seal may not return to the sea for three months, while a northern fur seal spends only about a month on land.

CORAL REEFS

LIKE TROPICAL RAINFORESTS, coral reefs teem with an astonishing variety of wildlife. They are found mainly in the sunlit, shallow water of tropical seas, where coral animals receive the light and warmth they need to grow. At first glance, a reef looks like a sculpture of strangely shaped rocks piled up underwater. These "rocks" are the skeletons of thousands of tiny coral animals, or polyps, which live joined together in colonies. Each polyp is about 0.04–0.4 in (1–10 mm) across and resembles a tiny sea anemone, with a ring of stinging tentacles that wave in the water to catch food. At its base is a hollow skeleton that protects the polyp's soft body. Over hundreds of years, the skeletons build up to form a coral reef.

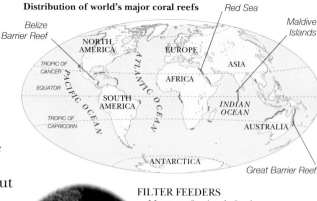

Distribution of world's major coral reefs

CORAL ATOLLS

An atoll is a ring-shaped coral reef surrounding a lagoon of shallow water. Parts of the atoll often rise above sealevel, forming flat islands covered with lush tropical vegetation. Most atolls are found in the Indian Ocean and the western Pacific Ocean. Unlike barrier reefs, atolls may be far from land. They vary in size from 0.4 miles (0.6 km) across to vast rings more than 19 miles (30 km) in diameter.

Kayangel Atoll in the Pacific Ocean

FILTER FEEDERS
Many reef animals feed on microscopic creatures that they filter out of the water. Sponges draw seawater through tiny holes that pepper their bodies, catching particles of food that flow in. Giant clams filter water through their gills to obtain food. They also absorb food from algae that live in their lips.

Organ pipe sponges on stagshorn coral

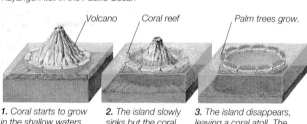

Volcano · Coral reef · Palm trees grow.

1. *Coral starts to grow in the shallow waters around a volcanic island.*

2. *The island slowly sinks but the coral continues to grow.*

3. *The island disappears, leaving a coral atoll. The high points form islands.*

HOW A CORAL ATOLL GROWS
Atolls develop from coral reefs around the shores of volcanic islands. Over millions of years, the volcanic islands slowly sink into the sea. However, coral reefs continually grow upward at about 0.4 in (1 cm) a year. Eventually, all trace of the volcano disappears. Sand may build up on parts of the reef to form land.

Nooks and crannies in the reef provide shelter for many different animals.

BARRIER REEFS

A barrier reef is found along a coastline, separated from the land by a wide and deep lagoon. Parts of a barrier reef may lie as far as 124 miles (200 km) from land. Reefs much closer to the shoreline are called fringing reefs. The Great Barrier Reef off the eastern coast of Australia is the largest coral reef on Earth. It runs in broken chains for more than 1,200 miles (2,000 km) and is visible from space.

Reef fish are often brightly colored. This may help them attract mates or it may warn predators that they are poisonous.

New Caledonia Barrier Reef, western Pacific Ocean

Whitetip reef sharks (*Triaenodon obesus*)

REEF PREDATORS
Predators find rich pickings in coral reefs. Octopuses lurk in dark crevices, ready to shoot out and snatch passing crabs, carnivorous snails stab small fish with poison darts, and starfish crawl over the coral, digesting polyps beneath them. The largest predators are reef sharks, which patrol deep water by the reef for stray fish.

GRAZERS
The algae that carpet coral reefs provide food for grazing animals, such as the colorful blue tang fish and the lettuce slug. The lettuce slug is a slow-moving distant relative of the garden snail. It has no shell to protect it, but its skin makes a foul-tasting substance to deter predators. Like a snail, the lettuce slug uses its abrasive tongue to scrape up food. Some of the algae it eats remain alive in the slug's skin, giving it a green color.

Lettuce slug
(*Tridachia crispata*)

Fleshy flaps help to camouflage the sea dragon within vegetation.

Weedy sea dragon
(*Phyllopteryx taeniolatus*)

CAMOUFLAGE
Some reef animals use camouflage to hide from danger. The sea dragon is a type of pipefish. Some sea dragons live in sea grass around coral reefs, others live in temperate seas. Their bodies are decorated by fleshy flaps to help them blend in with vegetation. Camouflage is not just used for defense – the predatory scorpionfish uses camouflage to hide as it waits to ambush prey.

Blue tang
(*Paracanthurus hepatus*)

These strange "rocks" are the skeletons of hundreds of tiny coral animals, or polyps.

Brain coral
(*Meandrina* sp.)

LIVING TOGETHER
Microscopic algae live inside the bodies of coral polyps. The algae make food by photosynthesis and pass some of this food on to the corals. They also help the corals make their limestone (calcium carbonate) skeletons. In return, the corals provide a safe place to live and a supply of nutrients in their waste products. The algae need sunlight to survive, which is why coral reefs only grow in shallow water.

WETLANDS

THE SALT AND FRESHWATER wetlands of the world contain a rich variety of wildlife. They are often found on coastal flats, alongside rivers, lakes, and estuaries, and in inland depressions where water cannot quickly drain away. Wetlands vary according to terrain, water conditions, and climate. Different types of wetland habitats include upland peat bogs, saltmarshes, mangrove swamps, and low-lying flooded meadows. Animals that live in wetlands have developed special ways to hunt and move around within their habitat and also to cope with the daily and seasonal changes in water level.

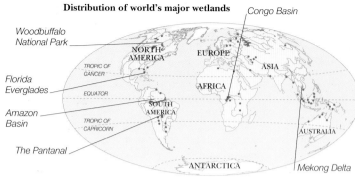

Distribution of world's major wetlands

Congo Basin

Woodbuffalo National Park

NORTH AMERICA

EUROPE

ASIA

TROPIC OF CANCER

Florida Everglades

EQUATOR

AFRICA

Amazon Basin

SOUTH AMERICA

TROPIC OF CAPRICORN

AUSTRALIA

The Pantanal

ANTARCTICA

Mekong Delta

How a peat bog forms

1. Lake sediment collects around plants on the edge of the lake.

2. Lake margins begin to fill in and can support larger plants such as willow trees.

3. Plant material slowly decomposes to form peat.

PEAT BOGS
Peat bogs form in cool, damp environments, where inland lakes slowly become filled in with sediment and then vegetation. There is a distinct order to the different groups of plants that grow over time, and each stage is adapted to the increasingly dry conditions. Peat bogs are typically dominated by sphagnum moss and cotton grass. A bog can take up to 5,000 years to form.

Red lechwes (Kobus leche) may wander into deep water in search of food.

Wetland in Okavango Delta, Botswana

SWAMPS
Swamps, such as parts of the Okavango Delta, are generally found in areas of slow-moving water that are permanently flooded and overgrown. Animals and plants that live here can cope with the changes in the water level as it rises and falls with the seasons. Some parts of the swamp may dry out completely. Emergent vegetation provides a safe haven for birds and small animals to nest and feed.

Goliath heron
(*Ardea goliath*)

SPREADING THE WEIGHT
Many wetland animals have evolved feet with widely splayed toes to prevent them from sinking into soft, waterlogged ground. Mammals such as the sitatunga (*Tragelaphus spekii*) and swamp deer (*Cervus duvauceli*) have long, splayed hooves, while birds such as herons, rails, and jacanas have long, slender, widely spread toes.

Hippopotamuses spend the day in water to save energy.

HIPPOPOTAMUSES
The largest swamp animal in Africa is the hippopotamus (*Hippopotamus amphibius*). It is a solitary feeder that rests by day in the water and grazes on land at night. Its eyes, ears, and nostrils are located on the top of its head, so it can see, hear, and smell while almost submerged.

Swamp forest in the Florida Everglades hides a wealth of animal life.

BITING INSECTS

Insects such as mosquitoes and midges breed in huge numbers in swamp habitats. Female mosquitoes feed by sucking the blood of mammals. They lay their eggs in water, where the eggs hatch into aquatic larvae. The larvae breathe through "siphons" at the tips of their abdomens. When they need air, the larvae rise to the water's surface and thrust their siphons through it.

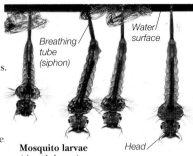

Breathing tube (siphon)

Water surface

Mosquito larvae
(*Anopheles* sp.)

Head

FLOODED FOREST

In some wetland habitats, such as the Florida Everglades, trees are partly submerged in water. These specialized trees have underwater roots that trap sediment and build up a firm base in an otherwise unstable habitat. This eventually creates a flooded forest. The Everglades covers a vast area that contains a variety of wetland habitats from cypress forests to marshy grasslands.

American alligator
(*Alligator mississippiensis*)

Waterbuck (Kobus ellipsiprymnus) *feed on a wide range of grasses including reeds and rushes.*

EVERGLADES WILDLIFE

The Everglades are home to more than 550 species of vertebrates including the rare Florida panther (*Felis concolor coryi*) and the American alligator – the most feared of all Everglades creatures. During the dry season alligators create "gator" holes by digging down into dry waterholes to reach the water below. These newly formed water hollows are also used by other animals.

Egyptian geese (Alopochen aegyptiacus) *feed on grasses and other plants.*

Stilt-rooted mangrove
(*Rhizophora* sp.)

MANGROVES

Mangrove swamps are found along tropical coasts. They are home to remarkable trees that can withstand changing water levels and high salt concentrations. Mangrove trees remove excess salt either by transporting it in the sap from their roots to old leaves that are then shed, or by excreting it from glands on their leaves. Some mangroves are supported by arching prop-roots that have breathing pores for taking in oxygen.

REPTILE PREDATORS

Many carnivorous reptiles thrive in swamps and marshes. These include crocodiles, alligators, and caimans. Snakes, such as the garter snake, often bask in the sunshine at the water's edge, or hunt for prey as they slither through vegetation and swim through shallow waters.

Garter snake
(*Thamnophis sirtalis*)

Mangrove swamp in Queensland, Australia

RIVERS, LAKES, AND PONDS

THE ANIMALS AND PLANTS OF FRESHWATER habitats are very different from those of the land or sea. Aquatic insects skate across the water's surface or crawl among rocks at the bottom, providing food for frogs, diving birds, and freshwater fish. Flowering plants such as reeds and rushes grow thickly at the water's edge, where the water is shallow and still. In lakes and ponds, floating plants such as waterlilies may flourish. Many freshwater animals spend only part of their lives in the water. Frogs, for example, develop underwater as larvae but live out of water as adults. Freshwater mammals, such as otters and water shrews, make their homes on land but hunt underwater.

Distribution of world's major rivers and lakes

The Great Lakes · Yangtze-Kiang River · NORTH AMERICA · EUROPE · ASIA · TROPIC OF CANCER · AFRICA · EQUATOR · SOUTH AMERICA · AUSTRALIA · TROPIC OF CAPRICORN · ANTARCTICA · River Nile · Amazon River · Lake Victoria

RIVERS

Rivers originate in mountains or hills, often springing from a water source underground. Near the river's source, the shallow, tumbling stream has plenty of oxygen but little plant food for animals to eat. As the stream enters the lowlands and becomes a river, increasing amounts of sediment build up and enable plants to establish themselves.

Trees and plants provide shelter and food for river animals.

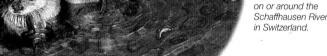

Ducks are among the birds that live on or around the Schaffhausen River in Switzerland.

North American otters (Lutra canadensis) eating fish

WATERSIDE MAMMALS

Various mammals, such as otters, mink, water shrews, and water voles, make their homes along the banks of rivers. They are adapted to hunt and live around watery habitats. Otters, for example, are excellent swimmers with thick, waterproof fur that protects them underwater. They propel themselves through the water using their flat tails and webbed hind feet.

LIFE IN THE FAST LANE

Creatures that live in fast-flowing rivers and streams often have bodies that are adapted to prevent them from being swept away or hurled against the rocks. Crayfish, for example, have flattened bodies that are streamlined to resist the current. Some caddisfly larvae glue sticks, sandgrains, and other materials around themselves to weigh them down against the force of the water.

White-clawed crayfish (*Austropotamobius pallipes*)

LAKES AND PONDS

The still water of lakes and ponds is home to many animals that would be quickly washed away in a river, such as tadpoles and pond skaters. Shallow lakes and ponds are often rich in nutrients, and contain large numbers of animals. In deeper lakes there may be fewer animals but a greater variety of species. Lakes and ponds may freeze over in winter, but the wildlife survives in a layer of cold water trapped under the ice.

Shallow lakes are often rich in wildlife.

Freshwater flea (*Daphnia* sp.)

The European common frog (Rana temporaria) uses webbed feet to push itself through water.

AMPHIBIANS

Frogs and other amphibians lay their eggs in rivers, lakes, and ponds. To protect the eggs, they cover them with a jacket of jelly that is unpalatable to most predators. Once hatched, however, the young are potential prey for a range of animals, including newts, water shrews, and ducks. As adults, frogs move onto land, returning to the water to breed.

LAKE PLANKTON

Lakes and ponds contain a wide variety of plankton (tiny organisms that float in the water). There are two main types of plankton. Phytoplankton are microscopic plantlike organisms, such as algae, that live near the water's surface and get their energy by photosynthesis. They are eaten by zooplankton, tiny animals such as water fleas and shrimp larvae. The zooplankton in turn provide food for fish.

DIVING BIRDS

A stretch of water acts as a magnet for all types of birdlife. Kingfishers perch or hover above the water's surface before plunging in and spearing fish with their daggerlike bills. Herons stand patiently until prey comes within reach, then dart out their long necks and stab the victim with their bills. Dippers are songbirds that can swim, dive, and even walk underwater along the bottom of the stream, where they snap up insects and other small prey.

Kingfisher has bright turquoise feathers.

Waterfalls and rapids stir oxygen into the water, helping aquatic animals to breathe.

Common kingfisher (Alcedo atthis) perches on a branch with its catch of fish.

STREAMLINED HUNTERS

In the sluggish rivers of South America there are some deadly hunters. Many fish eat plants, but some are ferocious predators. Armed with powerful jaws and razor-sharp teeth, the red-bellied piranhas hunt in packs and can strip the flesh off large prey in minutes. Although they attack animals that fall in the water, they usually eat fish.

Red-bellied piranha (*Serrasalmus nattereri*)

CONIFEROUS FORESTS

THE WORLD'S LARGEST FORESTS are spread across the far north, where winters can be up to eight months long. These dense northern, or boreal, forests are made up mainly of coniferous trees – such as spruce, pines, and larches – which are particularly good at coping with cold conditions. For animals, the northern forest is a demanding habitat. There is plenty to eat during the long days of summer when the sun shines almost around the clock, but summer is brief and the cold weather soon returns. To survive the winter, many animals migrate south, while others hibernate.

Distribution of northern coniferous forests

FORESTS AND LAKES

In northern regions, coniferous forests often grow on land once covered by ice age glaciers. These glaciers scoured the ground, scraping away the soil and creating rounded hills and hollows. When the glaciers melted, the hills became covered with trees, while hollows turned into lakes. In summer, this landscape can be difficult to cross. In winter the lakes freeze, and animals, such as bobcats, can travel across the ice.

CONIFER LEAVES

Most conifers have small, evergreen leaves that are tough enough to withstand the coldest winters. A narrow shape helps the leaves to cope with strong winds, while a leathery surface keeps them from drying out. The same features help conifers to thrive on high mountains, where broadleaved trees have difficulty surviving.

White spruce (*Picea* sp.)

Coniferous forest on formerly glaciated landscape in Sweden

Waterlogged soil beneath the trees is acidic and infertile.

Bobcat (*Felis rufus*)

PREDATORS

Mammals are relatively scarce in these northern forests, so predators, such as wolves, lynx, and bobcats, sometimes have to cover vast distances to find the food they need to survive. Bobcats roam 20 miles (30 km) in search of prey. They feed at night, mainly on small rodents, such as lemmings and voles, and on birds and carrion. Wolves hunt in packs for deer and other large mammals.

The interior of taiga forest in the far east of Russia

DEEP IN THE FOREST
The boreal forest in Siberia and North America is known as taiga, meaning "cold forest," and different types of trees grow across this vast space. In the western region, where the climate is warmer and more moist, spruces are the dominant trees. In central Siberia, and along the northern border with the tundra where conditions are harsher, spruces give way to the hardier larch trees. In mountainous regions and in the far east, Siberian stone pines dominate the landscape.

EATING WOOD
Several insects of the northern coniferous forests feed on wood. The horntail, or giant wood wasp (*Uroceras gigas*) – which is a sawfly and not a true wasp – lays its eggs by drilling deep beneath tree bark with its long ovipositor (egg-laying tube). The larvae that emerge from these eggs spend two to three years maturing within the bark while feeding on the wood.

How horntail larvae mature in tree bark

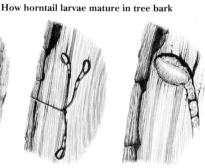

1. A horntail lays its eggs deep in the tree trunk.

2. Young larvae bore at right angles to their mother's drill-hole.

3. Each larva forms a pupation chamber just beneath the bark of the tree.

HIDE AND SEEK
Some birds in the northern forests, such as tits, jays, and some crows, are experts at storing food to see them through the long, harsh winter. One remarkable member of the crow family, Clark's nutcracker from North America, hides 4,000 or more conifer seeds each fall. It is able to remember the precise location of many of these stores for up to eight or nine months.

Clark's nutcracker (*Nucifraga columbianus*)

The nutcracker wedges conifer seeds into cracks in tree bark or in holes in the ground.

COPING WITH CONES
Crossbill finches have unique bills, with upper and lower mandibles that are crossed at the tips. This helps them remove seeds from closed conifer cones. The bird inserts its bill behind one of the tough scales, raising the scale with the upper mandible to release the seed beneath. It then scoops the seed out with its powerful, fleshy tongue.

Red crossbill (*Loxia curvirostra*)

Mandibles are crossed at the tips.

Crossbills feed on the seeds from spruce cones.

Cold lake water contains few nutrients, but is often rich in oxygen.

The caribou's splayed hooves spread the weight of the animal so that it does not sink in deep snow.

Caribou (*Rangifer tarandus*)

The woodchuck builds up fat reserves before hibernating.

SNOW SHOES
To help them to walk across thick layers of snow without sinking, caribou and elk have hooves with broadly splayed toes that help to distribute their weight. Lynx, snowshoe hares, and moose have similar adaptations. Some birds, such as the willow ptarmigan (*Lagopus lagopus*), rely on thickly feathered feet to help them spread their weight.

Woodchuck (*Marmota monax*)

COPING WITH COLD
To avoid the extreme winter temperatures, some mammals hibernate. During the fall, they build up a store of fat in their bodies that will last until spring. They then go into hibernation – slowing down their heartbeat, breathing, and other bodily functions to a minimum. The woodchuck, or groundhog, is a North American marmot that hibernates for several months in its extensive burrow home.

DECIDUOUS FORESTS

Distribution of temperate deciduous forests

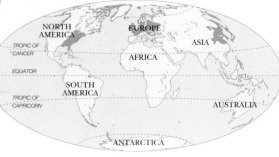

Distribution of temperate deciduous forests

ABOUT ONE QUARTER OF THE WORLD'S forests are made up of broadleaved, deciduous trees – such as oak, birch, and maple – that lose their leaves in winter. These forests flourish in places with moderate climates and distinct seasons. Summers are warm, winters are cool, and precipitation falls throughout the year. There are usually two or three layers of vegetation in a deciduous forest – ferns and small plants at ground level, the canopy of trees above, and, in some forests, a layer of shrubs in between. The soil is richer than in tropical forests, and the ground is littered with dead wood, which provides homes for small animals such as insects.

LEAF FALL

Deciduous trees lose water quickly from their wide, flat leaves. In winter, it is difficult for them to absorb water from the frozen ground so they shed their leaves and become dormant. The trees withdraw nutrients from the leaves in fall, which causes the leaves to change color and die. In spring, leaf and flower buds burst open and the trees appear to come back to life.

Oak tree (Quercus sp.) in full foliage during summer

Oak tree dormant in winter after shedding leaves

Tawny owl (Strix aluco)

WOODLAND PREDATORS

Tawny owls are nocturnal predators. They hunt at night, often preying on small mammals such as mice and voles. They have large eyes to see in the dark and special fringed feathers to swoop silently down on their prey. Many forest carnivores, such as wolves and bears, have been killed by people, but many smaller predators remain, such as weasels, martens, and polecats.

Fall colors in an aspen (Populus sp.) forest, US

NORTH AMERICAN FORESTS

Deciduous forests once covered the eastern half of North America, but most have now been cleared to make way for homes and farms. Tree species in these American forests are more varied than in Europe and include maple, aspen, oak, beech, linden, hickory, magnolia, and buckeye. In fall, many species turn golden, orange, and bright red before falling. Bobcats, foxes, raccoons, chipmunks, whitetail deer, and gray squirrels live among the trees.

The bell-shaped flowers of bluebells hang downward.

English bluebell
(*Hyacinthoides non-scripta*)

Primrose
(*Primula vulgaris*)

SPRING FLOWERS

In spring, wildflowers carpet the forest floor, such as the bluebells and primroses of British woodlands. These plants use the early spring sunshine to flower and set seed before the trees grow new leaves and cast the ground into shade again. Some plants, such as bluebells, grow from underground bulbs. A bulb contains a food supply that helps the plant grow quickly.

LIFE IN THE SHADE

Some plants are adapted to live in the shade. Ferns and mosses grow best on the forest floor, where it is dark and humid. Climbing plants, such as ivy, get nearer to the light by creeping up tree trunks with clinging roots. The toothwort plant (*Lathraea clandestina*) has no need for light. It steals its nutrients from the roots of trees.

Moss on rotting log

Ferns thrive in the shade.

SURVIVING THE WINTER
Winter is difficult for the mammals in deciduous forests because food is scarce and the weather is cold. Many mammals grow thick winter coats and rest in burrows, tree holes, or among fallen leaves. Groundhogs hibernate. Squirrels build winter nests, called dreys, out of sticks and leaves, and spend a lot of time asleep. They bury surplus food during the fall and dig it up for winter use.

View inside the winter drey of a gray squirrel

Creeper
(*Certhia* sp.)

INSECT CATCHERS
With millions of insects to hunt and many trees to nest in, woodlands make ideal homes for birds. The creeper preys on insects that live in bark. It hops nimbly up tree trunks, using its curved beak to pry its victims out of crevices. It usually climbs upward. When it reaches the top of a tree, it flies to the bottom of another tree and starts again.

The creeper uses its stiff tail to prop itself up on tree trunks.

Beech (Fagus sylvatica) *forest in late summer, UK*

EUROPEAN FORESTS
European deciduous forests are dominated by oak and beech, which grow taller and live longer than the other trees. Forest animals include foxes, badgers, squirrels, deer, mice, and birds. In spring, the trees grow leaves and flowers, insects hatch out, migrating birds arrive, and young mammals are born. In fall, leaves drop, nuts and berries ripen, mushrooms emerge from the ground, and animals gorge themselves on the glut of food to prepare for the coming winter.

Puss moth caterpillars lift their heads and tails to startle predators.

Puss moth
(*Cerura vinula*)

FOREST INSECTS
A mature oak tree can support as many as 40,000 caterpillars at once and is home to nearly 300 different species of insects. While the caterpillars munch away silently at the leaves, beetles and their larvae chew their way through bark and wood, aphids drink the tree's sap, and weevil larvae devour acorns from within. These plant-eating insects provide food for predatory insects, such as soldier beetles and ladybugs.

Red deer (Cervus elaphus) *in a forest clearing*

WOODLAND CLEARINGS
When an old tree falls down, sunlight suddenly strikes the forest floor and dormant seeds in the soil spring to life. Plants such as rosebay willowherb, knapweed, and vetch soon appear. Insects come to feed on their flowers and deer come to browse on the leaves. These natural clearings play an important role in woodland ecology because they increase the diversity of the wildlife.

TROPICAL RAINFORESTS

BEAUTIFULLY COLORED BIRDS, acrobatic monkeys, and noisy insects are just a few of the sights and sounds in a tropical rainforest – the richest plant and animal habitat in the world. Rainforests are found near the equator, where it is wet and warm enough for plants to grow all year round. Most rainforest trees are evergreen, and they produce food and shelter for a vast number of animals. However, despite this richness, rainforests are shrinking fast. Every year, huge areas are cut down for their lumber and to make way for pasture and crops.

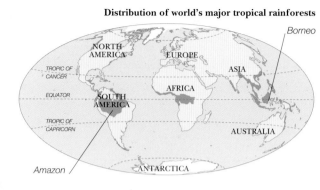

Distribution of world's major tropical rainforests

Borneo

Amazon

THE AMAZON RAINFOREST

The Amazon rainforest of South America is larger than all the other rainforests put together and is twice the size of India. The vegetation is dense and tall, and little light reaches the forest floor. Almost half the world's bird species are found here, including more than 300 species of hummingbirds. The many forest animals include sloths, jaguars, tapirs, snakes, and countless insects.

Very little sunlight penetrates the dense vegetation.

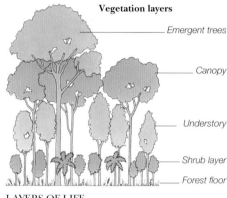

Vegetation layers

Emergent trees

Canopy

Understory

Shrub layer

Forest floor

LAYERS OF LIFE
Rainforest trees grow in distinct layers, each with its own plant and animal species. Life is richest in the canopy, which contains most of the leaves, flowers, and fruits. Under the canopy is an understory of smaller trees and a shrub layer of large-leaved plants that can tolerate shade. The forest floor is dark and cool with rotting leaves, which are quickly broken down by insects, worms, and fungi.

Tall trees, called emergents, poke above the rainforest canopy.

In this rainforest in Sarawak, Borneo, clouds constantly hang over the trees.

CLOUD FOREST
Cloud forests grow on tropical mountain slopes, where they trap and help create clouds. The cold air and mist favor different plants from those of lowland rainforest. The trees are short and gnarled, and the forest has fewer layers of vegetation. Nearly every branch is covered by mosses, ferns, lichens, orchids, and other epiphytes. Conifers, grasses, and alpine plants grow at higher altitudes.

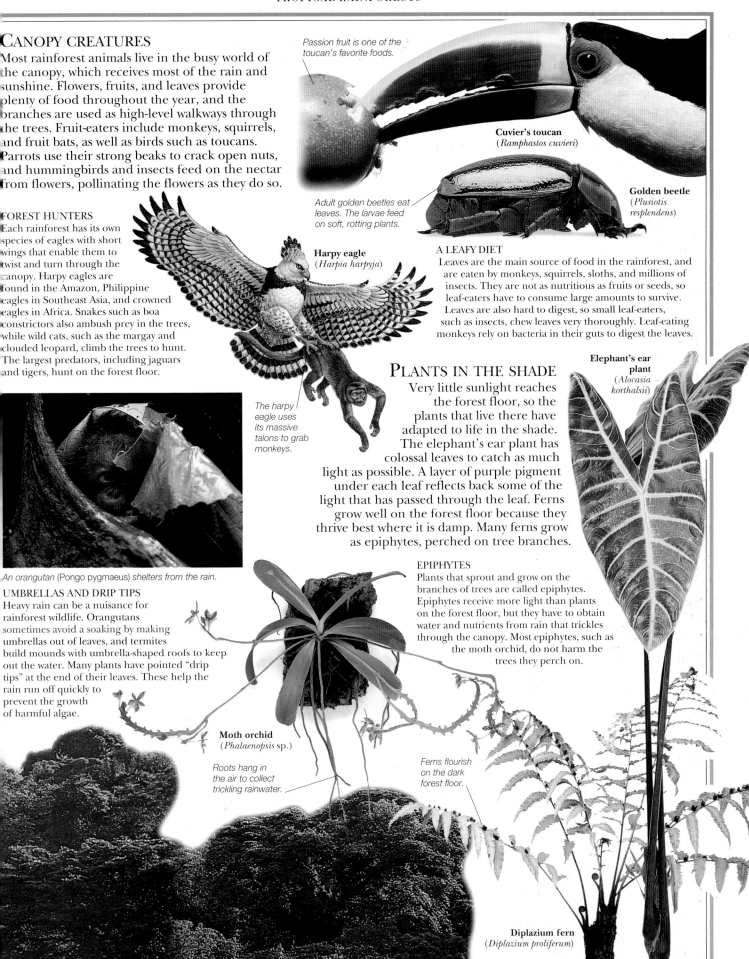

CANOPY CREATURES

Most rainforest animals live in the busy world of the canopy, which receives most of the rain and sunshine. Flowers, fruits, and leaves provide plenty of food throughout the year, and the branches are used as high-level walkways through the trees. Fruit-eaters include monkeys, squirrels, and fruit bats, as well as birds such as toucans. Parrots use their strong beaks to crack open nuts, and hummingbirds and insects feed on the nectar from flowers, pollinating the flowers as they do so.

Passion fruit is one of the toucan's favorite foods.

Cuvier's toucan
(*Ramphastos cuvieri*)

Golden beetle
(*Plusiotis resplendens*)

FOREST HUNTERS

Each rainforest has its own species of eagles with short wings that enable them to twist and turn through the canopy. Harpy eagles are found in the Amazon, Philippine eagles in Southeast Asia, and crowned eagles in Africa. Snakes such as boa constrictors also ambush prey in the trees, while wild cats, such as the margay and clouded leopard, climb the trees to hunt. The largest predators, including jaguars and tigers, hunt on the forest floor.

Harpy eagle
(*Harpia harpyja*)

The harpy eagle uses its massive talons to grab monkeys.

Adult golden beetles eat leaves. The larvae feed on soft, rotting plants.

A LEAFY DIET

Leaves are the main source of food in the rainforest, and are eaten by monkeys, squirrels, sloths, and millions of insects. They are not as nutritious as fruits or seeds, so leaf-eaters have to consume large amounts to survive. Leaves are also hard to digest, so small leaf-eaters, such as insects, chew leaves very thoroughly. Leaf-eating monkeys rely on bacteria in their guts to digest the leaves.

Elephant's ear plant
(*Alocasia korthalsii*)

PLANTS IN THE SHADE

Very little sunlight reaches the forest floor, so the plants that live there have adapted to life in the shade. The elephant's ear plant has colossal leaves to catch as much light as possible. A layer of purple pigment under each leaf reflects back some of the light that has passed through the leaf. Ferns grow well on the forest floor because they thrive best where it is damp. Many ferns grow as epiphytes, perched on tree branches.

EPIPHYTES

Plants that sprout and grow on the branches of trees are called epiphytes. Epiphytes receive more light than plants on the forest floor, but they have to obtain water and nutrients from rain that trickles through the canopy. Most epiphytes, such as the moth orchid, do not harm the trees they perch on.

An orangutan (*Pongo pygmaeus*) shelters from the rain.

UMBRELLAS AND DRIP TIPS

Heavy rain can be a nuisance for rainforest wildlife. Orangutans sometimes avoid a soaking by making umbrellas out of leaves, and termites build mounds with umbrella-shaped roofs to keep out the water. Many plants have pointed "drip tips" at the end of their leaves. These help the rain run off quickly to prevent the growth of harmful algae.

Moth orchid
(*Phalaenopsis* sp.)

Roots hang in the air to collect trickling rainwater.

Ferns flourish on the dark forest floor.

Diplazium fern
(*Diplazium proliferum*)

GRASSLANDS

NATURAL GRASSLANDS ONCE covered a quarter of the Earth's land surface, but large areas are now used for farming. Grasslands grow in places where it is too dry for forests but too wet for deserts. Grasses are firmly fixed in the soil by massive root systems but their tops bend so they are able to survive violent winds. If grass leaves are destroyed by drought, fire, grazing animals, or people, they can grow again from the base of the plant. There are two main kinds of grassland – tropical savanna grasslands and temperate grasslands, such as the pampas, prairie, or steppe. They all support a rich variety of grass-eating or seed-eating insects, birds, and mammals.

Distribution of world's major grasslands

Central Asian steppes

North American prairies

South American pampas

African savanna

The rare pampas deer (Ozotoceros bezoarticus) among termite mounds in the pampas, Brazil

SOUTH AMERICAN PAMPAS

The temperate grasslands of the South American pampas lie to the east of the Andes Mountains. The mountains prevent wet winds from reaching the area, so the climate is generally dry. Many pampas animals are unique to the area because they evolved after South America was cut off from the rest of the world. The main grazers are small mammals, such as cavies and maras, and insects such as termites. Insect-eaters include the giant anteater and armadillos, while hunters such as the maned wolf roam the plains.

AFRICAN SAVANNA

The word savanna means "treeless plain," although the African savanna usually has scattered trees, such as flat-topped acacias. The weather is hot all year round but there are long dry seasons separated by wet seasons. African savanna is home to vast herds of grazing animals, such as zebras and wildebeest, which move from place to place following the rains. Large predators, such as lions, prey on the grazers. At ground level there are millions of insects, as well as birds, reptiles, and small mammals.

Wildebeest migrate hundreds of miles across the savanna in search of fresh grass.

Zebras usually live in family groups but may gather into larger herds in the dry season.

GRAZERS AND BROWSERS

On the African savanna, many different species of plant-eating mammal can live in the same area because they feed on different plants or on different parts of the grasses. Elephants and giraffes, for example, browse on bushes and trees, while zebras and wildebeest graze on grass. Plants are less nourishing than meat, so grazers and browsers may have to spend all day feeding.

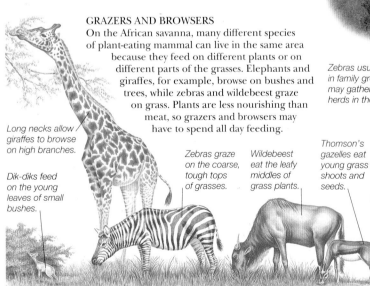

Long necks allow giraffes to browse on high branches.

Dik-diks feed on the young leaves of small bushes.

Zebras graze on the coarse, tough tops of grasses.

Wildebeest eat the leafy middles of grass plants.

Thomson's gazelles eat young grass shoots and seeds.

BURROWING ANIMALS

Many small grassland mammals live underground, where they can escape from predators or fires and survive the heat or cold. Some use their burrows to store food or to hibernate in winter. On North American prairies, prairie dogs live in huge colonies, called "towns." Their interconnected tunnels form a massive underground maze.

Prairie dog
(Cynomys sp.)

TREES AND SHRUBS

In savanna grasslands, scattered trees and shrubs shade and cool the ground, keeping the soil moist. Their fallen leaves enrich the soil and help grass to grow. Many trees and bushes, such as acacias, have thorns to deter grazing animals, and deep roots to reach water underground. Baobab trees store water in their swollen trunks and shed their leaves in the dry season. They also have tough bark for protection against fire.

Baobab trees (Adansonia digitata) have thick trunks to store water for the dry season.

Spotted hyenas are powerfully built and have jaws strong enough to crunch through bones.

Spotted hyena
(*Crocuta crocuta*)

Trees and bushes provide shade from the hot sun.

By living in large herds, grazing animals are more likely to spot a predator.

Sparse trees dot the landscape.

HUNTERS
The many plant-eaters on the savanna provide food for carnivores such as hunting dogs, lions, cheetahs, hyenas, and leopards. Lions, hunting dogs, and hyenas hunt in packs, preying on large mammals such as antelope and zebra. They also steal food from other carnivores. The North American prairies were once home to wolves, but coyotes are now the main hunters.

SCAVENGERS
No food is wasted on the savanna. Animals that die, and the remains of kills (carrion), are quickly devoured by scavengers such as vultures, jackals, marabou storks, and carrion beetles. Vultures often crowd around the same carcass, squabbling noisily as they fight for scraps. African white-backed vultures stick their heads right inside the carcass, while lappet-faced vultures rip open the skin and muscle.

White storks (Ciconia ciconia) hunt insects as they try to escape from a fire.

GRASSLAND FIRES
Fires, set off by lightning or by people, can suddenly sweep across the grasslands. The fire destroys trees, shrubs, and seedlings, which stops the grassland from turning into forest. Although the tops of the grasses are burned, the tufts quickly produce new shoots when the fire is over. Savanna birds, such as storks or secretary-birds, hunt at the edges of fires, snapping up small mammals and insects as they try to escape the flames.

White-backed vulture
(*Gyps africanus*)

DESERTS

DESERTS COVER ABOUT a quarter of the Earth's land surface and receive an average of less than 10 in (25 cm) of rain each year. During the day deserts can be scorchingly hot, but at night the temperature can sometimes plummet to below freezing. In addition, strong winds often send storms of sand and grit swirling through the air, while the occasional flash flood can carry rocks and boulders across the desert floor. In spite of this, many remarkable animals and plants are able to survive and even thrive in these hostile surroundings.

Distribution of world's major deserts

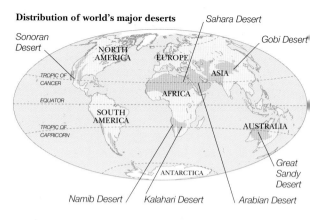

Sonoran Desert · Sahara Desert · Gobi Desert · NORTH AMERICA · EUROPE · ASIA · TROPIC OF CANCER · AFRICA · EQUATOR · SOUTH AMERICA · AUSTRALIA · TROPIC OF CAPRICORN · ANTARCTICA · Namib Desert · Kalahari Desert · Arabian Desert · Great Sandy Desert

Pin-tailed sandgrouse
(*Pterocles alchata*)

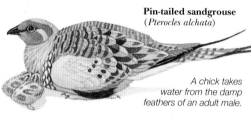

A chick takes water from the damp feathers of an adult male.

Fennec fox (Fennecus zerda) hides from the sun.

KEEPING COOL

Deserts have the greatest daily temperature range of any habitat. In the Sahara, the difference between day and nighttime temperatures can be more than 90°F (50°C). Desert animals have different ways of coping with the heat. The fennec fox, for example, loses heat through its large ears. It hides in a burrow during the day, and emerges at night when the air is much cooler.

THE WATER CARRIERS

Some desert animals get their water from their food, but most birds need a daily drink. In Africa's deserts, large flocks of sandgrouse gather at waterholes at dawn. During the breeding season, the males wade into the water and use their breast feathers as a sponge to soak up water to take back to their chicks.

ARID DESERTS

The Namib Desert, in southwest Africa, is a very arid desert. Some years there is no rainfall, but on average, 1 in (25 mm) of rain falls per year. Temperatures are usually low and there is frequent fog. Only a few plants and animals can survive in these extreme conditions. They include a plant called welwitschia (*Welwitschia mirabilis*), which has two tough, waterproof leaves that can absorb dew and retain moisture.

Tenebrionid beetle (Onymacris unguicularis) collecting water droplets

DRINKING FOG

In the Namib Desert, dense fog rolls in from the sea after dusk and then slowly thins after sunrise. Some desert beetles collect this moisture by standing head-down on the crests of sand dunes. The fog condenses onto their bodies, and the water droplets roll downward to their mouths, providing a much-needed drink.

Sand dunes in the Namib Desert can reach nearly 1,000 ft (300 m) high.

Sand dunes are piled up by onshore winds.

FEET OFF THE GROUND

In some deserts there is very little shade and the ground can get so hot that animals find it difficult to walk on. Many desert lizards display special behavior to avoid this problem. They lift their feet off the ground, either singly or two at a time, to cool them off. Once their feet are comfortable, they place them back down on the ground and then lift up the other pair.

Lizard cools its foot by lifting it off the hot surface.

Common collared lizard
(*Crotophytus collaris*)

The saguaro cactus (Carnegiea gigantea) is the largest plant in the Sonoran Desert. It reaches heights of up to 40 ft (12 m).

Some deserts feature rocky cliffs.

Waxy outer layer helps prevent water loss.

SEMIARID DESERTS

The Sonoran Desert straddles the border between Arizona and Mexico. It is a semiarid desert, with an average rainfall of about 8 in (20 cm) a year. This is enough rain for a wide range of plants to grow, including the saguaro cactus and various shrubs. These drought-resistant plants provide shelter and food for many animals including snakes, lizards, tortoises, and birds such as woodpeckers.

Tissue in stem retains water.

SURVIVING DROUGHT

Of all the plants that grow in deserts, cacti are among the best at surviving long periods without water. Their roots spread out around the plant, enabling them to collect water when it rains. Cacti store this water in a barrel-shaped stem that expands as it fills. The surface of a cactus is covered with a waxy layer that helps prevent water loss.

Golden barrel cactus
(*Echinocactus grusonii*)

Long roots tap water deep underground.

Some desert trees have small leaves, which help to reduce water loss.

During the heat of the day, many animals, such as Grant's golden mole, escape from the heat by burrowing down in the sand.

Shrubs sprout leaves after rain and lose them a few months later.

Sidewinder (Crotalus cerastes) leaps across the sand.

THE SAND DWELLERS

Sand is not easy to cross because it shifts under an animal's weight. Some animals, such as camels, have cushionlike feet that can cope with walking on soft sand. Sidewinding snakes have developed other ways to move over sand. Instead of slithering across the sand, they throw their bodies through the air in a series of sideways leaps.

MOUNTAINS AND CAVES

WILDLIFE HAS TO BE WELL adapted to survive in these extreme habitats. On mountains, there is plenty of light for plants to grow, but biting cold and fierce winds mean that only the toughest species can survive. Birds can soar effortlessly over the mountain slopes, but animals on the ground have to be agile to cross steep or rocky terrain. Caves provide more shelter than mountains, and offer steady conditions all year round. However, because there is no light, plants cannot grow and food is scarce. As a result, cave animals eat either food from outside or each other.

Distribution of major mountains and cave systems

Rocky Mountains
Alps
Carlsbad Caverns
Himalayas
NORTH AMERICA
EUROPE
TROPIC OF CANCER
ASIA
AFRICA
EQUATOR
SOUTH AMERICA
TROPIC OF CAPRICORN
AUSTRALIA
Andes Mountains
ANTARCTICA
Gunung Mulu Cave system

MOUNTAINS

A mountain is an extremely variable habitat. The temperature gets steadily colder toward the top, and the air gradually thins out. One side of a mountain is usually sunny, whereas the other lies in shadow. The side facing into the wind receives the most rain, while the other side is much drier. Most mountain animals do not roam freely up and down a mountain. Instead, they tend to stay in certain zones.

BIRDS OF PREY

Eagles can glide high over mountains by rising on warm updrafts of air (thermals). With their sharp eyes trained on the land below, they are quick to spot the movements of prey. They also scavenge the bodies of animals that have lost their footing on the steep slopes. Verreaux's eagle hunts in the rocky hills of Africa and the Middle East, preying on hyraxes and other small mammals.

Verreaux's eagle
(*Aquila verreauxii*)

MOUNTAIN ACROBAT

Sheep and goats are common on mountains because they are agile and sure-footed. The chamois of southern Europe has an incredible sense of balance. It will leap up rocky cliffs with death-defying ease to reach small patches of vegetation. Spongy pads under each hoof give it a good grip when the ground is slippery. Its leaps can be more than 20 ft (6 m) long and 6 ft 6 in (2 m) high.

Chamois
(*Rupricapra* sp.)

Mountain zones in the Alps

Snow and ice

Alpine tundra

Tree line (highest point trees grow)

Coniferous forest

Deciduous forest

LAYERS OF LIFE

Climbing a mountain in the Alps is like traveling from Europe to the North Pole in a single day. As the air gets steadily colder with height, the vegetation changes. Deciduous forest carpets the lower slopes, giving way to conifer trees farther up. Higher still is rugged grass like Arctic tundra, and above this is snow and ice.

Only the hardiest animals can survive on bare rocky slopes.

Coniferous trees grow higher up than deciduous trees.

CAVES

Most caves are formed by acidic water eating away at soft limestone rock. They can take thousands of years to form. Bats, insects, birds, fish, and amphibians have all adapted to cave life, and many other animals shelter in caves from time to time. In some caves, bat droppings build up in huge mounds on the floor. The droppings provide food for smaller animals, such as beetles, millipedes, and cockroaches. Cave predators include snakes, spiders, and blind salamanders.

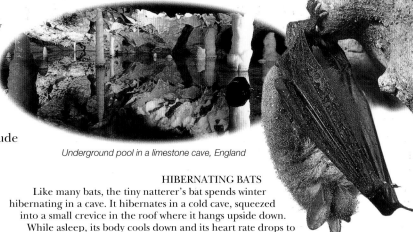
Underground pool in a limestone cave, England

Mexican blind cavefish
(*Astyanax mexicanus*)

Each eye is covered by fat and skin.

BLIND CAVEFISH
Creatures that spend their whole lives in the darkness of caves have no need for sight. They rely on their senses of touch, smell, or hearing to find their way around. Although Mexican blind cavefish hatch with eyes, a layer of skin slowly covers each eye as they grow. These unusual fish are related to piranhas. Like their relatives, they are predators with razor-sharp teeth.

HIBERNATING BATS
Like many bats, the tiny natterer's bat spends winter hibernating in a cave. It hibernates in a cold cave, squeezed into a small crevice in the roof where it hangs upside down. While asleep, its body cools down and its heart rate drops to save energy. The cooler the cave, the longer the bat's store of fat will last. It will not be able to eat again until spring.

Natterer's bat
(*Myotis nattereri*)

OILBIRDS
In some ways, oilbirds are more like bats than birds. They spend the day roosting deep underground in their breeding caves, emerging only at night to fly off in search of food. Like bats, they find their way around in pitch darkness by making special clicking noises and listening to the echoes (echolocation). Oilbirds eat only fruit and live in Central and South America.

Oilbird (Steatornis caripensis) nesting in cave

LIVING CUSHIONS
Mountain plants grow in low, dense cushions to protect themselves from the freezing wind. Fine hairs on the leaves trap moisture and warmth and protect the plants from the intense sunlight found at high altitude. The flowers are often bright and colorful to attract the few pollinating insects that live on mountaintops.

Rock spirea
(*Petrophyton caespitosum*)

Houseleek
(*Sempervivum tectorum*)

Thyme
(*Thymus cephalotos*)

The Alps, northern Italy. In winter, these peaks are covered with snow.

POLAR REGIONS

THE ICY POLAR REGIONS HAVE SHORT summers and dark, bitterly cold winters. There are fierce winds, water is locked up as ice, and snow and ice make it difficult for land animals to travel or find food. To help them survive, animals rely on adaptations such as thick fur or antifreeze in their blood. The two polar regions are very different. The region around the South Pole, called Antarctica, is a frozen continent, while the region around the North Pole, called the Arctic, is a frozen ocean. On the edge of the Arctic is a flat, frozen, treeless landscape, called the tundra. Small patches of tundra also occur on subantarctic islands.

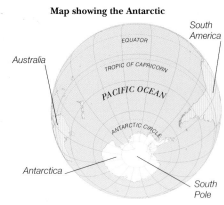

Map showing the Antarctic

South America

Australia

EQUATOR

TROPIC OF CAPRICORN

PACIFIC OCEAN

ANTARCTIC CIRCLE

Antarctica

South Pole

ANTARCTICA

Antarctica is the size of Europe and the US put together. It is covered by a layer of ice, in places 3 miles (4.8 km) deep. Only two percent of the land is free of ice and there is no proper soil. Lichens and mosses are dominant on land, and the largest resident animals are tiny insects and mites. However, the oceans around Antarctica are rich in nutrients, providing food for a variety of fish, seals, whales, and seabirds.

Ice floes move with the winds and currents.

Leopard seal
(*Hydrurga leptonyx*)

SOUTH POLE PENGUINS

Penguins live in the Southern Hemisphere, mostly in and around Antarctica. The only two penguins to breed on the Antarctic continent itself are the emperor and the Adelie, but king, gentoo, macaroni, chinstrap, and rockhopper penguins all breed within Antarctic waters. Dense, waterproof feathers and thick layers of fat under the skin keep penguins warm. They breed on land in huge colonies, called rookeries. The large numbers are useful for warmth and defense.

The "spring" catapults the insect to safety if danger threatens.

NATURAL ANTIFREEZE

Some polar animals survive the cold with the help of a natural chemical antifreeze in their body fluids. This allows them to survive at temperatures well below freezing without ice crystals forming inside their bodies. Antarctic springtails are tiny, wingless insects that can survive at temperatures as low as −22°F (−30°C). Other animals with antifreeze include the icefish (*Chaenocephalus aceratus*).

Crabeater seals (Lobodon carcinophagus) *under the ice*

HARDY SEALS

Seals spend most of their lives in the sea but have a thick layer of fat, called blubber, under the skin to keep them warm. Some seals, such as the ringed seal of the Arctic and the Weddell seal of the Antarctic, even manage to survive below the ice in winter. They must come to the surface to breathe air, and keep their breathing holes open by scraping the ice with their teeth. Other seals migrate to polar regions for the warmer summer months.

King penguins (Aptenodytes patagonicus) *in South Georgia*

ARCTIC AND TUNDRA

Most of the Arctic, including the North Pole, is a vast sheet of ice floating on the Arctic Ocean. Surrounding the Arctic are the northern edges of North America, Europe, and Asia. In these ice-free tundra lands, it is too cold for trees and the soil is always frozen 20 in (50 cm) below the surface. In summer, the tundra comes alive with flowers and insects, and many birds and mammals migrate there to feed and raise their young.

Map showing the Arctic

North Pole

Europe

ARCTIC OCEAN

ARCTIC CIRCLE

PACIFIC OCEAN

North America

Snowy owl (*Nyctea scandiaca*)

BIRDS OF THE ARCTIC AND ANTARCTIC

Dense feathers and reserves of fat help to keep birds warm in the Arctic and Antarctic, but few live there all year round. Most migrate there in spring when there is plenty of food and space for breeding. Bird predators such as eagles, skuas, owls, and falcons lurk around the crowded breeding colonies, taking easy meals of eggs and chicks. Snowy owls feed on small mammals, including lemmings and hares, which breed during the summer.

Brown bears (Ursus arctos) roam the tundra in summer.

North American alpine tundra in summer

Tundra plants flower quickly in the short growing season.

The hardy musk ox (Ovibos moschatus) has the longest coat of any mammal.

LAND MAMMALS

There are no land mammals in the Antarctic and only a few hardy mammals, such as musk oxen, polar bears, and Arctic foxes manage to survive all year round in the Arctic. These animals have thick fur coats, sometimes with two layers to trap warm air near the skin. A thick layer of fat under the skin traps extra warmth and also acts as a food store. Some mammals burrow under the snow where it is warmer and there is no wind to blow heat away from their bodies.

Falkland flower (*Calandria feltonii*)

POLAR PLANTS

The most successful Arctic and Antarctic plants are mosses, lichens, and algae. Lichens grow very slowly in cold climates and some Antarctic lichens the size of dinner plates may be over 1,000 years old. Polar plants tend to grow in low, rounded clumps, or "cushions," to combat the wind, trap moisture, and avoid being crushed by snow. Flowers burst open rapidly in the short summer, and many plants survive the winter as seeds in the soil.

Alpine azalea (*Loiseleuria procumbens*)

Garden tiger moth caterpillar (Arctia caja) feeding on Arctic willow

ARCTIC HUNTER

The polar bear is the only land mammal to venture over Arctic ice floes – almost to the North Pole. These animals can swim for many hours in freezing cold water, although they usually ride on pieces of ice to reach distant hunting grounds. Polar bears are powerful hunters that feed mainly on seals hidden in lairs under the ice. Females, especially pregnant females, will hibernate, but many males hunt right through the winter.

Polar bears (Ursus maritimus) hunt on melting ice packs. They can detect a seal lair from as far as half a mile away.

WOOLLY CATERPILLAR

The caterpillar of the European garden tiger moth, often called the woolly bear caterpillar, is one of many Arctic insects. Its dark colors absorb the warmth of the sun and its hairy coat traps body heat. It feeds on low-growing plants such as the Arctic willow, which sprouts in the spring. For the rest of the year, the caterpillar hibernates. The caterpillar grows slowly – it may be 1–2 years before it finally turns into a moth.

PEOPLE AND PLANTS

WITHOUT PLANTS, THERE WOULD be virtually no life on Earth. In addition to providing food crops, they also release oxygen into the air for people to breathe. Plants provide the raw materials for making clothes, perfumes, paper, and rubber – even toothpaste and ice cream can contain extracts from marine plants. Many of today's medicines are based on substances from plants, and their fossilized remains supply power in the form of coal. Over the centuries, people have selected and bred plants for different purposes. Many food plants, as well as ornamental plants and trees, are the result of these breeding programs.

The pith of the papyrus was cut into strips, placed in layers, and pounded to form a strong sheet of paper.

Making paper from papyrus in ancient Egypt

Pith inside the stem is used to make paper.

Papyrus (*Cyperus papyrus*)

PAPER FROM PLANTS

Most paper is produced from wood pulp, but it can also be made from nettles, bamboo, and other plants, or from cotton and linen rags. The ancient Egyptians made a type of paper from papyrus reeds. To make paper commercially, wood fibers are mashed up with water so they mesh together in a thin sheet. This is dried and pressed flat to make a large roll of paper. To save trees, more paper could be recycled and more alternatives to wood pulp, such as reeds and hemp, could be explored.

VERSATILE WOOD

Wood is used to make many items, from houses and furniture to toys and musical instruments. It is hard-wearing and can be cut into a variety of different shapes. Softwoods, such as spruce, pine, and fir, are light and easy to build with, while hardwoods, such as poplar, oak, and maple, are strong, but grow more slowly. Wood is also useful for burning as a fuel.

Logs may be floated from the forests to the sawmill.

PLANTS AS FOOD

People have cultivated plants as crops for thousands of years. Today, just three plants – wheat, rice, and corn – feed more than half the people in the world. As a result of breeding programs, these crops now have higher yields than when they grew in the wild. Other sources of food include the underground parts of plants, such as potatoes and cassava, the fruits and nuts of trees, such as apples, oranges, brazilnuts, and coconuts, and sugar from the stalks of sugarcane.

Nutmeg fruit

Mace

Nutmeg (*Myristica fragrans*)

HERBS AND SPICES

Today, herbs and spices, such as nutmeg and cloves, are used to add flavor to certain dishes. However, before refrigerators were available to preserve food, spices were often used as an antibacterial. In medieval times, spices were brought to Europe by camel caravan from East Asia. Today, most herbs and spices are grown on large plantations.

Cloves are the unopened flower buds.

Clove (*Syzygium aromaticum*)

The development of modern wheat

Small heads and grains

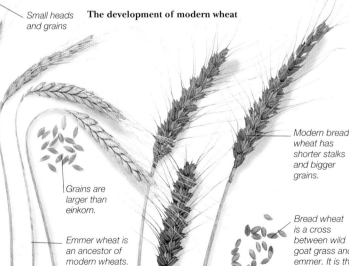

Long, thin stalks

Grains are larger than einkorn.

Modern bread wheat has shorter stalks and bigger grains.

Einkorn is a wild grass.

Emmer wheat is an ancestor of modern wheats. It was grown in Greek and Roman times.

Bread wheat is a cross between wild goat grass and emmer. It is the most widely grown modern wheat.

In Sri Lanka tea is picked by hand and collected in baskets.

PLANTS USED FOR DRINKS

Popular drinks, such as coffee, tea, and cocoa are all made from parts of plants. Coffee is produced from the seeds of *Coffea arabica*, a plant that originally grew in the forests of Ethiopia. Tea is made from the young leaves of the tea bush (*Camellia sinensis*), while cocoa is made from the seeds of the cocoa tree (*Theobroma cacao*), which bears fruit only after about seven years.

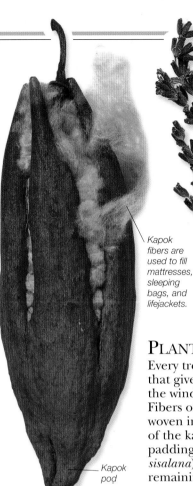

Kapok fibers are used to fill mattresses, sleeping bags, and lifejackets.

PLANTS AND PERFUMES
Although the modern perfume industry can make perfumes artificially, it still relies on essential oils extracted from flowers such as rose, lavender, jasmine, and orange for the purest fragrances. Fragrant plants have tiny sacs that make and store the substances that give them their distinctive smell. It is these substances that are known as essential oils. As many as 300 oils may be used in one perfume.

Lavender flowers

Lavender oil is obtained by distilling the flowers of the lavender plant (Lavandula angustifolia).

ALOE VERA

Aloe vera is a cactuslike plant of the lily family. It has sharp-tipped leaves arranged in rosettes at the base of flowering shoots. The jellylike sap from the leaves has been used since early times for healing and cosmetic purposes. Aloe oils are used to help keep the skin soft, while medical uses include aloe extracts to treat digestive problems.

Aloe vera has spiky, succulent leaves.

Cosmetic cream made from aloe vera

Scientific name: *Aloe vera*	
Size: 6 in (15 cm) to 50 ft (15.2 m) high	
Habitat: Warm and tropical dry regions	
Distribution: Believed to originate from the Mediterranean area, now widely cultivated	
Reproduction: By flowers and seeds	

PLANT FIBERS

Every tree and flowering plant contains fibers that give it strength and enable it to bend with the wind. These fibers can be used in many ways. Fibers of the flax plant (*Linum usitatissimum*) are woven into linen cloth, while those from the pods of the kapok tree (*Ceiba pentandra*) are used as padding. Fibers from the leaves of sisal (*Agave sisalana*) can be crushed between rollers and the remaining strands made into rope and twine.

Kapok pod

COTTON
Cotton, the most important vegetable fiber used for clothing, comes from flowering *Gossypium* plants. After each flower falls off the plant, a cotton boll begins to form. The boll, which contains seeds and hairs, ripens to reveal a fluffy white fiber ready for harvesting. Oil from the seeds can be used in cooking or in the manufacture of soap. Cotton is the sterilized fiber cleaned of its natural oils.

A ripe cotton pod, called a boll

This woman in Peru is putting picked cotton into bags.

Dead plants fall into the swamps and form layers of peat.

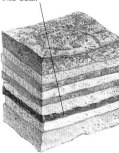

As the peat layers are compressed, they turn into coal.

How coal is formed from dead plants.

FROM PLANTS TO COAL
The coal that is burned as fuel today began to form about 300 million years ago in swamp forests during the Mississippian and Pennsylvanian periods. As plants died, they were buried in the swamps but did not rot away completely. Instead, they stuck together to form layers of peat. Gradually the peat was compressed and heated to form coal. Coal is a fossil fuel because it is made from fossilized, or preserved, plants.

PLANTS AS MEDICINE

In ancient times, plants played a vital role in healing, and many are still used by the modern pharmaceutical industry. For example, wild yam (*Dioscorea villosa*) is used in the medicines that are given for rheumatic diseases, and quinine, from the bark of the chinchona tree (*Cinchona officinalis*), can be used to treat malaria. Although the chemicals these plants produce may be poisonous in large doses, small amounts can be very useful. Plants are constantly being tested in the search for new medicines.

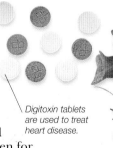

Digitoxin tablets are used to treat heart disease.

The poisonous leaves of the foxglove (Digitalis purpurea) are the source of digitoxin.

PEOPLE AND ANIMALS

SINCE THE EARLIEST TIMES, people have hunted wild animals for their meat, skins, and fur. Then, in about 10,000 BC, the first farmers began to tame and breed wild animals to feed the growing populations. This process, called domestication, played a vital role in the development of human civilization. Since then, people have continued to rear animals for food and clothing, as well as train them to work, breed them as pets, and even use them in their quest to combat disease. Some domesticated animals, including many breeds of dog, have been specially bred for so long that they look very different from their wild ancestors.

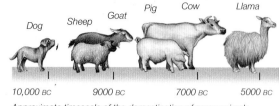

Dog Sheep Goat Pig Cow Llama

10,000 BC   9000 BC   7000 BC   5000 BC

Approximate timescale of the domestication of some animals

DOMESTICATED ANIMALS

When people selected animals to domesticate, they looked for certain desirable characteristics. Camels, for example, can travel without water and also provide milk and wool. Geese and ducks will supply meat and eggs as well as feathers for warm bedding. Animals as pets were often chosen for their docile behavior.

ANIMALS FOR FOOD

From the vast cattle ranches of South America to the cramped cages sometimes used for chickens, rearing animals for food today is big business. In the western world, technology makes the land highly productive, producing plenty of cheap food. However, to meet these needs, livestock (animals) are often reared intensively. Many of them are kept indoors in artificial conditions to encourage fast growth.

Cattle ranches take up a lot of space. In some places, such as South America, large areas of land have been cleared to make way for cattle ranches.

Beekeepers wear thick clothes and hats with veils to protect them from bee stings.

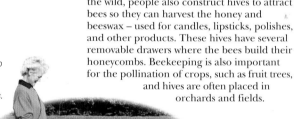

BEEKEEPING

Although honeybees normally build nests in the wild, people also construct hives to attract bees so they can harvest the honey and beeswax – used for candles, lipsticks, polishes, and other products. These hives have several removable drawers where the bees build their honeycombs. Beekeeping is also important for the pollination of crops, such as fruit trees, and hives are often placed in orchards and fields.

RESEARCH ANIMALS

Although many people consider it cruel, rabbits, mice, rats, and other animals are kept in laboratories and used to test new medicines, to help find cures for certain diseases such as cancer, and to increase human understanding of animal behavior. Some studies involve altering the genetic makeup of animals or producing clones – animals that are genetically identical. In 1997, British scientists cloned a sheep using body cells taken from an adult ewe. This was the first animal to be cloned directly from a body cell rather than from an animal embryo.

Some pets need a lot of exercise and have to be looked after for many years.

Identical sheep cloned from an embryo

KEEPING PETS

Many adults and children keep animals as pets. The most popular pets are cats, dogs, fish, and budgerigars, although some people have more unusual pets, such as spiders. Pets provide their owners with companionship and affection in return for food and shelter. Many schools keep animals as pets so that children can learn how they eat, sleep, and take care of their young. Studies have shown that people with pets suffer less from stress.

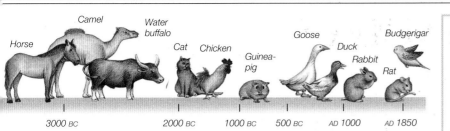

Horse · Camel · Water buffalo · Cat · Chicken · Guinea-pig · Goose · Duck · Rabbit · Budgerigar · Rat

3000 BC   2000 BC   1000 BC   500 BC   AD 1000   AD 1850

WORKING ANIMALS

Many animals are trained to work for people because of their strength or special skills. Elephants and llamas, for example, are used to carry heavy loads over long distances, while oxen, water buffalo, and horses can be used where a farmer has no tractor. Dogs are particularly intelligent animals and can be taught to guide blind people, control herds of sheep, sniff out drugs or explosives, and help police to track down criminals.

This farmer in Asia is using a water buffalo to pull his plow through the mud of a flooded paddy field.

MEDICINAL LEECH

Leeches feed by attaching themselves to the bodies of animals, piercing their skin and drinking their blood through an anterior sucker. The medicinal leech gives out a chemical substance called hirudin that thins the blood and prevents it from clotting (an anticoagulant). Doctors are interested in finding out more about this anticoagulant.

Anterior sucker

Scientific name: *Hirudo medicinalis*

Size: Swells up to 5 in (12 cm) in length after feeding

Habitat: Small, muddy ponds edged with plants

Distribution: Found wild in Europe and parts of Asia, introduced in North America

Reproduction: Hermaphroditic; cocoons, containing 5–15 eggs, are laid in cool, damp areas; eggs hatch 4–11 weeks later

Diet: Blood of other animals

ANIMALS IN ZOOS

Zoos allow people to see animals from all over the world and to learn about their behavior. In a good modern zoo or wildlife park, the emphasis is placed on educating the public about wild animals and helping to conserve them. Many zoos also try to breed endangered species and can sometimes release animals back into the wild.

At a zoo, visitors can see wild animals close up.

ANIMAL PRODUCTS

Animal furs were important for the survival of early peoples, but have now become fashion items in many countries. Other traditional animal products include wool from sheep, goats, and alpacas. Australia is the world's chief wool-producing country, where most of the sheep are Merinos that were introduced there in the 18th century. More unusual animal products include silk from silkmoths, and a red dye called cochineal from the Mexican scale insect.

Merino sheep can survive the heat in Australia and still produce a fleece of good wool.

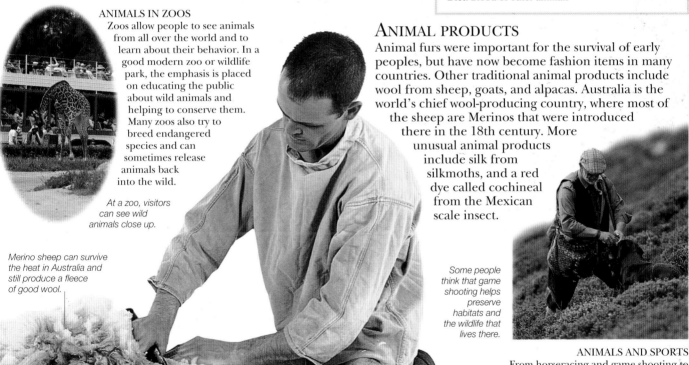

Some people think that game shooting helps preserve habitats and the wildlife that lives there.

ANIMALS AND SPORTS

From horseracing and game shooting to circuses and bullfighting, many sports and leisure activities involve animals. However, these animals are not always kept in the best conditions. Many modern circuses now have no animal acts because they do not want to keep wild animals in cramped cages. Sometimes the sport itself, such as bullfighting, may be cruel to animals.

Sheep-shearers work quickly – some can clip a lamb in less than a minute.

Find out more

ANIMALS IN DANGER: *100*
DOGS: *252*
ELEPHANTS AND HYRAXES: *266*
GAME BIRDS: *220*

PEOPLE AND NATURE

THE RAPID RISE IN THE human population and the corresponding demand for resources have had a dramatic impact on the natural world. While global warming, acid rain, and holes in the ozone layer affect the whole planet, other changes, such as habitat destruction and hunting, threaten individual species. Over millions of years, many species have adapted to natural changes, such as long-term variation in climate. However, it is more difficult for living things to adapt to the harmful materials released into the environment as a result of human activities.

MORE AND MORE PEOPLE

Modern humans have lived on Earth for about 300,000 years, but it took until 1960 for the population to reach 3 billion. However, in just 40 years, that figure has doubled – and by the year 2050 it is predicted that as many as 10 billion people may inhabit the Earth. One of the reasons for this rapid growth is that better health care means fewer babies now die and fewer women die in childbirth.

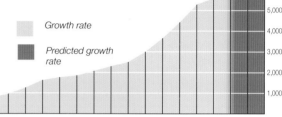

People (in millions)

Growth rate

Predicted growth rate

1750 1800 1850 1900 1910 1920 1930 1940 1950 1960 1970 1980 1990 1995 2000 2025 2050

NATURAL EXTINCTION

Since life first appeared on Earth more than 3.5 billion years ago, many living things have become extinct as a result of natural events. These have included the eruption of volcanoes as well as meteorite showers hitting the Earth. In 1980, the eruption of Mount St. Helens in Washington devastated nearby forests and killed 2 million birds, fish, and mammals.

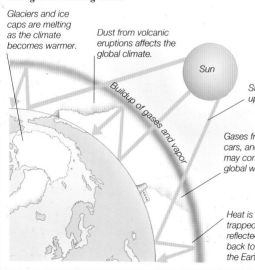

Active volcanoes, such as Hawaii's Kilauea, remain a threat.

HABITAT DESTRUCTION

As the human population grows, the natural areas where plants and animals live are shrinking. Tropical forests are disappearing at the rate of 6.9 million acres (17 million hectares) every year and more than half of the world's wetlands have now been destroyed. The Sahara Desert in northwest Africa is gradually increasing. Overgrazing in the Sahel, the grasslands at the edges of the Sahara, is turning the topsoil to dust. This process is known as desertification.

GLOBAL WARMING

World temperatures are currently rising by a fraction of a degree every year. This is known as global warming and is caused by the buildup of gases and water vapor in the atmosphere. These gases form a layer that reflects the heat back to Earth, rather than allowing it to escape into the outer atmosphere. As the planet warms up, the water in the oceans will expand (take up more space) and the water locked up in glaciers and the polar ice caps will start to melt. This could cause sea levels to rise and many habitats will disappear underwater.

As more land turns to desert there are fewer places for livestock to graze.

How global warming works

Glaciers and ice caps are melting as the climate becomes warmer.

Dust from volcanic eruptions affects the global climate.

Buildup of gases and vapor

Sun

Sunlight heats up the Earth.

Gases from factories, cars, and forest fires may contribute to global warming.

Heat is trapped and reflected back to the Earth.

The ozone hole (colored gray, red, and blue) covers the continent of Antarctica.

OZONE HOLES

High up in the atmosphere, a natural layer of ozone gas protects living things against harmful rays from the Sun. In the 1970s, scientists discovered that polluting gases, such as CFCs (chlorofluorocarbons), were destroying the ozone layer over the poles. Since then, the use of CFCs has been outlawed. But it will be many years before they disappear from the air, allowing the ozone layer to recover.

Satellite image of the ozone hole over the Antarctic

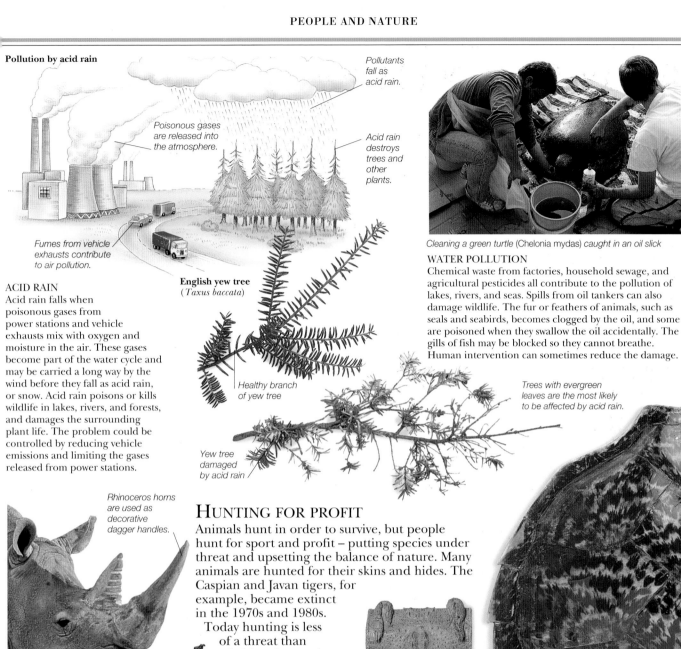

Pollution by acid rain

Poisonous gases are released into the atmosphere.

Pollutants fall as acid rain.

Acid rain destroys trees and other plants.

Fumes from vehicle exhausts contribute to air pollution.

English yew tree (*Taxus baccata*)

Cleaning a green turtle (Chelonia mydas) *caught in an oil slick*

ACID RAIN

Acid rain falls when poisonous gases from power stations and vehicle exhausts mix with oxygen and moisture in the air. These gases become part of the water cycle and may be carried a long way by the wind before they fall as acid rain, or snow. Acid rain poisons or kills wildlife in lakes, rivers, and forests, and damages the surrounding plant life. The problem could be controlled by reducing vehicle emissions and limiting the gases released from power stations.

WATER POLLUTION

Chemical waste from factories, household sewage, and agricultural pesticides all contribute to the pollution of lakes, rivers, and seas. Spills from oil tankers can also damage wildlife. The fur or feathers of animals, such as seals and seabirds, becomes clogged by the oil, and some are poisoned when they swallow the oil accidentally. The gills of fish may be blocked so they cannot breathe. Human intervention can sometimes reduce the damage.

Healthy branch of yew tree

Trees with evergreen leaves are the most likely to be affected by acid rain.

Yew tree damaged by acid rain

Rhinoceros horns are used as decorative dagger handles.

HUNTING FOR PROFIT

Animals hunt in order to survive, but people hunt for sport and profit – putting species under threat and upsetting the balance of nature. Many animals are hunted for their skins and hides. The Caspian and Javan tigers, for example, became extinct in the 1970s and 1980s. Today hunting is less of a threat than habitat destruction, but people continue to kill, tempted by the huge financial rewards.

Dried seahorses are used as an ingredient in Chinese medicine.

Crocodile skins are made into bags and belts.

The shells of hawksbill turtles are made into souvenirs for tourists.

TOURISM

As the demand for unusual holidays increases, more travel companies try to find original, unspoiled locations – often putting local wildlife under threat. Unless they are made aware of the risks, visitors can disturb or pollute these habitats. Ecotourists are encouraged to travel in small groups and to be sensitive to the needs of the local wildlife. A quarter of Costa Rica is made up of national parks. Visitors are charged a high entry fee and the money is then used to conserve rare animals.

Only a few tourists at a time visit a penguin rookery, Antarctica.

Find out more

ANIMALS IN DANGER: *100*
ECOLOGY: *62*
HABITATS IN DANGER: *104*
NUTRIENT CYCLES: *64*

PESTS AND WEEDS

PESTS ARE ANIMALS OR PLANTS that harm people, crops, or resources. Plant pests are often called weeds. There are two main types of pests: those that cause diseases in people, such as malaria, and those that cause economic problems, such as insects that eat crops. Pests are good at finding and colonizing new habitats. They move easily from place to place and multiply rapidly. Humans make it easier for pests to spread by destroying the natural balance of nature, which would otherwise keep their numbers in check. To control pests, people use chemicals called pesticides, biological controls, or a mixture of both methods, called integrated pest management.

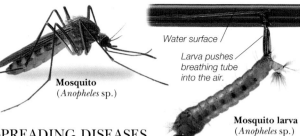

Mosquito
(*Anopheles* sp.)

Water surface

Larva pushes breathing tube into the air.

Mosquito larva
(*Anopheles* sp.)

SPREADING DISEASES

Many insects spread diseases. Some female mosquitoes, for example, transmit malaria by drinking blood before they lay their eggs. Mosquitoes can be controlled with chemical sprays, but they eventually become resistant to these chemicals and do not die. Alternative control methods include spraying oil onto water to keep the larvae from breathing air at the surface, or introducing fish to eat the larvae.

COCKROACHES

Some species of cockroach, such as the American cockroach (*Periplanata americana*), have become pests because of their natural scavenging habits. They damage more material than they eat and spread diseases such as salmonella with their droppings and their dirty feet as they move from sewage and waste systems to people's kitchens.

Oriental cockroaches (Blatta orientalis) *feeding on leftover food*

Electron micrograph of a carpet beetle (Anthrenus sp.)

A swarm of locusts attacking vegetation

LOCUSTS

The locust is able to breed quickly and migrate in vast groups, destroying all crops in its path, so it is dreaded throughout Africa and the Middle East. A swarm may cover 400 sq miles (1,000 sq km) and be made up of 50 billion locusts. Swarm locusts have more obvious markings, stronger wing muscles, and longer wings than other locusts. Control of these pests includes destroying eggs, using poisoned baits, or spraying insecticide on swarms or breeding grounds.

PESTS IN THE HOME

All the food and natural materials in people's homes attract a range of insects and fungi. The damage they cause as they feed makes them pests. Several types of beetle cause damage to wooden floors and furniture because their larvae eat into the wood, creating holes that undermine the structure. In tropical countries, termites and fungi can eat an entire house in just a few years. Other pests in the home include carpet beetles, clothes moths, and bedbugs.

BIRD PEST

The red-billed quelea from Africa is the world's worst bird pest. Flocks of queleas may contain up to 10,000 birds which move across fields of cereal crops like clouds of smoke, leaving a trail of devastation behind them. At night, they roost in groups of four million or more birds. Queleas migrate with the rains so they are always found in places where food is plentiful. They reproduce rapidly, breeding three or four times a year.

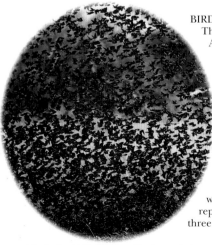

A flock of red-billed queleas (Quelea quelea)

INTRODUCED PESTS

Plants and animals introduced by people into new environments often become pests because there are no natural predators to control them. The South American water hyacinth, for example, spreads rapidly and in one growing season just 25 plants can produce 2 million new plants. Water hyacinths clog tropical waterways, using up valuable nutrients in the water and blocking out sunlight.

Life cycle of the spruce budworm

1. Scaly eggs on spruce needle

2. Caterpillar feeding

4. Adult moth

3. Pupa fastened to needles by silk threads

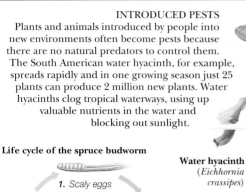

Water hyacinth (*Eichhornia crassipes*)

Dense, fibrous roots absorb oxygen and nutrients from the water.

TREE PEST

Caterpillars of a moth called the spruce budworm (*Choristoneura fumiferana*) are serious pests of North American conifers. They bore into needles and attack buds, cones, and twigs. The caterpillars cut off the needles and live in a large web on the bare branches. It is easier for pests to spread in plantations where only one species is grown, compared to an environment where different species grow side by side.

LARGE BINDWEED

This climbing weed twines around other plants, growing so strongly that it may smother them. It has creeping underground stems that send up new shoots at intervals, making it difficult to destroy. Large bindweed was first sold as a garden plant in northern Europe but it now thrives on wasteland.

Scientific name: *Calystegia silvatica*

Size: Up to 10 ft (3 m) high

Habitat: Cultivated land, wasteland, and hedgerows

Distribution: Western and Southern Europe

Reproduction: By seeds and underground stems that produce identical new plants

PEST MANAGEMENT

Integrated pest management is a way of controlling pests using natural methods together with minimal use of pesticides. In addition to spraying chemicals, some farmers plant different crops together to attract a greater variety of predators to reduce pests. On a smaller scale, gardeners will often use plants to control pests. For example, growing garlic between strawberries can prevent fungus, and lavender protects roses from aphids.

Marigolds (Tagetes sp.) attract hoverflies that eat aphids.

Control of aphids

1. Braconid wasp (Aphidius sp.) lays egg in aphid.

2. New wasp emerges from dead aphid.

3. Wasp leaves a hole in dead aphid.

NATURAL PREDATORS

A wide variety of creatures are used to control pests, such as aphids. Unlike chemical pesticides, these predators or parasites usually attack only one species, ignoring other animals. The natural enemies of pests must be able to reproduce quickly in order to limit the number of pests. Parasites introduced from one country to another must be able to survive in the climate of the new country.

Groundsel thrives on roadsides, railroads, and other open habitats.

Groundsel (*Senecio vulgaris*)

WEEDS

Weeds compete with garden plants and crops for light, water, and nutrients. They may contain diseases and viruses, and support insects that damage cultivated plants. Weeds thrive in a range of soils and reproduce easily. Some complete their life cycles in just a few months, while others last from year to year. Weeds can be controlled by physical removal, by chemicals, or by mulching with rotting vegetable matter to smother them.

Find out more

COCKROACHES, FLEAS, AND LICE: *164*

FLIES: *174*

GRASSHOPPERS AND CRICKETS: *166*

Spraying herbicide in a coffee plantation, Tanzania

PESTICIDES

Pesticides are chemicals designed to kill pests. They include insecticides, fungicides, and herbicides. Although they have successfully removed pests, pesticides have also caused pollution and killed many nonpest species. Today, fewer pesticides are used and they are based on the natural chemical pest repellents found in plants. They are targeted at specific pests and are soon broken down.

ANIMALS IN DANGER

EXTINCTION CAN BE A NATURAL process. Over millions of years, species gradually die out and new ones take their place. In recent times, however, species have been disappearing much faster than they would do naturally because people hunt animals and destroy their habitats. Most of the extinctions of the last 300 years have been influenced by people. Scientists believe that thousands of animal species are now endangered and may become extinct over the next 20 years or so. These include not only large animals such as mammals and birds, but countless smaller animals such as insects.

GORILLAS

There are two species of gorilla, and both are in serious trouble. Worst affected is the eastern gorilla, which lives in central Africa. It is directly threatened by hunting and deforestation, and also by successive wars that have flared up in this region. Until recently, the western gorilla was faring better, but it has been badly affected by the Ebola virus – a disease that is usually fatal.

Western lowland gorilla (Gorilla gorilla gorilla) standing in a treetop

African hunting dog
(*Lycaon pictus*)

Short, powerful muzzle

Long legs allow dog to run swiftly when chasing prey.

AFRICAN HUNTING DOGS

These intelligent pack-animals were once common in Africa, but now only about 2,000 remain. Hunting dogs have even disappeared from many wildlife reserves, where other large animals, such as lions, are thriving. Scientists think that the wild dogs are dying from diseases such as rabies and distemper spread by domestic dogs.

Tigers' coats are highly prized for their beautiful markings.

Tiger
(*Panthera tigris*)

TIGERS

Once widespread throughout Asia, tigers are now found only in small patches of wilderness. Until recently, there were eight subspecies of tigers, but three are extinct and the rest are endangered. There are now fewer than 2,500 breeding adult tigers left in the wild. These are threatened by loss of their habitat and by trade in their fur coats and body parts.

Illegal tiger skins, Calcutta, India

ELEPHANTS

In 1970, there were about two million elephants in Africa. Today, there are probably only 600,000 left. Asian elephants are even more threatened, with fewer than 30,000 remaining in the wild. Elephants are killed for their ivory tusks, which are made into ornaments and piano keys. Ivory trading is now strictly controlled, but elephants are still threatened by poaching.

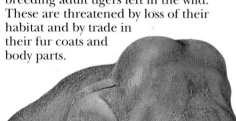

Asian elephant
(*Elephas maximus*)

Tusks grow at a rate of about 7 in (17 cm) per year.

Carved tusk from a young male elephant

Spanish moon moth
(*Graellsia isabellae*)

Large copper
(*Lycaena dispar*)

Homerus swallowtail
(*Papilio homerus*)

BUTTERFLIES AND MOTHS

Collecting butterflies was once a popular hobby. Enthusiasts caught specimens in nets and pinned them into cabinets. Few people collect butterflies today, but many species are still threatened now, by habitat loss. To survive, butterflies need large wild areas with plenty of plants for food and sites for laying eggs. Endangered species include the stunning Jamaican homerus swallowtail, the Spanish moon moth, and the large copper, which is now extinct in the UK.

GOLDEN LION TAMARIN

This species of monkey lives in remnant forest patches on the east coast of Brazil. Most of its natural habitat has been destroyed by the spreading human population. By 1980, only 100 golden lion tamarins survived in the wild. Conservation work has increased this number to about 600.

Seychelles paradise-flycatcher
(*Terpsiphone corvina*)

PARADISE-FLYCATCHER

Fewer than 300 Seychelles paradise-flycatchers now survive. Once found throughout the Seychelles, these birds have been killed in most of the islands by cats and rats brought by people. The eggs and chicks are particularly at risk. Like many island species, paradise flycatchers evolved in a habitat with few natural predators so they cannot defend themselves against the invaders.

CALIFORNIA CONDOR

This magnificent American vulture was once a common sight in the southwestern US. Shooting, egg-collecting, pesticides, and the spread of towns and cities may all have contributed to its downfall. In the 1980s, there were only 27 birds in captivity and none left in the wild. In 1992, scientists reintroduced California condors into the wild. By 2006, the total population had reached nearly 300, including more than 130 birds in the wild.

The condor lubricates its feathers with oil to keep them clean.

Scientific name:	*Gymnogyps californianus*
Size:	Wingspan 9 ft 6 in (2.92 m)
Habitat:	Mountain forest and scrub
Distribution:	Los Padres National Forest, 75 miles (120 km) north of Los Angeles, US
Reproduction:	One egg every two years
Diet:	Carcasses of dead animals, such as deer

RIVER DOLPHINS

These unusual dolphins live in fresh water and have suffered from close contact with growing human populations. Modern dams damage their habitats, and many dolphins are accidentally killed by fishing nets and by ships. The Yangtze River dolphin, from China, was last seen in 2004. Many experts think that it is now extinct.

Golden lion tamarin
(*Leontopithecus rosalia*)

White-finned dolphin
(Lipotes vexillifer)

Golden mantella
(*Mantella aurantiaca*)

Red ruffed lemur
(*Varecia variegata rubra*)

BLACK CAIMAN

The South American black caiman is endangered by poachers hunting for its valuable skin. This reptile needs a long period of growth before it reproduces, and many are killed before they can breed. Nearly half of all crocodilians are threatened, although American alligators are on the increase thanks to conservation measures.

Black caiman
(*Melanosuchus niger*)

VANISHING AMPHIBIANS

Amphibians are increasingly rare because of pollution, acid rain, low water levels, and the destruction of their habitats. Island species, such as Madagascar's golden mantella, are often more vulnerable because they are found only in small areas. Their future survival may depend on the establishment of nature reserves to protect their habitats.

RED RUFFED LEMUR

No one knows how many red ruffed lemurs remain in the rainforests of Madagascar because these animals are so seldom seen. The red ruffed lemur is now officially listed as critically endangered and may soon be extinct in the wild. Like all the lemurs of Madagascar, it is in decline becase its native rainforest is being destroyed to make way for farmland. Lemurs are also hunted and killed by animal traps.

PLANTS IN DANGER

A QUARTER OF ALL THE PLANTS in the world are known to be in danger or threatened with extinction. However, the true number of these plants is probably much higher because thousands of species have not yet been identified. The main dangers to plants throughout the world are habitat destruction, the spread of towns, and modern farming techniques, that include the use of pesticides. Two-thirds of the world's plants, including many endangered species, grow in the tropics where their rainforest habitat is threatened. Some plants are threatened by over-collection or the introduction of plant-eating animals such as goats. Plants that are introduced from other countries can also overwhelm native species.

South American slipper orchid
(*Phragmipedium besseae*)

OVER-COLLECTION

The collection of wild plants for private gardens in Europe and North America is a threat to many species. Rare orchids from South America and Southeast Asia, such as *Cattleya*, *Dendrobium*, and *Vanda*, have been collected almost to extinction. Some of these, such as slipper orchids, are worth hundreds of dollars each, which means that a lot of money can be made through smuggling. Millions of wild bulbs are uprooted each year and exported from countries such as Portugal or Turkey.

THREATENED CACTI
Cacti are popular with collectors because of their unusual appearance and ability to withstand heat and drought. In the United States and Mexico, cacti are dug up in the middle of the night by "cactus rustlers" who then sell them. Illegally collected cacti may be sold for as much as $500 each. It is not always easy to catch offenders and courts often treat plant theft as minor and impose only small fines.

Cactus
(*Melocactus matanzanus*)

Bottle palm
(*Hyophorbe lagenicaulis*)

The bottle palm grows only on Round Island off the coast of Mauritius. Its numbers are slowly increasing thanks to conservation measures.

THREATENED ISLAND PLANTS
About one-third of all threatened plants grow on islands. The bottle palm, for example, is particularly vulnerable because it lives only on one small island off the coast of Mauritius. Island plants can easily be destroyed by climate changes, disease, habitat destruction, and introduced species. Grazing animals, introduced to remote islands by European sailors, have eaten many rare plants. Garden plants have also been introduced to many islands and smothered the native plants.

The silversword (Argyroxiphium sp.) grows only on the Hawaiian island of Maui.

HAWAIIAN SILVERSWORD
A member of the daisy family, the Hawaiian silversword grows only on the slopes of the Haleakala volcano on the island of Maui. It can grow to a height of 8 ft (2.5 m), and flowers only once, after which it dies. There were no large plant-eating animals in Hawaii until livestock such as sheep were introduced. The silversword is threatened by these grazing animals and is one of more than 800 endangered plant species in Hawaii.

CAFE MARRON
The café marron plant comes from the remote island of Rodriguez, in the Indian Ocean. At one time it was common, but after centuries of deforestation and grazing, it was thought to have become extinct. In 1980, a schoolboy spotted a single living plant, and scientists managed to take cuttings from it a few years later. Today, café marron is back from the brink, though still endangered.

Café marron
(*Ramosmania heterophylla*)

HABITAT DESTRUCTION

The most serious threat to plants is the destruction of their habitat. This includes cutting down rainforests, draining wetlands, and overgrazing and plowing up grasslands. People continue to wipe out habitats as populations increase and demand more space. Tropical rainforests are being cleared at an alarming rate and in countries such as the Philippines, the logging industry has devastated many forests. Millions of animals die when the plants that they need for survival disappear.

Forest fires can destroy a habitat for many years.

TITAN ARUM

The titan arum has the largest flowering structure on Earth and is found only in a small pocket of rainforest in Sumatra. It grows from an underground tuber that lives for about 20 years but probably flowers only three times for no more than two or three days. There is concern over the future of the titan arum because so few of these plants remain and they grow in such a small area. They are also in danger from local people who dig up the huge tubers for food.

Titan arum (Amorphophallus titanum) growing in Sumatra, Indonesia

Rose periwinkle
(*Catharanthus roseus*)

ROSE PERIWINKLE

The rose periwinkle grows in the rapidly disappearing rainforests of Madagascar and it may soon become an endangered species. It is used to make drugs for treating certain types of childhood leukemia and Hodgkin's disease, a form of cancer. Drugs made from the rose periwinkle have contributed to the reduction in deaths from these cancers. Many other unknown rainforest plants could also contain useful drugs, but they may become extinct before they are discovered.

INTRODUCED SPECIES

Plants moved from one country to another, often by gardeners, may cause problems in their new home. They can swamp native plants by blocking out sunlight and using up water and nutrients in the soil. Kudzu (*Pueraria lobata*) was introduced into the US from Asia as a soil stabilizer. However, it is now a widespread and fast-growing pest. On the Galápagos islands, plants such as passion fruit (*Passiflora edulis*) have to be cut back regularly in order to safeguard the survival of native plants.

Kudzu (Pueraria lobata) is now a common pest in the US.

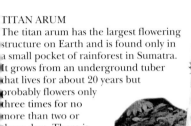

Cycads are palmlike plants with swollen trunks and crowns of spreading leaves.

Tree cycad
(*Encephalartos woodii*)

LAST MALE ON EARTH

Cycads have lived on Earth since the time of the dinosaurs but today they are the world's most threatened plant group – at least half of them face extinction. Only one male specimen of the cycad *Encephalartos woodii* has been found in the wild in southern Africa. No female has ever been found, but the surviving male plant has been successfully propagated. Young male plants are now being grown in botanical gardens in several parts of the world.

Find out more

CONIFERS AND CYCADS: *124*
CONSERVATION: *106*
PALMS: *130*
TROPICAL RAINFORESTS: *82*

HABITATS IN DANGER

WILD PLANTS AND ANIMALS are adapted to survive in a particular set of surroundings, called their habitat. As habitats change naturally over long periods of time, some species die out while others survive. But people are in a hurry to change habitats to suit their own needs – to create farmland or build cities, for example. The way people live also threatens the delicate balance between living things and their habitats. People create pollution, which travels through the air and water from one habitat to another. They also destroy wildlife habitats by digging the ground up for mining, or by building roads through them.

Magnificent frigatebird (*Fregata magnificens*)

This Galápagos hawk (Buteo galapagoensis) is used to photographers.

ISLAND HABITATS

Small islands are particularly at risk from habitat destruction because each one is home to unique wildlife which can be wiped out very quickly. Island species are threatened by introduced competitors, predators, or diseases, and by the spread of farming, towns, and tourism. Large numbers of tourists now visit the Galápagos Islands to see the giant tortoises, frigatebirds, and other wildlife. Tourism is carefully regulated there to minimize habitat destruction.

CORAL REEFS

Coral reefs are home to a huge range of creatures, from corals and anemones to fish and seahorses. These animals are threatened by pollution, overfishing, drilling for oil, mining coral for building materials, and dumping waste. Building operations on the coast may produce silt which drains into the sea, smothering and killing the coral. Tourists can damage reefs with their boat anchors or by collecting coral for souvenirs. Other dangers include increased water temperatures due to global warming.

Seahorse (*Hippocampus* sp.)

Emperor angelfish (*Pomacanthus imperator*)

Clownfish (*Amphiprion* sp.)

Logging for hardwood trees destroys large areas of forest.

DISAPPEARING RAINFORESTS

The destruction of rainforests is critical because nearly half of the world's species live there. The trees are cut down for timber or to make way for farms and mines, but forest clearance causes many long-term problems, such as soil erosion, floods, and droughts. About half of the rainforests have already been felled, and an area the size of a soccer field is cut down every second. If this continues, most of the world's rainforests are likely to vanish within the next 25 years.

Shoreline in 1960

Shoreline in 1989

The shrinking Aral Sea

ARAL SEA

This huge inland sea in Kazakhstan is disappearing fast. In 50 years it has shrunk by half and split into two, leaving some of its ports far inland. This ecological disaster was triggered in the 1960s, when the region's rivers were diverted to irrigate cotton and other crops. A rescue program has now been launched to help the lake refill. Without it, the Aral could disappear by 2025.

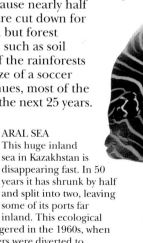

Salt bush
(*Atriplex nummularia*)

Atriplex *gets rid of surplus salt through its leaves.*

DAMS AND DELTAS
Many large-scale dams have been built around the world to generate electricity and control the irrigation of crops. But dams drown valleys and prevent silt in the water from flooding over the land and enriching the soil. Instead, the silt builds up behind the dam and clogs up reservoirs. Crops have to be fed with expensive fertilizers instead of free, natural silt. Dams and irrigation canals also reduce the amount of silt that reaches the river's delta. Silt normally builds up in the delta and helps protect the shoreline. With less freshwater coming down the river, saltwater from the sea is able to seep inland.

Reservoir behind the dam

Damming a river

Salt poisoning can occur in the delta as saltwater seeps in from the sea.

Coastline is slowly eroded because there is no silt to protect it.

Silt builds up behind the dam, reducing its lifespan and capacity.

Sea

SALTY AUSTRALIA
In Australia, farmers have removed many of the native bush plants which used to keep salt from sinking down into the ground. Now much of Australia's farmland is ruined by salt. One solution is to plant trees on higher ground. Their roots soak up water and prevent it from draining salt into the ground. On lower ground, salt-tolerant plants, such as *Atriplex*, can be grown. Salt builds up in the plants, which can then be harvested to remove some of the salt.

Nile perch are a good food catch for local fishermen.

LAKE VICTORIA
The introduction of an exotic species can affect the balance of nature within a habitat. Lake Victoria in East Africa, for example, used to be home to 300 species of cichlid fish. In the 1960s, Nile perch (*Lates niloticus*) were introduced. They fed on the cichlids and by the 1980s their numbers had increased so rapidly that they made up 70 percent of the fish caught in the lake. About 200 species of cichlid are now extinct.

Protection of Florida alligators has allowed their numbers to increase.

ARCTIC AND TUNDRA
The tundra is the largest wilderness and wildlife habitat left in the Northern Hemisphere, but mining, building roads, and laying pipelines have all damaged this fragile ecosystem. People driving vehicles over the tundra in summer churn up the ground and cause soil erosion, leaving permanent scars on the land. Roads have to be carefully constructed to avoid melting the frozen soil, called permafrost, that lies below the surface. Disposal of sewage, waste water, and garbage can also damage wildlife.

Polar bears are attracted to the food in waste dumps and can be injured or poisoned by the rubbish.

WETLANDS IN DANGER
Marshes, mangrove swamps, peat bogs, and other wetlands are important habitats. Coastal wetlands are spawning grounds for fish, lobsters, and shrimps and mangroves prevent coastal erosion. Half of the wetlands in the US and two-thirds of Europe's wetlands have been drained for agriculture, flood control, or tourism. Pollution from farms and towns also damages wetlands. Conservation laws, pollution control, and less intensive farming would help them recover.

Bison grazing in Badlands National Park, US

PRAIRIES
The North American grasslands, known as prairies, were once home to huge herds of bison and other grazing animals. Most of the prairies have now been plowed up for growing corn or ranching cattle and sheep. But the rich soils are easily ruined by overgrazing and wind erosion. In the 1930s, the wind eroded vast areas of topsoil, creating "dustbowl" conditions. To avoid this, farmers have to manage their land carefully, for example by planting grass as well as corn.

Find out more	
CORAL REEFS:	*72*
POLAR REGIONS:	*90*
TROPICAL RAINFORESTS:	*82*
WETLANDS:	*74*

CONSERVATION

CONSERVING INDIVIDUAL SPECIES and their habitats is important for the survival of life as a whole. Living things help to control the balance of gases, heat, and moisture in the atmosphere, and the flow of nutrients through the soil. Many rare and, as yet, undiscovered plants may also prove useful in the future. To conserve these resources, areas of natural habitat need to be protected and carefully managed to make sure that a variety of species can flourish. Conservation measures must also include the control of trade in endangered species, the introduction of breeding programs of rare species, and the reduction of pollution.

Botanist studying a fringed pitcher plant (Nepenthes tentaculata) *in Borneo*

FACT-FINDING

One of the first priorities in wildlife conservation is to find out which species are endangered. Millions of species have not yet been identified, especially those in the tropics. When an area is earmarked for development, there is often very little information about the plants and animals that live there. This makes it difficult to balance the demands of conservation and economic development.

Przewalski's wild horse
(*Equus caballus przewalskii*)

New Forest pony
(*Equus caballus*)

CAPTIVE BREEDING

Rare species, such as Przewalski's horse, have been bred in captivity to prevent them from dying out. However, this can bring its own problems such as inbreeding (mating between close relatives), which can increase susceptibility to disease. A species' survival may also be aided by artificial insemination (fertilization without mating), or the transfer of embryos from rare to common species, who act as surrogate mothers. This has been achieved by implanting a Przewalski's horse embryo into the womb of a New Forest pony.

CROSSING ROADS

Animals are often killed when crossing roads, especially where roads are built through nature reserves. Snakes are particularly at risk – they like to lie on warm roads at night. Animals that migrate across roads, or creatures such as toads, badgers, or bears that cross roads to reach breeding areas, often end up as roadkills. Special tunnels or underpasses are sometimes built to help animals cross roads safely.

Toad tunnel in England allows toads to cross a road to reach their breeding pond.

FARMING WILD ANIMALS

Some wild animals, such as salmon, crocodiles, and ostriches, are bred on farms and sold for their meat, hides, or feathers. This helps reduce the number of animals being taken from the wild, but it also uses up land where wild animals could be living. Fish farms are an efficient way of producing fish. However, diseases spread quickly when many fish are kept in a small space, and chemicals used to keep them healthy can pollute the surrounding waters.

Arabian oryx
(*Oryx leucoryx*)

OUT INTO THE WILD

The aim of captive breeding is not to keep the animals, but to release them back into the wild. This is not a simple process. Animals have to learn how to survive in their new environment, and there have to be enough animals to build up a new population without risk of inbreeding. A good example of this is the Arabian oryx, which was hunted to extinction in the wild by 1972. Those that had been bred in zoos, however, were successfully reintroduced into the Jiddah Desert of Oman.

Salmon are farmed in floating pens in freshwater and the sea.

SEED BANKS

A seed bank contains a collection of dried seeds stored in a deep freeze. The drying and freezing increases the length of time the seed can be stored – most will last for centuries, and some may even survive for millennia. This system also allows many different types of seeds to be stored in a very small space. Most seed banks specialize in seeds of crop plants, but the Royal Botanic Gardens at Wakehurst Place, UK, has a collection of seeds of more than 5,000 wild plant species.

Botanist at work at the seed bank, Wakehurst Place, UK

Propagation of plants

Carnivorous pitcher plants (Nepenthes rajah)

Sundew plants (Drosera granticola)

Royal Botanic Gardens, Sydney, Australia

BOTANICAL GARDENS

The 1,500 botanical gardens of the world play a valuable role in educating people about endangered plants. They can save plants which cannot be cold-stored and increase stocks of endangered species, some of which can be reintroduced into the wild. Using modern methods of propagation (reproduction), endangered plants can be bred and sent to other gardens.

NATIONAL PARKS

Today there are more than 1,200 national parks around the world. The first was Yellowstone in Wyoming, which was set up in 1872. National parks can make a vital contribution to the development of a country – they attract tourists, prevent soil erosion, protect water supplies, and conserve resources such as medicinal plants. But it is difficult to set aside large areas of land when people need land on which to live and farm. Inside the parks, animals need protection from poachers and may need to be culled if the numbers become too high to control.

Yosemite National Park in California

WORLD'S MAJOR NATIONAL PARKS		
NAME	LOCATION	SIZE SQ MILES (SQ KM)
Wood Buffalo	Canada	17,300 (44,807)
Salongar	Zaire	14,116 (36,560)
Bernardo O'Higgins	Chile	13,614 (35,260)
Kruger	South Africa	7,523 (19,484)
Kakadu	Australia	6,777 (17,552)
Yosemite	US	1,189 (3,079)

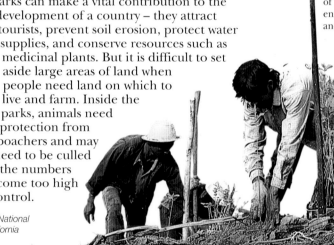

Planting eucalyptus trees in Kalimantan, Indonesia

PLANTING TREES

One solution to the problem of deforestation is to make sure that felled trees are always replaced with native species. Eucalyptus trees are often planted to provide wood for fuel because they reach maturity in only 10 years. But eucalyptus trees take nutrients and water from the soil, and poison other plants. Scientists believe it is better for the environment to plant trees that grow naturally in an area.

STOPPING THE TRADE

A great deal of money can be made from trade in endangered plants and animals. International cooperation is needed to enforce laws to prevent this. The Convention on International Trade in Endangered Species (CITES) is an organization that aims to regulate international trade in some 34,000 animals and plants. A monitoring group called Trade Records Analysis of Flora and Fauna in Commerce (TRAFFIC) recommends which species need extra protection.

Environmental Investigation Agency researcher filming in Quing Ping market, China

Find out more

ANIMALS IN DANGER: *100*
HABITATS IN DANGER: *104*
PEOPLE AND NATURE: *96*
TROPICAL RAINFORESTS: *82*

HOW LIVING THINGS ARE CLASSIFIED

No one knows exactly how many species there are on Earth, but the total runs into many millions. Some, like the giraffe, are unmistakable. Others, such as beetles or roundworms, exist in such a variety of forms that it is easy to confuse one kind with another. Scientists avoid this confusion by giving every type of living thing a scientific name. Unlike common names, scientific names are precise because each one identifies a single species and nothing else. Scientific names play a key part in biological classification. They show where a species fits in the natural world, and which other species are its closest relatives.

Carolus Linnaeus (1707–78)

DIVISIONS OF LIFE

Living things are organized into groups of increasing size. The groups show how closely related the different species are. On these two pages, you can see how this system works for one species – the golden jackal. Working from left to right, the illustrations show the seven major groups that the golden jackal belongs to, together with some other members of each group. The groups on the left, such as the dog family, contain the closely related species. Groups farther to the right include more distantly related species.

Kenilworth ivy
(*Cymbalaria muralis*)

MAKING NAMES

Scientific names are usually written in Latin, the language used by early naturalists. Unlike common names, Latin names can be understood all over the world. Each species name has two parts – a genus name, which comes first, and a species name. Kenilworth ivy, for example, is *Cymbalaria muralis*. *Cymbalaria* means "cymbal-shaped leaves," while *muralis* means "living on walls."

LINNAEUS

A Swedish botanist, Carolus Linnaeus, devised the system of giving species two-word scientific names. At first, this was a form of shorthand, but the system proved so useful that other naturalists soon began using it. Linnaeus classified thousands of plants and animals, and gave humans the scientific name *Homo sapiens*.

Asiatic short-clawed otter
(*Aonyx cinerea*)

Domestic cat
(*Felis catus*)

Stoat
(*Mustela erminea*)

Dingo
(*Canis familiaris*)

Golden jackal
(*Canis aureus*)

Gray wolf
(*Canis lupus*)

Maned wolf
(*Chrysocyon brachyurus*)

Golden jackal
(*Canis aureus*)

Dhole
(*Cuon alpinus*)

Raccoon dog
(*Nyctereutes procyonoides*)

Golden jackal
(*Canis aureus*)

Golden jackal
(*Canis aureus*)

American black bear
(*Ursus americanus*)

SPECIES

The scientific name for the golden jackal is *Canis aureus*. Like all other species, the golden jackal is unique. It normally breeds only with members of its own species and has its own special set of physical features, such as a distinctive golden-brown coat.

GENUS

A genus is a group of very similar species. The genus *Canis* contains eight species, including the golden jackal. All these species are hunters and scavengers with long legs and bushy tails. Each has a slightly different way of life.

FAMILY

The genus *Canis* belongs to the dog family (Canidae), which contains 36 species. All dogs have long jaws, pointed ears, and a bushy tail, but they behave in different ways. Some hunt in packs, while others find food on their own.

ORDER

The dog family belongs to the carnivore order (Carnivora), which contains 240 species in seven families. These include cats, bears, raccoons, hyenas, and otters. Carnivores have sharp teeth and strong jaws for eating flesh. Most find food by hunting, but some also eat plant food.

KINGDOMS

Scientists usually divide all living things except for viruses into five kingdoms – animals, plants, fungi, monerans (such as bacteria), and protists (single-celled organisms apart from monerans). The animal kingdom contains by far the most species, but the moneran kingdom contains the most individuals. So far, scientists have identified and described only a small fraction of the total number of species.

THE FIVE KINGDOMS

NAME	SPECIES DESCRIBED (APPROXIMATE)
Monerans	4,000
Protists	50,000
Fungi	70,000
Plants	300,000
Animals	1,000,000

This zebroid is a hybrid between a horse and a zebra.

WHAT IS A SPECIES?

A species is the basic unit of classification. Each species is a collection of similar living things that are capable of breeding together in the wild. Different species do not normally interbreed in nature, but when they do the resulting offspring are called hybrids. As such, they fall outside the system of classification. Hybrids may be healthy but are usually unable to have offspring of their own.

MODERN TECHNIQUES

Scientists once classified living things mainly by their shape and the way they develop. In recent years, a powerful new aid to classification has been developed. This involves comparing the genes (chemical "codes" passed from parents to offspring) of different species. By studying the differences in genes, scientists can work out how closely related two species are.

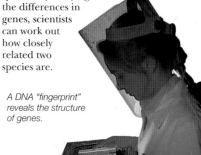

A DNA "fingerprint" reveals the structure of genes.

Noctule bat
(*Nyctalus noctula*)

Golden jackal
(*Canis aureus*)

Giraffe
(*Giraffa camelopardalis*)

Grivet
(*Cercopithecus aethiops*)

Red-necked wallaby
(*Macropus rufogriseus*)

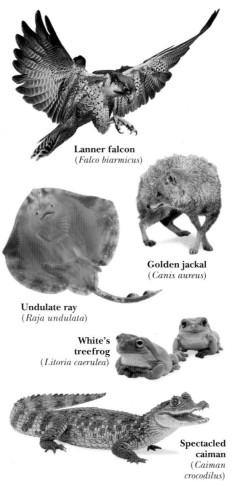

Lanner falcon
(*Falco biarmicus*)

Undulate ray
(*Raja undulata*)

White's treefrog
(*Litoria caerulea*)

Golden jackal
(*Canis aureus*)

Spectacled caiman
(*Caiman crocodilus*)

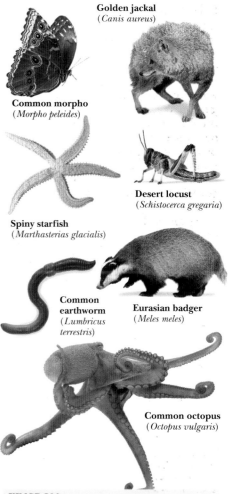

Golden jackal
(*Canis aureus*)

Common morpho
(*Morpho peleides*)

Desert locust
(*Schistocerca gregaria*)

Spiny starfish
(*Marthasterias glacialis*)

Common earthworm
(*Lumbricus terrestris*)

Eurasian badger
(*Meles meles*)

Common octopus
(*Octopus vulgaris*)

CLASS

The carnivore order belongs to a class called the mammals (Mammalia), which includes 22 separate orders. Despite their great differences in shape, size, and way of life, most of the animals in this class have hair and all raise their young by suckling them on milk. No other group of animals shows these features.

PHYLUM

Mammals belong to a higher group, or phylum, of animals called chordates (Chordata). At some stage in their lives, all chordates have a rod of strengthening tissue called a notochord, which runs along the body. Nearly all chordates are vertebrates – animals with backbones. The chordates include the largest animals alive.

KINGDOM

The chordate phylum is one of more than 30 phyla that make up the animal kingdom (Animalia). Animals are remarkably varied but share certain basic features – their bodies are made of many cells and they obtain energy by eating food. Animals respond quickly to their surroundings, and most can move around.

BACTERIA AND VIRUSES

BACTERIA ARE THE most abundant forms of life, and live in the air, on land, and in water. They consist of just one microscopic cell, without a nucleus. Some bacteria are known as "germs" because they cause disease. Most, however, are either harmless or extremely useful – for example, the bacteria used to produce foods and medicines. Viruses are even simpler than bacteria, and much smaller. They consist of tiny packages of chemicals that become active only inside living things. Like bacteria, some viruses do not cause disease, while others can be deadly.

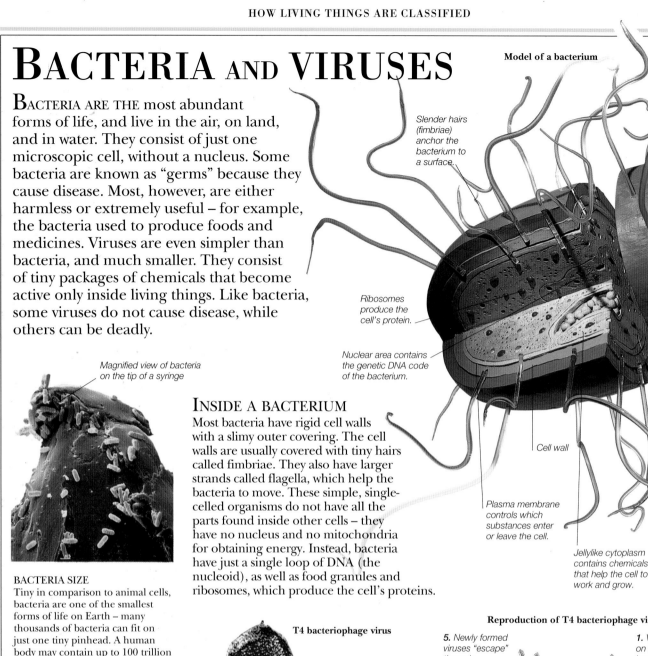

Model of a bacterium

Slender hairs (fimbriae) anchor the bacterium to a surface.

Ribosomes produce the cell's protein.

Nuclear area contains the genetic DNA code of the bacterium.

Cell wall

Plasma membrane controls which substances enter or leave the cell.

Jellylike cytoplasm contains chemicals that help the cell to work and grow.

Magnified view of bacteria on the tip of a syringe

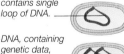

INSIDE A BACTERIUM

Most bacteria have rigid cell walls with a slimy outer covering. The cell walls are usually covered with tiny hairs called fimbriae. They also have larger strands called flagella, which help the bacteria to move. These simple, single-celled organisms do not have all the parts found inside other cells – they have no nucleus and no mitochondria for obtaining energy. Instead, bacteria have just a single loop of DNA (the nucleoid), as well as food granules and ribosomes, which produce the cell's proteins.

BACTERIA SIZE

Tiny in comparison to animal cells, bacteria are one of the smallest forms of life on Earth – many thousands of bacteria can fit on just one tiny pinhead. A human body may contain up to 100 trillion bacteria. They can only be seen in detail with an electron microscope.

How bacteria reproduce

Bacterium cell contains single loop of DNA.

DNA, containing genetic data, is copied.

Cell wall develops to form new cells.

Bacterium splits into identical cells.

HOW BACTERIA REPRODUCE

In favorable conditions, a bacterium may divide in two about once every 20 minutes. Bacteria usually reproduce by copying their DNA and then splitting into two identical cells. Some antibiotics work by preventing the development of a new cell wall as the bacterium divides.

T4 bacteriophage virus

Head contains a long, coiled strand of DNA (deoxyribonucleic acid).

Tail sheath contracts to inject virus's DNA into bacterium.

Tail fibers are made of proteins.

INSIDE A VIRUS

Viruses come in various shapes, from spheres to rods – and some have "heads" and "tails." They are not true living organisms because they are not made of cells. Viruses consist of nucleic acids (usually DNA), wrapped in a protective protein coat. This coat may help viruses invade other cells, which often leads to illness. Viruses invade all kinds of cells, including bacteria. A bacteria-invading virus is called a bacteriophage.

Reproduction of T4 bacteriophage virus

5. Newly formed viruses "escape" through the cell wall.

1. Virus lands on cell wall of bacterium and locks on.

2. Tail of virus injects genetic material into bacterium.

4. Parts of the new viruses come together.

3. Bacterium makes copies of the virus's genetic material and protein coating.

HOW VIRUSES REPRODUCE

A virus is inactive until it touches a living cell. Once this happens, the whole virus may enter the cell or, as in the case of the bacteriophage, just inject its genetic material through the cell wall. This material takes over the host cell, forcing it to build all the parts needed for new viruses. In this way, thousands of viruses are produced. They "escape" through the wall of the host cell.

USEFUL BACTERIA

Certain bacteria are vital for the well-being of all living things. For example, bacteria in human digestive systems destroy certain harmful bacteria, while bacteria in the stomachs of mammals such as cows and sheep help them digest grass. Some plants use bacteria in their root nodules to trap nitrogen from the air and turn it into nitrates – a form of nitrogen that plants can use. Bacteria also break down natural wastes, recycling elements such as carbon, nitrogen, and phosphorus.

Flagella propel bacteria through watery surroundings.

Bacteria in the root nodules of this sweetpea help it to survive in soils that are low in nitrogen.

Sticky, slimy, outer layer may help to protect bacterium.

INDUSTRIAL HELPERS

People use bacteria to make foods, medicines, and industrial products. Certain bacteria convert milk into other dairy products, such as buttermilk, yogurt, and cheese. Bacteria play an important part in waste disposal, and are also used to produce chemicals for the brewing, baking, and leather industries. Some bacteria are used to "grow" proteins, such as hormones and insulin, which are then used in medical research.

Bacteria help to curdle milk to make cheese.

HARMFUL BACTERIA

Bacteria are the main cause of infectious diseases such as cholera, tetanus, and typhoid. The symptoms of many of these diseases are caused by toxic proteins (toxins) which are produced by bacteria. Antibiotic drugs and good sanitation help fight bacterial diseases. However, in certain parts of the world, drug supplies and hygiene standards are poor, so serious epidemics spread rapidly.

Clostridium tetani bacteria produce tetanus toxins, which lead to convulsions and spasms.

PLANT VIRUSES

Most plant viruses are small and shaped either like filaments (hairs) or polygons (many-sided shapes). They cannot penetrate the rigid cell walls of plants, so they are transmitted by the piercing mouthparts of insects. Many plant viruses cause poor growth. Tulip viruses, however, can produce a lovely effect. By reducing the amount of pigment in the petals, they create vivid streaks of color.

The vibrant patterns of some tulips are created by viruses.

HIV

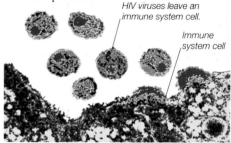

The human immunodeficiency virus (HIV) causes the disease AIDS (Acquired Immune Deficiency Syndrome). This virus stops the body's immune system from working properly, so it is unable to fight infections such as pneumonia. The incubation period of the virus is presently 8–10 years. There is no cure as yet, although drugs such as AZT may slow down the speed at which the virus reproduces.

HIV viruses leave an immune system cell.

Immune system cell

Scientific name: Human immunodeficiency virus

Size: 0.01 micrometer

Habitat: Human body; short life outside the body

Distribution: Worldwide

Reproduction: Uses the DNA of cells that it infects to replicate (copy) itself

DISCOVERIES WITH BACTERIA

The French scientist Louis Pasteur (1822–95) was one of the first scientists to show that bacteria helped break down organic matter. He boiled liquid in glass flasks to kill all the bacteria and then sealed the ends. The liquid remained unspoiled until the flasks were opened and bacteria could enter. Pasteur's work led to the development of pasteurization – killing bacteria in milk and other foods by heating them to very high temperatures.

Sealed flask of boiled liquid remains uncontaminated.

HARMFUL VIRUSES

Flu, mumps, rabies, and AIDS are just some of the diseases caused by viruses. Unlike bacterial diseases, few drugs can be used to fight viral infections because viruses invade cells. So any drug damaging the virus would also damage the host cell. When an animal suffers a viral disease, it develops a natural immunity. In the same way, injecting a human with dead or subdued viruses (vaccination) makes the body produce natural defences.

Vaccinations are given to some domestic animals.

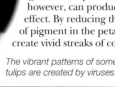

Find out more

CELLS: *20*
HOW LIFE BEGAN: *12*
NUTRIENT CYCLES: *64*
SINGLE-CELLED ORGANISMS: *112*

SINGLE-CELLED ORGANISMS

SINGLE-CELLED ORGANISMS far outnumber all other kinds of life. The most abundant of these organisms are bacteria, but there is also an immense variety of more complex single-celled organisms called protists. Protists are larger than bacteria, although they are too small to see with the naked eye. Most live in water or damp places. Some protists, called algae, are plant-like organisms that make food by photosynthesis. Others, called protozoa, behave like animals and take in food. Several behave in part like plants and in part like animals.

Paramecium

Waste being expelled

Nucleus

Groove leading to mouth

Food being digested

Detail of cell wall

Cilia

INDEPENDENT LIFE

This tiny, slipper-shaped organism is called *Paramecium*. It lives in ponds and puddles, and is just 0.01 in (0.25 mm) long. Although it has only a single cell, *Paramecium* is well adapted for survival. It darts around by beating tiny hairs (cilia), and it can shoot out sticky threads if attacked. *Paramecium* feeds on bacteria, which it sweeps into a groove on one side of the cell.

BEATING HAIRS
Paramecium is covered by thousands of microscopic hairs called cilia, which beat like tiny oars. They do not all beat at once, but move in rhythmic waves that flow across the cell.

Amoeba *moves by flowing like a liquid.*

Euglena *flicks a whiplike flagellum to pull it forward.*

MOVEMENT

Some single-celled organisms simply drift along in water, but many can propel themselves forward. *Amoeba* moves by flowing like a liquid, and takes about an hour to travel 1 in (2.5 cm). *Euglena* moves by flicking a tiny whip called a flagellum, and takes about 3 minutes to swim 1 in. *Paramecium* moves much faster – it takes only 10 seconds to swim 1 in.

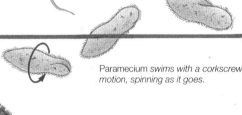

Paramecium *swims with a corkscrew motion, spinning as it goes.*

Bell animals
(*Vorticella*)

FEELING FOR FOOD
Bell animals, known scientifically as *Vorticella*, live in water, and each one is fastened in place by a long, slender stalk. Rings of cilia around the top of the cell sweep particles of food into the mouth. If anything touches a bell animal, its stalk suddenly coils up, pulling it out of danger.

Desmids *float near the surface of ponds and lakes.*

FEEDING

Like all living things, single-celled organisms need energy to survive. Desmids and diatoms collect energy directly from sunlight, and obtain their food by photosynthesis. Protozoa, or animal-like protists, cannot do this. Instead, they get their energy by eating food. Some protozoa sift particles of food from water, while others are active hunters that chase microscopic prey.

Didinium *devouring a Paramecium twice its size*

KILLER PROTIST
Some protists have phenomenal appetites. The freshwater predator *Didinium* eats protists that are much larger than itself. *Didinium* finds its victims by bumping into them, and attacks immediately by stunning its prey with an explosive dart. Its mouth then expands enormously to swallow the cell whole. *Didinium* can digest a single *Paramecium* every two hours.

PARTNERS AND PARASITES

Because they are so small, single-celled organisms can live in a wide range of habitats. Some form symbiotic partnerships with animals, which means that they help their hosts in return for a safe place to live. Others, called parasites, feed on their hosts and can cause disease.

View through a microscope of mouse blood cells infected by the parasites that cause malaria. The infected cells are pink.

SYMBIOSIS

Like many plant-eating animals, termites cannot digest cellulose, the tough substance that forms plant cell walls. Instead, they rely on protists to do this for them. Wood-eating termites carry huge numbers of a protist called *Trichonympha* in their hind guts. The *Trichonympha* cells break down the cellulose in wood, and the termites absorb the nutrients that are released.

Wood-eating termites

REPRODUCTION

Single-celled organisms reproduce in different ways. The simplest method, called asexual reproduction, involves a single parent. The parent either produces lots of young, or simply divides in two. In sexual reproduction, two parents come together and form new cells. Sexually produced cells are often specially adapted to withstand difficult conditions.

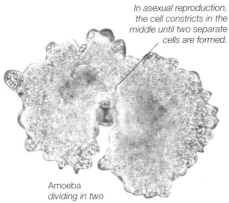

In asexual reproduction, the cell constricts in the middle until two separate cells are formed.

Amoeba dividing in two

DIATOMS

With their intricate silica shells, diatoms are among the most beautiful objects in the microscopic world. They live both in freshwater and the sea, and are amazingly abundant – a small jar of seawater contains several million diatoms. Like plants, diatoms use the energy in sunlight to make their food. Their shells are made of two parts that fit together like the halves of a box. In this species, the shell is oval, but other species are shaped like balls, wheels, triangles, or stars.

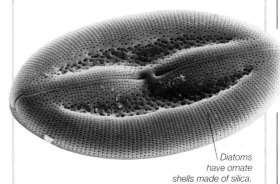

Diatoms have ornate shells made of silica.

Scientific name: *Navicula praetexta*

Size: 0.004 in (0.1 mm) long

Habitat: Creeps along the sea floor

Distribution: Shallow seas

Reproduction: Mainly by cell division

SHELLS AND SKELETONS

Despite their small size, many single-celled organisms have intricate shells or skeletons to protect them from enemies and help them float. Many of these shells are made of calcium carbonate. Over millions of years, calcium carbonate shells build up on the seabed and turn into rocks such as chalk and limestone. Other shells are made from silica, the glasslike mineral found in sand. Organisms called dinoflagellates have armor plating made of cellulose – the same substance that forms the tough walls of plant cells.

This dinoflagellate, called Ceratium, has armor plating and long "horns."

Cilia

A long stalk keeps Vorticella attached to a solid object.

DEADLY TIDES

Dinoflagellates are common single-celled organisms that live in freshwater and the sea. Most species are harmless, but some produce dangerous poisons. During a "red tide," a mass of dinoflagellates makes the sea look red. The poisons they produce kill fish and sea mammals.

A red tide off the coast of Alaska

Find out more

BACTERIA AND VIRUSES: *110*
CELLS: *20*
HOW LIFE BEGAN: *12*
PARTNERS AND PARASITES: *56*

FUNGI

NEITHER PLANTS NOR ANIMALS, fungi include mushrooms, toadstools, and molds. Unlike plants, fungi lack the green food-making compound – chlorophyll – so they cannot make their own food. Instead, they release enzymes that decompose living or dead organisms and absorb their nutrients. Fungi are usually invisible, either because they are microscopic single cells or because they are hidden inside their food as a mass of branching threads. It is only when they produce mushrooms for reproduction that they become noticeable.

The development of a mushroom

Mushroom starts to form.

Button elongates.

Outer skin splits.

Pores under cap exposed to air

Cap grows and pores shed spores.

Mycelium

LIFE CYCLE

The body of a fungus consists of tiny, threadlike cells called hyphae that are loosely woven into a mat called a mycelium. In many species of fungus the mycelium grows underground and gradually expands as the hyphae absorb nutrients. When conditions are right, the hyphae pack tightly together to make fruiting bodies, such as mushrooms, which push their way above the ground. The fruiting bodies make millions of spores that are blown away by the wind and may grow into new fungi.

SPORE TYPES

All fungi reproduce by spores, which are made up of one or more cells surrounded by a tough outer coat. The larger fungi are divided into two groups: spore droppers, called Basidiomycetes, and spore shooters, called Ascomycetes. In Basidiomycetes, such as the fly amanita, spores fall from club-shaped cells and are blown away by the wind. In Ascomycetes, such as morels, spores shoot out from a sac called an ascus.

The morel expels spores from special sacs.

FRUITS OF THE FOREST

The fruiting bodies of fungi produce and distribute spores. In many mushrooms, spores occur on the underside of the caps and are released from flaps called gills. One toadstool may discharge as many as a million spores a minute for several days. Many fungi form mushrooms and toadstools, but others produce fruiting bodies that look like antlers or even birds' nests. Some fungi are edible, but others, such as the death cap amanita, are extremely poisonous.

Common morel
(*Morchella esculenta*)

Bread mold
(*Mucor mucedo*)

Close-up of bread mold showing spore sacs

Mold thrives on moist bread and multiplies quickly in warm conditions.

Tawny grisette
(*Amanita fulva*)

This species is harmless when cooked.

Gills for shedding spores

Remains of the stem ring that appears on this fungus

Death cap
(*Amanita phalloides*)

The death cap is the world's most poisonous fungus. It can be mistaken for the field mushroom.

Antler jelly
(*Calocera viscosa*)

YEASTS

Yeasts are microscopic fungi that usually live as single cells. They are members of the Ascomycete group. Yeasts usually reproduce by budding. This involves new cells growing out like bubbles from the parent cell. These become larger and finally separate from the parent. One yeast cell can produce about 20 new cells. Yeasts convert sugar into carbon dioxide and alcohol and are used to produce wine and to make bread rise.

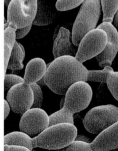

Yeast cells (Saccharomyces cerevisiae)

SIMPLE SPORES

The simplest groups of fungi produce spores in saclike structures called sporangia. Some spores have whiplike projections called flagella for swimming through water or moist habitats. However, fungi such as bread molds produce spores that cannot move. Hairlike hyphae spread through the bread and absorb nutrients from it. Spores develop on the end of thin hyphae that stick up from the food, producing the "furry" appearance of molds.

A puffball (Lycoperdon sp.) releases spores through a hole in the top of the cap.

SPORE DISPERSAL

Fungal spores are small and light, and many are carried by the wind. Mushrooms and toadstools form their spores above the ground, generally in gills, so they can be blown away by the slightest breeze. Many puffballs shed their spores internally and even a slight bump causes the spores to puff out of a hole in the cap. The spores of a bird's nest fungus are bounced out of the "nest" by raindrops, while stinkhorns rely on insects to distribute spores.

Bracket fungi grow on dead tree stumps and fallen logs.

Turkey-tail polypore (*Trametes versicolor*)

RECYCLING EXPERTS

Fungi and bacteria are the waste-disposal experts of the natural world. They break down the remains of dead plants and animals, releasing chemicals that can be recycled and used again by living things. Fungi and bacteria feed by releasing enzymes onto the surface on which they are growing. In fungi, these enzymes break down complex substances such as fats and sugars into simpler substances, which are absorbed through the walls of the hyphae.

FLY AMANITA

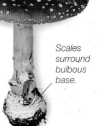

The bright red color of the fly amanita mushrooms warns that they are very poisonous. The spores are shed from vertical plates called gills that hang under the cap. This species has been used as a fly killer for centuries – mixed with milk and sugar it makes a deadly liquid that attracts flies.

Loose, white scales are the remains of the skin that covered the growing toadstool.

Scales surround bulbous base.

Scientific name:	*Amanita muscaria*
Size:	Cap is 2.5–6 in (6–15 cm) across
Habitat:	Under birch and pine trees, often in sandy soil
Distribution:	Widespread in temperate zones
Reproduction:	By white spores
Diet:	Sugars produced by tree roots

Dry-rot mushroom (Serpula lacrymans) on the wall of a house

PROBLEM FUNGI

Fungi cause problems when they eat people's food, clothes, and the wood used to build houses. Rusts, mildews, and smuts are all types of fungi that damage grain crops. Many human diseases, such as athlete's foot and ringworm, are the result of activity by parasitic fungi.

Dish containing bacteria

Penicillin tablet

Bacteria killed by penicillin in this area

Tablet without penicillin

USEFUL MOLDS

Penicillium molds are among the world's most common fungi and are found on decaying fruit. In 1928, Alexander Fleming discovered that one particular species, *Penicillium notatum*, produces a powerful antibiotic that kills bacteria. This substance – called penicillin – is extremely valuable because it combats infections without harming human cells.

Death of an eelworm

Eelworm moves toward fungus.

Noose of fungus traps worm and holds it tightly.

Hypha grows into worm and digests it.

FISHING FUNGI

A few microscopic fungi trap tiny animals with their hyphae. Some species of soil fungus, such as *Dactylaria*, produce rings on their hyphae that squeeze shut when an eelworm tries to pass through. A hypha then grows out of one of the ring cells, branches inside the worm's body, and kills it. The fungus can then feed on the animal's soft tissues.

Find out more

BACTERIA AND VIRUSES: *110*
FOOD CHAINS AND WEBS: *66*
NUTRIENT CYCLES: *64*
PESTS AND WEEDS: *98*

PLANTS

WHEREVER THERE IS WATER and light, plants are almost certain to grow, except in the coldest places on Earth. Most plants are rooted in the soil and use the energy in sunlight to make food from water and carbon dioxide. Unlike animals, plants lack complex sense organs and cannot move actively from place to place. Some are giants and others are tiny, but all play a key role in providing food for animals. So far, botanists have identified more than 300,000 plant species. These are divided into two groups – spore-bearing plants, such as algae, mosses, and ferns, and seed-bearing plants, such as flowering plants.

Tropical rainforest, Java

THE GREEN PLANET
The Earth's green landscapes get their color from a green pigment (colored chemical) called chlorophyll, which is present in the leaves and sometimes in the stems of plants. Chlorophyll traps the energy in sunlight, enabling plants to manufacture their own food. This process is called photosynthesis.

SPORE-BEARING PLANTS
Spore-bearing plants reproduce by means of spores – minute dustlike particles that are released in vast numbers and dispersed by wind or water. A spore is a simple structure. It consists of genetic material (DNA) encased in a protective coat. When a spore germinates, the young plant grows slowly at first and needs plenty of moisture. All spore-bearing plants need a damp habitat in order to reproduce.

Magnified view of a moss spore

ALGAE
Algae are simple plants that grow in water or wet places. Many are microscopic floating organisms, but others grow into large seaweeds. Unlike land plants, algae have no true roots, stems, or leaves, and so are unable to support themselves out of water. Scientists believe some groups of algae were the ancestors of all land plants.

The Chara alga growing in fresh water

MOSSES AND LIVERWORTS
Mosses and liverworts are small plants that usually grow in damp places. Most have slender stems and thin, simple leaves. Unlike more complex plants, mosses and liverworts have no transport systems and absorb water and nutrients directly through their leaves.

Liverwort **Moss**

FERNS AND HORSETAILS
Ferns and horsetails are the most advanced of all spore-bearing plants. A waxy coating on their leaves prevents water loss. Their stems contain transport tissue and strengthening tissue, enabling them to grow tall. Ferns and horsetails grow best in damp places, such as humid forests and river banks.

Fern

SEED-BEARING PLANTS
Seed-bearing plants can live in drier habitats than spore-bearing plants and are better adapted to life on land. A seed is a much larger and more complex structure than a spore. It contains a tiny embryo plant and a supply of food, all enclosed in a tough coat. Some seeds remain dormant for years before growing.

Broad bean
(*Vicia faba*)

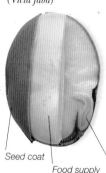

Seed coat
Food supply
Embryo

Flower

ANGIOSPERMS
Angiosperms are plants that produce flowers and fruits. They are the most abundant and successful group of plants, accounting for more than 80 percent of the world's plant species. Many have co-evolved with animals. Their colorful flowers attract animal pollinators, and their sweet fruits are eaten by animals, thus dispersing the seeds.

Maturing fruit

Nasturtium
(*Tropaeolum* sp.)

Douglas fir forest, Idaho

GYMNOSPERMS
Gymnosperms are plants that produce seeds but not flowers. Most are woody shrubs or evergreen trees, such as conifers, whose seeds usually develop inside cones. Gymnosperms were much more numerous during the age of the dinosaurs. Although vast conifer forests still exist, angiosperms are the dominant land plants in most parts of the world.

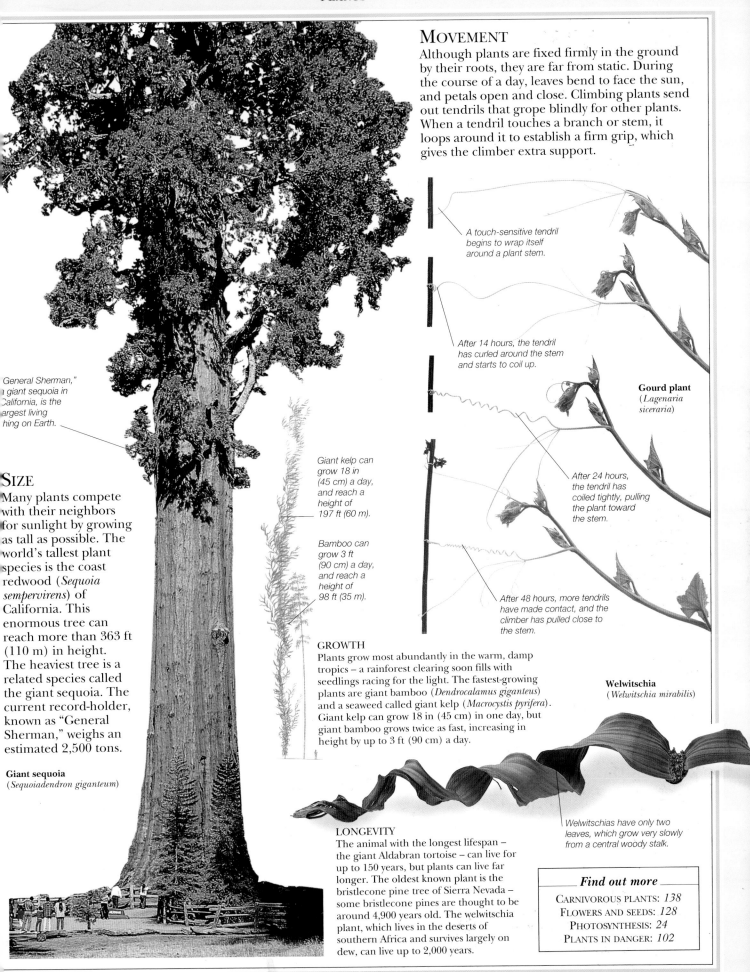

MOVEMENT

Although plants are fixed firmly in the ground by their roots, they are far from static. During the course of a day, leaves bend to face the sun, and petals open and close. Climbing plants send out tendrils that grope blindly for other plants. When a tendril touches a branch or stem, it loops around it to establish a firm grip, which gives the climber extra support.

A touch-sensitive tendril begins to wrap itself around a plant stem.

After 14 hours, the tendril has curled around the stem and starts to coil up.

Gourd plant
(*Lagenaria siceraria*)

After 24 hours, the tendril has coiled tightly, pulling the plant toward the stem.

After 48 hours, more tendrils have made contact, and the climber has pulled close to the stem.

"General Sherman," a giant sequoia in California, is the largest living thing on Earth.

SIZE

Many plants compete with their neighbors for sunlight by growing as tall as possible. The world's tallest plant species is the coast redwood (*Sequoia sempervirens*) of California. This enormous tree can reach more than 363 ft (110 m) in height. The heaviest tree is a related species called the giant sequoia. The current record-holder, known as "General Sherman," weighs an estimated 2,500 tons.

Giant sequoia
(*Sequoiadendron giganteum*)

Giant kelp can grow 18 in (45 cm) a day, and reach a height of 197 ft (60 m).

Bamboo can grow 3 ft (90 cm) a day, and reach a height of 98 ft (35 m).

GROWTH

Plants grow most abundantly in the warm, damp tropics – a rainforest clearing soon fills with seedlings racing for the light. The fastest-growing plants are giant bamboo (*Dendrocalamus giganteus*) and a seaweed called giant kelp (*Macrocystis pyrifera*). Giant kelp can grow 18 in (45 cm) in one day, but giant bamboo grows twice as fast, increasing in height by up to 3 ft (90 cm) a day.

Welwitschia
(*Welwitschia mirabilis*)

Welwitschias have only two leaves, which grow very slowly from a central woody stalk.

LONGEVITY

The animal with the longest lifespan – the giant Aldabran tortoise – can live for up to 150 years, but plants can live far longer. The oldest known plant is the bristlecone pine tree of Sierra Nevada – some bristlecone pines are thought to be around 4,900 years old. The welwitschia plant, which lives in the deserts of southern Africa and survives largely on dew, can live up to 2,000 years.

Find out more	
CARNIVOROUS PLANTS:	*138*
FLOWERS AND SEEDS:	*128*
PHOTOSYNTHESIS:	*24*
PLANTS IN DANGER:	*102*

ALGAE AND LICHENS

MOST SPECIES OF ALGAE live in the sea or in lakes and ponds, but a few are capable of living in damp places on land. Unlike other plants, algae have no roots, leaves, or flowers, although some of the seaweeds – algae that grow in the sea – have flexible stalks called stipes, leaflike structures called fronds, and branched holdfasts that anchor them to rocks. All algae contain the green pigment chlorophyll and make their food by photosynthesis. Many algae also contain other pigments that color them brown, red, or purple. Lichens are not plants, but living partnerships between fungi and algae.

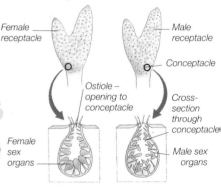

Kelp forest

ALGAL DIVERSITY

There are many types of algae, and they range in size from single-celled species to the giant kelps that grow at a rate of 18 in (45 cm) a day. Algae need moisture to survive, and they live in oceans, rivers, and lakes – and even under snow and ice. Algae are often called plants, but some scientists think they are so primitive that they do not belong in the plant kingdom. Instead, they are grouped with other simple organisms in the protist kingdom.

Bladder wrack
(*Fucus vesiculosus*)

Fronds

Gas-filled air bladders keep the fronds floating near the surface of the water.

Fronds are covered in a slimy mucus that keeps the seaweed from drying out when the tide goes out.

This bladder wrack may grow to more than 3 ft 3 in (1 m) in length.

Receptacle at end of frond

BROWN ALGAE

Brown algae contain green chlorophyll, and also the brown pigment fucoxanthin. This pigment gives them their brown or olive green color and enables them to photosynthesize in deeper water than chlorophyll would on its own. Many, such as the wracks and kelps, are tough and slippery and can survive for long periods out of water. Some wracks and kelps have air bladders that keep fronds near the surface of the water.

Receptacles of bladder wrack

Female receptacle

Male receptacle

Ostiole – opening to conceptacle

Conceptacle

Cross-section through conceptacle

Female sex organs

Male sex organs

REPRODUCTION

Like most algae, brown seaweeds of the *Fucus* genus reproduce sexually. At the ends of the fronds are fertile areas called receptacles. These are covered in chambers called conceptacles that contain sex organs. Here, male and female sex cells are produced and released into the sea to be fertilized. The fertilized egg settles on a rock to develop into a new seaweed. Bladder wrack has both male and female plants, whereas spiral wrack (*Fucus spiralis*) produces male and female cells in the same conceptacle.

Algae colors the snow red.

OUT IN THE COLD

A few algae contain a natural antifreeze that enables them to survive in the polar ice caps and on the permanent snow fields of mountain slopes. The single-celled alga, *Chlamydomonas nivalis*, is often found in mountainous regions. It lives below the snow's surface where it can absorb sunlight while remaining protected from the wind. It moves through the snow by beating two tiny hairs called flagellae.

Red pigment in the seaweed helps it photosynthesize in deep water where there is little light.

Hard, chalky structure

RED ALGAE

Almost all red algae are small- to medium-sized seaweeds, found in shady tidepools in temperate and tropical seas. Their red color comes from the pigment phycoerythrin. This pigment helps the algae photosynthesize in the dim blue light of deep water, thereby enabling it to grow at greater depths than other seaweeds. Some species produce chalky carbonates that make the plants rigid and abrasive.

Red seaweed
(*Phymatolithon* sp.)

Red seaweed
(*Corallina officinalis*)

Unbranched,
delicate fronds

GREEN ALGAE

Most green algae live in fresh water. Green seaweeds are found in tidepools and on coastal rocks in tropical and temperate regions. Some green algae form special partnerships with other organisms. For example, lichens and coral depend on the photosynthesizing green algae for carbohydrates. Land plants are believed to have evolved from green algae because they contain the same types of chlorophyll pigments.

FRESHWATER ALGAE
There are many forms of freshwater algae. Some consist of just one or a few cells and can be seen only under a microscope. Others, such as *Spirogyra*, are made of long chains of cells, and form the tangled masses seen floating on ponds. *Spirogyra* reproduces sexually – the contents of the cells of one filament pass into the cells of an adjacent filament to form zygotes. These later develop into new plants.

Holdfast
attaches
seaweed to
mussel shell.

Green seaweed
(*Enteromorpha linza*)

Freshwater green alga (*Spirogyra* sp.)

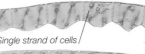
Single strand of cells

Two linked strands of cells

OARWEED

This large brown kelp has a flexible stalk, known as a stipe, and a tough, branched holdfast that attaches to rocks, allowing the frond to move freely in the water. Oarweed, otherwise known as tangle, can live for many years, and forms dense "forests" that provide shelter for many species of invertebrates and fish.

Flexible stalk is called a stipe, and ends in a holdfast that attaches the oarweed to rocks.

Scientific name: *Laminaria digitata*.

Size: Up to 6 ft 7 in (2 m) long

Habitat: Lower shoreline of rocky coasts

Distribution: Northwestern Europe

Reproduction: The large frond produces spores that develop into threadlike plants. These plants then produce male and female reproductive structures.

Soredia – powdery structures on end of lobe

Foliose thallus, or body

Foliose lichen
(*Hypogymnia physodes*)

Tree bark

Fungal threads surround the soredium.

Algal layer

A soredium is released into the air. If it lands in a suitable location, it will develop into a new lichen.

Fungal layer

Cross-section through foliose lichen

LICHENS

A lichen is made up of a fungus and either a green alga or a cyanobacterium. The algae or bacteria live beneath a protective layer of fungus. They provide the fungus with sugars from photosynthesis. In return, they receive protection from drying out and harmful levels of light. The three most common growth forms of lichen are fruticose (shrublike), foliose (leaflike), and crustose (flat and crusty). Lichens reproduce by releasing spores, called soredia, into the air.

Reindeer (*Rangifer tarandus*) *grazing*

POLLUTION MONITORS
Many species of lichen can grow only where the air is unpolluted. Since lichens are very sensitive to industrial pollutants, they are often used to monitor air quality. After the nuclear accident at Chernobyl, Russia, in 1986, reindeer moss (a type of fruticose lichen) absorbed much of the radioactive fallout. Caribou, or reindeer, feeding on the lichen produced radioactive milk and meat, and had to be destroyed.

Crustose lichen on quartz-rich rock

HARDY COLONIZERS
Lichens grow on all kinds of bare surfaces from rocks to tree trunks. They grow very slowly in some of the world's harshest environments. Some live in central Antarctica, just 4° north of the South Pole, others grow on mountain slopes, well above the treeline. Lichens, such as the black crustose lichen (*Verrucaria maura*), are often found encrusted on coastal rocks.

MOSSES AND LIVERWORTS

MOSSES AND LIVERWORTS are delicate, flowerless plants that grow in small clumps, or cushions. Together, they belong to the group Bryophyta. Mosses and liverworts have no true roots and depend on slender growths called rhizoids to provide them with limited anchorage. The small, thin leaves have no vascular tissues for transporting water and nutrients, so the plants quickly dry out. Because they are sensitive to water loss, and rely on a film of moisture for sexual reproduction, the majority of bryophytes grow in very moist habitats.

Moss-covered tree in a temperate forest

BRYOPHYTE HABITATS

Moss and liverwort habitats include tropical rainforests, wet, temperate forests, freshwater areas, and bogs. Certain types of mosses are found in drier environments such as heathlands. These may dry out and shrivel during the summer, but take up water and start to grow again in fall. Mosses can grow on stone walls, rock faces, trees, and bare soil.

Leaves of this moss are long and slender, and curve in the same direction.

Rootlike rhizoids anchor moss to ground.

Common moss
(*Dicranum* sp.)

MOSS STRUCTURE

Although most moss plants are very short, some tropical mosses, such as *Dawsonia*, can reach 28 in (70 cm) tall. Moss leaves are simple – only one cell thick in most species – and are usually arranged spirally around a slender stem. Rhizoids anchor the moss plant to soil, rock, or tree bark. Except for *Polytrichum* and related species, rhizoids do not play a role in taking up water. In some species of moss, male and female sex organs can be found on the same plant. In others, male and female plants are separate.

LIFE CYCLE

The life cycle of a moss plant occurs in two stages. First, the green, leafy plant (gametophyte) bears male (antheridia) and female (archegonia) sex organs, which produce sex cells (gametes). The mobile male gametes swim through droplets of water on the surface of the plant to fertilize the stationary female gametes. During the second stage, a fertilized cell develops into a plant called a sporophyte, which produces spores inside a capsule. Spores are released and germinate into new leafy plants.

These thin-stalked capsules are the sporophyte generation of the moss.

Life cycle of moss

A fertilized female sex cell grows into a sporophyte.

Thousands of minute spores are released from the capsule.

A threadlike plant, the protonema, grows from the germinating spore.

Male sex cells swim toward the female.

Male and female sex organs develop on the moss plants.

Leucobryum glaucum

Pseudoscleropodium

Polytrichum sp.

CUSHIONS, MATS, AND FEATHERS

Each kind of moss has a characteristic pattern of growth. *Leucobryum glaucum* forms dense cushions that can be almost spherical in shape. Taller species, such as *Polytrichum*, grow into loose clumps or tufts. Other mosses, such as *Pseudoscleropodium*, spread horizontally, producing a mat or weft of branching moss plants. Older parts of these mats die away, leaving the younger branches to grow into new plants.

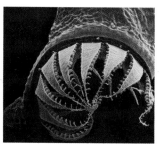

Spore-capsule showing rows of teeth

SPORE DISPERSAL

Most moss capsules have a mouth covered with a lid. When the spores ripen, the capsule lid falls off, revealing one or two rows of inward-curving teeth that block the mouth of the capsule. In dry conditions, these teeth fold outward, opening the capsule mouth and exposing the spores for dispersal by currents of air. Damp weather, unfavorable for dispersal, causes the teeth to fold in and close the mouth of the capsule.

PEAT BOGS

A peat bog is made up of a blanket of peatmoss (*Sphagnum* sp.) These mosses grow in areas where the climate is cool and there is plenty of rain. Over hundreds of years, the blanket becomes very deep, with a thin, living surface layer growing over thickening layers of old, dead moss plants. The lower layers become compressed to form blackish-brown peat.

Peat is cut and dried to use as domestic fuel in the Outer Hebrides, Scotland.

PEAT PRESERVATION

Because they do not have true roots, most mosses absorb water and minerals through their leaves. This makes them dependent on rainfall, which has a relatively low mineral content. To get all the minerals that they need, peatmosses use special chemical reactions that release acid by-products into the soil. This acidity kills bacteria, thereby helping to preserve human and animal remains.

In 1984, the mummified remains of a 2,300-year-old man was found in a peat bog in England.

The remains became known as "Pete Marsh."

SPHAGNUM MOSS

This moss grows on bog pools in clumps of weak-stemmed plants that support each other. Clusters of branches grow out from the main stem. Sphagnum leaves contain large, empty spaces that hold great quantities of water like a sponge.

Some branches in each cluster spread out horizontally.

Scientific name: *Sphagnum recurvum*

Size: 3–5 in (7–12 cm) high

Habitat: Bogs

Distribution: Throughout the Northern Hemisphere

Reproduction: Mostly asexual (vegetative) – parts of the moss grow into a new moss plant

COLONIZERS

Mosses and liverworts are often among the first plants to colonize damp, bare soil. Because they need little or no soil in which to root, they are able to grow on bare rock, bark, or even buildings. The granite mosses (*Andreaea* sp.) grow on hard, inhospitable granites. Some mosses are also very tolerant of the extremely low temperatures that occur on high mountain slopes, and in the Arctic and Antarctic.

Moss growing on rock in Antarctica

Liverwort (*Marchantia polymorpha*)

The flat plant body is called a thallus.

Gemmae cup

Rhizoids growing from the underside of the thallus anchor the plant to the ground.

Female branch (archegoniophore)

Male branch (antheridiophore)

LIVERWORT REPRODUCTION

Many species of lobed liverwort produce male and female sex organs on separate plants. In *Marchantia*, these are both stalked structures that resemble tiny umbrellas. The male is disc-shaped and the female has nine "leaves" or rays. After fertilization, small sporogonia develop on the underside of the female organ, between the rays. Each sporogonia bears a capsule that releases spores. *Marchantia* also reproduces asexually, producing tiny buds (gemmae) that develop into new plants.

LIVERWORTS

In medieval times, the appearance of a plant was thought to indicate the part of the body it could be used to cure. Although there are leafy as well as flat liverworts, these bryophytes take their name from the lobed kinds that resemble the liver. Flat, lobed liverworts grow on soil, trees, or wet rocks. The upper surface of some species has a waxy cuticle that helps to prevent water loss. Leafy liverworts have extremely thin, delicate leaves, which are often red, purple, or yellow in color.

Each tiny green gemma bud can grow into a new plant.

Nine-rayed structure housing female sex organs, seen from below.

Find out more

ALGAE AND LICHENS: *118*
FERNS AND HORSETAILS: *122*
PLANTS: *116*
REPRODUCTION: *28*

FERNS AND HORSETAILS

FERNS AND HORSETAILS ARE primitive plants. Most flourish in damp or shady places, such as humid forests and river banks. Ferns are distinguished by their graceful, tapering leaves, which uncurl slowly as they grow. Tropical rainforests are especially rich in ferns. There, some develop into magnificent trees. Horsetails are brushlike plants usually found near rivers and lakes, or in swamps. Ferns, horsetails, and their relatives make up a group of plants called pteridophytes. Like more complex plants, pteridophytes have rigid stalks containing transport vessels. However, they do not flower, but spread by releasing spores rather than seeds.

Bracken invading sheep pasture, Wales, UK

UNDERGROUND INVASION
Many ferns spread by sending out special stems that creep through the soil. The stems produce new plants that are genetically identical to the parents. A fern called bracken (*Pteridium aquilinum*) can spread over acres of farmland, ruining pasture.

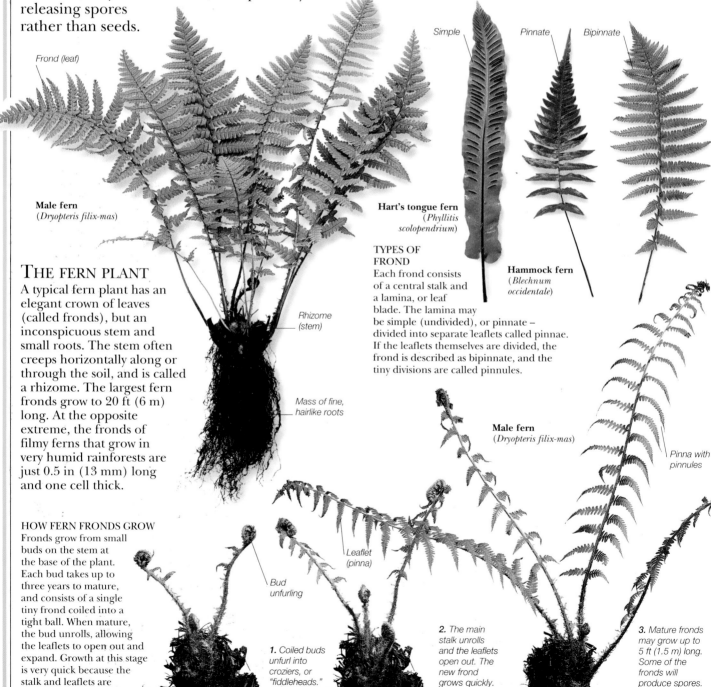

Frond (leaf)

Male fern
(*Dryopteris filix-mas*)

Simple

Pinnate

Bipinnate

Hart's tongue fern
(*Phyllitis scolopendrium*)

THE FERN PLANT
A typical fern plant has an elegant crown of leaves (called fronds), but an inconspicuous stem and small roots. The stem often creeps horizontally along or through the soil, and is called a rhizome. The largest fern fronds grow to 20 ft (6 m) long. At the opposite extreme, the fronds of filmy ferns that grow in very humid rainforests are just 0.5 in (13 mm) long and one cell thick.

Rhizome (stem)

Mass of fine, hairlike roots

TYPES OF FROND
Each frond consists of a central stalk and a lamina, or leaf blade. The lamina may be simple (undivided), or pinnate – divided into separate leaflets called pinnae. If the leaflets themselves are divided, the frond is described as bipinnate, and the tiny divisions are called pinnules.

Hammock fern
(*Blechnum occidentale*)

Male fern
(*Dryopteris filix-mas*)

Pinna with pinnules

HOW FERN FRONDS GROW
Fronds grow from small buds on the stem at the base of the plant. Each bud takes up to three years to mature, and consists of a single tiny frond coiled into a tight ball. When mature, the bud unrolls, allowing the leaflets to open out and expand. Growth at this stage is very quick because the stalk and leaflets are already fully formed.

Bud unfurling

Leaflet (pinna)

1. Coiled buds unfurl into croziers, or "fiddleheads."

2. The main stalk unrolls and the leaflets open out. The new frond grows quickly.

3. Mature fronds may grow up to 5 ft (1.5 m) long. Some of the fronds will produce spores.

SPREADING FROM SPORES

Ferns spread by making spores – microscopic particles of living material enclosed in tough coats. Mature spores are released into the air in thousands and float away like dust. They develop on the undersides of the fronds in structures called sori. Each sorus consists of a cluster of sporangia, and each sporangium contains 64 spores. Large ferns may produce millions of spores a year.

Sorus coat

Sporangium

A sorus viewed through an electron microscope

Life cycle of a fern

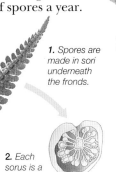

6. Fertilized egg cells grow into new fern plants.

1. Spores are made in sori underneath the fronds.

2. Each sorus is a cluster of sporangia.

5. Sperm swim to egg cells and fertilize (fuse with) them.

Egg cells develop here

Sperm develop here

4. Spores grow into tiny, heart-shaped plants that make sex cells.

3. Sporangia release spores into the air.

Spores

LIFE CYCLE OF A FERN

Ferns have a two-stage life cycle. When a spore lands in suitably wet soil it germinates, but it does not grow into a new fern plant. Instead, it grows into a tiny, heart-shaped structure called a prothallus, which produces sperm and egg cells. The sperm swim through moisture on the surface of the prothallus to reach the egg cells. When a sperm and egg cell fuse, the resulting cell grows into a new fern plant.

TREE FERN

Tree ferns grow in the tropics and subtropics. *Dicksonia antarctica* grows on the shady floor of Australian forests. It can tolerate quite cool conditions and may scorch in direct sunlight. The large, fibrous trunk supports a crown of spreading fronds, each of which is 5–8 ft (1.5–2.5 m) long. In suitable climates, tree ferns are grown as ornamental garden plants.

The bases of dead fronds build up around the trunk.

Scientific name:	*Dicksonia antarctica*
Size:	3–10 ft (1–3 m) tall
Habitat:	Cool, moist woodlands
Distribution:	Australia
Reproduction:	Releases spores into the air

FERNS IN TREES

The warm, humid air in tropical rainforests is ideal for ferns, but the forest floor can be too dark for new plants to grow. To get enough light, many tropical ferns grow as epiphytes – plants that take root on the boughs and trunks of trees. Epiphytic ferns obtain all the water they need from rain trickling through the forest canopy. They absorb nutrients from dead insects, leaves, and droppings that build up around their roots.

FILMY FERNS

The filmy ferns are a family of epiphytic ferns with extremely thin, delicate fronds. Since the fronds are only one cell thick, they dry out very easily. Filmy ferns are mostly restricted to tropical rainforests and cloud forests, but a few species survive in wet temperate countries. The rare Killarney fern grows on wet rocks near waterfalls in Ireland.

Killarney fern
(*Trichomanes speciosum*)

Epiphytic fern
(*Merinthosorus drynarioides*)

Horsetail
(*Equisetum* sp.)

Spore-producing tip

Leaf

Branch

Fertile stem

Sterile stem

HORSETAILS

Horsetails were very common millions of years ago, when they grew as large as trees. Today, only 23 species of small horsetails remain. They have stiff, upright stems with branches at intervals. The leaves are small, brownish scales, and photosynthesis takes place in the green stems and branches. Spores are produced at the top, sometimes on special fertile stems that have no branches.

Club moss
(*Lycopodium* sp.)

CLUB MOSSES

Club mosses are not mosses, but relatives of ferns and horsetails. They are small plants that have tiny, simple leaves arranged spirally around the stem. Club mosses are most abundant in the tropics, where they may grow on the ground or as epiphytes in trees.

Find out more

DECIDUOUS FORESTS: *80*
PHOTOSYNTHESIS: *24*
PLANTS: *116*
TROPICAL RAINFORESTS: *82*

CONIFERS AND CYCADS

DURING THE JURASSIC and Cretaceous periods, the world's forests consisted mainly of conifers and cycads. Today, conifers still form dense forests in many parts of the world, particularly in colder regions. Conifers, cycads, and a few other isolated species belong to a group called gymnosperms – plants that have seeds, but no flowers. The seeds of conifers are not enclosed inside fruits. Instead, they develop on the woody scales of cones or are embedded in fleshy cups. When cut or damaged, most conifers produce a sticky substance called resin that seals the wound and prevents decay.

Cedar of Lebanon
(*Cedrus libani*)

CONIFEROUS TREES

Typical conifer trees have tall, straight trunks with a leading shoot and regular branches. This type of growth pattern is known as apical dominance. Some conifers lose their symmetrical shape later in life, developing a more irregular outline as they mature. Almost all coniferous trees and shrubs are evergreen, which means that they keep their foliage throughout the year.

This young cedar is only about 20 ft (6 m) tall, but some conifers can grow to 300 ft (91 m).

White cypress (Chamaecyparis thyoides) has overlapping scalelike leaves.

CONIFER LEAVES

In cooler climates, conifers usually have flat, narrow leaves, sharply tipped needles, or tiny scalelike leaves. In warmer latitudes, conifers have broader, more oval-shaped leaves. Most conifer leaves are tough and leathery with a thick waxy outer layer, called a cuticle. This coating helps the long-lasting leaves withstand extreme temperatures and conserve water.

Western larch (Larix occidentalis) sheds its needles in fall.

Prince Albert's yew (Saxegothaea conspicua) has sharply tipped needles.

Stone pine cone
(*Pinus pinea*)

Stone pine seeds are spread by birds and small mammals.

CONES AND SEEDS

Most conifers bear seeds inside dry, woody, female cones. The seeds are protected by the cone's scales and may take up to three years before they are ripe. When the weather is warm and dry, the cone opens and releases its seeds. Most conifer seeds have papery brown wings that help to carry them away from the parent tree.

Unlike other cones, cedar and fir cones fall apart while still on the tree.

Cedar cones

Scots pine
(*Pinus sylvestris*)

Male cones grow at the base of short, weak shoots.

Leaves may be in pairs or clustered in threes.

Female cone matures and sheds seeds.

LIFE CYCLE

Conifer trees have separate male and female cones. The male cones produce pollen from sacs on the lower surface of each scale. Female cones contain the female sex cells (ovules), which usually lie on the upper surface of each scale. When ripe, a male cone opens to release clouds of pollen, which are carried by the wind to the open female cones. After the pollen is shed, the male cone falls to the ground. The seeds develop within the female cone, which may remain on the tree for several years.

DRY RELEASE

During wet weather, cones stay tightly shut. The seeds inside are protected by a waterproof layer of waxy resin. In hot, dry sunshine, the resin softens, and the scales crack open to release the seeds. Some species, such as the lodgepole pine (*Pinus contorta*), need scorching sunshine or forest fires to crack open their cones.

The scales on this damp cone are shut tight.

As the weather gets warmer, the cone opens.

Young female cones develop on the shoots.

Pollen grain from Scots pine

Air bladders help the pollen float through the air.

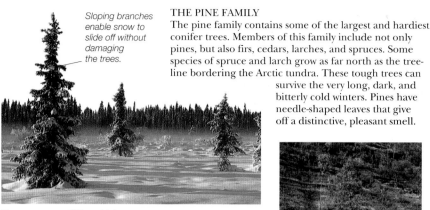

Sloping branches enable snow to slide off without damaging the trees.

Norway spruce (*Picea abies*)

THE PINE FAMILY

The pine family contains some of the largest and hardiest conifer trees. Members of this family include not only pines, but also firs, cedars, larches, and spruces. Some species of spruce and larch grow as far north as the tree-line bordering the Arctic tundra. These tough trees can survive the very long, dark, and bitterly cold winters. Pines have needle-shaped leaves that give off a distinctive, pleasant smell.

CONIFER DINOSAURS

Two conifers – the dawn redwood (*Metasequoia glyptostroboides*) and the Wollemi pine (*Wollemia nobilis*) – were discovered only recently. Both trees closely resemble tree fossils dating back to the Jurassic period. The dawn redwood was discovered in 1941, growing in remote valleys in southwest China. Wollemi pine trees were discovered in 1994, in a ravine in the Blue Mountains some 125 miles (200 km) outside Sydney, Australia.

Some of the Wollemi pine trees are 131 ft (40 m) tall.

THE YEW FAMILY

Yews are slow-growing, long-lived trees with poisonous foliage, bark, and seeds. Each seed is encased in a bright red, fleshy cup, called an aril. Although yew seeds can be fatal when eaten by people or cattle, birds feed on the sweet, juicy arils without coming to any harm. The toxic seeds remain intact as they pass through the bird's gut.

Common yew
(*Taxus baccata*)

The young aril is green at first.

CONIFERS IN INDUSTRY

Conifers grow tall and fast, and their wood is often used as a building material or pulped and made into paper. Conifers are often referred to as "softwoods," and broadleaved trees as "hardwoods." However, some conifers, such as the larch and yew, produce wood that is even harder than that of many broadleaved trees.

European larch
(*Larix decidua*)

The leaves turn yellow in fall.

MAIDENHAIR TREE

The maidenhair tree (*Ginkgo biloba*) is the sole survivor of a once large group of gymnosperms. Its fan-shaped foliage is identical to that of fossilized ginkgoes dating back 160 million years. This deciduous tree is native to China and is now planted in parks and gardens all over the world. It grows well in towns and cities because of its high tolerance of air pollution and resistance to pests and disease.

Maidenhairs by the roadside, Tokyo, Japan

Mexican cycad
(*Dioon spinulosum*)

The female cone can grow to more than 22 in (55 cm) in length.

This fossil cycad shows how little the leaves have changed over time.

CYCADS

The 160 species of cycads growing in the tropics and subtropics are descendants of an ancient group of plants that flourished about 250 million years ago. Many species have become extinct, and remaining cycads are under threat from over-collection and habitat loss. Cycads are distinguished by their stout stems topped with a crown of large compound leaves. More advanced species have large, often brightly colored cones.

Find out more
CONIFEROUS FORESTS: *78*
PLANTS: *116*
FLOWERING PLANTS: *92*
PLANTS IN DANGER: *102*

FLOWERING PLANTS

THE MOST ABUNDANT GROUP of vascular plants are the flowering plants, which make up the group known as angiosperms (angiosperm means "seed vessel"). These plants produce flowers, seeds, and fruits and account for more than 80 percent of all plant species. They are found in most parts of the world, although about two-thirds of all species of flowering plants occur in the tropics. Flowering plants grow as trees, shrubs, or herbaceous plants, whose stems die back after each growing season. They are divided into two main groups according to the number of their seed leaves, known as cotyledons.

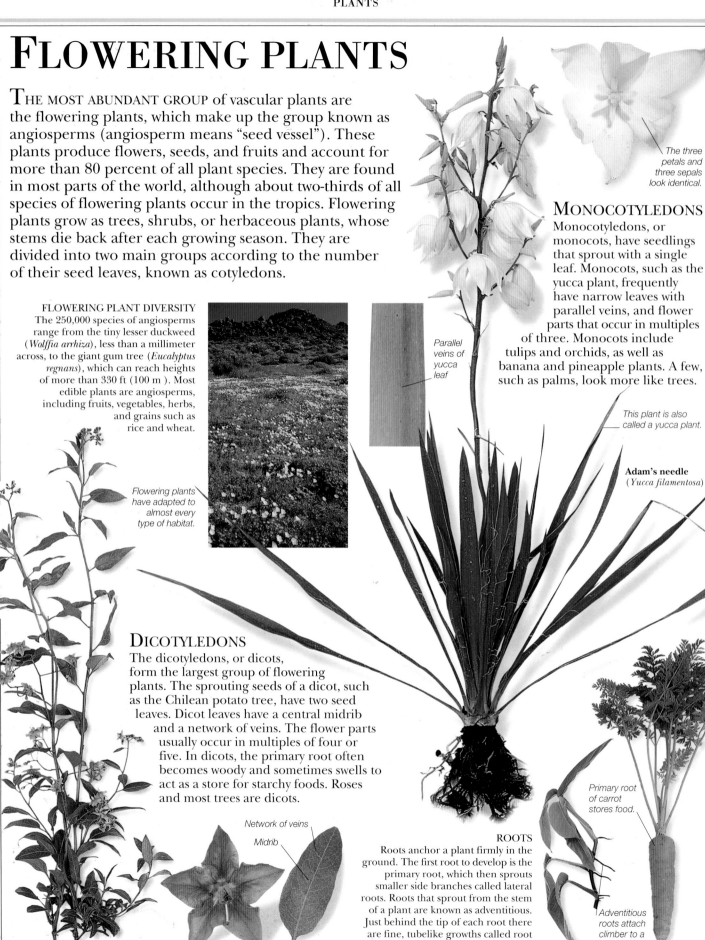

FLOWERING PLANT DIVERSITY
The 250,000 species of angiosperms range from the tiny lesser duckweed (*Wolffia arrhiza*), less than a millimeter across, to the giant gum tree (*Eucalyptus regnans*), which can reach heights of more than 330 ft (100 m). Most edible plants are angiosperms, including fruits, vegetables, herbs, and grains such as rice and wheat.

Flowering plants have adapted to almost every type of habitat.

The three petals and three sepals look identical.

MONOCOTYLEDONS
Monocotyledons, or monocots, have seedlings that sprout with a single leaf. Monocots, such as the yucca plant, frequently have narrow leaves with parallel veins, and flower parts that occur in multiples of three. Monocots include tulips and orchids, as well as banana and pineapple plants. A few, such as palms, look more like trees.

Parallel veins of yucca leaf

This plant is also called a yucca plant.

Adam's needle
(*Yucca filamentosa*)

DICOTYLEDONS
The dicotyledons, or dicots, form the largest group of flowering plants. The sprouting seeds of a dicot, such as the Chilean potato tree, have two seed leaves. Dicot leaves have a central midrib and a network of veins. The flower parts usually occur in multiples of four or five. In dicots, the primary root often becomes woody and sometimes swells to act as a store for starchy foods. Roses and most trees are dicots.

Network of veins

Midrib

Chilean potato tree
(*Solanum crispum*)

Flower parts are in fives

Dicotyledon leaf

ROOTS
Roots anchor a plant firmly in the ground. The first root to develop is the primary root, which then sprouts smaller side branches called lateral roots. Roots that sprout from the stem of a plant are known as adventitious. Just behind the tip of each root there are fine, tubelike growths called root hairs, which absorb water and dissolved minerals from the soil.

Primary root of carrot stores food.

Adventitious roots attach climber to a tree trunk.

Carrot
(*Daucus carota*)

STEMS

The petals of cacti flowers are usually arranged in a spiral.

True stems, found only in vascular plants, support the leaves and flowers. They also contain cells that carry nutrients and water up from the roots, and food away from the leaves to the rest of the plant. In some plants, such as cacti, the stems make food, rather than the leaves. Stems can grow above or below ground. Some, called rhizomes, help a plant spread over a wide area; others, called tubers and corms, store food for the next growing season.

Leaves are reduced to spines to lessen water loss.

Fat stem carries out photosynthesis and stores water.

Ginger
(*Zingiber officinale*)

Rhizome grows horizontally through soil.

Cactus
Gymnocalycium horstii

A tree's age can be calculated by counting the annual growth rings in its trunk.

Oak trunk

WOODY STEMS

The stems of shrubs and trees do not die back after each growing season. They are made of a tough tissue called wood. The stem, or trunk, of a tree gets thicker each year as a new layer of wood forms. This is called secondary growth. If the trunk of a dicot is cut, the layers can be seen as rings around the center.

FRINGED WATERLILY

The fringed waterlily grows on the surface of ponds and slow-moving rivers. Although its floating leaves closely resemble those of other waterlilies, this species belongs to a different family of flowering plants. Its name comes from the "fringe" around each of the yellow petals.

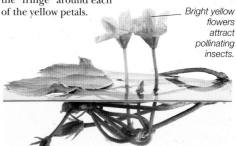

Bright yellow flowers attract pollinating insects.

Scientific name: *Nymphoides peltata*

Size: Clumps may be up to 5 ft (1.5 m) across

Habitat: Ponds, ditches, and slow-moving, fertile fresh water

Distribution: Europe, north and west Asia, and Japan. Introduced into North America, and now naturalized

Reproduction: By floating seeds

PLANT GROWTH

Roots and shoots grow from their tips. At every tip, there is a layer of thin-walled cells that are constantly dividing. This layer is called the meristem. The meristem at the tip of a shoot is protected by a tough casing. A covering called a root cap prevents the meristem on a root tip from being damaged as it pushes through the soil.

Tightly folded young leaves develop safely in scaly case.

Shoot

When conditions are right, the scales are shed and the shoots grow freely.

How plant hormones work

Hormones from central stem limit growth lower down.

Removing central stem encourages lower growth.

PLANT HORMONES

Plant growth is controlled by chemicals called hormones. In many plants, the main stem grows faster than the side branches, because the stem's tip produces hormones that inhibit growth lower down. This makes the plant tall and narrow. Cutting off the tip of the stem stops the production of these hormones, increasing lower growth and giving the plant a broad, bushy shape.

LEAVES

A leaf, often a flat structure, absorbs energy from the Sun's rays and uses it to make food by a process called photosynthesis. The leaves of some flowering plants have other uses. Some climbing plants have modified leaves that form tendrils to wrap around solid objects for support, while succulent plants have fat leaves that store water. A simple leaf consists of a stalk, or petiole, and a leaf blade. In a compound leaf, such as the rattan palm, the blade is subdivided into a number of separate leaflets.

Rattan palm
(*Calamus caesius*)

Succulent holds water in its swollen leaves.

Midrib

This large compound leaf is made up of more than 50 leaflets.

Hen and chickens
(*Echeveria* sp.)

Leaflets form tendrils that cling to other plants as the pea climbs up to the light.

Everlasting pea
(*Lathyrus latifolius*)

FLOWERS AND SEEDS

THE PRODUCTION OF SEEDS is the final stage in the life cycle of a flowering plant – and also the beginning of a new plant. A flowering plant has an advanced reproductive system whereby the seeds develop completely enclosed in a fruit, which nurtures and protects them. Before seeds can develop, however, pollination has to take place. Some plants can pollinate themselves in a process called self-pollination. Most, however, rely on receiving pollen from another plant of the same species. This is called cross-pollination. Wind or animals, such as insects and birds, carry pollen between flowers. Some flowers are pollinated by a wide variety of pollinators, but others rely on just one species.

Stigma at top of carpel collects pollen.

Style links stigma to ovary.

Ovary contains female sex cells.

Carpel

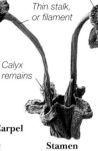

Sac, or anther, filled with pollen grains

Thin stalk, or filament

Calyx remains

Stamen

Dwarf Iceland poppy
(*Papaver croceum*)

Female sex organs (carpels)

Male sex organs (stamens)

Petals are arranged in a ring to form the corolla.

In the poppy, the sepals fall off as soon as the bud opens.

FLOWER STRUCTURE

Although flowers vary enormously in shape, color, and size, they are all based on four types of parts arranged around a central axis. An outer ring of sepals forms the calyx, which protects the flower when it is in bud. Within the calyx, an inner ring of petals forms the corolla. Within the corolla are the male sex organs, called stamens, and one or more female sex organs, called carpels.

Spike **Raceme** **Capitulum**

FLOWER HEADS
Some plants produce their flowers singly, but many develop clusters of flowers called inflorescences. There are many different types of inflorescence. A spike is an inflorescence of stalkless flowers attached to a common stem. A raceme has flowers on stalks that share the same stem. A capitulum looks like a single flower, but is typically a tightly packed cluster of two types of flowers, known as ray florets and disc florets.

Butterfly sipping nectar from a flower

POLLINATION
Flowers are pollinated by animals or by the wind, which blows pollen around. Wind-pollinated flowers are small – often with no petals – and tend to have small, smooth pollen grains. Flowers pollinated by insects and other animals have colored petals, strong scents, sugary nectar, and comparatively large, sticky pollen. Once attracted to a flower, the animal is dusted with pollen, which it then carries to another flower.

Stigma

Pollen grain

Pollen grain sprouts a tube that grows down into stigma.

Pollen tube

Male sex cells

Ovule

Stigma

Ovary

Female sex cells (ova)

1. Pollen grain lands on stigma and germinates.

2. Male sex cells pass down tube and enter ovary.

FERTILIZATION
A seed begins to develop when fertilization occurs – that is, when male and female sex cells fuse. If a pollen grain lands on a stigma of the same species, it sprouts a tiny tube that enters the stigma and grows into the ovary. One male sex cell passes out of the tube and fuses with a female sex cell, or ovum to form an embryo. A second male sex cell fuses with other cells to form endosperm, which will act as a food store for the germinating seed.

FRUITS AND SEEDS
Each fertilized seed contains an embryo and a food store (endosperm), enclosed in a special coat called a testa. Fertilized seeds develop and grow inside the ovary, where they are protected until they are ripe enough to be released. The ovary is now known as a fruit. The wall of the fruit becomes either thick and fleshy, or hard and dry. It grows larger, and its shape, color, and texture change as it matures.

1. Soon after pollination, the white petals of a pea plant shrivel and fall. The ovary begins to grow and to develop into a mature fruit.

Pea
(*Pisum sativum*)

TYPES OF FRUIT

A fruit is the part of the plant that contains the seeds. Fruits can be succulent (fleshy) or dry. The seeds of fleshy fruits, such as raspberries and peaches, are generally spread by animals, who are attracted by the sweet fruit. The seeds of dry fruits, such as love-in-a-mist and poppies, may be spread by the wind, by animals, or by the fruit wall splitting open. Many trees produce nuts – hard, dry fruits containing a single seed.

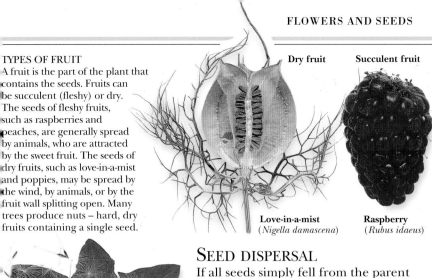

Dry fruit

Succulent fruit

Love-in-a-mist
(*Nigella damascena*)

Raspberry
(*Rubus idaeus*)

SEED DISPERSAL

If all seeds simply fell from the parent plant to the ground, many seedlings would die because they would all be competing for the same limited supplies of water, light, and nutrients. To avoid this competition, seeds are dispersed by various means. Many seeds are dispersed by the wind. They may be specially shaped or have downy "parachutes" to help them hang in the air. Some plants have fruits that burst open explosively, flinging the seeds out.

The fruits of the dandelion (Taraxacum sp.) have "parachutes" of hairs to aid wind dispersal.

Fleshy pod nurtures developing peas.

Growing peas

2. The fruit of the pea plant is a long green pod. The seeds (the peas) are arranged in a row inside the pod. Each is attached to the pod wall by a short stalk.

3. The plant provides the developing peas with water and nutrients via the stalks that hold them in the pod.

4. When the seeds are mature, the pea pod dries and splits to release the ripened peas.

BEE ORCHID

The bee orchid's color and shape make it resemble a particular species of bee. Male bees land on the flower, thinking it is a female. Having tried unsuccessfully to mate with the flower, they fly off, taking pollen to other flowers. In many cases the pollinated plant and the pollinator co-evolve so that the flowers resemble one particular insect pollinator.

Scientific name:
Ophrys apifera

Size: 6–20 in (15–50 cm)

Habitat: Pastures and banks on chalky or limy soils

Distribution: Europe and North Africa

Reproduction: By fine, dustlike seeds

The orchid's pollen forms clumps called pollinia.

WATER DISPERSAL

Some fruits rely entirely on water for their dispersal. They may be small, like alder fruits, which contain oil droplets to keep them afloat, or large, like coconuts, which have waterproof husks made of matted fibers.

A coconut may drift vast distances across the sea before germinating on a sandy shore.

Ants carry oily seeds back to their nest.

ANIMAL DISPERSAL

Some fruits have hooks that attach to an animal's body. These are carried away and fall in another place, where their seeds take root. Other fruits are eaten by animals, which excrete the seeds in their droppings. Many seeds are dispersed by animals that bury nuts for winter use but then forget to eat them. Ants carry some seeds back to their nests to eat the oily seed-casings.

Find out more

FLOWERING PLANTS: *126*
PLANTS: *116*
PLANTS IN DANGER: *102*
REPRODUCTION: *28*

PALMS

WITH ITS TALL, UNBRANCHED TRUNK, topped with a crown of fronds, the palm is probably one of the easiest plants to recognize. These distinctive plants form an ancient family of monocotyledons that have flourished on Earth for more than 110 million years. Today, there are about 2,800 species. Some palms are low-growing, but most are tall, slender, treelike structures, reaching heights of up to 130 ft (40 m). They are found throughout tropical and subtropical regions, but the greatest number of species lives in tropical Southeast Asia. Palms are most abundant where there is high rainfall, but can also survive in dry places. The leaves of palms are tough and leathery and can withstand heavy rains and hot winds.

Fronds emerge from the top of the tree only.

Trunk does not vary in diameter.

Coconut palm
(*Cocos nucifera*)

WHERE PALMS GROW
Palms grow naturally in a variety of different habitats, from warm, lowland rainforests to deserts and high mountain slopes. Some are cultivated and planted to provide shade along hot city streets. Only a few species, including the chusan palm (*Trachycarpus fortunei*), can survive in colder regions such as China and as far north as the British Isles.

Coconut palms thrive in a tropical climate.

PALM STRUCTURE
The majority of palms have a straight trunk and a crown of enormous leaves, called fronds. Unlike true trees, however, a palm has only a limited number of these radiating fronds, and a new leaf will not unfold until an old one dies. Some palm species retain a strawlike "skirt" of dead leaves that hangs down along their trunks. A palm trunk usually has the same diameter from top to bottom, although some may bulge slightly in the middle. Very few palms have branches.

Date palm
(*Phoenix dactylifera*)

Fragrant male flowers

FLOWERS AND SEEDS
Palm flowerheads are huge, modified branches that bear thousands of small flowers. A single flowerhead of the rattan palm, for example, may have up to 250,000 flowers. The palm's flowers are pollinated by insects and are either bisexual (both sexes in one) or unisexual (male or female). Male and female flowers often grow on separate trees – but sometimes they are found on the same plant. Palm fruits are mainly one-seeded berries or drupes – the name for fleshy fruits that have one central stone.

Flowerhead of chusan palm

PALM ROOTS
Palm roots do not thicken as they mature, and seldom form branches. Root systems can be extensive, especially in dry areas where the trees need to tap water deep underground. Roots grow from the base of the trunk and, as the plant matures, part of its roots may emerge above ground. Some species develop "stilt" roots. These help anchor palms such as *Verschaffeltia* in shallow or unstable soil.

Stilt roots emerge 3–6 ft (1–2 m) above ground level.

Long roots reach deep under the ground.

PALM FRONDS
Each large palm frond has a stiff leaf stalk and a leaf blade. A young blade is folded into pleats. As it unfolds, it splits to form the many leaflets that make up a frond. Fronds are usually feather- or fan-shaped, and are arranged in a crowded spiral. The raffia palm (*Raphia farinifera*) has the largest leaves of all flowering plants – with fronds that may be more than 66 ft (20 m) long.

Feather-shaped frond

Fan-shaped frond

Brazilian wax palm
(*Copernicia prunifera*)

HOW PALMS GROW

Although palms have tall, woodlike trunks, they are not true trees. This is because they do not have secondary thickening, so they do not get a little wider each year. Palm growth is from a single growing point called the apical bud. The seedling develops into a broad, squat structure, almost the final width of the trunk, before upward growth begins. If the apical bud dies or is removed, the whole plant dies.

Growth of a date palm

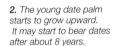

1. A date seed germinates within 2–3 months, first producing small, two-lobed fronds.

2. The young date palm starts to grow upward. It may start to bear dates after about 8 years.

3. Date palms reach heights of 66 ft (20 m) or more and can live for as long as 200 years.

COCONUT PALM

Found along tropical shores, just above the waterline, these palms have strong roots that anchor them in the ground so they can withstand strong coastal winds. The nut's husk is tough but light – it stays undamaged and allows the seed to float long distances. When a nut is washed up on a beach, it sprouts leaves and quickly puts down fibrous roots.

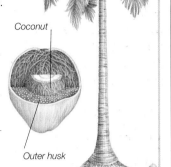

Coconut

Outer husk

Scientific name: *Cocos nucifera*

Size: Up to 60 ft (18 m) tall

Habitat: Coasts

Distribution: Tropical coasts all over the world

Reproduction: Female flowers produce clusters of large coconuts

SHORT- STEMMED PALMS

Some palms branch at, or below, ground level, forming a low-growing clump. The stems of these species may be short, as in the Mediterranean fan palm, or almost non-existent, as in the raffia palm (*Raphia* sp.), where only the leaves and flowerheads appear above ground. The Mediterranean fan palm is native to Europe. It can survive winter snows on stony mountainsides.

Mediterranean fan palm (*Chamaerops humilis*)

Hooked spines on rattan palm

CLIMBING PALMS

The rattans or rotangs (*Calamus* sp.) of Southeast Asia and Africa are climbing palms. Instead of forming a distinct crown, the leaves occur at widely spaced intervals along the stem. Rattans grow from the dimly lit jungle floor and wind their way up the trunks of tall rainforest trees. Their long, thin stems are armed with hooked spines that help them climb up to the light.

Oil palm (Elaeis guineenis) plantation

Cluster of oil palm fruits

USEFUL PALMS

Nothing from the palm is wasted. The trunks are used in construction, the fibers are woven into ropes, mats, fans, and thatched roofs, and some of the fruits, such as dates, have been enjoyed as healthy foods for thousands of years. Coconut, date, wax, and oil palms are important commercially. All kinds of products are made from the fatty seeds and fibrous fruits of the coconut palm. The oils from oil palms are used in margarine, soap, and candles, while the wax palm produces fine waxes used in various polishes.

Royal palms help shade the path.

ROYAL PALMS

Tall and stately, royal palms are a frequent sight in tropical America, where they are often used to form a decorative screen. Their gray-green trunks are about 24 in (60 cm) in diameter, and the tallest Caribbean royal palm (*Roystonia oleracea*) reaches 130 ft (40 m). The apical bud of the Caribbean royal palm is often used in a delicacy called Millionaire's salad. The removal of the bud results in the plant's death.

BROADLEAVED TREES

BROADLEAVED TREES ARE THE MOST numerous and varied of the world's trees, with more than 10,000 different species. Almost all have broad, flat leaves, and many are deciduous, shedding their leaves in the fall or in the dry season. Broadleaved trees belong to the group of flowering plants known as angiosperms. They have flowers that, after fertilization, develop into seeds enclosed in a fruit. Only the hardiest can compete with conifers in cold climates and high mountain slopes, but elsewhere broadleaved trees dominate the forests, especially in moist parts of the tropics.

Silver birch
(*Betula pendula*)

Sycamore maple
(*Acer pseudoplatanus*)

European ash
(*Fraxinus excelsior*)

CROWN SHAPES
Most broadleaved trees change shape as they mature. The leading shoot disappears as side branches grow out to form a rounded crown. Each type of tree has its own characteristic shape. This is based on the number and thickness of the smaller twigs, and the angle at which the twigs grow from the trunk.

TREE STRUCTURE

A mature broadleaved tree generally has a single, woody trunk, at least 20 ft (6 m) tall, which increases in thickness as the tree grows older. The trunk divides into spreading branches, forming a crown that supports twigs, foliage, flowers, and fruit. Long, woody roots fix the trunk into the ground and absorb water and minerals from the soil. Often fungi grow on the roots and supply the tree with nitrogen and further minerals.

Devil's walking stick
(*Aralia spinosa*)

Staghorn sumac
(*Rhus typhina*)

LEAVES
Broad, flat leaves have a large surface area, which makes them efficient at producing food from sunlight (photosynthesis). The leaves are concentrated at the edge of the tree's crown to maximize the amount of sunlight that falls on each leaf. Leaves range from fairly small, simple forms to the large, compound leaves that have two or more leaflets on the same stalk.

Indian bean tree
(*Catalpa bignonioides*)

Female flowers

Male flowers

Alder
(*Alnus glutinosa*)

Wind-pollinated flower

Insect-pollinated flower

REPRODUCTION
To reproduce, pollen from the male part of a flower must come in contact with the female part of a flower. Many broadleaved trees bear separate male and female flowers, frequently in long, dangling catkins. The pollen is carried to the female flowers on the breeze. Insect-pollinated trees generally have colorful flowers, often with sweet scents or generous supplies of nectar. In the tropics, some trees are pollinated by bats that are attracted by flowers with a strong, rancid smell and sturdy petals.

Apple (*Malus domestica*)

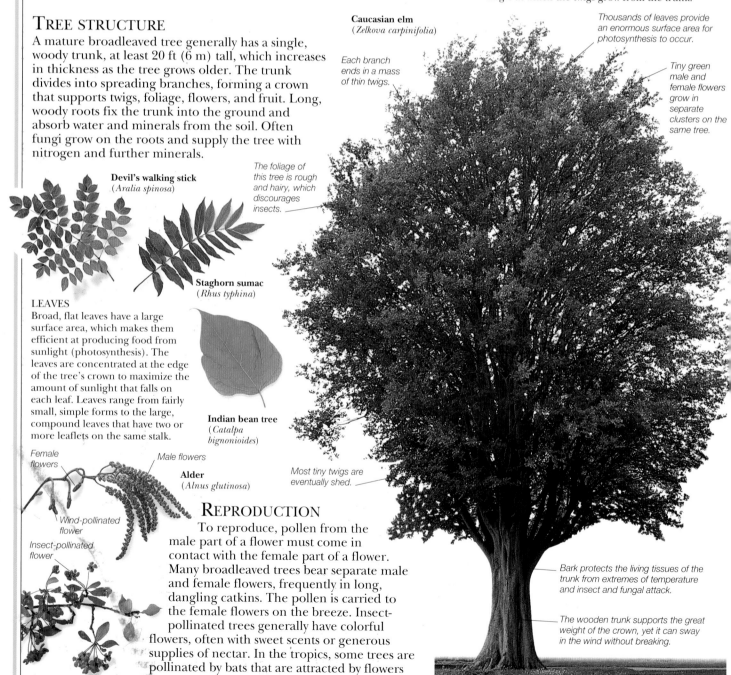

Caucasian elm
(*Zelkova carpinifolia*)

Each branch ends in a mass of thin twigs.

Thousands of leaves provide an enormous surface area for photosynthesis to occur.

Tiny green male and female flowers grow in separate clusters on the same tree.

The foliage of this tree is rough and hairy, which discourages insects.

Most tiny twigs are eventually shed.

Bark protects the living tissues of the trunk from extremes of temperature and insect and fungal attack.

The wooden trunk supports the great weight of the crown, yet it can sway in the wind without breaking.

DECIDUOUS OR EVERGREEN?

Broadleaved trees may be deciduous, shedding their foliage at certain times of year, or evergreens that retain foliage all year round. In colder latitudes, leaves drop in the fall. This avoids damage by wintry weather, and the low light levels in winter mean that little photosynthesis is possible. Keeping foliage supplied with water is also difficult, since trees cannot take up water from frozen ground. In warm climates, trees shed their leaves at the onset of the dry season to prevent excessive water loss.

Oak woodland in winter with leafless trees.

SUGAR MAPLE

In spring, the trunk of the sugar maple can be tapped for sap which is refined into maple syrup – once an important source of sugar for Native Americans. The large, five-lobed leaves turn brilliant fiery orange and red in fall.

Sap is extracted from the tree trunk and boiled to make syrup.

Scientific name: *Acer saccharum*

Size: 100 ft (30 m)

Habitat: Woodlands with rich, deep soil

Distribution: Eastern North America

Reproduction: Seeds are encased in a winged fruit

Dying leaves change color as chemical changes take place.

WINTER CHANGES

Before leaves drop in fall, a number of changes occur. Chlorophyll (the green pigment involved in photosynthesis), and any other useful substances, break down and flow back into the tree. Waste products such as tannins pass into the leaves. A layer of cork then forms across the base of the petiole (stalk) and the leaf eventually falls off. This leaves a scar on the twig. The following year's buds are protected by tough scales that prevent damage by frost and insects.

A corky leaf scar shows where the leaf has fallen off this horse chestnut tree.

Male catkins

OAKS

There are about 800 different species of oak trees (*Quercus* sp.). They are distributed in northern temperate regions, as well as in parts of tropical and subtropical Asia. Many types of oaks are deciduous, but in warmer places evergreen oaks are common. The fruit of the oak tree is a nut, which is enclosed in a cupule. Many wild birds and mammals, such as deer and squirrels, eat acorns.

Oaks produce single-seeded fruits called acorns.

Each acorn sits in its own woody cup.

Bamboo-leaved oak (*Quercus myrsinifolia*)

Upright female catkins

Himalayan birch (*Betula utilis*)

Many birches have bark that is deep-colored and glossy, or white and papery.

BIRCHES

Birch trees are often one of the first trees to colonize open areas. They thrive best on poor sandy soil, where the weeds that might otherwise choke them grow very slowly. There are about 40 different species of birches (*Betula* spp.). They are found in northern temperate regions and even high up on mountain slopes. Birches are fairly short-lived trees that have a number of local uses.

Many broadleaved trees are cultivated for their fruit.

Male catkins may be as long as 7.25 in (18 cm).

EUCALYPTUS

Almost all of the 550 or so species of eucalyptus trees (*Eucalyptus* sp.) come from Australia, where they are known as gum trees. The foliage of these trees contains aromatic oils, a number of which are extracted for commercial use. Eucalyptus trees are now grown in tropical and subtropical plantations in other parts of the world.

Urn gum (*Eucalyptus urnigera*)

The small, fluffy flowers attract insect, bird, and opossum pollinators.

FRUIT TREES

For more than two thousand years, many broadleaved trees – especially in the Northern Hemisphere – have been cultivated for their sweet, edible fruits. Today, fruit trees such as cherry, plum, apricot, peach, citrus fruit, apple, and pear are grown all over the world. They exist in numerous varieties that produce bigger, sweeter, and juicier fruit than their wild ancestors.

Apple trees in an English orchard

Find out more

CONIFERS AND CYCADS: *124*
DECIDUOUS FORESTS: *80*
FLOWERS AND SEEDS: *128*
PHOTOSYNTHESIS: *24*

GRASSES AND SEDGES

GRASSES ARE THE MOST widespread flowering plants on Earth, making up about 20 percent of the world's vegetation. There are about 9,000 species of grass. Three species – rice, wheat, and corn – provide the staple food for most of the world's population. At first glance, sedges look similar to grasses. Both types of plant have long, flat leaf blades, tall stems, and small, inconspicuous flowers that are pollinated by wind. Sedges tend to grow in damp or swampy places, and their stems are usually stiff and triangular in cross section.

Grass flowers are clustered at the top to catch the wind.

Yorkshire fog
(*Holcus lanatus*)

THE GRASS PLANT

A typical grass plant is made up of a clump of short branches and stems. Left uncut, the stems grow tall and produce clusters of tiny flowers at the top. Each leaf consists of a tubelike sheath that clasps the stem, and a long, narrow blade. New branches (tillers) grow from ground level, sometimes running along the ground to take root elsewhere. A fibrous mass of tangled roots grows under the ground. Grass plants often grow close together to form a sod.

New branches (tillers) grow from ground level.

Horses grazing

HOW GRASS GROWS

Grass can tolerate the pressures of grazing and mowing because of the way it grows. New branches grow from buds at ground level. When foliage is bitten off or mowed, the buds remain unharmed. Each leaf has a growing point at the base and continues to grow if the upper part is removed. Growing points on the stems enable them to bend upright after being trampled.

FROM FLOWERS TO SEEDS

Each tiny grass flower consists of several greenish scales enclosing male and female reproductive organs. The male organs (anthers) produce a fine powder called pollen, which is blown away by the wind. If a pollen grain lands on the female part (stigma) of another grass flower, it fertilizes an egg cell in the ovary, and a seed will develop. This process is called pollination.

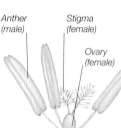

Anther (male)

Stigma (female)

Ovary (female)

Whole grass flower of Yorkshire fog plant

Inside a grass flower

GRASS POLLEN

When a grass flower is blown by wind, millions of microscopic pollen grains fly into the air. Nearly all will die within a day, but a tiny fraction may land on other flowers and pollinate them. Pollen is usually released before the female parts of the flower are ripe. This prevents the flower from pollinating itself.

Yorkshire fog shedding pollen and dead anthers

Grass roots form an interwoven mat in the soil.

SOIL BINDING

Grass roots form an interwoven mat that binds loose or dry soil. The deep roots of marram grass (*Ammophila arenaria*), for example, make coastal sand dunes more stable. Marram grass also has tall, spiky leaves that trap windblown sand around them. The grass then grows up through the sand and traps more sand. Gradually, a sand dune builds up. Cordgrass grows in wet estuary mud, eventually turning the mud into land fit for grazing.

The tough leaves of marram grass can survive in sand.

Marram grass grows in coastal sand.

The tough leaves trap wind-blown sand.

Eventually, the sand builds up into a dune, stabilized by the grass roots.

USEFUL GRASSES

Cultivated grasses (cereals) have been grown for thousands of years for their nutritious seeds. The seeds can be boiled and eaten whole, like rice, or ground into flour for cooking, like wheat. Wheat, oats, barley, and rye are grown in temperate parts of the world. Rice, corn, millet, and sorghum are the most important tropical cereals. The flowers and seeds of modern cultivated cereals are often much bigger than those of wild grasses.

Corn is used to make popcorn, cooking oil, and breakfast cereals.

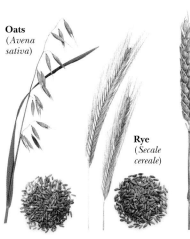

Oats
(*Avena sativa*)

Wheat
(*Triticum* sp.)

Rye
(*Secale cereale*)

Corn
(*Zea mays*)

SUGARCANE

Sugarcane is the source of most of the sugar we eat and has been cultivated for at least 3,000 years. It grows quickly, and can reach a height of 15 ft (4.5 m) in a single year. After harvesting, the large stems (canes) are crushed between steel rollers to yield a sweet juice. The juice is then boiled to make syrup and further refined to make pure sugar crystals.

Sugarcane being harvested, Barbados

Bamboo scaffolding, Hong Kong

BAMBOOS

Unlike most other grasses, bamboos have strong, woody stems and can grow very tall. The tallest of these – *Dendrocalamus giganteus* – can reach 115 ft (35 m) in height. Since their stems are strong, hollow, and light, bamboos are useful for building huts, scaffolding, and small boats. There are about 830 species of bamboo.

The hollow stem of a bamboo plant

RICE

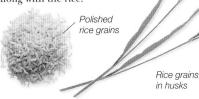

The grain from this grass provides the staple diet of half the world's population. People have grown rice in Thailand, China, and India for at least 5,000 years, and the plant now covers about 11 percent of the world's arable land. Farmers plant it in waterlogged fields called paddies and harvest the crop by hand. Some farmers release fish in the paddies and harvest them along with the rice.

Polished rice grains

Rice grains in husks

Scientific name: *Oryza sativa*	
Size: From 3–20 ft (1–6 m) tall	
Habitat: Wet and waterlogged soils	
Distribution: Originated in India, southern China, or Southeast Asia, but now grown throughout the tropics	
Reproduction: Wind-pollinated flowers produce seeds (rice grains). The plant then dies.	

TROUBLESOME WEEDS

Some grasses grow as weeds on farmland, depriving crops of moisture, light, and nutrients. Quack grass, for example, spreads quickly in plowed fields from shoots that creep horizontally just below the surface. It is difficult to remove because even broken fragments of the shoots can grow into new plants.

Quack grass
(*Elytrigia repens*)

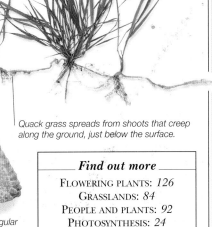

Quack grass spreads from shoots that creep along the ground, just below the surface.

SEDGES

Sedges are found all around the world, especially in wet and marshy places. Of the 4,000 or so species in the sedge family, about a quarter are called "true sedges." These have creeping underground shoots from which new leaves and flower stems grow. The flower stems are usually tall, with small male and female flowers at the top, often on separate spikes. The sedge family includes the papyrus plant, which the ancient Egyptians made into paper by pressing the stems together.

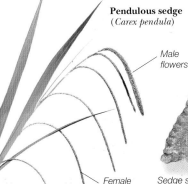

Pendulous sedge
(*Carex pendula*)

Male flowers

Female flowers

Sedge stems are triangular in cross section.

Find out more

FLOWERING PLANTS: *126*
GRASSLANDS: *84*
PEOPLE AND PLANTS: *92*
PHOTOSYNTHESIS: *24*

PARASITIC AND EPIPHYTIC PLANTS

MOST PLANTS COLLECT water and nutrients from the soil and make their food by photosynthesis. Parasitic plants, however, have evolved different methods of survival. Instead of getting their own nutrients and mineral supplies, they steal them from other plants, known as host plants. Many parasitic plants attach themselves to their hosts using suckers called haustoria. A few live buried deep inside the host and are visible only when they flower. Epiphytes also live on other plants, but do not use them as a source of food. Instead, they grow on the branches and stems of their host plants to get nearer the sun. Epiphytes are particularly common in tropical rainforests.

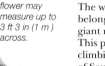

A rafflesia flower may measure up to 3 ft 3 in (1 m) across.

GIANT PARASITES

The world's largest flower belongs to a plant called the giant rafflesia (*Rafflesia arnoldii*). This parasite usually lives on climbing plants in the forests of Southeast Asia. The rafflesia flower is huge and weighs up to 15 lb (7 kg). Its powerful smell attracts pollinating flies, which are essential for the plant's reproduction. Unlike most parasitic plants, the giant rafflesia and its relatives are usually hidden inside their hosts. They are seen only when they flower.

Dodder stem

Stem of host plant

Hairlike stems of dodder attack host plant.

PARASITIC PLANTS

About one percent of the world's flowering plants live as parasites. Some parasitic plants attack a wide range of host plants; others only survive on a single species. Dodder (*Cuscuta* sp.) is a typical parasitic plant. It does not have green leaves so it is unable to carry out photosynthesis. Instead, its slender stems wind their way around the host like strands of hair. At intervals, each strand breaks into the host so it can steal essential supplies and food.

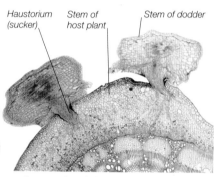

Haustorium (sucker)   *Stem of host plant*   *Stem of dodder*

Cross section of plant with dodder stems

BREAKING IN

Dodder stems wrap around and penetrate the host plant using suckerlike haustoria. They grow very quickly, absorbing water, minerals, and food from the host. Dodder stems stretch from one plant to another in a tangled, hairlike mass.

Ghost orchid
(*Epipogium aphyllum*)

SAPROPHYTIC PLANTS

Some plants feed on dead plant remains rather than from a living host. These saprophytic plants do not carry out photosynthesis, but often form partnerships with fungi, which help them absorb nutrients from the soil. Saprophytes usually spend most of their lives underground until they flower. The rare ghost orchid is a typical saprophyte that grows in leaf-litter on the floor of beech woods.

HEMIPARASITES

Plants called hemiparasites steal water and mineral nutrients but, unlike true parasites, they have green leaves and can therefore make their own food. Some hemiparasites live off their hosts underground by growing onto their roots. Others attack them above ground and grow out of their stems. Common mistletoe (*Viscum album*) is a typical hemiparasite found on trees. It grows on branches, and spreads by producing sticky berries that are carried away by birds. There are 1,200 species of mistletoe worldwide.

Green leaves trap the sun's energy to make food by photosynthesis.

Mistletoe grows on branches of trees such as apple, hawthorn, and fir.

EPIPHYTES

Epiphytes make their own food by photosynthesis, but use other plants as living platforms to get a better share of the light. Normally they do not harm the host plant, but in some habitats, such as rainforests, they become so numerous that their host's branches collapse under their weight. In warm parts of the world, epiphytes include many flowering plants such as orchids, bromeliads, and even some kinds of cacti. In cooler regions, common epiphytes include mosses and ferns.

Bromeliads growing on tree branches in a Brazilian rainforest

GETTING SUPPLIES

Rainforest plants must compete for water and mineral nutrients. Bromeliads solve part of this problem by making watertanks with their leaves. When it rains, water runs down the leaves and collects in the tank. These tree-top tanks provide homes for many small animals, such as mosquito larvae and tree frogs. Rotting debris and droppings from these animals accumulate in the tank, providing nutrients for the bromeliad.

Epiphytic bromeliad
(*Aechmea miniata*)

Water collects in the spaces formed by overlapping leaf bases.

Epiphytic orchid
(*Oncidium* sp.)

Epiphytic orchid is clamped in place by thickened roots.

TREETOP FLOWERS

In tropical rainforests, some of the most beautiful flowers are often perched high above the ground. They include epiphytic orchids, which clamp their specially thickened roots around the host plant's branches. These roots absorb water and also nutrients from dust. There are about 18,000 species of orchid in the world, half of which are epiphytes. Some have been over-collected and are now very rare.

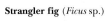

Small fig plant begins to send roots down tree.

Fig takes root and quickly smothers tree.

Fig kills host tree.

Strangler fig (*Ficus* sp.)

FATAL EMBRACE

Tropical strangler figs start life as harmless epiphytes but become deadly when mature. A young strangler fig germinates high up in a tree and grows a long root that reaches the ground. The strangler then grows a tangled network of stems that slowly entwines its host. Eventually its leaves become so dense that the host tree dies. Its trunk slowly rots away and the strangler takes its place.

STAGHORN FERN

Staghorn ferns are found high up on trees. These epiphytes grow two quite different kinds of fronds (leaves). One type spreads out like a deer's antlers, giving the plant its name; the other is rounded and grows around the tree's trunk. These rounded fronds hold the fern in place. They also form a basket, which collects dead leaves that fall from above. The leaves turn into a form of compost, which the fern uses as a source of essential nutrients.

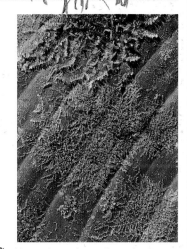

Scientific name:
Platycerium superbum

Size: Up to 5 ft (1.5 m) across

Habitat: Humid, tropical forests

Distribution: Northern Australia and New Guinea

Reproduction: Releases millions of microscopic spores that drift through the air to other trees

---

Liverworts growing on damp plant leaves that lie close to the forest floor

EPIPHYLLS

In dense, tropical rainforests the competition for light is intense, especially near the forest floor. Here, tiny plants called epiphylls survive by living on the leaves of other plants, often where it is very damp. A range of liverworts, for example, are found on single leaves in the forests of Costa Rica.

Find out more

PARTNERS AND PARASITES: *56*
PHOTOSYNTHESIS: *24*
PLANTS: *116*
TROPICAL RAINFORESTS: *82*

CARNIVOROUS PLANTS

NEARLY ALL PLANTS PRODUCE food by photosynthesis, and most obtain essential nutrients from fertile soils. However, some plants grow in infertile areas that lack important minerals, particularly nitrates. These plants get their nutrients by catching insects and small vertebrates in their leaves. Carnivorous plants capture their victims using a range of methods, including pitfall traps, snapping traps, and sticky secretions. The insects are usually digested by special juices secreted by the leaves, or by bacterial and fungal processes.

Carnivorous plants survive in nutrient-poor soils.

NUTRIENT-POOR HABITATS

Bogs and marshes have poor soil that often lacks nutrients. Organisms that break down plant matter, such as bacteria and fungi, cannot survive in these waterlogged soils. Without the help of bacteria and fungi, dead plants decompose slowly, keeping their nutrients locked up. Carnivorous plants survive in these conditions by absorbing extra nutrients from trapped insects.

Marsh pitcher
(*Heliamphora tatei*)

AMERICAN PITCHERS

These plants are the simplest of all pitfall traps. Their leaves form tall, narrow cups that fill with rainwater. At the tip of each pitcher is a brightly colored hood, covered with nectar-secreting glands. Insects, attracted by the color and nectar, land on the slippery rim. The downward-pointing hairs inside the pitcher guide insects down to a lower region with smooth walls. Here, the insects lose their grip and fall into the water where they drown.

Insects that fall into the pitfall trap of the marsh pitcher are decomposed by bacteria.

Cross section of a pitcher

The slippery rim is colored red, yellow, or purple.

Loose flakes of wax make it impossible for insects to climb back up the wall.

Thin-walled cells in the lining of the pitcher absorb vital nutrients from digested insects.

Each hair secretes a sticky droplet at its tip that attracts insects.

TRAPS FOR THE UNWARY

Pitcher plants catch their victims using pitfall traps. Their colored rims lure insects into the traps. Inside the pitcher, loose, waxy flakes covering the pitcher's walls clog the insects' feet, so that they tumble into the water. As the victims fall into the pitcher, they stimulate the secretion of enzymes, which digest the insects' body tissues. Bacteria also help to decompose trapped victims. Liquid nutrients obtained from digested insects are absorbed through the pitcher's walls.

Trap is similar to flypaper because the fly cannot free itself.

Sundew plant
(*Drosera* sp.)

PITCHER DEVELOPMENT

Some pitcher plants grow in the tropical rainforests of Southeast Asia and northern Australia. A few grow on the ground, but most are climbers or epiphytes. A new pitcher appears as a swelling at the tip of a leaf tendril. As the tendril gets longer, the swelling gradually enlarges. The "lid" of the pitcher stays closed as it develops. Once the pitcher is fully mature the lid opens, allowing water to collect inside.

Monkey cup pitcher
(*Nepenthes mirabilis*)

Immature pitcher becomes hollow and fills with air.

When mature, the lid opens and the pitcher collects rainwater. It is ready to trap prey.

Not yet full-sized, the lid remains tightly closed.

The midrib of the leaf develops into a tendril. A new pitcher will start to grow at its tip.

STICKY TRAPS

The leaves of sundew plants are covered with red glandular hairs that secrete droplets of clear, sticky liquid. Insects are attracted by the glistening droplets and get stuck on the hairs. As the insect attempts to escape, its struggle stimulates adjacent leaf hairs to curl around its body. As the leaf encloses its prey, the plant releases digestive enzymes that break down the insect's body tissues.

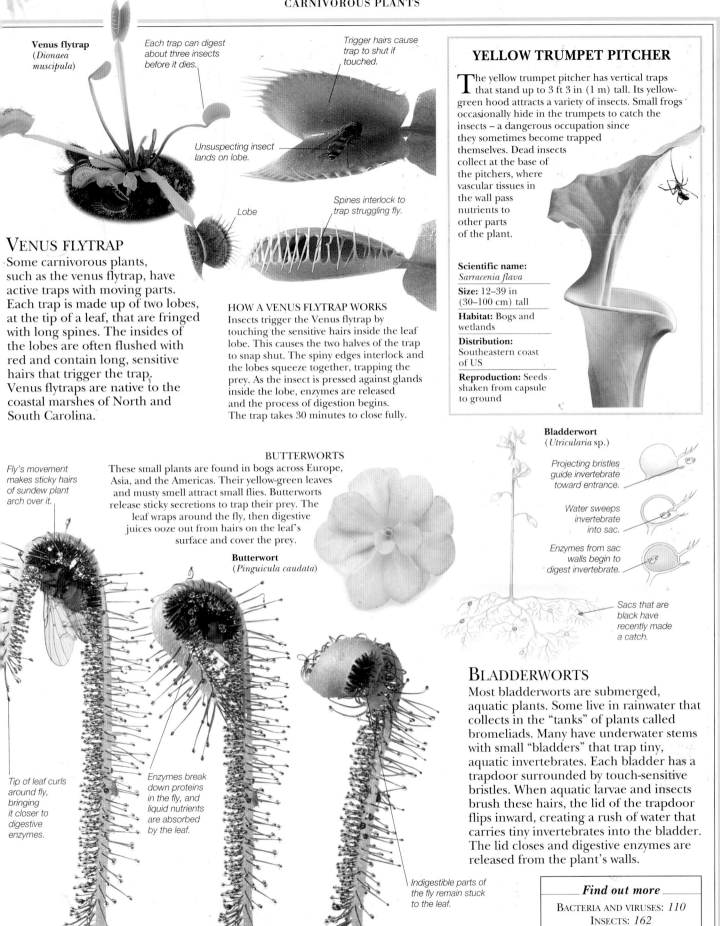

Venus flytrap
(*Dionaea muscipula*)

Each trap can digest about three insects before it dies.

Trigger hairs cause trap to shut if touched.

Unsuspecting insect lands on lobe.

Lobe

Spines interlock to trap struggling fly.

VENUS FLYTRAP

Some carnivorous plants, such as the venus flytrap, have active traps with moving parts. Each trap is made up of two lobes, at the tip of a leaf, that are fringed with long spines. The insides of the lobes are often flushed with red and contain long, sensitive hairs that trigger the trap. Venus flytraps are native to the coastal marshes of North and South Carolina.

HOW A VENUS FLYTRAP WORKS
Insects trigger the Venus flytrap by touching the sensitive hairs inside the leaf lobe. This causes the two halves of the trap to snap shut. The spiny edges interlock and the lobes squeeze together, trapping the prey. As the insect is pressed against glands inside the lobe, enzymes are released and the process of digestion begins. The trap takes 30 minutes to close fully.

YELLOW TRUMPET PITCHER

The yellow trumpet pitcher has vertical traps that stand up to 3 ft 3 in (1 m) tall. Its yellow-green hood attracts a variety of insects. Small frogs occasionally hide in the trumpets to catch the insects – a dangerous occupation since they sometimes become trapped themselves. Dead insects collect at the base of the pitchers, where vascular tissues in the wall pass nutrients to other parts of the plant.

Scientific name:
Sarracenia flava

Size: 12–39 in (30–100 cm) tall

Habitat: Bogs and wetlands

Distribution: Southeastern coast of US

Reproduction: Seeds shaken from capsule to ground

Fly's movement makes sticky hairs of sundew plant arch over it.

BUTTERWORTS
These small plants are found in bogs across Europe, Asia, and the Americas. Their yellow-green leaves and musty smell attract small flies. Butterworts release sticky secretions to trap their prey. The leaf wraps around the fly, then digestive juices ooze out from hairs on the leaf's surface and cover the prey.

Butterwort
(*Pinguicula caudata*)

Bladderwort
(*Utricularia* sp.)

Projecting bristles guide invertebrate toward entrance.

Water sweeps invertebrate into sac.

Enzymes from sac walls begin to digest invertebrate.

Sacs that are black have recently made a catch.

Tip of leaf curls around fly, bringing it closer to digestive enzymes.

Enzymes break down proteins in the fly, and liquid nutrients are absorbed by the leaf.

Indigestible parts of the fly remain stuck to the leaf.

BLADDERWORTS

Most bladderworts are submerged, aquatic plants. Some live in rainwater that collects in the "tanks" of plants called bromeliads. Many have underwater stems with small "bladders" that trap tiny, aquatic invertebrates. Each bladder has a trapdoor surrounded by touch-sensitive bristles. When aquatic larvae and insects brush these hairs, the lid of the trapdoor flips inward, creating a rush of water that carries tiny invertebrates into the bladder. The lid closes and digestive enzymes are released from the plant's walls.

Find out more

BACTERIA AND VIRUSES: *110*
INSECTS: *162*
NUTRIENT CYCLES: *64*
WETLANDS: *74*

ANIMALS

ANIMALS MAKE UP THE largest of the five kingdoms of nature. Despite their diversity, all animals share certain features that set them apart from the other four kingdoms. Unlike plants, which use sunlight to manufacture their food, animals obtain their food by eating other living things. To do this, they use a variety of senses to detect their food, and most animals have to move around actively to find it. Unlike bacteria and single-celled organisms, animals have complex bodies made of specialized cells. Many animals have skeletons to support their weight, and most – but not all – have brains to control the way they respond to their surroundings.

ANIMAL OR NOT

Many people use the word animal just to mean mammal. However, animals include birds, reptiles, amphibians, and fish, as well as the vast and varied world of invertebrates (animals without backbones) – from sponges and jellyfish to crabs, insects, and starfish. Scientists have identified about 1.5 million animal species. Of these, more than 90 percent are invertebrates. Some scientists believe there may be another 15 million invertebrates yet to be identified.

European John Dory (*Zeus faber*)

Slowworm (*Anguis fragilis*)

Rhinoceros beetle (*Chalcosoma atlas*)

SENSES

Without senses, animals would not be able to find food, locate each other, identify predators, or navigate. It is the five main senses – vision, hearing, smell, taste, and touch – that enable animals to survive in their habitats. Some animals have additional senses, such as the infrared vision of a rattlesnake that allows it to see the warmth of its prey. The sense organs, such as the eyes, ears, and whiskers of a rabbit, are linked to a nervous system and brain.

Large eyes for night-time vision

Long, mobile ears for pinpointing distant sounds

Sensitive whiskers for feeling the way in dark tunnels

Barrel sponge (*Petrosia* sp.)

PRIMITIVE ANIMALS

Sponges are among the simplest organisms in the animal kingdom. Their bodies are made of two layers of cells and have no organs. Most sponges are found in the sea, where they live attached to rocks or the seabed. They feed on tiny food particles filtered from the water. Some sponges have an internal skeleton made of a fibrous substance called spongin. Bath sponges are spongin skeletons without the living tissue.

FINDING FOOD

Animals use an impressive variety of ways to find food. Filter feeders, such as barnacles, simply stay in one place and filter food from the water around them. However, most animals have to search out their food. For animals that eat plants (herbivores), finding food is relatively easy. Animals that prey on other animals (carnivores) need special skills or weapons to catch food. Most pelicans, for example, use their huge, pouched beaks to scoop fish from water.

BRAINS AND NERVES

Simple animals, such as hydras, have a network of nerve cells throughout the body but no brain. More complex animals, such as flatworms, have some of their nerve cells concentrated together to form a primitive "brain," which communicates with the rest of the body via distinct nerve pathways. The vertebrates (animals with backbones) have the most complex nervous systems, with a large brain controlling many body processes.

A hydra has a simple nerve network with no brain.

In a flatworm, nerve cells in the head form a simple "brain."

Vertebrates, such as frogs, have complex nervous systems and brains.

Great white pelicans (Pelecanus onocrotalus) feeding

SKELETONS

Many animals have a skeleton to hold up the body, to protect internal organs, and to provide anchorage for muscles. Skeletons are especially important for animals that live on land. Tigers, for example, have internal skeletons that are made of bones. Without its skeleton, a tiger would be a heap of soft flesh, unable to move. Other animals, such as spiders, have external skeletons (exoskeletons) made of a hard substance called chitin.

The skeleton provides a supporting framework for the body and anchorage for muscles.

Tiger
(*Panthera tigris*)

Spiders have to shed their exoskeletons, or molt, in order to grow.

Old exoskeleton after molting

Tarantula
(*Ceratogyrus* sp.)

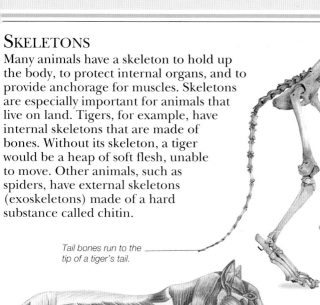

Tail bones run to the tip of a tiger's tail.

Powerful muscles cover a tiger's skeleton.

TIGER MUSCLES

About half the weight of a tiger's body is taken up by muscles that enable it to move. Most of these muscles are attached to the bones of the skeleton. The tiger's muscles are controlled by its brain, which sends rapid signals along nerve cells running to each muscle when the tiger moves. The muscles work by contracting and relaxing in a coordinated way, pulling certain bones as they do so. Joints between the tiger's bones make its skeleton highly flexible.

A Bengal tiger chasing its prey

PARENTAL CARE

Although most animals abandon their young soon after reproducing, others stay and care for them. Parental care is most common in birds and mammals. A chimpanzee may spend up to seven years in the care of its mother before becoming fully independent. During this time it learns how to find food, how to avoid danger, and who to trust in chimpanzee society. Apart from cockroaches, earwigs, and scorpions, few invertebrates look after their young.

Female chimpanzees are devoted parents.

Common chimpanzee
(*Pan troglodytes*)

MOVEMENT

While plants spend their lives rooted in one spot, most animals move around in order to find food and mates or to escape from danger. Some animals seem to spend their whole lives on the move. Young swifts may spend up to two years in nonstop flight after leaving their nest – they eat, mate, and even sleep on the wing. Like most cats, tigers are experts at stealthy movement. They creep up on their victims before making a dash for the kill.

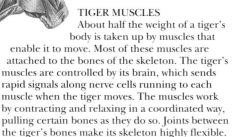

Anemones wave their tentacles to trap prey.

MOVING PARTS

Some animals, such as sea anemones, do not usually move around as adults. However, they do have moving parts for capturing food. When submerged by the tide, sea anemones extend their tentacles in the water. The tentacles are armed with lethal stinging capsules that trap and kill prey. Although adult sea anemones usually stay fixed in one place, their larvae can swim.

Snakelocks anemone
(*Anemonia viridis*)

Find out more

APES: *284*
CATS: *256*
INVERTEBRATES: *142*
VERTEBRATES: *182*

INVERTEBRATES

WHEN PEOPLE THINK of animals, they usually
think of mammals, birds, reptiles, and fish.
Yet these creatures make up only a tiny fraction
of the animal kingdom and belong to just one of
the 34 major groups of animals – vertebrates
(animals with backbones). The other 33 groups
are known collectively as invertebrates (animals
without backbones). The invertebrates are an
incredibly diverse group of animals that share
few features in common and are only distantly
related to each other. They display every
imaginable way of life and come in all shapes
and sizes. Many are found only in the sea, but
certain groups, such as insects, live on land
and are extremely common worldwide.

Sponges
(Porifera)
15,000 species

Echinoderms
(Echinodermata)
6,000 species

Segmented worms
(Annelida)
11,000 species

Roundworms
(Nematoda)
12,000 species

Cnidarians
(Cnidaria)
10,000 species

Mollusks
(Mollusca)
150,000 species

Arthropods
(Arthropoda)
3–15 million species

Flatworms
(Platyhelminthes)
100,000 species

INVERTEBRATE GROUPS

Some invertebrates are familiar – insects, crabs, worms, and
snails, for example – but many are so tiny, inconspicuous,
or numerous that biologists have not yet given them names.
There are thought to be between 3 million and 15 million
invertebrate species (far more than the 40,000 or so
vertebrate species). These are classified into 33 groups,
or phyla. Some of the best-known invertebrate phyla are
shown above with an estimate of the number of species.

AN UNCERTAIN HISTORY
No one is certain when the first invertebrates
appeared. The fossil record goes back only about
600 million years, and the animal groups we
know today had already evolved by then. Over
time, some invertebrate groups diversified more
than others – the phylum Arthropoda is now
the largest, and contains at least a million
named species, most of which are insects.

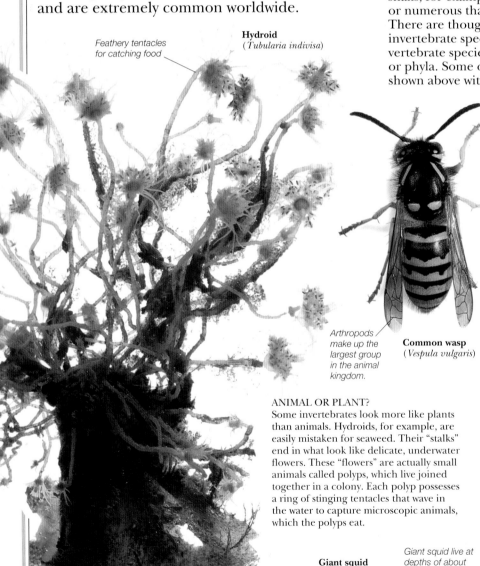

Hydroid
(*Tubularia indivisa*)

Feathery tentacles
for catching food

Arthropods
make up the
largest group
in the animal
kingdom.

Common wasp
(*Vespula vulgaris*)

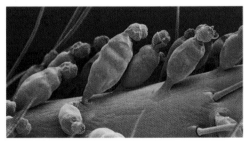

Magnified view of Symbion pandora on a lobster bristle

ANIMAL OR PLANT?
Some invertebrates look more like plants
than animals. Hydroids, for example, are
easily mistaken for seaweed. Their "stalks"
end in what look like delicate, underwater
flowers. These "flowers" are actually small
animals called polyps, which live joined
together in a colony. Each polyp possesses
a ring of stinging tentacles that wave in
the water to capture microscopic animals,
which the polyps eat.

NEW ARRIVALS

For biologists, the discovery of a new
species of animal is a noteworthy event,
and finding a new family of animals is a
cause of major excitement. As recently as
1994, biologists discovered a completely
new phylum – a group equivalent in
status to the arthropods or mollusks.
The only known member of the new
phylum is *Symbion pandora*, a tiny
creature that lives exclusively around
the mouth of the Norway lobster and
feeds on scraps of the lobster's food.

Giant squid
(*Architeuthis* sp.)

Giant squid live at
depths of about
3 miles (5 km).

BODY SYMMETRY

Apart from sponges, nearly all invertebrates have symmetrical bodies. There are two main types of body symmetry: radial and bilateral symmetry. Radially symmetrical animals have circular bodies, and can be cut across the middle in many directions to make two equal halves. All live in water and none has a brain. Bilaterally symmetrical animals have distinct front and back ends. They can be cut across the middle in only one direction to make two equal halves.

Jellyfish
(*Cassiopea andromeda*)

Radially symmetrical animals can be cut in many directions to make two equal halves.

FACING FORWARD

Most invertebrates have distinct front and rear ends. This arrangement has many advantages. The sense organs are clustered at the front near the mouth, ready to meet new challenges and find food. Body parts are specialized for movement in one direction only, making movement faster and more efficient. This body plan is the most successful produced by hundreds of millions of years of evolution, and is now found in most animals, including ourselves.

Garden slug
(*Arion ater*)

Bilaterally symmetrical animals can be cut in only one direction to make two equal halves.

SPONGY LIFE

Most invertebrates have symmetrical bodies divided into parts – legs, head, eyes, and so on. Sponges, however, have no body symmetry and no distinct parts. All the parts of a sponge's body appear to be the same, and there is no "right way up." Despite this apparent simplicity, sponges have specialized cells dedicated to different tasks, and are made up of distinct layers. Some sponges grow to more than 3 ft 3 in (1 m) wide.

Most sponges, such as this tube sponge (Aplysina archeri), grow on the seafloor.

FILTER FEEDING

The simplest sponges have small, tube-shaped bodies, peppered with tiny pores. Lining the inner surface of the tube are special cells called collar cells. These have whip-like hairs that beat to make water flow into the pores, through the tube, and out of a hole at the top. The collar cells also have a "collar" of tiny tentacles that trap tiny pieces of organic matter as the water flows past. These food particles are then digested.

Seawater leaves.

Pore

Cross section of the wall of a sponge

Seawater enters pores.

Collar cell

Flagellum *Collar hairs*

Centipedes use their long antennae to feel around and "taste" objects.

SEGMENTS

Many invertebrates have bodies divided into separate segments. This allows the animal to change its shape and move in complex ways. Earthworms, for example, have separate muscles in each segment and can squirm through soil by coordinating the way the muscles contract. Centipedes have a pair of legs on most of their segments and can run very quickly to chase prey or escape from predators.

Woodland centipede
(*Lithobius* sp.)

Poison claw

Hind legs act as extra antennae.

INVERTEBRATE GIANTS

Invertebrates are found in virtually all the Earth's environments, but most of the main invertebrate groups are restricted to the seas, where the first invertebrates evolved. Many are microscopic and drift along with ocean currents, but others are powerful swimmers. With their bodies buoyed up by the salty water, some invertebrates reach great sizes. Giant squid can grow up to 59 ft (18 m) long.

Human diver shown to scale

> ### Find out more
> ANIMALS: *140*
> HOW LIVING THINGS WORK: *18*
> INSECTS: *162*
> VERTEBRATES: *182*

WORMS

FOR MOST PEOPLE, THE WORD "WORM" describes the familiar soft-bodied, legless animal found in garden soil. But in fact, there are thought to be more than one million species of worms, living in a wide range of different habitats. Some, such as the earthworm, live in burrows, feeding on broken-down plant matter. Others live in the sea or in freshwater, filtering food particles from the water around them. Some are predators, while many are parasitic and cause diseases that kill millions of people each year. The three most important groups of worms are flatworms, segmented worms, and roundworms.

Planarian flatworm (*Bipalium* sp.)

FLATWORMS

Planarians, or flatworms, are the simplest animals with a distinct "head." Their bodies are flattened and ribbonlike, giving them a large surface area. This is vital because they have no lungs, and they breathe and pass dissolved waste directly through their skins. There are about 80,000 species of flatworms. Many live as parasites in or on other animals. Others live in soil or in fresh or saltwater.

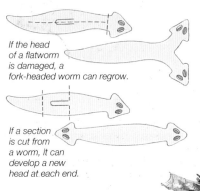

If the head of a flatworm is damaged, a fork-headed worm can regrow.

If a section is cut from a worm, it can develop a new head at each end.

SPLITTING UP

Most flatworms are hermaphrodites – they have both male and female sexual organs – although they still pair up to reproduce sexually. Some species can also reproduce asexually, by splitting into two. Flatworms have an amazing ability to regenerate from small sections of the "parent." If the worm is cut into pieces, each fragment will grow into a new worm, complete with head and sensory organs.

SEGMENTED WORMS

Segmented worms, or annelids, include the most familiar types of worm, such as earthworms, leeches, and the clam worms used as bait by anglers. Most, such as the parchment worm, have elongated bodies divided into fluid-filled segments. Segmented worms have well-developed nervous, circulatory, and waste-disposal systems. Many species also have a pair of leg-like appendages attached to every segment.

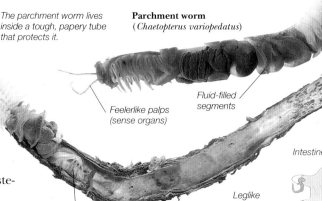

The parchment worm lives inside a tough, papery tube that protects it.

Parchment worm (*Chaetopterus variopedatus*)

Feelerlike palps (sense organs)

Fluid-filled segments

The end of the tube sticks out above the mud's surface.

The worm feeds by drawing water containing food into its tube.

Intestine

Muscle layer

Leglike appendage

Cross section through a segmented worm

ROUNDWORMS

Nematodes, or roundworms, are possibly the most numerous animals in the world. They are found almost everywhere and many live as parasites in animals and plants. Some areas of sand in shallow waters contain more than one million of these tiny worms per square yard. Roundworms are fairly uniform in appearance – most are less than 0.125 in (3 mm) in length, with long, cylindrical bodies tapered at each end, and elastic, muscular walls.

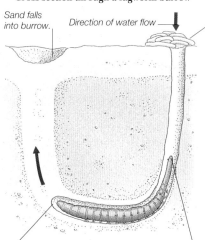

Marine nematode worm (*Draconema* sp.)

Flattened head with tentacles and mouth

Pointed tail

Cross section through a lugworm burrow

Sand falls into burrow.

Direction of water flow

Pile of waste sand and mud

A lugworm swallows sand and mud that falls into the burrow.

The lugworm squirts waste material out from its anus.

BURROWS

Many worms live in tubes or burrows in soil or sand. Some are active predators that crawl through networks of burrows opening out on to the seabed. When they detect disturbance in the water above, they lunge out and grab passing prey. Others, such as lugworms, feed on organic material in the sand. They expand and contract their bodies to draw oxygen-rich water through the burrow.

HORSEHAIR WORMS

Some parasitic worms, such as horsehair worms, swim and lay their eggs in freshwater. When the eggs hatch, the larvae live as parasites in the bodies of animals such as crabs and insects. They will then feed on the host until it eventually dies. They are called horsehair worms because they are found in animal watering troughs, and were once thought to be horses' hairs brought to life.

Horsehair worm
(*Chordodes verrucosus*)

Horsehair worms can grow to 3 ft 3 in (1 m) long.

The thick trunk looks like a peanut when the whole body retracts.

Peanut worm

BULBOUS WORMS

Not all worms have a classic "wormlike" shape. Peanut worms, in particular, have bizarre bulbous forms. Most live in burrows on the seabed, have thick, muscular body walls, and breathe by extracting oxygen from the water through their skins. They feed by extending a proboscis, which can be up to ten times the length of the body, to collect particles of food from the sand.

Mouth surrounded by tentacles

PEACOCK FANWORM

The elegant, feathery gills of the peacock fanworm act as a net, trapping particles of food that drift past in the sea. The fanworm's soft body is hidden in a long, protective tube, which it makes from mud and mucus. In times of danger the worm pulls its head and gills rapidly into the tube.

The worm's mouth is hidden in the center of its gills.

Scientific name: *Sabella penicillis*

Size: Up to 8 in (20 cm) long

Habitat: Mud and sandy seabeds

Distribution: Temperate waters of Atlantic Ocean

Reproduction: Each fanworm sheds both sperm and eggs into the sea; after fertilization, developing larvae drift with the current before settling on the seabed

Diet: Filter feeder; extracts minute organisms and other organic matter from the sea

A mucous covering helps the earthworm move and keeps it from drying out.

1. Circular muscles contract and body stretches forward.

2. Hairs anchor segments.

MOVEMENT

Segmented worms, such as earthworms, have a fluid-filled body with two layers of muscle – an inner layer of longitudinal muscles (which run along the length of the body), and an outer layer of circular muscles (which run around the body). To move forward, the worm contracts its circular muscles and elongates its body. Tiny bristles extend from its front portion to anchor it to the soil. Next, the worm contracts its longitudinal muscles to draw up the rest of its body behind the front section.

3. Longitudinal muscles contract and drag up rest of body.

Tiny bristles called setae on an earthworm's skin

Earthworm
(*Lumbricus terrestris*)

Most of the earthworm's segments have four pairs of tiny, almost invisible bristles.

Most tapeworms grow hundreds of identical segments.

The tapeworm's head carries a ring of hooks to grip on to its host.

Tapeworm (*Amirthalingamia macracantha*)

PARASITES AND DISEASES

Many worms live as parasites in other animals. Some, especially flatworms and roundworms, are serious pests of animals and cause a variety of human diseases. For example, tapeworms are flatworms that live as parasites in the guts of vertebrates, including humans. They lack mouths, but absorb food through the entire surface of their body. They anchor themselves to the gut using hooks and suckers at the head end and can grow to lengths of 100 ft (30 m) or more.

INSECT ANCESTORS

The carnivorous velvet worms have features in common with both segmented worms and insects. Some biologists think they form an evolutionary link between worms and insects. Reaching lengths of up to 6 in (15 cm), velvet worms may have as many as 43 pairs of legs, which allow them to crawl like caterpillars. Unlike insects, their outer layer is thin and not very waterproof, so they can only survive in damp places.

A velvet worm (Peripatus sp.) searching for prey in a rainforest

Find out more

ANIMAL HOMES: *58*
PARTNERS AND PARASITES: *56*
REPRODUCTION: *28*
SEASHORES AND TIDEPOOLS: *70*

JELLYFISH and CORALS

WITH BODIES MADE UP of just two layers of tissue – and only a few distinct organs – jellyfish and corals are among the simplest of invertebrates. They are classified as cnidarians (or coelenterates), a group that also includes hydras and sea anemones. Most live in seawater. Some, such as jellyfish, swim freely while others, such as corals, live anchored to rocks on the seafloor. Many cnidarians are carnivorous, capturing their prey with the help of stinging cells called cnidocytes. The sting of some species is strong enough to paralyze or even kill a human swimmer.

ANATOMY

The body of a cnidarian has two "ends." At one end is the mouth, which is surrounded by a ring of tentacles studded with stinging cells. The other end may form a stalk that anchors the animal to the ground, or in the case of jellyfish, forms its dome-shaped umbrella. The mouth leads into a closed gut. There is no anus, so undigested waste passes back out through the mouth. All cnidarians are characterized by symmetrical bodies with tentacles radiating from a large digestive cavity.

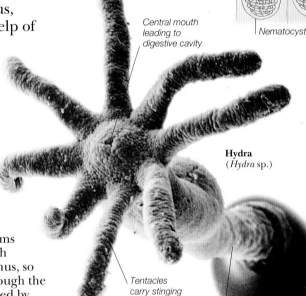

Cross section of tentacle

The barbed capsule punches a hole in the prey's skin.

Poison is injected through the hollow thread.

Barb

Skin of prey

Stinging cell

Nematocyst | Coiled thread

Central mouth leading to digestive cavity

Hydra
(*Hydra* sp.)

Tentacles carry stinging cells, known as cnidae.

Stalk anchors the hydra.

Hydras may attach themselves to rocks, shells, or even algae.

STINGING CELLS

Small cnidarian species feed on tiny plankton, but larger jellyfish and anemones catch bigger prey, including fish and mollusks. They immobilize their prey using stinging cells located on their tentacles. Inside each cell is a bulblike nematocyst (cnida), which contains a coiled thread studded with spines. When prey makes contact with the stinging cell, it explodes outward, pushing the barbed thread into the skin of its victim. The tentacles then draw the prey back toward the predator's mouth.

If the bell stops opening and closing, the jellyfish will sink.

POLYPS AND MEDUSAE

Polyp

Epidermis Gastrodermis

Mesoglea

Medusa

Epidermis

Mesoglea | Gastrodermis

Cnidarians exist in two basic forms – polyps and medusae. Polyps, such as hydras and sea anemones, are cylindrical in shape, and live anchored to the seafloor with their mouths and tentacles pointing upward to trap their prey. Medusae, such as jellyfish, are umbrella-shaped and their mouths and tentacles point downward when they swim. Some species alternate between the two forms during their life cycle.

In both a polyp and a medusa, the outer epidermis and inner gastrodermis are separated by a jellylike layer called mesoglea.

Movement in the jellyfish is coordinated by a simple nervous system.

GENTLE JETS

A jellyfish uses a gentle form of jet propulsion to propel it through the water. Muscle contractions force water out from the "bell" shape made by its body. The force of the water leaving its body pushes the jellyfish in the opposite direction. Because its body is "elasticized," it pulls back into shape after each contraction, ready for the next push forward.

DEADLY JELLIES

The stinging cells of some jellyfish and anemones are capable of injecting some of the most poisonous chemicals in nature. The sting of the sea nettle (*Chrysaora* sp.) may be just a nuisance to swimmers, but box jellyfish are very dangerous, and can be lethal. One type of box jelly, the sea wasp (*Chironex fleckeri*), is found off the coast of Australia.

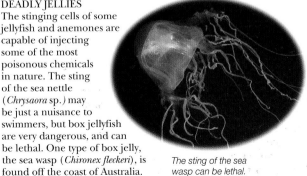

The sting of the sea wasp can be lethal.

Specialized organs detect gravity, telling the jellyfish if it is swimming up or down.

Hydra (Hydra fusca) budding off a "daughter" hydra

REPRODUCTION

The life cycles of cnidarians are very complex. Most can reproduce asexually (without mating) by splitting or budding from the body, or by regenerating from fragments. At other times they reproduce sexually, by shedding sperm and eggs into the water – fertilization occurs either in the water or in the body cavity of an adult. Many species may pass through one or two larval stages, as well as both polyp and medusa forms.

Lion's mane
(*Cyanea capillata*)

Coral reef, Fiji, in the Pacific Ocean

PORTUGUESE MAN-OF-WAR

The Portuguese man-of-war can be considered a single jellyfish, or a colony of individual polyps and medusae adapted for different tasks. One polyp makes up the prominent "float." Other polyps catch and digest food; medusae are involved in reproduction.

The "float" is filled with gas.

Scientific name:	*Physalia physalis*
Size:	Float 12 in (30 cm) long; tentacles 33 ft (10 m)
Habitat:	Floats on the surface of water
Distribution:	Warm and tropical seas worldwide
Reproduction:	*Physalia* is a colony of cnidarians, which reproduce sexually
Diet:	Fish and crustaceans

SEA SKELETONS

The chalk (calcium carbonate) skeletons of corals can create many elaborate patterns. These distinctive shapes are formed by the different arrangement of coral polyps within a colony. Some coral skeletons are upright, resembling the veins of a leaf; others are low and crustlike or folded into sheets. Depending on the species, coral skeletons can grow at rates of about 5 percent a year.

CORALS

Most corals resemble tiny sea anemones. A few are solitary, but most live in large colonies, with each one connected to its neighbor by a sheet of tissue. Corals generally secrete a hard skeleton, which supports and protects the living polyps. Most hard corals are found in clear, shallow, tropical waters, where their skeletons can form huge reefs and become a habitat in their own right.

Blue coral
(*Heliopora coerulea*)

Sea fan
(*Gorgonia flabellum*)

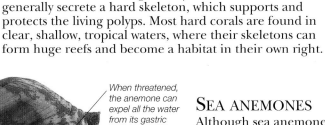

When threatened, the anemone can expel all the water from its gastric cavity, and flatten itself against the rock.

SEA ANEMONES

Although sea anemones look like harmless underwater plants, they are active predators that catch fish and small invertebrates with stinging tentacles. Despite the fact that they are polyps, they can move slowly across their habitat – typically the rocky floor of a shallow sea. By taking in or expelling water from their digestive cavities, they are capable of dramatic changes in size. The largest anemones can measure more than 3 ft 3 in (1 m) across.

Dahlia anemone (red form)
(*Urticina eques*)

A feeding anemone with its tentacles extended

Find out more	
CORAL REEFS:	*72*
MOVEMENT IN WATER:	*38*
OCEANS:	*68*
STARFISH AND SEA URCHINS:	*154*

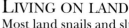

SNAILS AND SLUGS

SNAILS AND SLUGS BELONG to a group of animals called gastropods. Although gastropods are most familiar as plant-eating garden pests, most of the 72,000 or so species live in the world's seas and oceans. A large proportion are carnivorous hunters, some stunning their prey with potent toxins. Gastropods belong to a group of animals called mollusks, together with squid, octopuses, clams, and oysters. Like other mollusks, most gastropods have soft bodies protected by shells. A gastropod also has a muscular "foot" for moving, and a tongue covered in tiny teeth for scratching at food. There are three main types of gastropod: sea snails, sea slugs, and snails and slugs that live on land.

Eye

Tentacle

Short tentacle

Columella

Muscular foot

Giant African snail
(*Achatina fulica*)

Shell made of calcium carbonate

Breathing hole leading to lung

Land slug
(*Arion ater*)

Slimy skin

Eye

LIVING ON LAND

Most land snails and slugs come out to feed at night and spend the day hiding in dark, damp places to conserve moisture and avoid predators. They move by sliding over slime secreted by a large, muscular foot. Snails can withdraw into their shells when in danger, but slugs have to rely on their sticky, offensive slime for protection. Land snails and slugs usually have eyes at the tips of long tentacles, and smaller tentacles to feel nearby objects. Unlike aquatic species, they have lungs and can breathe air.

TWISTED HOMES

Snail shells are coiled into a clockwise spiral over the right side of the snail's body. Coiling makes the shell compact and portable, but the snail's body has to twist around to fit inside. As a result, one side of the body is smaller than the other, and in most species the right kidney and the right side of the heart are small or absent. The snail's body is attached to the central axis of the shell (the columella) by a powerful muscle.

Trapezium horse conch
(*Pleuroploca trapezium*)

SEASHELLS

The colorful and exotic shells of marine gastropods wash up on beaches all over the world. While the shells of land snails are light and delicate, those of species that live between the tides are robust to withstand constant battering by the waves. Gastropod shells are usually coiled, but there are exceptions – limpets, for example, have shieldlike shells to deflect the relentless pounding of the sea.

The Eloise
(*Acteon eloisae*)

Japanese wonder
(*Thatcheria mirabilis*)

Fly-spotted auger
(*Terebra areolata*)

EMERGING FROM A SHELL

Snails may be slow movers, but when threatened, they withdraw their tentacles and disappear into the shell in seconds. Aquatic snails have an extra form of protection – a hard, round plate called an operculum, which blocks the shell's entrance. When danger has passed, the snail slowly emerges, using its muscular foot to flip over if left upside down.

1. The snail is hiding in its shell for protection.

2. As the foot emerges, the snail rolls over.

3. Tentacles extend to check for danger.

4. The snail moves off on its muscular foot.

SLEEPY SUMMER

Snails that live on land are constantly losing water through evaporation and the production of slime. Not surprisingly, most species live in humid places and avoid drying out by moving around only at night. However, some species have adapted to life in hot, dry countries, and even semideserts. They survive the heat by estivating (remaining dormant) during the hottest part of the year.

A mass of snails remains dormant over the summer (estivating) on a fence post.

A snail using its radula (tongue) to scrape at a leaf

Radula

Snail "teeth" seen through an electron microscope

FEEDING

Snails and slugs obtain food in all sorts of ways – some "graze" on algae or plants, others harpoon fish with poisonous stings, and several species drill holes though the shells of bivalves. No matter what they eat, most gastropods use a special tongue called a radula to scrape away at their food. The radula is covered with thousands of tiny, hook-shaped teeth that scratch and scoop up matter.

GREAT POND SNAIL

Although it spends all of its time in the water, the great pond snail breathes air. It has a single lung under the widest part of its shell and breathes through a small hole that it can open or close. The snail feeds on carrion or algae scraped from water plants. It is often kept in an aquarium because it removes algae that grow on glass.

Sharply pointed spiral shell

Scientific name: *Lymnaea stagnalis*

Size: Up to 2 in (5 cm) long

Habitat: Ponds, lakes, and slow-flowing streams

Distribution: North America and Europe

Reproduction: Female lays ribbons of jelly-covered eggs on water plants; eggs hatch into miniature snails

Diet: Carrion and algae on surface of water plants

SEA SNAILS

The sea snails make up the largest group of gastropods. Unlike land snails, they often have eyes at the base of their tentacles, and they have gills rather than lungs. Sea snails breathe by drawing water over the gills via a tube called a siphon. The water also passes over a special "scent" organ called the osphradium, which helps carnivorous and scavenging sea snails detect their food. Conches, whelks, and winkles are all types of sea snails.

Barnacles on shell

Common whelk
(*Buccinum undatum*)

Eye

Siphon

Operculum

FLOATING YOUNG

Some gastropods, especially land snails and slugs, are hermaphrodites – they have both male and female reproductive organs. The majority of aquatic species, however, have separate sexes that come together to mate, producing clumps of eggs within protective cases. The eggs typically hatch into tiny snails, but in some species they hatch into floating larvae that can be carried great distances by ocean currents.

The floating larva of a sea snail

CHITONS

Chitons are unusual mollusks that have lived in the Earth's seas for over 500 million years. Although related to the gastropods, they are placed in a class of their own. Like snails and slugs, chitons have a single muscular foot and a rasping tongue. However, they have flat shells made up of eight overlapping plates. If a chiton is pulled from a rock, it can roll into a tight ball to protect itself.

Outside surface of a chiton shell (Chiton marmoratus) showing eight interlocking plates

SEA SLUGS

Despite their unpromising name, sea slugs and their close relatives, the sea hares and bubble shells, are among the most beautiful of all invertebrates. There are more than 2,000 species, ranging in size from tiny creatures that can crawl between grains of sand to giants weighing over 2.2 lb (1 kg). Since they have no protective shells, sea slugs use camouflage or poison to defend themselves. Unlike sea snails, they breathe through gills on their surface. Sea slugs are also known as nudibranchs.

Feathery gills

Clown nudibranch (Chromodoris norrisi)

Tentacle

TOXIC SLUGS

Vivid colors and bold patterns make many sea slugs conspicuous underwater. The bright display is a warning to predators that the slug's body is poisonous or dangerous to touch. Some sea slugs obtain their poisons in an unusual way – they eat sea anemones and "steal" the anemones' stinging cells, incorporating them into their own skin.

Homburg's sea slug
(*Tritonia hombergi*)

Find out more

CORAL REEFS: 72
INVERTEBRATES: 142
MOVEMENT ON LAND: 34
SEASHORES AND TIDEPOOLS: 70

BIVALVES

CLAMS, MUSSELS, AND oysters are all bivalves – so called because they have shells made up of two hinged plates, or valves. Most live in seawater, either on the shore or in the depths of the oceans, but about 15 percent of the 25,000 or more species are found in freshwater. Like snails, slugs, octopuses, and squid, bivalves are part of the large animal group (or phylum) called mollusks. Their bodies are adapted to life spent anchored to one place, or burrowing in mud or sand and filtering food from the silt that surrounds them. Some species are harvested for food or to produce pearls used in jewelry.

Giant cockle
(*Plagiocardium pseudolima*)

West African tellin
(*Tellina madagascariensis*)

Chorus mussel
(*Choromytilus chorus*)

SHELLS

The valves of a bivalve shell are made of calcium minerals embedded in organic "glue." They are joined by an elastic hinge, and sockets or hinge teeth prevent the two halves from slipping apart. To close its shell, the bivalve contracts a pair of adductor muscles that link the valves. Shells vary in size and shape – many are thick and ridged to deter predators, some have spines for gripping loose sand, and others are brightly colored by the food that the bivalve ingests.

BIVALVE ANATOMY

The soft, flat body of a bivalve is protected by the two valves (plates) of the shell. Lining the inner surface of both plates is a thin layer of tissue, called the mantle. This contains cells that secrete hard minerals that make up the shell. The cavity within the mantle contains organs for feeding, breathing, and circulation. There is also a muscular "foot" that protrudes when the shell is open, and which the animal uses for movement and for making burrows. Bivalves have no heads, and there are only a few sense organs, usually on the edges of the mantle.

Shiny lining of shell

Muscular "foot"

Banded carpet shell
(*Venerupis rhomboides*)

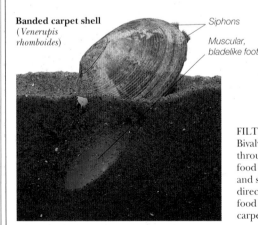

Siphons

Muscular, bladelike foot

Gills absorb oxygen from the water.

A layer of tissue called the mantle lines the shell.

Adductor muscle for closing the shell

Digestive gland takes in food particles.

Great scallop
(*Pecten maximus*)

FILTER FEEDING

Bivalves are mostly filter feeders. They get food, as well as oxygen, through a muscular tube called a siphon. The siphon draws water and food particles through the gills, which are covered in sticky mucus and studded with beating hairs (cilia). Food is trapped in the gills and directed to the animal's mouth. The siphon can be stretched to reach food and water if the animal is buried in mud or sand. The banded carpet shell uses its muscular foot to burrow and anchor it in the mud.

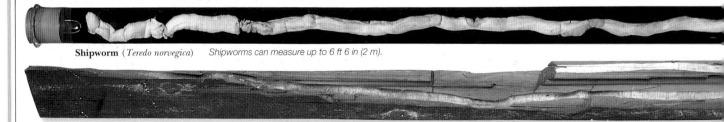

Shipworm (*Teredo norvegica*)   *Shipworms can measure up to 6 ft 6 in (2 m).*

GIANT WITH NO BACKBONE

Bivalves vary enormously in size. The smallest freshwater species are less than 0.08 in (2 mm) across, while the giant clam is one of the largest invertebrates in the world. Living only in the shallow waters of the tropical Pacific Ocean, this clam can measure up to 4 ft 6 in (1.4 m) across, and its thick, defensive shells can weigh up to 882 lb (400 kg). Giant clams live permanently in one spot, anchored by their own weight.

Giant clam
(*Tridacna gigas*)

PEARLS

The shell of a bivalve is secreted by the mantle, and consists of several layers – a thick, watertight outer layer and several inner layers of calcium laid down in thin sheets, called nacre. If a piece of grit works its way into the space between the mantle and the shell of an oyster, it is also covered by nacre and may grow into a pearl. Pearls grow at a rate of about 0.04 in (1 mm) in five years.

Oyster shell with pearl

Mother of pearl

Burrowing technique of razor clam

The razor clam (Ensis sp.) extends its muscular foot into soft mud on the floor of an estuary.

Blood is pumped into the foot to make it expand and grip the walls of the burrow.

Muscles contract, pulling the body and shell down into the mud.

PORTUGUESE OYSTER

Like all oysters, this bivalve uses the left valve of its shell to cement itself to muddy rocks or other oyster shells. The Portuguese oyster is often used in commercial farming because it is easy to rear in warm water and is larger than its relative, the edible oyster.

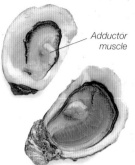

Adductor muscle

Scientific name:	*Crassostrea angulata*
Size:	Shell up to 7 in (18 cm) long
Habitat:	Firm ground in estuaries and creeks
Distribution:	Atlantic, English Channel, North Sea
Reproduction:	Fertilized eggs develop into larvae
Diet:	Planktonic algae

LIFE AT THE BOTTOM

Most bivalves live on the seabed, burrow into sediment, or anchor themselves to rocks. The burrowing species use contractions of the muscular foot to pull them into the sediment where there is greater protection from predators. To feed and breathe, they raise two tubes (siphons) above the sediment. One siphon draws in water and food particles and the other pumps water out. In some burrowing species, these tubes may be up to 3 ft 3 in (1 m) long.

GETTING A GRIP

Instead of burrowing, some bivalves attach themselves to a hard surface, such as a rock or sea wall. Oysters secrete shell material that fuses them to rocks, while mussels produce tough threads to anchor them in place. These bivalves often cluster together, which can cause problems. For example, if many bivalves gather in the same pipe, it may become blocked.

Bivalves on an underwater oil rig

A FAST MOVER

A few bivalves live on the surface of marine sediment and do not dig burrows. Some use their muscular feet to jump and even swim. Queen scallops can swim surprisingly quickly by "clapping" the two valves of their shells together, forcing out a jet of water. Unlike other bivalves, they are very active and need detailed information about their surroundings. Their "eyes" are visible as black dots along the edges of their shells.

Queen scallop
(*Aequipecten opercularis*)

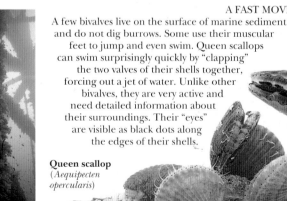

Shipworms (Teredo norvegica) live outside their shells, which are only used for drilling. They line their long burrows with shell material.

Shipworm

Shell of shipworm

Shipworms are adapted to live in wood. They cause serious damage to ships' hulls.

HARD TIMES

For some bivalves, the protection of a burrow in soft mud is not sufficient. These animals drill homes in wood, coral, and even sandstone and limestone rocks. Using their feet as suckers to pull hard against the rock, they scrape their shells on the surface, and may even use chemical secretions to soften the rock. Shipworms burrow into wood – often in the hulls of ships – and eat the sawdust that they produce.

Find out more

INVERTEBRATES: *142*
OCEANS: *68*
SEASHORES AND TIDEPOOLS: *70*
SENSES: *42*

OCTOPUSES AND SQUID

WITH THEIR STREAMLINED, jet-propelled bodies, squid are among the fastest animals in the oceans. Their relatives, the octopuses, are the most intelligent of all invertebrates, with highly developed brains and nervous systems. Amazingly, these fast-swimming hunters are related to such slow-moving animals as slugs and snails. Squid, octopuses, cuttlefish, and nautiluses make up the class of mollusks called cephalopods. There are 600 species, ranging from the 0.8 in (2 cm) long Antarctic squid to the giant squid, which reaches a staggering 59 ft (18 m). Many cephalopods hide in caves or crevices during the day, emerging at night to feed.

SQUID

Squid live at almost every level of the ocean. In the course of evolution, the bulky external shell has been reduced to an internal shell, or "pen," and the mantle – a layer of tissue below the shell in other mollusks – has developed into a muscular jacket over the body. Squid are clever, active creatures, with good eyesight, large brains, and fast reactions.

Two long tentacles

Side fin acts as a stabilizer.

Eight arms

Soft, muscular outer mantle

Common squid
(*Loligo pealeii*)

Eye

Shell, or pen, normally lies in the center of the squid's body.

Body sac

Large eyes help octopus to find its prey.

Eight arms, or tentacles, are joined by webs of skin.

OCEAN HUNTERS

Both octopuses and squid are formidable hunters. They use their armlike tentacles to seize prey such as fish, mollusks, and crabs. They can outswim most marine animals, both to catch their prey and to avoid being caught themselves. Some species of squid can reach speeds of 22 mph (35 kmh), and can leap 13 ft (4 m) out of the water to avoid a predator. When swimming, they face backward and propel themselves along by squirting a jet of water through a funnel called a siphon.

The octopus has a crab inside its jaws.

Arms for swimming, gripping prey, and fighting.

Common octopus
(*Octopus vulgaris*)

Suckers grip rock to pull octopus along.

Powerful, bill-shaped jaws are used to bite off pieces of prey.

Sharp, pointed ends

ARMS AND SUCKERS

An octopus has eight muscular, flexible "arms" with suction caps on the lower surface. They use their arms to grip prey and to hold onto the seafloor. The arms are covered with touch and taste sensors that help the octopus to determine whether its catch is edible. In addition to their eight sucker-studded arms, squid have two longer tentacles. These are used for hunting and can be extended in less than one hundredth of a second to snatch passing prey.

JAWS AND FEEDING

Octopus and squid have sharp, bill-shaped jaws to defend themselves and to cut and tear prey. They also have a toothed tongue, called a radula, that acts like a conveyor belt, drawing food into the mouth. Some species inject their prey with toxic substances produced by their salivary glands.

REPRODUCTION

Before mating, a male squid changes color to attract a female and warn off rivals. The male and female then embrace face to face, in a tangle of arms that can sometimes result in one partner being strangled. The male uses a modified arm to reach into his mantle for a packet of sperm, called a spermatophore. He places this inside the female's mantle, where the sperm fertilize the female's eggs. The eggs are usually laid on the seabed.

Opalescent squid (Loligo opalescens) mating

CHANGING COLOR

Siphon   *Eye*

Cephalopods may be black, red, orange, yellow, blue, green, or violet depending on the species. They can change color almost instantly to startle predators, blend with their surroundings, or signal to other members of their species. Their skin contains pigment-filled cells, or chromatophores, surrounded by rings of muscle. When the chromatophores expand, the skin darkens in color, and when they shrink, it lightens.

Blue rings are pale when octopus is relaxed.

Center of ring turns a dark mustard color.

Rings turn a vibrant blue when the octopus is agitated or feeding.

Bright blue color warns predators that the octopus has a poisonous bite.

Blue-ringed octopus
(Hapalochlaena maculosa)

CUTTLEFISH

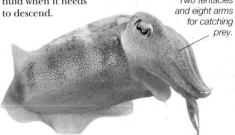

With shorter bodies than squid, cuttlefish are agile but not fast swimmers. They have an internal shell – the cuttlebone – that contains gas-filled spaces. These help keep the animal buoyant, and can be flooded with fluid when it needs to descend.

Two tentacles and eight arms for catching prey.

Scientific name: *Sepia* sp.

Size: Up to 12 in (30 cm) long

Habitat: Shallow waters, where it swims close to the seafloor

Distribution: East Atlantic and the Mediterranean

Reproduction: Lays clusters of grapelike eggs

Diet: Small fish, crustaceans, and mollusks

The squid lights up and shimmers during bioluminescence.

LIGHTING UP

Many cephalopods can produce light – a phenomenon called bioluminescence. They use this light display to communicate with others or to attract prey. The light is produced by a chemical reaction within organs called photophores. The photophores are complex, with lenses to focus the light, shutters to switch the light on and off, and filters to produce colored light. The fire squid (*Lycoteuthis* sp.) can produce flashes of white, blue, yellow, and red light.

INKY DIVERSIONS

Squid and octopuses produce an inky liquid from large sacs connected to their digestive systems. The black or brown ink is made by glands that empty into the sac. When threatened, the cephalopod squirts the contents of the sac through its anus, confusing its attacker. The ink sometimes has a mild numbing effect that helps disorientate the predator. Some deep-sea squid eject luminescent particles.

Giant Pacific octopus (Octopus dofleini) ejecting ink

NAUTILUS AND ITS ANCESTORS

The six species of nautilus are the only cephalopods with external shells. As the nautilus grows, it adds a new chamber to its spiral shell. These chambers are filled with gas and help the nautilus control its buoyancy. The nautilus is thought to be primitive compared to octopuses and squid, and closely resembles fossils of ammonites (cephalopods that became extinct in the Cretaceous period).

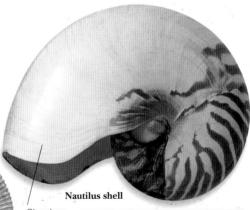

Nautilus shell

Chambers inside the shell contain gas to provide buoyancy.

Ammonite fossil

Find out more

DEFENSE 2: *50*
INVERTEBRATES: *142*
MOVEMENT IN WATER: *38*
OCEANS: *68*

STARFISH AND SEA URCHINS

WITH THEIR DISTINCTIVE spiny skeletons, starfish and sea urchins are perhaps the most familiar marine invertebrates. Both are members of a group of animals known as echinoderms (from the Greek words for "spiny-skinned"). The 6,000 species in this group include other exotic creatures, such as sea cucumbers, brittle stars, sand dollars, and sea lilies. All echinoderms live in the sea and have a unique internal hydraulic system that helps them move, eat, and breathe. Their bodies are usually divided into five equal parts, arranged around a central disk. Most echinoderms have bodies that are protected by chalky plates.

Spiny starfish
(*Marthasterias glacialis*)

Podia
(tube feet)

Oral (lower)
surface

Mouth

Suction disks
at tip of feet

Arm

Aboral
(upper)
surface

NO FRONT OR BACK

Most animals, including humans, have a distinct "head" and "tail" and are more or less bilaterally symmetrical along the length of their bodies. Echinoderms are very different. Their bodies have five symmetrical parts, radiating from a central disk like the spokes of a wheel. They have no head or brain, and without a "front" or "back," can often move in any direction. The mouth is on the underside (oral surface) and the anus is on the upper side (aboral surface).

HYDRAULIC ANIMALS

An echinoderm body contains a hydraulic system of water-filled canals. The canals connect to tubelike "feet" (up to 2,000 in some species) that stick out through tiny perforations in the skeleton on the body's underside. By pumping water into the suckerlike feet, the starfish is able to crawl along the sea floor. The tube feet are also used to take in food and to extract oxygen from the water.

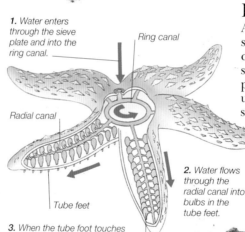

1. Water enters through the sieve plate and into the ring canal.

Ring canal

Radial canal

Tube feet

2. Water flows through the radial canal into bulbs in the tube feet.

3. When the tube foot touches the surface, it contracts and water is forced back into the bulb, pulling the starfish forward.

Bulb

Some starfish have many more than five arms.

Sea star (*Heliaster* sp.)

Sea cucumbers can pull these tentacles back inside for protection.

Sea cucum
(*Stichopus s*

SKIN AND SKELETON

Starfish have a hard internal skeleton made up of thousands of tiny fragments of calcium carbonate (chalk) embedded in a "glue" of connective tissue. The fragments (ossicles) can slide past one another, so although the skeleton is tough, it allows the starfish to move its "arms." Some ossicles are spine-shaped. In most starfish, these spines are fairly blunt, but in others they are painfully sharp. The starfish's skin is stretched over its spiny skeleton.

SEA CUCUMBERS

The hard ossicles in a sea cucumber's skeleton are very small, making its body soft and flexible. Sea cucumbers live on the ocean floor, where they feed by filtering simple life forms from mud and sand. Their tube feet are modified into long, feathery tentacles that surround the mouth. Some species can grow more than 3 ft 3 in (1 m) long.

FEEDING

Most echinoderms live on the sea floor, primarily on sand, mud, or rock. Others, including sea cucumbers and sand dollars, burrow down into the sediment. They have a variety of diets – a few species "graze" on algae and animals encrusted on rocks. Some are scavengers or filter food from the water or sand, others eat live mollusks and crustaceans. Most species feed with the mouth facing down toward the seabed.

Common sea urchin (Echinus esculentus) *grazing on algae*

Starfish about to devour its mussel prey

Common starfish
(*Asterias rubens*)

PRYING APART

Starfish of the genus *Asterias* feed mainly on mollusks. To get at their food, they use their tube feet to pry open a mussel's shell, creating a gap about 0.08 in (2 mm) wide. Then they push their stomachs through their mouths and into the mussel's shell. Starfish can be serious pests, causing damage to commercial oyster beds.

SELF-PROTECTION

Echinoderms are eaten by many marine animals, including fish and spider crabs. Those exposed by the tide also make tasty food for seabirds, which crack open sea urchins by dropping them from a height onto rocks. Many echinoderms, such as the tropical sea urchin (*Diadema*), possess additional defenses in the form of sharp, venomous spines. Starfish and brittle stars, however, deliberately shed the arm that the predator grabs.

Palmer's sea urchin (*Diadema palmeri*)

Sea lily
(*Ptilocrinus pinnatus*)

SEA LILIES

Sea lilies are not plants, but primitive echinoderms. Unlike their relatives, which are free to move around, sea lilies are anchored to the sea floor by a long stalk. Their five feathery arms gather food particles in the water and transfer these particles to the mouth, which, unlike most animals, faces upward. Some biologists believe that echinoderms evolved from ancestors of the sea lily.

If a brittle star's arm snaps off it will grow again.

Central disc

BRITTLE STARS

These creatures are close relatives of the starfish, but have much longer arms attached to a small central disk. They are particularly well adapted to life in rock crevices or on coral reefs, where they scavenge for animals or extract food from the sediment. Tending to hide during the day, they emerge at night to feed in their thousands. They move by making snakelike movements with their arms.

Common black brittle star (*Ophiocomina nigra*)

CROWN OF THORNS STARFISH

This well-armed starfish is protected by rows of long spines. It feeds on coral by protruding its stomach through its mouth onto coral polyps, pouring digestive juices on the polyps and absorbing them. In parts of Australia's Great Barrier Reef, this starfish's population has greatly increased, devastating large areas of coral.

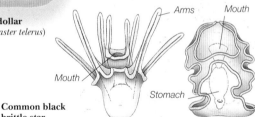

Starfish is protected by poisonous spines

Scientific name: *Acanthaster planci*

Size: About 16 in (41 cm) across

Habitat: Coral reefs

Distribution: Pacific Ocean, Indian Ocean

Reproduction: Sperm and eggs are released into the water; larvae are free-floating

Diet: Coral polyps

SAND DOLLARS

Like sea urchins, sand dollars are echinoderms that have no arms. The tiny mineral particles (ossicles) that make up their skeleton are fused together, making their bodies rigid and inflexible. These animals burrow through sand, propelled by the movement of the tiny spines that cover their surface.

Sand dollar
(*Clypeaster telerus*)

Arms

Mouth

Mouth

Stomach

Brittle star larva

Starfish larva

REPRODUCTION

Echinoderms reproduce by releasing sperm and eggs into the water. Once fertilized, the eggs hatch into larvae that look very different from the adults. Larvae are dispersed by ocean currents with the help of tiny beating hairs (cilia). Echinoderms can also regenerate from fragments of themselves that have broken away (as long as the fragment contains part of the central disk).

Find out more

INVERTEBRATES: *142*
JELLYFISH AND CORALS: *146*
MOVEMENT IN WATER: *38*
OCEANS: *68*

ARTHROPODS

THE ARTHROPODS MAKE UP the largest group in the animal kingdom, accounting for more than 75 percent of all animal species. Insects, millipedes, spiders, mites, and crustaceans are all arthropods and the group also includes the strange-looking horseshoe crabs and sea spiders. They range in size from the microscopic ocean-dwelling copepods to lobsters that reach lengths of more than 29 in (75 cm). All arthropods have an external skeleton (exoskeleton), which covers a segmented body with jointed legs.

Crustaceans

Shrimp

Insects

Red-spotted longhorn beetle

Armored millipede

Arachnids

Crab spider

Chilopods

Woodland centipede

Diplopods

ARTHROPOD EVOLUTION

The bodies of most arthropods are made up of a row of segments. This characteristic has led most scientists to believe that millions of years ago annelid worms with unspecialized segments slowly evolved into insects. Gradually they developed legs, and over the course of evolutionary time, their segments have become fused together to serve specialized functions, such as excretion and reproduction.

Possible evolution from worm to insect

Segmented worm

Eyes and antennae form.

Legs develop.

Segments fuse to form head and mouthparts.

Legs develop joints.

Only six legs remain.

MAJOR GROUPS

The evolution of arthropods stretches back at least 600 million years. Biologists are not sure which species evolved first because the main groups had already appeared by the Cambrian period (570 million years ago) – the earliest period from which fossils survive for identifying different species. Today, five major classes of arthropods are recognized: crustaceans (crabs, shrimps, and their relatives); arachnids (spiders, scorpions, ticks, and mites); insects; chilopods (centipedes); and diplopods (millipedes).

TRILOBITES

One group of arthropods – the trilobites – is known only from fossils. About 500 million years ago these seabed dwellers were very common, with fossils of at least 4,000 species discovered. Most trilobites were about 2 in (5 cm) long, but some reached more than 3 ft 3 in (1 m). Some may have burrowed into the seabed, while others could walk and swim. Many species had large compound eyes. Fossils of their flattened, oval bodies show a primitive arthropod structure with many similar segments.

Large eyes

Thorax with short spines

Eyes

Moderately large tail shield

Fossil of trilobite (*Xystridura*)

Pacific lobster (*Enoplometopus occidentalis*)

The new external skeleton will take several days to harden.

Lobster's old skeleton is discarded.

LIVING IN A BOX

All arthropods have an external skeleton, or cuticle, which is made of a chemical substance called chitin. In crustaceans, this is strengthened by calcium carbonate, while in many insects and arachnids it is "tanned" – molecules of chitin are bonded together for extra strength. The cuticle protects soft tissues, provides attachment points for muscles, and reduces the amount of water that evaporates from the body. As the animal grows, the cuticle becomes tight and must be replaced. Lobsters grow throughout their adult lives and regularly need to molt their hard external skeletons.

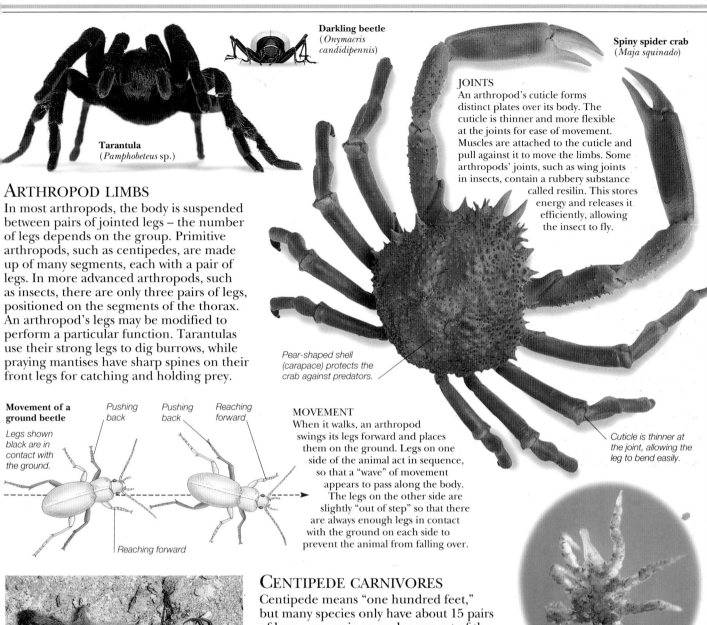

Tarantula
(*Pamphobeteus* sp.)

Darkling beetle
(*Onymacris candidipennis*)

Spiny spider crab
(*Maja squinado*)

ARTHROPOD LIMBS

In most arthropods, the body is suspended between pairs of jointed legs – the number of legs depends on the group. Primitive arthropods, such as centipedes, are made up of many segments, each with a pair of legs. In more advanced arthropods, such as insects, there are only three pairs of legs, positioned on the segments of the thorax. An arthropod's legs may be modified to perform a particular function. Tarantulas use their strong legs to dig burrows, while praying mantises have sharp spines on their front legs for catching and holding prey.

JOINTS

An arthropod's cuticle forms distinct plates over its body. The cuticle is thinner and more flexible at the joints for ease of movement. Muscles are attached to the cuticle and pull against it to move the limbs. Some arthropods' joints, such as wing joints in insects, contain a rubbery substance called resilin. This stores energy and releases it efficiently, allowing the insect to fly.

Pear-shaped shell (carapace) protects the crab against predators.

Cuticle is thinner at the joint, allowing the leg to bend easily.

Movement of a ground beetle

Legs shown black are in contact with the ground.

Pushing back

Pushing back

Reaching forward

Reaching forward

MOVEMENT

When it walks, an arthropod swings its legs forward and places them on the ground. Legs on one side of the animal act in sequence, so that a "wave" of movement appears to pass along the body. The legs on the other side are slightly "out of step" so that there are always enough legs in contact with the ground on each side to prevent the animal from falling over.

CENTIPEDE CARNIVORES

Centipede means "one hundred feet," but many species only have about 15 pairs of legs – one pair on each segment of the body. These arthropods are active, fast-running carnivores that feed mostly on insects. Some tropical species grow to lengths of 12 in (30 cm), and may feed on prey as large as frogs and mice. Centipedes have poisonous, fanglike claws just behind the mouth, which are used to seize and paralyze their prey.

Anemone sea spider
(*Pycnogonum littorale*)

Giant centipede (Scolopendra gigantea) eating a mouse

SEA SPIDERS

Despite having legs that may be 15 times the length of their bodies, sea spiders move very slowly, feeding on animals such as sponges. They range in size from a fraction of an inch to 4 in (10 cm) across. Sea spiders have an unusual anatomy. They do not have any specialized organs for breathing or excretion, and their intestines and reproductive organs are packed inside their legs.

POISON PILL

Some millipedes have as many as 300 legs, which give them great pushing power as they bulldoze through soil and leaf litter. They feed mainly on plants, although some are carnivores. Most millipedes are slow moving and have special defenses against predators. Some produce poisons such as cyanide and quinone from glands on their segments, while others coil into tight balls, presenting potential predators with the thick armor of their upper cuticles.

Fragile body parts are tucked away as the millipede rolls up.

Pill millipede
(*Glomeris marginata*)

Find out more

EVOLUTION: *14*
INSECTS: *162*
INVERTEBRATES: *142*
WORMS: *144*

CRUSTACEANS

IT IS EASY TO SEE HOW crustaceans, such as crabs and lobsters, got their name. Their bodies are enclosed by hard, chalky plates that seem to cover them like a crust. Crustaceans belong to a group of animals called arthropods, which also includes insects and spiders. Like other arthropods, crustaceans are protected by their external skeleton and move about with jointed legs. There are nearly 40,000 species of crustaceans. Although a few species live on land, the majority of crustaceans live in fresh water or the sea. The smallest are not much bigger than a period, but the largest are more than 1 m (3 ft 3 in) across.

ANATOMY OF A CRUSTACEAN

Crustaceans vary a great deal in size and shape, but they have certain features in common. All have an external skeleton, which they periodically shed as they grow. They also have two pairs of antennae and often have compound eyes. Crustaceans usually breathe through gills at the base of their legs. Some have special legs for swimming. Crabs and lobsters have walking legs and a front pair that end in powerful pincers.

Long antenna

Compound eye

Short antenna

Pincer for handling food

Tail fan for rapid swimming

Rigid body case (exoskeleton)

European lobster (*Homarus gammarus*)

Jointed leg

Life-cycle of a crab

1. A female crab carries a mass of eggs under her body.

2. This egg is ready to hatch.

4. The megalopa settles on the sea floor to mature.

Claw

3. The zoea lives floating in the sea.

Eye

CRUSTACEAN LIFE CYCLES

Like many insects, crustaceans start life as eggs and change shape completely as they grow up. A female crab guards her eggs carefully until they hatch. The eggs produce tiny floating larvae, called zoea, which drift away in the water. These slowly change into megalopa larvae, which eventually settle on the seabed. These larvae slowly take on the adult shape and make their way toward shallow water and the shore.

Land hermit crab (Coenobita sp.) feeding on dead fish

FEEDING TECHNIQUES

Crustaceans feed in two quite different ways. Most crabs and lobsters clamber over the seabed or the shore and use their claws to pick up pieces of food or smash open the shells of other animals. They often find their food by its smell. Instead of searching for things to eat, swimming crustaceans usually wait for it to drift by. They use their legs or antennae as tiny filters to sift particles of food from the water around them.

Wood lice (*Armadillidium* sp.)

Wood lice usually live in damp, dark habitats to avoid drying out.

LIVING ON LAND

Land is a hostile environment for most crustaceans. Unlike other arthropods, their bodies do not have a waxy surface to prevent water loss. Some crabs survive on land, but most have to return to water to breed. The most successful land crustaceans are wood lice. They live in damp habitats and can breed out of water by using a special pouch that holds their eggs.

CLEANING UP

Some crustaceans get their food by teaming up with other animals. The cleaner shrimp (*Lysmata amboinesis*) uses its slender pincers to pick dead skin and parasites – which it eats – from the skin of fish. Fish recognize the shrimp's colors and often line up to be cleaned.

A cleaner shrimp attends to one of its "customers."

MOLLUSK LOOK-ALIKES

On many shores, millions of barnacles cover the rocks. Naturalists once thought that these animals were mollusks, but they are actually crustaceans shaped for a special way of life. A barnacle starts life as a tiny larva that drifts through the sea until it touches a rock. It then fastens itself in place and grows a case. It spends the rest of its life inside its case, sifting food from the water.

Northern rock barnacles (Balanus balanoides) on coastal rocks

LIFE IN A CASE

Some barnacles have fleshy stalks, but most are fastened directly to the rock. Their cases are made of separate plates and some of the plates hinge together to form a lid. At low tide, the barnacle keeps the lid closed, but at high tide it opens it to feed. The barnacle sweeps its feathery legs through the water and traps particles of food that drift past.

Legs withdrawn

Legs extended to catch food

Mouth

KRILL

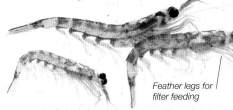

These small, shrimplike animals are a major source of food for many sea animals, such as whales. Krill are most common in the nutrient-rich waters of the Antarctic Ocean. Here, they form vast swarms containing up to 1,700 adults per cubic foot (0.3 cubic meter) of water. Blue whales feeding on the swarms can eat up to 5,500 lb (2,500 kg) of krill a day.

Feather legs for filter feeding

Scientific name: *Euphasia superba*

Size: 2.4 in (60 mm) long

Habitat: Oceans, usually near the surface

Distribution: Antarctic Ocean

Reproduction: Females release 2,000–3,000 eggs into the water each year; larvae (nauplii) hatch out

Diet: Plankton filtered from the water by feathery legs

PLANKTONIC CRUSTACEANS

In fresh water and the seas, tiny crustaceans form a vast but hidden realm of animal life. Most are just a fraction of an inch and make up part of the plankton – a mass of tiny floating organisms near the sea surface. Among them are copepods. These crustaceans feed on microscopic algae and are probably the most common animals on Earth.

The decorator crab camouflages its body with seaweed and animals from the seabed.

Claw

Eye

Decorator crab
(*Camposcia retusa*)

Crab

Copepod

Shrimp

Crab larva

CRAB CAMOUFLAGE

Most crabs use their pincers if they are threatened, but some have other ways of avoiding attack. The decorator crab covers itself with seaweed and small marine animals such as sponges. Held in place by tiny hooks, these living decorations grow to form a cover that camouflages their owner. Other crabs hold shells above them to hide, and some place stinging sea anemones on their claws.

FINDING A HOME

Hermit crabs have soft abdomens, which makes them vulnerable to attack. They protect themselves by living in seashells, where their soft body parts are safe. As the crab grows, it has to search for a bigger shell. Once found, the crab cautiously puts a pincer inside to see if it is empty. Suitable shells are hard to find, and hermit crabs fight for the chance to own them.

Hermit crab moving home

A hermit crab (Pagurus sp.) prepares to leave its old home.

Outside the shell, the crab is vulnerable to predators.

The crab checks the size of a glass model shell.

It curls into the shell, leaving its antennae sticking out.

Find out more

ANIMAL HOMES: *58*
ARTHROPODS: *156*
HOW LIVING THINGS WORK: *18*
OCEANS: *68*

SPIDERS, SCORPIONS, AND MITES

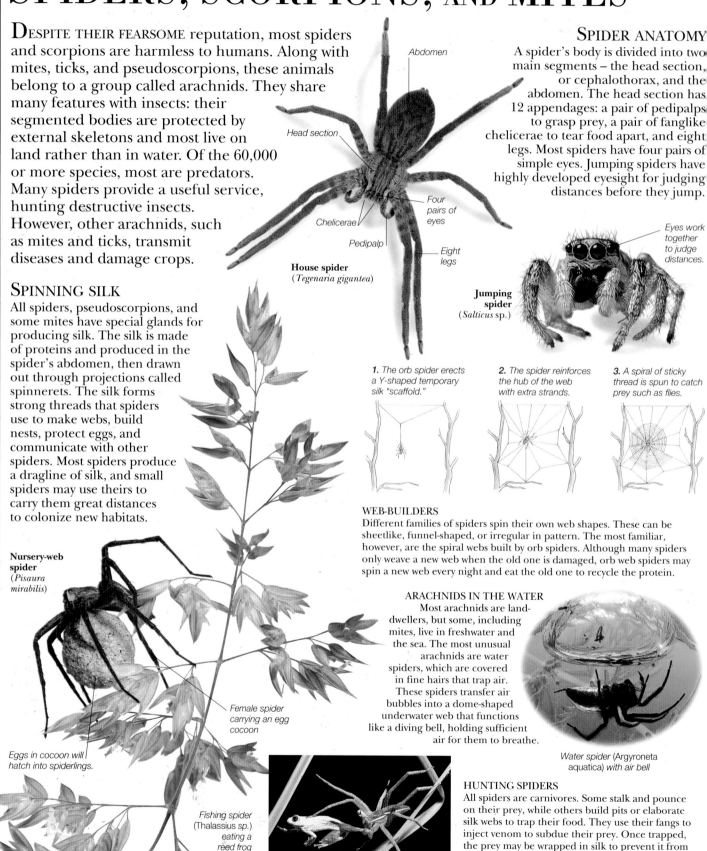

DESPITE THEIR FEARSOME reputation, most spiders and scorpions are harmless to humans. Along with mites, ticks, and pseudoscorpions, these animals belong to a group called arachnids. They share many features with insects: their segmented bodies are protected by external skeletons and most live on land rather than in water. Of the 60,000 or more species, most are predators. Many spiders provide a useful service, hunting destructive insects. However, other arachnids, such as mites and ticks, transmit diseases and damage crops.

Abdomen

Head section

Chelicerae

Pedipalp

Four pairs of eyes

Eight legs

House spider
(*Tegenaria gigantea*)

SPIDER ANATOMY

A spider's body is divided into two main segments – the head section, or cephalothorax, and the abdomen. The head section has 12 appendages: a pair of pedipalps to grasp prey, a pair of fanglike chelicerae to tear food apart, and eight legs. Most spiders have four pairs of simple eyes. Jumping spiders have highly developed eyesight for judging distances before they jump.

Eyes work together to judge distances.

Jumping spider
(*Salticus* sp.)

SPINNING SILK

All spiders, pseudoscorpions, and some mites have special glands for producing silk. The silk is made of proteins and produced in the spider's abdomen, then drawn out through projections called spinnerets. The silk forms strong threads that spiders use to make webs, build nests, protect eggs, and communicate with other spiders. Most spiders produce a dragline of silk, and small spiders may use theirs to carry them great distances to colonize new habitats.

1. The orb spider erects a Y-shaped temporary silk "scaffold."

2. The spider reinforces the hub of the web with extra strands.

3. A spiral of sticky thread is spun to catch prey such as flies.

WEB-BUILDERS

Different families of spiders spin their own web shapes. These can be sheetlike, funnel-shaped, or irregular in pattern. The most familiar, however, are the spiral webs built by orb spiders. Although many spiders only weave a new web when the old one is damaged, orb web spiders may spin a new web every night and eat the old one to recycle the protein.

Nursery-web spider
(*Pisaura mirabilis*)

ARACHNIDS IN THE WATER

Most arachnids are land-dwellers, but some, including mites, live in freshwater and the sea. The most unusual arachnids are water spiders, which are covered in fine hairs that trap air. These spiders transfer air bubbles into a dome-shaped underwater web that functions like a diving bell, holding sufficient air for them to breathe.

Female spider carrying an egg cocoon

Eggs in cocoon will hatch into spiderlings.

Water spider (Argyroneta aquatica) with air bell

HUNTING SPIDERS

All spiders are carnivores. Some stalk and pounce on their prey, while others build pits or elaborate silk webs to trap their food. They use their fangs to inject venom to subdue their prey. Once trapped, the prey may be wrapped in silk to prevent it from escaping before the spider begins to digest it with juices from its gut. Most spiders feed on other arthropods, but some – such as the fishing spider – can catch small vertebrates, including fish and frogs.

Fishing spider (Thalassius sp.) eating a reed frog

MITES AND TICKS

Mites and ticks are usually smaller than spiders, with many species less than 0.04 in (1 mm) long. They have eight legs and their bodies are fused into a single segment. Vast numbers of mites live in soil and leaf litter and account for about 10 percent of all invertebrates found there. They thrive in many freshwater and land habitats, and also attach themselves to animals, where many live as parasites.

Scanning electron micrograph showing the whole animal

Dust mite (*Dermatophagoides pteronyssinus*)

Three-host tick (*Ixodes* sp.)

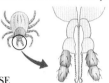

Close-up of mouthparts as tick searches for a place to feed on an animal's skin.

Tick makes a wound in animal's skin and inserts its feeding tube to suck the blood.

MINIATURE UNIVERSE

The tiny size of mites allows them to invade the smallest of microhabitats. Some mites ride on the backs of insects, while others live on human eyelashes. Because of this huge diversity of habitats and their small size, it is likely that many mite species have not yet been discovered. Ticks feed by sucking the blood of animals such as cows, goats, and sheep.

Tail is jointed so that it can bend.

Cross section of tail showing venom gland

Desert scorpion (*Androctonus amoreuxi*)

SCORPIONS

Scorpions are large arachnids that live in warmer regions, where they feed mainly on other arthropods. Some grow to lengths of 6 in (15 cm) or more, excluding their pincers, which are highly developed pedipalps. Their bodies have many segments, the last of which ends in a sting used for self-defense and to kill prey held firm in the pincers. Scorpions are nocturnal and use the comblike sensory organs on their undersides to detect the vibrations of their prey.

Legs used as feelers

Tailless whip scorpion (*Amblypygi* sp.)

WHIP SCORPIONS

In addition to scorpions, spiders, and mites, arachnids include some less familiar members. Whip spiders have wide bodies carried on long, spindly legs, and tend to run sideways when hunting their insect prey. Vinegarones are tropical animals with huge pincerlike pedipalps. They walk on just six of their eight legs, using the first, thinner pair to feel their way around.

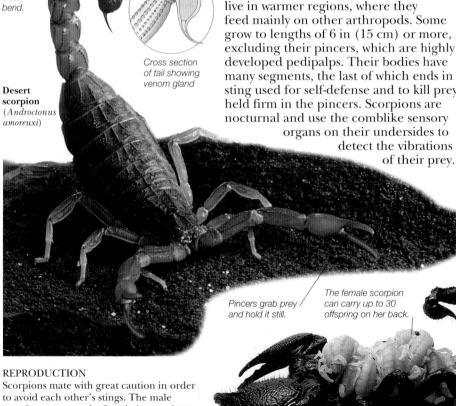

Pincers grab prey and hold it still.

The female scorpion can carry up to 30 offspring on her back.

REPRODUCTION

Scorpions mate with great caution in order to avoid each other's stings. The male transfers sperm to the female in a package called a spermatophore. Unusually for arthropods, the young are born live. In some species, the young scorpions are carried on the female's back for about two weeks until they are strong enough to fend for themselves.

Imperial scorpion (*Pandinus* sp.)

Find out more

ARTHROPODS: *156*
INSECTS: *162*
INVERTEBRATES: *142*
PESTS AND WEEDS: *98*

INSECTS

INSECTS COLONIZE ALMOST every imaginable habitat, and are the most numerous and diverse animals on Earth. Scientists have so far named about a million insect species, and some believe that there may be 10 million more species waiting to be identified. Many insects have complex life cycles and go through several stages of growth before they become adults. Some insects undergo a dramatic change called complete metamorphosis. Others go through a gradual transformation called incomplete metamorphosis.

Hot-springs flies laying eggs

INSECTS EVERYWHERE
Insects are found in almost every habitat, except the open sea. Land and air are the most common habitats, but many species live among vegetation or beneath the soil. One of the strangest insect habitats is that of the hot-springs fly (*Ephydra bruesi*). This fly lays its eggs in salty water around hot springs in the Yellowstone National Park, Wyoming.

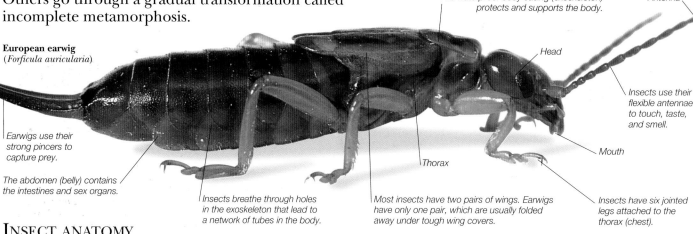

The waterproof body casing (exoskeleton) protects and supports the body.

Antenna

Head

European earwig
(*Forficula auricularia*)

Insects use their flexible antennae to touch, taste, and smell.

Earwigs use their strong pincers to capture prey.

Mouth

Thorax

The abdomen (belly) contains the intestines and sex organs.

Insects breathe through holes in the exoskeleton that lead to a network of tubes in the body.

Most insects have two pairs of wings. Earwigs have only one pair, which are usually folded away under tough wing covers.

Insects have six jointed legs attached to the thorax (chest).

INSECT ANATOMY
Insects are air-breathing animals that have six jointed legs and a hard skeleton (exoskeleton) outside the body. The body is divided into three parts: a head, thorax (chest), and abdomen (belly). The head has a single pair of antennae (feelers) and a mouth specialized for a particular diet. The thorax bears the legs and wings. The abdomen contains the intestines and reproductive organs. Insects belong to a group called the arthropods, which also includes spiders, centipedes, and crabs.

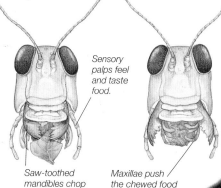

Mouthparts of a locust

Sensory palps feel and taste food.

Saw-toothed mandibles chop up leaves.

Maxillae push the chewed food into the mouth.

ADAPTABLE FEEDERS
Insects have evolved incredibly diverse mouthparts to suit their particular diet. Locusts chew leaves with a pair of large jaws called mandibles. They use hairy feelers (palps) to taste the food, and a second pair of jaws (maxillae) to push the food into the mouth. Other insects have special mouthparts for stabbing into food or sucking up liquids.

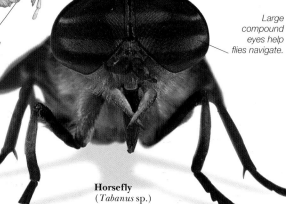

Large compound eyes help flies navigate.

Horsefly
(*Tabanus* sp.)

An ant stumbles into a pit made by an ant lion larva.

BRAIN POWER
The insect brain is a complex cluster of nerve cells that controls the insect's behavior. Although tiny, it can generate surprisingly complex behavior. An ant lion larva, for example, instinctively knows how to dig a small, conical pit in sand, and then hide at the bottom. If an ant stumbles into the pit, the ant lion flicks sand at it so that the ant falls down farther, toward its captor's waiting jaws.

The ant lion larva waits in its trap.

INSECT SENSES
The main insect sensory organs are the antennae, the eyes, and sensory bristles on the body. Insects use their antennae to sense the shape and texture of objects and to detect scents and tastes. The large eyes are made of hundreds of separate units, each with its own lens. Together, these produce a simple picture of nearby objects. Insects can see colors invisible to humans, and their eyes are very sensitive to rapid movement.

REPRODUCTION

Many invertebrates, such as crustaceans, reproduce by releasing their sperm and eggs into water. Fertilization only occurs if these sex cells meet by chance. Insects, however, practice internal fertilization – the male puts his sperm directly into the female's abdomen, where the eggs are fertilized. Some insects choose their mates very carefully. Female hangingflies, for example, mate only with males that bring them a gift of food.

Hangingflies (Harpobittacus sp.) mate while the female eats a fly brought by the male.

Ladybug life cycle

1. An adult 7-spot ladybug (Coccinella septempunctata)

2. Ladybugs lay groups of eggs on leaves.

6. A new adult (at first yellow) emerges after a week.

3. After a week, the larvae hatch.

Metamorphosis takes place inside the pupa.

5. A month after hatching, the larva forms a dormant pupa.

4. The wingless larva preys on other insects, such as aphids.

INCOMPLETE METAMORPHOSIS

Some insects, including damselflies, grow by a process called incomplete metamorphosis. The eggs hatch out into miniature versions of the adult (nymphs), which often have no wings. In order to grow, a nymph must shed the hard skin (exoskeleton) that encases its body. In some species, nymphs shed and regrow their skin (molt) up to 20 times before becoming adults.

1. Damselfly nymphs climb out of the pond for their final molt.

2. The old skin splits and the adult pulls itself out.

3. Over a couple of hours, the wings fill with blood and expand.

4. Several days later, the damselfly has developed its brilliant adult colors.

COMPLETE METAMORPHOSIS

The life cycle of many insects involves a process called metamorphosis. The egg hatches into a larva, which looks very different from the adult and has no wings. When the larva has grown large, it stops moving and produces a tough coat that forms a pupa. The pupa then stays dormant for several days or weeks. Inside, its body tissues are broken down and then completely rebuilt to form an adult insect.

Claw

Silverfish are considered primitive because they have no wings.

Silverfish
(*Lepisma saccharina*)

PRIMITIVE AND ADVANCED

Biologists call some insect species "primitive" because they have changed little in certain ways since the first insects evolved. Insects are usually considered to be primitive if they are wingless, if they cannot fold their wings over their bodies, or if they do not undergo full metamorphosis. A "primitive" insect is not inferior to an "advanced" insect – it may be just as well adapted to survive.

Long antenna

South American longhorn beetle
(*Titanus giganteus*)

BEYOND COUNTING

Insects sometimes mass together in vast numbers. In Africa, a swarm of desert locusts may contain up to 30 billion individuals. African driver ants form swarms with hundreds of thousands of blind soldiers and workers. Following scent trails laid by scouts, the ants march through the undergrowth, hunting any small animals in their path.

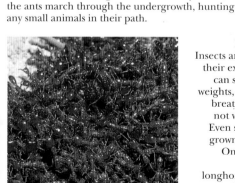

Swarm of African driver ants (Dorylus nigricans)

INSECT GIANT

Insects are small because their external skeletons can support only light weights, and because their breathing systems would not work in large bodies. Even so, some species have grown to giant proportions. One of the largest insects is the South American longhorn beetle, which grows up to 6 in (15 cm) long. The longest is the stick insect *Pharnacia kirbyi*, which can grow to 14 in (36 cm) long, although it is very thin.

South American longhorn beetle shown in scale with ladybug

Find out more

ARTHROPODS: *156*
BEES AND WASPS: *180*
GROWTH AND DEVELOPMENT: *32*
INVERTEBRATES: *142*

COCKROACHES, FLEAS, AND LICE

ALTHOUGH COCKROACHES, fleas and lice are not related, they are commonly reviled as human and animal pests. Cockroaches are renowned for infesting human homes, where they thrive in the artificial warmth and feast on leftover scraps of food. Fleas and lice are parasites that live on the bodies of mammals and birds: they irritate the skin and can weaken their hosts as they suck their blood. By far the most serious damage, however, is caused by the fact that these insects spread fatal diseases, such as typhus and the bubonic plague.

The fossil of the cockroach Archimylacris dates back 300 million years to the Pennsylvanian period.

Anus

BORN SURVIVORS
Cockroaches are among the most adaptable of all insects, and can survive in almost any environment. Their simple chewing mouthparts enable them to feed on a wide range of foods including plant and animal remains. Cockroaches have existed for 340 million years, in a more or less unchanged form, making them the oldest surviving winged insects.

COCKROACHES AT HOME
Cockroaches evolved long before humans, but some species have adapted well to living in homes. They eat almost anything, including kitchen scraps and droppings. Mostly active at night, cockroaches are often difficult to spot. They have flattened bodies that allow them to squeeze into crevices if they are disturbed. To alert them to danger, cockroaches have appendages on their abdomens called cerci. Hairs on the cerci detect even the tiniest vibrations, so the insects can run off on their long legs.

Long, sensitive antennae help the cockroach to feel its way in the dark.

Parchment-like forewings cover delicate hind wings.

Flattened, oval body

American cockroach
(*Periplaneta americana*)

AWAY FROM HOME
The vast majority of cockroach species are not human pests, but live as scavengers in leaf litter, under the bark of trees, and in vegetation. Some, including *Cryptocercus*, are unusual because they can digest wood. Termites are the only other insects that can do this, and experts think that termites evolved from cockroachlike ancestors.

Australian mountain cockroach
(*Polyzosteria viridissima*)

Fertilized female American cockroach

The hard egg purse contains about 18 eggs.

Short, reduced antennae

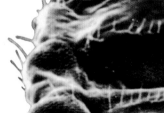

FAST BREEDER
One of the reasons for the success of cockroaches is their ability to breed quickly. A female American cockroach can live for up to two years, during which she may lay about 1,000 eggs in hard protective capsules, known as egg purses. The eggs hatch after about 45 days, and the nymphs that emerge live for about one year before reaching maturity.

FLEA LIFE
Fleas spend their lives on the bodies of warm-blooded animals, such as birds and mammals. Only a few of these animals – mainly primates and aquatic mammals – are untroubled by these pests. Fleas thrive in a "forest" of fur, where they can feed undetected on the blood of their hosts. Their body parts are covered with backward-pointing bristles to keep them from falling off their host while they move around.

Hind legs store energy in resilin (a rubberlike substance).

Backward-pointing bristles

Rat flea
(*Xenopsylla cheopis*)

1. Like a stretched elastic band, energy is stored in the resilin in the flea's hind legs.

2. When the flea jumps, the resilin "twangs" back with a release of energy.

3. The power in the hind legs produces a huge leap.

FLYING WITH THEIR LEGS
Many species of fleas are capable of jumping long distances to escape danger or to move from one host to another. A flea that is 0.1 in (2–3 mm) long can jump 3 ft 3 in (1 m) in 0.002 seconds with a degree of acceleration of about 200 gravities. A human, by comparison, cannot survive acceleration of more than 20 gravities.

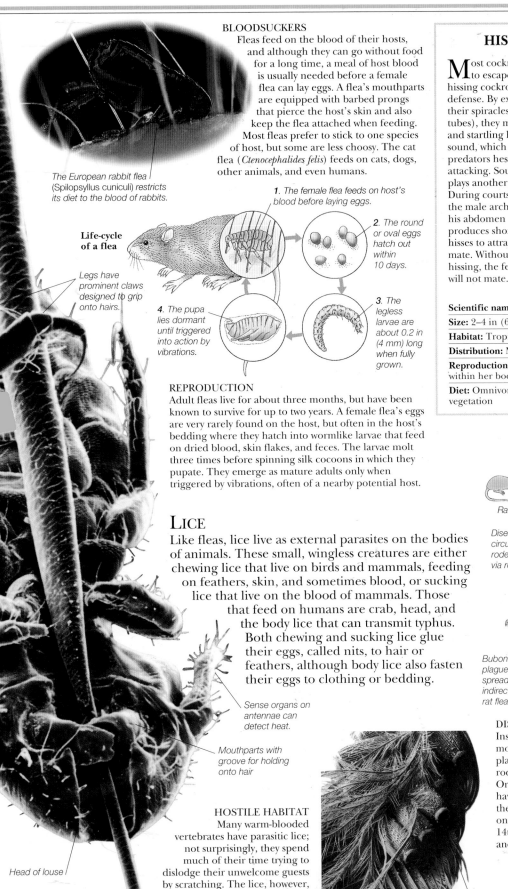

BLOODSUCKERS

Fleas feed on the blood of their hosts, and although they can go without food for a long time, a meal of host blood is usually needed before a female flea can lay eggs. A flea's mouthparts are equipped with barbed prongs that pierce the host's skin and also keep the flea attached when feeding. Most fleas prefer to stick to one species of host, but some are less choosy. The cat flea (*Ctenocephalides felis*) feeds on cats, dogs, other animals, and even humans.

The European rabbit flea (Spilopsyllus cuniculi) restricts its diet to the blood of rabbits.

Life-cycle of a flea

Legs have prominent claws designed to grip onto hairs.

1. The female flea feeds on host's blood before laying eggs.

2. The round or oval eggs hatch out within 10 days.

4. The pupa lies dormant until triggered into action by vibrations.

3. The legless larvae are about 0.2 in (4 mm) long when fully grown.

REPRODUCTION

Adult fleas live for about three months, but have been known to survive for up to two years. A female flea's eggs are very rarely found on the host, but often in the host's bedding where they hatch into wormlike larvae that feed on dried blood, skin flakes, and feces. The larvae molt three times before spinning silk cocoons in which they pupate. They emerge as mature adults only when triggered by vibrations, often of a nearby potential host.

LICE

Like fleas, lice live as external parasites on the bodies of animals. These small, wingless creatures are either chewing lice that live on birds and mammals, feeding on feathers, skin, and sometimes blood, or sucking lice that live on the blood of mammals. Those that feed on humans are crab, head, and the body lice that can transmit typhus. Both chewing and sucking lice glue their eggs, called nits, to hair or feathers, although body lice also fasten their eggs to clothing or bedding.

Sense organs on antennae can detect heat.

Mouthparts with groove for holding onto hair

Head of louse

Louse (*Damalinia meyeri*) found on roe deer

HOSTILE HABITAT

Many warm-blooded vertebrates have parasitic lice; not surprisingly, they spend much of their time trying to dislodge their unwelcome guests by scratching. The lice, however, hold on by means of claws and mouthparts. Many species found on birds live on the head or neck – parts the bird cannot reach with its bill.

HISSING COCKROACH

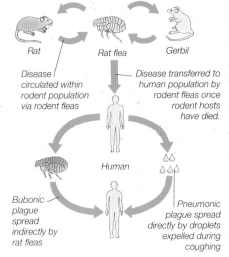

Most cockroaches rely on speed to escape their enemies, but hissing cockroaches have another defense. By expelling air through their spiracles (breathing tubes), they make a loud and startling hissing sound, which makes predators hesitate before attacking. Sound also plays another role. During courtship, the male arches his abdomen and produces short hisses to attract a mate. Without the hissing, the female will not mate.

Scientific name: *Gromphadorhina portentosa*

Size: 2–4 in (6–9 cm)

Habitat: Tropical forest

Distribution: Madagascar

Reproduction: Female produce eggs which hatch within her body

Diet: Omnivorous – small animals as well as vegetation

How fleas spread disease

Rat

Rat flea

Gerbil

Disease circulated within rodent population via rodent fleas

Disease transferred to human population by rodent fleas once rodent hosts have died.

Human

Bubonic plague spread indirectly by rat fleas

Pneumonic plague spread directly by droplets expelled during coughing

DISEASE CARRIERS

Insects carry numerous human diseases, the most destructive of which is the bubonic plague – a bacterial infection transmitted to rodents and indirectly to humans, by the Oriental rat flea (*Xenopsylla cheopis*). There have been several epidemics of the plague, the largest of which destroyed an estimated one-quarter of Europe's population in the 14th century. The plague destroys its rat and flea hosts – as well as killing humans.

Louse eggs (nits) are glued to the bird's feathers.

Find out more

GRASSHOPPERS AND CRICKETS

DESPITE THEIR RELATIVELY large size and distinctive appearance, grasshoppers and crickets are more likely to be heard than seen. Although well camouflaged, they often betray their presence by loud chirping "songs." The 20,000 or so species of grasshopper and cricket make up the order Orthoptera (from the Greek words for "straight wings"). Orthopterans are common worldwide, especially in the Tropics. In addition to the familiar species that live and feed on vegetation, the group includes wingless cave-dwellers, species that burrow in soil, aquatic forms, and even a few carnivorous predators.

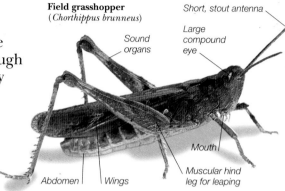

Field grasshopper
(*Chorthippus brunneus*)

Sound organs

Short, stout antenna

Large compound eye

Mouth

Muscular hind leg for leaping

Abdomen

Wings

GRASSHOPPERS

Grasshoppers have large eyes to watch out for predators, and powerful hind legs to leap away if disturbed. They feed on leaves, using their sideways-moving jaws to cut and chew. Many species are camouflaged to look like vegetation, but tropical grasshoppers are often poisonous and brightly colored to warn off predators.

Peg

Close-up of pegs on a grasshopper's leg

SOUND SYSTEMS

Grasshoppers live concealed in vegetation, so they rely on sound to communicate. Males use different "songs" to attract females, and to warn other males to keep away. They sing by scraping tiny pegs on the hindleg against stiff veins on the wing. Crickets sing by rubbing their forewings together.

Long antenna

Oak bush cricket
(*Meconema thalassinum*)

Desert locust
(*Schistocerca* sp.)

CRICKETS

Like grasshoppers, crickets have long hind legs for jumping, and chewing mouthparts for eating leaves. They are mostly active at night, and use long, hairlike antennae to feel their way in the dark. While grasshoppers are herbivores, crickets sometimes eat other animals as well as plants. Many females have long, pointed ovipositors (egg-laying tubes). When a female lays her eggs, she uses the tip of her ovipositor to stab a tiny hole for each egg in a plant or in soil.

Ovipositor

Immature acorn

Front legs are tucked in to make the body streamlined.

2. The hindlegs extend to push the locust into the air.

1. With its hindlegs folded, this desert locust is ready to leap.

HEARING LEGS

Grasshoppers and crickets have keen hearing to listen to the songs of potential mates or rivals, and to detect approaching predators. The "ear" of a grasshopper or cricket consists of a thin membrane attached to sensitive receptors. In grasshoppers, the ears are located on the abdomen, but crickets have ears on the knees of their front legs.

Magnified view of a cricket's "ear" on its front leg

TAKING FLIGHT

Like most insects, grasshoppers and crickets have two pairs of wings (although some species are flightless). When the insect is resting, tough forewings protect the delicate hindwings folded beneath like a fan. The hindwings may be brightly colored to provide a flash of color when the insect leaps into the air – this display helps to confuse predators. Some grasshoppers can close their wings in mid-flight and dive to the ground in order to escape their enemies.

LIFE CYCLE

Grasshoppers and crickets usually produce just one new generation a year. After mating, the female lays small clusters of eggs in the soil or vegetation. Some species produce a special foam to protect the eggs. When they hatch, the young (nymphs) look like miniature adults. They shed their skin between five and 15 times before reaching maturity.

Mating rainforest grasshoppers (Rhopsotettix consummatus)

3. Wings open and flap to propel the locust farther.

Mole cricket (Gryllotalpa gryllotalpa) *digging a burrow*

UNDERGROUND, OVERGROUND

Some grasshoppers and crickets have unusual habitats and diets. Some species live in ants' nests or caves, while others, such as the slender groundhopper (*Tetrix subulatua*), can swim underwater. The mole cricket lives underground, using its shovel-shaped front legs to dig tunnels in the soil. It feeds on beetle larvae, other invertebrates, and roots.

TREE WETA

Wetas are giant crickets found only in New Zealand. The tree weta takes shelter in tree holes made by beetles or moths during the day, and emerges to feed only at night. Its uses its powerful jaws to make the holes big enough for its large body. Males are aggressive, raising their heavily spined hind legs when threatened. Wetas are long-lived insects – some can survive for five years.

Spined hind leg

Scientific name:	*Hemideina thoracica*
Size:	Around 4 in (10 cm)
Habitat:	Holes bored in trees
Distribution:	New Zealand
Reproduction:	Males look after a number of females and young. Eggs are laid on or near vegetation.
Diet:	Omnivorous

LIVING STICKS

Grasshoppers and crickets are masters of disguise. Many resemble leaves, and some mimic stones or even lichen. The most spectacular impostors, however, are the stick grasshoppers, which not only look like twigs, but also sway gently as though caught in a light breeze. Stick grasshoppers look similar to true stick insects (phasmids), but they have large, muscular hind legs like other orthopterans.

Muscular hind legs

South American stick grasshopper (*Microcoema camposi*)

Malaysian stick insect (*Lonchodes brevipes*)

LOCUSTS

Locusts are grasshoppers that have a well-earned reputation as crop pests. They are usually harmless, solitary creatures that live well camouflaged in dry places, such as deserts. Only when unusually heavy rains cause a flush of plant growth do they begin to form groups, and then swarms, to take advantage of the food glut. Young locusts are called hoppers, and are unable to fly until they grow into adults. They change color when they band together, turning bright yellow-orange and black.

Hoppers have undeveloped wings and cannot fly.

Desert locust (*Schistocerca gregaria*)

CROP PESTS

The migratory and desert locusts (*Locusta migratoria* and *Schistocerca gregaria*) have caused devastating famines in parts of Africa and the Middle East by destroying vast areas of grains and other crops. A swarm can number more than 10 billion individuals. Its path depends largely on the direction of the winds – if the winds blow out to sea, the whole swarm may drown.

Locust swarm in Mauritania, West Africa

Find out more

ANIMALS: *140*
INSECTS: *162*
RESPIRATION: *26*
SENSES: *42*

DRAGONFLIES, MAYFLIES, AND MANTIDS

DELICATE AND OFTEN spectacularly colored, dragonflies are familiar insects although their numbers are relatively small. Dragonflies – together with damselflies – form the order Odonata and are considered to be cousins of mayflies. They are fast-flying predators whose speed and shape have earned them the name "devil's darning needles." Mantids belong to the order Mantodea and have more in common with crickets. These insects appear to be "praying" while lying in wait for passing insects. Although it is generally thought that female mantises always eat their partners after mating, this usually happens only in captivity.

Emperor dragonfly
(*Anax imperator*)

GIANT ANCESTORS

Dragonflies and damselflies are usually seen flying low over freshwater lakes or rivers where they lay their eggs. Of the 5,000 or more living species, most live in tropical or subtropical regions. Their wingspans range from 0.8 in (2 cm) to 8 in (20 cm). Even the emperor dragonfly, the largest British species, is dwarfed by its prehistoric relatives. Many ancestors of dragonflies from the Pennsylvanian period had a wingspan of 25 in (65 cm), making them the largest insects ever known.

This fossilized dragonfly wing and the emperor dragonfly – wingspan up to 4 in (10 cm) – are shown to scale.

Dragonfly fossil (Typus sp.) showing the giant wingspan of an early species

DRAGONFLY ANATOMY

The dragonfly's slender body and long, thin wings make it one of the swiftest fliers in the insect world. Unlike most insects, the forewings and hind wings beat alternately for better flight control. The dragonfly's huge multifaceted eyes often meet at the back of the head and enable it to see prey from up to 39 ft (12 m) away. The position of the legs at the front of its body prevents a dragonfly from walking but enables it to shape its legs into a "basket" to catch prey.

Southern hawker
(*Aeshna cyanea*)

Forewing

The narrow, lacy wings are often brightly colored.

The male of this species has a striking blue, green, and black coloring.

Hind wing

Long abdomen with 10 segments

Hind wing

Forewing

Large eyes

Legs set forward on thorax

Black-tailed skimmer (Orthetrum cancellatum) eating a damselfly

DAMSELFLIES

Damselflies and dragonflies are usually classified as separate suborders within the order Odonata. Although they seem very similar there are several important differences between them. Damselflies have thinner bodies and are weaker in flight. A damselfly's front and hind wings are roughly equal in size with rounded ends. Unlike the dragonfly, it folds them over its back when resting.

Beautiful demoiselle
(*Calopteryx virgo*)

Wingtips are rounded.

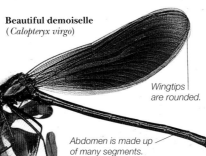

Abdomen is made up of many segments.

The male uses a pair of claspers to hold onto the female during mating.

DAYTIME HUNTERS

Because they locate prey exclusively by sight, most adult dragonflies and damselflies hunt during daylight hours. They feed on a range of insects, such as midges, mosquitoes, and moths. Their wings beat as much as one hundred times per second and before these insects can become airborne, they must raise their body temperature. Some species generate heat by "shivering" their flight muscles and many bask in the sun.

COURTSHIP AND REPRODUCTION

Male dragonflies claim a territory near water and fiercely defend it against all rivals. On the arrival of a female, the male changes his flight pattern and performs a courtship display before grasping the female's head with special claspers on the tip of his abdomen. The female then arches her abdomen forward to bring their sexual organs together and fertilization takes place. The eggs are laid in or near water.

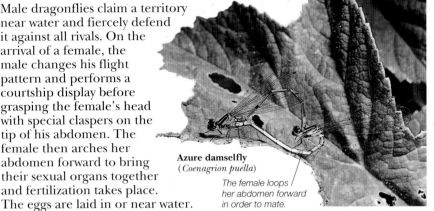

Azure damselfly
(*Coenagrion puella*)

The female loops her abdomen forward in order to mate.

NYMPHS

Dragonfly eggs hatch into nymphs that develop in the water. The nymphs breathe through gills on the tips of their abdomens and feed mainly on aquatic invertebrates, although some species catch small fish. They have a special lower jaw, called a mask, which shoots forward to grab prey. Nymphs shed their skins several times before emerging as adults between one and five years later.

Dragonfly nymph (Aeshna sp.) grabbing a three-spined stickleback (Gasterosteus aculeatus)

MAYFLY SWARMS

Mayflies are relatives of dragonflies and damselflies. They are members of the order Ephemeroptera, which means "one-day wings." The adults do not live for long, cannot feed, and their sole function is to reproduce. Most of their lives – between one and three years – are spent in the water as nymphs, feeding on plants and small invertebrates. Adults gather in swarms over rivers to mate, although this sight is now less common due to water pollution.

A swarm of mayflies gathering over a lake to mate

MANTIDS

Mantids, or mantises, are solitary insects that do not actively hunt down their prey. Instead they ambush grasshoppers, flies, and even small birds. They are able to remain almost motionless, observing their prey until it comes into striking distance. To avoid detection themselves, their bodies are camouflaged to resemble twigs and leaves.

The mantis is well camouflaged against the leaf.

— Large eyes

Spines on forelegs for gripping prey.

Praying mantis
(*Mantis religiosa*)

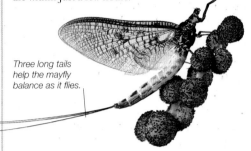
PREYING NOT PRAYING

Mantids are sometimes called "praying" mantises because their forelegs are raised as if in prayer. This posture prepares the mantis to strike out and grab its prey. The insect's front legs are positioned far in front of the other four "walking" legs, ready to shoot forward and grab a passing insect. These legs are covered with spines to grip struggling prey.

Ambush technique of mantis

1. The mantis waits for an insect to land within striking distance.

2. The mantis leans forward, keeping a grip on the twig with its rear legs.

Mantis
(*Sphodromantis* sp.)

3. The mantis shoots its front legs forward to grip the fly.

BUGS

PEOPLE OFTEN USE the word "bug" to describe any type of insect. However, zoologists use the term to describe the 80,000 or so members of the major order known as Hemiptera. This group, which is remarkably diverse in appearance and size, contains species ranging from less than 0.004 in (1 mm) to more than 4.3 in (11 cm). Bugs also have varied diets; some live as carnivores in water or on land, while others survive by sucking sap from green plants. All have long, strawlike feeding tubes through which they suck plant and animal juices.

Black bean aphid (Aphis fabae) with rostrum

TYPES OF BUG

Some specialists divide bugs into two distinct groups. The "true bugs," such as water boatmen, assassin bugs, and pond skaters belong to the suborder Heteroptera. Their forewings are always divided into two parts – a leathery front and a membranous back. They are either aquatic or terrestrial, and feed on plants and other animals. The second suborder, the Homoptera, includes aphids, scales, and cicadas. They live on land and feed exclusively on plant juices.

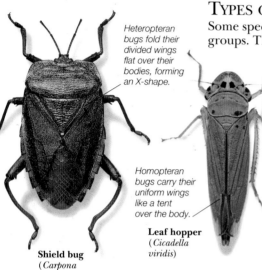

Heteropteran bugs fold their divided wings flat over their bodies, forming an X-shape.

Homopteran bugs carry their uniform wings like a tent over the body.

Leaf hopper (*Cicadella viridis*)

Shield bug (*Carpona imperialis*)

FEEDING

The most prominent feature on a bug's head is its feeding tube (rostrum), which consists of two thin channels. Enzymes are pumped down one tube to help liquefy the insect's food, while the other tube sucks up the food into the digestive system. Most bugs feed on plants, and many are significant crop pests. Some feed on animal blood or tissues, and may transmit human and animal diseases.

Thorax

SHIELDED STINKERS

Shield bugs and their relatives are mostly plant-feeding pests. Some species, such as the seed-eating chinch bug (*Blissus leucopterus*), cause massive damage to cereal crops worldwide. Shield bugs are sometimes called "stink bugs" because, when handled, they produce a repugnant odor. This smell is produced by special glands on the sides of the thorax and helps deter predators.

Striped shield bug (*Graphosoma italicum*)

WATER BUGS

Toad bugs, water scorpions, and water boatmen are carnivorous bugs that live in fresh water. They have all developed unique ways of breathing underwater. Water scorpions (*Nepa cinerea*) breathe through a long siphon that projects above the surface. Water boatmen take air from the surface through holes called spiracles, at the tip of their abdomens. They trap this air, in the form of tiny air bubbles, beneath water-repellent hairs on their bodies.

Backswimmers are so called because they swim on their backs.

Backswimmer (*Notonecta* sp.)

Bedbug (*Cimex lectularius*)

LIVING ON A FILM

Pond skaters live on the surface of ponds, lakes, and slow-flowing rivers. Some tropical and subtropical species live on the sea. They rely on the surface tension of the water to keep them from sinking. Pond skaters feed mainly on invertebrates that fall into the water from the air and overhanging plants. Ripples produced from a struggling insect alert the skater to potential food.

Water skaters (Gerris najas) feeding on surface

BEDBUGS

A small number of bugs are parasites. These insects use their sucking mouthparts to feed on blood from birds and mammals. Three species, commonly known as bedbugs, hide in clothing during the day, and are known to feed on humans at night. These inconspicuous, wingless parasites are more of an inconvenience than a threat – there is no evidence that they transmit disease.

HOPPERS AND CICADAS

Plant hoppers and cicadas include some of the largest species of bugs. Some cicadas have wingspans of more than 8.5 in (22 cm). Like all homopterans, hoppers and cicadas feed by sucking plant sap, which provides them with sugars, minerals, and water. Although they are not as destructive to crops as some aphids, these bugs may carry viruses from plant to plant. In common with most bugs, courtship is initiated by sound signals. Cicadas, in particular, are notorious for their piercing "song," which they make by clicking lidlike structures on their abdomen.

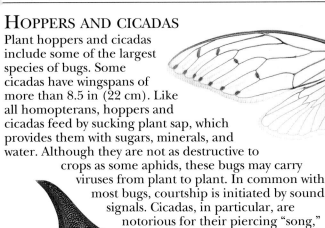

Cicadas (Pomponia sp.) are among the loudest of all insects.

Some plant hoppers such as the thorn bug (Umbonia sp.) have developed elaborate camouflage.

A projection on the thorax makes this thorn bug look like part of a prickly stem.

SPITTLE BUGS

The immature stages (nymphs) of some plant-sucking bugs protect themselves from predators, disease, and the environment by enclosing themselves in a frothy jacket, sometimes called cuckoo spit. This froth is released through the anus. When they reach maturity, the small adult spittle bugs leave the safety of their spit and assume a more active lifestyle, jumping from leaf to leaf.

Froth surrounding froghopper's larva gives the insect the more common name of spittle bug.

Adult scale bugs on leaf

LAZY SCALES

Scale insects are tiny bugs that are pests of many tropical and greenhouse plants. The adults resemble scales and seldom move. Although many scale bugs are destructive, some are used to make useful products. For example, the food dye cochineal is made from the bug *Dactylopius coccus*, and chewing gum is derived from the bug *Cerococcus quercus*.

Cochineal coloring

ASSASSIN BUG

Assassin bug is the common name for the 3,000 or so species of carnivorous bugs that feed on other animals. The *Eulyes illustris* feeds exclusively on other insects. It ambushes its prey and injects a paralyzing venom into its victim. This venom helps digest the prey's tissues, allowing liquefied food to be sucked up through the bug's rostrum.

Bright spots warn predators to stay away.

Scientific name: *Eulyes illustris*

Size: 1.2 in (30 mm) long

Habitat: Commonly found in forests

Distribution: Philippines

Reproduction: After hatching, nymphs (adultlike young without wings) undergo five molts

Diet: Other arthropods

Mother shield bug (Elasmucha grisea) protects young.

REPRODUCTION

Unlike other insects, bugs do not undergo metamorphosis. Instead, eggs hatch out into miniature, usually wingless, replicas of adults. As these nymphs grow, they shed their hard exoskeletons several times before reaching maturity. In sap-feeding species, such as shield bugs, the eggs are usually laid on the host plant, or injected into the plant through the female's swordlike ovipositor (egg-laying tube). After hatching, the emerging nymphs are usually left to fend for themselves.

Aphids live in large numbers on plant buds, where sap is easy to reach.

APHID ARMIES

Aphids have devastating effects on crops and plants. They rob plants of nutrients and also transmit plant diseases. Plant sap is rich in sugar, but low in protein. Aphids feed until they have extracted enough protein, and get rid of the "excess" sap as sugary droplets. Other insects, such as ants and bees, feed on these droplets. Some ants even stand guard over their "flock" of aphids to ensure a steady supply of food.

Find out more

DEFENSE 2: *50*

INSECTS: *162*

PEOPLE AND ANIMALS: *94*

PESTS AND WEEDS: *98*

BEETLES

WITH MORE THAN 360,000 known species, beetles account for 40 percent of all insect species, and include the brightly spotted ladybug. Beetles belong to the order Coleoptera, and range in size from the tiny feather-winged beetle, which grows to a length of 0.01 in (0.25 mm) to the titan longhorn beetle measuring 6 in (16 cm). Beetles live in almost every imaginable habitat and feed on a wide range of foods including plants, fungi, insects, and dead animals. Some beetles are considered pests, but others perform a valuable role by breaking down dead animal and plant matter, and returning nutrients to the soil.

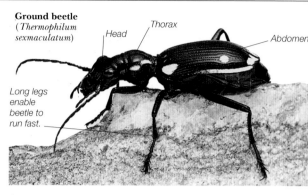

Ground beetle
(*Thermophilum sexmaculatum*)

Head

Thorax

Abdomen

Long legs enable beetle to run fast.

ANATOMY

A beetle's body is divided into three parts – the head, thorax, and abdomen. All beetles have biting mouthparts, and antennae that they use for touch and smell. Most have two pairs of wings. The front wings have developed into tough leathery covers, called elytra, that protect the delicate hindwings and the abdomen when the insect is at rest. The wings, elytra, and six legs are joined to the thorax.

Red-colored elytra held clear of beating hind wings

Cardinal beetle
(*Pyrochroa coccinea*)

Beetles use an elaborate system of hooks to fold their delicate hindwings under the elytra, or wing cases

BEETLING ALONG
Like all insects, beetles have six jointed legs used for walking, jumping, digging, or swimming. Ground beetles and tiger beetles have long legs to run away from predators and to chase prey over soil and leaf litter. Dung beetles have toothed, spadelike legs to help them roll and bury balls of dung. Diving beetles have flattened legs fringed with hairs that push them through water in pursuit of prey.

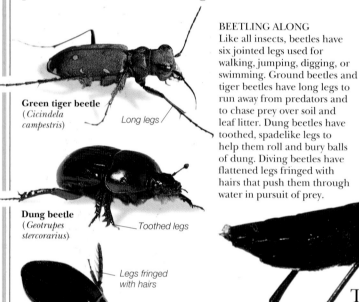

Green tiger beetle
(*Cicindela campestris*)

Long legs

Dung beetle
(*Geotrupes stercorarius*)

Toothed legs

Legs fringed with hairs

Great diving beetle
(*Dytiscus marginalis*)

TAKING FLIGHT

Some beetles, such as the cockchafer, are relatively poor fliers. Their front wings, or elytra, have become little more than covers that protect the insect's delicate hindwings as it runs on the ground. In flight, the elytra are held up, out of the way of the beating hindwings. They provide little aerodynamic lift although they do help stabilize the insect in the air. Most beetles are able to fly, but some have fused elytra and are completely flightless.

MOUTHPARTS

The structure of a beetle's mouthparts usually reflects its diet. Many beetles have mouths that are adapted for feeding on leaves, seeds, or nectar. Others are scavengers that feed on rotting vegetation, dead animals, and dung. The carnivorous tiger beetles have sharp sickle-shaped jaws (mandibles), while weevils and seed beetles, which feed on plants or bore into seeds, tend to have long snouts with hard, biting jaws at the tip.

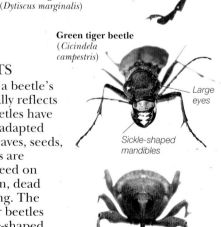

Green tiger beetle
(*Cicindela campestris*)

Large eyes

Sickle-shaped mandibles

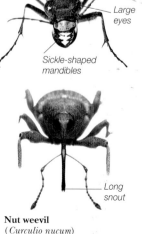

Long snout

Nut weevil
(*Curculio nucum*)

GIANT JAWS
Male stag beetles have large, powerful jaws that look like branched "antlers." The impressive jaws suggest that these beetles catch large prey, but in fact they feed on honeydew and tree sap. The jaws are often used in fights between males over territory, mates, or food.

Stag beetles (Lucanus cervus) *fighting*

Male stag beetles can grow up to 3 in (7 cm) long.

Firefly sending "flashes" to attract a mate

FINDING A MATE

Beetles use a variety of signals to attract a mate of the same species. Some attract mates by their bright colors or patterns, while others, such as chafer beetles, release special chemicals called pheromones. Deathwatch beetles tap the walls of their wooden burrows with their heads, while fireflies use a special organ in their bodies to "flash" signals to potential mates. The signals are sent out in specific frequencies to lure the right partner.

REPRODUCTION

Most beetles undergo a form of development called complete metamorphosis. The female lays her eggs on or near a food source – usually in the soil or on a plant. The larvae look completely different from the adults, and often eat other types of food so they are not in competition with their parents. Most beetles show little or no care for their offspring. A few species of dung beetle, however, construct brood chambers for their young.

A dung beetle's brood chamber

Female beetle fills chamber with pellets of dung.

Beetle digs into a dung pile, rolling it into pellets.

Eggs are laid in dung, giving the young an instant food source when they hatch.

Lunate ladybug (Cheilomenes lunata) feeding on green aphids

COSTS AND BENEFITS

Many beetles are harmful – they eat crops, stored seeds, fabrics, and dried animal products. Others, however, are of great benefit. Some are important pollinators, others feed on animal dung or rotting plants and animals, recycling the nutrients for new generations of plants. Ladybugs are helpful to gardeners because they help to control pests such as aphids and scale insects.

Soft-bodied aphids move slowly and are vulnerable.

CLICK BEETLE

Like other click beetles, the South American click beetle has a hard body and wing-case, short, thin legs, and toothed antennae. When alarmed, it slips to the ground and lands on its back. To right itself, it bends its body backward until it rests on its head and tail tips; then it lets go suddenly, springing upward with a clicking sound. The "click" is also used to startle predators.

Hard body and wing case

Scientific name: *Chalcolepidius limbatus*

Size: 0.16–0.7 in (4–18 mm)

Habitat: Woodlands and grassland

Distribution: South America

Reproduction: Larvae develop in wood or soil

Diet: Plants, insects, dead plant or animal matter

Chafer beetles
(*Hoplia caerulea*)

Shining flower chafer
(*Plusiotis optima*)

Frog beetle
(*Sagra buqueti*)

Leaf weevil
(*Eupholus schoenherri*)

Jewel beetle
(*Chrysochroa chinensis*)

Longhorn beetle
(*Sternotomis bohemani*)

COLORFUL COLEOPTERA

Contrary to popular belief, not all beetles are drab. Many species, including scarabs and wood-boring beetles, have bright, metallic colors. The beetles' colors are caused either by iridescence – the effect of sunlight shining on the elytra – or by colored pigments present in the body.

Bark of elm tree shows damage caused by large elm bark beetles.

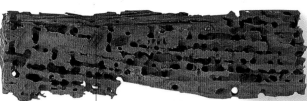

The deathwatch beetle (Xestobium rufovillosum) can reduce structural timbers to a skeleton.

PESTS

Some beetles damage plants directly, while others cause destruction indirectly by acting as vectors (carriers) for disease. The most celebrated example is the large elm bark beetle (*Scholytus scholytus*). The adults and larvae excavate burrows under the bark of living trees and transmit spores of the fungus *Ceratocystis ulmi* – the cause of Dutch elm disease in the US. This disease has wiped out much of the elm population.

Find out more

COCKROACHES, FLEAS, AND LICE: *164*

INSECTS: *162*

PESTS AND WEEDS: *98*

FLIES

FLIES ARE GENERALLY despised because they transmit diseases and contaminate food. Nevertheless, many species play a vital role in the chain of decomposition by breaking down dead organic matter. Flies are members of the order Diptera, which means "two wings" – all other insects have four wings. With more than 120,000 species, they are the fourth largest insect group and can be found in almost every habitat. Many are opportunists that feed on a wide variety of foods, while others, such as the female mosquito, feast on the blood of human and animal hosts.

Large, furry body and back legs

Distinctive brown spots on abdomen

Slender body

Mosquito
(*Culex* sp.)

House fly
(*Musca domestica*)

South American robber fly
(*Mallophora atra*)

DIVERSE DIPTERA

Flies range in size from robber flies that may reach lengths of more than 3 in (7 cm) to mosquitoes that are sometimes difficult to see. In general, the more primitive flies, such as mosquitoes, midges, and fungus gnats, are fragile insects with delicate wings. The more advanced flies, such as bluebottles and house flies, are generally squat, sturdy, and bristly, and they fly in a faster and stronger way than midges and gnats.

PIERCING, SUCKING, AND SPONGING

Flies do not have biting jaws to eat solid food. Instead, their mouthparts are adapted for sucking or sponging up liquid food, such as nectar, blood, living body tissues, or decomposing organic matter. A female mosquito will pierce the skin of her victim before sucking the blood. Flies, such as bluebottles and other blow flies, squirt digestive enzymes onto meat and take up the partly digested food through special spongelike mouthparts.

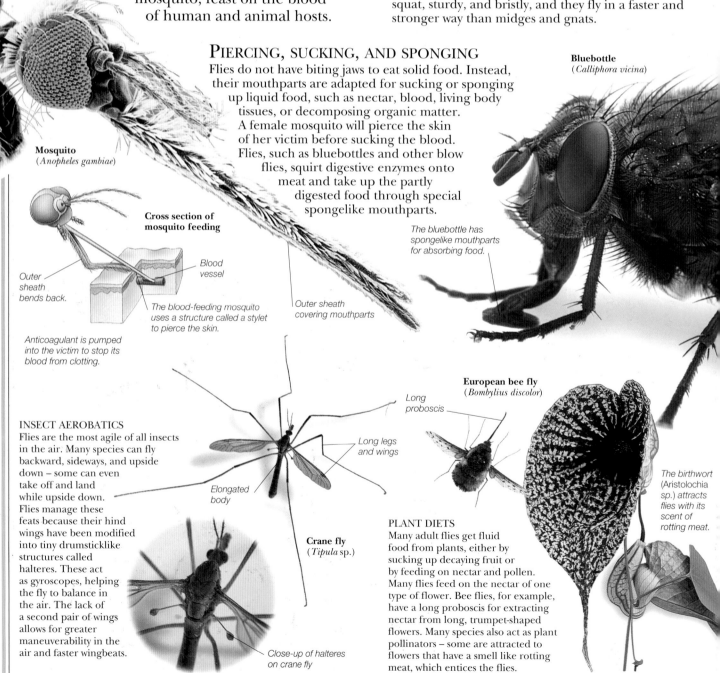

Mosquito
(*Anopheles gambiae*)

Cross section of mosquito feeding

Outer sheath bends back.

Blood vessel

The blood-feeding mosquito uses a structure called a stylet to pierce the skin.

Anticoagulant is pumped into the victim to stop its blood from clotting.

Outer sheath covering mouthparts

Bluebottle
(*Calliphora vicina*)

The bluebottle has spongelike mouthparts for absorbing food.

INSECT AEROBATICS

Flies are the most agile of all insects in the air. Many species can fly backward, sideways, and upside down – some can even take off and land while upside down. Flies manage these feats because their hind wings have been modified into tiny drumsticklike structures called halteres. These act as gyroscopes, helping the fly to balance in the air. The lack of a second pair of wings allows for greater maneuverability in the air and faster wingbeats.

Elongated body

Long legs and wings

Crane fly
(*Tipula* sp.)

Close-up of halteres on crane fly

Long proboscis

European bee fly
(*Bombylius discolor*)

PLANT DIETS

Many adult flies get fluid food from plants, either by sucking up decaying fruit or by feeding on nectar and pollen. Many flies feed on the nectar of one type of flower. Bee flies, for example, have a long proboscis for extracting nectar from long, trumpet-shaped flowers. Many species also act as plant pollinators – some are attracted to flowers that have a smell like rotting meat, which entices the flies.

The birthwort (*Aristolochia* sp.) attracts flies with its scent of rotting meat.

CARNIVOROUS FLIES

Some adult flies are ferocious predators. Robber flies have acute vision and are daytime hunters that live by chasing down other insects, usually catching them in flight. The robber fly has long, spiny legs that hold prey while piercing it with a powerful proboscis and sucking it dry. A tuft of stiff hairs on its head may protect the fly against the struggling limbs of its victims. An individual robber fly may patrol a regular beat in search of prey.

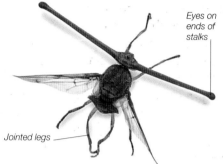

Robber fly
(*Machimus atricapillus*)

This robber fly is devouring a lacewing.

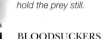

Long, spiny legs hold the prey still.

STALK-EYED FLY

This tropical fly is distinctive because its eyes are located on the ends of long stalks. In territorial battles, competing males measure each other's size by comparing the lengths of their eyestalks. They advance toward each other until their eyestalks are touching and the fly with the closer-set eyes normally withdraws his challenge.

Eyes on ends of stalks

Jointed legs

Scientific name: *Achias rothschildi*

Size: 0.1–0.25 in (4–6 mm)

Habitat: Wetlands

Distribution: Papua New Guinea

Reproduction: Eggs are laid in wet plant material where the larvae grow and pupate.

Diet: Plant matter

BLOODSUCKERS

Some adult flies are parasitic – that is, they feed exclusively on the blood or flesh of other animals. Examples include the tiny wingless bat fly that survives on the blood of bats. In mosquitoes and other "biting" flies, such as gnats and horseflies, only the females feed on blood. They do this to get extra protein before laying their eggs.

Horsefly (Tabanus barbarus) sucking blood

FLIES AND DISEASE

Throughout history, diseases spread by flies, such as malaria and yellow fever, have killed millions of people. Tsetse flies (*Glossina* sp.) spread a fatal sleeping sickness that can affect both humans and cattle. The danger from tsetse flies has prevented the development of vast areas of tropical Africa. Nonbiting, scavenging flies also transmit a range of diseases because they carry bacteria from dung and rotting flesh to food.

Tsetse fly
(*Glossina* sp.)

Before sucking blood – abdomen is empty.

Blood-sucking insects, such as tsetse flies, have stomachs that shrink when empty.

A tsetse fly can drink two or three times its own weight in blood at one sitting.

After sucking blood – abdomen is swollen.

LARVAL LIFE

All flies undergo a process called metamorphosis in which they change their body form and shape. Each egg hatches into a flightless "grub" that does not resemble the adult. Unlike flies, the larvae have biting mouthparts so they can eat while they grow. As it grows, the larva sheds its skin until it finally produces a pupa with a hard skin. At this stage the larva's body is reorganized and it emerges as an adult with wings.

Bluebottle larvae or maggots feed on carrion. They become adult flies after about 3 weeks.

The larvae of the leaf-mining fly (Agromyzidae sp.) are herbivores that tunnel through leaves.

Color-enhanced scanning electron micrograph of a mutant fruit fly (Drosophila melanogaster)

GENETIC LABORATORIES

Fruit flies are among the most important organisms in the study of genetics. They are quick and easy to breed in the laboratory, and have "giant" chromosomes that can be examined under the microscope. Much of what is known about the way genes work comes from studies of this fly and its mutant forms, some of which have four wings.

Find out more

FOOD CHAINS AND WEBS: 66
MOVEMENT IN AIR: 36
PARTNERS AND PARASITES: 56
PESTS AND WEEDS: 98

BUTTERFLIES AND MOTHS

BUTTERFLIES AND MOTHS are unique among insects because every part of their bodies is covered by thousands of tiny scales. In many moths these scales are drab, but in butterflies the wing scales are often brilliantly colored. The 135,000 or more species in this large group of insects make up the order Lepidoptera (from the Greek words for "scaled wing"). All butterflies and most moths feed through a long, tubelike proboscis, which normally coils neatly away when not in use. Both start life as caterpillars that usually feed on plants; only as adults do they live on liquid food. Butterflies and moths can generally be distinguished by the shape of their antennae and by the way they hold their wings.

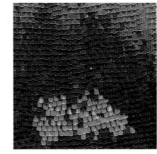

Magnified view of a butterfly's wing

SURFACE OF SCALES

The wings of a butterfly are brightly colored with scales that overlap like tiles on a roof. Butterflies get these colors in two different ways. Some – particularly yellow and orange – are produced by chemical pigments stored in the wings. Others are produced by microscopic ridges on the surface of the scales, which reflect the light in a special way.

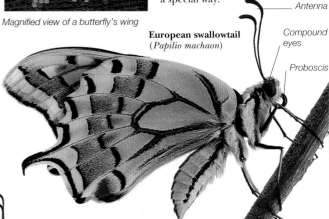

European swallowtail (*Papilio machaon*)

Antenna

Compound eyes

Proboscis

LIFE CYCLE

Butterflies and moths have a life cycle that consists of several stages. They begin life as small, hard-shelled eggs that are usually laid on plants. Each egg hatches into a caterpillar, which spends most of its time feeding. When fully grown, the caterpillar's skin splits to reveal the pupa. During this stage, the body changes completely – a process known as metamorphosis – until the butterfly emerges.

1. These butterfly eggs have been laid on a milk parsley plant.

2. The caterpillar emerges by chewing through the egg's shell.

Pupa

Pupal case

3. For about four weeks the caterpillar feeds hungrily, and periodically sheds its skin.

4. When it is ready to pupate, the caterpillar fastens itself to a stem.

5. The pupa has a hard case that is held in place by a thin loop of silk.

6. Eventually, the pupal case splits open and the adult butterfly emerges.

ANATOMY OF A BUTTERFLY

The European swallowtail belongs to a family of large, fast-flying butterflies. It has two pairs of large wings, six working legs, compound eyes, a tongue (proboscis), and long antennae that help it find food. However, not all butterflies and moths are built this way. Some females are wingless and cannot fly. Brush-footed butterflies, or nymphalids, have only four walking legs – the other pair, held close to the head, are tiny and end in brushes.

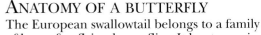

Clubbed antenna

Feathered antenna

Butterflies have antennae that are clubbed.

Some moths have antennae that are feathered.

ANTENNAE

Butterflies and moths use their antennae, or feelers, to detect scents drifting through the air. This enables them to track down food plants and also to identify other members of their species. Most butterflies have slender antennae that end in a "club," or small knob. Many moths also have slender antennae, but others have antennae with filaments like tiny feathers.

Sunset moth (*Chrysiridia riphearia*)

BUTTERFLY OR MOTH?

Most butterflies have colorful wings and fly by day, while moths are usually drab and fly at dusk or during the night. However, there are some species that do not follow this simple rule. The sunset moth, for example, is as colorful as any butterfly, but is actually a diurnal moth. Another way to tell Lepidoptera apart is that most butterflies rest with their wings held upright over their back, while moths generally hold theirs flat.

Tongue is 12 in (30 cm) long.

Morgan's sphinx
(*Xanthopan morgani*)

A LIQUID DIET

Adult butterflies and moths feed almost entirely on liquids, which they suck up through their hollow tongues. Most of them drink nectar, a sugary fluid produced by plants. Some, such as Darwin's hawkmoth, have tongues that are long enough to reach into the deepest flowers. Many butterflies also feed on the slushy remains of rotting fruit, while some moths have more unusual diets. They settle around the eyes of large animals, such as water buffalo, and drink their tears.

ROLLING TONGUE

A butterfly's tongue is flexible and very sensitive. It can probe straight down into a flower, but it can also bend sharply so the butterfly can feed from different angles without having to move its body. Once a butterfly has finished feeding, it stows its tongue away. The tongue coils up like a spring and fits neatly under the butterfly's head.

Butterfly tongue is tucked away.

Sulphurs drinking from a puddle

GATHERING ON THE GROUND

It is quite a common sight, especially in the tropics, to see a group of butterflies such as the sulphurs (*Eurema* sp.) congregate at muddy puddles where they sip water. This water contains essential mineral salts that the butterflies cannot always obtain from their food.

MOTH DISGUISE

Although moths are often dull-looking, this can provide a useful camouflage. Some, such as carpenter moths (*Cossus* sp.), have wings that look like the tree bark on which they rest. The large tolype has a hairy body and broken wing pattern that helps it blend with its surroundings.

Large tolype
(*Tolype velleda*)

Camouflaged hind wings hide the morpho when it is at rest.

Common morpho
(*Morpho peleides*)

QUEEN ALEXANDRA'S BIRDWING

This magnificent insect is the world's largest butterfly – and also one of the rarest. It lives in dense forest and hardly ever comes down to the ground. Like other birdwings, it has narrow wings and is a powerful flier that moves by means of flapping flight and long glides. The caterpillars of this butterfly have long spikes that protect them from attack by predators.

Scientific name: *Ornithoptera alexandrae*

Size: Wingspan up to 11 in (28 cm)

Habitat: Humid tropical forest

Distribution: Southeast New Guinea

Reproduction: Eggs are laid high in the forest canopy.

Diet: It has just one foodplant, a pipevine called *Aristolochia schlecteri*

Bright upperwings create a startling display when the morpho takes off.

CATERPILLAR DEFENSES

Because caterpillars cannot run away, they are in constant danger of attack. Many species, such as the postman butterfly caterpillar (*Heliconius melpomene*), have long spines or hairs that make them difficult to eat. Others are superbly camouflaged. By looking like twigs or bird droppings, they escape notice.

Long spines to deter predators

AVOIDING PREDATORS

Butterflies have many enemies, but few are more dangerous than birds. Birds are generally fast fliers, so butterflies cannot use speed to escape attack. Instead, some have chemicals that make them taste unpleasant. These butterflies usually have bright colors that warn they are distasteful or inedible. Other species, such as the blue morphos, have patterned hind wings that help to break up their outline. When the morpho takes off, the sudden flash of its upper wings may help to startle its attacker.

Find out more

DECIDUOUS FORESTS: *80*
DEFENSE 2: *50*
FEEDING AND NUTRITION: *22*
INSECTS: *162*

ANTS AND TERMITES

ANTS AND TERMITES ARE PROBABLY the most numerous insects on Earth. In tropical South America alone, their combined weight exceeds that of all other animals – including humans. All species live in close-knit societies, called colonies, that are sometimes made up of several million individuals. Within an ant or termite colony, the tasks of feeding, defense, rearing young, and reproduction are split between different castes (social classes) of insects. Both types of insects have developed complex communication systems. Despite their similarities, ants and termites are not closely related.

Termite king

Major soldier

Minor soldier

Major worker

Termite queen

Enlarged abdomen full of eggs

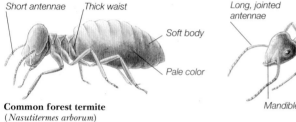

Common forest termite
(*Nasutitermes arborum*)

Short antennae — Thick waist — Soft body — Pale color

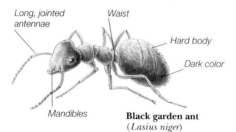

Long, jointed antennae — Waist — Hard body — Dark color — Mandibles

Black garden ant
(*Lasius niger*)

CASTES
In almost all termite and ant colonies, members are divided into castes. The queen and king spend all their life in the nest. A termite queen can lay up to 30,000 eggs a day, and can grow to more than 6 in (15 cm) long. The wingless workers forage for food, rear the young, and maintain the nest, while major and minor soldiers defend the colony. Soldiers are equipped with enlarged jaws (mandibles) adapted for biting.

ANT OR TERMITE?
Termites evolved at least 250 million years ago from their cockroachlike ancestors. Ants are of more recent origin and are related to bees and wasps. Like bees and wasps, most ants have a distinct "waist" and long, jointed antennae. They are dark in color and hard-bodied. By contrast, termites are pale and soft-bodied. They have no real waist and their antennae are beaded and short. Termites tend to be confined to tropical or subtropical regions, whereas ants live almost anywhere.

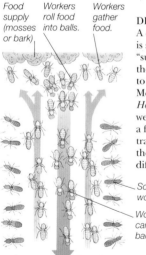

Food supply (mosses or bark)

Workers roll food into balls.

Workers gather food.

Soldiers guard workers.

Workers carry food back to nest.

Foraging team of termites

DIVISION OF LABOR
A colony of termites or ants is sometimes described as a "superorganism" because of the way the individual insects work together to feed and protect the colony. Members of the termite species *Hospitalitermes umbrinus* move in a well-ordered column to and from a feeding area by following odor trails. Workers and soldiers divide their labor by performing different roles.

Chimneys disperse warm, moist air given off by termites and their fungus gardens.

The mound can be more than 20 ft (6 m) tall.

Food stores

Ground level

King and queen in royal chamber

Magnetic termite mounds in Australia

MAGNETIC TERMITES
The magnetic (or compass) termite (*Amitermes meridionalis*) from Australia builds tall, ridged mounds that run north to south. In the morning and evening, the sun on the wide surface helps keep the nest warm. The narrow side is orientated towards the midday sun, thus preventing overheating when the sun is hottest.

Termites grow fungus that helps them digest their food.

Nurseries containing eggs

Weaver ants building a nest

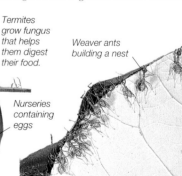

MADE TO MEASURE
Several species of ants build homes in trees. The most remarkable of these are the Old World weaver ants (*Oecophylla* sp.). They stitch together the edges of a leaf to create an inside chamber. The silk thread is produced by glands in the ant larvae. The ants pass the larvae back and forth like shuttles until the leaf is held together.

TERMITE MOUNDS
Both ants and termites build elaborate homes to house their huge colonies. Some termites construct huge mounds out of soil particles which they mix with their own saliva. The mound is divided into several chambers and in the center is a cell where the king and queen mate. The queen lays several thousand eggs a day. Workers carry the eggs away and look after them in specially constructed cells where they hatch into larvae.

Cross section of a termite mound (*Macrotermes*)

FEEDING

Termites feed on plant matter (especially wood), and usually build nests near their food supply. A large termite colony is capable of stripping a dead tree within days. However, since termites cannot distinguish between trees and building materials, they can cause serious damage. Ants are usually carnivores or scavengers and have more varied diets. Some store food, such as seeds, but the most extraordinary hoarders are the North American honeypot ants. The workers of this species store nectar within their abdomens.

Swollen abdomen

Honeypot ants
(*Camponotus inflatus*)

TENDING THE GARDEN

Some ants always have enough food because they grow their own. Central American leafcutter ants (*Atta* sp.) bite off pieces of leaf (sometimes several times their own weight) and carry them back to a special chamber in their underground nest. Here, the leaves are thoroughly chewed and regurgitated to provide an ideal compost for growing fungi. Members of the colony then eat the fungus once it has grown.

Antennae identify scent of other ants.

Worker ant with piece of leaf following scent trail

Close-up of fungus garden

Termites being captured by ants

FIGHTING FOR SURVIVAL

Although ants and termites fight each other, they also attack any other predators that attack their nests. Ants defend themselves by spitting out corrosive formic acid, whereas termite soldiers are armed with a variety of weapons. Most have powerful jaws; some paint a poison onto their enemies with a brush-tipped snout; others squirt a quick-setting glue to immobilize their foes.

WOOD ANT

Wood ants nest at the base of conifer trees in colonies of up to 300,000 ants. The ants keep the nest warm by building a large mound of conifer needles, dry grass, and twigs above the ground. Below ground is a maze of chambers and tunnels. Wood ants catch huge numbers of insects and bring them to their nest in pieces as food for their young.

A wood ant can squirt acid from its abdomen, killing other insects.

Scientific name: (*Formica rufa*)

Size: Up to 0.5 in (6 mm) long

Habitat: Woods and forests

Distribution: Europe

Reproduction: Queen lays eggs, which develop into larvae

Diet: Seeds, invertebrates, and honeydew from aphids

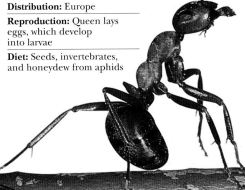

Ants use chambers with smooth walls as living quarters.

Some chambers contain droppings and leftovers from insect meals.

Ants benefit from the sugary nectar produced by the plant's flowers.

ANTS IN PLANTS

In tropical regions, competition between ant species is fierce, so many species have teamed up with plants to gain food or shelter. In return, the ants protect the plant by attacking any browsing herbivorous insects. The relationship between *Iridomyrmex* ants and the ant plant is slightly different. As the plant ages, its stems become pitted with cavities that provide homes for ants. When the ants defecate, their mineral-rich droppings are absorbed by the plant.

Ants enter and leave through holes in the surface of the swollen stem.

Ant plant
(*Myrmecodia* sp.)

NEW COLONIES

Some termite colonies are more than 70 years old. New colonies are formed when the parent colony produces winged reproductive males and females. These winged members fly off at the same time to pair up and find a new nest site. Many birds and mammals feast on the flying termites, and probably no more than one in a thousand makes it through to start a new colony. Winged ants pair off in a similar way to mate and form new colonies.

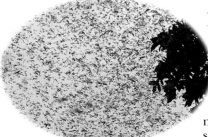

Male and female termites leaving a nest

Find out more
BEES AND WASPS: *180*
COCKROACHES, FLEAS, AND LICE: *164*
INSECTS: *162*

BEES AND WASPS

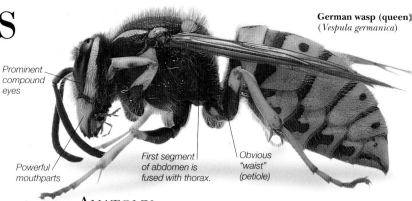

German wasp (queen)
(*Vespula germanica*)

Prominent compound eyes

Powerful mouthparts

First segment of abdomen is fused with thorax.

Obvious "waist" (petiole)

BEES AND WASPS ARE among the most advanced of all insects. Many species live in highly organized social groups, display complex behavior, and use effective methods of communication. Together with ants, they make up the order Hymenoptera – the second largest insect group after beetles. Bees and wasps are important in many ways. Honeybees produce honey and wax and certain wasps destroy pests such as aphids. Bees and wasps are major pollinators of all kinds of plants – experts have speculated that if these insects were wiped out, it could have a catastrophic impact on the production of many crops.

ANATOMY

With at least 150,000 species, bees and wasps are a diverse group of animals. The common image of a large insect with black and yellow stripes applies to several families, such as the Vespidae (including paper wasps and hornets) and the Apidae (honeybees and bumblebees). Other species differ widely in size and color, although most have a narrow "waist" between the first and second abdominal segments, fairly large compound eyes, and biting mouthparts.

WAYS OF LIFE

Some bees and wasps are social insects that cooperate to build nests, gather food, and rear their young. Many wasps, however, are solitary hunters, taking prey such as spiders and insects as food for their larvae. Some even feed on the immature stages of other wasps. These species tend to have a thick, armored casing to protect them against the stings of their prey. One characteristic common to many wasps is that they are parasites, laying their eggs on living prey.

A wasp (Vespidae sp.) seizing an orb-web spider (Araneus sp.)

GROWING FOOD

Some wasps feed directly on plant material, such as pollen or nectar, but others use plants in a different way. Female gall wasps deposit eggs inside the buds of oak trees. When they hatch, a chemical is released that causes a swelling, or gall, on the twig. This gall contains enough plant tissue to nourish the developing larvae (see also below).

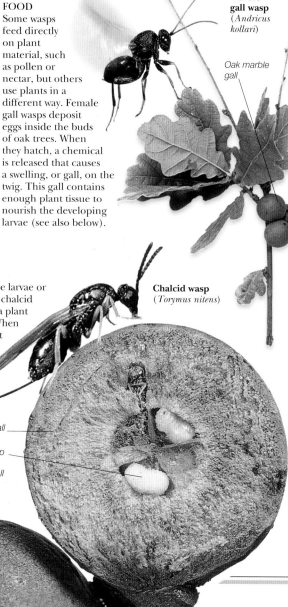

Marble gall wasp
(*Andricus kollari*)

Oak marble gall

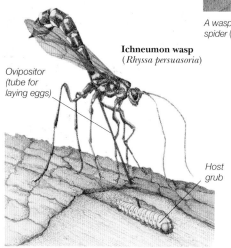

Ichneumon wasp
(*Rhyssa persuasoria*)

Ovipositor (tube for laying eggs)

Host grub

PARASITIC PRACTICES

The larvae of some wasps live off the larvae or pupae of other insects. The female chalcid wasp, for example, bores a hole in a plant gall and deposits her eggs inside. When the eggs hatch, the young larvae eat the gall wasp larvae already within the gall. Wasps that eat other insects are known as parasitoids rather than parasites, because they eventually kill their host (a parasite does not).

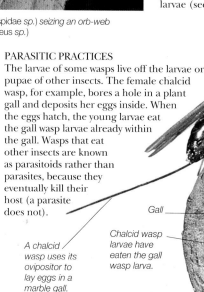

Chalcid wasp
(*Torymus nitens*)

Gall

A chalcid wasp uses its ovipositor to lay eggs in a marble gall.

Chalcid wasp larvae have eaten the gall wasp larva.

DRILLS AND DEFENSES

Most female wasps have a long egg-laying tube, called an ovipositor. This may be used to drill holes in wood where the eggs can be laid in safety. In parasitic species, the tube may also be used like a needle to inject eggs into the tissues of a host animal, where larvae then develop. In many species, the tube has evolved into a defense tool – the insect's sting.

The papery nest of the Saxon wasp (Dolichovespula saxonica) is made from chewed-up wood fibers.

BUILDING A HOME

With the exception of parasitoid wasps, most bees and wasps build some type of nest. Its main purpose is to protect developing larvae rather than the adults (which usually die before their offspring become mature). Eggs are laid in the nest – they may be sealed inside protective cells – and supplied with a "larder" of food, such as nectar and insects. Nests range from simple burrows in the ground and old beetle tunnels in wood to complex, impressive structures made from paper, wax, or clay.

Cells for storing food and raising larvae

Cross section of wasp nest

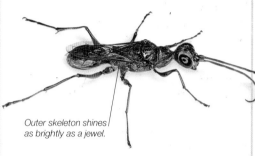
SOCIAL LIVING

The social bee and wasp species live in colonies of up to 75,000 insects. Bee societies are highly ordered, with three distinct classes, or castes – queens, drones, and workers. Each caste differs in appearance and has a specific role. Workers are small females that build and repair the nest, and take care of the queen and larvae. They use special "baskets" on their legs to take pollen back to the nest. The male drones exist only to fertilize the queen – the mother of all the workers.

Honeybee
(*Apis mellifera*)

Worker   *Drone*   *Queen*

Cross section of a beehive

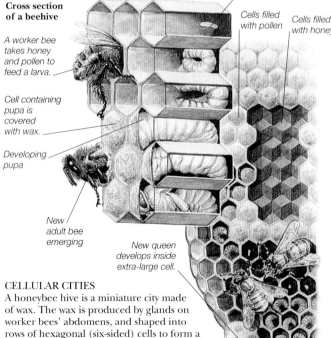

A worker bee takes honey and pollen to feed a larva.

Cell containing pupa is covered with wax.

Developing pupa

New adult bee emerging

New queen develops inside extra-large cell.

Egg hatches into larva

Cells filled with pollen   *Cells filled with honey*

CELLULAR CITIES

A honeybee hive is a miniature city made of wax. The wax is produced by glands on worker bees' abdomens, and shaped into rows of hexagonal (six-sided) cells to form a honeycomb. Some cells are filled with nectar and saliva (a mixture that becomes honey); others store collected pollen or hold developing larvae. The temperature inside the hive is kept cool by bees that fan their wings or bring in water. They can also "shiver" to produce more heat.

Honeybees' waggle dance

Honeybees' round dance

DANCING BEES

Honeybees have a system that enables one bee to tell many others where nectar-rich flowers can be found. After the first worker bee finds food, it returns to its hive and performs a special dance. A "round dance" signals that flowers are near the hive. The "waggle dance" means that flowers are farther away and also pinpoints their exact position.

A swarm of honeybees

A COMPLETE CYCLE

Bees and wasps undergo complete metamorphosis while developing – eggs hatch into grubs, grubs become pupae, and pupae turn into adults. In social species, such as honeybees, unfertilized eggs develop into drones and fertilized eggs into workers and queens. When new queens emerge, the old queen may leave with a group of workers to find a new nest site – moving in a large swarm.

Find out more

ANIMAL HOMES: *58*
COMMUNICATION: *44*
INSECTS: *162*
SOCIAL ANIMALS: *54*

VERTEBRATES

VERTEBRATES MAKE UP only a small fraction of the animal kingdom, yet they are the animals we know the best. Their most important distinguishing feature is a backbone, or vertebral column. A typical vertebrate also has an internal skeleton attached to muscles, four limbs, complex sense organs, and a relatively large brain. The flexible internal skeleton allows vertebrates to grow much larger than most invertebrates, while staying highly mobile – whether on land or in the water. Scientists divide the vertebrates into nine classes: fish (which are broken down into five classes), amphibians, reptiles, birds, and mammals.

EVOLUTION

The first vertebrates evolved more than 500 million years ago from small, wormlike animals that burrowed in mud on the sea floor. Those wormlike ancestors may have looked similar to modern sea animals called lancelets, which are closely related to the

Lancelets (Branchiostoma lanceolatum) *half buried in coarse sand*

vertebrates. With their heads poking out of the sand, lancelets filter small particles of food out of seawater. Although a lancelet has no skeleton, it has the beginnings of a backbone – a rod of supporting tissue, called a notochord, that runs along its back.

UNLIKELY RELATIVES

Sea squirts, or tunicates, are unlikely looking relatives of the vertebrates. As adults, they live fixed to the seabed and filter water through their bag-shaped bodies to obtain food. However, their larvae look like tadpoles, and have distinctive rods of supporting tissue along their backs. Sea squirt larvae also have brains and a nerve cord along the body, but these disappear when the larvae turn into adults.

A colony of sea squirts (tunicates) attached to rocks on the seafloor

FISH

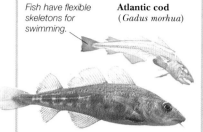

Fish have flexible skeletons for swimming.

Atlantic cod (*Gadus morhua*)

Fish were the first vertebrates to evolve. They have streamlined, muscular bodies, protective coats of scales, and gills for breathing underwater. There are more species of fish than all the other vertebrate classes combined.

AMPHIBIANS

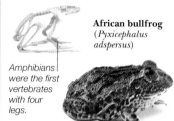

African bullfrog (*Pyxicephalus adspersus*)

Amphibians were the first vertebrates with four legs.

Amphibians live partly on land but usually have to breed in water. Most move on four legs and have lungs for breathing air. Almost all lack scales and have loose-fitting, moist skin that can absorb oxygen to supplement their breathing.

BACKBONE

The backbone runs from the neck to the tail and is the main supporting part of the vertebrate skeleton. It also protects nerves running from the brain to the body. It is not a single bone, but a row of interlocking pieces called vertebrae. An elephant's backbone is arched to carry its body weight.

Vertebrate characteristics of Asian elephant (*Elephas maximus*)

Vertebra

SKIN

Vertebrate skin may be scaly, slimy, furry, or feathered. Elephant skin is up to about 1 in (3 cm) thick on the back, and almost hairless. Skin protects the body from injury and parasites.

Close-up of elephant skin

SKELETON

All vertebrates have a strong, internal skeleton made of bone or cartilage. This supports the body and gives it shape. Muscles are anchored to the skeleton, and joints make it flexible, allowing the animal to move around.

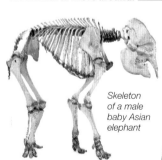

Skeleton of a male baby Asian elephant

The backbone runs to the end of an elephant's tail.

LIMBS

Most vertebrates have four limbs. In fish the limbs are fins, but in other vertebrates they may be legs, arms, or wings. Some vertebrates, including many snakes, have lost all trace of external limbs. Elephants have pillarlike legs to support their immense weight.

REPTILES

Reptiles usually have low bodies and splayed legs.

Nile crocodile
(*Crocodylus niloticus*)

Reptiles were the first vertebrates to live entirely on land. Unlike amphibians, they have dry, scaly skin to reduce water loss. The eggs of many have thick, leathery shells and can be laid on land. Most reptiles live in warm parts of the world.

BIRDS

Birds have lightweight skeletons for flight.

Common starling
(*Sturnus vulgaris*)

Birds evolved from reptiles. The front limbs became wings and the scales became feathers. As well as helping birds to fly, feathers help to keep their bodies constantly warm. Flight has enabled birds to spread to every corner of the earth.

MAMMALS

Eurasian badger
(*Meles meles*)

Mammals walk on upright legs.

Mammals also evolved from reptiles. Like birds, they have constantly warm bodies, but most mammals have fur instead of feathers. Mammals have special glands for suckling their young. Most give birth to live young and do not lay eggs.

SENSE ORGANS
Sense organs are concentrated around the head and are used to spot danger and to find food and mates. The senses are highly developed in vertebrates and include vision, hearing, touch, taste, smell, echolocation, magnetic and electrical senses, and sensitivity to heat, gravity, and pain. An elephant's trunk has two main senses – touch and smell. It can also hold and manipulate objects with "fingers" at the tip.

"Fingers"

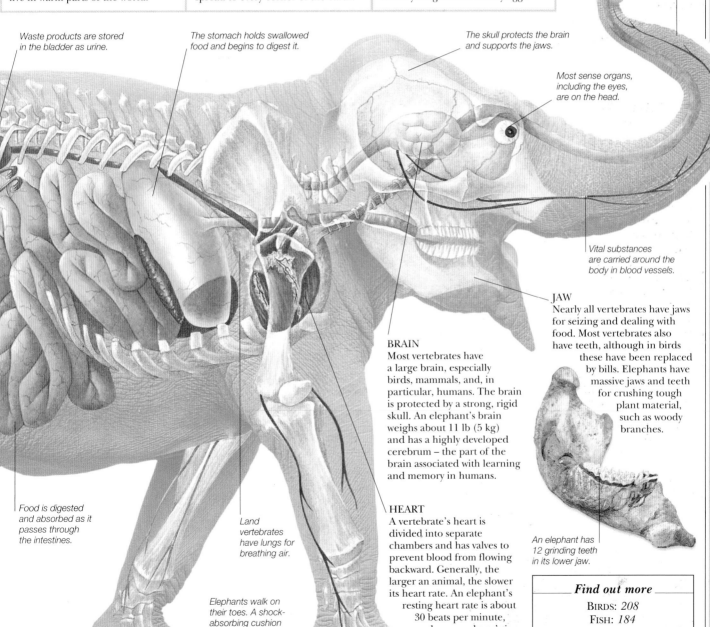

Waste products are stored in the bladder as urine.

The stomach holds swallowed food and begins to digest it.

The skull protects the brain and supports the jaws.

Most sense organs, including the eyes, are on the head.

Vital substances are carried around the body in blood vessels.

JAW
Nearly all vertebrates have jaws for seizing and dealing with food. Most vertebrates also have teeth, although in birds these have been replaced by bills. Elephants have massive jaws and teeth for crushing tough plant material, such as woody branches.

BRAIN
Most vertebrates have a large brain, especially birds, mammals, and, in particular, humans. The brain is protected by a strong, rigid skull. An elephant's brain weighs about 11 lb (5 kg) and has a highly developed cerebrum – the part of the brain associated with learning and memory in humans.

HEART
A vertebrate's heart is divided into separate chambers and has valves to prevent blood from flowing backward. Generally, the larger an animal, the slower its heart rate. An elephant's resting heart rate is about 30 beats per minute, whereas a shrew's is about 600 beats per minute.

An elephant has 12 grinding teeth in its lower jaw.

Food is digested and absorbed as it passes through the intestines.

Land vertebrates have lungs for breathing air.

Elephants walk on their toes. A shock-absorbing cushion under the heel helps carry their weight.

Find out more
BIRDS: *208*
FISH: *184*
MAMMALS: *232*
REPTILES: *198*

FISH

THE FIRST FISH APPEARED ON EARTH almost 500 million years ago. Today, more than 25,000 species live in the world's rivers, lakes, and oceans. Most fish are "cold-blooded"; consequently they are unable to alter their body temperature to compensate for changes in the environment. Some species, however, can survive in extreme conditions. Some Antarctic fish have a natural antifreeze in their blood that helps them survive sub-zero temperatures, while desert pupfish live in hot springs at temperatures of 104°F (40°C).

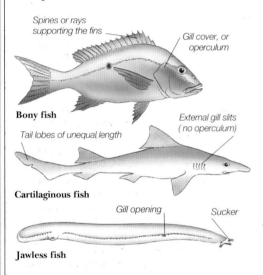

Spines or rays supporting the fins

Gill cover, or operculum

Bony fish

Tail lobes of unequal length

External gill slits (no operculum)

Cartilaginous fish

Gill opening

Sucker

Jawless fish

ANATOMY OF A FISH

Most fish are covered with a protective coat of scales and are generally streamlined in shape. Their internal organs are similar to those of other vertebrates, but they have gills for breathing in water, rather than lungs. Most fish have several fins to steer them through water, including a caudal fin, or tail, at the end of the body, a dorsal fin on the back, and an anal fin underneath. The pectoral and pelvic fins correspond to the limbs of other vertebrates.

Stomach

Spinal cord

Kidney

Brain

Swim bladder

Ureter

Mouth

Gills

Leptoid scales overlap to cover the body.

Urinary bladder

Heart

Anus

Spleen

Liver

Ovary

Intestine

Pancreas

Cross section of a bony fish

TYPES OF FISH

There are three main groups of fish. More than 95 percent of these are bony fish, such as cod and trout. Their backbones, skulls, ribs, jaws, gill arches, and fin supports are made of bone. Most also have a gas-filled chamber called a swim bladder, which inflates or deflates to control buoyancy. Cartilaginous fish, such as sharks, have skeletons made of tough cartilage and no swim bladder. Jawless fish include two groups (lampreys and hagfish), which have funnel-shaped, sucking mouths, and lack proper gills.

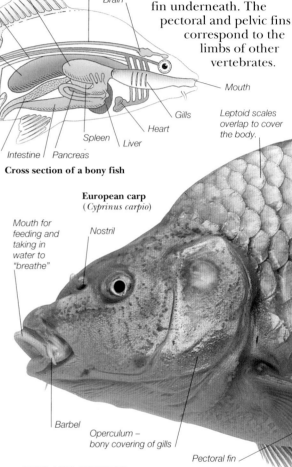

European carp
(*Cyprinus carpio*)

Mouth for feeding and taking in water to "breathe"

Nostril

Barbel

Operculum – bony covering of gills

Pectoral fin

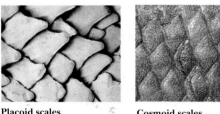

Placoid scales

Cosmoid scales

Ganoid scales

A COAT OF SCALES

There are four basic types of fish scales. Most bony fish have leptoid scales – overlapping, flexible scales, covered by a thin skin. Sharks and their relatives have placoid scales – toothlike structures embedded in the skin that give the surface a sandpaper-like texture. The coelacanth has four-layered cosmoid scales, while garfish have ganoid scales that are diamond-shaped and interlock. Some fish, such as catfish, have no scales at all.

FISH OUT OF WATER

Some fish can live partially out of water. Mudskippers spend more time on mud flats than in the water, but they need to keep their skin moist. They breathe through modified gills, and when on land can hold water in their mouths and gill chambers. Lungfish breathe through lungs that are modified swim bladders, while the European eel (*Anguilla anguilla*) breathes through its skin when migrating overland.

Mudskippers can breathe through their skin as well as their gills.

Stiff rays dig into sand when the fish walks.

Mudskipper
(*Periophthalmus barbarus*)

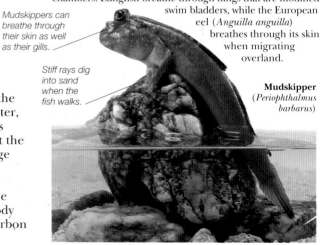

BREATHING UNDERWATER

Like other animals, fish need to breathe oxygen to survive. The fish draws water, containing dissolved oxygen, into its mouth and pumps it over the gills at the back of the head. The gills have a huge surface area to absorb the oxygen, which passes from the water through the gill membranes and into the fish's blood. The oxygen is then distributed around the body in the blood vessels. Wastes, including carbon dioxide, are expelled with the water.

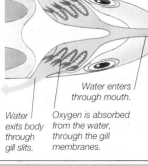

Water enters through mouth.

Water exits body through gill slits.

Oxygen is absorbed from the water, through the gill membranes.

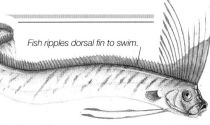

SWIMMING STYLES

Many long-bodied fish, such as dogfish, swim by undulating the body and tail in S-shaped waves. Each wave begins at the head and becomes more pronounced as it reaches the tail. The surrounding water is pushed sideways and backward to propel the fish forward. Oarfish and ribbonfish move up and down by rippling their dorsal fins, while fish encased in rigid "armor," such as boxfish, swim by beating their pectoral fins.

Fish ripples dorsal fin to swim.

Oarfish
(*Regalecus glesne*)

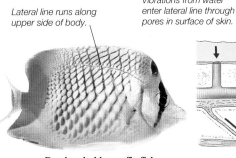

Male sockeye salmon (Oncorhynchus nerka) at spawning ground

REPRODUCTION

Many fish gather together to spawn (release their eggs and sperm into the water). The female lays her eggs in the water to be fertilized by a male's sperm. Only a few of the millions of eggs laid develop into adults – the majority remain unfertilized or are eaten by predators. Most fish leave their eggs and young to fend for themselves. Others take care of their offspring and protect them from predators.

Lateral line runs along upper side of body.

Pearl-scaled butterfly fish
(*Chaetodon xanthurus*)

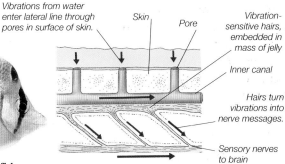

Vibrations from water enter lateral line through pores in surface of skin.

Skin

Pore

Vibration-sensitive hairs, embedded in mass of jelly

Inner canal

Hairs turn vibrations into nerve messages.

Sensory nerves to brain

Cross section of lateral line

WATERY SENSES

Sound vibrations are carried easily through water. Fish can sense movements caused by currents, predators, and prey using a series of sensitive organs called the lateral line. The lateral line is a fluid-filled tube that runs along each side of the body below the skin. Vibrations from the water are transmitted through pores in the skin. The vibrations shake small lumps of jelly inside the tube. These movements are detected by tiny hairs that turn them into nerve messages and send them to the brain.

Dorsal fin

Fin rays

Anal fin

Two-lobed caudal fin or tail

Covering of slimy mucus, produced by glands in the skin, helps to protect against parasites and fungi.

Deeply cleft tail helps catfish to swim fast.

Belly

Pelvic fin

Erect dorsal fin

Large eyes set high on head

Angel catfish
(*Synodontis angelicus*)

Barbels are used to feel for food on the riverbed.

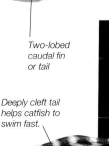

Four-eyed fish (*Anableps anableps*)

SEEING UNDERWATER

Fish focus in a different way from land vertebrates. Instead of changing lens shape, the fish focuses by moving its lens toward or away from the retina (like the focusing action of a camera). Unlike most cartilaginous fish, many bony fish can see in color. Four-eyed fish, which live at the water's surface, have remarkable eyes, divided into two halves, enabling them to see in air and water at the same time.

OTHER SENSES

Although they have no external ears, most fish can hear well and have a good sense of smell, which helps them to navigate and detect food, predators, and mates. Fish have taste buds in the mouth, lips, fins, and skin, for identifying food and avoiding toxic substances. Many bottom-dwellers, such as catfish, also have taste buds on whiskerlike projections around the mouth, called barbels.

Find out more

BONY FISH 1: *188*
BONY FISH 2: *190*
MOVEMENT IN WATER: *38*
OCEANS: *68*

SHARKS AND RAYS

ALTHOUGH FAR LESS diverse than the bony fishes, sharks and rays are successful predators found in oceans worldwide. The 800 species in the shark and ray group are cartilaginous fishes. Their skeletons are not made of bone, but of strong, flexible cartilage. In some sharks, part of the skeleton is strengthened with mineral deposits, particularly in the bones of the back, jaws, and braincase. A shark's skin is covered by tiny teethlike scales called "dermal denticles," which give the surface a sandpaperlike texture. Unlike bony fish, sharks have gill slits behind the head instead of a gill cover, or operculum.

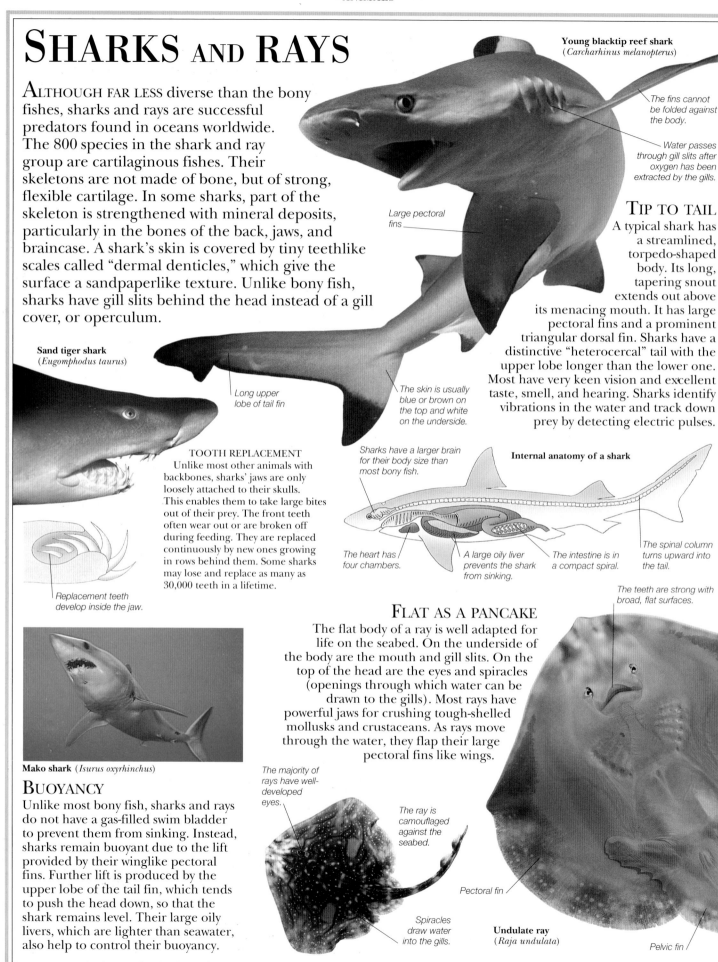

Young blacktip reef shark (*Carcharhinus melanopterus*)

The fins cannot be folded against the body.

Water passes through gill slits after oxygen has been extracted by the gills.

Large pectoral fins

TIP TO TAIL
A typical shark has a streamlined, torpedo-shaped body. Its long, tapering snout extends out above its menacing mouth. It has large pectoral fins and a prominent triangular dorsal fin. Sharks have a distinctive "heterocercal" tail with the upper lobe longer than the lower one. Most have very keen vision and excellent taste, smell, and hearing. Sharks identify vibrations in the water and track down prey by detecting electric pulses.

Sand tiger shark (*Eugomphodus taurus*)

Long upper lobe of tail fin

The skin is usually blue or brown on the top and white on the underside.

TOOTH REPLACEMENT
Unlike most other animals with backbones, sharks' jaws are only loosely attached to their skulls. This enables them to take large bites out of their prey. The front teeth often wear out or are broken off during feeding. They are replaced continuously by new ones growing in rows behind them. Some sharks may lose and replace as many as 30,000 teeth in a lifetime.

Replacement teeth develop inside the jaw.

Sharks have a larger brain for their body size than most bony fish.

Internal anatomy of a shark

The heart has four chambers.

A large oily liver prevents the shark from sinking.

The intestine is in a compact spiral.

The spinal column turns upward into the tail.

The teeth are strong with broad, flat surfaces.

Mako shark (*Isurus oxyrhinchus*)

FLAT AS A PANCAKE
The flat body of a ray is well adapted for life on the seabed. On the underside of the body are the mouth and gill slits. On the top of the head are the eyes and spiracles (openings through which water can be drawn to the gills). Most rays have powerful jaws for crushing tough-shelled mollusks and crustaceans. As rays move through the water, they flap their large pectoral fins like wings.

BUOYANCY
Unlike most bony fish, sharks and rays do not have a gas-filled swim bladder to prevent them from sinking. Instead, sharks remain buoyant due to the lift provided by their winglike pectoral fins. Further lift is produced by the upper lobe of the tail fin, which tends to push the head down, so that the shark remains level. Their large oily livers, which are lighter than seawater, also help to control their buoyancy.

The majority of rays have well-developed eyes.

The ray is camouflaged against the seabed.

Pectoral fin

Spiracles draw water into the gills.

Undulate ray (*Raja undulata*)

Pelvic fin

WHITE SHARK

The huge jaws of the white shark (*Carcharodon carcharias*) contain a terrifying armory of sharp, triangular teeth, each about 2.5 in (6 cm) long. White sharks hunt tuna, squid, turtles, seals, and dolphins, as well as other sharks. They occasionally attack humans, usually mistaking them for seals. Over the years, huge numbers of great whites have been slaughtered for food and sport. They are now a protected species in many parts of the world.

Teeth of white shark

PLANKTON-EATING GIANTS

Surprisingly, the largest species of sharks feed on the smallest creatures. At up to 40 ft (12 m) long, the basking shark is the second largest shark after the whale shark (*Rhincodon typus*). These harmless plankton-feeders swim along near the ocean surface, as though basking in the sunshine. They use their long, fine gill rakers to strain out plankton from the surrounding seawater.

Basking shark (*Cetorhinus maximus*)

ELECTRIC SENSES

Most underwater animals create electrical signals as they move. Sharks and rays can sense these signals using an electrical detection system. Pores, called the ampullae of Lorenzini, on the underside of the shark's snout are connected to sensory nerve cells. These cells detect minute electrical fields that lead the shark toward a meal.

Electric field created by fish

ANGEL SHARK

The sandy-colored angel shark (or monkfish) lies well camouflaged on the seabed. It darts up to snatch passing fish with its long, sharp teeth. Angel sharks have very large pectoral fins, which make them look like rays. However, they swim like sharks using their large tails for propulsion.

The large muscular tail propels the shark forward

Scientific name: *Squatina squatina*

Size: Up to 7 ft (2.5 m) long

Habitat: Shallow, warm seas

Distribution: Eastern North Atlantic

Reproduction: 7–25 young per live litter

Diet: Fish (especially flatfish), mollusks, and crabs

ELECTRIC SHOCKS AND POISONOUS STINGS

Electric rays have evolved large organs for generating electricity. Situated on either side of the head, these can deliver shocks of up to 200 volts, capable of stunning prey and scaring off predators. Stingrays are armed with one or more large spines on the tail. The venom, supplied from a gland at the base of the spine, causes predators great pain, but is rarely fatal.

The stingray lashes out with its tail and drives its spine into the body of an attacker.

The European stingray (Dasyatis pastinaca) has a serrated spine about 5 in (12 cm) long.

— *Spine*

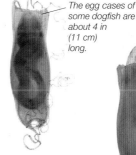

The egg cases of some dogfish are about 4 in (11 cm) long.

Abandoned egg cases or "mermaid's purses" are often washed up on the shore.

After 6–9 months, the dogfish wriggles out of the case.

Hammerhead shark (*Sphyrnidae* sp.)

HAMMERHEAD SHARKS

Hammerhead sharks hunt as individuals at night and swim together in groups during the day. The eyes and nostrils of the shark are set far apart at either side of the "hammer." As the shark swims along, it swings its head back and forth, searching for stingrays – its favorite prey. The hammer-shaped head may protect the shark from the stingray's venomous spines. The head also serves as an extra fin, giving the shark more lift at the front of its body.

The tail is used for balance, steering, and defense.

REPRODUCTION

Most sharks give birth to fully developed baby sharks called pups. Female dogfishes and some other sharks, as well as skates and rays, lay tough egg cases within which the embryos develop. The egg case is safely attached to seaweed by long, curling tendrils. Inside, the embryo absorbs its yolk sac, and hatches after about 6–9 months.

Find out more

CORAL REEFS: *72*
DEFENSE 1: *48*
FISH: *184*
PARTNERS AND PARASITES: *56*

BONY FISH 1

WITH MORE THAN 24,000 species, there is an amazing variety of bony fish – from streamlined barracudas that speed through the water to flatfish that lie motionless on the sea floor. Some fish cruise the surface waters of the oceans, others survive the freezing temperatures, crushing pressures, and inky blackness of the deepest ocean trenches. Many bony fish are fierce predators – archerfish shoot down insects with a jet of water, while angler fish catch their prey with a "fishing rod" complete with "bait."

Coelacanth (*Latimeria chalumnae*)

LIVING FOSSIL
The coelacanth is the last survivor of a primitive group of fish that were in abundance as far back as 300 million years ago. This ancient fish was thought to have become extinct 90 million years ago. However, in 1938, the first live specimen was dredged up in a trawler's net off the coast of South Africa.

CAMOUFLAGE
Many fish are camouflaged to avoid detection by predators. Some have spots or stripes that help to break up their outline against rocks and plants. Surface-dwellers are dark on top and pale underneath. From above, they blend into the darker colors of deep water, and from below, they merge into the shimmering surface water. Many bottom-dwellers are dull in color, resembling mud or sand. Flatfish, such as plaice, bury themselves under sand and gravel, and change color to blend in with their background.

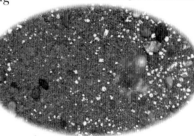

Plaice (*Pleuronectes platessa*)

The fish has started to flick gravel onto itself.

Only a small part of the fish is now visible.

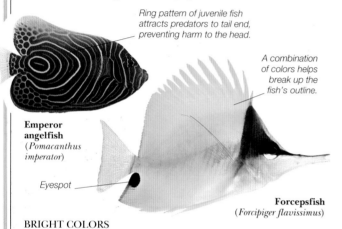

Ring pattern of juvenile fish attracts predators to tail end, preventing harm to the head.

A combination of colors helps break up the fish's outline.

Emperor angelfish (*Pomacanthus imperator*)

Eyespot

Forcepsfish (*Forcipiger flavissimus*)

BRIGHT COLORS
Many bony fish, particularly those living in coral reefs, are brightly colored. The colors help the fish attract mates, to defend their territories, and signal their presence to members of the same species. Some fish have eyespots, or "false eyes," at the rear of the body. As a predator moves to attack the "head end," the fish suddenly darts off in the opposite direction.

DIFFERENT DIETS
Many fish, such as tuna and barracudas, are active predators, hunting down large, fast-moving prey. Others, including the elephant-noses (*Gnathonemus* sp.), use their long, curved snouts to probe for tiny food particles in mud and crevices. South American piranhas usually feed on fish, fruit, and seeds, but their razor-sharp teeth can also strip the flesh from animals in minutes. Some fish eat plants – parrotfish use their beaklike mouths to scrape algae from rocks and corals.

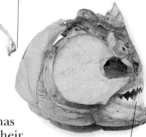

This fish pokes its long snout between stones into mud to find small water creatures.

Elephant-nose skull

Piranha skull

Sharp, triangular teeth are capable of stripping flesh from a mammal.

Parrotfish skull

Horny beak, made of fused teeth, for scraping seaweed off rocks

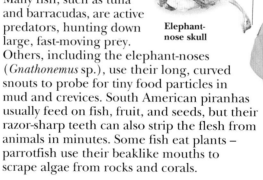

Rockling lies in wait, hidden by seaweeds.

Once sighted, the rockling will pounce on prey such as crabs, and other fish.

LYING IN WAIT
Some fish, such as the pike and the five-bearded rockling, are "lie-in-wait" predators. Pikes lurk among water plants waiting for a young bird or fish to approach, then dash out to snap up their prey. A pike's ambush is aided by good camouflage, a strong tail for sudden acceleration, and forward-facing eyes for judging distances accurately.

Five barbels

Five-bearded rockling (*Ciliata mustela*)

FLYING FISH

To escape predators, flying fish propel themselves out of the water by rapidly moving their strong tails from side to side. They then glide above the waves for up to 164 ft (50 m) while beating their large pectoral fins. In contrast to these gliders, freshwater hatchetfish can leap from the water and actually fly for short distances. Their deep body shape helps keep them steady.

Flying fish

Large pectoral fins are held out like wings when gliding.

ATLANTIC COD

These voracious feeders swim in schools near the water's surface, but look for their food on the seabed at depths of up to 1,970 ft (600 m). They prefer cold water with temperatures of 36–50°F (2–10°C) , and sometimes migrate to follow cool currents out of their normal range. Most of the millions of eggs laid by the female cod are eaten by other fish; only a few out of every million survive to develop into adults.

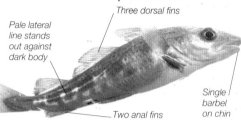

Three dorsal fins

Pale lateral line stands out against dark body

Single barbel on chin

Two anal fins

Scientific name: *Gadus morhua*

Size: Up to 5 ft (1.5 m) long

Habitat: Coastal waters up to 1,000 ft (305 m) deep

Distribution: North Atlantic Ocean, Baltic Sea, and Barents Sea

Reproduction: Female cod lays up to 9 million eggs in February or April; eggs and the newly hatched young float freely in the water

Diet: Sea worms, crustaceans, mollusks, and fish, including herring, capelin, and sand eels

A GARDEN OF EELS

Garden eels live in colonies in warm, shallow, tropical waters. As they sway in the current, they look more like a field of sea grass than a group of fish. Each eel lives in a separate burrow dug out of the sandy seabed. The eels are up to about 3 ft (0.9 m) long. By day, they extend their bodies vertically from their burrows to feed on drifting plankton. If danger threatens, they swiftly sink into their burrows.

Garden eels (*Gorgasia sillneri*)

Teeth hinge backward to allow large prey into the mouth.

Lure on the top of the head contains luminous bacteria to attract prey and mates.

Small eye, typical of all anglers

Leaves of mangrove tree hang over the water.

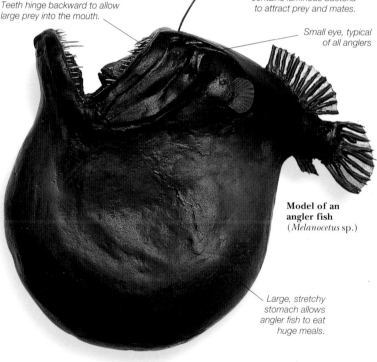

Model of an angler fish
(*Melanocetus* sp.)

Large, stretchy stomach allows angler fish to eat huge meals.

SHOOTING DOWN PREY

The six species of archerfish live in the mangrove swamps of Southeast Asia, Australia, and the Pacific Islands. These remarkable predators can shoot down prey from overhanging branches with precisely aimed jets of water. They can knock spiders out of their webs more than 3 ft 3 in (1 m) away. The fish presses its tongue against a groove along the roof of its mouth. On spotting its prey, it snaps its gill covers shut, forcing a jet of water out of the mouth to its target.

Insects are attracted to the shady environment of the mangrove swamp, and act as sitting targets for archerfish.

Fish directs a jet of water upwards to knock the fly off the leaf.

Archerfish
(*Toxotes* sp.)

DEEP-SEA DWELLERS

Deep-sea fish, such as the angler fish, are bizarre-looking creatures. They lurk at the bottom of the ocean at depths of more than 9,000 ft (2,750 m), waiting for the chance of a meal. Prey is attracted to a lure on the fish's head, which contains luminous bacteria and glows in the dark. The fish's jaws can open remarkably wide to take in prey much larger than itself. The prey is not chewed up, but is swallowed whole.

Large eyes and excellent eyesight help the fish aim accurately.

Find out more
DEFENSE 2: *50*
FEEDING AND NUTRITION: *22*
FISH: *184*
OCEANS: *68*

BONY FISH 2

IN THE UNDERWATER WORLD, fish are always on the lookout for predators. Many bony fish rely on camouflage to hide from their enemies, others have evolved spines or prickles that can inflict great damage on an unwary predator. Several species are poisonous, while some eels can deliver an electric shock. Most bony fish reproduce by depositing their eggs and sperm in the water. The eggs are fertilized and then left to hatch and develop into fish. Although the parents usually leave the eggs and young to look after themselves, some species protect their young in pouches, or nests, or even in their mouths.

Shoal of fairy basslets (Pseudanthias sp.) on coral reef

SCHOOLS AND SHOALS
Many species of fish swim together in large groups called schools or shoals. Grouping helps fish to find mates and food, and to navigate when migrating. It also reduces the risk of being caught. Predators find it hard to single out individuals, and many eyes are more likely to spot enemies. Schools confuse predators by darting off in all directions, or splitting in two.

Spines inject potent venom if stepped on, causing pain or even death.

Porcupine fish before it inflates.

Fish gulps water and becomes too large for most predators to swallow.

Spines stick out as fish inflates itself.

Long-spined porcupinefish
(*Diodon holocanthus*)

DEFENSE
Some fish, including stonefish and lionfish, defend themselves by injecting venom, while puffers have poisonous toxins that can cause illness or death in humans. Other fish use physical weapons. Surgeonfish have sharp structures, called lancets, in front of the tail. If threatened, the fish flicks out its tail, slicing the lancets into the enemy's flesh. Triggerfish have a sharp spine on the back, held erect by a spur on a smaller spine called the trigger. They use the stiff spine to wedge themselves into crevices from which they cannot be extracted.

PORCUPINEFISH AND PUFFERS
One of the most ingenious methods of defense is that used by porcupinefish and their relatives the puffers. When threatened, these fish inflate their bodies with water, or when at the surface, with air. They increase greatly in size, frightening their attackers and making themselves difficult or impossible to swallow. Porcupinefish and some puffers are also armed with sharp spines, which are erected when the fish inflates.

Hornlike growths

PROTECTIVE ARMOR
Some fish have a suit of armor for protection. Boxfish, including cowfish and trunkfish, are encased in a rigid shell made of flat, bony plates. They are inefficient swimmers, propelling themselves forward by moving their tail and pectoral fins. However, they have little need to swim fast because most predators are deterred by their tough armor.

Wide pectoral fins for fanning and aerating the eggs.

Salmon leaping up waterfall

Pectoral fin

Long-horned cowfish
(*Lactoria cornuta*)

Bony projections at rear

Bullhead
(*Cottus gobio*)

SALMON MIGRATION
Like lampreys and sturgeons, salmon are anadromous fish – they spend most of their lives in the ocean, but migrate upriver to breed. Salmon begin their lives in rivers, before migrating to the sea. After one to four years at sea, mature salmon return to the river or stream of their birth to spawn. They recognize their home stream using their sense of smell. Salmon are powerful swimmers and can leap out of the water to ascend waterfalls.

BREEDING AND COURTSHIP

Many fish go through dramatic courtship rituals to attract a mate. Some species, such as the three-spined stickleback, change color and perform elaborate dances. Others make sounds or spread their fins to show off special markings. The male sockeye salmon (*Oncorhynchus nerka*) indicates that he is ready to mate by changing from silver to red. He also develops hooks on his jaw and a prominent hump.

1. The male zigzags toward a female to attract her attention.

Male

Female

2. He then displays his red belly and leads the female to his nest on the riverbed.

3. The male strikes female's tail to provoke her to lay eggs.

4. The female lays up to 100 eggs, which the male fertilizes and then guards.

Courtship behavior of the three-spined stickleback (Gasterosteus aculeatus)

ZEBRA MORAY EEL

Unlike most species of moray eel, which have long, sharp teeth, the zebra moray eel and many of its tropical relatives have flattened, blunt teeth adapted for crushing their hard-bodied prey. Moray eels hide in crevices and caves among underwater rocks and coral reefs. If provoked, they can inflict serious bites to divers. The zebra moray's bold black and white markings break up the fish's outline.

Scientific name: *Gymnomuraena zebra*

Size: Up to 5 ft (1.5 m) long

Habitat: Coastal waters and coral reefs up to 250 ft (75 m) deep

Distribution: Indian and Pacific Oceans

Reproduction: Female lays a large number of eggs which float to the surface; the eggs hatch to produce transparent larvae

Diet: Mainly crabs, but also crustaceans, sea urchins, and other hard-bodied animals

PREGNANT FATHERS

Found in shallow marine waters worldwide, the remarkable looking seahorses, and their relatives the pipefish, have an unusual method of reproduction. The female lays up to 400 eggs in a brood pouch at the front of the male's body. The male fertilizes, then incubates, the eggs and protects the babies in his pouch until they can fend for themselves. When they are ready to hatch, his body convulses and the young pop out of the pouch in batches of five or so.

Fish is camouflaged by lumpy skin and blotchy colors.

Seahorse
(*Hippocampus* sp.)

Young seahorses swim close to their father.

Tail anchors seahorse to vegetation to prevent it being buffeted by the waves.

Reef stonefish
(*Synanceia verrucosa*)

Male protects the eggs from predators and other hazards.

Round clump of about 250 yellow eggs

If some of the eggs are late in hatching, the father will eat them.

Baby cichlid being blown out of its mother's mouth.

FISHERIES
Fishing is one of the oldest methods of obtaining food. Commercial fisheries provide employment and food for millions of people worldwide, and fish make up 85 percent of the harvest from the sea. Today many fish stocks, including those of herring and cod, are being exhausted.

Commercial fishing boat hauling in a net of herring

Cichlid
(*Melanochromis joanjohnsonae*)

MOUTH-BROODERS
Some fish, such as cichlids, give the ultimate protection to their offspring. The female keeps the eggs and young in her mouth or throat, where they receive a good supply of oxygen-rich water. Occasionally, she blows the babies out of her mouth. This gives both the mother and young a chance to feed. Until they become independent, the young return to her mouth at night or if danger threatens.

LOOKING AFTER THE EGGS
Some fish lay millions of eggs, which are left to fend for themselves. Despite the large numbers, only a few survive to develop into adults. Other fish, such as the bullhead, lay only a few hundred eggs, which the male guards fiercely for up to a month. He fans the eggs until they hatch.

Find out more
COURTSHIP, MATING, AND PARENTAL CARE: *30*
FISH: *184*
MIGRATION AND NAVIGATION: *46*

AMPHIBIANS

MOST AMPHIBIANS CAN live on both land and in water – the name "amphibian" comes from the Greek words "amphi" and "bios" meaning "double life." Amphibians undergo a process called metamorphosis as they develop from tadpoles or larvae into adults. There are three groups of amphibians: frogs and toads, salamanders and newts, and caecilians. All amphibians are "cold-blooded," which means that their body temperatures vary with their surroundings. Most species return to the water to mate and lay their eggs, but some make nests on land.

Eryops lived in the swamps of Texas, about 200 million years ago. It grew to a length of 6 ft 6 in (2 m).

EARLY AMPHIBIANS

Amphibians were the first vertebrates to live both on land and in water. Early amphibians may have evolved from lobe-finned fish or from lungfish, which can breathe air. They moved out of the water because there were few enemies on land and good food supplies. Early terrestrial amphibians developed strong limbs for walking around on land.

LEGLESS CAECILIANS

Caecilians are legless, wormlike amphibians. Some species have tiny scales embedded in the rings on their bodies. Caecilians live in the tropics, spending their lives in water or underground. They use their blunt heads to dig in the mud for worms, termites, and lizards, and they have sharp teeth for cutting and holding their prey. Some caecilians lay eggs that hatch into larvae, others produce live young.

Caecilian
(*Dermophis mexicanus*)

The common frog has complex lungs.

Oxygen absorbed through the skin into the bloodstream

Carbon dioxide expelled

BREATHING

Most adult amphibians can breathe through their skin as well as through their lungs. Some can also take in oxygen through the lining of their mouth. Mucous glands under the skin keep the surface damp, allowing oxygen to pass through easily. About 200 species of salamander have no lungs and breathe only through the skin and mouth. Amphibian larvae breathe through gills. These gills are fleshy and feathery with a large surface area and a good blood supply to take in oxygen from the water.

Blood capillaries

Mucous glands

Cross section of skin

American bullfrog
(*Rana catesbeiana*)

Large eardrum

Large, bulging eyes

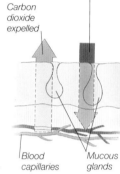

Individual lateral-line sense organs are called plaques.

SWIMMING

Salamanders, newts, and aquatic caecilians swim like fish, using "S-shaped" movements. Many salamanders and newts have well-developed, flattened tails for swimming. Frogs and toads have webbed feet, but they do not bend their bodies when they swim. Their hind legs kick out to propel their bodies through the water. Tadpoles, however, swim by lashing their tails from side to side.

African clawed toad
(*Xenopus laevis*)

EYES AND EARS

Most frogs, toads, newts, and salamanders have good eyesight, but caecilians have tiny eyes and are almost blind. Cave salamanders have lost the use of their eyes, but land-living salamanders need good eyesight to spot slow-moving prey. Frogs have large eyes that help them to look out for danger and food. Many amphibians, such as frogs and toads, have very sharp hearing that helps them identify mating calls and approaching predators.

SENSES

Creatures that live in water have a very good sense of touch. Aquatic amphibians use a lateral-line system – a set of sensitive organs along the sides of the body that respond to movements in the water. Many species smell by means of a pair of tiny holes, called the Jacobson's organ, in the roof of the mouth. Caecilians have a sensory tentacle on the head, which may help them to smell or find their way around.

Salamanders and newts swim by moving their body in "S-shaped" waves.

Frog inflating its body, making itself difficult to swallow

AVOIDING PREDATORS

Amphibians make an ideal meal for a predator because they have no fur, feathers, or scales. They are prey to a wide variety of animals, including lizards and mammals. Many species have skin colors and markings that help to camouflage them against their surroundings, others escape attack by diving into water. Most adult amphibians have poison glands. These glands ooze an unpleasant-tasting substance that can poison a predator.

In hot sunshine, White's tree frogs (Litoria caerulea) are a light green color to reflect heat.

COLORS

Amphibians have evolved a wide range of shapes and colors to suit their environment. Many species change color to attract a mate in the breeding season or to regulate their body temperature. They become pale-colored in warm weather and darker in cold, wet weather. Some amphibians have bright colors and patterns to warn predators that they are poisonous.

1. Embryos are developing inside the eggs.

Frog spawn

LIFE-CYCLES

Most amphibians mate and lay their eggs in water. They lay their eggs singly in clumps or in strings of clear jelly called spawn. The larvae undergo a series of changes, called metamorphosis, before becoming adults. Tadpoles, the larvae of frogs and toads, look very different from the adults. In the early stages, they breathe through gills, or spiracles, and have no legs. Before they become adults, they develop lungs and legs and lose their tails.

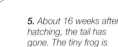

2. On hatching, tadpoles have a weak tail, and gills outside the body. After 10 days, they begin to swim and feed.

3. The outside gills have grown over and lungs form inside. After nine weeks, the back legs appear. The tadpole changes to a meat-eating diet.

4. The front legs appear about 12 weeks after hatching. The eyes become more prominent, and the mouth gets wider.

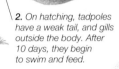

The tail will soon start to recede.

5. About 16 weeks after hatching, the tail has gone. The tiny frog is about 0.4 in (1 cm) long and is ready to leave the water.

BREEDING MIGRATION

Each spring, many salamanders, newts, frogs, and toads migrate up to 3 miles (5 km) from their hibernation sites to the ponds or streams where they breed. To find the way, they use familiar landmarks, scent, the position of the sun, and the Earth's magnetic field. Frogs may "home in" on the calls of other frogs when they near the breeding site. Amphibians often return to the pond or stream where they grew up.

Golden toads (Bufo periglenes) at a breeding pool

Salamanders use their legs like oars to row themselves along.

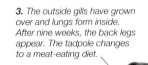

European fire salamanders mating

LIVE YOUNG

Although most amphibians lay eggs, some species such as the European fire salamander (*Salamandra salamandra*) give birth to live young. After mating, the fertilized eggs develop inside the female's body for about eight months. She can give birth to as many as 60 young, which are like tiny adults, but with gills. The larvae develop lungs and leave the water after three months.

When the toad draws its back legs up, it holds its arms by its side to form a streamlined shape.

The toad floats and glides forward with its arms and legs stretched out.

The toad draws its knees up ready for the next kick.

Find out more

FROGS AND TOADS: *196*
LIZARDS: *202*
RIVERS, LAKES, AND PONDS: *76*
SALAMANDERS AND NEWTS: *194*

SALAMANDERS AND NEWTS

SALAMANDERS ARE MOSTLY SMALL, long-tailed amphibians that live in a variety of damp habitats. Some live permanently in water, others live entirely on land – there are even a few species that prefer dark, damp caves. Whether terrestrial or aquatic, they all breed in the water. They often have smooth, slimy skin with fins along the edges of their tails to help them swim. Salamanders have adapted to living in cold areas by hibernating in winter. In warmer regions, they estivate (remain dormant) during hot, dry periods. Salamanders and newts undergo a process called metamorphosis in their development from larvae to adults.

Spotted salamander (*Ambystoma maculatum*)

WHERE SALAMANDERS LIVE
Salamanders and newts have porous skin that allows water and air to pass through it. In hot, dry conditions, the skin must be kept moist to avoid drying out. Most species live in damp places, or only emerge at night when it is cooler and wetter. Aquatic species live in streams, lakes, ponds, and caves. Terrestrial species lurk below rocks and logs or burrow into the soil – a few climb trees.

COURTSHIP AND MATING

Most male salamanders lay a packet of sperm, called a spermatophore, on land that the female picks up with an opening called the cloaca. The eggs are fertilized internally and laid on land. Male newts deposit their spermatophore in water. The male attracts the female with his prominent crest. He may also perform a courtship dance or release special scents, called pheromones. He then guides the female over the spermatophore by nudging against her side.

Courtship behavior of the great crested newt

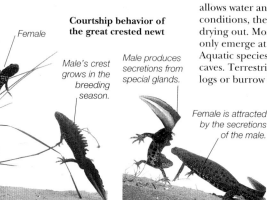

Female

Male's crest grows in the breeding season.

Male produces secretions from special glands.

Female is attracted by the secretions of the male.

The female takes the spermatophore into her body.

The male newt is attracted to the egg-carrying female, by her swollen belly.

The male lashes his silvery tail to waft secretions towards the female.

The male lays his spermatophore and guides the female over it.

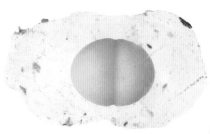

1. Day 1 – the egg cell has divided into two cells.

Development of the great crested newt

Gills are forming behind the head.

2. Day 12 – the egg has developed into an embryo with a head, tail, and small bumps where the legs will grow.

EGGS AND DEVELOPMENT

Salamanders and newts undergo a period of larval development called metamorphosis. Terrestrial salamanders lay their eggs on land. The larval development occurs inside the eggs, and the young, when hatched, look like tiny versions of the adults. Aquatic salamanders and newts lay their eggs in water. Tadpole-like larvae, which later lose their gills, hatch out of the eggs. Some salamanders do not lay eggs, but give birth to fully formed young.

The tadpole still has feathery, external gills.

Eye is not yet fully developed.

Salamander in the unken reflex position

DEFENSE

To deter predators such as birds and snakes, salamanders and newts have many defense tactics. Some keep still and adopt the "unken reflex" position, holding the tail and chin upright to show off their brightly colored undersides. Many have poisonous skin and are brightly colored to warn predators. Spanish ribbed newts (*Pleurodeles waltl*) have sharp ribs tipped with toxic substances that give predators a shock. Some salamanders can shed their tails if attacked.

3. Day 14 – the newt tadpole makes a hole in the jelly and wriggles out.

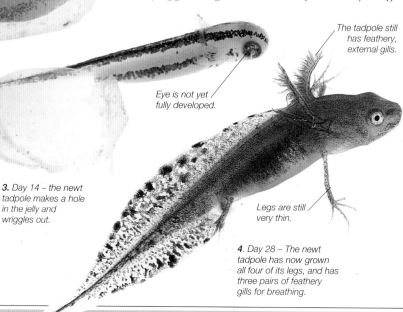

Legs are still very thin.

4. Day 28 – The newt tadpole has now grown all four of its legs, and has three pairs of feathery gills for breathing.

FEEDING

Salamanders and newts are carnivores that feed on slow-moving animals, such as snails, slugs, and worms. They move slowly toward their prey, then make a quick grab with their sharp teeth and jaws. Some species can flick the tongue forward to capture small prey. Salamanders need little food because they move slowly. When they do feed, they can store a large part of their meal as fat. Giant salamanders feed mainly at night, relying on smell and touch to detect prey.

Mandarin salamander
(*Tylototriton verrucosus*)

Greater siren (*Siren lacertina*)

AMPHIUMAS AND SIRENS
These North American amphibians look like eels. They live buried in sand or mud at the bottom of water, and feed on frogs, snails, worms, and fish. Amphiumas have lungs and four tiny legs. Sirens retain their gills throughout their lives, and have small, weak front legs, but no hind legs. Sirens may estivate (remain dormant) during hot, dry periods.

LUNGLESS SALAMANDERS
Most salamanders and newts breathe both through their skin and lungs, but there are also about 250 species that have no lungs at all. Lungless salamanders breathe only through their skin and mouth lining. Some live in fast-flowing streams, where the water is rich in oxygen. Land-living species must keep their skin moist at all times so oxygen can pass to the blood from the film of water on top of the skin.

Cave salamander
(*Eurycea lucifuga*)

FIRE SALAMANDER

This terrestrial salamander has brightly colored spots or stripes on its body. The markings warn potential predators that the salamander's skin glands produce a secretion that will irritate their mouth and eyes if they attempt to eat it. The poison is even powerful enough to kill small mammals. Fire salamanders hunt their prey by night and shelter during the day.

Poison glands are located on top of the head.

Scientific name: *Salamandra salamandra*

Size: Males up to 7 in (17 cm) long; females up to 12 in (30 cm) long

Habitat: Damp areas in forests and on mountains

Distribution: Europe (excluding the UK), northwestern Africa, parts of southwestern Asia

Reproduction: Female gives birth to 10–50 tadpoles in the water, after about 8 months' gestation

Diet: Slow-moving invertebrates, such as earthworms

Frilly gills allow the axolotl to breathe underwater.

Five toes on back legs

Four toes on front legs

Gills have disappeared because the newt can now breathe through its lungs as well as through its skin.

Great crested newt
(*Triturus cristatus*)

5. The male newt is now fully grown. Great crested newts reach sexual maturity at 3–4 years. The female lays up to 300 eggs which she wraps individually in the leaves of water plants.

STAYING YOUNG
Some water-dwelling salamanders, such as the axolotl and olm, do not develop fully into adults. They retain some of their larval features, including gills and a lateral line, despite being sexually mature and able to breed. This condition is called neotony, and may have a genetic or environmental cause, such as a low level of iodine in the water, or a low water temperature. The axolotl develops into an adult if given hormones, or if iodine is added to the water; the olm does not change if treated the same way.

Axolotls may be albino like this one, or black, yellow, or speckled.

Axolotl
(*Ambystoma mexicanum*)

___ *Find out more* ___

AMPHIBIANS: *192*
DEFENSE 2: *50*
GROWTH AND DEVELOPMENT: *32*
MOVEMENT IN WATER: *38*

FROGS AND TOADS

FROGS AND TOADS ARE BY FAR the largest and most diverse group of amphibians. There are more than 3,900 different species, many of which live in tropical rainforests. Their wide variety of shapes, sizes, and colors helps them adapt to a range of habitats including deserts, grasslands, and mountains. Frogs and toads can live both on land and in water. Those that live mainly in water tend to have long, slender bodies, while those that spend most of their time on land have rounder bodies and short legs. Nearly all frogs and toads are meat-eaters and have large mouths for swallowing their food whole.

Unlike other amphibians, adult frogs and toads have no tail.

Green toad (*Bufo viridis*)

European common frog (*Rana temporaria*)

FROG OR TOAD?

Frogs and toads share many characteristics, and it is often difficult to tell them apart. Many biologists use the word "frogs" to refer to both frogs and toads. Frogs and toads have evolved different characteristics to suit their environments. In general, frogs have smooth skins, long back legs, webbed feet, and live in or near water. Toads tend to have dry, warty skins, little or no webbing between the toes, and prefer to live on land.

TREE FROGS

These frogs have small, lightweight bodies that help them to balance on branches and leaves. The sticky pads on their long, thin fingers and toes give them a good grip, while the loose skin around their bellies enables them to cling tightly to tree trunks. Tree frogs also have large, forward-facing eyes that help them to judge distances when climbing or attacking prey.

Red-eyed tree frog (*Agalychnis callidryas*)

Tree frogs are agile climbers. They curl their toes around branches for extra grip.

Each finger- and toe-pad produces a sticky mucus that "glues" the frog to smooth, slippery leaves and branches.

JUMPING AND SWIMMING

Short-legged frogs and toads walk, crawl, or make short hops, while long-legged species leap or make long jumps. In order to leap, a frog quickly straightens its legs and pushes itself forward in an arc through the air. When swimming, the frog pulls its hind legs up to its body then kicks them out backward. It propels itself through the water using its webbed feet.

1. The frog presses its feet back against the ground to push itself forward.

FLYING FROGS

In the rainforests of Southeast Asia, some tree frogs glide between trees to escape predators. They spread their webbed feet wide and can "fly" up to 49 ft (15 m) from one tree to another. Their big feet and long webbed toes act like parachutes, helping to slow their descent.

Flying frog (*Agalychnis spurrellii*)

Spadefoot toad (*Pelobates fuscus*)

FEEDING

All adult frogs and toads swallow their food whole, so the size of their prey depends on the size of their mouth. Most eat insects, slugs, snails, and worms, but larger species may eat mice, birds, young snakes, and even other frogs and toads. Frogs tend to be more active hunters than toads and often catch flying insects by flicking out their long, sticky tongues. Toads usually creep up slowly on a meal, then snap it up.

THE BURROWERS

Some frogs and toads burrow into the ground to escape predators, to lie in wait for a passing meal, or to avoid extreme temperatures. Burrowing frogs dig down backward into the soft ground with a sideways shuffle of the back feet. Their heels have a special hard scraper, or scoop, to move the soil out of the way.

1. Green toad watching a wriggling mealworm

2. The toad snatches up the worm with its sticky tongue.

3. As the toad swallows, it blinks. Its eyeballs push downward, squeezing food down its throat.

CAMOUFLAGE

Frogs and toads have many enemies, including snakes, birds, and spiders. Their skin colors and markings help to camouflage them against their surroundings. Some species can change color, others have fringes to disguise their shape. The African square-marked toad is so well camouflaged that it simply "disappears" against the bark and leaves on the forest floor.

African square-marked toad
(*Bufo regularis*)

DARWIN'S FROG

This strange-looking frog is a mouthbrooder – its tadpoles develop inside its mouth. The female lays her eggs on bare ground. After about 15 days, males gather round and gulp down several eggs each. The males' vocal sacs act as a nursery until the tadpoles have metamorphosed into tiny frogs.

The vocal sac runs right along the underside of the male frog's body.

From above, the Darwin's frog looks like a green leaf.

Scientific name: *Rhinoderma darwinii*

Size: 1 in (2.5 cm) long

Habitat: On land near forest streams

Distribution: Southern Chile and southern Argentina

Reproduction: Eggs laid on land hatch and complete their development in male's vocal sac

Diet: Insects

DEFENSE

Although frogs and toads cannot bite or sting their enemies, they use several other devices to avoid predators. When threatened, the Chilean four-eyed frog turns its back to reveal poisonous glands that look like staring eyes. This confuses and startles an attacker, giving the frog a chance to leap away.

Chilean four-eyed frog
(*Pleurodema bibroni*)

2. As the frog takes off, it straightens its body into a streamlined shape. The frog leaps with its legs at full stretch.

If startle tactics do not work, the glands produce a foul-tasting poison, which will repel most predators.

The eyes are closed for protection.

FROG CALLING

Frogs were probably the first animals to develop a true voice. They call by moving air across a series of vocal cords to their large, inflatable throat pouch. Each species of frog has its own distinctive call. Males call to attract females and to warn off other males.

The throat pouch, or vocal sac, is formed from stretchy skin on the floor of the mouth.

Painted reed frog (*Hyperolius marmoratus*)

Once in the water, the frog is safe from many enemies.

Male frogs are smaller than females.

3. The front legs act as a brake and cushion the impact of landing.

MATING AND EGG-LAYING

Most frogs and toads mate in the water, with the male clasping the female with his forelegs. The female's eggs are fertilized by the male as she releases them. Some frogs and toads lay their eggs in clumps, others lay long strings of eggs. The surrounding jelly protects the embryos from predators and keeps them from drying out. Many frogs and toads lay large numbers of eggs – as many as a quarter of a million in a lifetime.

European common frog (*Rana temporaria*)

CARING FOR THE EGGS

Not all frogs and toads leave their eggs to hatch by themselves. Some species guard their eggs, keeping them moist and protecting them from predators. The male midwife toad (*Alytes obstetricans*) carries a string of eggs on his back, wrapped around his legs. When the eggs are ready to hatch he releases them into water.

Poisonous, warty glands protect this toad from predators.

Male midwife toad

Find out more
AMPHIBIANS: *192*
HUNTING: *52*
TROPICAL RAINFORESTS: *82*
VERTEBRATES: *182*

REPTILES

SNAKES, LIZARDS, TORTOISES, turtles and crocodiles are all reptiles. Inside their bodies, reptiles have a bony skeleton with a backbone. On the outside, they have a covering of tough, protective scales, that keeps their bodies from drying out. They lay eggs with waterproof shells or give birth to live young. Their young are usually born on land and look like tiny versions of their parents. Reptiles are able to live in many different environments on land. They are most common in warmer places because they rely on their surroundings for warmth. Since they do not need to eat to keep warm, reptiles can survive well in barren areas, such as deserts, where there is little food.

REPTILE ANCESTORS

The first reptiles lived about 340 million years ago. They developed from amphibians that crawled out of the water onto land. Reptiles dominated the Earth from about 250 to 65 million years ago. Dinosaurs inhabited the land, and flying reptiles called pterosaurs ruled the sky.

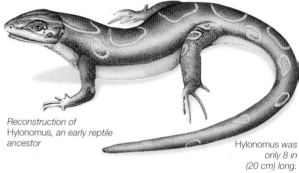

Reconstruction of Hylonomus, an early reptile ancestor

Hylonomus was only 8 in (20 cm) long.

SCALY SKIN

A reptile's scales are thickenings of the outside layer of skin and are mostly made of a horny substance called keratin. Human nails are made of a similar material. Some reptiles have scales with bony plates called osteoderms. The scaly skin protects the reptile's body from drying out and from damage caused by predators. The outside skin is shed from time to time to allow reptiles to grow and to replace worn-out skin. The scales may be smooth, bumpy, or ridged and can form crests or spines.

Crosssection of reptile skin

Each scale is made of the hard material keratin.

Osteoderm

Lower layer of skin contains nerves and blood vessels.

A snake's scales may overlap for extra protection.

The scales pull apart when the skin stretches.

LIVING FOSSIL

Tuataras are the sole survivors of a group of reptiles that lived during the days of the dinosaurs. Today, these reptiles live only on a few islands off the coast of New Zealand. They are active in cool temperatures and live, move, and grow very slowly.
A tuatara breathes only once every seven seconds when moving, and once an hour when resting.

Tuatara
(*Sphenodon punctatus*)

SENSES

Reptiles rely on their senses of sight, smell, and hearing to find food and avoid danger. Some reptiles have poorly developed senses. Burrowing reptiles, for example, have poor eyesight and snakes cannot hear very well. But some reptiles have special senses. Snakes, and some lizards, taste and smell the air with their tongue and a sense organ in the roof of the mouth called the Jacobson's organ. Pit vipers, and some pythons and boas, have heat pits on their faces to detect heat given off by prey.

Snake's forked tongue picks up tiny scent particles in the air.

The tip of each fork is pressed against the Jacobson's organ in the roof of the mouth.

Nostril   Eye

Jacobson's organ "tastes" and "smells" chemical particles in the air.

Tongue

Red-tailed rat snake
(*Elaphe oxycephala*)

TEMPERATURE CONTROL

Reptiles are cold-blooded, or ectothermic, which means that they depend on the sun or on warm surfaces to heat their bodies. By moving between warm and cool places, reptiles can control their body temperature. A reptile often basks in the sun to absorb enough energy for hunting and then digesting its food. As the day becomes hotter, the reptile will move into the shade to cool down.

Turtles bask in the sun to warm their bodies.

Galápagos marine iguana submerged in water

DIET

Most reptiles, such as snakes and crocodiles, are carnivores. Many lizards eat meat in the form of insects. A house gecko, for example, can eat half its own weight in small insects in just one night. Some lizards are herbivores – the Galápagos marine iguana (*Amblyrhynchus cristatus*) feeds only on seaweed, and tortoises feed mainly on plants.

Looking after turtle eggs in Sri Lanka

PROTECTING REPTILES

The future of many reptiles is in danger. Their habitats have often been destroyed, and they have been hunted for food or to make objects such as leather bags and tortoiseshell combs. Laws now protect some species, such as turtles, whose eggs may be moved to safety.

EGGS

Reptiles usually dig holes in the sand or soil or make nests in which they lay eggs. Some guard the eggs until they hatch. Most reptile eggs have soft, leathery shells but tortoises, crocodiles, and geckos lay eggs with hard shells. Inside the egg, the embryo is cushioned by a water-filled sac called the amnion.

HATCHING

To help them break free of the egg, baby lizards and snakes have a sharp, pointed egg tooth on the tip of the upper lip. This drops off soon after hatching. Tuataras, tortoises, turtles, and crocodiles have a horny growth that does the same job. From the moment they hatch, most young reptiles have to fend for themselves. Crocodiles may carry their young to water and protect them from predators, but they do not feed them.

The stripes on this young leopard gecko's body will gradually change into spots as it grows older.

LIVE YOUNG

Some lizards and snakes give birth to fully formed young. Their eggs are protected inside the female's body, and the developing young may get their food from the yolk sac or sometimes from the mother. Many reptiles that live in cold places give birth to live young, probably because the eggs are warmer inside the mother's body than they would be in the soil. Reptiles that live in watery places produce live young.

Ground python egg

Matamata turtle egg

Alligator egg

Inside an egg

Embryo
Amnion
Yolk sac

The shell of a reptile egg protects the embryo but also allows it to breathe.

Leopard gecko hatching

1. A gecko develops for 2–3 months before the egg splits open.

2. Five minutes later, the baby gecko starts pushing its head out of the egg.

3. After about 20 minutes, the gecko's head emerges.

4. The gecko rests briefly before struggling free.

5. In just 40 minutes, the young gecko is free of its shell.

Leopard gecko
(*Eublepharis macularius*)

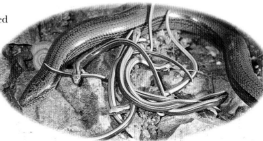

A female slowworm (Anguis fragilis) and her newborn young

Lizard worm heads

Round head

Keel head

Chisel head

Shovel head

WORM LIZARDS

Neither lizards nor snakes, worm lizards are strange reptiles. They burrow underground to hunt for insects, which they find by touch. Worm lizards tunnel by pushing their heads through the soil. They have different burrowing techniques according to the shape of the head. Their eyes are under the skin and their nostrils close when they burrow.

Amphisbaenid
(*Amphisbaena fuliginosa*)

The pattern on this worm lizard helps it blend with its forest habitat.

Find out more

ANIMALS IN DANGER: *100*
CROCODILES AND ALLIGATORS: *206*
DESERTS: *86*
SNAKES: *204*

TORTOISES AND TURTLES

THESE HARD-SHELLED REPTILES belong to a group called chelonians. There are more than 250 species of chelonian, including tortoises, turtles, and terrapins. The shell protects their soft bodies from predators and adverse weather, and it can also provide camouflage. Most tortoises and turtles lack teeth. Instead, their jaws have sharp edges that can tear food. Tortoises usually live on land, while turtles live in the water. Freshwater turtles are known as terrapins. All reproduce by laying eggs on land, usually in sand, leaf litter, or other animals' burrows. Tortoises can live for more than 100 years.

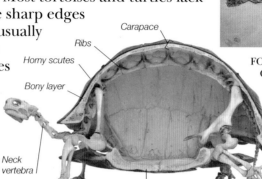

Carapace

Ribs

Horny scutes

Bony layer

Neck vertebra

Plastron

FOSSIL RELATIVES
Chelonians are the oldest living group of reptiles. Fossilized remains show that turtles may have lived on Earth as early as the first dinosaurs, about 200 million years ago. They have not changed much over the years, and still look similar to their ancient fossil relatives. However, early turtles had small teeth and could not withdraw their heads inside their shells.

Head pulled in sideways

Head retracted straight back

Starred tortoise (Geochelone elegans) has starlike patterns on its knobbly carapace.

SHELL ARMOR
The strong shell of a chelonian consists of two parts – a domed carapace covering the back, and a flat plastron under the belly. The shell is made from bony plates that are fused to the ribs and vertebrae to form a solid box of armor. It is covered by large scales called scutes, made of a horny material known as keratin. Growth rings on the plates help to determine the age of a chelonian.

NECK POSITIONS
Chelonians are divided into two groups according to the way they draw their heads into their shells. Side-necked chelonians bend their necks sideways, curling their heads under the upper shell. Most straight-necked turtles and tortoises have shorter necks and can pull their heads straight back into the shell.

SHELLS AND LEGS
The shape of a chelonian's shell usually reflects its environment. Land-living tortoises have either high-domed or knobbly shells to protect them from predators. They need strong, thick legs, like pillars, to support their weight. Turtles tend to have flatter, lighter shells, which are streamlined for easy movement. Their long front legs are wing-shaped to enable them to "fly" through the water.

The flat shell of this red-eared slider (Trachemys elegans scripta) is a typical feature of most aquatic turtles.

Spiny soft-shell turtle (*Apalone spinifera*)

BREATHING
A chelonian's ribs form part of its shell so, unlike other reptiles, it is unable to move its ribs and pump air in and out of the lungs. Instead, muscles at the tops of the legs and in the abdomen draw fresh air into the lungs and expel stale air. Turtles can also breathe through the skin, the lining of the throat, and through an opening near the anus. Some can survive underwater for weeks without coming to the surface to breathe.

Snapping turtles stretch to breathe air above the water.

Some turtles breathe through the skin and throat lining.

Snapping turtle (*Chelydra serpentina*)

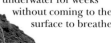

SOFT SHELLS
Soft-shelled turtles have shells with a leathery texture and no horny plates. The bony part of the shell contains large air spaces, which makes the turtle lighter, helping it float and swim with ease. The flat shape of the shell enables the turtle to hide from predators in the mud at the bottom of rivers, lakes, and ponds.

FEEDING

Most chelonians are too slow to catch prey, so they feed on plants or small animals such as worms and insect larvae. Sea turtles eat fish, sponges, seaweed, and crabs. Some chelonians have special ways of catching prey. The camouflaged alligator snapping turtle lures fish into its mouth with a wormlike "bait" on its tongue. The matamata turtle (*Chelus fimbriatus*) opens up its throat and sucks up food like a vacuum cleaner.

Wormlike appendage attracts prey.

Alligator snapping turtle
(*Macroclemys temmincki*)

Once hatched, baby green turtles dash for the open sea to escape predators.

EGGS AND YOUNG

Chelonians lay eggs on land so that the developing embryos can breathe oxygen from the air. Without this oxygen, they would suffocate. In a nesting season, most species lay two or more clutches of eggs, and there may be between four and more than a hundred eggs in each clutch. Most females lay their eggs in nests that they dig out with their back feet. Others, such as the stinkpot turtle (*Sternotherus odoratus*), lay their eggs under rotting vegetation. Some species, such as the Florida redbelly (*Pseudemys nelsoni*), use the nests of other animals.

HATCHING OUT

Baby chelonians hatch out of their eggs using a peg, or egg tooth, on the front of their snouts. Initially, the baby still has a supply of yolk in its body and may not need to feed for a while. Some species stay in the nest after hatching, usually waiting for winter to end.

Egg tooth drops off soon after hatching.

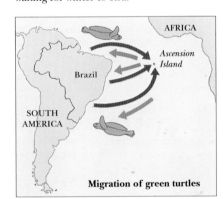

AFRICA

Ascension Island

Brazil

SOUTH AMERICA

Migration of green turtles

➡ *Turtle route to feeding grounds off Brazilian coast*

➡ *Turtle route to nesting grounds on Ascension Island*

GALAPAGOS GIANT TORTOISE

This giant tortoise is one of several species living on the Galápagos Islands, off the west coast of South America. It has adapted to living in areas where it is dry, and is able to go for long periods without food or water. Its long neck enables the tortoise to reach high-growing plants.

Long neck

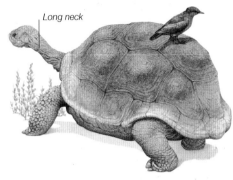

Scientific name:	*Geochelone nigra*
Size: Shell up to 4 ft (1.3 m) long; weight up to 550 lb (250 kg)	
Habitat: Dry, rocky ground	
Distribution: Galápagos Islands	
Reproduction: Female lays clutches of up to 15 eggs in dry, sandy soil	
Diet: Plants, including cacti	

MIGRATION

Sea turtles often make long journeys between their feeding grounds and the beaches where they nest. The most common species is the green turtle (Chelonia mydas), which breeds on coasts in many warm parts of the world. Green turtles have a strong homing instinct, and they swim back to the beaches where they hatched. Some migrate from eastern Brazil all the way to Ascension Island – a tiny speck in the mid-Atlantic, less than 9 miles (15 km) across.

Streamlined shell allows turtle to swim easily through the water.

Turtles come to the surface to breathe through their nostrils.

Front legs are flipper-shaped so the turtle can glide through water.

Green turtle
(*Chelonia mydas*)

Back feet are used as rudders for steering.

SEA TURTLES

The seven species of sea turtle all have flat, lightweight, streamlined shells and large front flippers. The largest is the leatherback turtle (*Dermochelys coriacea*), which is found in warmer oceans. Some species of sea turtles are very fast swimmers and can reach speeds of up to 18 mph (29 kmh). They swallow a lot of seawater as they feed, so they produce salty tears to get rid of excess salt.

Sea turtles, such as the green turtle, swim gracefully in the sea, but are clumsy on land.

Find out more

DEFENSE 2: *50*
MIGRATION AND NAVIGATION: *46*
MOVEMENT IN WATER: *38*
REPTILES: *198*

LIZARDS

THERE ARE NEARLY 4,000 SPECIES of lizards – more than any other group of reptiles. Lizards live in almost every type of environment, but most are found in tropical or subtropical countries where they spend much of their time basking in the sunshine. Others live in trees or have adapted to living in caves or underground burrows. Typical lizards have four legs, feet with sharp claws, scaly bodies, and long tails. Most are swift, agile hunters that prey on small animals, such as snails. To reproduce, most lizards lay leathery-shelled eggs in leaf litter or sandy holes; a few give birth to live young.

Leopard gecko
(*Eublepharis macularius*)

The skin can peel off in one piece.

SCALY SKIN

All lizards have a tough, scaly skin, which acts as a waterproof covering and helps retain body moisture. Burrowing lizards have smooth scales that help them slide through the soil. In some lizards, the scales have developed into sharp spines for defense. As lizards grow, they shed (slough) their scaly skin about once a month. The old skin comes off in large flakes, although some species peel it off with their mouths and then swallow it.

Geckos cling upside down with their special toe pads.

Tokay gecko
(*Gekko gekko*)

Geckos can climb vertically and even hang horizontally.

LEGLESS LIZARDS
Some lizards look like snakes. They have long, thin bodies and very small legs, or no legs at all. They move easily underground, or through thick vegetation, by twisting their bodies from side to side. Unlike snakes, however, legless lizards have small ear openings and pointed tongues.

The glass lizard has no front legs and only tiny back legs.

Glass lizard
(*Ophisaurus* sp.)

GETTING ABOUT
Lizards are extremely agile and many have specially adapted feet and toes. Climbing lizards, such as girdled lizards, have very sharp claws for extra grip. A gecko has sharp claws and pads on its toes that are covered with millions of tiny hairlike structures. These microscopic hairs cling to any bumps and dips in a surface, allowing the gecko to walk up walls and even upside down on ceilings. The powerful legs and feet of monitor lizards and plated lizards are specially adapted for digging.

Head

LIZARD TAILS
Several lizards, such as chameleons, have prehensile tails, which they curl around plants like an extra leg to help them climb. Some lizards, such as gila monsters and shinglebacks, store fat in their thick tails – they use the fat later as a source of energy. If attacked by a predator, some lizards can shed their tail and run away, leaving the tail wiggling on the ground. A new tail will grow to replace the old one.

Australian shingleback
(*Trachydosaurus rugosus*)

Plated lizard feet are good for digging.

Girdled lizard feet have sharp claws.

Geckos have five wide toe pads.

The head-shaped tail confuses predators.

This Madagascan chameleon has a strong tail that it curls around branches for a good grip.

Flying gecko
(*Ptychozoon kuhli*)

FLYING LIZARDS
Lizards, such as flying geckos and flying dragons, can glide between rainforest trees to escape from predators. The skin along the sides of the gecko's body spreads out like a parachute to slow the lizard down as it falls through the air. The "wings" of the flying dragon are extensions of their ribs. They normally lie folded against the body, but can be spread out wide for gliding flights.

The tokay gecko from eastern Asia is one of the best lizard climbers.

WALKING ON WATER

The extraordinary basilisk lizard escapes predators by running quickly across the surface of water on its hind legs. Its feet have very broad soles, and the extra strips of skin on the sides of its toes give more support. As the lizard loses speed, it sinks down through the water and swims or dives to safety.

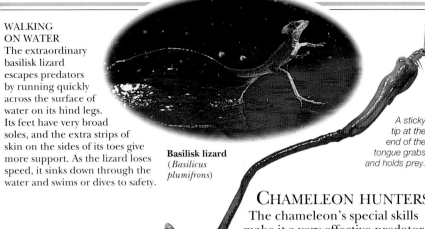

Basilisk lizard
(*Basilicus plumifrons*)

A sticky tip at the end of the tongue grabs and holds prey.

Jackson's chameleon
(*Chamaeleo jacksoni*)

The eyes can swivel in different directions at the same time.

CHAMELEON HUNTERS

The chameleon's special skills make it a very effective predator. As it lies in wait for prey, its skin changes color to blend with the surroundings. When searching for food, a chameleon can swivel its eyes in all directions. Its muscular tongue is as long as its body and ends in a large, sticky tip. When it spots a potential meal, the chameleon shoots out its tongue with lightning speed. The insect is trapped on the end of the sticky tongue and is drawn into the mouth.

Chameleon toes and feet can grip a branch securely.

KOMODO DRAGON

This ferocious animal is a type of monitor lizard and is the largest lizard in the world. A heavy, but fast-moving predator, it has powerful legs and sharp claws to bring down its prey. It feeds mainly on carrion, but is capable of killing small deer. Komodo dragons have become fairly rare and are found only on certain Indonesian islands.

Scientific name:	*Varanus komodonsis*
Size:	Up to 3 m (10 ft) long
Habitat:	Grassland, riverbanks
Distribution:	Komodo and neighboring islands in Indonesia
Reproduction:	Female lays about 12 eggs in sandy ground
Diet:	Reptiles, birds, and medium-sized mammals including deer and wild pigs

Madagascan day gecko
(*Phelsuma quadriocellata*)

GECKO VISION

Geckos are mostly active at night, and their eyes are very sensitive to daylight. Most geckos do not have movable eyelids. Instead, each eye is covered by a transparent scale called a spectacle. Without eyelids, geckos cannot blink to clean their eyes. Many, such as the Madagascan day gecko, use their tongue to wipe over their eyes.

SCARY LIZARDS

Most lizards are well camouflaged and hide from predators, such as birds and mammals. Others use surprise tactics to frighten predators and give themselves a chance to escape. The frilled lizard suddenly expands the collar of skin around its neck to make itself look bigger, and then bobs its head, hisses, and waves its tail around. Other lizards also extend the neck or throat crest and swallow air to puff up their bodies and make themselves look too large to swallow.

Frilled lizard
(*Chlamydosaurus kingi*)

Tail is used to grasp branch.

Anole lizards
(*Anolis* sp.)

Male anole lizard flashing its red throat

LIZARD DISPLAYS

Most lizards come into contact with other lizards to mate and to fight over territory. To signal their mood, lizards may change color, raise their crest, or open their throat fan. Male chameleons change color to threaten rivals, while male anole lizards flick down their large, brightly colored throat fans to attract females.

Find out more

DEFENSE 1: *48*
HUNTING: *52*
REPTILES: *198*
TROPICAL RAINFORESTS: *82*

SNAKES

SNAKES ARE AN UNUSUAL GROUP of reptiles: they have no legs, eyelids, or external ears. There are about 2,700 species living on all continents except Antarctica. Snakes vary in size from the thread snake, which is only 4.3 in (11 cm) long, to the reticulated python, which grows to 33 ft (10 m). Snakes are meat-eaters, feeding on everything from ants and snails, to goats and caimans. Most snakes immobilize their prey before eating it, either with venom or by suffocation.

Python skeleton

Skull

Vertebra

Rib

Backbone

SNAKE INSIDES
A snake's skeleton consists of a skull and a long backbone, with a pair of ribs attached to each vertebra. Small snakes have about 100 vertebrae; larger snakes can have up to 400. Muscles attached to the ribs and vertebrae enable a snake to twist into smooth coils. Organs, such as the heart and lungs, are long and thin and fit one behind the other.

Tree boa
(*Corallus hortulanus*)

Long tail coils around branch.

Lightweight body moves easily through branches.

Small head and smooth scales for burrowing

Sunbeam snake
(*Xenopeltis unicolor*)

Forked tongue is used to sense taste, smell, and touch.

Rattle

Prairie rattlesnake
(*Crotalus viridis*)

SNAKE SHAPES
All snakes are similar in shape, but many species have special adaptations to suit their environment. Tree snakes, such as tree boas, have long tails to help them climb. Burrowing snakes have rounded, tube-shaped bodies to slide through the soil, while ground snakes have heavy bodies with large belly scales to grip soil and rock. Sea snakes have oarlike tails for swimming.

Skin starts to shed at the head.

SEA SNAKES
Most sea snakes live in the Pacific and Indian Oceans and eat fish, such as eels. They can dive to 330 ft (100 m) on one lungful of air and close their nostrils to keep out water. Sea snakes include the most venomous snakes in the world. All species give birth to live young.

Olive sea snake
(*Aipysurus laevis*)

Flattened tail forms a powerful oarlike paddle.

Thick, heavy body of ground snake

SHEDDING SKIN
A snake's scales are covered by a thin layer of skin. This outer layer peels off up to six times a year, often in one piece. This process, called sloughing, allows the snake to grow. A new layer of skin grows below the old layer before it peels off. When the process is finished an entire transparent skin may be left.

Burmese rock python
(*Python molurus bivittatus*)

S-shaped curves

Body wriggles from side to side.

Front of body thrusts forward.

Accordion locomotion

Rear acts as an anchor.

Rectilinear crawling

Snake raises and flattens scales on its belly to move forward.

ON THE MOVE
Snakes move gracefully without arms, legs, fins, or wings. Some snakes wriggle from side to side in S-shaped curves, others bunch up and straighten like an accordion. Heavy snakes move by crawling slowly forward in a straight line. Snakes that live on loose, slippery surfaces, such as sand, move by "sidewinding." They move diagonally, throwing their bodies forward a section at a time.

JAWS AND DIET

All snakes are carnivorous, feeding mainly on birds, mammals, frogs, and reptiles. A few snakes eat snails or eggs, while king cobras feed on other snakes. Snakes eat infrequently and may consume large amounts at each meal. Their teeth cannot cut up flesh, but are sharp and point backward, which helps them hold their prey still during the kill. Snakes' jaws are elastic and stretch wide, allowing them to swallow some animals whole.

Jaws stretch wide.

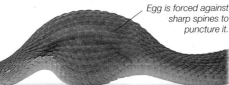
1. The African egg-eating snake (Dasypeltis inornata) starts to eat an egg that is larger than its head.

Egg is forced against sharp spines to puncture it.

2. The egg passes down the snake's throat, taking up to one hour to be swallowed completely. The snake then regurgitates the eggshell.

GREEN VINE SNAKE

An expert at ambush, the green vine snake stalks its prey, moving slowly backward and forward, holding its tongue still to avoid being seen. It strikes at its prey, snatching a lizard in a fraction of a second. It can judge distances accurately by looking down special grooves along its snout.

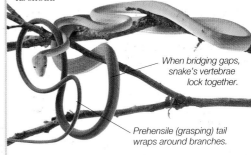

When bridging gaps, snake's vertebrae lock together.

Prehensile (grasping) tail wraps around branches.

Scientific name:	*Ahaetulla prasina*
Size:	3 ft 10 in (1.2 m) long
Habitat:	Forest borders and woodland
Distribution:	From the eastern Himalayas and India through China into Indonesia and the Philippines
Reproduction:	7–10 live young, born once a year
Diet:	Mainly lizards, small birds, and tree frogs

EGGS AND YOUNG

Most snakes lay eggs. They bury the eggs in damp, warm places, such as rotting vegetation and soil. A few snakes, including pythons, coil around their eggs to incubate them; most snakes leave the eggs to hatch by themselves. Some species, such as boas, give birth to live young. Snakes do not care for their young after hatching – the baby snakes fend for themselves immediately.

Green tree python (Morelia viridis) with eggs and young

Hood displayed in threat posture

Venom is produced in a gland in the roof of the mouth.

Nostril

VENOMOUS SNAKES

There are about 600 species of venomous snakes. They kill with a poison called venom, which they inject into prey through grooved or hollow teeth called fangs. Some snakes have fangs at the back of the mouth, others have them at the front. A cobra's venom affects the nervous system of its prey, stopping the heart and lungs from working, and paralyzing muscles.

Egyptian cobra (*Naja haje*)

DEFENSE

Snakes are hunted by many predators, including birds of prey, crocodiles, and mammals. To defend itself, a snake may hide, make itself look bigger, hiss, or pretend to be dead. A few snakes shed their tails when attacked. Some snakes, such as gaboon vipers (*Bitis gabonica*), use camouflage to avoid detection, others, such as coral snakes, are brightly colored to warn predators that they are venomous. Some harmless snakes mimic the colors of venomous ones.

Patterned skin of gaboon vipers camouflages them against leaves.

CONSTRICTORS

Constricting snakes, such as pythons and anacondas, squeeze their prey to death. After seizing an animal with its sharp teeth, the constrictor wraps its body around the victim. Every time the animal breathes out, the snake squeezes more tightly, until eventually, the animal dies of suffocation. Prey such as rats may die in seconds; larger animals such as caimans, take longer. The snake does not relax its coils until the prey is dead.

Yellow anaconda (Eunectes notaeus) constricts a caiman.

Body coiled up, ready to strike

Find out more

DEFENSE 2: *50*
DESERTS: *86*
HUNTING: *52*
REPTILES: *198*

CROCODILES AND ALLIGATORS

LURKING BENEATH THE WATER, crocodiles and alligators look like scaly logs with huge teeth. However, they are some of the world's most dangerous predators. They belong to a group of reptiles called crocodilians, which includes crocodiles, alligators, caimans, and gharials. All are meat-eaters that feed on prey such as fish, buffaloes, and sometimes even humans. Despite their aggressive behavior, they are very protective of their young. Crocodilians live in rivers and lakes in warmer parts of the world, although a few prefer estuaries and coastal waters.

FOSSIL RELATIVES

Crocodiles evolved about 200 million years ago and have changed little since then. They are the closest living relatives of dinosaurs, apart from birds. Early crocodiles were similar to modern gharials with long, narrow snouts and pointed teeth for catching fish. Modern crocodiles have broader snouts to suit their more varied diet.

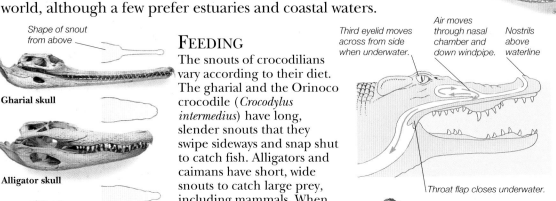

This crocodilian lived 180 million years ago.

Long, slender snout

Fossil of Steneosaurus bollensis

FEEDING

The snouts of crocodilians vary according to their diet. The gharial and the Orinoco crocodile (*Crocodylus intermedius*) have long, slender snouts that they swipe sideways and snap shut to catch fish. Alligators and caimans have short, wide snouts to catch large prey, including mammals. When crocodiles close their mouths, the fourth tooth in the lower jaw is visible, distinguishing them from alligators and caimans.

Shape of snout from above

Gharial skull

Alligator skull

Crocodile skull

Fourth tooth is visible.

AQUATIC ADAPTATIONS

A crocodilian's nostrils and eyes are placed high on its head, allowing it to see and breathe as it lies in the water. It can breathe while half-submerged by closing a throat flap to prevent water entering the lungs. When below water, the nostrils and ears close and a transparent third eyelid moves across to protect the eyes.

Third eyelid moves across from side when underwater.

Air moves through nasal chamber and down windpipe.

Nostrils above waterline

Throat flap closes underwater.

Crocodiles lie almost motionless for most of the day.

HUNTING

Young crocodilians eat crabs, insects, and frogs. Larger crocodilians chase fish, feed on dead animals, or lie in wait for hours, ready to ambush prey such as mammals and water birds. They seize prey with their powerful jaws and sharp teeth, pulling it below the water until it drowns. Crocodilians cannot chew, so they dismember prey by shaking and tearing it with their teeth. New teeth grow to replace broken or lost ones.

Crocodile twisting and shaking its prey

LAZY LIVES

Crocodilians lead fairly inactive lives. In the morning, rivers warm up slowly and crocodiles often heat themselves by basking in the sun at the river's edge. At night, the water cools slowly so crocodiles spend the night in the river to keep warm. Opening their mouths wide helps them to warm up in the morning or to cool down at midday. Blood vessels in the mouth lie close to the skin's surface, allowing heat to pass quickly to or from the blood.

Tail lashes from side to side to propel alligator through the water.

American alligator (*Alligator mississippiensis*)

Front legs are held close to the body.

CAIMANS

Caimans are alligators that live in Central and South America. There are six species, ranging from the 5 ft (1.5 m) long dwarf caiman (*Paleosuchus palpebrosus*), which lives in forest creeks, to the 15 ft (4.5 m) black caiman (*Melanosuchus niger*) of the Amazon River.

Spectacled caiman
(*Caiman crocodilus*)

Short, broad snout and sharp teeth for feeding on frogs, snails, and insects

Large scales help to protect against predators.

COURTSHIP

Male crocodilians bellow to attract mates and to warn off other males. Male Nile crocodiles try to impress females by blowing bubbles below the water. If interested, the female lifts her head, opens her mouth, and arches her back. The male scrapes his jaw on her back and places his legs over her body, before sinking to the river bed to mate. About 30 days later, the female lays her eggs.

American alligator bellowing

GANGES GHARIAL

The long snout and jagged, slender teeth of the gharial reflect its diet: it preys almost exclusively on fish. It swims alongside a shoal of fish, chasing them forward before swinging its jaws into the shoal to capture its prey. This reptile spends more time in the water than any other crocodilian. Its legs are relatively weak, but its hind feet are heavily webbed, making it an excellent swimmer.

Scientific name: *Gavialis gangeticus*

Size: Up to 23 ft (7 m) long

Habitat: Rivers and large streams

Distribution: Northern India, Nepal, Pakistan, Bangladesh, and Burma

Reproduction: Lays 28–43 eggs in a nest on the river bank

Diet: Primarily fish, but will also eat invertebrates, amphibians, and young mammals

Most adult males have bulbous tips on the ends of their snouts.

CARING PARENTS

Female crocodilians are very protective of their young. They guard their eggs from predators, and keep them warm in a hole in the ground or in a mound of mud and plants. After two to three months, the young call from inside the eggs. Their mother gently cracks the shells with her teeth, then carries her young to a nursery area, where she protects them.

Nile crocodile (Crocodylus niloticus) *guarding young*

Crocodile swings its rear end from side to side as it walks.

Crocodile lifts its body off the ground in a "high walk."

West African dwarf crocodile (*Osteolaemus tetraspis*)

The alligator uses its front legs to help it descend slowly.

Alligator pushes down with webbed back feet to brake as it descends.

MOVEMENT ON LAND

Some crocodilians, such as the gharial (*Gavialis gangeticus*), rarely move far from water. Others, such as the mugger crocodile (*Crocodylus palustris*) wander many miles if their river dries up. On land, crocodilians slide on their bellies, pushing with their feet. For longer distances, they adopt a a "high walk," lifting their bodies off the ground and dragging their tails behind them. Smaller species and young crocodilians can "gallop" at speeds of up to 11 mph (17 kmh).

American alligator (*Alligator mississippiensis*)

SWIMMING

Crocodilians are powerful, fast swimmers. They sweep their strong, flat-sided tails from side to side to propel themselves through the water. They also use their tails to steer when changing direction. Crocodilians rarely use their legs when swimming. Instead, they hold them tightly against their streamlined bodies.

SINKING IN WATER

Crocodilians have four webbed toes on their hind feet; the front five toes are only partially webbed. If danger threatens, a crocodilian can sink quickly backward and downward by pushing its back feet down with the webbed toes spread wide.

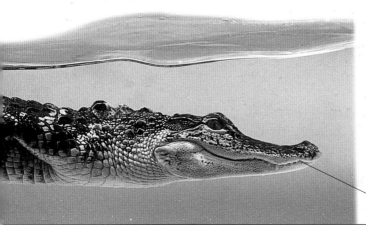

The streamlined body of the American alligator allows it to swim with ease.

Find out more	
ANIMALS IN DANGER:	*100*
HUNTING:	*52*
MOVEMENT IN WATER:	*38*
REPTILES:	*198*

BIRDS

SINCE BIRDS FIRST TOOK TO THE AIR, their mastery of flight has enabled them to migrate, colonize new habitats, and reach otherwise inaccessible nest sites. With their lightweight skeletons, efficient respiratory systems, and strong, flexible feathers, birds are the largest, fastest, and most powerful flying animals. During the course of evolution, some birds, such as emus, lost the need to fly and eventually became flightless. There are about 9,600 species of birds, ranging in size from the tiny bee hummingbird to the ostrich – the world's largest bird.

FEATHERS

Birds are the only animals that have feathers. They use them to fly, and also to keep warm and dry. Some birds have special feathers for display. There are three main types of feathers: flight feathers of the wings and tail, contour feathers that cover the body and give it a streamlined shape, and down feathers that grow close to the skin. The flight feathers have a rigid quill bearing hundreds of barbs. Each barb has hooks that lock together to form a smooth surface. Down feathers are fluffy and help to trap warm air.

Keel on breastbone for anchorage of flight muscles

Tern skeleton

Ribcage

Long toe bones

Lightweight, toothless bill

Holes in bone make it much lighter.

Large wing bones for attachment of powerful flight muscles

Honeycomb structure of bird bone

Outer flight feathers provide lift in flight and help the bird to steer.

ADAPTATIONS FOR FLYING

Birds' skeletons combine great strength with extreme lightness. To save weight, many of the larger bones are hollow. Others have air spaces and are reinforced with internal struts. The major wing and leg bones are fused for strength, and the powerful flight muscles are attached to a large ridge on the breastbone called the keel.

Hummingbird

BILLS

The size and shape of a bird's bill depends mainly on its diet. Birds use their bills, or beaks, for seizing and manipulating food, preening their feathers, and building their nests. A few birds, notably parrots, use their bills to help them climb.

Long slender bill to probe flowers

African gray hornbill

Rigid quill runs along each flight feather.

Tiny strands called barbs are connected to the quill.

Large bill to dig animals out of the ground

Pigeon wing

Covert feathers form a smooth surface for air to flow over.

Very strong curved bill to crack nuts and seeds

Scarlet macaw

Chestnut-eared aracari
(*Pteroglossus castanotis*)

Bird uses its bill to pick up oil from the preen gland.

PREENING

Birds regularly preen their plumage to condition the feathers and remove parasites, such as feather lice. Some birds bathe in water, while other species take dust baths. When preening, birds use their bill like a comb to zip together the barbs and hooks of the feathers. Many birds spread an oily liquid over their feathers to keep them waterproof. The oil is released from the preen gland at the base of the tail.

Partly webbed feet to spread load on mud and for swimming

Sharp talons to seize prey

Webbed feet for swimming

Three toes in front and one behind – typical of a perching bird

Strong toes

Flamingo foot

Eagle foot

Duck foot

Warbler foot

FEET FIRST

Birds' feet come in a great variety of shapes. Some wading birds, such as flamingos, have partly webbed feet and long legs for striding in deep water. Highly aerial birds, such as warblers and swifts, have tiny feet that reduce their weight in the air. Ducks, gannets, and gulls have fully webbed feet for swimming, while birds of prey have powerful feet armed with strong, sharp talons for seizing and killing prey.

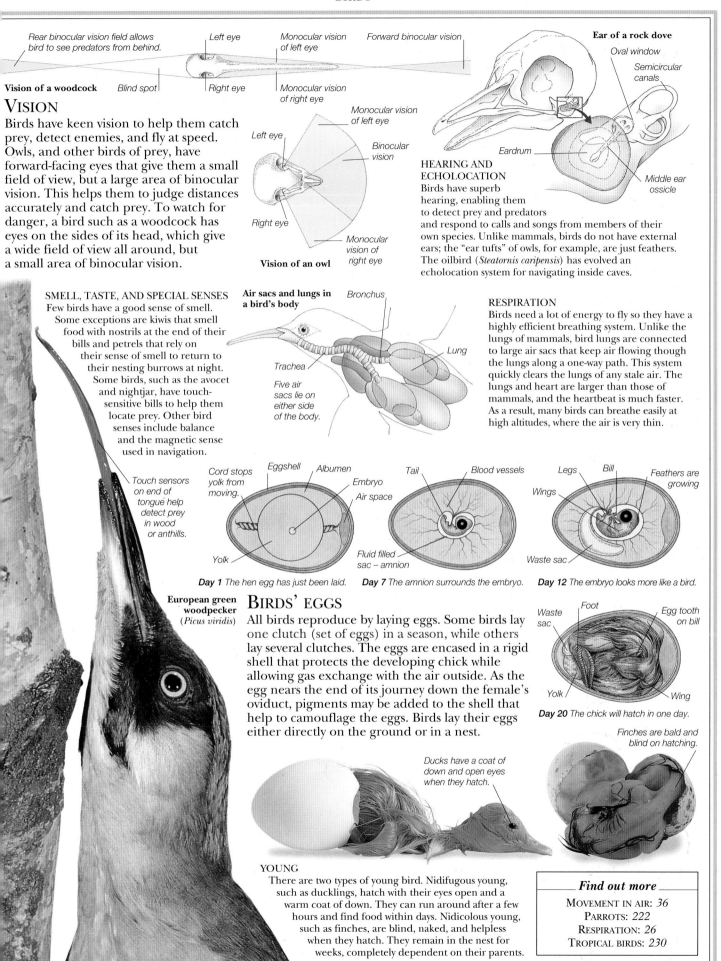

Rear binocular vision field allows bird to see predators from behind.

Vision of a woodcock   Blind spot

Left eye   Monocular vision of left eye   Forward binocular vision

Right eye   Monocular vision of right eye

VISION

Birds have keen vision to help them catch prey, detect enemies, and fly at speed. Owls, and other birds of prey, have forward-facing eyes that give them a small field of view, but a large area of binocular vision. This helps them to judge distances accurately and catch prey. To watch for danger, a bird such as a woodcock has eyes on the sides of its head, which give a wide field of view all around, but a small area of binocular vision.

Monocular vision of left eye

Left eye

Binocular vision

Right eye

Monocular vision of right eye

Vision of an owl

Ear of a rock dove

Oval window

Semicircular canals

Eardrum

Middle ear ossicle

HEARING AND ECHOLOCATION

Birds have superb hearing, enabling them to detect prey and predators and respond to calls and songs from members of their own species. Unlike mammals, birds do not have external ears; the "ear tufts" of owls, for example, are just feathers. The oilbird (*Steatornis caripensis*) has evolved an echolocation system for navigating inside caves.

SMELL, TASTE, AND SPECIAL SENSES

Few birds have a good sense of smell. Some exceptions are kiwis that smell food with nostrils at the end of their bills and petrels that rely on their sense of smell to return to their nesting burrows at night. Some birds, such as the avocet and nightjar, have touch-sensitive bills to help them locate prey. Other bird senses include balance and the magnetic sense used in navigation.

Air sacs and lungs in a bird's body

Bronchus

Lung

Trachea

Five air sacs lie on either side of the body.

RESPIRATION

Birds need a lot of energy to fly so they have a highly efficient breathing system. Unlike the lungs of mammals, bird lungs are connected to large air sacs that keep air flowing though the lungs along a one-way path. This system quickly clears the lungs of any stale air. The lungs and heart are larger than those of mammals, and the heartbeat is much faster. As a result, many birds can breathe easily at high altitudes, where the air is very thin.

Touch sensors on end of tongue help detect prey in wood or anthills.

Cord stops yolk from moving.   Eggshell   Albumen   Embryo   Air space

Yolk

Fluid filled sac – amnion

Day 1 The hen egg has just been laid.

Tail   Blood vessels

Day 7 The amnion surrounds the embryo.

Legs   Bill   Feathers are growing

Wings

Waste sac

Day 12 The embryo looks more like a bird.

European green woodpecker (*Picus viridis*)

BIRDS' EGGS

All birds reproduce by laying eggs. Some birds lay one clutch (set of eggs) in a season, while others lay several clutches. The eggs are encased in a rigid shell that protects the developing chick while allowing gas exchange with the air outside. As the egg nears the end of its journey down the female's oviduct, pigments may be added to the shell that help to camouflage the eggs. Birds lay their eggs either directly on the ground or in a nest.

Waste sac   Foot   Egg tooth on bill

Yolk   Wing

Day 20 The chick will hatch in one day.

Finches are bald and blind on hatching.

Ducks have a coat of down and open eyes when they hatch.

YOUNG

There are two types of young bird. Nidifugous young, such as ducklings, hatch with their eyes open and a warm coat of down. They can run around after a few hours and find food within days. Nidicolous young, such as finches, are blind, naked, and helpless when they hatch. They remain in the nest for weeks, completely dependent on their parents.

Find out more

MOVEMENT IN AIR: *36*
PARROTS: *222*
RESPIRATION: *26*
TROPICAL BIRDS: *230*

FLIGHTLESS BIRDS

FLYING USES A LOT OF ENERGY and is only possible for light-bodied animals. Over time, some birds have lost the ability to fly, and they run or swim instead. Today there are more than 40 species of flightless birds, including emus, kiwis, cassowaries, rheas, penguins, and the world's largest bird, the ostrich. Most are fast runners, with sturdy legs that help them escape predators. Penguins became flightless during their adaptation to life in the sea. Other birds lost the need to fly after living on islands with no predators; these include the kakapo, a New Zealand parrot, and the famous dodo, which is now extinct.

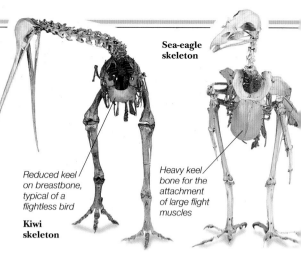

Sea-eagle skeleton

Reduced keel on breastbone, typical of a flightless bird

Kiwi skeleton

Heavy keel bone for the attachment of large flight muscles

PENGUINS
Penguins are flightless marine birds of the Southern Hemisphere that use their flippers (modified wings) to "fly" underwater. Unlike most flightless birds, they still have the strongly keeled breastbone of their flying ancestors, for the attachment of the powerful muscles that move the flippers.

LOSS OF FLIGHT
The loss of flight in some birds has led to the reduction in size of some muscles and bones, which are normally well developed in flying birds. Flightless birds have reduced wing bones and chest muscles, and a far smaller keel on the breastbone. The legs are sturdy and powerful, enabling ostriches, rheas, emus, and cassowaries to run quickly.

Sleek body is streamlined for swimming.

Humboldt penguin
(*Spheniscus humboldti*)

Bony casque may give protection when the animal dashes through dense vegetation.

CASSOWARIES
The three species of cassowary live in the tropical rainforests of Australia and New Guinea, where they feed mainly on fallen fruit, as well as some fungi and small animals. The female may mate with several males, laying a clutch of eggs for each. The chicks are cared for by their father for nine months. Cassowaries are dangerous birds and can kill people in the wild. They inflict terrible wounds by leaping into the air, kicking out with their stout, strong legs, and ripping open the intruder's body with sharp, daggerlike claws.

CHAMPION RUNNERS
The ostrich is the fastest runner of all birds, reaching speeds of up to 45 mph (72 kmh). It can even outpace some mammals, including lions. The large, powerful legs are powered by much larger leg muscles than in flying birds. This enables the ostrich to travel long distances to find sparsely distributed food. Ostriches are unique among birds because they have just two toes, reducing the surface area in contact with the ground, for fast, efficient running.

Coarse feathers, some of which end in hairlike filaments.

Southern cassowary
(*Casuarius casuarius*)

Ornamental neck wattle

Large outer claw is used when fighting.

Cassowary claws

Ostriches can maintain an average speed of 31 mph (50 kmh) for 30 minutes or more.

Ostrich
(*Struthio camelus*)

Long strides of about 11 ft 6 in (3.5 m), enable these birds to outpace predators.

A VERY VARIED DIET

Emus, ostriches, and rheas all have varied diets. They feed on the leaves, roots, flowers, fruits, and seeds of plants, as well as on a range of small animals, such as frogs, lizards, snakes, birds, and insects. Ostriches in captivity have swallowed a remarkable range of items, including coins, pieces of wire, alarm clocks, combs, rope, and gloves.

Emus (Dromaius novaehollandiae) grazing

THE BIGGEST EGGS

The ostrich's egg is the largest of any living bird, at up to 8 in (20 cm) long, and 5 lb (2.3 kg) in weight. It is equivalent in volume to 24 chickens' eggs. The shell, although only 0.06 in (1.5 mm) thick, can support the weight of a human. The largest egg ever laid was 15 in (39 cm) long and belonged to the extinct elephant bird; it was equivalent in volume to 220 chickens' eggs.

Elephant bird egg

Ostrich egg

Cassowary egg

Chicken egg

BROWN KIWI

The nocturnal kiwi is one of the most reclusive flightless birds, and is rarely seen in the wild. Kiwis have poor eyesight, but an excellent sense of smell, which they use to find food. They nest in underground burrows dug out with their strong claws. Relative to her body, the female kiwi lays the largest eggs of all birds.

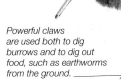

Powerful claws are used both to dig burrows and to dig out food, such as earthworms from the ground.

Scientific name: *Apteryx australis*

Size: Up to 20 in (50 cm) long

Habitat: Forest, scrub, and farmland

Distribution: New Zealand

Reproduction: Female usually lays one egg up to 5 in (13 cm) long, which is incubated for 11–12 weeks

Diet: Earthworms, insect grubs, spiders, and fruit

GIANT EXTINCTIONS

Two large groups of flightless birds became extinct due to hunting and habitat destruction. The 11 species of moa from New Zealand ranged from hen-sized birds to the giant moas, while the seven species of elephant bird from Madagascar and southern Africa were all giants. The dodo, a large, flightless pigeon from Mauritius, was extinct by the 1600s – killed off by introduced animals.

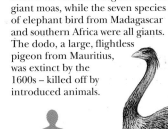

Giant moas stood up to 11 ft 6 in (3.5 m) tall.

Human

Dodo (*Raphus cucullatus*)

Elephant bird (*Aepyornis maximus*)

Giant moa (*Dinornis maximus*)

Feathers are shaggy because flightless birds do not need to have a smooth flying surface to their feathers.

The male rhea protects his offspring, defending them fiercely against predators.

Greater rhea (*Rhea americana*)

CARING FATHERS

Many male flightless birds incubate the eggs and care for the young. For example, male rheas mate with a harem of 2–12 females, then build a nest on the ground. The females lay the eggs in the nest, returning every 2–3 days to lay more eggs. Once they have finished laying their eggs, they depart to mate with another male, leaving the male to look after the eggs and young.

Young rheas are looked after by their father for up to five months.

Find out more

BIRDS: 208
MOVEMENT ON LAND: 34
PARROTS: 222
SEABIRDS: 212

SEABIRDS

MANY SEABIRDS SPEND MUCH of their lives out on the open oceans, and return to land only to breed and raise their young. They nest in colonies along the shoreline or on cliff ledges away from predators. Most seabirds have webbed feet to help them swim, and bills adapted to catch slippery prey. The sea is a rich source of food for birds – the surface water is full of fish, and the shoreline provides worms, crabs, and other shellfish. Some seabirds can remain at sea for more than five years without coming back to land.

Rockhopper penguin
(*Eudyptes chrysocome*)

SUPREME SEABIRDS
Of all seabirds, penguins are the most fully adapted for life in the water. They have lost the power of flight completely and their wings have been modified into flattened flippers to propel them through the water. Penguins have heavier bones than other birds to reduce buoyancy and to make diving easier. Their bodies have become smooth and streamlined to reduce the water's drag, and their thick plumage enables them to survive in very cold waters.

Flattened flippers aid swimming.

Skin when normal

Feathers lying normally

Insulating layer (blubber)

ALL-WEATHER OUTFIT
Penguins have a dense covering of feathers, which provides waterproofing and protection from the cold. Beneath the skin is a thick layer of fat (blubber) that insulates the penguin. To make its feathers more waterproof the bird applies a special oil with its bill. In hot weather, blood vessels in the blubber swell, bringing body heat to the skin's surface.

Skin when hot

Fluffy aftershafts open

Feathers ruffled

Blood vessels swell

Body is smooth and streamlined.

Salt glands above the eye

Salty fluid runs down grooves in the bill.

SALT GLANDS
Seabirds have large salt glands, connected to the nostrils, which remove salt from seawater. Although seabirds need some salt in their diets, too much can be harmful. The excess salt runs out of the nostrils and down grooves in the bill, before dripping off the bill tip.

King penguin dives underwater.

SWIMMING
Most seabirds land on the water's surface to feed, rest, or preen. Only a few can swim any distance. Penguins can swim long distances underwater, but every so often they leap in and out of the water. This technique (called "porpoising") enables the penguin to breathe while traveling at high speeds. Penguins are the fastest swimmers of all birds; gentoo penguins (*Pygoscelis papua*) can reach speeds of up to 19 mph (30 kmh).

King penguin
(*Aptenodytes patagonicus*)

Powerful flippers propel the penguin through the water.

SEABIRD CITIES
Many seabirds nest in huge, noisy colonies on cliffs. Colonies provide safety in numbers – there are plenty of eyes to watch for danger, and the mass of birds makes it hard for predators to pick out a single target. Various groups of seabirds nest at different levels on a cliff, dividing the seabird "city" vertically like an apartment building. Gannets and kittiwakes nest near the top, while shags and cormorants nest lower down.

Kittiwakes nesting close together

Heavy blotching on cream background

GUILLEMOT EGGS
The common murre, or guillemot, does not build a nest. Instead it lays a single egg on a very narrow cliff ledge. The egg's pear shape helps to prevent it from rolling off the ledge. Individual colors and markings on each egg help the parent bird recognize it among thousands of others.

Intricate markings on buff background

Sparse scribbles on grey background

Brown pelican plunge-diving from midair

Prion using both feet to skim over ocean surface

Albatross feeding from the ocean surface

Gull dipping down to ocean surface in flight

Storm-petrel pattering on webbed feet across ocean surface

Cormorant diving underwater from ocean surface

FEEDING

Seabirds catch food in a variety of ways. Gulls fly close to the surface and snatch prey from the water. Gannets and brown pelicans plunge into the water from great heights to catch fish. Air-sacs under their skin cushion them from the impact as they hit the water. Cormorants dive from the ocean surface, propelling themselves with their feet underwater, where they seize fish. Penguins and auks are deep divers, chasing small fish and other marine animals as they "fly" through the water.

ATLANTIC PUFFIN

With their brightly colored bills and feet, Atlantic puffins are among the world's most distinctive seabirds. They have webbed feet and small wings, which they use like fins to propel themselves through the water. Puffins breed in large colonies, and raise their chicks in the safety of underground burrows.

The puffin carries fish cross-wise in its beak.

Scientific name:
Fratercula arctica

Size: Up to 12 in (31 cm) long; weight up to 1 lb 2 oz (510 g)

Habitat: Rocky coasts

Distribution: North Atlantic

Reproduction: Female lays single egg, which hatches after 40 days

Diet: Small fish

ALBATROSSES

Albatrosses breed mainly on sub-Antarctic islands, then glide across the open ocean until they return to land to breed again. The wandering albatross has the longest wingspan of any bird at up to 11 ft (3.4 m). It glides close to the water's surface and often circumnavigates the globe in search of food. Its long, narrow wings are ideally suited for soaring for hours on end without a wingbeat.

Wandering albatross
(*Diomedea exulans*)

Common murre
(*Uria aalge*)

PENGUINS OF THE NORTH

Although they are not related, the auks of the northern hemisphere bear a striking resemblance (both in appearance and in swimming techniques) to the penguins of the southern hemisphere. Auks include murres, razorbills, and puffins. Like penguins, they live in large, densely populated colonies.

Migration Route

Breeding colony

North Atlantic

Skokholm

AFRICA

SOUTH AMERICA

Brazil

Migration of Manx shearwater

MIGRATION

Some seabirds make migrations that require astonishing powers of navigation. The Manx shearwater (*Puffinus puffinus*) migrates from breeding colonies in the North Atlantic to the waters off eastern South America. One of these birds migrated from the Welsh island of Skokholm to the coast of Brazil in only 17 days, traveling almost 6,200 miles (10,000 km).

In water, penguins look dark from above, and pale from below for camouflage.

Webbed feet and stiff tail steer like a rudder.

Find out more
BIRDS: *208*
MIGRATION AND NAVIGATION: *46*
OCEANS: *68*
SEASHORES AND TIDEPOOLS: *70*

DUCKS, GEESE, AND SWANS

KNOWN COLLECTIVELY as waterfowl, ducks, geese, and swans form a large group of mainly aquatic birds. They are excellent swimmers, with strong legs and large, webbed feet to propel them through the water. Swans and geese spend much of their time on land, while some ducks live on the water for most of the year, coming ashore only to breed and to rest. There are about 150 species of waterfowl throughout the world, ranging from the Hottentot teal, at 1 ft (30 cm) long, to the trumpeter swan that reaches lengths of 6 ft (1.8 m). For centuries, humans have hunted waterfowl for their meat, eggs, and feathers.

ANATOMY

Waterfowl have broad, boat-shaped bodies with flattened bellies to improve buoyancy on the water. The plumage is dense, with a well-developed layer of down that provides good insulation in cold water. Some species, such as swans and geese, have long necks that help them reach down under the water for food. Most waterfowl walk awkwardly on land, although swans and geese can move more easily.

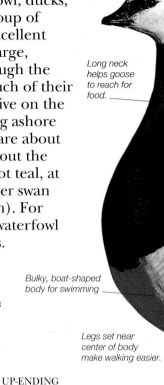

Long neck helps goose to reach for food.

Short, pointed wings for strong, fast flight

Broad bill adapted for grazing

"Nail" for tearing tough grass

Bulky, boat-shaped body for swimming

Goose skull

Flattened bill is dabbled through surface water.

Dabbling duck skull

Legs set near center of body make walking easier.

Webbed feet propel goose through water.

Barnacle goose
(*Branta leucopsis*)

Slender bill with lamellae to grip fish underwater

Merganser skull

ADAPTABLE BILLS

Waterfowl have broad, cone-shaped bills that are flattened from top to bottom. There is a shield-shaped horny tip on the upper mandible, called the "nail," which is harder than the rest of the bill. A row of toothlike projections, called lamellae, are found along the sides of the bill. The tongue is covered with horny spines that help the bird to grasp food. Some species have modified bills that help them cope with specialized diets.

UP-ENDING

To reach food under the water, many waterfowl "up-end" into a vertical position. Their buoyant bodies allow them to float with just over half of their bodies submerged. From this position they reach down to find food, using their legs and feet to keep their heads under the water.

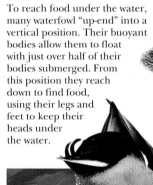

Mallard (Anas platyrhynchos) *searching for food*

DIVING

Some waterfowl specialize in diving for food. To do this, they reduce their buoyancy by squeezing out the air trapped between their feathers. Their feet, set at the back of their bodies, propel them under the water. Among the deepest divers is the old squaw (*Clangula hyemalis*), which can dive to 180 ft (55 m).

Common merganser (Mergus merganser) *diving*

Mute swan
(*Cygnus olor*)

Swan patters with feet across surface of the water.

Powerful wing strokes help swan into the air.

Swan takes off into the wind to gain extra lift.

TAKING OFF

Some ducks, especially the dabbling ducks, can take off very rapidly, flying up almost vertically. They push downward with their feet and flap their wings so strongly that the tips often hit the water. By contrast, the pochards, eiders, and sea ducks as well as the heavy swans, need to run across the water, pattering with their feet, before they can become airborne.

Eclipse plumage – male has drab feathers for temporary camouflage.

Mandarin duck (*Aix galericulata*)

Normal plumage – male has brightly colored feathers.

MOLTING

Waterfowl are unusual because all their main flight feathers molt at the same time. Most ducks, geese, and swans are unable to fly while their new feathers grow. During this vulnerable period, male ducks, which have bright feathers for the rest of the year, molt into a special "eclipse" plumage. These temporary feathers are similar to the females' drab plumage and help camouflage the males from predators.

COMMON GOLDENEYE

This dumpy, large-headed sea duck has golden-yellow irises in the eyes of both sexes. These birds are mostly silent, but make soft, nasal calls during display. Numbers of common goldeneyes have declined in many areas due to forest clearance and the disappearance of their nesting holes.

Row of drooping, black-and-white shoulder feathers

Scientific name: *Bucephala clangula*	
Size: 18–20 in (46–50 cm)	
Habitat: Spends summer beside inland water in northern forests; winters on estuaries and inland lakes	
Distribution: North America and Asia	
Reproduction: Female lays 8–12 eggs in a tree hole lined with chips of rotten wood and down	
Diet: Mainly shellfish, crustaceans, and insects	

COURTSHIP DISPLAY

Most ducks find a new mate each winter, and the males use their bright plumage in dramatic courtship displays. They often interrupt these displays to chase away rivals. The performances include a series of ritualistic movements, accompanied by special calls. This elaborate sequence is unique for each species. The ducks are already paired when they reach their breeding grounds in the spring.

Male northern pintail (Anas acuta) rapidly raising and lowering his head in a courtship display

Female mute swan (Cygnus olor) carrying cygnets on her back

SNUG NESTS

Most waterfowl nest on the ground among vegetation and near water. The female makes a hollow in the earth, then constructs a nest from vegetation before adding a lining of downy feathers plucked from her belly. This layer of down keeps the eggs warm while the mother goes off in search of food. Before leaving, she covers the eggs with more down, which helps disguise them from hungry predators. Humans use the soft downy under-feathers of the eider duck to make quilts, sleeping bags, and winter jackets.

Nest and eggs of common eider (Somateria mollissima)

FAST LEARNERS

Waterfowl hatch with their eyes open, and after their camouflaged, downy plumage has dried out, they are able to stand, walk, and swim almost immediately. They soon leave the nest, following their mother to a safe stretch of water where they feed for themselves right away. This is a vital period in which the young learn from their mother (and their father in the case of geese and swans), following her wherever she goes.

Find out more

BIRDS: *208*
MIGRATION AND NAVIGATION: *46*
MOVEMENT IN AIR: *36*
RIVERS, LAKES, AND PONDS: *76*

WADING BIRDS

THE TERM WADING BIRDS refers to a group of unrelated birds that live in a variety of watery habitats, ranging from rivers and shorelines to swamps and marshes. Some, such as herons, have long legs and necks, and can wade deep into the water without getting their feathers wet. Many wading birds have long bills, adapted for a variety of feeding methods, from the stabbing spears of herons to the filtering devices of flamingos. Others probe soft ground for food, and some, such as oystercatchers, have strong beaks used to hammer or pry open shells.

Long, down-curved bill

Scarlet ibis
(*Eudocimus ruber*)

Long, widely spaced toes help bird to balance.

ANATOMY

Wading birds have specialized beaks for reaching a particular type of food. Many have long, slender bills that they use to probe in soft mud for buried invertebrate prey. Waders may also have long legs with widely spaced toes that help them walk on marshland, mud, or other soft ground without sinking. Some have webs of skin between their toes, which help them balance and obtain food. Most have keen eyesight that helps them watch out for predators.

HERONS

There are about 65 species of herons. They usually live close to the water and often nest in groups. Many are solitary feeders that hunt by waiting patiently before suddenly seizing their prey. Their necks are highly specialized with a distinct S-shape. When a heron darts its neck out to catch prey, the kink in the neck acts like a spring, giving the thrust extra strength and force.

Neck held back in S-shape

Herons wade in wetlands, lake edges, and coastal regions.

Gray heron
(*Ardea cinerea*)

STORKS

Storks live mainly in tropical and subtropical areas. Some species have the unusual habit of defecating on their legs to cool themselves – as the urine evaporates from their legs, heat is lost from their bodies. Most storks feed on fish, frogs, insects, and small mammals. The giant marabou stork from Africa is a scavenger that feeds on dead animals as well as on live prey.

Heron thrusts out its neck to seize prey.

Marabou stork
(*Leptoptilos crumeniferus*)

Herons have a varied diet that includes fish and other aquatic animals.

Lesser flamingos (Phoeniconaias minor) feed together.

FILTER FEEDERS

Flamingos live in large colonies, sometimes containing thousands of birds. They wade into salty lakes and hold their bills upside down in the water. This enables them to filter algae and small plants and animals from just beneath the water's surface. Their tongues pump water into their bills, forcing the water through comblike plates called lamellae, which sieve suspended food particles from the water.

DIFFERENT BILLS

Many waders feed together on estuaries and mudflats. Individual species have developed bills of various lengths and shapes. They can feed on different prey and avoid competing for the same food. Birds with shorter bills, such as plovers, usually pick or probe for food on, or just below, the muddy surface. Others, such as oystercatchers, have blunter, more blade-like bills, which can pry open bivalve mollusks such as mussels. Deeper probers, such as curlews, use their long, sensitive bills to feel for buried creatures.

The common curlew's (Numenius arquata) long downcurved bill enables it to probe for prey. Touch-sensitive cells on the bill help it identify different types of prey.

The strong bill of the oystercatcher (Haematopus ostralegus) hammers open cockles and mussels.

Cranes dance to attract mates. They usually stay with the same partner all their lives.

Red-crowned cranes (*Grus japonensis*)

CRANES

Cranes have very long legs and are the tallest flying birds in the world – the sarus crane (*Grus antigone*) stands at 5 ft 9 in (1.76 m). Cranes communicate with one another using remarkable dances, which are performed during courtship ceremonies and to communicate with one another. They are also renowned for their trumpeting calls. In most species the long windpipe is coiled within the breastbone – the extra length probably serves to amplify the calls.

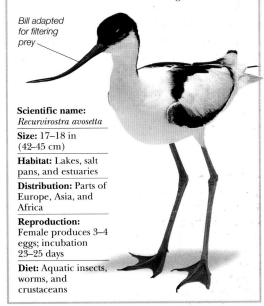

Bill adapted for filtering prey

Scientific name: *Recurvirostra avosetta*

Size: 17–18 in (42–45 cm)

Habitat: Lakes, salt pans, and estuaries

Distribution: Parts of Europe, Asia, and Africa

Reproduction: Female produces 3–4 eggs; incubation 23–25 days

Diet: Aquatic insects, worms, and crustaceans

FLOCKS TOGETHER

Outside the breeding season, waders usually form huge flocks along the coasts. They feed, fly, and roost together to increase their chances of survival. Predators, such as peregrine falcons, find it harder to pick out a victim from a large, tightly packed flock. Some species, such as red knots and dunlins (*Calidris alpina*), perform amazing coordinated aerial maneuvers, which look like wave movements in the air.

A flock of red knots takes to the air.

The oystercatcher's eggs are difficult to see among pebbles on the beach.

JACANAS

The African jacana is renowned for its long legs, toes, and claws that enable it to walk over lily pads and other floating plants without sinking. Despite its long legs, the jacana can swim and will occasionally fly. Male jacanas make simple nests on top of floating vegetation. After mating, the male incubates the clutch of eggs, and feeds and rears the chicks.

African jacana (Actophilornis africanus) on lily pad

CAMOUFLAGE

Like many waders, oystercatchers lay eggs that are well camouflaged against their surroundings. They lay clutches of three or four eggs in a shallow dip on the shoreline. The pear-shaped eggs have pointed ends that fit neatly together in the nest. The chicks hatch covered in down that blends in with their background. They look for their own food soon after hatching.

The common plover (Charadrius hiaticula) takes food from near or on the surface.

A red knot (Calidris canutus) often feeds in groups probing for food near the surface.

The ruddy turnstone (Arenaria interpres) lifts individual rocks or clumps of weed to find small crabs and mollusks.

NATURAL SPOONS

Spoonbills have long, straight, flattened bills with broad, spatula-shaped tips. Unlike herons, which rely on their eyesight to find food, these birds use their sense of touch. They sweep their unique bills from side to side in shallow waters, detecting small fish and crustaceans with special touch-sensitive cells.

African spoonbill (*Platalea alba*)

Find out more

COURTSHIP, MATING, AND PARENTAL CARE: *30*
SEASHORES AND TIDEPOOLS: *70*
WETLANDS: *74*

BIRDS OF PREY

WITH THEIR HOOKED BILLS, large wings, and sharp talons, birds of prey make formidable hunters. Most hunt a wide range of creatures, which they kill with their powerful feet. Birds of prey are called raptors, from the Latin word *raptare*, which means "to seize." Their lethal talons can pierce tough animal hides, strike birds in midflight, and snatch fish from water. As adults, they have few enemies except other birds of prey and humans. This diverse group includes condors, hawks, eagles, falcons, and vultures. Vultures are unusual because they depend mainly on carrion – the flesh of dead animals – rather than killing prey themselves.

Hooked tip acts like scissors to strip off small pieces of flesh.

Toral tooth severs the spinal cord of its prey

Andean condor bill
(*Vultur gryphus*)

Saker falcon bill
(*Falco cherrug*)

BILLS
Although they are usually hooked, the bills of birds of prey are adapted for catching specific prey. The Andean condor, for example, has a deeply hooked bill to rip into the hides of large dead animals, such as llamas, and to shear the meat from the carcass. The saker falcon has a "toral" tooth on each side of the bill to break the neck of birds that it strikes down with its feet.

Feathers fan out for landing.

Long, broad, narrow-based wings for soaring and swooping on prey

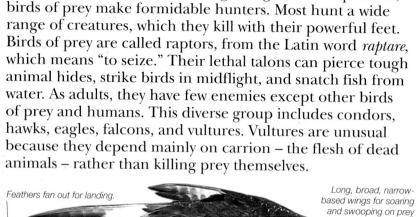

Verreaux's eagle
(*Aquila verreauxii*)

BUILT TO KILL
With the exception of vultures and a few other species, birds of prey survive by hunting down and killing other animals. Their bodies are built for hunting. They have well-developed wings for active flight and soaring, and sharp vision (up to eight times as acute as human eyesight) for locating prey. Once they have spotted potential prey, they seize it with their strong legs and sharp talons, then use their powerful, hooked bill to tear up the flesh.

Powerful feet for tightly gripping prey

Toes as well as talons exert force.

Gripping small prey

LEGS AND FEET
Most birds of prey have powerful legs and feet with sharp claws, or talons. Verreaux's eagle has strong legs and feet, with long talons for seizing prey such as rabbits. A bird's toes and talons are used in different ways depending on whether it is gripping large or small prey.

Tips of talons exert force.

Gripping large prey

A male eagle dives down to meet his partner.

Bald eagle courtship display

The female eagle turns upside down to link toes with her partner.

Once joined, the eagles spiral downward before releasing each other.

Female eagle

DRAMATIC DISPLAYS
Many birds of prey perform dramatic aerial displays during courtship, while established pairs also perform for each other to strengthen the bond. During the courtship display of the bald eagle (*Haliaeetus leucocephalus*), the male flies above the female, who turns on her back in midair as he passes over her. They extend their legs and link talons before tumbling downward over each other in a series of cartwheels, letting go before they reach the ground.

Osprey (Pandion haliaetus) catching a fish

UNUSUAL BIRDS OF PREY
Ospreys catch and eat fish. Their pale bellies help camouflage them as they swoop down to seize fish from the water. Horny spines on their toes, long talons, and a special toe that can swivel backward, all help ospreys to grip their slippery, struggling prey. Unlike other birds of prey, secretary birds hunt on the ground. They have long legs and run through the grass to catch snakes.

VARIED DIETS

The prey, or diet, of these large birds varies greatly. Some eat mammals and birds, others feed on insects or fish. Several species have more unusual tastes. The European honey-buzzard (*Pernis apivorus*) eats honeycombs, and wasp and bee larvae, the lammergeier (*Gypaetus barbatus*) drops bones onto rocks to expose the marrow inside, and the snail kite (*Rostrhamus sociabilis*) uses its long, hooked bill to eat freshwater snails.

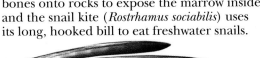

The sparrowhawk takes its blackbird prey to a favorite plucking site before eating it.

Hunting technique of peregrine falcon
(*Falco peregrinus*)

Eurasian sparrowhawk
(*Accipiter nisus*)

The falcon dives at up to 124 mph (200 kmh) or more, making it the fastest bird in the world.

The falcon hits a grouse with great force in midair. Its powerful feet and sharp talons stun or kill its prey.

HUNTING TECHNIQUES

Birds of prey hunt in many different ways. The peregrine falcon is a spectacular hunter that dives on its bird prey from great heights in a breathtaking "stoop." A sparrowhawk hunts by stealth, flying low along one side of a hedge, out of view of small birds on the other side. Without warning, it flies over the hedge and seizes the victim from safety with its talons.

Strong beak to rip open the bodies of large animals.

Bald head keeps bird free from becoming matted with blood as it feeds.

Vulture tears pieces of flesh from a dead goat.

White-backed vulture
(*Gyps bengalensis*)

GOLDEN EAGLE

This majestic eagle is one of the largest and most powerful birds of prey. It has a wingspan of up to 7 ft 6 in (2.3 m), enabling it to soar effortlessly. Golden eagles prey on many kinds of animals, and fully grown birds can pick up prey weighing up to 10 lb (4.5 kg).

Large eyes for spotting prey

Huge talons

Scientific name:
Aquila chrysaetos

Size: Female up to 3 ft (90 cm) long; male slightly smaller

Habitat: Mountains, and other open wild habitats

Distribution: North America, Europe, North Africa, Middle East, and northern Asia

Reproduction: Female lays 1–3 eggs in nest on rocky ledge or in tree; eggs hatch after about 45 days

Diet: Small mammals and carrion

Common buzzard (Buteo buteo) in search of prey

HOVERING

Some birds of prey, particularly kestrels, have mastered the art of hovering in midair while searching for prey. They use their sharp eyesight to scan the ground for voles or mice. Their heads remain steady while their bodies, wings, and tails are constantly making tiny adjusting movements to maintain their position in the air.

SCAVENGERS

Vultures are specialized carrion-eaters. Their broad, rectangular wings help them soar high in the sky as they look out for carrion far below. They have deep, strongly hooked beaks with sharp edges for cutting and tearing skin and flesh, and rough tongues for rasping flesh from bones. Vultures lack the strong feet and sharp talons of other birds in this group because they do not kill or carry off live prey.

Find out more
BIRDS: *208*
HUNTING: *52*
MOVEMENT IN AIR: *36*
OWLS: *224*

GAME BIRDS

GENERALLY HUNTED for sport, hence their name, game birds live mainly on the ground. They are strong runners that rarely fly, except when they burst from cover to escape danger. From the order Galliformes, these plump birds feature a versatile range of plumage displays. Males sport brilliant colors to attract mates, while others, such as the willow ptarmigan, change color with the seasons. Most game birds have strong, blunt claws with three forward-facing toes used for scratching at food on the ground. Some roost in trees to avoid predators.

Hill partridge
(*Arborophila torqueola*)

Hooked bill

Rounded wings used in short flights

Strong claws for scratching at food

GAME BIRD ANATOMY

Game birds have plump bodies that are supported by their strong, sturdy legs. Their large feet have tough, blunt claws that they use for scratching at seeds and other food on the ground. They also use their hooked bills to dig up roots and buried insects. Although game birds do not make long flights, their powerful breast muscles, attached to a large keel on the breastbone, enable them to take off rapidly, especially when in danger.

SKIN SIGNALS

During courtship, many game birds rely on changing skin colors to attract mates or to warn off rivals. The temminck's tragopan, for example, has a brightly colored flap of skin called a lappet that dramatically expands after meeting a mate. At the height of the courtship display, two fleshy horns above the head become erect.

Temminck's tragopan
(*Tragopan temminckii*)

Fleshy lappet expands over breast during courtship.

Mountain peacock-pheasant
(*Polyplectron inopinatum*)

Spurs may be used in fighting.

Food passes through the esophagus.

Digestive organ secretes enzymes which help break down foods.

Well-developed gizzard is able to digest tough foods.

TOUGH DIGESTIVE SYSTEMS

Game birds have a gizzard which is specially adapted to grind tough foods such as insects and grains. This muscular part of the stomach has a folded inner lining that helps the bird crush and digest its food. Game birds also swallow grit and small stones, which help grind the food.

ARMED WITH SPURS

Males of some groups of game birds, such as turkeys and pheasants, have one or more spurs on each leg. It is generally thought that spurs act as weapons in fights between males, or that they serve to attract females – the larger the spur, the greater the male's fitness. Some species, such as the Malayan peacock-pheasant (*Polyplectron malacense*), can have as many as seven spurs.

Sensing danger, the pheasant rockets into the air.

The wings flap rapidly, producing a loud noise that startles the predator.

The body is held at a steep angle for a near-vertical ascent.

EXPLOSIVE TAKEOFF

When in danger, game birds can rocket to safety from the ground or a tree. Their broad wings and powerful flight muscles enable them to accelerate upward, while the noisy whirring sounds of their wings may frighten off the predator. The ring-necked pheasant (*Phasianus colchicus*) is able to rise faster than any other bird of comparable size and weight. Game birds tend not to fly long distances, since they prefer to run to cover when threatened.

A male pheasant walks across ground in search of food.

Reeves's pheasant
(*Syrmaticus reevesii*)

Pheasant alternates burst of noisy, flapping flight with glides, before returning to cover.

Wing shape and powerful breast muscles give fast flight, but the bird soon tires.

Long tail trails behind.

RED JUNGLEFOWL

The red junglefowl is the wild ancestor of the domestic chicken, its wide diet enabling it to live in a range of habitats. In spring, the males mate with several females, enticing their mates with dramatic displays of their magnificent plumage. The females nest on the ground, hidden in dense undergrowth. Junglefowl often congregate in large numbers at feeding sites, scratching the ground in search of plants, roots, and invertebrates.

Males have colorful plumage.

Scientific name: *Gallus gallus*

Size: Males 26–30 in (65–75 cm) long; females 16–18 in (42–46 cm) long

Habitat: Forest edge, open wood, scrubland

Distribution: Northeast India and Southeast Asia

Reproduction: Lays 4–9 eggs in a hollow in the ground. Eggs incubated for 18–20 days

Diet: Seeds, plant foods, and insects

COURTSHIP DISPLAYS

The strutting display of the male sage grouse (*Centrocercus urophasianus*) is typical of many grouse attempting to attract females at communal grounds (leks). They fan their long, sharply pointed tail feathers upward and inflate huge air sacs beneath their necks. At the height of this remarkable demonstration, the male shows off his bright yellow neck patches, then suddenly empties his air sacs, causing an incredible noise that sounds like a whip cracking.

Male sage grouse during courtship

MOUND-BUILDERS

A small family of game birds are known as mound-builders because they incubate their eggs inside mounds of vegetation and sand, rather than under their bodies. As the vegetation rots, it gives off heat, which keeps the eggs warm. Some species use their sensitive bills as thermometers to monitor the temperature inside the nest, and make adjustments by adding or removing sand. Some species lay their eggs in holes on sandy beaches heated by the sun or in soils near volcanic areas.

Crosssection of incubation mound

Sandy soil covers incubating eggs.

Incubation temperatures inside the mound are about 93°F (34°C).

Rotting vegetation gives off heat to warm the eggs.

Malleefowl (*Leipoa ocellata*)

Sixteen eggs laid by the gray partridge (Perdix perdix)

CHAMPION EGG LAYERS

Some game birds are renowned for the huge number of eggs that they lay. The gray partridge regularly lays up to 16 eggs in a clutch, and may lay as many as 20 eggs – the largest single clutch laid regularly by any bird. The northern bobwhite (*Colinus virginianus*) has laid as many as 28 eggs on rare occasions. Domestic chickens may lay up to 360 eggs a year, usually for human consumption.

Summer plumage

Willow ptarmigan (*Lagopus lagopus*)

CAMOUFLAGE THROUGH THE YEAR

Willow ptarmigans molt their feathers three times a year, revealing different plumages for each season. In summer, their reddish-brown color helps conceal the females against the foliage surrounding their nests. White plumage in winter hides the birds against the snow, while in spring and fall their patchy appearance provides superb camouflage against the melting snow, rocks, and vegetation.

Fall plumage

Winter plumage

Find out more

BIRDS: *208*
COURTSHIP, MATING, AND PARENTAL CARE: *30*
DEFENSE 2: *50*

PARROTS

SOME OF THE WORLD'S most colorful, noisy, and endangered birds belong to the parrot family. There are about 330 species of parrots, and nearly all of these live in warm places. They feed almost entirely on plant food, such as fruit, seeds, pollen, and sugary nectar. Parrots are strong fliers and good climbers. They often clamber around in the treetops, using their bills to grasp branches while shifting their sturdy feet. They use their feet to hold up food – a feature that is unique in the bird world. The smallest parrots are the pygmy parrots of Southeast Asia, which can be just 3 in (7.5 cm) long. The largest are the brilliantly colored macaws.

PARROT ANATOMY

One of a parrot's most distinctive features is its hooked bill. Both parts of the bill hinge against the skull, allowing a parrot to open its bill wide when it feeds. Most parrots have small eyes, which are often surrounded by a patch of bare skin. A parrot's feet are short but powerful, with two toes pointing forward and one pointing backward. In many species, males and females look the same, although males are often slightly bigger.

Peach-fronted parakeet
(*Aratinga aurea*)

Crest raised to signal alarm

Short legs for stability while climbing and perching

Most parrots are brightly colored, and many are green.

Large feet with flexible toes to grip branches

DIET AND FEEDING

Almost all parrots are herbivores (plant-eaters), typically feeding high up in trees, where they search for fruit, nuts, and other seeds. They collect food with their bills but often hold nuts in their feet while they crack open the hard shells. A few species of parrots have given up life in the trees and feed on the ground. Budgerigars, for example, live in the dry grasslands of Australia, where they often gather on the ground in huge flocks.

Hinged beak allows parrot to open its mouth wide to pick fruit.

Bill has scissorlike cutting edges.

Amazon parrot
(*Amazona* sp.)

COLORFUL SIGNAL

Cockatoos are unusual parrots because of the feathery crests on their heads. They can raise and lower these crests to signal alarm or aggression to each other. Unlike most parrots, these birds are plainly colored. The sulphur-crested cockatoo (*Cacatua galerita*) is pure white except for its yellow crest.

HOLDING FOOD

Many birds grip their food with their feet, but parrots are the only birds that can hold food up to their bills. Using one foot to perch on a branch, the parrot lifts the food up with its other foot. The fleshy toes work like fingers.

Fleshy toes fold around food and hold it tightly.

FEEDING AT FLOWERS

Some parrots specialize in feeding on flowers, often gathering in large flocks where trees are in bloom. Small, brilliantly colored parrots called lorikeets feed on pollen and nectar inside flowers. Their tongues have brushlike tips that they use to lap up their food. Lorikeets live in Australasia and islands in the Pacific Ocean. They are aggressive birds and often squabble at feeding sites.

Brush-tipped tongue mops up pollen and nectar.

Yellow-streaked lory
(*Chalcopsitta scintillata*)

Powerful feet allow parrot to perch on one leg.

Fischer's lovebirds (Agapornis fischeri) *gather together in Tanzania, Africa*

PARROT BEHAVIOR

Compared to many other birds, parrots are constantly active, noisy, and very sociable. Instead of living on their own, they generally gather together in flocks. When parrots fly, they keep in contact with each other by screeching loudly as they speed over the treetops. Communication is important because it helps them find food that is sometimes widely scattered. When one parrot locates food, its excited calls soon attract the rest of the flock.

TREETOP NESTS

A few parrots nest in branches or on the ground, but for most species, life begins inside a hollow tree. The parents search for a suitable hole high up in a tree trunk, often taking over old nest holes made by woodpeckers. Parrots sometimes enlarge the hole, but they do not use any nesting material. The female lays 2–5 pure white eggs. In all species (except cockatoos), she alone incubates the eggs.

Four-week-old chicks with mother

Orange-bellied parrot
(*Neophema chrysogaster*)

SCARLET MACAW

This spectacular bird is one of the world's largest parrots. Like other macaws, it feeds mainly on fruit and nuts high in the forest canopy, and is rarely seen near the ground. Macaws are sociable birds. They travel in pairs or small groups, often making loud, screeching noises as they fly. Capture by humans and deforestation has made this species scarce.

The macaw's brilliant colors have made it a target for trappers.

Scientific name: *Ara macao*

Size: Up to 2 ft 10 in (86 cm) long

Habitat: Tropical rainforest at low altitude

Distribution: Central America, tropical South America

Reproduction: Nests in tree holes; female lays two or three eggs, which hatch after 20–28 days

Diet: Fruit, large nuts

NESTING MONK PARAKEETS

The monk parakeet from South America builds an unlined, domed nest made of twigs, perferably thorny, with a low upward-slanting entrance. Each pair builds its nest up against the next, gradually forming a large colony in a tree. The birds use the colony as a communal roosting place, which makes it the permanent center for all their activity.

Monk parakeet
(*Myiopsitta monachus*)

Hatching and early development

The kakapo has broad wings but cannot fly.

The kea uses its long beak to tear up meat.

HATCHING

Parrot eggs take 2–14 weeks to hatch. Newly hatched parrots are blind and have no feathers. The mother bird feeds them for the first few days, but later the father also helps. The young often stay with their parents until the next breeding season.

Parrots are blind when they first hatch.

After one week, gray feathers begin to grow.

At four weeks, green feathers start to grow.

UNUSUAL PARROTS

Two of the world's strangest parrots are found in New Zealand. The kakapo (*Strigops habroptilus*) feeds at night and is the only parrot that does not fly. It is now extremely rare. The kea (*Nestor notabilis*) is much more common. It is bold and inquisitive, and is the only parrot that feeds partly on animals and their remains.

PARROTS IN DANGER

Parrots have been kept as pets for centuries. This is partly because they are brightly colored and partly because some can imitate human speech. A few species – including budgerigars and cockatiels – breed very successfully in captivity, but many others are collected from the wild. Over-collection and deforestation have brought several species to the brink of extinction.

Caged rose-ringed parakeets (Psittacula krameri) on sale in India

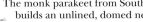

Find out more	
ANIMALS:	*140*
BIRDS:	*208*
MOVEMENT IN AIR:	*36*
VERTEBRATES:	*182*

OWLS

WHEN THE SUN SETS, most birds stop feeding and find a safe place to spend the night. Owls are different because many species emerge at dusk and set off to find food. These stealthy hunters track down food with a combination of excellent vision and hearing. Once they have located their prey, they use their sharp claws to grasp the animal. Some owls catch creatures as small as moths, but the largest – called eagle-owls – can tackle prey the size of a small deer. Although most owls are nocturnal, a few hunt by day. One such animal is the snowy owl. It lives in the Arctic where it is never completely dark during the summer months.

Tawny owl (Strix aluco) has a flat face that channels sound to its ear openings.

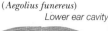

Skull of boreal owl
(*Aegolius funereus*)
Lower ear cavity

Higher ear cavity

SIGHT AND SOUND

To make a successful attack, an owl must pinpoint the exact position of its prey. Most find prey by sight and sound, although some, such as the barn owl, can locate small animals just by sound. The shape of an owl's face channels sounds toward the ear openings, and into the skull, where the inner parts of each ear differ in size and position. This arrangement helps an owl locate the source of any sound with extraordinary precision.

LOOKING AROUND

Instead of being round, an owl's eyes are shaped like funnels, with the widest part set deep inside the head. This shape means that the eyes cannot swivel in their sockets and the owl must turn its head to look around. Owls can swivel their heads through more than 180 degrees to look over their shoulders.

Rock eagle-owl
(*Bubo bengalensis*)

Owls have broad wings that help them to fly slowly as they search for prey.

Cape eagle-owl
(*Bubo capensis*)

Fanned-out feathers control speed of descent.

The owl uses its wings as brakes, and drops quietly toward the ground.

NIGHT-TIME STRIKE

All owls are carnivorous, and rely on their exceptionally keen senses and almost silent flight to swoop on their victims. The rock eagle-owl, for example, flies fairly close to the ground before attacking a small mammal. Like most owls, if it hears the sound of potential prey, it glides downward and swings its feet forward. The owl grabs the animal with its talons and flies away to a tree, where it can eat without being disturbed.

Owl flight feather

DAYTIME CAMOUFLAGE

During the day, this collared scops-owl roosts in a tree, where its camouflaged plumage helps it hide. If another animal ventures too close, the owl opens its eyes wide and hisses at the intruder. Some owls roost in gardens and even in city parks, but because they are so well hidden, people very rarely notice they are there.

Collared scops-owl (Otus lempiji) roosting

FRINGED FEATHERS

Many owls have velvety fringes around their flight feathers that help to silence the wings as they move through the air. This stops wing noise interfering with the owl's hearing, and makes it easier to catch prey.

Sharp talons grab prey before it can escape.

FEEDING

Once an owl has caught its prey, it usually carries the dead animal to a tree before eating it. Owls have large mouths and most can swallow mice and small birds in a single gulp. When owls catch larger animals they feed like birds of prey, tearing up food with their hooked bills and powerful talons. In Africa, Pel's fishing-owls feed on pike, bream, and catfish, always starting at the head end. They also eat frogs and crabs.

Pel's fishing-owl (Scotopelia peli) *has spiny toes that grip its prey.*

Little owl (Athene noctua) *with centipede prey*

A VARIED DIET

Owls are well known for attacking mice, but their diet includes many other kinds of animals. Some species are fast enough to catch other birds in flight while many smaller owls catch moths in midair. In many places, earthworms make up most of the little owl's diet. However, if it is fortunate enough to catch one, it will even swallow a wriggling centipede.

BARN OWL

This owl is one of the most widespread birds in the world, but because it is nocturnal it is not seen very often. Unlike other owls, the barn owl has a heart-shaped face, formed by a ring around each eye. It usually hunts by flying low over open ground.

Powerful talons for snatching prey

Scientific name: *Tyto alba*

Size: Female up to 13 in (33 cm); male slightly smaller

Habitat: Open ground, grassland, farmland, often near buildings

Distribution: Worldwide, except far north and south

Reproduction: Nests in tree holes or in buildings; female lays and incubates 4–7 eggs, which hatch after about 30 days

Diet: Small mammals, such as mice, voles, and shrews

Inside an owl pellet

Complete pellet

Vole skull

Jaws

Hipbones

Matted fur

Shoulder blades

Parts of backbone

Ribs

OWL PELLETS

Owls cannot chew their food, so they usually swallow it whole. After feeding, they cough up any indigestible remains in a soft lump, called a pellet. Owl pellets are like a record book because they show exactly what the bird has eaten. On the left, a pellet has been pulled apart. The remains show that the owl has been feeding on voles.

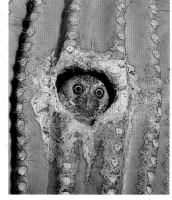

Elf owl nesting in a saguaro cactus

READY-MADE NESTS

Most owls nest in holes, but the type of hole they use varies from one species to another. Some owls nest in hollow trees or in ruined buildings, but smaller species often use holes that have been made by woodpeckers. The tiny elf owl (*Micrathene witneyi*), the smallest species of owl in the world, lives in the deserts of the American southwest. It nests in saguaro cacti, using holes made by gila woodpeckers (*Melanerpes uropygialis*).

NESTING UNDERGROUND

The American burrowing owl lives in open grassland where there are no trees. It nests underground, and although it can dig with its feet and beak, it often takes over tunnels made by prairie dogs. Burrowing owls are active during the day as well as at night. They often stand outside their tunnels like sentries, watching for signs of danger.

Burrowing owl (*Speotyto cunicularia*)

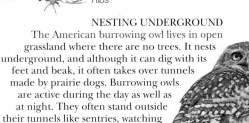

Barn owl chicks

RAISING A FAMILY

Unlike most birds, owls start incubating their eggs as soon as the first one is laid. This means that their eggs hatch in sequence, producing chicks a few days apart. The oldest chick is always the biggest and the youngest the smallest. If food is scarce, the youngest chick often dies, but the older ones stand a good chance of survival. If the chicks were all the same size, they might all fail to survive.

Find out more
BIRDS: *208*
BIRDS OF PREY: *218*
HUNTING: *52*
SENSES: *42*

SWIFTS AND SWALLOWS

SWIFTS, SWALLOWS, and nightjars are acrobatic fliers that can twist and turn in the air with amazing speed and agility. Although they are not closely related, these birds look similar and obtain food in the same way. They prey on flying insects, which they catch with great skill in midair. Many swifts and swallows are migrants that travel huge distances between their breeding sites and wintering quarters. Some are well adapted to living near people and build their nests on walls, chimneys, or under roofs. Swifts are the most aerial of all birds – some even roost while flying.

ANATOMY

Swifts and swallows have small bodies with long, slender wings. Their streamlined shape helps them to turn quickly and brake easily when chasing fast-flying insects. Swifts can beat each wing at a different rate, which helps them to maneuver at high speed. Swallows also have forked tails and some have long tail streamers that make them more agile. Male barn swallows have extra-long tail streamers to attract females.

Alpine swift
(*Apus melba*)

Narrow wings

European nightjar
(*Caprimulgus europaeus*)

Sensitive bristles help to trap insect prey.

Swallow chasing insect in midair

GAPING MOUTHS

Aerial insect-eaters have very small, fragile bills that open wide to reveal huge, gaping mouths. The wide gape allows them to trap as many insects as possible while in flight. Some species, such as the European nightjar, have a fringe of touch-sensitive bristles around the bill. The bristles trap insects and funnel them into the mouth.

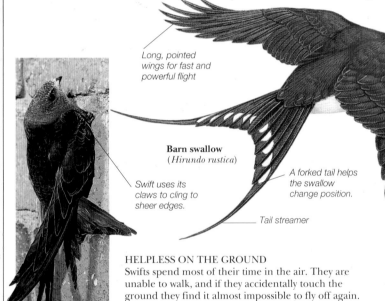

Long, pointed wings for fast and powerful flight

Barn swallow
(*Hirundo rustica*)

A forked tail helps the swallow change position.

Swift uses its claws to cling to sheer edges.

Tail streamer

Common swift
(*Apus apus*)

HELPLESS ON THE GROUND

Swifts spend most of their time in the air. They are unable to walk, and if they accidentally touch the ground they find it almost impossible to fly off again. This is because their tiny legs and feet are too weak to support them when they try to take off from the ground. However, their four sharp claws are well adapted for clinging onto tree hollows, walls, and other vertical surfaces.

FEEDING IN MIDAIR

Swifts and swallows feed on different insects, and usually hunt at varying heights. This helps them to avoid competing for the same food. However, in cold, wet weather, many insects stay close to the ground or over water, and house martins (*Delichon urbica*) and bank swallows (*Riparia riparia*) need to fly lower than usual to catch them. Barn swallows (*Hirundo rustica*) eat flies during the summer in North America, but feed mainly on other insects during winter in South America.

30 m
98 ft

Common swifts catch small insects, such as aphids and moths.

25 m
82 ft

20 m
66 ft

House martins feed mainly on small flies and aphids.

15 m
49 ft

10 m
33 ft

Bank swallows trawl for insects such as mayflies.

5 m
16 ft

Barn swallows eat larger insects such as bluebottles.

Ground level

A barn swallow swoops down to drink from a garden pond.

ON THE WING

Various species of swift and swallow, notably the common swift (*Apus apus*), spend most of their lives in the air. Once young swifts have left the nest, some may fly for up to two years before landing to breed and build their own nests. They mate, collect nest material, and even sleep in the air. Swallows obtain nearly all their food while flying and-often take a drink on the wing. However, in bad weather they may land to catch insects on the ground.

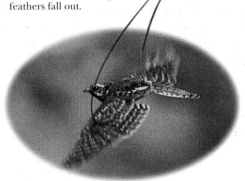

STANDARD-WINGED NIGHTJAR

The standard-winged nightjar roosts and nests on the ground by day and flies in search of insect prey at night. Males have greatly elongated wing feathers, which grow up to 20 in (50 cm) in length. They use their spectacular feathers during courtship displays, which take place at dusk. When the breeding season is over, the long feathers fall out.

Scientific name:	*Macrodipteryx longipennis*
Size:	11 in (28 cm)
Habitat:	Open woodland, savanna, coastal plains, sandy or stony wasteland
Distribution:	Africa, from Senegal to western Ethiopia
Reproduction:	Lays one or two eggs on bare ground
Diet:	Small flying insects, such as beetles and moths

NEST SITES

The common swift and the house martin often find nesting sites in cities, towns, and villages. They collect mud pellets to make shallow, cup-shaped nests, which they stick to walls or under the eaves of houses. Bank swallows make their nests by digging out burrows in the soft earth of river banks or cliffs. Great dusky swifts have the most spectacular nesting sites – they nest in rocky crevices behind waterfalls, and have to fly through the cascading water every time they visit the nest.

House martin (Delichon urbica) feeding young in nest

EDIBLE NESTS

The edible-nest swiftlets of Southeast Asia build their nests in large colonies on the roofs and walls of caves. They use their sticky saliva to make cup-shaped nests. As the saliva dries, the nests stick to the walls. In some countries, such as Borneo, people collect these nests to make an oriental delicacy called "bird's nest soup."

Edible-nest swiftlet
(*Aerodramus fuciphaga*)

PALM SWIFTS

Some species of swifts build their nests on palm leaves. African palm swifts use sticky saliva to stick their nests to the undersides of leaves. They also glue their eggs to the nest to stop them from falling out. Other species, such as the pygmy swift (*Tachornis furcata*) hang bag-shaped nests from palm trees, glueing the tip of the "bag handle" to the palm.

A palm swift (Cypsiurus parvus) on its nest under a coco palm leaf

Migration routes of barn swallows

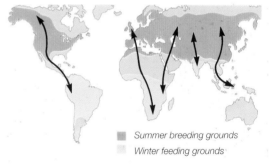

■ *Summer breeding grounds*
■ *Winter feeding grounds*

MIGRANTS

Many swifts and swallows are long-distance migrants. They breed in temperate parts of the Northern Hemisphere during summer, and in winter fly south to tropical countries where food is more abundant. Before each migration, swallows form flocks that will travel thousands of miles together. When returning to their breeding grounds, their amazing navigational skills enable them to locate their old nesting sites.

Brown colors camouflage the nightjar.

SUPERB CAMOUFLAGE

Nightjars have soft, loose plumage and intricate patterns in mottled brown, buff, gray, cream, and black. These markings provide superb camouflage because they mimic the bird's surroundings of dead leaves, bracken, and heather. By day, nightjars remain very still on the ground, while at night they fly around catching insects.

Find out more
BIRDS: *208*
DEFENSE 2: *50*
MIGRATION AND NAVIGATION: *46*
MOVEMENT IN AIR: *36*

SONGBIRDS

THERE ARE MORE THAN 4,000 species of songbirds – a name also given to most of the passerines, or perching birds. Songbirds have well-developed voiceboxes, called syrinxes, which enable most of them to produce beautiful sounds – although some, such as the crow, utter harsh notes. In most species, the male is the main singer. He sings to attract females during the courtship season and to warn intruders to stay out of his territory. Many songbirds have small bills adapted to feed on a variety of foods, including insects and seeds. Some, such as the shrike, feed on small animals.

House sparrows (*Passer domesticus*) grow up to 5.5 in (14 cm) long.

Carrion crows (*Corvus corone*) grow up to 18 in (46 cm) long.

GREAT RANGE OF SIZE
Most songbirds are small and compact with small bills. They range in size from the tiny short-tailed pygmy-tyrant (*Myiornis ecaudatus*), which weighs less than 0.2 oz (5 g) and is less than 3 in (7 cm) long, to the common raven (*Corvus corax*), which grows up to 57 in (65 cm) and weighs up to 3 lb 5 oz (1.5 kg).

PERCHING FEET
Songbirds are also known as perching birds. This is because they are able to grip slender perches such as twigs, reeds, or grass stems with their feet. Songbirds have feet with three toes pointing forward, and one pointing backward. Their feet maintain a firm grip even when they are asleep. When they prepare to sleep, they lower their body by bending their legs. As they do this, their leg tendons tense and their claws flex, triggering a locking mechanism. Their four toes automatically grip fast and lock around the perch.

Chaffinch
(*Fringilla coelebs*)

This fledging will learn to produce a loud, musical song.

Small head with powerful bill

Gouldian finch
(*Chloebia gouldiae*)

Toes clamp around perch when bird rests its weight on foot.

Tendons pull tight, drawing in the toes.

Three toes point forward, hind toe points backward.

Hind toe is longer than front toes.

LEARNING TO SING
Each kind of songbird has its own distinctive song. Young chicks learn to sing by listening to adults of the same species. Some learn the basics of their song within the first two months of their lives. Others, such as the chaffinch, can take as long as a year. The northern mockingbird (*Mimus polyglottos*) is unusual in that it is able to add new elements to its song repertoire throughout its life.

Syrinx

The windpipe helps amplify sounds made by the syrinx.

Lungs

SYRINX
Songbirds produce varied songs using their syrinxes. This unique structure is positioned at the junction of the windpipe (trachea) and the two bronchi (tubes leading to the lungs). The syrinx has a thin membrane that vibrates to produce complex sounds. The membrane is triggered by air moving through the syrinx. Special muscles control the syrinx action, enabling the birds to produce a variety of different sounds.

REMARKABLE MIMIC
European marsh warblers (*Acrocephalus palustris*) are the most accomplished bird mimics in the wild. They are capable of reproducing the sounds of as many as 99 other European species, and 113 African species. They hear the songs of other birds along their migration routes, and also in their winter feeding grounds. Marsh warblers copy a rich medley of fluty phrases, ringing notes and nasal sounds from other birds. By combining these sounds, they can produce an amazing range of imitated songs and calls.

Marsh warbler in song

White-throated dipper (Cinclus cinclus) enters the water and moves forward and downward by moving its wings.

Dives last an average of 3 seconds.

WALKING UNDERWATER

One of the few songbirds that is able to dive underwater is the dipper. It lives along shallow, fast-running rivers and catches most of its prey underwater. To propel itself forward and downward in the water, it makes small flicking movements with its wings. It also walks along the river bed, gripping firmly onto stones with its large claws.

Northern shrike (Lanius excubitor) with prey

SHRIKE'S LARDER

Shrikes have strong legs and feet and sharp claws for holding prey. Some members of the shrike family have the nickname "butcher birds." This is because they impale and store small prey on thorns and barbed wire. Some even squeeze their victim between twigs. This "larder" provides a store of food for the birds, especially during cold weather when prey is hard to find.

MOUNTAIN BLUEBIRD

The mountain bluebird is a member of the thrush family. The female is duller than her beautiful blue mate, and has only a trace of color on her gray-brown plumage. The male has a quiet warbling song. Bluebirds prefer open areas, such as mountain meadows that are dotted with trees. In winter, they migrate as far south as Mexico.

Scientific name: *Sialia currucoides*

Size: Up to 7 in (18 cm) long

Habitat: Woody and grassy mountains

Distribution: Mexico, and along western US up to southern Alaska

Reproduction: Nest usually built in tree hole; female lays five or six eggs, which hatch after about 14 days

Diet: Insects, and fruit during winter

INTRICATE NESTS

During the breeding season, songbirds spend much of their time making elaborate nests. Many, such as the warblers, build neat cup-shaped nests. Others, such as penduline tits, weave intricate hanging nests using grasses and mosses. To keep predators away, they conceal the way into the nest by building a false entrance. Other ingenious nest-builders include tailor birds (*Orthotomus* sp.). They sew together leaves using strips of plant fibers in their bills. This forms a snug cavity in which to build their nests.

Nests are made of reed flowers, grasses, and feathers.

Tit enters through a slit just above the false entrance.

Reed warblers (Acrocephalus scirpaceus) build nests between dried stems in reed beds.

This hanging nest belongs to the penduline tit (Remiz pendulinus).

Although this looks like the main entrance, it only leads to a small, empty chamber.

European starling (*Sturnus vulgaris*)

Sharp bill helps starling probe for different types of food.

THE SUCCESSFUL STARLING

Common starlings are well adapted to life in towns and cities, as well as rural areas. Although they originally came from Asia, they were introduced to countries such as the USA in the 19th century. Today, starlings live in many parts of the world. They compete with native species for nest-holes and for food. Starlings have a varied diet, which includes seeds, worms, and insects.

Marsh warbler removing fecal sac from nest

HELPLESS YOUNG

When songbirds hatch, they are naked, blind, and helpless. They are cared for and fed by their parents until they are old enough to fend for themselves. The young excrete their feces in neat gelatinous sacs, which their parents can easily pick up and drop well away from the nest. This helps keep their nests clean and deters predators.

Find out more

ANIMAL HOMES: *58*
COURTSHIP, MATING, AND PARENTAL CARE: *30*
DEFENSE 2: *50*

TROPICAL BIRDS

TROPICAL RAINFORESTS ARE HOME to a rich variety of birds. The warm, wet climate of these regions is ideal for the growth of thick, lush vegetation that provides plenty of leaves, fruits, and insects for birds to feed on, and bushes and trees to nest in. Birds are found at all levels of the tropical rainforest. Toucans live high in the forest canopy where there is more light, warmth, and fruit. Birds such as the trumpeter hornbill tend to stay within the middle layers of the forest. Here, they remain hidden from predatory birds that swoop through the trees in search of food. On the forest floor, larger birds, such as cassowaries, push their way through the dense undergrowth to find seeds, berries, and fruits.

Small head has a long, erect, bristly crest.

Hoatzin (*Opisthocomus hoazin*)

THE HOATZIN
Hoatzins live in groups along quiet riverbanks in Amazonia. They feed mainly on mangrove leaves and have a huge crop (storage organ) that grinds up the tough leaves. Young hoatzins are good swimmers and drop into the water below their nest when danger threatens. They then climb back, using special claws on the front of their wings to haul themselves up the tree.

Huge, lightweight bill has serrated edges to cut through large fruit.

TOUCANS
Famous for their massive bills, toucans are found only in the tropical forests of Central and South America. They use their bills to reach fruit on the tips of branches or to pluck young birds from deep within a nest cavity. The brightly colored bill probably helps the toucan to recognize others of its own kind.

Bony casque helps signal the bird's status.

BIG BILLS
Many tropical birds, including toucans and the hornbills of Africa and Asia, have huge bills. These bills mean the birds can reach food on the ends of slender branches that would not support their weight. Despite their size, the bills are hollow and extremely light.

Rhinoceros hornbill (*Buceros rhinoceros*)

Hollow bill, strengthened by bony struts

Red-billed toucan (*Ramphastos tucanus*)

Feet have two toes pointing forward and two backward giving a firm grip on tree trunks and branches.

NECTAR SPECIALISTS
Various groups of tropical birds have specialized bills for feeding on nectar. They include the sunbirds of southern Asia and Africa, the honeyeaters of Australasia, and various parrots. Many nectar-feeders have bills that can reach inside flowers. Hummingbirds have a long, thin bill and an equally long, thin tongue to push inside tubular-shaped flowers and lap up the nectar.

The hummingbird hovers as it feeds.

Honeyguide leads the honey badger to a bees' nest.

Honey badger (*Mellivora capensis*)

Honeyguide waits while the honey badger breaks into the bees' nest.

WORKING TOGETHER
Honeyguides have developed mutually beneficial relationships with various mammals, including honey badgers and humans. To attract the attention of a honey badger, the bird chatters noisily and flicks its tail. It then leads the honey badger to a bees' nest and waits silently while its "helper" breaks open the nest to get at the honey. When the nest is open, the bird swoops down to feed on the larvae and wax. Honeyguides are among the few birds able to digest wax.

Long bill can probe deep into tubular flowers to obtain nectar.

Sparkling violet-ear (*Colibri coruscans*)

COURTSHIP DISPLAYS

Many tropical birds, including some manakins from Mexico and South America, perform spectacular courtship displays. Pairs or trios of males are watched by females as they hop along a branch, then take turns leaping up and fluttering their feathers. The subordinate males eventually fly away, leaving the dominant male to mate with the females. Male birds-of-paradise perform either alone or in groups. They fan out their feathers and vibrate their bodies, while making loud calls.

Male leaps and flutters feathers.

Female

Blue-backed manakins (*Chiroxiphia pareola*)

Female stands in the bower.

Male collects blue objects.

Satin bowerbird (*Ptilonorhynchus violaceus*)

BOWERBIRDS

Male bowerbirds are the supreme architects of the bird world. They build structures called bowers from sticks and vegetation to entice females to mate with them. Some species, such as the satin bowerbird, paint the walls of their bowers with a paste of chewed fruit or charcoal. They apply the "paint" with a "brush" consisting of a wad of plant fibers held in the bill. They even decorate the bower with brightly colored flowers, feathers, and stones.

TURACOS

Turacos are distant relatives of cuckoos that live in the forests and open woodlands of Africa, where they feed mainly on fruit. The feathers of the red-crested turaco contain pigments called turacin and turacoverdin. These copper-containing pigments give the feathers their red and green colors. It takes about a year for the young to acquire the full adult plumage.

Akiapolaau
(*Hemignathus munroi*)

Iiwi (*Vestiaria coccinea*)

HAWAIIAN FINCHES

The Hawaiian finches are thought to have evolved from a single ancestor. Each of the 28 species has a differently shaped bill, adapted for eating different types of food. The bill of the akiopolaau is unique, with a straight, stout lower mandible used to hammer into soft bark, and a long, curved upper mandible that extracts the exposed insect larvae. Iiwis feed on nectar and have bills matching the shape of certain flowers, while akohekohes have bills that enable them to feed on insects and nectar.

Akohekohe
(*Palmeria dolei*)

Many turaco species have green body plumage and red on the wings and crest.

Red flight feathers flash as the bird takes off.

Red-crested turaco
(*Tauraco erythrolophus*)

RESPLENDENT QUETZAL

Male *Female*

Despite its brilliant colors, the resplendent quetzal is well camouflaged in the leafy shade of the upper canopy. The male's tail coverts can grow up to 3 ft 3 in (1 m) long; he flutters his long tail during courtship displays. This spectacular bird is is now rare due to the destruction of its cloud forest habitat. Although legally protected, some quetzals are still captured for the caged-bird trade.

Scientific name: *Pharomachrus mocinno*

Size: Up to 1 ft 3 in (38 cm) long, excluding tail

Habitat: Humid cloud forest, mainly at an altitude of about 4,000–10,000 ft (1,200–3,000 m)

Distribution: Southern Mexico to Panama

Reproduction: Female lays two pale blue eggs in a tree hole. Both parents share incubation.

Diet: Mainly fruit, but young also eat insects and other invertebrates and small vertebrates

Helmeted hornbill (*Buceros vigil*)

THREATENED TROPICAL BIRDS

Many tropical birds, such as the helmeted hornbill from Indonesia and Malaysia, are threatened by the destruction of their forest home. The parrot family is the most threatened group, with more than 70 species at risk. Island birds face the additional threat of introduced species – the native birds have no defense against the new intruders, which spread disease and compete with them for food and space.

Find out more
ANIMALS IN DANGER: *100*
BIRDS: *208*
FLIGHTLESS BIRDS: *210*
TROPICAL RAINFORESTS: *82*

MAMMALS

BATS, KANGAROOS, WHALES – and even humans – fall into the class of animals known as mammals. What sets this diverse group apart from other animals is that the female of each species suckles her young on milk produced in mammary glands. Mammals are also endothermic (warm-blooded) and most have a covering of hair. The 4,000 or more species of mammal – which are found on land, in the air, and in water – are divided into three groups according to the way they reproduce. Placental mammals, such as gorillas, give birth to well-developed young. Marsupials, found in Australasia and the Americas, produce young that complete their development in a pouch. Monotremes, found only in Australasia, lay eggs.

European common shrew (Sorex araneus)

MAMMAL EVOLUTION
Mammals evolved from mammal-like reptiles, called therapsids, about 220 million years ago. The first mammals were small, shrewlike insect eaters. They survived in a world dominated by dinosaurs because they were endothermic (warm-blooded) and able to remain active and feed at night when the temperature fell. Mammals became more diverse and widespread 65 million years ago when the dinosaurs died out.

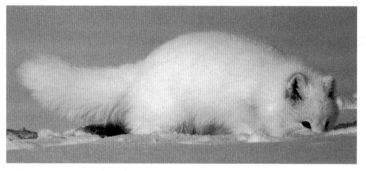

The thick fur of the Arctic fox (Alopex lagopus) insulates it in freezing conditions.

The hare's large external ears pick up the sounds of approaching predators.

European brown hare (*Lepus europaeus*)

KEEPING WARM
Because of their warm blood, mammals are generally able to maintain a constant body temperature regardless of how cold it is. Most species are also kept warm by a covering of fur. Thousands of hairs, made of a tough protein called keratin, grow from pits (follicles) in the skin to form a layer of fur. Short underfur traps a layer of air next to the skin to keep out cold air and water, while longer guard hairs form an outer covering. Animals in cold climates generally have thicker fur than those in warm climates.

Short, water-repellent fur covers the seal's streamlined body.

The thick fur of the beaver has long guard hairs.

EXTERNAL EARS
Most mammals have external ears, or pinnae, that direct sound into the part of the ear inside the skull. External ears can usually be moved in order to pinpoint the precise location of a sound. This enables mammals, many of which have a good sense of hearing, to detect noises made by an approaching predator or potential prey, or to listen for calls made by another member of the same species.

Dog teeth from upper jaw

Molar   *Carnassial premolar*   *Premolar*   *Canine*   *Incisor*

MAMMAL TEETH
Unlike other animals, mammals have teeth that vary according to their use. The chisel-like incisors are used for cutting, the canines for gripping and tearing, and the premolars and molars for grinding and crushing. The shape and size of these teeth varies according to the animal's diet. In meat-eating mammals, such as dogs, pointed canines are used for killing prey, while carnassial teeth are used to slice through flesh.

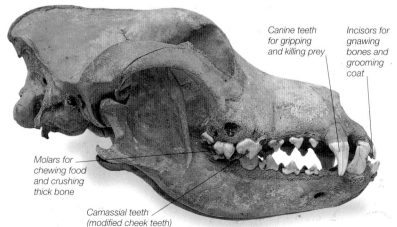

Canine teeth for gripping and killing prey

Incisors for gnawing bones and grooming coat

Molars for chewing food and crushing thick bone

Carnassial teeth (modified cheek teeth) for slicing through flesh

Skull of wolf (*Canis lupus*)

REPRODUCTION

In all mammals fertilization takes place inside the female's body. The fertilized egg divides many times and eventually becomes a fetus. In placental mammals the fetus develops inside the uterus nourished by the placenta, an organ attached to the wall of the uterus and connected to the fetus by an umbilical cord. The blood supplies of the mother and baby come into close contact inside the placenta allowing food and oxygen to be passed to the fetus and waste to be removed. The fetus grows inside the uterus until it is ready to be born.

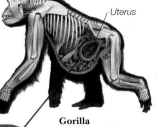
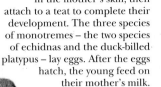

Uterus

Gorilla
(*Gorilla gorilla*)

The baby gorilla develops inside the uterus for about 260 days until it is ready to be born.

Placenta

Gorilla fetus is linked to the placenta by an umbilical cord.

HOW MARSUPIALS AND MONOTREMES REPRODUCE

Unlike the majority of mammals, marsupials, which include koalas, kangaroos, and opossums, do not have a placenta. They give birth to tiny, poorly developed young that find their way to a pouch in the mother's skin, then attach to a teat to complete their development. The three species of monotremes – the two species of echidnas and the duck-billed platypus – lay eggs. After the eggs hatch, the young feed on their mother's milk.

Coppery brush-tailed possum (Trichosurus vulpecula) with offspring in her pouch

BRAINY ANIMALS

Mammals have larger brains, relative to their body size, than other vertebrates. In addition, a larger part of the brain is taken up by the cerebrum, the "thinking" part of the brain. This is very noticeable in primates, a group that includes monkeys, apes, and humans. With larger brains, mammals have more complex behavior than other animals. They can also learn and adapt their behavior to suit changing circumstances.

SUCKLING

Female mammals produce a nutritious fluid called milk to feed their young during the early part of their lives. Milk is made by mammary glands in the skin and when the young mammal sucks, milk is released through projections called teats. Suckling is an important part of parental care. Milk is rich in proteins and fats, which speed growth, and contains antibodies that protect the young mammal against disease.

Japanese macaque monkeys (Macaca fuscata) washing food to remove dirt

SMALLEST MAMMAL

Kitti's hog-nosed bat is the world's smallest mammal. Found in limestone caves in southwest Thailand, this tiny bat is 1.3 in (33 mm) long, and weighs just 0.07 oz (2 g). Small mammals lose body heat very rapidly and some, such as shrews, eat almost constantly to generate heat. When resting, Kitti's hog-nosed bats go into a state of torpor – during which body temperature falls – in order to save energy.

Kitti's hog-nosed bat
(*Craseonycteris thonglongyai*)

Young monkeys suck their mother's teats to release the milk.

Lowe's monkey
(*Cercopithecus lowei*)

LARGEST MAMMAL

With an average length of 86 ft (26 m) and a weight of about 120 tons, the blue whale is the largest animal that has ever existed on Earth. On land, the size of all mammals is limited by how much weight their limbs can support. In the sea, however, their weight is supported by water, which allows many species of whales to grow to a large size. Also, larger mammals lose body heat more slowly – an advantage in cold marine environments. Marine mammals have streamlined bodies that help them move easily in water.

As it surfaces, the whale breathes out and in through its blowholes.

Blue whale (Balaenoptera musculus) breathing at the water's surface

Find out more

MARSUPIALS: 236
MONOTREMES: 234
PRIMATES: 280
WHALES: 262

MONOTREMES

MOST MAMMALS REPRODUCE by giving birth to live young. Monotremes are unique in being the only mammals that lay eggs. There are three species of monotreme: the duck-billed platypus, and the short- and long-nosed echidnas. Their soft-shelled eggs hatch after only ten days, and the naked, underdeveloped young are dependent on their mothers for feeding and protection. Although monotremes are regarded as "primitive" animals because they lay eggs, they have all the other features of mammals – warm blood, fur, and young that suckle.

Small eyes

Body is covered with soft fur.

Large bill is very sensitive to touch.

Webbed front feet for swimming

SWIMMING
The platypus is well adapted for swimming and diving. It has a streamlined body, with dense, waterproof fur and webbed front feet. It swims by "rowing" with its broad front feet – pulling first on one side, then on the other to propel itself through the water. Its partially webbed back feet are used as rudders to steer through the water.

Duck-billed platypus
(*Ornithorhynchus anatinus*)

DUCK-BILLED PLATYPUS
This semiaquatic mammal lives in burrows by ponds and streams in eastern Australia and Tasmania. It is territorial by nature and each platypus tries to secure a stretch of river for itself. The platypus is 18–24 in (45–60 cm) long, including its bill and tail. The ducklike bill, which is soft and pliable, is used to probe for prey on river beds. It is sensitive to weak electrical fields generated by prey.

Hollow spurs project from the ankle of each hind foot.

VENOMOUS SPUR
The male platypus is one of the few venomous mammals. It has a spur, connected to a venom gland, on the ankle of each hind foot. The platypus erects the spur to inject venom into its victim. The spur is probably used both to deter rivals and as a defense against predators.

Oval-shaped nesting chamber

Grass and eucalyptus leaves line the nesting chamber.

After leaving the water, the platypus grooms itself.

The platypus uses its rear claws as a comb.

Young suckle milk that seeps from milk-secreting glands in their mother's fur.

BURROWS
The platypus uses its powerful front legs to dig burrows in the banks of rivers or ponds. Both sexes excavate tunnels for shelter, but only the female builds the breeding burrow with a nesting chamber at the far end. Platypuses breed from August to October, and the female usually lays two eggs, 14 days after mating. To keep the eggs moist, the female carries wet leaves into the chamber with her tail. She then incubates the eggs for ten days. When they hatch, the blind and naked young are 1 in (2.5 cm) long. Four months later, they are 13 in (33 cm) long, covered with fur, and ready to venture outside.

The tunnel of a breeding burrow generally follows the slope of the bank. It can be up to 100 ft (30 m) long.

The female platypus builds two or three plugs of earth to prevent water and predators from entering the tunnel.

The entrance usually lies above the waterline.

SPINY ANTEATERS

Both species of echidna have muscular bodies covered with fur and spines. The head narrows to a slim snout. They have no teeth, but the back part of the narrow tongue is horny and rubs against the inside of the mouth to grind up food. Echidnas have poor eyesight but an acute sense of smell. The short-nosed echidna lives in Australia, Tasmania, and New Guinea. It is solitary and active mainly at dusk and at night. It moves with ease across most terrain and can swim using its snout as a snorkel.

Broad, beaverlike tail for storing fat reserves

Sharp, hollow spines cover the back and sides, growing out through the dense coat of fur.

The egg has a soft shell.

The female echidna lays a single egg into her pouch. After 7–10 days, the baby hatches.

Small eyes

Nostrils and mouth are at the end of the hairless snout.

Very long claw for scratching between its spines

Short-nosed echidna
(*Tachyglossus aculeatus*)

Broad feet and curved claws for digging

LONG-NOSED ECHIDNA

The long-nosed echidna is larger than its short-nosed relative, and has more hair, but fewer, shorter spines. It feeds almost exclusively on earthworms, which it finds by sniffing the ground. Once found, the worm is hooked by spines on the tongue and pulled into the mouth.

Snout is two-thirds the length of the head.

Large feet

Scientific name: *Zaglossus bruijni*

Size: Head and body length 18–35 in (45–90 cm)

Habitat: Humid mountain forests

Distribution: New Guinea

Reproduction: Breeds in July. Single egg transferred to temporary abdominal pouch. After hatching, the young echidna remains in the pouch for 6–8 weeks.

Diet: Earthworms

Echidnas use their strong legs and claws to dig into soft earth with amazing speed.

The echidna sits on top of a mound of earth.

ANT DIET

The short-nosed echidna feeds almost exclusively on ants and termites, which it locates by smell. Once it finds a nest, the echidna breaks it open with its broad front feet and flat claws. It uses its snout to probe into rotten logs and to plow through soil to uncover nests. Ants and termites are swept up by the echidna's tongue, which can be up to 7 in (18 cm) long and coated with sticky saliva.

The echidna forages for termites with its pink, sticky tongue.

Within a minute, the echidna is almost out of sight, leaving only its erect spines above the soil's surface.

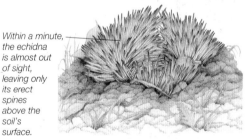

Only the echidna's spines remain visible.

ECHIDNA DEFENSE

If threatened, an echidna erects its spines and rolls up into a spiky ball. On soft ground it may dig straight down into the soil. However, this does not protect it from dingoes, which can dig out the buried echidna. An echidna may also avoid predators by using its spines and feet to wedge itself into a crevice so it cannot be dislodged.

UNDERWATER HUNTERS

At dawn and dusk, the platypus leaves its burrow to hunt for food. It dives to the bottom of the stream or pond and can stay underwater for up to five minutes. Its eyes and ears close underwater, sealed by a fold of skin. The platypus locates its prey by probing the mud with its bill. It snatches up prey and stores it in cheek pouches. When these are full, the platypus surfaces and grinds the food up between horny plates in its bill.

The platypus sweeps its bill from side to side in search of food.

The platypus hunts crayfish, insect larvae, and snails, which live near the riverbed.

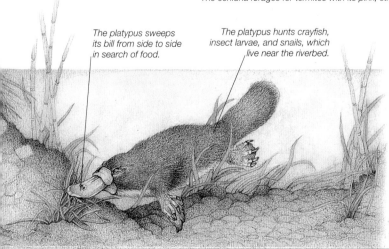

Find out more

ANIMAL HOMES: *58*
MAMMALS: *232*
MOVEMENT IN WATER: *38*
REPRODUCTION: *28*

MARSUPIALS

THIS DIVERSE GROUP of pouched animals contains more than 270 species, most of which live in Australasia and South America. They range in size from the tiny Pilbara ningauis – which may weigh as little as 0.07 oz (2 g) – to large kangaroos weighing 198 lb (90 kg). Marsupials reproduce in a different way from other mammals. Young are born in an immature state and complete their development in the mother's pouch.

Spotted cuscus (*Spilocuscus maculatus*)

Ecuadorian opossum (*Caluromys lanatus*)

AUSTRALASIAN AND AMERICAN MARSUPIALS

Australian marsupials, such as the spotted cuscus, evolved in isolation from the rest of the world. This diverse group is made up of 16 families and includes wombats, kangaroos, bandicoots, opossums, and the koala. American marsupials are less diverse and include three families: shrew opossums, opossums, and the monito del monte (colocolo). Most are small, ground- or tree-dwelling omnivores, and many are good climbers.

REPRODUCTION

Most mammals develop in their mother's uterus, receiving nourishment via the placenta. Marsupial embryos remain in the uterus for only a brief period. For example, when a kangaroo is born, it is underdeveloped apart from its mouth and forelimbs. It crawls up its mother's abdomen and climbs into a pouch, where it stays for several months to continue its development.

1. The blind newborn wallaby crawls up its mother's stomach fur to reach her pouch.

2. Inside the pouch, the newborn attaches itself to a nipple and starts to feed.

READY TO LEAVE

A young wallaby or kangaroo may spend up to 11 months developing in its mother's pouch. After a month or so, its hind limbs and tail have grown and it is still attached to the nipple. Several months later, the joey (young kangaroo or wallaby) looks like a small adult and may push its head out of the pouch or leave the pouch temporarily. Eventually, it leaves the pouch permanently but continues to put its head in to suckle, until it is weaned.

Red-necked wallaby (*Macropus rufogriseus*)

The joey sticks its head out of its mother's pouch.

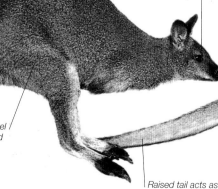

Virginia opossum (Didelphis virginiana) with brood

LARGE BROOD

Kangaroos and wallabies usually give birth to one baby at a time. Other marsupials, especially the smaller species, such as opossums, pygmy possums, and dasyurids, have larger broods. The cat-sized Virginia opossum is North America's only marsupial. Female Virginia opossums often have litters of over 20 young. Most offspring do not survive because their mothers do not have enough nipples to feed the entire litter.

MARSUPIAL MOVEMENT

Most kangaroos and wallabies cannot walk. Instead, they use their powerful hind legs and long feet like springs to hop. Some tree-dwelling marsupials glide between branches by extending a membrane that stretches between their legs. The water opossum (*Chironectes minimus*) can swim using its webbed hind feet, while marsupial moles (*Notoryctes typhlops*) have shovellike feet to tunnel through soil.

How a wallaby makes a move

Wallaby pushes off the ground with its large back feet.

It leans forward as it takes off from the ground.

Wallabies can travel at great speed and for long distances when leaping.

Wallaby looks directly forward as it leaps.

Raised tail acts as a counterbalance.

TREE-DWELLERS

Some marsupials, including many opossums, possums, tree kangaroos, and the koala, are adapted for life in the trees. Many have grasping hands and sharp claws to grip tree bark, and some have a prehensile (gripping) tail that acts as an extra "foot" while climbing. Tree kangaroos, such as the Doria's tree kangaroo, live in rainforests where they feed on leaves and fruit. They have longer forelimbs and shorter hind limbs than their ground-dwelling relatives.

KOALAS

These tailless marsupials live in the eucalyptus trees of eastern Australia. Their diet of eucalyptus leaves is not particularly nutritious, so they rest for up to 18 hours a day on forked branches to conserve energy. Koalas use their strong legs, sharp claws, and grasping hands to grip tree trunks. They climb by bringing up their hind legs in a series of jumps.

Long, curved claws and cushioned pads on feet grip branches.

Doria's tree kangaroo
(*Dendrolagus dorianus*)

Koala
(*Phascolarctos cinereus*)

RED KANGAROO

The red kangaroo is the largest of all marsupials. The males usually have reddish-brown fur, and may be twice the size of the females, which are usually blue-gray in color. By day, small herds of kangaroos shelter under trees, emerging in the evening to feed. Male red kangaroos can reach speeds of 35 mph (56 kmh) over short distances.

Scientific name: *Macropus rufus*

Size: Males up to 6 ft 6 in (2 m) tall

Habitat: Scrub and grassland

Distribution: Australia

Reproduction: Single young born which climbs into its mother's pouch, where it remains for eight months

Diet: Grass

Tail may be up to 3 ft 3 in (1 m) long.

FEEDING

Marsupials have varied feeding habits. Many are herbivorous: the honey possum uses its brush-tipped tongue to extract nectar from flowers, while kangaroos graze on grass and other plants. Omnivorous marsupials feed on fruit, insects, small vertebrates, and carrion. The Australian numbat (*Myrmecobius fasciatus*) feeds on ants and termites. It rips up their nests with its sharp claws and extracts the insects with its long, sticky tongue.

Common wombat (Vombatus ursinus) *with baby*

BURROWERS

Resembling small bears, wombats use their powerful front legs to dig burrows up to 100 ft (30 m) long. By resting in their burrows during the day, they keep cool in summer and warm in winter. Boodies, small relatives of kangaroos, live in burrows in large social groups.

Honey possum
(*Tarsipes rostratus*)

Long whiskers help the Tasmanian devil detect objects and find its way around at night.

Sharp teeth and powerful jaws to rip apart meat and skin and crush bones.

Short legs for foraging in dense undergrowth

Tasmanian devil
(*Sarcophilus harrisii*)

The Tasmanian devil is the size of a small dog.

Back legs are extended forward, ready to land.

MARSUPIAL CARNIVORES

Many carnivorous marsupials belong to the Australasian dasyurid family. The majority of dasyurids are small, mouselike animals that eat mainly insects and other invertebrates, but may also catch small lizards and mammals. The Tasmanian devil is a larger dasyurid that feeds on reptiles, mammals, and carrion, including dead sheep and wallabies. It eats all parts of the animal, including the skin and bones.

Find out more

GRASSLANDS: *84*
MAMMALS: *232*
MOVEMENT ON LAND: *34*
REPRODUCTION: *28*

INSECTIVORES

THE THIRD LARGEST order of mammals – the insectivores – includes some members that retain primitive features. Most are small, nocturnal, solitary, and feed mainly on invertebrates, especially insects. They are found on land and in semiaquatic habitats with the exception of Australasia and parts of South America. The group includes about 400 species in six families – tenrecs and otter shrews; solenodons; hedgehogs and moonrats; shrews; golden moles; and moles and desmans. Some insectivores have specialized features, such as the defensive spines of hedgehogs.

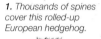

1. Thousands of spines cover this rolled-up European hedgehog.

2. If the predator retreats, the hedgehog begins to unroll.

3. The head emerges and the hedgehog sniffs its surroundings.

PRICKLY DEFENSES

Hedgehogs live in Europe, Asia, and Africa, and defend themselves against predators with their sharp spines. During the course of evolution, the soft hairs on the backs of their ancestors modified to form stiff, sharp spines, each 0.75–1.25 in (2–3 cm) long. If a hedgehog is threatened, it erects its spines to deter the enemy. As a further line of defense, the hedgehog tucks in its head, feet, and tail, arches its back, and rolls into a tight ball, protecting its soft underparts.

European hedgehog
(*Erinaceus europaeus*)

4. It turns over to protect its soft underparts.

5. The hedgehog returns to its normal state.

INSECTIVORE ANATOMY

The greater moonrat, from Southeast Asia, is a typical insectivore. It has a flattened head and a small brain, fairly small ears and eyes, and a long, highly mobile snout with sensitive whiskers. The moonrat also has sharp cheek teeth so that it can easily bite through the tough outer casing of insects. Like most insectivores, this animal depends on smell and touch, rather than sight and sound, to find its prey.

Short, dense underfur covered by long, coarse hair

Greater moonrat
(*Echinosorex gymnurus*)

Sensitive snout and sharp teeth

Short legs and feet with five toes

UNDERWATER INSECTIVORES

Otter shrews, desmans, and water shrews are adapted for life in ponds and streams. When they dive, their dense fur traps air, which provides insulation. The water shrew's large feet are fringed with stiff hairs to propel it underwater, while the tail acts as a rudder. Water shrews bite prey, such as frogs and fish, which they possibly also immobilize with poisonous saliva.

Water shrew (Neomys fodiens) diving underwater

A shrew uses its acute senses of smell and hearing to detect prey such as earthworms.

FREQUENT FEEDER

Shrews belong to the largest family of insectivores. These small, very active creatures need to eat every two to three hours, and they consume more than their own weight in food every day. Because they are so tiny, shrews have a large surface area compared to their internal volume, so they lose heat easily. To compensate, they digest food quickly and generate the extra warmth needed to maintain their body temperature.

Eurasian pygmy shrew
(*Sorex minutus*)

TRAVELING BY CARAVAN

When they are old enough to leave the nest, some species of shrew travel around in a type of "caravan," or line. The first shrew grasps its mother's rump with its teeth, and the others copy, each holding onto the shrew in front. The mother then sets off, with her offspring following, to explore their surroundings or to move to a new nest site.

Shrews form a line by hanging onto each other tightly.

Cross section through a mole burrow

Large molehill is formed where a vertical tunnel reaches the surface.

Main nest is lined with vegetation.

A mole patrols the tunnel, which acts like a trap for its prey.

LIFE UNDERGROUND

Since moles spend most of their lives underground, they are specially designed for burrowing. They have long, cylindrical bodies covered with short, dense fur, broad, spadelike forelimbs, a highly sensitive, mobile snout with whiskers, and small eyes and ears. Moles dig extensive burrow systems up to 3 ft 3 in (1 m) deep, with a central nest, interconnecting tunnels, and vertical shafts. They devote much of their time to maintaining these burrows. They feed on earthworms, insect larvae, and slugs that fall into the tunnels.

European mole
(*Talpa europaea*)

Spadelike forelimbs, with long claws and powerful muscles, are adapted for digging.

TREE SHREWS

Although called shrews, tree shrews are more closely related to primates and belong to a separate mammal order. These small, squirrellike mammals live in the tropical forests of Southeast Asia and are excellent climbers among the branches of trees. Most species forage on the forest floor, using their snouts and clawed front feet to root out prey from leaf litter.

Common tree shrew
(*Tupaia glis*)

STAR-NOSED MOLE

This North American mole is distinguished from other moles by the fleshy tentacles at the end of its snout that act as sensitive feelers. Star-nosed moles spend less time burrowing than other moles. They are good swimmers, and use their spadelike front legs as paddles when they hunt for prey.

Tentacles act as sensitive feelers.

Scientific name: *Condylura cristata*	
Size: Head and body length, up to 5 in (13 cm); tail length, up to 3.25 in (8.5 cm)	
Habitat: Riverbanks, lake shores, marshes, and wet fields	
Distribution: Eastern Canada and the USA	
Reproduction: Females produce a single litter of 2–7 offspring each year, between mid-April and mid-June	
Diet: Insects, earthworms, crustaceans, small fish	

SOLENODON SNOUT

Solenodons have remarkable long, flexible snouts. They use them to search crevices in dead wood for food such as insects, earthworms, and small vertebrates. Once it has trapped an animal, the solenodon uses its toxic saliva to immobilize its prey. The two species of solenodon, found on the Caribbean islands of Cuba and Hispaniola, are among the most endangered of all mammals. They are hunted by species introduced to the islands, in particular cats, dogs, and mongooses.

Haitian solenodon
(*Solenodon paradoxus*)

Pygmy white-toothed shrew
(*Suncus etruscus*)

SMALLEST LAND MAMMAL

With a head and body length of just 2 in (5 cm), and a tail length of 1 in (2.5 cm), the pygmy white-toothed shrew is the smallest ground-living mammal. These shrews live in forests and scrubland in southern Europe, Asia, and northern Africa. They search for food by day and night, feeding on insects, spiders, and other invertebrates.

Find out more

ANTEATERS
AND ARMADILLOS: *242*
MAMMALS: *232*
MONOTREMES: *234*

BATS

ALTHOUGH SOME MAMMALS can glide, bats are the only ones that are capable of sustained, flapping flight. There are about 925 species of bats, which belong to the order Chiroptera. Bats live in both temperate and tropical parts of the world and are divided into two groups. Microchiropterans make up the majority of species. They are mainly insect-eaters, but also include species that feed on fruit, pollen, fish, blood, and small mammals. Megachiropterans, or fruit bats, include the largest bats that feed on fruit and nectar. Most bats are nocturnal. Fruit bats use their keen eyesight to navigate and find food in the dark, while other species use a form of "animal radar" called echolocation.

Eurasian long-eared bat
(*Plecotus auritus*)

Tent-building bat
(*Uroderma bilobatum*)

Old world fruit bat
(*Pteropus* sp.)

BAT HEADS

Bats have a variety of head shapes and features, some of which are specially adapted to help them hunt prey. Some insect-eating bats have large ears that detect an insect's flapping wings; others have elaborate noseleafs that help with echolocation. Pollen-feeding bats, such as the fruit bats, usually have long snouts and very long tongues.

Clawed thumb

Forearm bone

The wing's membrane (patagium) is supported by the finger, arm, leg, and tail bones.

Upper arm

Franquet's fruit bat
(*Epomops franqueti*)

Large eyes

ANATOMY

Bats' wings are modified forelimbs, covered by an extension of the skin called the patagium (wing membrane). The first finger, or thumb, is short and has a claw that is used for grooming, crawling, climbing, and sometimes handling food. When flying, bats use their chest and upper arm muscles to pull their wings down, and their back muscles to raise the wings. Other muscles retract and extend the wings.

Lightweight body covered in fur

Clawed foot

Noctule bat
(*Nyctalus noctula*)

FRUIT BATS

Fruit bats, or flying foxes, are found in tropical and subtropical parts of Australia, Asia, and Africa. Most eat fruit, although some species feed on flowers, nectar, and pollen. These bats usually have doglike faces with a snout, simple ears, and large eyes that enable them to see in dim light. Unlike other bats that use echolocation to navigate and find food, fruit bats rely on their excellent senses of smell and vision.

ECHOLOCATION

Bats use echolocation to navigate and to hunt in the dark. To do this, a bat produces ultrasonic sounds in its larynx (voicebox), which are sent out in pulses or clicks through its mouth or nose. These ultrasonic pulses bounce off static objects and moving prey, and returning echoes are picked up by the bat's ears. These echoes are relayed to the brain, which creates a "sound picture" of the bat's surroundings. When bats detect prey, the number of pulses produced increases as they get nearer to their target.

A bat uses its broad wings to deflect up insects toward its mouth.

Some bats, such as horseshoe bats, focus sounds through an outgrowth called a noseleaf.

Ears channel returning echoes into the internal ear.

Ultrasonic pulses travel through air.

Echoes bounce off moving prey.

Pollinating bat feeding on banana flower

POLLINATORS

Some bats pollinate flowers. These bats, which live in tropical and subtropical regions, use their long tongues to feed on flower nectar and pollen. As they feed, their fur becomes dusted with pollen. When they visit another flower of the same species, the pollen falls onto the flower's stigma and pollinates it.

BREEDING

Most bats breed once a year and usually give birth to single offspring. In many species, females gather to give birth and bring up their young in a nursery colony. Mothers leave the infant bats huddled together in the nursery, while they go in search of food. When they return, each infant makes unique sounds that enable its mother to pick it out from the huddled mass.

Infant bat roosts close to its mother.

ROOSTING

Most bats feed at night and rest during the day in roosts. Fruit bats roost in trees. Many insect-eating species roost in caves and mines, rock overhangs, tombs, ruins, and buildings. Inside a roost, bats sleep hanging upside down. They also wash and groom themselves by hanging from one foot and using the other as a "comb." Bats need to roost in damp places so they do not dry out.

Cluster of Rousettes fruit bats (Rousettus sp.) roosting in cave

Bat uses echolocation to detect ripples in water made by fish.

Fisherman bat
(*Noctilio leporinus*)

TENT-BUILDING BATS

These bats from Central and South America create a tentlike roost under the leaves of palm and banana trees. They partially bite through the rib and veins of a leaf, so that its edges bend over to provide protection from the sun, rain, and wind, as well as from predators. Several bats may roost under the folded leaf, using the bitten holes as toe holds.

Tent-building bats roosting

Long toes and sharp claws pull fish out of water.

FISHERMAN BATS

Fisherman, or bulldog, bats catch fish that swim just below the surface of lakes and rivers. These bats have long legs, large feet, and long flattened toes, ending in sharp claws. They rake their feet through the water, grab the fish, and lift it quickly to their mouths where they hold it with their teeth. The bats either carry the fish back to the roost or eat it while in flight.

Bats swoop silently to avoid alerting prey.

FLESH EATERS

While most bats are insect eaters, a few species, such as the false vampire bat, are carnivores that prey on small mammals, birds, lizards, frogs, and even other bats. False vampire bats hunt at night, flying close to the ground through trees and undergrowth, before swooping silently to catch prey on the ground. They kill their victim with a bite on the head or neck, then carry it back to the roost to be eaten.

Great false vampire bat
(*Megaderma lyra*)

Mice are tasty prey for flesh-eating bats.

Unlike other bats, flesh-eating bats use both sight and echolocation to find prey.

Find out more

FLOWERS AND SEEDS: *128*
MAMMALS: *232*
MOUNTAINS AND CAVES: *88*
MOVEMENT IN AIR: *36*

ARMADILLOS AND ANTEATERS

ARMADILLOS, ANTEATERS, AND SLOTHS make up the order of mammals called Xenarthra. All 29 species live only in Central and South America, but the nine-banded armadillo also lives in southern North America. The animals that make up this order are quite distinct. Armadillos are burrowing animals, anteaters are ground- and tree-dwellers, while sloths spend most of their lives hanging upside down in trees. Two other groups – the pangolins and aardvarks – are unrelated to the xenarthrans, despite having much in common with them. Like anteaters, they use their long, sticky tongues to feed on ants and termites.

Bony plate on rear protects armadillo as it digs.

Burrow of pink fairy armadillo

ARMADILLOS

Armadillos are distinguished by their protective body armor, formed by bands of hinged bony plates capped with horn. The head is protected by a shield consisting of several plates; only the belly remains unprotected. The 20 species of armadillos live in a range of habitats including forests, deserts, and savannas. Most species rest in burrows during the day, emerging at night to feed on small vertebrates, invertebrates, plants, and carrion.

Bands of bony plates protect the body.

Grass lines the burrow.

Pink fairy armadillos (Chlamyphorus truncatus) are just 7 in (18 cm) long.

Screaming hairy armadillo (*Chaetophractus vellerosus*)

Large claws for finding food and digging tunnels

RAPID BURROWERS
Armadillos dig into the ground to find food, make burrows, and escape predators. They loosen the earth with their front feet, then kick the soil out backward with their hind feet. Fairy armadillos spend most of the day underground. As they dig a burrow, they block the entrance with their armor-plated rear.

Long, bristly tail covers body when the anteater is asleep.

Giant anteater (*Myrmecophaga tridactyla*)

Powerful front legs and sharp claws break open ant and termite nests.

ANTEATERS
Of the four species of anteater, three are mainly forest-dwellers, while the fourth, the giant anteater, lives in grassland and swampy areas. It is unmistakable with its long, probing snout, small eyes and ears, and striped coat. Anteaters have a good sense of smell and constantly sniff the air to find food. Once it has found an ant or termite nest, an anteater uses its front claws to open the nest and feeds briefly before moving on. It does not demolish the nest as it may return later for more food.

Forepaw of giant anteater

Long, strong claws of second and third fingers.

CLAWS
The giant anteater uses the long curved claws on its front feet to dig into ant and termite nests and to defend itself. When moving, the anteater protects its claws by walking on the knuckles of its front feet with its claws tucked inward – this gives it a limping gait.

STICKY TONGUE
Anteaters consume about 30,000 insects a day. The giant anteater's tongue is about 2 ft (60 cm) long, and is covered with backward-pointing spines and sticky saliva. As the anteater flicks its tongue into a nest, ants and termites become trapped and are drawn into the mouth. Anteaters do not have teeth, but crush their prey with horny projections in the mouth, and with their muscular stomachs.

A giant anteater can extend its long, sticky tongue to probe into an ants' nest.

A giant anteater can flick its tongue in and out 150 times a minute.

Ants are trapped by the spines and saliva on the anteater's tongue.

TREE-LIVING ANTEATERS

The silky anteater (*Cyclopes didactylus*) and the two species of tamandua are all tree-dwellers. They use their long claws for breaking open insect nests, defending themselves, and climbing. They also have a prehensile tail, which acts as an "extra leg" when moving through the trees. Silky anteaters are nocturnal and rarely descend from the forest canopy. They feed mainly on ants. Tamanduas may be active by day or night. They often rest in tree hollows, emerging to feed on ants, termites, and bees.

Baby clings to its mother's back.

Southern tamandua (Tamandua tetradactyla) breaks into an ants' nest.

If threatened, the three-banded armadillo rolls into a tight ball.

Three-banded armadillo
(*Tolypeutes tricinctus*)

DEFENSE

Xenarthrans have many defense tactics. The giant anteater rears up on its hind legs and slashes at predators with its long claws. Sloths avoid detection by using camouflage and remaining motionless during the day. If attacked, they bite and lash out with their claws. Despite its armor, an armadillo's underside is soft and vulnerable. To escape attack, some species run away, others burrow rapidly, and the three-banded armadillo curls up into a ball.

GIANT ARMADILLO

This sheep-sized insect-eater is the largest of the armadillos. The giant armadillo avoids the daytime heat by resting in a burrow, but emerges at night to feed. It uses its powerful claws to dig into the center of termite mounds on the forest floor, seemingly oblivious of the bites of the angry termites.

Middle claw may be 8 in (20 cm) long – the largest in the animal kingdom.

Scientific name: *Priodontes maximus*

Size: Body 3 ft 3 in (1 m) long; tail 20 in (51 cm) long

Habitat: Forest

Distribution: Venezuela to northern Argentina

Reproduction: Female produces 1 or 2 offspring

Diet: Ants, worms, termites, spiders, and snakes

Green algae may grow in the grooved hairs of the sloth's coat, helping to camouflage it.

Sloths eat, mate, and give birth upside down.

Long claws grip around branch.

Pale-throated three-toed sloth
(*Bradypus tridactylus*)

Aardvark (*Orycteropus afer*)

AARDVARK

The aardvark is a solitary mammal found in the savanna and open forests of Africa. It can dig a burrow very quickly, and spends most of the day resting inside it. At night, the aardvark travels long distances in search of food, sniffing the ground with its piglike snout. It uses its strong feet and large claws to dig into ant and termite nests before extracting the insects with its sticky tongue and crushing them in its mouth.

Sloths can rotate their heads through a 270° angle, so they can see all around them while hanging upside down.

SLOTHS

The five species of sloth live in the rainforests of Central and South America. They have three toes on their hind feet and two or three on their front feet, depending on the species. Each toe ends in a long claw. Sloths spend most of the day upside down, hanging by their claws from a branch. At night they move slowly through the trees to feed on leaves. Every week or so, they descend from the trees to defecate, but they move with difficulty on the ground.

PANGOLINS

Pangolins, also called scaly anteaters, use their short limbs and long claws to dig out termite mounds and ant hills. They have no teeth, but grind up their insect prey with small stones in the horny stomach. As it feeds, the pangolin defends itself from attacking insects by closing its nostrils; it also has protective membranes over its eyes. If attacked by larger animals, the pangolin will run for shelter or curl up into a tight ball, protected by its sharp scales.

Overlapping, horny scales protect the upper side of the body.

Long, saliva-coated tongue extends into insects' nests.

Malayan pangolin
(*Manis javanica*)

Find out more

DEFENSE 1: *48*
FEEDING AND NUTRITION: *22*
MAMMALS: *232*
TROPICAL RAINFORESTS: *82*

RABBITS AND HARES

THESE FAST, GROUND-DWELLING mammals are found in most parts of the world. In some countries, such as Australia, rabbits were introduced to be hunted. Rabbits, hares, and a smaller group called the pikas, belong to the order Lagomorpha, or "hare-shaped" mammals. They feed on soft plants and grasses, but also eat the bark of young trees and shrubs when other food is in short supply. Rabbits and hares have large hind limbs for bounding and they depend on speed to escape predators. Pikas look like guineapigs, with short legs adapted for rocky terrain.

European rabbit
(*Oryctolagus cuniculus*)

Long hind legs help rabbits to run from predators.

Rabbits have a good sense of smell.

Long ears listen for possible danger.

RABBIT ANATOMY
Rabbits have sharp eyesight and their bulging eyes help give them all-round vision to scan their surroundings. Their large ears are very sensitive to sound and act as an early warning system by detecting approaching danger. Rabbits can also pick up the scent of nearby enemies using their slitlike nostrils. Rapid escape is important. Their hind legs, longer than the front legs, enable them to race to their burrows or the cover of vegetation.

Skull of rabbit

Incisor teeth grow continuously.

EVER-GROWING TEETH
Rabbits, hares, and pikas have long, sharp incisor teeth which grow constantly throughout their life. They use these teeth to gnaw and crop grass and other vegetation. Their teeth also enable them to graze very close to the ground. Their large premolar and molar cheek teeth at the back of their jaw grind the food before it is swallowed.

Cross section through a rabbit warren

Entrance leads to tunnels within the rabbit warren.

JACK RABBITS
Jack rabbits are generally larger than rabbits and have black tips on their ears. They do not burrow, but rest in a slight dip on the ground shaped by their bodies. This dip in the soil or vegetation is called a "form." The 30 species of jack rabbits are faster and more powerful runners than rabbits. They reach speeds of up to 50 mph (80 kmh) over short distances in order to find cover and escape predators. In Europe jack rabbits are called hares.

Gray-brown fur provides hare with camouflage

Warrens in stony soil last longer than those dug in sandy soil.

Most tunnels are only wide enough for one rabbit.

A nest is made of grass and fur.

BURROWING
Most species of rabbits dig burrows to provide protection from predators during the day, to shelter in cold weather, and to give birth. The type of burrow made depends on the species and on whether the soil is soft and sandy, or hard and stony. Some species of rabbit make their homes in existing burrows. European rabbits live in large colonies in a system of burrows called a warren. Each warren has many entrances and may contain burrows up to 10 ft (3 m) deep and 150 ft (45 m) long.

BREEDING IN RABBITS

European rabbits breed regularly and have large litters – some giving birth to as many as 30 offspring each year. The young are born underground in nests lined with hair and grass. Newborn rabbits are called kittens. They are hairless, helpless, and blind until their eyes open after about 10 days. The doe (female rabbit) leaves her young in the nest, returning for just a few minutes each day to feed them. Young rabbits leave the nest when they are about three weeks old.

Tiny newborn domestic rabbits stay warm in their fur-lined nest.

LEVERETS

Young brown hares are called leverets. They are born in the open and at a more advanced stage than baby rabbits. They have fur, their eyes are open, and they are able to move around soon after birth. About three days after birth, each of the leverets is moved to its own hiding place, usually concealed by vegetation. Each day at sunset, the leverets return to the original birth site, where they suckle from their mother.

Leverets stay under cover in dense vegetation.

BLACK-TAILED JACK RABBIT

Like most animals that live in the desert, the jack rabbit takes shelter from the intense daytime heat and becomes active at night when the temperature drops. Its long ears detect predators, and also give off heat, helping to keep the jack rabbit cool. Jack rabbits use their powerful hind limbs to run if danger threatens. They can bound across the desert at speeds of up to 35 mph (56 kmh) for short distances.

Scientific name: *Lepus californicus*

Size: 18–24 in (46–61 cm)

Habitat: Desert, semidesert, and prairie

Distribution: Western United States

Reproduction: Gestation period 40 days. Female produces four or more litters a year

Diet: Grass in summer; twigs and shrubs in winter

European brown hare
(*Lepus europaeus*)

Hare's ears move like a radar to detect nearby enemies.

When pursued, hares run in a zigzag line to throw predators off their scent.

Some hares grind their teeth to indicate danger.

Hares drum their back feet on the ground to warn others of danger.

TWILIGHT FEEDERS

Most rabbits and hares emerge at dusk, dawn, or during the night to feed on grasses, shoots, and other vegetation. Feeding under the cover of darkness gives them some protection against predators, but they still need to be alert. Their large eyes enable them to see well in dim light so that they find their way around. They can also sense predators approaching from behind, even as they feed.

Rabbit feeding at night

COLOR CHANGE

Hares living in northern regions show a remarkable adaptation to changing seasons. The snowshoe hare has a gray-brownish coat in spring and summer, but as winter approaches it becomes thicker and turns white. This change provides camouflage against the snowy landscape, and helps protect hares from attack by predators such as lynxes.

Snowshoe hare
(*Lepus americanus*)

Summer coat is gray-brown.

PIKAS

Pikas live among rock debris in remote mountainous areas of North America and most of Asia. They are active, busy animals that forage during daylight hours. Pikas usually live alone or with a mate. They make characteristic sounds to defend their territory, and if danger threatens they quickly disappear into rock crevices. During the summer and fall months they "harvest" plants and hoard them in haypiles to provide food during the lean winter months.

Pika
(*Ochotona* sp.)

Pika calls out to deter enemies from entering its territory.

White winter coat helps to conceal hare from predators.

Find out more	
ANIMALS:	*140*
ANIMAL HOMES:	*58*
DEFENSE 1:	*48*
SENSES:	*42*

RODENTS

RATS AND MICE are among the many animals that belong to the order Rodentia – the most numerous, diverse, and widespread group of all mammals. The three main types are squirrel-like rodents, mouselike rodents, and cavylike rodents. They are able to survive in a range of habitats from hot, dry deserts to waterlogged marshes. Typically, rodents are small and compact, and have two pairs of constantly growing, chisel-like incisor teeth. Some species produce large numbers of offspring, and may even breed several times a year. They are very protective of their young, and many species build special burrows or nests from grass, leaves, or sticks.

Black-tailed prairie dogs emerging from their burrows

SOCIAL RODENTS

Many rodents, especially ground-dwellers, live in social groups. For example, black-tailed prairie dogs (*Cynomys ludovicianus*) live in underground burrows in small groups called coteries. Each coterie consists of a male, several females, and their young. Tunnels connect coteries with one another to form huge prairie dog "towns," containing thousands of individuals.

Norway rat
(*Rattus norvegicus*)

Tail is covered in protective scales.

Mole rats have very poor eyesight.

MOUSELIKE RODENTS

Common rodents, such as mice and rats, belong to the mouselike group of rodents, together with lemmings, voles, hamsters, and gerbils. They make up a quarter of all mammal species. Most are small, nocturnal animals that generally feed on seeds. They produce large numbers of offspring during their relatively short lifespan. Some species of rats and mice are regarded as pests because they raid human food stores and spread disease.

Naked mole rat
(*Heterocephalus glaber*)

NAKED MOLE RATS

These hairless rodents live in complex tunnel systems, and behave in a similar way to social insects such as bees. A single breeding female, or "queen," produces "castes" of workers and nonworkers. Workers, which make up the majority, dig tunnels, feed and defend the colony, and look after the young. Nonworkers stay close to the queen.

Gray squirrel
(*Sciurus carolinensis*)

SQUIRREL-LIKE RODENTS

Familiar tree-dwelling squirrels are members of this group, as well as ground squirrels, prairie dogs, and marmots. All have distinctive heads, long, cylindrical bodies, and bushy tails. Tree squirrels have keen eyesight, useful for judging distances when jumping from branch to branch. Flying squirrels can glide longer distances, using a membrane (patagium) that extends between their fore- and hind limbs.

Capybara
(*Hydrochaeris hydrochaeris*)

CAVYLIKE RODENTS

Cavylike rodents form the most diverse rodent group. They include agoutis, guinea pigs, porcupines, and the largest rodent – the capybara. Most have large heads, plump bodies, short tails, and slender legs. They produce small litters of well-developed young. Although most of these animals live on land, the capybara spends much of its life in or near rivers or swampy areas.

Bushy tail helps squirrel to balance while jumping from tree to tree.

FAST BREEDERS

Rodents are fast breeders. Many, especially mouselike rodents, have a short gestation period (the time taken for babies to develop inside their mother), and produce large litters. Most young are able to breed at a very early age. The house mouse (*Mus musculus*) can breed at just six weeks old and have up to 10 litters a year, with between five and seven young in each litter. Its gestation period is 20 days.

Blind, naked mice are born in straw nests.

Fur starts to grow at around six days old.

Development of house mice

At 14 days old, young mice start leaving their nests.

DESERT JERBOA

These desert rodents walk and hop on their long hind legs, and can leap several yards to escape predators. They use their front feet to hold food and to dig burrows where they rest during the heat of the day, emerging at night to feed on seeds and other vegetation. Their large eyes enable them to see in dim light, while their ears help them detect approaching enemies. Jerboas rarely drink since they get the water they need from their food.

Large eyes for seeing in dim light

Scientific name:	*Jaculus orientalis*
Size:	Head and body length up to 6.5 in (16 cm); tail length up to 10 in (25 cm)
Habitat:	Flat sandy deserts and rocky valleys
Distribution:	North Africa and Middle East from Morocco to Israel
Reproduction:	Breed twice a year, with between 2–6 young in each litter
Diet:	Seeds, grains shoots, and roots

FEEDING

Most rodents feed on plant food, including seeds, flowers, leaves, stems, and roots. Some may also catch and eat insects, spiders, and other invertebrates. Rodents feed by holding food with their forepaws and gnawing it with their incisor teeth. Many store food for future use. Some species, such as golden hamsters (*Mesocricetus* sp.), carry food in their cheek pouches and store it until they reach the relative safety of their nest.

The hamster empties nuts from its cheek pouches using its front paws.

Skull of rat

Razor-sharp incisor teeth

GNAWING TEETH

A rodent's upper and lower incisor teeth grow continuously throughout its life. Its upper teeth are kept razor-sharp for gnawing by rubbing them against its lower teeth. Behind the incisors is a gap called the diastema. The rodent's lips are drawn into this gap while it is gnawing to keep hard, inedible materials out of its mouth. Cheek teeth grind up food before it is swallowed.

Cross section through a beaver lodge

A vent allows fresh air in, and stale air out of the lodge.

Underground entrance to lodge

Food is kept in a separate store.

A pond is created by the dam.

Dam is made from sticks, branches, stones, and mud.

Beavers live in lodges surrounded by water to help protect them from predators.

DAM BUILDERS

Beavers (*Castor* sp.) are large rodents that live in small family groups in or near streams and rivers. They have webbed feet, a streamlined body, and a flat, scaly tail that acts as a rudder, pushing and steering them through the water. Beavers use their large front teeth to cut down trees and branches, which are used to build dams across streams. These dams create ponds in which the beavers build nests called "lodges" from sticks and mud.

Find out more

ANIMAL HOMES: *58*
MOVEMENT IN AIR: *36*
PESTS AND WEEDS: *98*
REPRODUCTION: *28*

BEARS

THE POLAR BEAR AND brown bear are the world's largest land carnivores. There are seven species of bear, plus the panda, which has recently been reclassified as a close relative. Most bears live in the Northern Hemisphere, although some species, such as the sloth bear and the sun bear, also inhabit the south. Bears that live in cooler climates sleep in dens during winter, but those in warmer climates are active all year round. The number of bears in the world has been considerably reduced as a result of habitat destruction and hunting, and they now live mainly in remote areas.

Brown bear
(*Ursus arctos*)

Small rounded ears

Snout with sensitive nose

Strong body covered with thick hair

Bear walks on the soles of its feet.

Five sharp claws

MIXED FEEDERS

Most bears are omnivores, which means they eat both plants and meat. They generally feed on whatever they can find, including plants, fruits, honey, insects, fish, and carrion (dead animals). Because of their poor eyesight and hearing, bears usually detect their food by smell. Those that live near tourist areas feed on food scraps left by visitors and can become a danger. American black bears are mainly forest dwellers that feed on plants, fruits, and insects.

American black bear (Ursus americanus) *feeding on dandelions*

BEAR ANATOMY

All bears share the same basic features. They have strong, heavily built bodies with powerful legs. Each of their feet has five sharp claws, which they use for digging, tearing food apart, and climbing. Their strong jaws contain a set of relatively unspecialized teeth, which enables them to eat a wide range of food. Bears walk on the soles of their feet, usually shuffling along at a steady pace, but they can move quickly when in pursuit of prey. They can also stand on their hind legs.

FISHING BEARS

Brown bears take advantage of the summer migrations of salmon swimming upriver to breeding sites. Normally solitary, the bears gather in groups by the sides of rivers as the salmon migration begins. The bears wade into the shallows to catch the large fish with their teeth or claws. They then return to the riverbank where they skillfully fillet and eat their catch.

Bears catch salmon as they leap from the water, Kodiak Island, Alaska

Sloth bear (Ursus ursinus) *sucks up termites using its lips and long tongue.*

TERMITE EATERS

The sloth bear, found in India and Sri Lanka, feeds mainly on insects, particularly termites. It has long, flexible lips and a long tongue, but lacks four upper incisor teeth. To feed, the bear uses its extra-long claws to break open a termite mound. Forming its lips into a tube, it blows the dirt off the termites, and then, using its tongue, noisily sucks them up through the gap in its front teeth.

White or cream rings around eyes

Spectacled bear
(*Tremarctos ornatus*)

SOUTH AMERICAN BEAR

Spectacled bears get their name from the white or cream rings around their eyes. They are the only bears that live in South America and are found in the humid forests and grasslands on the lower slopes of the Andes Mountains. Active at night, they feed on fruit and other vegetation, effortlessly climbing high trees in search of food. By day, they rest in rough nests in the tree branches or under a tangle of roots.

BEAR HUGS

Bears are aggressive animals and males compete with each other for females during the mating season. Bear fights are usually violent and, in some cases, can result in a death. When they are young, play fighting between males helps improve their fighting skills. Female bears with cubs avoid large males and any other potential threats, including humans.

By opening its mouth, the bear reveals its large canine teeth.

Young bear, play fighting, stands up to make itself look bigger.

Asiatic black bear
(*Ursus thibetanus*)

BROWN BEAR

Known in parts of North America as the grizzly bear, the brown bear is a large, powerful animal. It feeds on small mammals, fish, insects, and plants, but can also kill an animal as big as a moose. A brown bear can run very fast over short distances, and may stand up on its back legs to get a better view of its surroundings.

Standing on its hind legs, the bear warns off enemies.

Scientific name: *Ursus arctos*

Size: Average of 8 ft (2.4 m) in length

Habitat: Tundra, alpine meadows, woodlands, and forests

Distribution: Northwestern North America, Europe, and Asia

Reproduction: Female produces a litter of up to four cubs. Gestation period 26–35 weeks

Diet: Tubers, fruit, insect grubs, rodents, fish, young deer, and carrion

American black bear mother watches over her cubs.

FAMILY LIFE

Male and female bears only associate during the mating season. Females then give birth in a secluded den the following spring. Smaller species have one or two young that are born very small, helpless, and almost naked. Cubs remain with their mother during the first, and often the second, winter after their birth. During this period they are protected from enemies and learn to fend for themselves. The male plays no part in their upbringing.

Cubs develop quickly, but remain with their mother until nearly full-grown.

WINTER SLEEP

Bears that live in cooler parts of the world – except for male polar bears – enter a period of dormancy during the winter months. They remain relatively inactive in order to conserve energy for when food is in short supply. In summer and early fall bears prepare for their winter sleep by eating enough to build up fat reserves. They then make their den in a tree hollow.

A black bear spends winter in a den lined with dry vegetation.

Polar bear
(*Ursus maritimus*)

Polar bear swimming underwater

ICY SWIM

Despite the cold water, polar bears can swim for hours across open water from one piece of pack ice to another, at speeds of up to 4 mph (6.5 kmh). Protected by thick, water-repellent fur, they swim using their oarlike front feet. Polar bears have longer necks than most bears, so they are able to swim with their head and shoulders above the water. They also swim underwater and beneath ice sheets to catch seals.

ARCTIC SURVIVOR

The polar bear is one of the few mammals that is able to survive the harsh, freezing conditions of the Arctic. It is protected against the biting cold by an insulating layer of fat, called blubber. For additional warmth, its dense, white fur consists of hollow hairs that conduct warming ultraviolet rays from the sun onto its black, heat-absorbing skin. The white fur also provides camouflage in snow and icy conditions, concealing the bear from seals and other potential prey.

Find out more

GROWTH AND DEVELOPMENT: *32*
POLAR REGIONS: *90*
RACCOONS AND PANDAS: *250*
RHYTHMS OF LIFE: *40*

RACCOONS AND PANDAS

THESE TWO GROUPS of mammals share so many of the same characteristics that, in the past, they have been classified in the same family. Today, many scientists divide the raccoons into two subfamilies: one includes the common raccoon, cacomistle, ringtail, and kinkajou, the other contains the lesser panda. The giant panda is generally placed in the bear family. All members of the raccoon family live in the Americas, except for the red panda, which together with the giant panda, is found in remote parts of Asia. Scientists believe that because the two species of panda evolved in the same habitat, they developed similar features.

Ringtail
(*Bassariscus astutus*)

Foxlike face with large ears and eyes

Like all members of the raccoon family, ringtails have five toes on each foot.

Long, ringed tail

RACCOONS AND RELATIVES

Members of the raccoon family, which includes the ringtail, are small animals with foxlike faces, limber bodies, and long tails, which are ringed in many species. They have short legs with five toes on each foot, which they use for climbing trees and catching prey. Most species are solitary hunters that search for food at night, both on the ground and in trees. Apart from the kinkajou, most species have distinctive coat patterns with brown, red, gray, or white colors.

Mainly nocturnal, the lesser panda spends most of the day in the trees.

Lesser panda
(*Ailurus fulgens*)

LESSER PANDA
Like the giant panda, the lesser panda feeds on bamboo. It also has an extra "thumb" on its paw – not as well-developed as that of the giant panda's. Lesser pandas eat fruits, plants, and insects. They are nocturnal, usually solitary, animals that live in the forests of Nepal, Myanmar, and China. They are agile animals that climb trees using their sharp claws to reach the higher branches.

Skull of raccoon

OMNIVORE TEETH
Most raccoon species are omnivores – they eat both animals and plants. Typically, they have incisors at the front of their jaws for gripping and tearing their prey. Their long canines pull at plant roots or dig into animal flesh. At the back of the jaw, flattened cheek teeth grind vegetation or crush insects.

Incisor teeth enable raccoon to grip and tear at food.

Thick fur coat keeps raccoon warm during winter months.

Agile, catlike body

RACCOON SUCCESS
Notorious for their inquisitive nature, raccoons are highly successful inhabitants of North and Central America. They can eat almost anything and live anywhere, even close to, or in, people's homes. In their natural habitat they usually feed alone, using their dextrous forepaws to pick up and hold prey such as crayfish and frogs from swampy pools. Their amazing ability to survive means that the total area they inhabit is extending.

Raccoon
(*Procyon lotor*)

Raccoons raiding a trash can

URBAN BANDITS
Raccoons are commonly referred to as bandits because of their "masked" faces and because they raid food stores, garbage dumps, and farmers' crops. They are nocturnal animals that sometimes congregate at food sources, often leaving a trail of destruction behind them. They have adapted so well to living near humans that they even take food from people.

Ring-tailed coati
(*Nasua nasua*)

Coatis rummage for food using their long, sensitive snouts.

COATIS

Coatis are expert foragers that live in the forests of Central and South America. They hunt for food during the day, using their long snouts to probe the forest floor, and their strong claws to dig up plant roots and tubers. They also climb high into tree canopies in search of fruits. The females form social groups and hunt together with their young. The males are solitary, and are only permitted near the females during the mating season.

Tails may be used to help balance in trees.

RINGTAILS

Found in dry areas of western US, ringtails favor rocky areas and are able to climb cliffs with ease. They usually feed on mice, birds, grasshoppers, and other small prey. They pounce on their victims, killing them with a single bite, then slice up their food using their cheek teeth. Ringtails were once tamed by miners to rid their camps of mice and other pests.

Ringtail kills its prey instantly.

Giant panda
(*Ailuropoda melanoleuca*)

The giant panda is one of the rarest mammals in the world.

GIANT PANDA

Giant pandas are recognized by their bearlike shape and distinctive black and white markings. They live in remote areas of mountain forests in central China, among the bamboo thickets. They feed on bamboo shoots and roots while in a sitting position, which frees their front feet to wrench off pieces of bamboo. As bamboo is not particularly nutritious, giant pandas lead a leisurely lifestyle in order to conserve energy. The giant panda is an endangered species, although its numbers are slowly on the increase.

Female panda nurses single cub.

Cub is born pink and hairless.

SLOW BREEDERS

Giant pandas are slow breeders, and until recently, zoos found it almost impossible to persuade them to mate. However, in the last few years, Chinese researchers have become much more successful at breeding them in captivity. As a result, the total number of pandas is at last starting to grow. However, the panda's habitat also needs to be protected if the species is to thrive.

EXTRA THUMB

The giant panda's forepaws are unusual because they have an extra "thumb." This is a modified wrist bone that is enlarged. It acts like a thumb and can touch each of the panda's other digits, in much the same way that people can touch each of their fingers with their thumb. This enables the panda to grip bamboo stems while it is feeding.

Panda's extra digit is also known as a "false thumb."

Find out more

ANIMALS IN DANGER: *100*
BEARS: *248*
MAMMALS: *232*
SOCIAL ANIMALS: *54*

DOGS

THE TERM "DOG" IS most often used to describe one of the many breeds of domestic pet. However, there are 34 other related species of doglike carnivores that include foxes, wolves, coyotes, and jackals. Known collectively as canids – because they belong to the family Canidae – these animals are found worldwide. Some dogs, such as wolves, are carnivorous, while bat-eared foxes mainly eat insects. Many are opportunist feeders that eat whatever is available, including lizards, birds, small mammals, carrion, and fruit. Their excellent hearing and keen sense of smell make them efficient hunters.

Long, pointed ears

Large, forward-facing eyes

Slender, muscular body

Long, bushy tail is used for balance and communication.

Dhole
(*Cuon alpinus*)

Long legs enable dog to run fast.

Nonretractable claws provide grip when running.

DOG DESIGN

A dog's anatomy reflects its ability to pursue prey at speed over long distances. Most canids, including the dhole (an Asiatic wild dog), have a lithe body with a bushy tail. They have long legs and walk on their toes, which increases their stride length and speed. The long snout has a highly sensitive nose, and the jaws contain 42 teeth (a dhole has 40), including four stabbing "canines" that pierce through flesh. A dog has large, forward-facing eyes and pointed ears that can be moved to pick up sounds.

Howling warns rival wolf packs to stay away.

LIVING IN PACKS

Some canids are solitary, while others, such as red foxes, are sociable but find food on their own. Gray wolves (*Canis lupus*) live and hunt in social groups, or packs, that can contain 20 or more members. Living in a group enables wolves to hunt large prey cooperatively, to share care of their young, and to protect each other from attack by other wolves. Each pack defends a territory large enough to provide sufficient food, and its boundaries are scent-marked with urine to ward off rival packs.

KEEPING ORDER
Wolf packs have distinct social hierarchies. One pair of male and female wolves dominates the whole pack, and are the only animals who breed. Below them, there is a clear-cut organization of dominant and subordinate animals. This hierarchy is maintained by recognized postures and behaviors – such as baring the teeth or lowering the ears. These indicate threat or submission, and make sure that every animal knows its place.

Defensive teeth posture with teeth bared

Submissive greeting posture with ears, tail, and body lowered

Offensive threat posture with ears and tail erect

Play posture indicates that this is not a threat but the wolf wants to play.

Each African hunting dog (Lycaon pictus) plays a distinct role in bringing down the wildebeest.

HUNTING STRATEGIES

By hunting together in packs, gray wolves, African hunting dogs, and dholes are able to kill prey larger than themselves. African hunting dogs hunt at least once a day and pursue prey tirelessly over long distances until it is exhausted. After bringing down a prey animal cooperatively, the pack shares the kill and allows pups to feed as well. Feeding as a pack keeps most other predators away from the kill – although lions and hyenas are usually able to drive the dogs away.

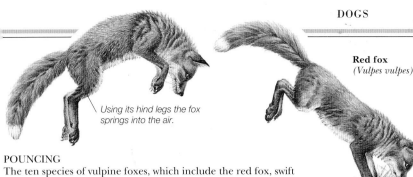

Using its hind legs the fox springs into the air.

Red fox
(*Vulpes vulpes*)

The fox stretches out its front paws, dives onto the prey, and squashes it.

POUNCING

The ten species of vulpine foxes, which include the red fox, swift fox (*Vulpes velox*), and the kit fox (*Vulpes macrotis*), have a special strategy for catching rodents and other small prey. Once the prey animal is spotted, the fox leaps in the air and lands on top of it. The unwary rodent is taken by surprise, and is squashed by the fox's front paws before it can jump out of the way.

A DOG'S DINNER

All canids have a keen sense of smell, sight, and hearing, which they use to track down their prey. The average dog has 200 million scent receptors in its nasal folds, whereas a human has five million. Red foxes hunt rodents and rabbits by listening and watching. At night, foxes locate earthworms by listening for the rasping sound that worms make as they move along the soil's surface. Red foxes have also moved into inner city areas where they forage at night for scraps of food.

A trashcan is a prime food source for the urban fox.

DINGO

Also known as the Australian wild dog, the dingo is a feral species – a domesticated species that has become wild again. It is descended from the earliest tamed dogs, and was introduced to Australia about 4,000 years ago. Dingos usually hunt alone but form packs to hunt for prey larger than themselves, such as kangaroos.

Scientific name:
Canis familiaris

Size: Body 4 ft (1.2 m)
Tail 10–12 in (25–30 cm)

Habitat: From tropical forest to semiarid regions

Distribution: Australia

Reproduction: Female produces litter of 4–5 offspring; gestation is nine weeks

Diet: Small mammals, lizards, invertebrates, kangaroos

Bush dog
(*Speothos venaticus*)

BREEDING

Most canids breed once a year. Their offspring, called pups or cubs, are born blind and helpless, often in a concealed den. After weaning, wolves, wild dogs, and dholes feed their young on regurgitated food, while foxes carry food to their dens. Usually, both parents look after pups. The African black-backed jackals (*Canis mesomelas*) live in family groups but gain extra assistance from juvenile jackals who act as "nannies."

A black-backed jackal with pups

BUSH DOG

The bush dog, which lives in the forests of Central and South America, looks more like a badger than a dog. Its small ears, short legs, and stumpy tail enable it to move easily through the dense vegetation of the forest floor. Bush dogs live and hunt in packs of up to 10 individuals. They hunt large rodents such as agouti and pacas. Being capable swimmers, they also pursue capybaras (large, semiaquatic rodents) into water.

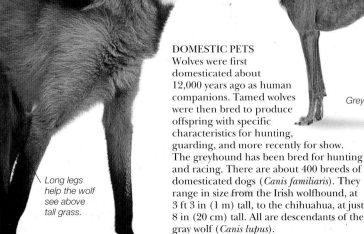

Long mane stands up to make the wolf look larger if it is threatened.

Maned wolf
(*Chrysocyon brachyurus*)

LONG LEGS

The solitary and elusive maned wolf lives in the open grasslands of South America. Its long legs are not an adaptation for fast movement. Instead, they enable it to see over the tops of tall grasses as it moves around its territory. The maned wolf is mainly active at night when it goes in search of small prey such as small mammals, birds, reptiles, insects, eggs, and fruit. It stalks and pounces on prey in much the same way as a fox.

Long legs help the wolf see above tall grass.

DOMESTIC PETS

Wolves were first domesticated about 12,000 years ago as human companions. Tamed wolves were then bred to produce offspring with specific characteristics for hunting, guarding, and more recently for show. The greyhound has been bred for hunting and racing. There are about 400 breeds of domesticated dogs (*Canis familiaris*). They range in size from the Irish wolfhound, at 3 ft 3 in (1 m) tall, to the chihuahua, at just 8 in (20 cm) tall. All are descendants of the gray wolf (*Canis lupus*).

Greyhound

These very different dogs belong to the same species.

Chihuahua

Find out more

COPING WITH EXTREMES: *60*
HUNTING: *52*
MAMMALS: *232*
SOCIAL ANIMALS: *54*

BADGERS, WEASELS, AND OTTERS

THE FAMILY MUSTELIDAE, which includes badgers, weasels, and otters, is one of the largest of the seven carnivore families. Mustelids live in many habitats, including rivers, lakes, and seas, and are found on all continents except Australia and Antarctica. This family includes some of the smallest of all carnivores. Some mustelids have long, cylindrical bodies, and short legs, adapted for hunting in trees, burrows, or underwater. Badgers, skunks, and wolverines have larger, stockier bodies. Mustelids may have anal scent glands that produce pungent, often foul-smelling secretions for marking territory, social communication, or defense against predators.

Wedge-shaped body with coarse outer fur

Eurasian badger
(*Meles meles*)

Long, striped snout

BADGERS

Badgers are nocturnal animals that spend most of their daylight hours underground. They have stocky bodies and small heads, with long snouts to root out prey, and powerful jaws with large cheek teeth for crushing food. Many species use their strong forelimbs and claws for digging multitunneled burrows called sets. They have poor eyesight and rely on their excellent sense of smell to locate food, which consists of small vertebrates, invertebrates, and fruit.

Dung pit

Mound of earth and old bedding thrown out during cleaning of tunnels

Bedding material such as bracken or grass is dragged into the nest.

A badgers' set

Sleeping chamber

SOCIAL ANIMALS

Eurasian badgers live in social groups with up to 12 members that share the same burrow (set) but forage for food on their own. The set is a maze of passages, chambers, and entrances, and provides shelter for badgers during the daytime and in winter. Generations of badgers may live in the same set for hundreds of years. When digging, they close their ears and nostrils to keep out dirt and mud.

AMERICAN BADGER

The habitat of the American badger (*Taxidea taxus*) stretches from southern Canada to the Mexican border. Its diet is more carnivorous than that of other badgers, and it uses its powerful front legs and claws to dig out burrowing mammals, such as chipmunks and ground squirrels.

SMALL BUT FIERCE

Weasels and their relatives, which include stoats, martens, polecats, minks, and wolverines, have a fierce reputation. Most are carnivorous, with teeth adapted for killing and cutting up prey, such as rabbits. All hunt on their own, and can kill prey much larger than themselves with a lethal bite to the neck. Weasels and polecats chase their prey on the ground or down burrows; minks hunt on land and in water. The wolverine is both a hunter and a scavenger.

The common weasel has a reddish brown back and a white underside.

Common weasel
(*Mustela nivalis*)

TREE HUNTERS

The eight species of marten, which include the pine marten (*Martes martes*) and sable (*Martes zibellina*), are adapted for life in the trees. They have large paws with sharp claws for gripping branches, and long tails for balancing. They can leap from branch to branch with ease, following pathways through the trees marked with scent from the anal gland. Martens catch squirrels and young birds in the trees, and hunt on the ground for rabbits, small rodents, and insects. They also forage for wild fruit and berries.

Sharp claws help the pine marten to grip branches.

Pine marten
(*Martes martes*)

Summer coat is chestnut-colored with white underparts

Stoat
(*Mustela erminea*)

In winter, when its coat is white, the stoat is known as an ermine.

WINTER CHANGES

Stoats live in the northern forests and tundra of North America, Europe, and Asia. In cold regions, a stoat's fur changes from a chestnut color to white during winter. This provides camouflage against the snow, helping the stoat avoid detection by prey, such as rodents, or predators, such as owls.

EUROPEAN POLECAT

Polecats have long, low bodies with bushy tails. They are solitary hunters that are active mainly at night. They will kill any animal they can find, including rats, mice, and rabbits, birds, toads and frogs, lizards, and snakes. Sometimes they wipe out whole litters of young animals, but eat only one or two. A domesticated polecat, used for catching rabbits, is known as a ferret.

Characteristic white mask

Scientific name: *Mustela putorius*	
Size: 12–18 in (30–45 cm) long	
Habitat: From woodlands to sand dunes	
Distribution: Europe from the Atlantic Ocean to the Ural Mountains, and from Norway to the Mediterranean Sea	
Reproduction: Female gives birth to a litter of 5–10 young	
Diet: Small mammals, reptiles, amphibians, insects, ground-nesting birds, and worms	

Brownish-gray soft coat

Small head and streamlined body

Stiff whiskers help otter find food.

Thick tail and webbed feet provide power for swimming.

Asiatic short-clawed otter
(*Aonyx cinerea*)

Skunks can spray accurately over 6 ft 6 in (2 m).

Spotted skunk
(*Spilogale putorius*)

OTTERS

Otters are semiaquatic mustelids. They are graceful swimmers with lithe, cylindrical bodies, short limbs, webbed feet, and a tapering tail. Their fur is dense and water-repellent. Some otters swim only in freshwater, others are exclusively sea creatures, while several species are at home in both habitats. Most have sleeping dens, called holts, on land. They mark their territory with scented droppings, known as spraints, which they leave on high points such as rocks. Otters are playful creatures, with dexterous forepaws that they use to hold food while eating.

SKUNKS

Found in North and South America, skunks are ground foragers that feed on small mammals, birds, eggs, and fruit. Their black and white markings warn predators to stay away. If threatened, they stamp their feet and walk stiff-legged or, in the case of the spotted skunk, stand on their front legs. If warnings fail, skunks squirt a foul-smelling liquid from their anal glands, severely irritating the predator's eyes.

TOOL USER

The sea otter (*Enhydra lutris*) is one of the few mammals that can manipulate tools. The otter dives down to the seabed, where it collects clams, mussels, and sea urchins. On the water's surface, it lies on its back, puts a flat stone on its chest, and smashes its prey against the stone to break open the shell. The stone "tool" is sometimes kept in a fold of skin under the sea otter's armpit.

UNDERWATER HUNTERS

Otters use their tails and hind feet to swim rapidly, and can twist and turn when chasing prey. When diving, they close their ears and nostrils. They locate prey, such as fish, frogs, crustaceans, and waterbirds, by sight and with their stiff, highly sensitive whiskers. When they come out of the water, the guard hairs (outer fur) of their coat form spiky clumps, enabling the water to run off easily.

The otter's body is streamlined as it swims underwater

Find out more	
ANIMALS IN DANGER:	*100*
MAMMALS:	*232*
MOVEMENT IN WATER:	*38*
RIVERS, LAKES, AND PONDS:	*76*

CATS

CATS ARE NATURE'S MOST efficient hunters. These carnivorous (meat-eating) animals feed almost entirely on vertebrates, and use cunning and stealth to stalk their victims silently before attacking. Most wild cats are solitary and secretive. They are most active at night, and have acute hearing and vision to hunt in darkness. The 37 species in the cat family are often divided into two groups – small and big cats. Small cats crouch to eat, rest with their paws tucked under them, and can purr (but not roar). Big cats lie down to eat, rest with their paws in front, and can roar (but not purr). There are seven big cat species – the lion, tiger, jaguar, leopard, snow leopard, clouded leopard, and cheetah.

CAT ANATOMY

Cats have lithe, muscular bodies that enable them to move with speed, strength, and flexibility. Unlike dogs, however, they are not equipped for long-distance running. Most cats live in forests, and are agile climbers thanks to their strong forelimbs and chest muscles, and their razor-sharp claws. They use their powerful hindlimbs to pounce, and their long tails to balance when leaping or climbing.

An ocelot (Felis pardalis) hiding in undergrowth

CHAMPIONS OF DISGUISE

A cat's fur acts as a camouflage so that it can hide from both prey and potential enemies. The lion's sandy-colored coat, for example, helps to conceal it in the dry grasses of the African savanna. Like many cats, the ocelot has a striped and spotted coat. Ocelots live in forests and thick brush in Central and South America. Their patterned coats provide excellent camouflage in the dappled light of the forest, making them almost invisible when they keep still.

TEETH AND SKULL

A cat's teeth and skull are adapted to give a powerful, killing bite, and to rip and cut flesh. The jaws can only move up and down, and are controlled by powerful muscles that provide a vicelike grip. The long, pointed, canine teeth bite into the prey's neck. The smaller teeth pull flesh off bones or slice up meat with a scissorlike action.

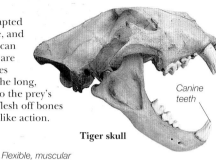

Canine teeth

Tiger skull

Flexible, muscular body

Sensitive ears

VISION

Cats have excellent vision for hunting at night. In dim light, their eyes are six times more sensitive than human eyes. At night, a cat's pupils open wide to let in as much light as possible. During the day, they close to narrow slits to keep out dazzling sunlight.

Pupils narrowed to slits

Pupils wide open

Whiskers for feeling objects in the dark

Rasping tongue for stripping flesh off bones

RETRACTABLE CLAWS

A cat's claws are usually retracted (pulled back) into protective sheaths to keep them sharp. When the cat attacks its prey, the toes spread out and special tendons tighten to extend the claws. Cats also use their claws to defend themselves and to climb.

Puma
(*Felis concolor*)

Pads on the feet cushion puma's landing after a jump.

Tendon loose   *Claw retracted*

Tendon tight   *Claw extended*

SOCIAL CATS

Lions are social cats that live in groups called prides. The males are easily distinguished by their manes. Lions were once widespread throughout Europe, Africa, and Asia, but are now found only in African grassland south of the Sahara Desert, and in a small forest reserve in northwest India. They hunt anything they can kill, including large herbivores such as zebras and wildebeest. Lions usually hunt at night, and spend most of the day resting.

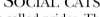

Black panther
(*Panthera pardus*)

HUNTING

Most cats hunt by stalking their prey with their bodies close to the ground. When the prey is not looking, the cat creeps up on it with low, fast movements. Once the cat has moved close enough to attack, it pounces on the prey and delivers a fatal bite to the neck before the victim can kick out or bite back. Big cats normally kill larger prey with a suffocating bite to the throat or mouth.

Panthers are leopards with black coats.

HIDING PREY

Cats may conceal their prey after a kill in order to hide the meat from scavengers – especially if there is too much to eat at one sitting. Some cats cover the prey to conceal it. Canadian lynxes, for example, bury hares in the snow. Leopards drag their prey up a tree and wedge it in a fork in the branches, out of reach of lions, hyenas, and other rival predators.

Fishing cat
(*Felis viverrina*)

A leopard (Panthera pardus) dragging its prey up a tree

FISHING CAT

Unlike most other cats, the fishing cat will readily enter water to catch prey such as fish, frogs, and mollusks. Found in the forests and swamps of southern and Southeast Asia, this cat waits by streams and ponds on the lookout for prey. If a fish or other prey appears, the cat grabs it with its teeth or flicks it out of the water with a paw.

FALLING

Cats are renowned for their instinctive ability to land safely on their feet even when they fall from a height. This skill allows them to climb high in trees in search of prey or to escape from danger. If a cat slips off a branch, it can right itself in mid-fall and land on its feet. This protects the cat's head and soft parts from damage, and enables it to survive a fall that would kill other animals.

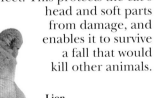

Lion
(*Panthera leo*)

The cat twists around as it falls.

The front legs stretch out to absorb the impact of landing.

Domestic cat
(*Felis catus*)

JAGUAR

The jaguar is the largest South American cat, and the only big cat found in the Americas. Jaguars are good swimmers and climbers, but they hunt mainly on the ground. Most hunting is done at night, and jaguars either stalk prey or lie in wait and ambush it.

Jaguars look similar to leopards, but have a more stocky build.

Scientific name: *Panthera onca*

Size: Head and body length up to 6 ft (1.8 m)

Habitat: Tropical forest, swamps, grassland

Distribution: From Belize to northern Argentina

Reproduction: Females have 1–4 offspring per litter

Diet: Peccaries, capybaras, agoutis, deer, sloths, birds, turtles, fish

Tiger
(*Panthera tigris*)

TIGERS

Tigers were once widespread in Asia, but their numbers have fallen drastically because of the loss of their natural habitat. There are several different types of tiger. The Siberian tiger is the largest member of the cat family – adult males weigh about 584 lb (265 kg). Tigers occupy large territories in forests, and may have several dens where they hide their prey. They normally avoid contact with people, but in rare cases may attack humans.

Find out more

ANIMALS IN DANGER: *100*
HUNTING: *52*
MOVEMENT ON LAND: *34*
SOCIAL ANIMALS: *54*

CIVETS, MONGOOSES, AND HYENAS

RENOWNED FOR THEIR SKILLFUL hunting, civets, mongooses, and hyenas are flesh-eating mammals that belong to the order Carnivora. Most species live in Africa, Madagascar, and Asia, although civets are also found in the forests of southwest Europe. The civet group includes civets, genets, and palm civets. These catlike animals are mostly nocturnal and usually make their homes in trees. Mongooses are small with long, cylindrical bodies. They are fast-moving killers that feed on insects, scorpions, and small vertebrates. There are four members of the hyena family, three of which – the true hyenas – are scavengers with powerful bone-crunching jaws. The fourth species, the aardwolf, feeds mainly on insects.

Malagasy civet (Fossa fossa) foraging for food at night

CIVETS

Civets are solitary mammals that rest by day and hunt at night. Most are foragers that ambush prey and sometimes feed on fruit. They mark their territory and communicate with other animals by rubbing strong-smelling secretions from their anal glands onto vegetation. The secretions of the African civet (*Viverra civetta*) are collected to produce a fragrant perfume additive called "musk."

Meerkats stand on termite mounds to scan their surroundings.

Sharp eyes look out for potential danger.

SOCIAL GROUPS

Unlike most mongooses, meerkats (*Suricata suricatta*) and dwarf mongooses (*Helogale parvula*) live in large social groups. Some hunt during the day when insect prey is most abundant, while others take turns to act as sentries (guards), scanning the landscape for predators. If danger threatens, they bark a noisy warning to alert other members of the group. Social mongooses also work together to drive away predators, such as birds of prey, that attack a member of their colony.

Common genet
(*Genetta genetta*)

GENETS

These long-bodied carnivores have large, forward-facing eyes that enable them to see in dim light and to judge distances accurately. They use their sharp claws to climb and their long, ringed tails to balance.

The mongoose taunts the snake by darting backward and forward and from side to side.

The snake prepares to attack.

BABYSITTERS

Meerkats, and some other mongooses, rear their young in highly organized social groups. One or more adults look after the young while the rest of the group is hunting. Babysitters remain near the group's underground dens, protecting the young from predators.

Dwarf mongoose protecting young

SNAKE-KILLERS

Mongooses have long, slender bodies, pointed faces, short legs, and long tails. Some chase prey down burrows; others hunt for insects and other small prey. Larger species are skilled snake-killers. They use their agility to outwit the snake and kill it with a swift, powerful bite to the back of the neck. Mongooses have a greater immunity to snake venom (poison) than other animals.

Sloping
shoulders

Striped hyena
(*Hyaena hyaena*)

Bushy tail

Spotted hyena
(*Crocuta crocuta*)

Long,
powerful
front legs

Short
hind legs

Four-toed
front feet with
blunt claws

HYENAS

Hyenas are
sturdy animals with sloping
backs, large heads, and bushy tails. They
are mostly nocturnal, resting by day in dense vegetation
or in burrows abandoned by other animals. At dusk, these
expert scavengers emerge to feed on the remains of dead
animals, eating and digesting body parts left by other
carnivores. Hyenas communicate with each other by leaving
scent markings on vegetation within their territory. Spotted
hyenas also make loud, whooping calls, which sound like
manic laughter, to alert others of their presence.

BINTURONG

A member of the civet family, the shaggy-coated
binturong (or bear cat) is a nocturnal forest-
dweller that spends most of its time in trees. It uses
its prehensile (grasping) tail as a "fifth foot" to hold
onto branches as it moves slowly through the trees.
Although binturongs are most agile when in trees,
they also forage for food on the ground.

Scientific name:	*Arctictis binturong*
Size: Body length 33 in (85 cm); tail 29 in (75 cm)	
Habitat: Tropical and subtropical forests	
Distribution: Myanmar, Thailand, Malaysia, and Indonesia	
Reproduction: Females produce two litters a year	
Diet: Mainly fruit	

Bony crest
anchors
powerful jaw
muscles

Spotted hyenas scavenging on a zebra carcass

PACK POWER

The spotted hyena is the largest and most powerful member of the
hyena family. A large pack of hyenas is sufficiently intimidating to drive
larger predators, such as lions, away from their own kill. Spotted hyenas
not only scavenge for dead animals, but also hunt live prey. They
occasionally hunt on their own, but when in a pack, they can bring
down a zebra or even a wildebeest with ease.

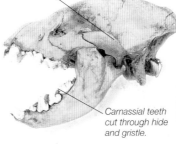

Carnassial teeth
cut through hide
and gristle.

POWERFUL JAWS

A hyena's short jaws, strong teeth,
and massive jaw muscles give it a
more powerful grip than any other
carnivore. The premolar teeth
crack and crush bones, while the
molar carnassial teeth slice through
hide, flesh, and tendons. The
digestive system dissolves most
material (including bone),
although hoofs, horns, hair, and
ligaments are regurgitated.

Aardwolf feeding on termites

AARDWOLVES

The aardwolf (*Proteles cristatus*) lacks
the strong jaws of the hyena and
feeds exclusively on termites. When
these insects emerge at night to find
food, the solitary aardwolf locates
the trail of termites by sound. It
licks them up using its long tongue
and sticky saliva. In one night an
aardwolf can eat more than 300,000
termites, and is apparently
unharmed by the defensive poisons
that termites squirt at attackers.

*As the tired
snake withdraws
to strike again, the
mongoose pounces.*

Even if the
mongoose is
bitten, it is usually
resistant to venom.

The mongoose kills
the snake with a
quick bite to the neck.

Find out more
DOGS: *252*
HUNTING: *52*
MAMMALS: *232*
SOCIAL ANIMALS: *54*

SEALS AND MANATEES

ALTHOUGH SEALS AND MANATEES are both adapted for life in water, with streamlined bodies and limbs in the form of flippers, they lead very different lives. Seals are fast-moving, acrobatic hunters that prey mainly on fish and squid. Unlike other marine mammals, they come ashore to breed, gathering in groups called rookeries. Seals are most common in cooler oceans, especially around the Arctic and Antarctic. There are three families: eared seals, earless seals, and the walrus. Manatees are the only plant-eating aquatic mammals. They are slow and bulky and live in tropical and subtropical coastal waters.

EARED SEALS

Eared seals (sea lions and fur seals) move more easily on land than true seals because they can bring their hind flippers forward and walk on all fours. In the sea, they are skillful swimmers, using their strong front flippers to row themselves through the water. Unlike true seals, eared seals have visible outer ears. The males are much larger than the females, and weigh up to five times as much. In true seals, this size difference is seen only in elephant seals.

Outer ear

Sensitive whiskers for navigating in murky water

Smooth, streamlined body

Hind flippers brought forward for walking

Large, muscular front flippers

California sea lion
(*Zalophus californianus*)

Harbor seal pups
(*Phoca vitulina*)

TRUE SEALS

True seals (earless seals) are better adapted to life in water than eared seals. They are completely streamlined, with no outer ears, torpedo-shaped bodies, and backward-pointing hind flippers that cannot turn forward. They swim by bringing their hind flippers together – like hands clapping – and by swinging them from side to side. Unable to walk on land, true seals shuffle along the ground on their bellies. The 19 species of true seals include harp, harbor, leopard, and elephant seals.

Doglike face

Strong shoulders

Hind flippers used for steering

Large front flippers for propulsion

Long hind flippers for propulsion

Eared seal (sea lion)

True seal (elephant seal)

SEAL SKELETONS

Seal skeletons reveal many adaptations to their aquatic life. The backbones are flexible, allowing seals to twist and turn underwater. The leg bones are short and the toe bones long, forming broad flippers for swimming. True seals use their long hind flippers for propulsion and steer with their front flippers. In contrast, eared seals use their powerful front flippers for propulsion and steer with their hind flippers.

PLAYFUL PUPS

Just like carnivores such as cats and dogs, seals learn many of the skills they need to survive by playing together when they are young. In pairs or threesomes, seal pups chase each other underwater, practicing high-speed turns and other maneuvers. They seek out fish and other prey to practice their hunting skills and they play-fight, rehearsing possible future battles over territory or mates.

A pair of young harbor seals play-fighting

Walrus
(*Odobenus rosmarus*)

BREEDING

Seals come ashore each year to breed, usually in spring. They gather in large breeding colonies, or rookeries, at sites that are safe from predators. Once ashore, females give birth to pups that grow quickly on fat-rich milk. The mothers soon become ready to mate again. In many species, males fight to win a territory in the rookery – the winning male mates with all the females in his territory. Male elephant seals fight so violently that pups are often crushed to death if they get in the way.

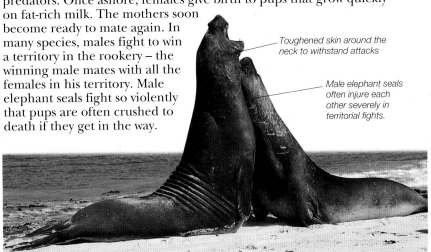

Toughened skin around the neck to withstand attacks

Male elephant seals often injure each other severely in territorial fights.

Southern elephant seal (*Mirounga leonina*)

WEST INDIAN MANATEE

Manatees swim slowly through warm and muddy waters, driving themselves forward by swinging their paddle-shaped tails up and down. They feed on submerged or floating plants, sometimes using their flippers to push food into their mouths. They are mostly solitary and live for about 30 years.

Sensitive bristles around mouth

Scientific name:	*Trichechus manatus*
Size:	8–15 ft (2.5–4.5 m)
Habitat:	Lagoons, bays, estuaries, rivers
Distribution:	Florida, Caribbean, South America
Reproduction:	Female has a calf about every two years
Diet:	Sea grass and freshwater aquatic plants

Ringed seal at breathing hole in ice

Female digging into snow over hole

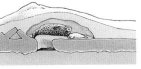

Female suckling pup in snow cave

SNOW CAVE

Ringed seals (*Phoca hispida*) give birth and rear their pups in snow caves on floating ice. In winter, snow builds up above breathing holes in the ice. Between February and March, the female ringed seal pushes her front flippers through a suitable hole and digs out a cave in the snow. Her pup will spend its first two months of life in the cave. Despite being protected and hidden from view, ring seal pups are sometimes killed by polar bears that crash into their caves.

The Hawaiian monk seal (Monachus schauinslandi) is now an extremely rare sight.

ENDANGERED SEALS

Monk seals are the only seals that live in warm waters. Of the three species, two are endangered and one is probably extinct. These seals are easily disturbed by people, especially when the seals come ashore to breed. Fishing and pollution have also taken their toll. There are now fewer than 1,000 Hawaiian monk seals and fewer than 500 Mediterranean monk seals (*Monachus monachus*) left. The Caribbean monk seal (*Monachus tropicalis*) was last seen in 1952.

Dugong
(*Dugong dugon*)

The dugong has a tail instead of hind flippers.

WALRUSES

With their large tusks, blubbery bodies, and wrinkly skin, walruses are unmistakable. These gregarious animals live in large colonies in Arctic coastal waters. A walrus's tusks reveal its social rank – the longer the tusks, the higher the rank. Walruses feed on invertebrates such as crabs and sea urchins on the sea floor. Like pigs, they use their snouts to root around for food in the mud. Their sensitive whiskers help them find food in dark or murky water.

Tusks removed.

DUGONGS

Dugongs live in the warm coastal waters of the Indian and Pacific oceans. Unlike manatees, dugongs are entirely marine. The dugong's broad snout ends in a U-shaped upper lip that grasps sea grasses or grubs up nutritious roots. Its tail is shaped like that of a whale. Dugongs are docile animals with few natural predators and poor defenses against human hunters, who kill them for meat. Like manatees, they are endangered.

COOLING OFF

Walruses emerge from the water in large numbers to rest, shed, or breed. The thick layer of blubber (fat) under a walrus's skin keeps it warm in freezing water, but when the sun is shining a basking walrus risks overheating. To cool down, it loses heat through special blood vessels that widen in its skin. These turn the walrus pink, in stark contrast to the pale brown of walruses emerging from the cold sea.

Walruses basking on a rocky coast. They turn pink when they need to cool down.

Find out more

MAMMALS: *232*
MOVEMENT IN WATER: *38*
POLAR REGIONS: *90*
SEASHORES AND TIDEPOOLS: *70*

WHALES

WHALES EVOLVED FROM four-legged mammals that left the land to live in the sea millions of years ago. Over time, they gradually adapted to their watery habitat, becoming sleek and streamlined. The tail became a powerful paddle, the front limbs became flippers, and the nostrils moved to the top of the head to make breathing easier. There are now 79 known whale species in two main groups: baleen whales and toothed whales. Baleen whales are the world's largest animals. They feed by straining tiny shrimplike animals from the sea. Toothed whales are hunters that prey mostly on fish and squid.

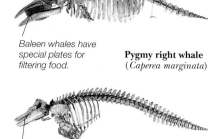

Baleen whales have special plates for filtering food.

Pygmy right whale
(*Caperea marginata*)

Toothed whales have teeth for seizing prey.

Killer whale
(*Orcinus orca*)

WHALE SKELETONS
The skeletons of whales have a streamlined, fishlike shape that tapers to the end. The flexible backbone is powerfully built to support strong tail muscles, which drive the whale forward. The front limbs form broad flippers for steering, and the hind limbs have nearly disappeared over the course of evolution. In baleen whales, the arched upper jaw holds the baleen plates, used for feeding. In toothed whales the jaws are lined with teeth.

BALEEN WHALES
Despite its vast size, a baleen whale feeds on tiny prey. Instead of teeth, its large mouth is filled with horny baleen plates that hang from the upper jaw and are fringed by bristles. These plates are used to filter huge amounts of shrimplike animals called krill and small fish from the water. Unlike a toothed whale, a baleen whale has two blowholes, or nostrils, on top of its head. There are 10 species of baleen whales.

Blowhole

Barnacles and parasites on skin

Broad flippers for steering

Right whale
(*Eubalaena glacialis*)

Whales and diver shown to scale

Cross section of a Sei whale's mouth

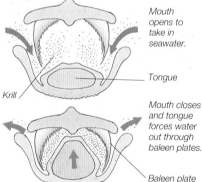

Mouth opens to take in seawater.

Tongue

Krill

Mouth closes and tongue forces water out through baleen plates.

Baleen plate

FEEDING
Baleen whales filter huge amounts of krill and other small animals from the water with their baleen plates. A blue whale can eat 2.5 tons of krill each day. A Sei whale feeds by taking in a huge mouthful of seawater, which it then pushes out through the baleen plates with its tongue. Any animals in the water remain on the inner surface of the plates. The Sei whale scrapes these animals off with its tongue and swallows them.

Human

The blue whale is the largest animal on Earth.

Blue whale
(*Balaenoptera musculus*)

Sperm whale
(*Physeter catodon*)

Pygmy right whale
(*Caperea marginata*)

Killer whale
(*Orcinus orca*)

Goose-beaked whale
(*Ziphius cavirostris*)

TOOTHED WHALES
The toothed whales include dolphins, porpoises, and sperm whales. As the name suggests, these whales have sharp teeth that they use to capture prey such as fish and squid. Toothed whales usually locate their prey by producing special sounds and then listening to the echoes (echolocation). In most species, the large forehead contains a waxy organ, called a melon, that helps with echolocation. A toothed whale has a single blowhole on top of its head. There are 69 toothed whale species.

School of beluga whales (Delphinapterus leucas)

WHALE SIZE
Some whales, especially baleen whales, grow to an enormous size. The blue whale can reach 98 ft (30 m) in length, making it the longest animal ever to have existed on Earth. It is so large that an adult elephant could stand on a blue whale's tongue. Whales reach such great sizes because their bodies are supported by water. If a whale is stranded on land, the weight of its own body will crush its internal organs and kill it.

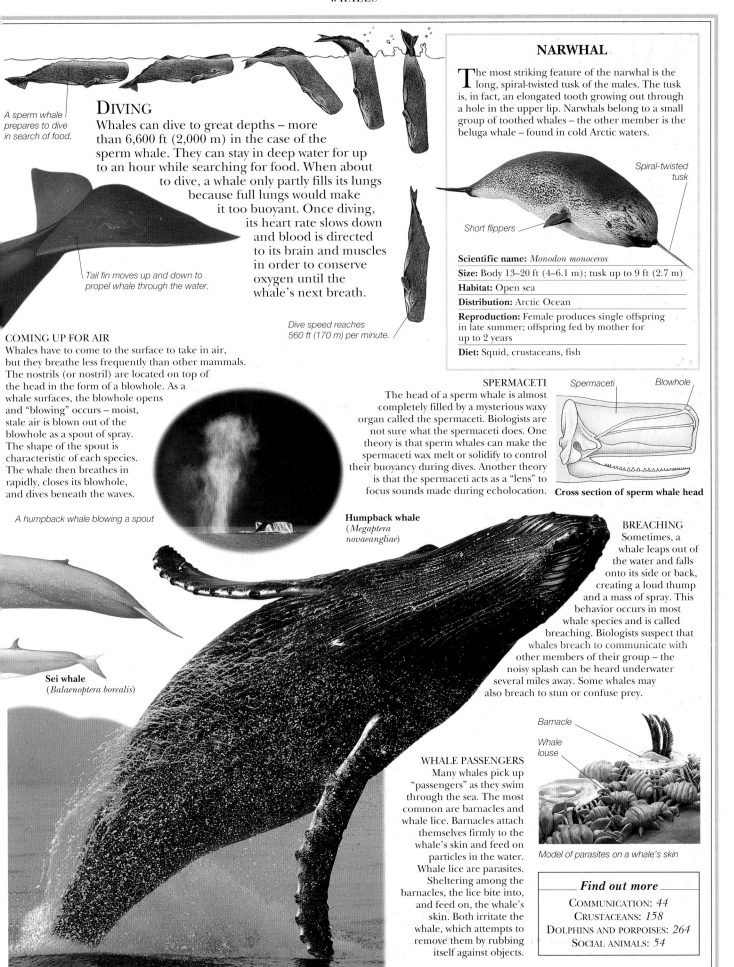

A sperm whale prepares to dive in search of food.

DIVING

Whales can dive to great depths – more than 6,600 ft (2,000 m) in the case of the sperm whale. They can stay in deep water for up to an hour while searching for food. When about to dive, a whale only partly fills its lungs because full lungs would make it too buoyant. Once diving, its heart rate slows down and blood is directed to its brain and muscles in order to conserve oxygen until the whale's next breath.

Tail fin moves up and down to propel whale through the water.

Dive speed reaches 560 ft (170 m) per minute.

NARWHAL

The most striking feature of the narwhal is the long, spiral-twisted tusk of the males. The tusk is, in fact, an elongated tooth growing out through a hole in the upper lip. Narwhals belong to a small group of toothed whales – the other member is the beluga whale – found in cold Arctic waters.

Spiral-twisted tusk

Short flippers

Scientific name: *Monodon monoceros*

Size: Body 13–20 ft (4–6.1 m); tusk up to 9 ft (2.7 m)

Habitat: Open sea

Distribution: Arctic Ocean

Reproduction: Female produces single offspring in late summer; offspring fed by mother for up to 2 years

Diet: Squid, crustaceans, fish

COMING UP FOR AIR

Whales have to come to the surface to take in air, but they breathe less frequently than other mammals. The nostrils (or nostril) are located on top of the head in the form of a blowhole. As a whale surfaces, the blowhole opens and "blowing" occurs – moist, stale air is blown out of the blowhole as a spout of spray. The shape of the spout is characteristic of each species. The whale then breathes in rapidly, closes its blowhole, and dives beneath the waves.

A humpback whale blowing a spout

SPERMACETI

The head of a sperm whale is almost completely filled by a mysterious waxy organ called the spermaceti. Biologists are not sure what the spermaceti does. One theory is that sperm whales can make the spermaceti wax melt or solidify to control their buoyancy during dives. Another theory is that the spermaceti acts as a "lens" to focus sounds made during echolocation.

Spermaceti *Blowhole*

Cross section of sperm whale head

Humpback whale (*Megaptera novaeangliae*)

BREACHING

Sometimes, a whale leaps out of the water and falls onto its side or back, creating a loud thump and a mass of spray. This behavior occurs in most whale species and is called breaching. Biologists suspect that whales breach to communicate with other members of their group – the noisy splash can be heard underwater several miles away. Some whales may also breach to stun or confuse prey.

Sei whale (*Balaenoptera borealis*)

WHALE PASSENGERS

Many whales pick up "passengers" as they swim through the sea. The most common are barnacles and whale lice. Barnacles attach themselves firmly to the whale's skin and feed on particles in the water. Whale lice are parasites. Sheltering among the barnacles, the lice bite into, and feed on, the whale's skin. Both irritate the whale, which attempts to remove them by rubbing itself against objects.

Barnacle

Whale louse

Model of parasites on a whale's skin

Find out more

COMMUNICATION: *44*
CRUSTACEANS: *158*
DOLPHINS AND PORPOISES: *264*
SOCIAL ANIMALS: *54*

DOLPHINS AND PORPOISES

Skeleton of killer whale
(*Orcinus orca*)

THESE FAST-SWIMMING, AQUATIC mammals belong to the group of whales called the toothed whales. Within this group are the dolphins, river dolphins, and porpoises. Dolphins are the most abundant whale group and they live in coastal waters and oceans. This family includes the killer whale, which can grow to 30 ft (9 m) in length. River dolphins have limited sight and are found in some river systems of Asia and South America. Porpoises inhabit shallow coastal waters. Many dolphin and porpoise species live in social groups called schools or pods. They navigate and find food by emitting sound vibrations that bounce off obstacles in their path. This is known as echolocation.

SKELETON
The killer whale's skeleton shows its streamlined, tapering, fishlike shape. There are no hind limbs and the forelimbs have shortened arm bones and extra finger bones that support the paddlelike flippers. The neck is short, and the skull is elongated with pointed, conical teeth. The long, flexible backbone anchors the powerful swimming muscles that move the tail flukes up and down.

DOLPHIN ANATOMY
Dolphins have streamlined, torpedo-shaped bodies, smooth, hairless skin, and no external ears or hind limbs. Their powerful tail fins move up and down to push them through the water, while their paddlelike flippers steer. The dorsal fin acts as a stabilizer. Dolphins have a single nostril, or blowhole, on top of their heads, through which they breathe at the water's surface. Most species have a well-defined beak or snout with sharp teeth, and a rounded forehead.

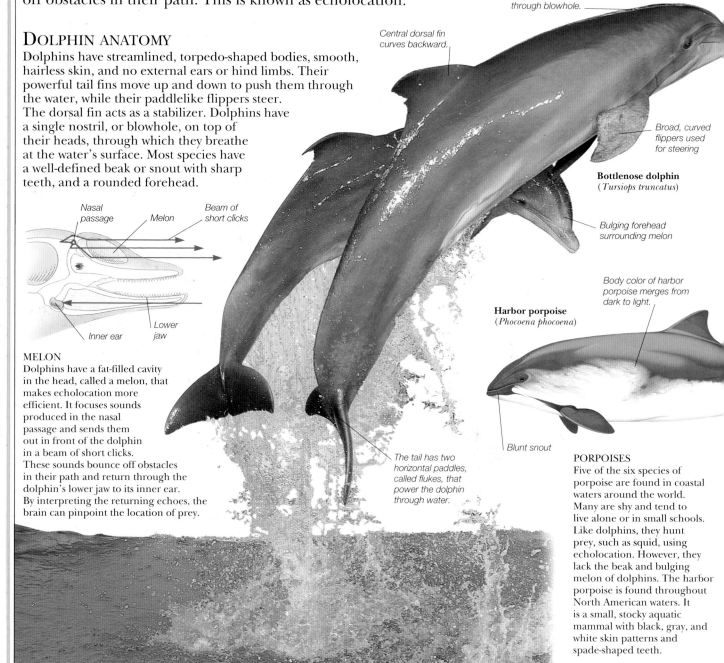

Dolphin breathes through blowhole.

Central dorsal fin curves backward.

Nasal passage

Melon

Beam of short clicks

Inner ear

Lower jaw

Broad, curved flippers used for steering

Bottlenose dolphin
(*Tursiops truncatus*)

Bulging forehead surrounding melon

Body color of harbor porpoise merges from dark to light.

Harbor porpoise
(*Phocoena phocoena*)

Blunt snout

The tail has two horizontal paddles, called flukes, that power the dolphin through water.

MELON
Dolphins have a fat-filled cavity in the head, called a melon, that makes echolocation more efficient. It focuses sounds produced in the nasal passage and sends them out in front of the dolphin in a beam of short clicks. These sounds bounce off obstacles in their path and return through the dolphin's lower jaw to its inner ear. By interpreting the returning echoes, the brain can pinpoint the location of prey.

PORPOISES
Five of the six species of porpoise are found in coastal waters around the world. Many are shy and tend to live alone or in small schools. Like dolphins, they hunt prey, such as squid, using echolocation. However, they lack the beak and bulging melon of dolphins. The harbor porpoise is found throughout North American waters. It is a small, stocky aquatic mammal with black, gray, and white skin patterns and spade-shaped teeth.

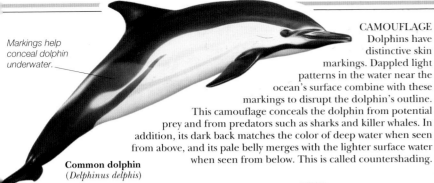

Markings help conceal dolphin underwater.

Common dolphin
(*Delphinus delphis*)

CAMOUFLAGE
Dolphins have distinctive skin markings. Dappled light patterns in the water near the ocean's surface combine with these markings to disrupt the dolphin's outline. This camouflage conceals the dolphin from potential prey and from predators such as sharks and killer whales. In addition, its dark back matches the color of deep water when seen from above, and its pale belly merges with the lighter surface water when seen from below. This is called countershading.

INDUS RIVER DOLPHIN

This blind freshwater dolphin is one of the world's most endangered mammals. It has a narrow snout packed with small teeth, and it uses echolocation to hunt for food. In the last 50 years, the Indus River has been divided up by dams, making it much harder for the river dolphin to survive.

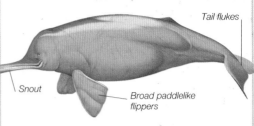

Tail flukes

Snout

Broad paddlelike flippers

Scientific name:	*Platanista minor*
Size:	Length 5.5 ft (1.7 m) females; 5 ft (1.5 m) males
Habitat:	Rivers from the estuary to the headwaters
Distribution:	Indus river system of Pakistan and India
Reproduction:	Births peak at the beginning of the dry season; a single calf is born and suckled for a year
Diet:	Freshwater shrimps and fish

BREEDING

Female dolphins and porpoises produce a single calf every two or three years, usually during the warmer months of the year. The newborn calf may be helped to the surface to take its first breath by its mother or by other females in the pod. Suckling takes place underwater. The milk, which is squirted into the calf's mouth from the mother's teats, has a high fat and protein content, which helps the calf to grow quickly.

Calf remains close to its mother for several months after birth.

Increasing its speed, the dolphin breaks the surface.

Sounds bounce off shoals of fish.

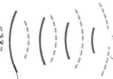

Dolphin sends out click sounds to locate prey.

Dolphin picks up returning echoes from prey in its path.

Dolphin glides for a few seconds in the air.

Dolphin re-enters the water with a splash.

SKIMMING THE WAVES

Dolphins and porpoises are fast, agile swimmers. They often leap out of the water and glide just above the surface for short distances. This is called porpoising and enables the dolphin to breathe while traveling at high speeds. Dolphins also perform graceful leaps and somersaults. They do this in order to breathe and to communicate with other members of the pod.

FEEDING

Dolphins feed mainly on fish and squid that they catch with their cone-shaped teeth and swallow whole. They hunt their fast-moving food by sending out rapid click sounds, which bounce off schools of fish in their path. Dolphins often work together to "round up" fish before feeding on them. Some use loud sounds to disorient or even stun fish. This makes the fish easier to catch.

Killer whale "spy-hopping"

Killer whale patrolling the shoreline

BEACH PATROL
Killer whales feed on warm-blooded prey such as seals, penguins, and dolphins as well as on fish and squid. Members of the pod often patrol the shoreline waiting to snatch an unwary sea lion pup from the beach. Killer whales are the only members of the whale group that can "beach" themselves in this way and then return safely to the ocean.

LOOKING OUT
Many species of whales survey the scene above the water's surface by "spy-hopping." The whale thrusts its head out of the water, rests vertically, and then slowly sinks downward. "Spy-hopping" enables whales to spot distant fish schools and look for signs of land to help them navigate.

ELEPHANTS AND HYRAXES

African elephant
(*Loxodonta africana*)

Flattened forehead

Larger ears than Asian elephant

Back dips in the middle

DESPITE THE DIFFERENCES IN APPEARANCE, elephants and hyraxes are descended from a common ancestor. Both are plant-eaters, have toes with flattened nails, and grinding cheek teeth. Elephants are the largest of all land animals. There are two species: the African elephant and the smaller Asian elephant, found in India and Southeast Asia. Both species are endangered as a result of human pressures. Hyraxes, by contrast, are much smaller, furry mammals that live in Africa and the Middle East. The seven species include rock and bush hyraxes, which live in rocky terrain, and tree hyraxes, which live in woodland.

Asian elephant
(*Elephas maximus*)

Domed forehead

Ears are smaller than on African elephant.

Straight or humped back

The African elephant's trunk has more rings and is less rigid than that of the Asian elephant.

ELEPHANT ANATOMY

The elephant's massive, robust body is supported by four pillarlike legs. The head, also large, supports the trunk and the tusks. The ivory tusks are extended upper incisor teeth, and are used for display, defense, and digging for food or water. Inside the mouth, large vegetation-grinding cheek teeth are replaced from the rear as they wear out. The large, flapping ears help to keep the elephant cool, and may also be used for communication.

Asian elephants do not always have tusks.

Strong, pillarlike legs

Cross section through elephant's foot

Fatty pad supports foot bones

ELEPHANT FEET

Surprisingly, elephants walk nearly on tiptoe with their heels off the ground. The bones of the foot are spread out and supported by a fatty pad that contains elastic fibers. This arrangement produces a wide, rounded foot which spreads and absorbs the elephant's weight, and enables it to move quietly.

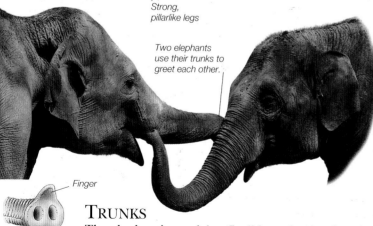

Two elephants use their trunks to greet each other.

FEEDING

Elephants use their trunks to grasp vegetation and push it into the mouth. Elephants feed on grasses and other ground vegetation. They also reach up into trees with their trunk to pull down leaves, branches, and bark. In times of food shortage, elephants use their bulk to push over trees in order to reach the highest foliage. Their feces contain swallowed tree seeds which grow to replace the fallen trees.

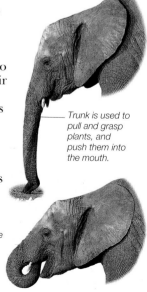

Trunk is used to pull and grasp plants, and push them into the mouth.

Finger

TRUNKS

The elephant's trunk is a flexible and muscular extension of the nose and upper lip. Its tip, equipped with one or two "fingers," is very sensitive and acts like a hand to grasp vegetation and pick up small objects. The trunk is also used for sucking up water to drink, for squirting water when showering, for communicating by touch and smell, for amplifying sounds, and to show aggressive behavior.

Asian elephants have one "finger"

African elephants have two "fingers"

Acacia seeds pass out in the elephant's feces and grow into new plants.

Elephants cool off in a muddy waterhole

AT THE WATERHOLE

When elephants are thirsty they congregate at river banks or waterholes, or dig for water using their tusks. Elephants drink by sucking up water in their trunk and squirting it into their mouth. They consume 40–80 gallons (155–305 liters) a day. Water is also squirted over the back to keep the skin cool. Dust settles on the wet skin forming a dry mudpack that protects the skin from sunlight and parasites.

Elephant mothers shade their young from the sun.

HERDS

Elephants usually live in family units of 8–10 members. These are often composed of related females and their offspring and are dominated by a senior female. Males may live singly or in bachelor herds. Sometimes family units congregate in large herds made up of hundreds of animals. Elephants communicate by touch, smell, or visual signals using the trunk or ears. In addition to trumpeting calls, they produce low-frequency sounds that travel over long distances and help keep the herd together.

A female Asian elephant lifts a heavy log

WORKING ELEPHANTS

For thousands of years, elephants (especially Asian elephants) have been tamed and used for carrying heavy loads, pulling plows, lifting and moving logs, and for ceremonial purposes. Elephants are intelligent animals that can learn simple skills quickly and are able to remember them. Asian elephants are still widely used in southern Asia to shift lumber over terrain that is too rough for trucks or tractors.

AFRICAN ELEPHANT

The largest living land animals, African elephants can weigh up to 6.6 tons (6,000 kg). Sensitive to the intense heat of the African savanna, these elephants regularly break from feeding to cool off in waterholes or under the shade of a tree. African elephants have long been hunted for their ivory, and this, together with pressure for more land, has made the species endangered.

Scientific name: *Loxodonta africana*

Size: Shoulder height: up to 13 ft (4 m)

Habitat: Semidesert, swamp, savanna, forest

Distribution: Africa south of the Sahara desert

Reproduction: Females have single calf every 5–6 years

Diet: Leaves, grasses, flowers, fruit, roots, tree bark

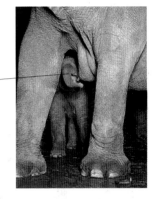

Young elephant lifts its trunk in order to suckle milk from its mother's teats.

CARING FOR YOUNG

Like other mammals with long life spans, elephants invest many years in nurturing their young. Elephant calves are tended by other females in the herd, as well as their mother. This care begins at birth, when herd females may act as "midwives." Calves feed on milk from their mother's teats, which are situated between her front legs.

HYRAXES

Rock and bush hyraxes live in dry areas, and typically have short fur, a short tail, and long incisor teeth that are used for defense. They also have cheek teeth for cropping vegetation. Their legs are short and sturdy, and their feet have bare pads that, when moist with sweat, grip rocks and tree branches. This helps the hyrax to climb and jump over its terrain.

Rock hyrax
(*Procavia capensis*)

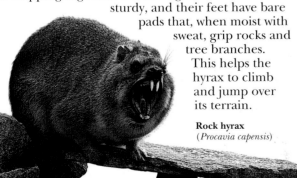

SOCIAL GROUPS

Rock and bush hyraxes may live in single family units or colonies of up to 100 individuals. Sometimes, unusually for mammals, members of different hyrax species will congregate together. Although they can survive dry conditions with little water, hyraxes have difficulty regulating their body temperature. At night and in the early morning they huddle together on their kopje, or rocky outcrop, to keep warm.

Bush hyraxes (Heterohyrax brucei) huddle together and bask in the early morning sun to warm themselves.

Find out more

ANIMALS IN DANGER: *100*
HORSES, ASSES, AND ZEBRAS: 268
MAMMALS: *232*
VERTEBRATES: *182*

HORSES, ASSES, AND ZEBRAS

OUT ON THE OPEN PLAINS, herds of horses graze freely on grasses and shrubs, using speed to outrun potential predators. Over millions of years, horses have evolved from forest-dwelling mammals to become powerful, high-speed gallopers. The domestic horse belongs to the family called Equidae, which also includes Przewalski's horse – recently reintroduced into the wild – three species of ass, and three species of striped zebra. The horses now living in areas such as the American west and Australian outback are not true wild species, but are feral animals – descendants of escaped domestic stock, which have returned to a natural state.

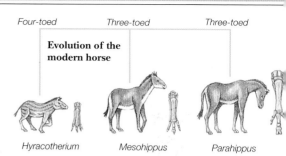

Four-toed   Three-toed   Three-toed

Evolution of the modern horse

Hyracotherium   Mesohippus   Parahippus

EVOLUTION

Over the course of time, horses have evolved from having four toes on each foot to having just one toe on each foot. The earliest horse, *Hyracotherium*, was a dog-sized, scampering mammal that lived in the forests of North America some 55 million years ago. Its four toes splayed out to stop it from sinking into the ground. As the climate changed, and grasslands became more widespread, larger, faster-moving species, such as *Parahippus*, evolved. With fewer foot and toe bones their limbs were lighter so they could run faster and escape predators. Modern horses have one toe on each foot, protected by a hoof.

HORSE ANATOMY

Horses and other equids share features that reflect their fast-moving, herbivorous lifestyle. Typically, a horse has a long head with wide-set eyes that help it look out for predators while grazing. The muscular body has a long neck topped with a mane of stiff hairs. Each leg is slender and ends in a single hoofed toe. Equids have large teeth for grinding food and tails that whisk away flies.

Stiff mane

Pale muzzle

Przewalski's horse
(*Equus caballus przewalskii*)

Single toe is protected by a horny hoof.

African wild ass (*Equus asinus*)

ASSES

Generally smaller than horses, asses have longer ears and are more sure-footed. The African wild ass, the kulan, and the kiang are adapted to live in dry locations. The African wild ass is now rare and lives in the rocky deserts of northeast Africa, although the donkey, its domesticated descendant, is still common.

Zebra kicking its back legs at an attacking cheetah

ZEBRAS

Zebra is the name given to three species of black-and-white striped equids from Africa. The stripes – once thought to confuse predators – are now thought to aid recognition within the herd, helping to keep it together. Grevy's zebra (*Equus grevyi*) and the mountain zebra (*Equus zebra*) live in semiarid areas and are endangered. The more numerous Burchell's zebra is found in savanna, light woodlands, and scrub.

DEFENSE

Horses, asses, and zebras all use the same strategy to defend themselves when fighting each other or when attempting to deter a predator. Rival males will push and bite each other on the neck and legs. They may also turn and lash out with their powerful hind legs, kicking an opponent or predator with their sharp hooves. Equids tend to live in large herds for added protection – zebras sometimes live in mixed herds with antelopes.

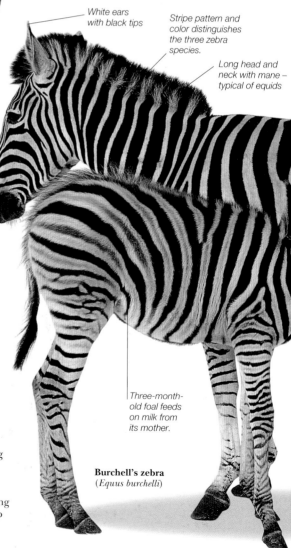

White ears with black tips

Stripe pattern and color distinguishes the three zebra species.

Long head and neck with mane – typical of equids

Three-month-old foal feeds on milk from its mother.

Burchell's zebra
(*Equus burchelli*)

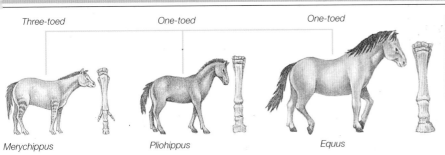

Three-toed
One-toed
One-toed

Merychippus

Pliohippus

Equus

GREVY'S ZEBRA

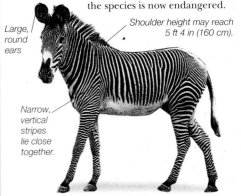

The largest of the zebras, Grevy's zebra is no more closely related to the other zebras than it is to the horses and asses. Hunting for its skin, and competition with domestic animals for water, have reduced its numbers severely, and the species is now endangered.

Large, round ears

Shoulder height may reach 5 ft 4 in (160 cm).

Narrow, vertical stripes lie close together.

Scientific name: *Equus grevyi*

Size: Head and body length up to 9 ft 10 in (3 m)

Habitat: Semidesert areas

Distribution: NE Africa, Somalia, Kenya, Ethiopia

Reproduction: Single young born after 390 days' gestation; foal remains with female for up to 3 years

Diet: Tough grasses

HERDS

Horses, asses, and zebras live in family groups of a male, several females, and offspring. The male defends his territory and the females when they are ready to breed. Such herds are permanent in horses and Burchell's and mountain zebras, but are loose associations in asses and Grevy's zebras. Living in a herd provides some protection from predators, especially for young animals.

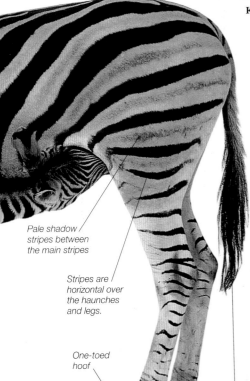

Herd of Camargue feral horses (Equus caballus)

COMMUNICATION

Communication helps to keep a herd together, alert members to danger, and define friendships and rivalries. Equids have acute senses of sight, smell, and hearing – all used in communication. They convey their mood by changes in posture, the position of their ears, tail, or mouth, and by making sounds. For example, if a horse is startled, it raises its head and tail, arches its neck, and flares its nostrils, alerting the others to run.

Flattened ears indicate aggression.

Kulans are a subspecies of the wild ass from Asia.

Kulans (*Equus hemionus kulan*)

Mare rests after giving birth to her foal.

Foal is still covered in the amniotic sac.

Mare licks amniotic sac from foal.

GIVING BIRTH

Life in open grasslands is full of dangers for horses – particularly for a young foal. As soon as a foal is born, its mother licks it to remove the birth membranes and to stimulate its circulation and breathing. Within one hour, it can struggle to its feet, wobbling at first on its long legs. Soon it is able to walk and run, and to follow its mother if danger threatens.

The foal will soon take its first steps.

Pale shadow stripes between the main stripes

Stripes are horizontal over the haunches and legs.

One-toed hoof

Tail has long hairs at the tip.

Lean muscular body

DOMESTICATION

Horses (*Equus caballus*) were first domesticated about 6,000 years ago for use as food, beasts of burden, to send into war, and to race and ride for pleasure. Today, there are 300 breeds of domestic horse, divided into three groups: heavy horses, such as Shire horses, light horses, including thoroughbreds, and smaller ponies, such as Shetland ponies. Mules (the offspring of male donkeys and female horses) have been bred as domesticated animals by humans.

Thoroughbred horses are bred for stamina and strength in horse racing. They can reach speeds of 40 mph (65 kmh).

Find out more

DEFENSE 1: *48*

MAMMALS: *232*

MOVEMENT ON LAND: *34*

PEOPLE AND ANIMALS: *94*

RHINOS AND TAPIRS

Black rhinoceros
(*Diceros bicornis*)

RHINOCEROSES ARE MASSIVE, bulky mammals with thick skins and distinctive horns on their snout – the name rhinoceros comes from the Greek word for "nose-horned." Like tapirs, they are herbivorous mammals that have hooved toes on each foot. There are five rhino species: the black and white rhinos from Africa, and the Sumatran, Indian, and Javan rhinos from Asia. While most rhinos are solitary animals, white rhinos sometimes live in groups of related females and their young. Tapirs are related to rhinos. They are nocturnal, shy, forest-dwelling animals with short mobile trunks. There are three South American tapir species and one Asian species.

Horn made of keratin fibers – the same material found in human nails and hair

Upper lip is prehensile (capable of grasping).

Short, stocky legs support bulky body.

Hair on belly and legs

Sumatran rhinoceros
(*Dicerorhinus sumatrensis*)

TOUGH SKIN AND HORN

A rhino has a large head with one or two horns on the snout, depending on the species. The horn is not made of bone but of a mass of keratin (hairlike) fibers. Most rhinos have tough, thick skin that is virtually hairless. The Sumatran rhino from Southeast Asia is the smallest rhino and is very rare. It differs from all other rhinos by having a hairy coat when young.

Indian rhinoceros
(*Rhinoceros unicornis*)

BROWSERS AND GRAZERS

Rhinos need to eat plenty of vegetation each day in order to maintain their large bulk. The rhino family includes both browsers that pluck leaves and fruit from trees and plants, and grazers that crop grasses. The black, Sumatran, and Javan rhinos are browsers, and have specialized upper lips adapted for feeding on shrubs. The Indian rhino can extend its upper lip to grasp leaves when browsing, and can fold its lip away when grazing.

White rhinoceros
(Ceratotherium simum) at a waterhole

SUNBLOCK

With so little hair, a rhino's skin is vulnerable to sunlight. Living in hot climates, rhinos often become overheated and need to cool off by lying in water or by wallowing in mud. As the mud dries on a rhino's skin, it forms a sunblock and may also help to deter tormenting skin parasites.

This rhino's single horn has been removed.

Upper lip can be extended to grasp long grass, and folded away when feeding on short grass.

PECULIAR PARTNERS

African rhinos and oxpeckers make unusual feeding partners. Oxpeckers clamber over rhinos with their sharp claws, and use their flattened bills to feed on ticks and other parasites from the rhinos' skin. The birds also help rhinos by screeching if danger threatens. In return, the oxpecker secures a constant food supply.

Oxpeckers on the back of a black rhinoceros

*White rhinos
clashing horns*

CONFRONTATION

Male rhinos defend their territory to protect their food, water, and females. They mark out boundaries with feces and urine, and may charge at any unwary intruders at high speeds. Conflicts with other rhinos are usually resolved through ritual gestures, such as the clashing of horns. Sometimes real fights erupt that can result in gaping wounds.

*Leathery hide falls
in distinct folds.*

ARMOR
Rhinos have few natural predators – but humans and other rhinos are a serious threat. Rhinos' horns, thick skin, and massive bulk are all part of their defense. The Indian rhino seems particularly well protected – its heavily folded, bumpy skin has the appearance of armor plating.

Indian rhinoceros
(*Rhinoceros unicornis*)

CONSERVATION
Habitat destruction and demand for rhino horn have dramatically reduced the number of rhinos. In Asia, the horns are crushed to produce medicinal "remedies," and in North Yemen they are used to make dagger handles. Conservationists try to prevent rhino slaughter by shearing off the animals' horns before poachers can get to them. This is a painless process for the rhinos.

Conservationists removing horns

MALAYAN TAPIR

The only tapir species outside South America, the Malayan tapir lives in the densest parts of the rainforests of Southeast Asia. It is easily distinguished from its South American relatives by its distinctive black and white patterned coat. This helps break up its outline and conceal it from possible predators. Hunting and destruction of its rainforest habitat have made the Malayan tapir an endangered species.

*Black and
white coat*

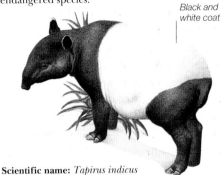

Scientific name:	*Tapirus indicus*
Size: Up to 3 ft 3 in (1 m) high	
Habitat: Rainforests	
Distribution: Southeast Asia	
Reproduction: Female gives birth to one offspring	
Diet: Leaves, shoots, buds, and fruits	

Long, flexible snout

Brazilian tapir
(*Tapirus terrestris*)

TAPIRS
Tapirs are shy, solitary animals with short, stout bodies. Their snout and upper lip are joined together to form a short, fleshy trunk called a proboscis. Tapirs use their trunk to "smell" their way around the forest and to pull forest vegetation and fruit into the mouth. Tapirs have very good senses of smell and hearing, but poor eyesight.

*Splayed feet help prevent tapirs
from sinking into soft ground.*

A young Brazilian tapir (Tapirus terrestris)

TAPIR CAMOUFLAGE
The dark-brown coat of the Brazilian tapir gives it excellent camouflage. Baby tapirs of all species have striped and spotted coats that blend in with the dappled light of the forest. When they are about six months old, the spots and stripes fade and the young tapir begins to look like its parents.

*Tapirs plunge into
the water to escape
from enemies.*

SWIMMERS
Tapirs are able swimmers and divers, and are nearly always found near water or swampy ground. They spend long periods splashing in water or wallowing in mud in order to cool off during the heat of the day. They feed on shoots, leaves, and succulent water plants. In times of danger, tapirs can escape from predators by submerging themselves in water – sometimes for several minutes at a time.

Find out more
ANIMALS IN DANGER: *100*
ELEPHANTS AND HYRAXES: *266*
GRASSLANDS: *84*
HORSES, ASSES, AND ZEBRAS: *268*

HIPPOS AND PIGS

HIPPOPOTAMUSES AND PIGS are distinguished by their short legs, stocky bodies, and large heads. Hippopotamuses are nocturnal plant-eaters found only in wet parts of Africa. There are two species – a large species called the hippopotamus and a smaller forest-dweller called the pygmy hippopotamus. The hippopotamus lives mostly in water to keep cool and to support its massive body weight. Pigs are intelligent, nimble animals with sensitive snouts that they use to root for food in forests and grassland. Most are omnivores – they eat animals as well as plants. There are 9 pig species, native to Europe, Africa, and Asia. The peccaries of South and Central America are similar to pigs, but are placed in a family of their own.

HIPPOPOTAMUSES

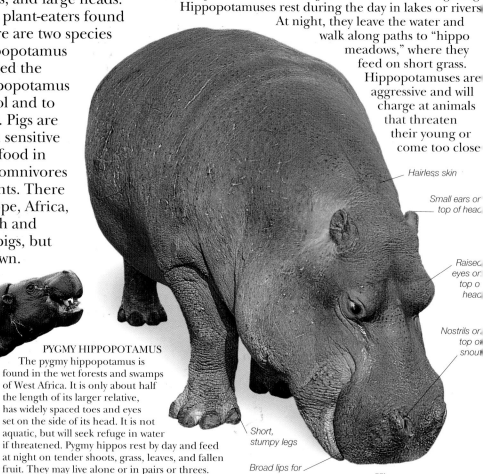

The hippopotamus is a massive animal with a barrel-shaped body, stumpy legs, and a huge, wide-opening mouth. The mouth conceals a pair of large, razor-sharp teeth in the lower jaw that are used for fighting Hippopotamuses rest during the day in lakes or rivers At night, they leave the water and walk along paths to "hippo meadows," where they feed on short grass. Hippopotamuses are aggressive and will charge at animals that threaten their young or come too close

Hairless skin

Small ears or top of head

Raised eyes or top o head

Nostrils or top o snout

Short, stumpy legs

Broad lips for plucking short grass plants

Hippopotamus (*Hippopotamus amphibius*)

PYGMY HIPPOPOTAMUS

The pygmy hippopotamus is found in the wet forests and swamps of West Africa. It is only about half the length of its larger relative, has widely spaced toes and eyes set on the side of its head. It is not aquatic, but will seek refuge in water if threatened. Pygmy hippos rest by day and feed at night on tender shoots, grass, leaves, and fallen fruit. They may live alone or in pairs or threes.

Pygmy hippopotamus (*Choeropsis liberiensis*)

LIFE IN WATER

Hippopotamuses live in water to avoid the heat of the day and to save energy. They can see and breathe when their bodies are submerged because their eyes, ears, and nostrils are set on top of their heads. They are sociable creatures, and live in herds of 10–15 animals. Staying together protects them from attack by predators. The young are especially vulnerable, and sometimes crawl onto their mothers' backs to avoid crocodiles. Nearly half die in their first year.

Hippos keep their eyes above water to watch out for danger.

TERRITORIAL CONFLICT

Some male hippopotamuses fiercely defend their territory. These dominant males have exclusive mating rights to females in the territory. If a dominant male is challenged, the two rivals threaten each other by grunting, showing their huge teeth, or scattering dung with their tails. If neither retreats, they fight fiercely, using their sharp teeth to inflict wounds until one submits. The fight may be fatal.

MOVING UNDERWATER

Although hippos spend most of their time resting when in water, they are also excellent swimmers and divers. Water flows easily over their smooth skin, and their webbed toes act like paddles. When underwater, the hippo's slitlike ears and nostrils close to keep water out. Hippos can remain submerged for up to five minutes, and sometimes longer. In deeper water, they may walk along the bottom of rivers and lakes.

PIGS

Pigs are sure-footed, fast runners with agile, powerful bodies. Their most prominent feature is the mobile snout, which is flattened and sensitive at the tip. They also have a pair of upturned tusks. Most pigs have a varied diet, and use their snouts to turn over soil in search of roots, insect larvae, and other food. Pigs usually forage in small family groups, and communicate using grunts and squeaks.

Bristly coat

African bushpig
(*Potamochoerus porcus*)

Sensitive snout

A female wild boar with her family of striped piglets

LARGE FAMILIES

Tropical pig species breed throughout the year, while temperate species produce their litters in the spring. Piglets are born in a grass nest, where they stay for several days before following their mother. Some species, such as the wild boar (*Sus scrofa*), have large litters of up to 12 piglets. In most species, the piglets are striped to camouflage them against their surroundings.

BABIRUSA

This hairless pig has tusks that grow upward through its snout and curve toward its eyes. Babirusas live in small groups, preferring dense cover within forests. When foraging, the male does most of the rooting, while females and young follow behind and feed on unearthed items. Babirusas are good swimmers, and sometimes venture out to sea.

Tusks growing through snout

Scientific name: *Babyrousa babyrussa*

Size: Body up to 3 ft 3in (1 m) long

Habitat: Forests and thickets, always near water

Distribution: Several islands in Indonesia

Reproduction: Females have 1 or 2 young each year

Diet: Leaves, grass, fallen fruit, roots

SELF-DEFENSE

Pigs use their acute senses of smell and hearing to detect approaching enemies. If threatened, they hide in vegetation and keep still until danger passes. Alternatively, a pig may charge at a predator and try to injure the animal with its tusks. The pig's broad head has thickened skin and some species, such as the warthog, have growths to protect the face.

Warthog
(*Phacochoerus aethiopicus*)

Warthogs have large growths, or warts, around the face.

FIGHTING

Male pigs come into conflict when competing for females. They use their heads and tusks as weapons to overcome their rivals. The shape of a pig's head and tusks reflects the way it fights. The wild boar tries to slash its rival's shoulders with sharp tusks, and has matted hair on its shoulders for protection. Warthogs clash head-on, and try to injure their opponent's head with wide, curving tusks.

Male wild boars fight by gashing each other's shoulders with their tusks.

Warthogs clash head-on. Their "warts" protect against the other's fearsome tusks.

Males confront each other in a territorial dispute.

Hippopotamuses open their mouths wide to display aggression.

Fighting hippopotamuses try to injure each other with their teeth.

Collared peccaries
(Tayassu tajacu)
foraging for food

PECCARIES

These slender-legged animals are found in the forests of South and Central America. Although similar to pigs, they are not members of the pig family. Peccaries are omnivores but feed mainly on roots, fruits, and seeds. They live in herds in well-defined territories, which they defend from rival peccaries. The rarest of the three peccary species is the Chacoan peccary (*Catagonus wagneri*), which was discovered in South America by scientists in 1975.

Find out more

ANIMALS: *140*
GRASSLANDS: *84*
MAMMALS: *232*
WETLANDS: *74*

GIRAFFES AND CAMELS

THE WORLD'S TALLEST ANIMAL, the giraffe roams in small herds through the savanna of Africa, taking its pick from the treetop vegetation. The okapi, the giraffe's only living relative, is a solitary forest-dweller. The camel family (camelids) is another of the 10 families that make up the order Artiodactyla. It includes the Bactrian and dromedary camels of Asia and Africa, and the smaller South American camelids – the guanaco, vicuña, and the domesticated alpaca and llama. Camels can survive in harsh deserts and for long periods without water, while the South American camelids thrive at high altitude and in dry conditions.

DRINKING

Because it has such long legs, a giraffe is unable to drink without getting into an awkward position. To reach the water, a giraffe needs to splay its front legs and bend its knees, a position that leaves it vulnerable to attack. For this reason, giraffes usually visit waterholes in small herds, so that one can keep a lookout while the others drink.

Giraffe splays its front legs to drink at a waterhole.

Thick lips protect the giraffe from thorns.

TREETOP BROWSERS

Giraffes use their height to feed on leaves, twigs, shoots, and other vegetation at the tops of trees. Trees provide food all year, unlike grasses which die out in the dry season. The giraffe uses its long tongue and grooved canine teeth to strip off leaves, while its thick lips provide protection from the sharp thorns of acacias and other trees. Female giraffes tend to feed on lower trees and shrubs at body level, while males stretch up to feed on leaves in taller trees.

Giraffes walking and galloping

CANTERING AND GALLOPING

Despite their size, giraffes move both gracefully and at speed, supported by their robust, two-toed hoofed feet. When cantering or running slowly, giraffes swing the legs on the same side of the body forward at the same time. When galloping, they bring their hind legs forward at the same time, outside the front legs. When on the move, giraffes usually travel in small groups.

GIRAFFE ANATOMY

Giraffes are easy to identify with their long, graceful necks and legs and their unmistakable patterned coat. Both sexes are born with short horns on their heads. These are used by the males when fighting, but are not shed each year. Like other mammals, the giraffe's flexible neck contains just seven vertebrae, but these bones are greatly elongated. The tail, tipped with long hairs, is used as a fly whisk to keep insects and other pests away.

A single horn may grow from the middle of the forehead, in addition to the horns on the crown.

The patterned coat helps to camouflage the giraffe.

Horns are covered with hairy skin.

Reticulated giraffe

Rothschild's giraffe

Masai giraffe

COAT PATTERN

The eight subspecies of giraffe are most easily distinguished by variations in their coat pattern. The background color may vary and the blotches range from bright chestnut to a very dark brown, with either a fuzzy or distinct outline. There is also considerable variation within each subspecies, and an individual giraffe's pattern is as unique as a human fingerprint. While coat pattern does not change with age, its colors tend to darken.

Thick hide protects giraffe from insect bites.

Calves are weaned at 15–17 months of age.

Forelegs are longer than the hind legs.

Large hooves may be used to kick out at predators.

Giraffe
(*Giraffa camelopardalis*)

OKAPI

"Discovered" only in 1901, the okapi is one of the last large mammals to become known to science. It is much smaller, and has a shorter neck and legs than its relative, the giraffe. The okapi's patterned coat provides camouflage in the dense tropical forests of central Africa. Okapis are reclusive animals and feed mainly at night using their long tongues – which can be up to 20 in (50 cm) in length – to pull leaves from the trees. The okapi has poor eyesight but depends on its senses of smell and hearing to detect predators.

Striped legs provide camouflage.

Okapi
(*Okapia johnstoni*)

The humps contain a fat store that is used up when food is scarce.

Dromedary camel
(*Camelus dromedarius*)

Dromedaries have one hump.

CAMELS

The largest of the even-toed mammals, both camel species are adapted for survival in hot, dry conditions. Their splayed, two-toed feet prevent them from sinking into soft sand. Fur keeps them warm during cold desert nights, while their body temperature can increase during the heat of the day without causing them harm. Long eyelashes keep sand from getting into the eyes, while slitlike nostrils prevent sand from blowing up the nose.

Flexible pads on feet

Bactrian camel
(*Camelus bactrianus*)

VICUÑA

The smallest members of the camel family, vicuñas live in the alpine grasslands of the Andes Mountains, where they graze on grasses. Vicuñas live in family groups consisting of a male, several females, and their young. Once prized by the Incas for their wool, vicuñas were hunted to near extinction in recent times. Numbers have now increased because of conservation programs.

Vicuñas have long legs and can run at up to 31 mph (50 kmh).

Scientific name:	*Vicugna vicugna*
Size: Head and body length up to 5 ft 4 in (1.6 m)	
Habitat: Semiarid mountain grasslands and plains 11,500–18,800 ft (3,500–5,750 m) in altitude	
Distribution: Andes Mountains in South America	
Reproduction: Single young, born after 11 months	
Diet: Grasses	

The packs are tied securely around the llamas' bodies.

Llamas (Lama glama) carrying corn in Bolivia

WATER LOSS

Camels have an extraordinary ability to go without water. When not working, they may go for months without drinking, as long as there are plants to eat, from which they can extract moisture. To reduce water loss, camels produce dry feces and little urine. Despite these adaptations, camels lose a significant amount of their body mass if without water. When water is available they quickly make up the loss, consuming up to 30 gallons (135 litres) in minutes.

A camel may lose 40 percent of its body mass after long periods without water.

A camel can drink enough water to make up huge losses in just 10 minutes.

BEASTS OF BURDEN

Llamas and camels have been domesticated as pack animals for thousands of years and have played a crucial role in enabling people to inhabit harsh areas in mountains and deserts. Llamas can carry loads of up to 220 lb (100 kg) at high altitude over long distances, while camels can travel more than 19 miles (30 km) a day in searing heat and without water. Many nomadic peoples survive in deserts by using camels to transport loads, as well as using their milk, meat, and skins. Domesticated alpacas and llamas also provide wool, milk, meat, and other products.

GUANACO

Close relatives of the domesticated llamas and alpacas, guanacos are the largest South American camelids. They need little water and are able to live on the dry grass and shrublands in the foothills of the Andes Mountains. They are found grazing and browsing on grasses and shrubs at altitudes of up to 13,900 ft (4,250 m). They live in small family groups overseen by a single male. The male bleats a warning if a predator approaches so the herd can make its escape.

Fur is thick and shaggy, and helps to keep the guanaco warm in the mountains.

Guanacos have long necks and camel-like faces, typical of all camelids.

Guanacos live in small family groups.

Guanaco
(*Lama guanicoe*)

Find out more

DEFENSE 2: *50*
DESERTS: *86*
FEEDING AND NUTRITION: *22*
MAMMALS: *232*

DEER

FINELY BUILT AND fast-moving, deer are shy animals that often spend daylight hours hidden away in forests. They belong to a group of even-toed, hoofed mammals that includes pigs, camels, cattle, and antelope. Deer graze on grasses and shrubs and roam wild in Europe, the Americas, Asia, and North Africa. Some species have been introduced into Australasia and New Guinea. There are about 40 species of deer including red deer, wapiti, moose, and reindeer. The mouse deer and musk deer are related to true deer, but belong to different families.

Female red deer
(*Cervus elaphus*)

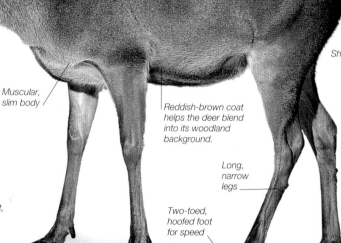

ANATOMY

Deer have slender, muscular bodies with long, thin legs ending in twin toes that help them to run quickly from predators. Male deer, called stags, have branched antlers that are shed each year. Deer are very alert animals. Their triangular ears can move to pinpoint the quietest noise. Large eyes on the sides of their head provide good, all-round vision and help deer to keep a constant lookout for potential enemies.

Short tail

Muscular, slim body

Reddish-brown coat helps the deer blend into its woodland background.

Long, narrow legs

Two-toed, hoofed foot for speed

ANTLERS

Deer are the only mammals to have antlers. They are carried on the heads of all male deer as well as female reindeer. Antlers are made of bone and are shed and regrown every year. They range in size and shape from the simple spikes of the pudu to the massive, complex branching structures found in moose and red deer. Male deer use their antlers to attract females and to fight rival males during the rutting (breeding) season.

Flattened palmate (handlike) region of antler

Tine, or point, of antler

Skull of a fallow deer

ANTLER GROWTH

A deer's antlers start as bumps on the skull that gradually extend and become more complex. At first, the antlers are quite soft and are covered by a layer of skin, called velvet, that contains the blood vessels that carry blood to the growing antlers. In late summer, the velvet dries up and falls off, revealing the bony core.

Deer speed up the removal of the velvet by rubbing their antlers against trees. In winter or early spring, at the end of the rutting season, the antlers fall off.

1. Antler buds start to grow on the skull.

2. In early summer, the antlers grow and branch rapidly.

3. In late summer, the antlers are fully grown and the velvet is shed.

ALARM SIGNAL

Grazing or browsing deer are constantly on guard. If a deer spots an approaching predator, it can warn the rest of the herd by performing a tail "flash." The rumps and short tails of most deer are white on the underside. As a deer runs away from danger, it raises its tail to give a clear white flash that can be seen from a distance.

A reindeer running from danger

SMALLEST AND LARGEST

The smallest true deer is the pudu, which lives in the foothills of the Andes in Chile and Argentina. Pudus reach only about 15 in (38 cm) at the shoulder. The largest deer is the moose or elk, as it is known in Europe. Moose are found in Alaska, Canada, Greenland, Scandinavia, and eastern Siberia and can reach 7 ft 6 in (2.3 m) in height and weigh 1,750 lb (800 kg).

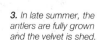
The moose can weigh up to 100 times as much as the pudu.

FEEDING

Most deer are woodland animals that feed in small herds. Their diet varies according to species and the time of year. Some graze on grasses in forest clearings, while others browse on the shoots, leaves, twigs, or bark of shrubs and trees. While feeding, a deer uses its acute senses of hearing and smell to keep a lookout for predators, and will raise its head periodically to scan the surroundings.

A herd of red deer grazing

A male moose wading into water in search of food

WATER-FEEDER
The moose lives in woodland and browses on trees and shrubs. During the warm summer months, the moose wades into lakes or streams to feed on aquatic plants such as pond weeds and water lilies. These provide it with sodium, a mineral needed for growth. A strong swimmer, the moose may even submerge itself completely in deep water to eat the stems and roots of water plants.

RUTTING

For most of the year, male deer remain separate from the females. During the fall rutting (breeding) season, males round up groups of females to protect them from rival males. All males mark their territories by scraping the soil with their hooves and antlers. A stag starts a challenge by roaring at his rival, who then roars back. The ability to roar loudly is an indication of fighting ability, although the competition between males does not necessarily lead to a fight.

1. A red deer stag bellows out his challenge.

2. The two stags walk next to each other to assess one another's strength.

3. The stags turn and lower their antlers.

4. Antlers locked, the stags push against each other.

5. The losing stag pulls away and runs off.

REINDEER

Also known as the caribou, the reindeer is the only species of deer in which both males and females have antlers. In the summer, reindeer herds consist mainly of females and young. In the fall, they are joined by the more solitary adult males who compete with rival males to gather groups of females in preparation for mating.

Female reindeer are the only female deer with antlers.

Broad hooves

Scientific name: *Rangifer tarandus*

Size: Body length 6 ft (1.8 m)

Habitat: Tundra

Distribution: Alaska, Canada, Greenland, northern Europe, Russia

Reproduction: Female produces one or two offspring; gestation period of 33–35 weeks

Diet: Summer: grasses, sedges; winter: lichens

Mouse deer (*Tragulus javanicus*)

MOUSE DEER
Mouse deer, or chevrotains, live in the forests of tropical Africa and southern Asia. There are four species, and all are solitary, nocturnal animals about the size of rabbits. Unlike true deer, they do not have horns or antlers.

MUSK DEER
These shy, solitary animals live in the hilly forests of Central and Eastern Asia. Musk deer reach no more than 23 in (60 cm) in height. They move by bounding, but can also climb nimbly on rocky crags. Males have long, pointed teeth that project beneath the lips, and they produce a brownish secretion called musk that is used in perfume production. The hunting of musk deer led to a decline in their numbers, but they are now farmed, and the musk is removed without killing them.

Musk deer (*Moschus moschiferus*)

The pronghorn is named after the male's horns that have forward-pointing prongs.

PRONGHORN
The pronghorn (*Antilocapra americana*) is a North American species that shares some of the characteristics of both deer and antelope. Pronghorns live in small herds in open grassland and scrub. They have long, slender legs and can run fast over long distances. Pronghorns have been hunted to near extinction, but are now protected and their numbers are increasing.

CATTLE AND ANTELOPE

KNOWN COLLECTIVELY AS BOVIDS, cattle and antelope form one of the 10 families of even-toed, hoofed mammals. Bovids are found in many habitats. Most species live in herds, which gives them some protection from predators. Bovids are herbivores and ruminants – they have a four-chambered stomach in which vegetation is partially digested before being regurgitated, chewed, and swallowed again. This diverse family is divided into five smaller groups: wild cattle and spiral-horned antelopes; duikers; grazing antelopes, such as oryx; gazelles and dwarf antelopes; and goats, sheep, and their relatives.

CATTLE ANATOMY

Cattle are large bovids with stocky bodies and wide skulls. Both males and females have a pair of horns that are used for defense or for fighting. Cattle have strong legs that enable them to move with speed when threatened. Like other bovids, most cattle have sharp senses of smell and vision.

Horns splay out from the side of the head.

American bison (*Bison bison*)

Shaggy hair on front of body makes the bison look larger.

Strong, slender legs end in two toes tipped with hooves.

Skull of a four-horned antelope (*Tetracerus quadricornis*)

BOVID SKULL
Bovids have long skulls with large cheek teeth that cut and grind tough vegetation before it is swallowed. Like deer, bovids have a tough pad at the front of the upper jaw rather than incisors. The lower incisors push against this pad to cut and crush vegetation. The bony cones on top of the skull form the central cores of the horns. The position of the eye sockets on the sides of the skull allows good all-around vision.

Large, ridged cheek teeth

Pad in place of upper incisor teeth

A herd of wildebeest crossing the Mara River in Kenya

ANTELOPE HORNS
Unlike deer, which lose their antlers regularly, cattle and antelope have permanent horns. The shape and size of the horns vary with different species. In most species, males use their horns when competing with rivals to assert their dominance.

The male greater kudu (Tragelaphus strepsiceros) *has long horns that corkscrew backward from its head.*

GRASSLAND MIGRATORS
Although they look similar to cattle, wildebeest (*Connochaetes gnou*) are in fact grazing antelope. They live in the savanna of southern Africa. At the start of the wet season, wildebeest migrate in vast numbers to find water and new vegetation. Many perish as they cross rivers – they may be crushed by the rest of the herd, swept away by swollen waters, or seized by waiting crocodiles.

AGILE CLIMBERS
Mountain sheep and goats are sure-footed and can climb easily on rock faces in order to find food and escape predators. Barbary sheep from the mountains of North Africa have shock-absorbing legs and rubbery hoof pads that cushion heavy landings. The mountain goat and the ibex have hollow hooves that allow them to scramble over the craggiest of rocks with ease.

Both male and female roan antelope (Hippotragus equinus) *have backward-curving horns.*

Barbary sheep (*Ammotragus lervia*)

Royal antelope
(*Neotragus pygmaeus*)

SMALLEST ANTELOPE

The royal antelope is the smallest ungulate (hoofed mammal) with horns. This rabbit-sized mammal measures just 20 in (50 cm) in length and 11 in (28 cm) in height to the shoulder. It weighs about 4 lb 6 oz (2 kg). It is a shy, secretive animal living in the tropical forests of West Africa, where it is small enough to dart away into the dense vegetation at the first sign of danger.

FEEDING

Some bovids are browsers that feed on trees and leaves above the ground, while others graze and crop vegetation at ground level. One species of gazelle, the gerenuk, has adapted to life in the hot, dry savanna with its unique ability to feed while standing on its back legs. This enables it to browse on the shoots and leaves at the top of shrubs when vegetation on the ground has dried up.

Bighorn sheep (Ovis canadensis) *banging their heads together*

BREEDING

During the breeding season, male bovids compete to determine which of them will mate with the females in the herd. The competition may be a fight, or it may take the form of ritualized movements that signal to a male whether his rival is stronger. If fighting does take place, males lock horns and push against each other until one of them gives in. Some species, such as bighorn sheep, run at each other head-on. The impact is absorbed by their thickened skulls.

Gerenuk (*Litocranius walleri*)

ASIAN WATER BUFFALO

Most Asian water buffalo have been domesticated and are used to pull plows in wet paddy fields. However, some herds of wild water buffalo still roam the swampy grasslands of Borneo, Malaysia, Thailand, and India. They graze mainly at night, drink water each morning and evening, and rest in the shade during the heat of the day. The buffalo's ferocity generally protects it from tigers and other predators.

Scientific name: *Bubalus arnee*

Size: Body length of up to 9 ft (2.8 m)

Habitat: Swampy grasslands

Distribution: Borneo, Malaysia, Thailand, and India

Reproduction: Female produces a single calf; gestation period is 47 weeks

Diet: Mainly grasses and sedges; needs to drink daily

GIVING BIRTH

Female bovids give birth to large young that are typically able to struggle to their feet and move with the herd shortly after birth. Newborn bovids are in danger of attack by predators, which are always ready to pick off vulnerable members of the herd. The mother and other members of the herd cannot always drive away attackers, so the ability to run within the herd helps the newborn's chances of survival.

Blue wildebeest giving birth

The young wildebeest staggers to its feet 15 minutes after birth.

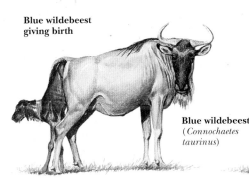
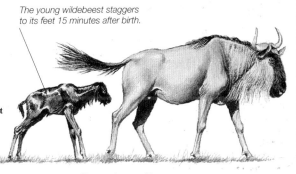

Blue wildebeest (*Connochaetes taurinus*)

A female wildebeest gives birth standing up. She licks her offspring to remove the birth membranes.

The newborn calf is soon ready to follow its mother.

Auroch   *Jersey cow*

FAST MOVERS

Bovids are preyed upon by animals such as large cats, wild dogs, and hyenas. Living in a herd provides some protection from attack. Fast-moving bovids, such as antelope and gazelles, also depend on speed to escape their enemies. When threatened, gazelles may "stot" or "pronk." This involves making sudden vertical leaps while running to show a predator that the gazelle is very fit and likely to escape.

Springbok stotting in the Kalahari Desert, Africa

DOMESTICATION

Wild cattle, sheep, and goats were domesticated thousands of years ago to provide products such as meat, milk, wool, and leather. Modern cattle breeds are descended from the wild auroch, which used to roam the plains of Europe and Asia. Sheep were domesticated about 10,000 years ago in the Near East, and goats about 9,000 years ago in southwestern Asia.

Find out more

PRIMATES

THE PRIMATE FAMILY IS of special interest to scientists because it includes humans. There are about 180 primate species, most of which live in forests in warm parts of the world. Most primates are agile climbers, with long limbs and flexible fingers and toes. They also have wide, forward-facing eyes and larger brains than other mammals of the same size. Scientists divide the primates into two main groups – anthropoids, which include monkeys and apes, and prosimians, which include lemurs, lorises, and bushbabies. Prosimians tend to be smaller than anthropoids, and many are nocturnal.

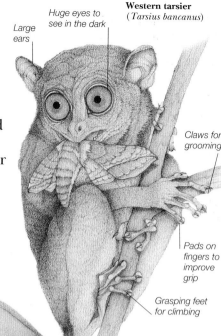

Western tarsier
(*Tarsius bancanus*)

Large ears

Huge eyes to see in the dark

Claws for grooming

Pads on fingers to improve grip

Grasping feet for climbing

TARSIERS
Tarsiers live in forests on the islands of Southeast Asia. They hunt at night, leaping through the trees and grabbing insects in their hands. In addition to eating insects, some tarsiers also hunt lizards, birds, scorpions, and snakes. The prey is usually eaten head first. Tarsiers are unusual because they can turn their heads around to see backward. There are four tarsier species. Some scientists classify them as anthropoids, but others place them in a group of their own.

Common chimpanzee
(*Pan troglodytes*)

ANTHROPOIDS
Sometimes called the "advanced primates," this group includes apes, monkeys, marmosets, and tamarins, as well as humans. Anthropoids are adaptable, intelligent animals that often live in social groups. Most are good climbers, but some live mainly on the ground. Chimpanzees are anthropoids, and are also our nearest relatives.

Long tail for balance when leaping

AMAZING BRAINS
Primates have much larger brains relative to their body size than most other animals. The "thinking" part of the brain – the cerebrum – is especially large and complex. Having a large brain makes primates fast learners, and allows them to communicate with each other in complex ways. A considerable part of a primate's brain deals with vision, and with making precise movements with the hands and fingers.

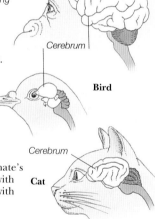

Gorilla

Cerebrum

Bird

Cerebrum

Cat

Opposable toe and thumb for gripping

Long toe and thumb for grasping tree trunks

Claws for clinging

Thin middle finger for probing wood

Chimpanzee foot | Chimpanzee hand

Indri foot | Indri hand

Aye-aye foot | Aye-aye hand

GETTING A GRIP
Compared to other mammals, primates have very flexible fingers and toes. Their exact shape varies according to their way of life. A chimp has quite short fingers and toes, but it can press its thumb against its fingers to achieve a very precise grip. An indri's hands and feet are shaped for gripping branches and tree trunks, while an aye-aye's extraordinary hands have evolved to help it pry insects out of bark.

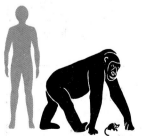

LARGEST AND SMALLEST
Primates vary enormously in size. The largest is the male gorilla (*Gorilla gorilla*), which can weigh up to 385 lb (175 kg) in the wild, and even more in captivity. The smallest are western mouse lemurs (*Microcebus* spp.). They measure about 7.5 in (19 cm) from the nose to the tip of the tail, and weigh about 1.2 oz (35 g). By comparison, an average American man weighs about 154 lb (70 kg).

Human | Gorilla | Mouse lemur

Black lemur (Lemur macaco) feeding

FEEDING
Some primates live almost entirely on leaves, but most eat a wide variety of other foods. The black lemur, for example, feeds on leaves as a large part of its diet, but also eats eggs, small birds, and insects, as well as flowers and fruit. Monkeys are often untidy eaters. When they feed on fruit high up in the treetops, they usually drop half-eaten scraps onto the ground below, and this attracts other animals, such as deer and wild pigs.

LEMURS

Lemurs live only on the island of Madagascar, off the east coast of Africa. There have never been apes or monkeys here, and instead lemurs have evolved in their place. The largest species of lemur are active by day. They look similar to monkeys, but have sharply pointed muzzles and are not as good as monkeys at using their hands. The smallest lemurs look more like rodents than primates and are active at night.

AFRICA

Madagascar

Ring-tailed lemur
(*Lemur catta*)

Sharply pointed muzzle

Scent gland

AYE-AYE

Active at night, the aye-aye is a secretive and endangered animal that lives in the forests of Madagascar. It uses its long, thin middle finger for extracting grubs from branches and for grooming its fur. This primate's strange appearance and eerie calls have led to its persecution by local people, who believe that it brings bad luck.

Scientific name: *Daubentonia madagascariensis*

Size: Up to 3 ft 3 in (1 m) long, including tail

Habitat: Tropical rainforest, bamboo thickets, and mangrove forest

Distribution: Isolated areas of Madagascar

Reproduction: Single offspring born in October or November; raised in a stick nest until it can accompany its mother into the open

Diet: Fruit, insects, leaves, shoots, birds' eggs, and young coconuts

LIFE ON THE GROUND

The ring-tailed lemur spends a lot of time on the ground compared to other lemurs. It lives in rocky scrubland, and its leathery hands and feet give it a good grip when running over boulders. These lemurs usually hold their long, striped tails upright, which helps them keep in contact as they forage for food. Males have scent glands on the inside of their arms and often rub scent onto their tails to warn off rivals.

LEAPING IN THE DARK

Bush babies are nocturnal creatures that live in the forests of Africa. They have huge eyes for night vision, large ears that can fold up, and long hind legs for leaping. A bush baby's call sounds rather like a baby crying. The bush baby is a skilled jumper that has no difficulty leaping in the dark. Its long, silky tail helps it balance as it moves from branch to branch.

The back legs swing forward, ready to land.

Forward-facing eyes help it judge distance.

The bush baby grabs a branch with its hands and feet.

The bush baby takes off with a kick from its powerful back legs.

Bushbaby
(*Galago* sp.)

CAUTIOUS MOVER

The slow loris is a methodical and unhurried climber found in the rainforests of Southeast Asia. Like the bush baby, this animal comes out to feed after dark. The loris's hands and feet give it a good, firm grip on tree branches, and it often climbs upside down as it searches for food. Completely adapted to a life among the trees, lorises very rarely come down to the ground.

A slow loris (Nycticebus coucang) *climbing*

Find out more
APES: *284*
COMMUNICATION: *44*
MONKEYS: *282*
SOCIAL ANIMALS: *54*

MONKEYS

MONKEYS BELONG TO the primates, the group of mammals that also includes lemurs, apes, and humans. They are intelligent, very social animals that live mostly in close groups, although some live alone. Monkeys feed mainly on fruit and other vegetation, but also on meat. There are two main types of monkeys. New World monkeys, which include marmosets and howlers, have widely spaced nostrils that face to the side, and live in the tropical forests of Central and South America. Old World monkeys, which include baboons, macaques, and colobus, have nostrils that are close together and point downward. They are found in a range of habitats in Africa and Asia.

MARMOSETS

Marmosets are small, squirrel-like monkeys that live in the tropical forests of South America. They have soft, dense coats, long tails, and often have prominent manes, crests, or tufts. Marmosets are active in the day, feeding on fruit, flowers, insects, and tree sap. They live in small family groups, made up of adults and their offspring. Female marmosets give birth to up to three young, and males help with the care of infants.

Tufted-ear marmoset (*Callithrix jacchus*)

Ear tufts of long, white hair

The marmoset feeds on an insect.

Capuchin monkey (*Cebus* sp.)

Forward-facing eyes provide excellent vision.

Short snout with sideways-pointing nostrils

ANATOMY

Monkeys are active, agile animals with long limbs and muscular bodies. Most monkeys have long tails that help them to balance when clambering among the branches. Some South American species have prehensile (grasping) tails that can wrap around a branch and act as an extra limb. Monkeys often have short-snouted, hairless faces with forward-facing eyes. Their strong flexible hands and feet are perfect for gripping branches. Monkeys also use their hands for grooming, holding food, and catching insect prey as it flies past.

Lithe, athletic body with long limbs

Grasping hands and feet for climbing trees and holding food

Prehensile tail is used to grip the branch.

Tail and arms outstretched, a red colobus monkey (Piliocolobus badius) leaps from tree to tree.

LEAPING
Tree-dwelling monkeys are able to move quickly and with great agility through the forest canopy, running along the branches and leaping from tree to tree. A monkey uses its strong back legs to propel itself into the air, helped by the natural flexibility of the tree branches. Its long tail acts as a rudder, enabling it to balance and steer in the air. As it lands, the monkey grips the twigs and branches with its long, grasping fingers and toes.

WALKING ON ALL FOURS
All South American monkeys are tree-dwellers, but some African and Asian species, such as baboons and macaques, spend much of their time on the ground. Ground-dwelling monkeys walk on all fours, placing their hands and feet flat on the ground. They can also run at high speed to escape predators. Long tails would get in the way on the ground; these monkeys usually have short or stumpy tails.

Celebes ape (*Macaca nigra*)

Infant monkeys can cling on tightly to their parents.

SOCIAL LIFE

Monkeys live in groups, called troops. Depending on the species, the troops range in size from one male and female with their young, to several hundred monkeys. Living in a group helps monkeys guard their feeding grounds and protect their young, and provides better defense against predators. Monkeys are intelligent animals, and social interactions within a group are complex. Each monkey has a social rank that marks it as more or less powerful than other monkeys.

Baboons can live in large groups of up to 750 animals.

Grivet monkeys (Cercopithecus aethiops) grooming each other

GROOMING

Monkeys scratch and pick their fur with their nails to comb and clean it, and to remove any irritating skin parasites. Mutual grooming – two monkeys grooming each other's fur – forms an important part of social life for all monkey species. The friendly contact involved in grooming helps to reduce tensions between members of a social group and to reinforce the bonds between them.

COMMON WOOLLY MONKEY

There are two species of woolly monkeys which are thus named because of their short, woolly fur. They spend most of their lives in tropical forests, but often descend to the ground. Woolly monkeys live in groups of four or more individuals. During the day, they move from tree to tree in search of new food sources.

Scientific name: *Lagothrix lagotricha*

Size: Head and body length 20–28 in (51–70 cm); tail length 24–28 in (60–70 cm)

Habitat: Tropical forest

Distribution: South America from Colombia to Bolivia

Reproduction: Females produce only one offspring at a time

Diet: Fruit, seeds, and some insects

This monkey can hang from a branch using its prehensile tail when feeding.

ENTWINED TAILS

Titi monkeys are tree-dwellers that live in the tropical forests of South America. The 13 species of titi monkeys (*Callicebus* sp.) live in small family groups consisting of two adults and their offspring. Like other monkeys, titis communicate with each other using both sounds and body language. When titi monkeys rest together on a branch, they often link their long tails. This entwining helps to strengthen family ties and friendships.

Titi monkeys with their tails entwined

Red howler (*Alouatta seniculus*)

COMMUNICATION

Communication is of vital importance within a troop. It holds the group together, and is used to give warning of approaching predators and to warn off rival troops. Monkeys communicate using visual signals, such as facial expressions and gestures. They also use vocalization (calling), touch and grooming, and scent. Troops of howlers signal their presence to other troops with howls that can be heard several miles away.

JAPANESE MACAQUES

The 16 species of macaque, most of which are found in Asia, are heavily built and spend a lot of time on the ground as well as in trees. While most monkeys live in tropical areas, the Japanese macaque with its thick, shaggy, gray coat is adapted for survival in cold conditions. In the winter, Japanese macaques living in the mountains of northern Japan take dips in hot volcanic springs to keep warm.

Japanese macaques (Macaca fuscata) bathing in hot volcanic springs

Howlers are among the loudest animals on Earth. They howl in chorus to warn other troops to keep their distance.

Find out more	
APES:	*284*
COMMUNICATION:	*44*
PRIMATES:	*280*
SOCIAL ANIMALS:	*54*

APES

APES ARE LARGE, INTELLIGENT primates that live mainly in forests and feed predominantly on vegetation. There are two families of apes. The gibbons, or lesser apes, are small, slender apes that move rapidly through the trees of the Southeast Asian forests. The great apes include the Asian orangutan, and the African gorilla, common chimpanzee, and pygmy chimpanzee, as well as humans. The great apes are capable of using tools and solving problems. Most ape species are threatened by human persecution and habitat destruction.

GIBBONS

The nine species of gibbons are found in the tropical rainforests of Southeast Asia and Indonesia. Gibbons spend their life in the trees, feeding on fruit and shoots. Their very long arms, fingers, and toes, and mobile shoulder and wrist joints, enable them to swing rapidly, hand over hand, through the forest canopy. Gibbons live in small family groups. The parents defend a territory by calling loudly at dawn and dusk to ward off intruders.

Gibbon hangs from one hand and reaches for the next branch with the other hand.

ANATOMY

Like other primates, apes have forward-facing eyes and excellent eyesight. Their hands and feet have thumbs and toes adapted for gripping, and nails rather than claws. But they differ by having no tail, forelimbs longer than hindlimbs, and very mobile wrists and shoulders. Apes also have larger, more complex brains. While all apes can sit or stand upright, some that live mainly on the ground, such as chimpanzees and gorillas, generally walk on all fours with their weight on their knuckles.

Skull contains a large, complex brain.

Common chimpanzee
(*Pan troglodytes*)

Forelimbs are longer than hind limbs.

Apes lack a tail.

Feet are placed flat on the ground during walking.

Chimp leans on knuckles of hand during walking.

ORANGUTANS

Meaning "man of the forest," orangutans (*Pongo pygmaeus*) are large, tree-dwelling, red-haired apes that live in the forests of Borneo and Sumatra. They lead solitary lives, moving slowly and deliberately from branch to branch in search of fruits such as rambutans and durians. Male orangutans are much larger than females, and have big cheek flaps which make them look more impressive.

An orangutan's long arms can span 7 ft (2.1 m).

GORILLAS

The largest and most powerful of the apes, gorillas live in the mountain and lowland forests of central Africa. Gorillas are massively built with prominent brow ridges, a flattened nose, and a covering of black hair. Mature males, which are much larger than females, are called silverbacks because their hair turns silvery-gray with age. Gorillas live in small groups, which consist of a dominant silverback male, females, offspring, and subordinate males. They move within large territories and feed on leaves, shoots, and fruit.

Prominent brow

Male silverback gorilla (Gorilla gorilla) rests on its knuckles

A young chimpanzee (Pan troglodytes) extracts termites from their nest using a twig as a tool.

TOOLMAKERS

Chimpanzees use their high intelligence and natural inquisitiveness to make and use tools. In order to catch termites to eat, a chimp will take a twig, pull off its leaves, and carefully push the twig into the termites' nest. The chimp then pulls out the twig laden with termites, which it removes with its lips. Chimps also use chewed-up leaves to soak up drinking water, and stones to crack open nuts.

Body twists around to allow free hand to grab branch.

Long arms allow far reach and fast swing

Siamang gibbon
(*Hylobates syndactylus*)

Grasping feet reach for branch as gibbon comes to a halt.

PYGMY CHIMPANZEE

Despite their name, pygmy chimpanzees, or bonobos, are about the same size as common chimpanzees although they have a smaller head and slender body. Bonobos are forest dwellers that spend most of their time in the trees. Bonobos live in close-knit communities in which females play a dominant role.

Body is lighter in build than the common chimpanzee.

Scientific name:	*Pan paniscus*
Size:	Head and body length 23–33 in (70–83 cm)
Habitat:	Tropical rainforest
Distribution:	Central Africa: Congo (Zaire)
Reproduction:	Females have single young; offspring stays with mother for 7–9 years
Diet:	Vegetation, and rarely, small animals

SOCIAL GROUPS

While orangutans usually lead a solitary life, most apes live in social groups. Chimpanzee communities can number more than 60 individuals that defend territories against rival groups. Living in a social group provides greater security against attack, enables apes to defend feeding sites, and helps protect the young. Apes constantly communicate with each other using sounds, body language, and facial expressions; grooming helps strengthen bonds.

Gorillas constantly interact within their social group.

Male chimpanzee stands on two legs and "swaggers."

He begins to charge, beating his chest.

He stops, slaps the ground and charges again.

AGGRESSION

In chimpanzee communities males tolerate each other and will form temporary alliances, but are sometimes aggressive toward each other. Aggressive behavior, such as charging, often serves to establish the position of both males in the group hierarchy: a chimp that "submits" in the face of aggressive behavior is subordinate to the other, dominant male. Once each male's position has been established, tension is reduced and the males groom each other.

GROWING UP

Apes, like humans, put a lot of effort into caring for their young. Newborn apes are born small and weak. They cling to their mother for warmth and protection, and are carried around by her. Young apes take a long time to grow up and maternal protection can last for several years. Chimpanzees stay with their mothers until they reach full maturity at about 13 years of age. The older offspring help to look after their younger siblings.

A baby white-handed gibbon (Hylobates lar) clings to its mother's fur for warmth and protection.

PLAY

Play is vitally important for young apes to learn and to practice adult skills and behavior patterns. As they chase each other, wrestle, climb trees, swing from branches, and manipulate objects, young apes exercise their muscles and rehearse essential survival skills. Play also enables young apes to learn the "rules" of their group and find their place within it.

Play helps young apes to find their place in the group.

Find out more

ANIMALS IN DANGER: *100*
MAMMALS: *232*
MONKEYS: *282*
PRIMATES: *280*

CLASSIFICATION 1

CLASSIFICATION IS A WAY OF identifying and grouping living things together. These two pages cover four of the kingdoms of living things: monerans, protists, fungi, and plants. The fifth kingdom, which contains animals, is shown on pages 288–89. In classification, as in all other branches of science, new discoveries are being made all the time and ideas are constantly changed and updated. As a result, the details of classification often change. The system shown here, based on five kingdoms, is widely accepted by most biologists, but is not the only one in use today. Some experts, for example, divide monerans into two separate kingdoms, each containing different kinds of bacteria.

Classification groups

The charts on these two pages are color-coded to indicate different kinds of classification groups. The largest groups shown are kingdoms. These are divided into smaller groups: phylum or division, class, order, and family. A division, which is the equivalent of a phylum, is used in plant classification.

	Kingdom
	Phylum/Division
	Class
	Order
	Family

FIVE KINGDOMS OF LIVING THINGS

Living things are divided into overall groups, called kingdoms, based on the different ways they work. At one time naturalists divided the entire living world into just two kingdoms: plants and animals. Scientific research later showed that this system was too simple, and more kingdoms were devised. Today biologists divide the living world into at least five kingdoms, and sometimes more.

MONERANS
This kingdom contains bacteria – microscopic organisms that have a simple, single cell. Most monerans get their energy from substances around them. Some, such as cyanobacteria, carry out photosynthesis to gather their energy from sunlight.

PROTISTS
The protist kingdom contains a variety of complex but mainly single-celled organisms. Some eat food, while others carry out photosynthesis. Multicellular algae, particularly seaweeds, are sometimes treated as plants.

FUNGI
This kingdom contains organisms that absorb food and that reproduce by making spores. Many are microscopic, but some make their spores in large fruiting bodies such as mushrooms and toadstools.

PLANTS
Plants have many cells and most carry out photosynthesis. Simple plants have no specialized roots or water-carrying tissue, and reproduce by making spores. More advanced plants have roots and stems, and reproduce by making seeds.

ANIMALS
The animal kingdom probably contains more species than all the other kingdoms put together. All members of this kingdom have bodies made of many cells, and they live by eating food. Unlike fungi, most animals ingest or swallow their food instead of digesting it externally. Compared to other forms of multicellular life, animals are often highly mobile.

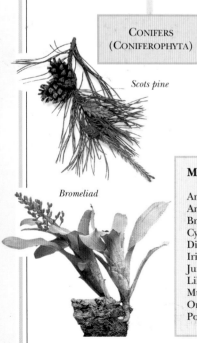

Scots pine

Bromeliad

CONIFERS (CONIFEROPHYTA)	CYCADS (CYCADOPHYTA)	FLOWERING PLANTS (ANTHOPHYTA)	HORSETAILS (SPHENOPHYTA)	FERNS (PTEROPHYTA)

MONOCOTYLEDONS (MONOCOTYLEDONEAE)

DICOTYLEDONS (DICOTYLEDONEAE)

Fern

Major families include

Amaryllidaceae (e.g., daffodil)
Arecaceae (palms)
Bromeliaceae (bromeliads)
Cyperaceae (e.g., sedges)
Dioscoreaceae (e.g., yams)
Iridaceae (e.g., iris, crocus)
Juncaceae (rushes)
Liliaceae (e.g., lily, tulip)
Musaceae (e.g., banana)
Orchidaceae (orchids)
Poaceae (grasses)

Major families include

Apiaceae (e.g., carrot)
Asteraceae (e.g., daisy)
Brassicaceae (e.g., cabbage)
Cucurbitaceae (e.g., melon, cucumber)
Fabaceae (e.g., pea)
Lamiaceae (e.g., mint)
Magnoliaceae (e.g., magnolia, tulip tree)
Ranunculaceae (e.g., buttercup)
Rosaceae (e.g., apple, rose)
Rubiaceae (e.g., coffee)
Solanaceae (e.g., potato, tomato)

Red seaweed

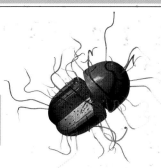
Model of a bacterium

MONERANS
(MONERA)

ARCHAEBACTERIA
(ARCHAEBACTERIA)

TYPICAL BACTERIA
(EUBACTERIA)

PROTISTS
(PROTISTA)

FUNGAL PROTISTS
(OOMYCOTA &
CHYTRIDOMYCOTA)

FLAGELLATES
(ZOOMASTIGINA &
PHYTOMASTIGINA)

AMOEBAE
(RHIZOPODA)

FORAMINIFERANS
(FORAMINIFERA)

HELIOZOANS
(HELIOZOA)

CILIATES
(CILIOPHORA)

APICOMPLEXANS
(APICOMPLEXA)

CNIDOSPORIDIANS
(CNIDOSPORIDIA)

GOLDEN ALGAE
(CHRYSOPHYTA)

EUGLENOID ALGAE
(EUGLENOPHYTA)

DIATOMS
(BACILLARIOPHYTA)

DINOFLAGELLATES
(DINOPHYTA)

RED ALGAE
(RHODOPHYTA)

BROWN ALGAE
(PHAEOPHYTA)

GREEN ALGAE
(CHLOROPHYTA)

Bread mold

Fly amanita

FUNGI
(FUNGI)

MOLDS
(ZYGOMYCOTA)

SAC FUNGI
(ASCOMYCOTA)

FUNGI IMPERFECTI
(DEUTEROMYCOTA)

CLUB FUNGI
(BASIDIOMYCOTA)

*Leaves from
maidenhair tree*

Welwitschia

PLANTS
(PLANTAE)

GINKGO
(GINKGOPHYTA)

CLUB MOSSES
(LYCOPHYTA)

BRYOPHYTES
(BRYOPHYTA)

WHISK FERNS
(PSILOPHYTA)

WELWITSCHIA,
EPHEDRA, GNETUM

LIVERWORTS
(HEPATICAE)

HORNWORTS
(ANTHOCEROTAE)

MOSSES
(MUSCI)

Liverwort

Moss

CLASSIFICATION 2

THE CHART ON THESE TWO pages shows how animals are classified by biologists. It includes all the major phyla, or animal groups, together with some of the classes and orders that they contain. The animal kingdom is by far the most diverse in the living world and scientists have identified only a small proportion of the animals that exist. The majority of vertebrates – particularly those that live on land – have been described and catalogued, but huge numbers of invertebrates have yet to be discovered and studied.

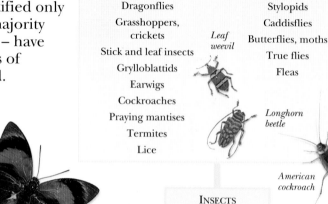

Springtails
Proturans
Diplurans
Silverfish
Mayflies
Stoneflies
Webspinners
Dragonflies
Grasshoppers, crickets
Stick and leaf insects
Grylloblattids
Earwigs
Cockroaches
Praying mantises
Termites
Lice

Thrips
Zorapterans
Bugs
Beetles
Ants, bees, wasps
Lacewings, ant lions
Scorpionflies
Stylopids
Caddisflies
Butterflies, moths
True flies
Fleas

Common wasp

House fly

Leaf weevil

Longhorn beetle

American cockroach

INSECTS
(INSECTA)

Classification groups

The charts on these two pages are color-coded to indicate different kinds of classification groups. The largest groups shown are kingdoms, while the smallest are orders. A subphylum is part of a phylum.

Kingdom
Phylum
Subphylum
Class
Order

ANIMALS (ANIMALIA)

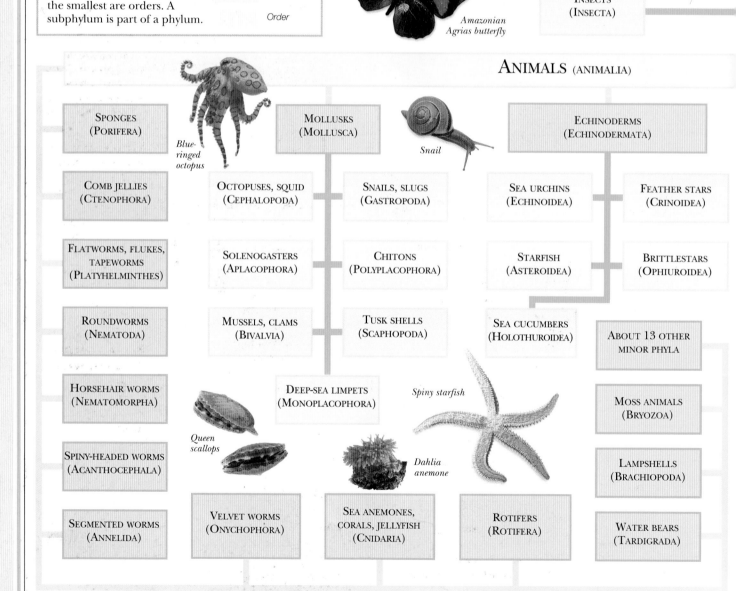

Amazonian Agrias butterfly

SPONGES
(PORIFERA)

Blue-ringed octopus

MOLLUSKS
(MOLLUSCA)

Snail

ECHINODERMS
(ECHINODERMATA)

COMB JELLIES
(CTENOPHORA)

OCTOPUSES, SQUID
(CEPHALOPODA)

SNAILS, SLUGS
(GASTROPODA)

SEA URCHINS
(ECHINOIDEA)

FEATHER STARS
(CRINOIDEA)

FLATWORMS, FLUKES, TAPEWORMS
(PLATYHELMINTHES)

SOLENOGASTERS
(APLACOPHORA)

CHITONS
(POLYPLACOPHORA)

STARFISH
(ASTEROIDEA)

BRITTLESTARS
(OPHIUROIDEA)

ROUNDWORMS
(NEMATODA)

MUSSELS, CLAMS
(BIVALVIA)

TUSK SHELLS
(SCAPHOPODA)

SEA CUCUMBERS
(HOLOTHUROIDEA)

ABOUT 13 OTHER MINOR PHYLA

HORSEHAIR WORMS
(NEMATOMORPHA)

DEEP-SEA LIMPETS
(MONOPLACOPHORA)

Spiny starfish

MOSS ANIMALS
(BRYOZOA)

SPINY-HEADED WORMS
(ACANTHOCEPHALA)

Queen scallops

Dahlia anemone

LAMPSHELLS
(BRACHIOPODA)

SEGMENTED WORMS
(ANNELIDA)

VELVET WORMS
(ONYCHOPHORA)

SEA ANEMONES, CORALS, JELLYFISH
(CNIDARIA)

ROTIFERS
(ROTIFERA)

WATER BEARS
(TARDIGRADA)

House spider

Verreaux's eagle

HORSESHOE CRABS
(MEROSTOMATA)

SAND SHRIMPS
(CEPHALOCARIDA)

MYSTACOCARIDANS
(MYSTACOCARIDA)

Whip spiders
Whip scorpions
Scorpions
Ricinuleids
Micro-whip scorpions
Camel spiders
Pseudoscorpions
Harvestmen
Mites and ticks
Spiders

SEA SPIDERS
(PYCNOGONIDA)

SPINY SAND
SHRIMPS
(BRANCHIURA)

CRABS, LOBSTERS,
SHRIMPS
(MALACOSTRACA)

Ostriches
Rheas
Cassowaries, emus
Kiwis
Tinamous
Penguins
Loons
Albatrosses, petrels,
shearwaters, fulmars

CENTIPEDES
(CHILOPODA)

BARNACLES
(CIRRIPEDIA)

SEED SHRIMPS
(OSTRACODA)

Gouldian finch

ARACHNIDS
(ARACHNIDA)

MILLIPEDES
(DIPLOPODA)

BRANCHIOPODS
(BRANCHIOPODA)

COPEPODS
(COPEPODA)

ARTHROPODS
(ARTHROPODA)

CRUSTACEANS
(CRUSTACEA)

Armored millipede

Reef hermit crab

Grebes
Pelicans, gannets,
cormorants, anhingas,
frigate birds
Herons, storks, ibises,
spoonbills, flamingos
Ducks, geese, swans
Eagles, hawks, vultures
Pheasants, partridges,
grouse, turkeys
Cranes, rails, coots,
bustards
Waders, terns,
gulls, auks
Sandgrouse
Pigeons, doves
Parrots
Turacos, cuckoos,
roadrunners
Owls
Frogmouths, nightjars
Swifts, hummingbirds
Trogons, quetzals
Kingfishers, bee-eaters,
rollers, hornbills
Woodpeckers, barbets,
honeyguides, puffbirds,
toucans
Perching birds

BIRDS
(AVES)

European rabbit

CHORDATES
(CHORDATA)

MAMMALS
(MAMMALIA)

Frog

Red kangaroo

AMPHIBIANS
(AMPHIBIA)

Frogs, toads
Newts, salamanders
Caecilians

Monotremes (egg-laying mammals)
Marsupials (pouched mammals)
Insectivores
Elephant shrews
Colugos
Bats
Tree shrews

Salamander

Primates
Sloths, anteaters, armadillos
Pangolins
Hares, rabbits, pikas
Rodents
Whales and dolphins
Carnivores
Seals, sealions, walruses
Aardvarks
Elephants
Hyraxes
Manatees and dugongs
Odd-toed hoofed mammals
Even-toed hoofed mammals

REPTILES
(REPTILIA)

Lizards and snakes
Turtles, terrapins, tortoises
Crocodilians
Tuatara

JAWLESS FISH
(AGNATHA)

Milk snake

CARTILAGINOUS FISH
(CHONDROICHTHYES)

Sharks, skates,
rays

Blacktip reef shark

More than 20 orders including:

Eels
Herrings, anchovies
Salmon, trout
Characins, carps
Catfish
Flying fish, garfish
Perches, cichlids, gobies, wrasses

BONY FISH
(OSTEICHTHYES)

European carp

SEA SQUIRTS
(ASCIDIACEA)

Tiger

Scarlet ibis

GLOSSARY

Abdomen: the part of an animal's body that contains digestive and reproductive organs. An insect's abdomen is at the rear of its body.

Adaptation: a special feature of a living thing that makes it better suited to its particular way of life.

Advanced: possessing characteristics that appeared later in evolution.

Aerobic respiration: a chemical process that uses oxygen to release energy from food.

Algae: simple, plantlike organisms that make their food by photosynthesis.

Amnion: a membrane that surrounds the developing embryos of reptiles, birds, and mammals.

Amphibian: a cold-blooded vertebrate that lives partly in water and partly on land.

Anaerobic respiration: a chemical process that releases energy from food without the need for oxygen.

Angiosperm (flowering plant): a plant that reproduces by bearing flowers, fruits, and seeds.

Animal: one of the five kingdoms of nature, composed of multicellular living things that live by taking in food.

Antennae (feelers): long sensory organs on an arthropod's head. They feel and "taste" objects in addition to sensing vibrations and smells.

Anther: the part of a flower that produces pollen (male sex cells).

Arachnid: an invertebrate with four pairs of legs.

Arthropod: an invertebrate with a jointed body case, such as an insect or spider.

Asexual reproduction: production of offspring by a single parent.

Autotroph: a living thing that makes its own food, such as a plant.

Backbone (spine): a flexible chain of bones running from the head to the tail of a vertebrate.

Bacteria: a group of microscopic, single-celled organisms. Bacteria are the most abundant living things on Earth.

Baleen plates: the fringed plates that hang from the roof of the mouth of the largest types of whales. Baleen plates filter small animals from seawater.

Barbel: a long, thin feeler near the mouth of certain fish. Catfish use barbels to help find food.

Barbs: the thin strands that make up a bird's feather. Barbs are held together by tiny hooklike structures called barbules.

Bark: the tough outer layers of a tree or shrub.

Binocular vision: a kind of vision that uses two eyes facing forward to produce a three-dimensional image.

Bioluminescence: production of light by a living thing.

Biosphere: all the parts of the Earth that make up the living world, including the land, ocean, and air.

Bivalve: a mollusk with a shell made of two parts, or valves, such as an oyster or mussel.

Blood: a complex liquid that carries substances around an animal's body.

Blowhole: the nostrils of a whale or dolphin, located on the top of its head.

Breeding: producing offspring by mating. In birds and mammals, breeding also involves raising the young.

Browse: to feed by continual nibbling on twigs, leaves, and other vegetation.

Bud: an undeveloped shoot on a plant.

Bulb: a shortened underground plant stem that stores food.

Camouflage: the way animals hide by blending in with their surroundings. Stick insects, for example, are camouflaged as twigs.

Canine: a pointed tooth that grips and pierces.

Canopy: the top layer of branches in a forest.

Carapace: the hard shield that covers the body of crabs, lobsters, and shrimp. The top part of a turtle's shell is also called a carapace.

Carnivore: a mammal with specially shaped teeth that feeds mainly on meat. Carnivore can also mean any meat-eating predator.

Carpel: a female reproductive organ in a flower.

Carrion: dead or rotten animal flesh. Carrion is eaten by scavengers.

Cartilage (gristle): a tough, flexible tissue found in the skeleton of vertebrates. In cartilaginous fish the skeleton is made entirely of cartilage instead of bone.

Caterpillar: the wingless larva (immature form) of a butterfly or moth.

Cell: a tiny unit of living matter. Cells are the basic units of all living things, other from viruses.

Cephalopod: a mollusk with a large head and a ring of tentacles, such as an octopus or squid.

Chlorophyll: the green chemical that gives most plants their color. It traps the sunlight energy that plants use to make food.

Chloroplast: a tiny structure inside a plant cell that contains the green chemical chlorophyll.

Chrysalis: the resting stage in the life cycle of a moth or butterfly. A caterpillar becomes a chrysalis before turning into an adult.

Cilia: tiny, hairlike structures on the surface of a cell. Cilia can beat to make a cell move or to move things nearby.

Classification: a way of identifying and grouping living things.

Cloven: hooves divided into two parts in certain plant-eating mammals, such as pigs and deer.

Cnidarian: an aquatic animal with stinging cells and a digestive cavity that has only one opening, such as a jellyfish.

Cocoon: a hard case made of silk that protects certain insects as they change from larvae into adults.

Colony: a number of related living things that live closely together.

Compound eyes: eyes made up of many small units, such as the eyes of insects.

Cone: a conifer's reproductive structure. Male and female cones usually grow separately.

Conifer: a plant that reproduces by making cones. Most conifers are evergreen trees or shrubs.

Coral: a small sea animal that catches food with stinging tentacles. Many corals live in large colonies on coral reefs.

Cotyledon: a small leaf inside a seed.

Courtship: behavior that forms a bond between a male and a female before mating.

Crop: a pouch in a bird's digestive system where swallowed food is stored.

Crustacean: an invertebrate with jointed legs and two pairs of antennae, such as a crab or woodlouse.

Cyanobacteria: a group of bacteria that make their food by photosynthesis.

Deciduous: plants that shed their leaves during some part of the year.

Decomposer: a living thing that obtains food by breaking down the remains of other living things. Many fungi are decomposers.

Deforestation: removal of forests by felling or burning.

Development: the formation of a more complex body as a living thing matures.

Dicot: a flowering plant that has two cotyledons (seed leaves). Dicots make up the larger group of flowering plants. Most deciduous trees are dicots.

Digestion: the process of breaking down food into chemicals that cells can absorb. In most animals, digestion takes place in a tube running through the body.

Diurnal: active during the day but inactive at night.

DNA (deoxyribonucleic acid): the chemical that carries all of the genetic information. It is passed from one generation to the next when living things reproduce, whether sexually or asexually.

Domestic: animals and plants kept by humans for food or other uses.

Drag: the resistance to motion that occurs when an animal travels through air or water.

Echinoderm: a sea animal with an internal skeleton and a body divided into five equal parts, such as a starfish, brittle star, or sea urchin.

Echolocation: a way of sensing objects by using high-pitched sounds. Bats, dolphins, and some whales use echolocation to "see" in the dark or in water.

Ecology: the study of the relationships between living things and their environment.

Ecosystem: a collection of living things and their environment. An ecosystem can be anything from a puddle to a vast forest.

Ectotherm: an animal whose temperature varies with its surroundings. Ectothermic animals are also called cold-blooded.

Egg cell (ovum): a female sex cell. When an egg cell fuses with a male sex cell (sperm), a zygote is produced.

Embryo: the early stage of development of an animal or plant. The embryo of a flowering plant forms inside a seed.

Endangered: at risk of extinction.

Endoskeleton: a hard skeleton located inside an animal's body.

Endotherm: an animal with a constant temperature. Endothermic animals are also called warm-blooded.

Environment: a living thing's surroundings. The environment includes nonliving matter, such as air and water, as well as other living things.

Epinephrine: a chemical that prepares an animal's body for danger.

Equator: an imaginary line that encircles the Earth halfway between the North and South Poles. The climate at the equator is hot because the Sun is almost directly overhead.

Evaporation: the change of a liquid into a gas as it warms up. Water evaporates into the air when warmed by the Sun.

Evergreen: a plant that keeps its leaves throughout the year.

Evolution: change occurring in a species over many generations.

Exoskeleton: a hard, outer skeleton that surrounds an animal's body.

Extinction: the permanent disappearance of a species.

Fang: a long, sharp tooth. Venomous snakes have hollow fangs that inject poison into their prey. Carnivorous mammals normally have two pairs of fangs called canines.

Fertilization: the joining of a male sex cell and a female sex cell to produce a zygote.

Fetus: an unborn mammal in the later stages of development.

Filter-feeding: feeding by sieving food from water.

Flagellum: a long, whiplike projection on a cell that beats to make the cell move. Sperm cells use flagella to swim.

Fledgling: a young bird at the time it leaves the nest.

Fluke: one of the two flat paddles that make up a whale's tail. Also, an invertebrate related to flatworms and tapeworms.

Food chain: a process whereby energy passes along a chain of living things. In a simple food chain, energy passes from a plant to a caterpillar and then to a bird that eats caterpillars.

Food web: a collection of interconnected food chains.

Fossil: the preserved remains or trace of a living thing.

Frond: the leaf of a fern or palm.

Fruit: a ripened ovary that contains a flower's seeds. Some fruits have a juicy wall to attract animals.

Fruiting body: a part of a fungus that produces spores. Mushrooms and toadstools are fruiting bodies.

Fungi: one of the five kingdoms of nature. A fungus is a living thing that absorbs food from living or dead matter around it.

Gastropod: a mollusk with a suckerlike foot, such as a snail or slug.

Gene: the basic unit of heredity. Genes are passed from parents to offspring and help determine the characteristics of each living thing. Most genes are made of DNA.

Germination: the start of growth in a seed or spore.

Gill: an organ used to breathe underwater. The flaps on the undersides of mushrooms and toadstools are also called gills.

Gizzard: a chamber in an animal's stomach that grinds up food. The gizzards of birds often contain grit or small stones to grind food.

Graze: to eat vegetation, usually grass or other low-growing plants.

Greenhouse effect: the trapping of heat by gases in the Earth's atmosphere, such as carbon dioxide.

Grub: an immature beetle, wasp, or bee.

Gymnosperm: a plant that produces seeds but not flowers. Most gymnosperms are trees that make seeds in cones, such as conifers.

Habitat: the natural home of a species.

Halteres: small, club-shaped organs that help flies to maintain their balance during flight.

Heart: a hollow muscular organ that pumps blood around an animal's body.

Hemisphere: one of the halves of the Earth created by an imaginary division along the equator. This divides the Earth into the Northern and Southern Hemispheres.

Herbivore: an animal that eats only plant food.

Hermaphrodite: a living thing that has both male and female reproductive organs, such as an earthworm.

Heterotroph: a living thing that eats other living things. Animals are heterotrophs.

Hibernation: a resting state somewhat like very deep sleep, which occurs in some animals in winter.

Host: a living thing that provides food for a parasite.

Hybrid: the offspring of parents from two different species.

Incisor: a chisel-shaped tooth with a cutting edge. Rodents use their incisors to gnaw through food.

Incubate: to hatch eggs by sitting on them.

Instinct: a behavior that occurs automatically in an animal and does not need to be learned.

Insulation: reduction of heat loss by a body layer such as fat, fur, or feathers.

Invertebrate: an animal without a backbone, such as an insect. Most animals are invertebrates.

Kingdom: the highest category into which living things are classified. There are five kingdoms – plants, animals, fungi, monerans, and protists.

Larva: a young animal that develops into an adult by a complete change in body shape (metamorphosis). A tadpole is the larva of a frog.

Lichen: a plantlike partnership between a fungus and an alga.

Life cycle: the pattern of changes that occurs in each generation of a species.

Limb: an arm, leg, flipper, or wing.

Lung: an organ used to breathe air.

Mammal: a warm-blooded animal with hair that feeds its young on milk, such as a hamster.

Mammary gland: the milk-producing organ of a female mammal.

Mandible: one of a pair of biting external mouthparts in arthropods.

Marsupial: a mammal that develops inside its mother's pouch, such as a kangaroo.

Mating: the coming together of male and female animals during sexual reproduction.

Medusa: the umbrella-shaped, swimming stage in the life cycle of jellyfish and certain other cnidarians.

Meiosis: a form of cell division that produces sex cells.

Membrane: a thin layer of animal tissues surrounding internal organs, or a thin barrier that separates a cell from its surroundings.

Metabolism: all the chemical processes that take place in a living thing.

Metamorphosis: a major change in an animal's body shape during its life cycle. Maggots turn into flies by metamorphosis.

Microorganism: a living thing that can be seen only by using a microscope, such as a bacterium.

Migration: a journey by an animal to a new habitat. Many birds migrate each year between their summer and winter homes.

Mineral: an inorganic chemical that is needed by living things.

Mitosis: division of a cell nucleus to produce two identical cells.

Molecule: a chemical unit made of two or more atoms linked together. Nearly all matter is made of molecules.

Mollusk: a soft-bodied invertebrate that is often protected by a hard shell. Snails, slugs, bivalves, and octopuses are mollusks.

Molting: the shedding of the outer covering of an animal's body. Insects and crustaceans have to molt in order to grow. Birds molt their feathers, which are then replaced by new ones.

Monerans: one of the five kingdoms of nature. A moneran is a single-celled organism that has no cell nucleus, such as a bacterium.

Monocot: a flowering plant that has one cotyledon (seed leaf). Palms, orchids, and grasses are all monocots.

Monotreme: a mammal that lays eggs, such as a duck-billed platypus.

Muscle: a tissue that contracts to produce movement.

Mushroom: the fruiting body of a fungus.

Mutation: A sudden change in a gene or group of genes. Mutations may be harmful but some bring accidental benefits.

Mutualism: a close relationship between two species in which both partners benefit.

Nectar: a sugary liquid produced by flowers to attract pollinating animals.

Nerve: a bundle of specialized cells that carry signals rapidly around the body of an animal.

Nervous system: the network of nerve cells in an animal's body, including the brain.

Nitrogen fixation: the conversion of nitrogen gas from air into a chemical that living things can absorb. Nitrogen is a vital part of all proteins.

Nocturnal: active at night but inactive during the day.

Nucleus: the control center of a cell. The nucleus is the largest structure in most animal cells. It contains most of the cell's genes.

Nutrient: any material that is taken in by a living thing to sustain life.

Nymph: an immature insect that resembles an adult but has no wings.

Omnivore: an animal that eats both plant and animal food.

Operculum (gill cover): a flexible flap of skin covering the gills of most fish, or a horny cover on the foot of a snail, used to close its shell.

Organ: a specialized part of an animal or plant, such as a brain or leaf.

Organelle: a tiny structure inside a cell that has a particular function.

Organism: a living thing.

Ovary: an organ in a female animal that produces egg cells, or the part of a flower that contains ovules.

Ovule: the part of a flower that develops into a seed.

Ovum: an egg cell (female sex cell).

Oxygen: a gas that makes up 21 percent of the atmosphere. Animals and plants take in oxygen from the air and use it to release energy from food in a process called respiration.

Parasite: a living thing that lives on or inside the body of another species, called a host.

Pedipalps: a pair of appendages on the head of an arachnid. Scorpions use their huge pedipalps as pincers to catch prey.

Permafrost: permanently frozen ground below the surface of the tundra.

Petal: a leaflike part of a flower that is often large and colorful to attract pollinating animals.

Pheromone: a chemical released by an animal that has an effect on another of the same species.

Phloem: microscopic vessels that carry sugars and other nutrients around a plant.

Photosynthesis: a process that uses light energy to make food from simple chemicals. Photosynthesis occurs in nearly all plants.

Phytoplankton: plantlike microorganisms that live in the oceans and fresh water.

Pigment: a colored chemical.

Placenta: an organ in mammals that allows substances to pass between the bloodstream of a mother and that of her fetus.

Plankton: tiny organisms that float in water.

Plants: one of the five kingdoms of nature. A plant is a multicellular living thing that makes its own food by photosynthesis.

Pollen: dustlike plant particles that contain male sex cells.

Pollination: the transfer of pollen from the male part of a plant's flower to the female part. Pollination is essential for sexual reproduction in flowers.

Pollution: the disruption of the natural world by the release of chemicals or other agents.

Polyp: a small sea animal with a hollow cylindrical body and a ring of tentacles around its mouth. A polyp is one of the two stages in the life cycle of cnidarians, such as corals.

Pore: a tiny hole in the surface of a living thing. In humans, sweat comes out of pores in the skin.

Predator: an animal that kills and eats other animals.

Prehensile: able to wrap around and grasp objects. Monkeys, for example, often have prehensile tails.

Prey: an animal that is killed and eaten by another animal.

Primate: a mammal with flexible fingers and toes and forward-pointing eyes. Humans are primates.

Primitive: similar in a certain way to an early ancestor in evolution.

Proboscis: a long, flexible snout or mouthpart. A butterfly uses a proboscis to suck nectar from flowers.

Protein: a substance made by all cells that is essential for life. There are millions of different proteins. Some control chemical processes in cells, while other are used as building materials. Spider's webs, muscles, and hair are all made of protein.

Protists: one of the five kingdoms of nature. Protists are single-celled organisms that have a cell nucleus.

Protozoa: single-celled organisms that live by taking in food.

Pupa: the resting stage in the life cycle of certain insects, during which they develop into adults by a complete change in body shape (metamorphosis).

Regeneration: the regrowth of a missing body part, such as a leg or tail.

Reproduction: the production of offspring.

Reptile: a cold-blooded vertebrate with scaly skin.

Resilin: an elastic protein in fleas' legs. Resilin is normally compressed like a spring. When released, it makes the flea jump.

Respiration: a chemical process in which food is broken down to release energy.

Retina: a membrane in the back of an animal's eye that receives the image formed by the lens.

Rhizome: a horizontal underground stem.

Rodent: a mammal with sharp incisor teeth used for gnawing. Rats, mice, and squirrels are all rodents.

Rookery: a colony of seals or penguins that have come ashore to breed.

Roosting: settling on a perch or other place to rest and sleep. Birds often roost in trees and bats roost in caves.

Ruminant: a plant-eating mammal with a three- or four-chambered stomach. Deer, cattle, and camels are ruminants.

Sap: a liquid that transports nutrients in plants.

Scales: small, overlapping plates that protect the skin.

Scavenger: an animal that feeds on the remains of dead animals or plants, such as a vulture.

Seed: a reproductive structure containing a plant embryo and a food store.

Sepal: an outer flap that protects a flower bud. Most sepals are green, but some flowers have big, colorful sepals that look like petals.

Sex cell: a special cell that is involved in sexual reproduction.

Sexual reproduction: the production of offspring by two parents.

Silk: the very thin fiber some insect larvae produce to make cocoons, or spiders produce to make webs.

Snout: an elongated part of an animal's head including the mouth and nose.

Species: a group of living things that can breed together in the wild.

Sperm: a male sex cell. When a sperm fuses with a female sex cell (egg cell), a zygote is produced.

Spiracle: a tiny air hole that allows air to circulate inside an insect's body.

Spore: a microscopic package of cells produced by a fungus or plant that can grow into a new individual.

Stamen: a male reproductive organ in a flower. A stamen consists of an anther and a stalk called a filament.

Stigma: the pollen-collecting tip of a female reproductive organ in a flower.

Stomata: microscopic pores that allow air to circulate inside leaves.

Streamlined: shaped to move easily through air or water. Seals are streamlined to help them swim faster.

Succession: an orderly change of species in an ecosystem. For example, if an area of forest is cleared of vegetation, the land will gradually turn back into forest by succession.

Swim bladder: a gas-filled bag that helps a fish to float in water.

Swimmeret: a small limb on the underside of many crustaceans, including lobsters and shrimp. Swimmerets can be used for swimming, carrying eggs, moving water over the gills, and burrowing.

Symbiosis: a close ecological relationship between two different species.

Tadpole: the immature form of a frog or toad.

Taproot: a large, main root growing straight down.

Tentacle: a long, flexible organ near an animal's mouth. Sea anemones use their stinging tentacles to catch food in seawater.

Territory: an area defended by an animal.

Thorax: the central body part of an arthropod (between the head and the abdomen) or the chest of a vertebrate.

Toxin: a poisonous substance.

Transpiration: the loss of water vapor from a plant through evaporation.

Tuber: a swollen stem growing underground. A potato is a tuber.

Tundra: cold, treeless areas of the world found around polar regions.

Tusk: a tooth that projects beyond the jaw.

Umbilical cord: a long, cord-like structure that carries blood between an unborn mammal and the placenta.

Uterus: the organ in female mammals in which offspring develop before birth.

Vascular: a system of interconnecting vessels to move fluids within a living organism, present in many plants and animals.

Vegetation: the plants found in a particular habitat.

Venom: a poisonous substance in an animal's bite or sting.

Vertebrate: an animal with a backbone. There are five main types of vertebrates: fish, amphibians, reptiles, birds, and mammals.

Virus: a package of chemicals that can reproduce itself by infecting living cells.

Xylem: microscopic vessels that carry water and nutrients from a plant's roots to its leaves.

Yeast: a microscopic, single-celled fungus.

Zooplankton: tiny animals, as well as animal-like microorganisms, that live in the oceans and freshwater.

Zygote: the cell formed by the union of male and female sex cells at the first stage of development.

INDEX

Main entries are shown in **bold** type.
Scientific names are given in *italics*.

PICTURE CREDITS

The publisher would like to thank the following for their kind permission to reproduce their photographs:

t=top, a=above, b=below, l=left, r=right, c=center, f=far.

Aquila Photographics: N. J. Bean 101tc; Abraham Cardwell 70cl; B. L. Hanne & Jens Eriksen 229cla, 274ca; Hans Gebuis 228bc; Robert Maier 250cl, 269cla; Richard T. Mills 70tr; Sage 261c; M. C. Wilkes 221crb, 227cl.

Ardea London Ltd: 125ca, 255cb, 265bl; A. E. Bomford 191crb; Jean-Paul Ferrero 65bl, 65cl, 268cl, 269cr, 269crb; Kenneth W. Fink 86cl, 101tr, 215cl; Pascal Goetgheluck 167ca; Francis Gohier 44bc, 118clb, 263bl; C. Clem Haagner 74–75; C. & J. Knights 217ca; Ferrero-Labat 223cl, 268bl; Peter Lamb 229bl; B. Mc Dairmant 96crb; P. Morris 238crb, 247tr; Starin 282bl; Ron & Valerie Taylor 146bl, 187tc; Warden Weisser 221cra, 258bl.

Auscape: Jean-Paul Ferrero 213c, 234c, 235tr; Hellio-Can Ingen 167bl; D. Parer & E. Paper-Cook 29tc.

Barnaby's Picture Library: 94cl.

BBC Natural History Unit: 59cb; Jeff Foott 113bc, 129crb; Jurgen Freund 77tc; David Kjaer 44–45b; Thomas D. Mangelsen 276crb; Dietmar Nill 54cra; N. O'Connor 86–87; Ron O'Connor 42cr; Pete Oxford 230tr; Jeff Rootman 118tr; 153clb; Tom Vezo 213tr.

Biofotos: Heather Angel 19tc, 84–85, 85bl, 93crb, 115cr, 116ca, 125bl, 131cb, 133tl, 135c, 182cl, 242clb, 248cl, 272cb; C. A. Henley 178br, 181crb; P. Herring 69bl; J. M. Pearson 46cl; Paul Simons 103cl; Slim Sreedharan 201cla; Jason Venus 66c.

Anthony Blake Photo Library: 27bc.

Booth Museum: 8–9ca, 256tl.

British Museum: 121cl; Natural History 51cb.

Edmund D. Brodie, Jr: 194clb.

David Burnie: 32crb.

The J. Allan Cash Photolibrary: 88–89, 92br.

Bruce Coleman Ltd: Franco Banfi 140cr; Trevor Barrett 270cr; Erwin & Peggy Bauer 141bl, 277bc; Mark N. Boulton 109tc; Thomas Bucholz 125tl; Jane Burton 232tr; John Cancalosi 87tc, 196c, 245br; Steven Ckaufman 283bl; Luiz Claudio Marigo 137tl, 275cr; Alain Compost 107cr, 136cl, 243bc, 277cr; Gerald Cubitt 281bc; Peter

Davey 284bc; Francisco J. Erizo 90c; M. P. L. Fogden 51ca; Jeff Foott Productions 162tc, 185tl, 262bc, 279ca; Christer Fredriksson 134clb; HPH Photography 9bc, 30clb; Paul van Gaalen 94cr; Carol Hughes 160bc; Johnny Johnson 91bc, 190bl, 270bc; Felix Labhardt 193clb; George McCarthy 106cr; Joe McDonald 91ca; Scott Neilson 198bc; Flip de Nooyer 9crb, 31clb; Allan G. Potts 261tl; Michael P. Price 83cl; Andrew J. Purcell 279clb; Hans Reinhard 102cb, 248crb; John Shaw 61tl; Kim Taylor 175tc, 176tc, 181tl; Norman Owen Tomalin 69tr; Uwe Walz 60tr; Rod Williams 243cl.

Colorific: Enrico Ferorelli 285bc.

Phillip Dowell: 257tr.

Ecoscene: W. Lawler 75br.

Mary Evans Picture Library 108tr.

FLPA: K. Aitken/Panda 63bl; Lee Batten 71tc; L. Gamlin 32crb; M. Gore 227tr; E. & D. Hosking 100tc, 24bl; S. Jonasson 191cr; David K. Jones 105ca; F. W. Lane 185crb; S. Maslowski 194tr, 250crb; Mark Newman 105bc; E. van Nostrand 104tr; Panda/M. Melodia 199cl; Phillip Perry 215cr, 253cl; Don Smith 227cb; R. Tidman 71crb; John Tinning 239bl; Roger Wilmshurst 77cr, 81tl; W. Wisniewski 78–79.

Michael & Patricia Fogden: 11cr, 60bl, 86c, 192ca, 193tl, 231cla.

Rachael Foster: 277tc.

John Hall: 272bl, 273c.

Robert Harding Picture Library: Nigel Francis 133br; Schaffhausen 76–77.

Hutchison Library: Sarah Murray 135clb.

Images of Africa Photobank: 54cr.

Microscopix: Andrew Syred 166bl, 170crb.

NASA: 10tr.

National Museums of Scotland: 16crb.

Natural History Musem, London: 11br, 16bl, 16c, 17tc, 17crb, 17cfrb, 17cb, 29c, 29cr, 29cfr, 98clb, 100crb, 113tr, 120bc, 145clb, 145cr, 146c, 149tc, 161tl, 164bc, 170tr, 174cla, 177ca, 192cr.

Natural Image: Michael Woods 18bc.

Natural Science Photos: D. Allen Photography 266tl, 274clb; Ken Cole 254cr; Beth Davidow 221cl; Simon Everett 95crb; Carol Farneli Foster 205cl; Ken Hoppen 15c; Pete Oxford 98bc; C. & T. Stuart 163bl; I. West 47cr.

Nature Photographers: Geoff du Feu 55clb;

Nicholas Phelps Broam 147tc; Paul Sterry 59cl, 82cl, 138tr; Roger Tidman 74br.

NHPA: A.N.T. 14ca, 37tr, 41cl, 63tr, 64c, 223tl, 237cr; Dan Balfour 14cb; Anthony Bannister 18br, 17 cl, 259cr, 279bc; G. I. Berhard 137crb; Stephen Dalton 169cla, 203tl, 226crb, 227tl, 238crb, 241bc; Nigel J. Dennis 217clb; Ron Fotheringham 57cr; Martin Harvey 140br; Brian Hawkes 89ca; Ken Griffiths 178cr; Gerard Lacz 261bc; David Middleton 117l; Dr. Ivan Polunin 173tl; Onon Press 233ca; Christophe Ratier 52tr, 99clb; Steve Robinson 272–273b; Andy Rouse 141cra; Jany Sauvanet 61bl; John Shaw 75tl, 249tr; Martin Wendler 104cl, 205cb, 271bcl; Alan Williams 225ca; David Woodfall 121tc.

Oxford Scientific Films: Animal Animal/Breck P. Kent 41tr; Kathie Atkinson 13ca, 139tr, 147cra, 235cb; Lloyd Beesley 236cr; Niall Benvie 119cr; G. I. Bernard 56c, 160crb, 165tl; Tony Bomford 97tr; Deni Bown 131cl; Derek Bromhall 241ca; Scott Camazine 113cla/CDC 110bc; John Cheverton 28bl; Densey Clyne/Mantis Wildlife Films 164cb; Martyn Colbeck 266ca, 285tr; Conservation International © Merlin D. Tuttle, Photo Researchers Inc. 36bl; Richard Davies 64br; Mark Deeble & Victoria Stone 189tc; Jack Dermid 195c, 195cla; Phil Devries 56br; Gregory G. Dimijian 144tr; Fredrik Ehrenstrom 48br; Douglas Faulkner 8cflb, 72cl; Kem & Finzel/Survival 48tr; David B. Fleetham 38tr, 42tr; Michael Fogden 82–83, 145bl, 196cr, 197cra, 197clb; Paul Franklin 103tc; Jim Frazier 175bl; Max Gibbs 129cr; Nick Gordon 255bl; Karen Gowlett-Holmes 27tr; Mark Hablin 81crb; Howard Hall 46tr, 199tl; Mike Hall 206cb; Richard R. Hansen 47tc; David Haring 280bc; Terry Heathcote 11tl; Richard Herrmann 48c; Rudie Kuiter 45tr; Michael Leach 253cae; London Scientific Films 13crb, 170bc; Tom McHugh 186cl; Colin Milkins 29bc; Owen Newman 22tr; Okapia 130r/Robert Maier 255tl/Hans Reinhard 273tl; Ben Osbourne 121c; Stan Osolinski 22br, 207ca, 277cl; Peter O'Toole 111c; Peter Parks 39bl, 149cl; Photo Researchers Inc./Phil A. Dotson 251ca/Craig K. Lorenz 225cr; Andrew Plumptre 285c; Alan Root 243tc; Krupaker Senari 266cb; Rafi Ben-Shahar 177cla; Alastair Shay 168crb; Tim Shepherd 136bcr; Survival Anglia/Des & Jen Bartlett 210b, 259cl/Tony & Liz Bomford 225tl/Richard & Julia Kemp 214crb/ David Shale 98cr; Victoria Stone 207cl; Harold Taylor 159tl/ABIPP 89tc; David Tipling 220cl; Ronald Toms 87tr; Tom Ulrich 218bc; Babs & Bert Wells 237cl; Ian West 41cla, 41cra, 63tl; Belinda Wright 9cl, 100c, 257cl.

Panos Pictures: Magnus Rarshagen 10cr.

Papilio Photographic: 120tr.

Partridge Films/Inframetics Infrared Systems Ltd: 53c.

Pictor International: 126cl.

Planet Earth Pictures: K. & K. Ammann 42bl; Peter Atkinson 68cra; Gary Bell 12bc, 67crb, 147c, 237cb, 249cb; J. Bracegirdie 125clb; Franz Camenzind 271cl; Mary Clay 79tc, 233tr; Colour Library Books 105crb; M. & C. Denis-Huot 231cr; Georgette Douwma 155tr, 158c; James Dwaff 187bl; Geoff du Feu 9cfrb, 31c; Richard Foster 8crb, 256clb; Jennifer Fry 35c; Martin King 245ca; P. Kumar 117crb, 223bc; Jiri Lochman 258tr; John Lythgoe 95cl, 96ca; John & Gillian Lythgoe 131cr; Paulo de Oliveira 69br, 175cl, 193crb; Nikita Ovsyanikov 232cl; Doug Perrine 55tc, 68–69c, 265cla; Mike Read 214tr; Carl Roessler 204clb; David Rootes 90crb; Peter Scoone 90bc, 188tc, 189cla, 190tr, 263cb; Jonathan Scott 9cb, 257c, 283tc; Seaphoto Ltd/Richard Matthews 84cl; Anup Shah 266br; Yuri Shibner 79tl; Martin Snyderman 8cb, 73tl; James D. Watt 153cr; Margaret Welby 148br; Doc White 233bl; Norbert Wu 28 cl.

Premaphotos Wildlife: 23cl, 103br, 180c, 211tc; K. G. Preston-Mafham 51tc, 85tc, 163tl, 167tl, 179cl.

RBG Kew: 107tl.

Royal British Columbia Museum: 17bc.

Royal Scottish Museum: 64clm.

Science Photo Library: Biophoto Associates 112bc; Dr. Tony Brain 110cl; Dr. Jeremy Burgess front jacket cr, 25cla, 25cra; C.N.R.I. 20cr; John Durham 115bc; Ken Edward 11cl; Eye of Science 49bc, 110bc, 111cb; Dr. Gene Feldman/NASA GSFC 24br; Astrid & Hanns-Frieder Michler 20bl; Frances Gohier 17clb; K. H. K. Jeldsen 112–113; Dr Kari Lounatmaa 13tr; Microfield Scientific Ltd 69car; Professor P. Motta/Dept. of Anatomy/University "La Sapienza," Rome 21cl; Dr. Gopal Murti 21bl; NASA 13bl; N.O.A.A. 96bc; Claude Nuridsany & Marie Perennou 42tc, 42cra, 113br; D. Phillips 26cr; J. C. Revy 77cla, 109tr; David Scharf 114bl, 144br, 175bc; Sinclair Stammers 21cr, 24cb; T. Stevens & P. McKinley, Pacific Nothwest Laboratory 11bc; Andrew Syred 25bc, 69cla; Geoff Tompkinson 94bc.

Still Pictures: Mark Carwardine 101c.

Tony Stone Images: Dave Jacobs 80clb; Mark Lewis 130ca; James Martin 116tr; Tom Tracy 116crb; John Warden 92cl.

Warren Photographic: Jane Burton 156bl, 199crb, 228tr; Kim Taylor 245cr.

Barry Watts: 140cl.

Wild Images: Rupert Barrington 169c; Sue Bennett 128cb; Peter Blackwell 206cr; Martin Dohrn 8bl, 72–73; John Downer 278cr; Dutcher Films Productions 252cl; Frank Krahmer 62c; Howard Hall 186bl, 187cla; T. Martin 157clb; Louise Murray 158bc; Tony Phelps 122tr; Samantha Purdy 87crb, 252crb.

The Wildlife Collection: Martin Harvey 216bl; Richard Herrman 153tl; Chris Huss 149crb; Tom Vezo 212bl.

Simon Wilkins/Imperial College, London: 113tr.

Woodfall Wild Images: Paul Kay 8clb, 72ca; Mike Lane FRPS 219cr.

Jerry Young: 100cra.

Additional photography by: Peter Anderson, Sue Barnes (NHM), Philip Blenkinsop, Geoff Brightling, Jane Burton, Peter Chadwick, Gordon Clayton, Andy Crawford, Geoff Dann, Richard Davies (OSF), Philip Dowell, Mike Dunning, Andreas von Einsiedel, Neil Fletcher, Pete Gardner, Steve Gorton, Derek Hall, Peter Hayman, John Heseltine, Gary Higgins, Alan Hills, Colin Keates, Dave King, Cyril Laubscher, Mike Linley, Andrew McRobb, Sue Oldfield, Stephen Oliver, Roger Phillips, Tim Ridley, Kim Sayer, Tim Shepard (OSF), Karl Shone, Kim Taylor, Mike Walker, Matthew Ward, Alan Williams, Jerry Young,

Models by: Gary Staab; Chris Reynolds, BBC; Peter Minister, Model FX:

The publisher would also like to thank the Norfolk Rural Museum.

ILLUSTRATORS

David Ashby: 241cr

Fiona Bell Currie: 131bl

Richard Bonson: 13cla, 32br, 33bl, 93bl, 117c, 143bc

Louise Boulton: 137cb, 178tr, 178cla

Peter Bull: 2bc, 16c, 20br, 22cr, 23clb, 26tr, 30cb, 30crb, 36crb, 37tl, 37ca, 37clb, 40tr, 42cl, 42br, 43cl, 43c, 43cr, 45cr, 46clb, 47tl, 47cb, 51cl, 57ca, 57cl, 60cr, 60br, 61cb, 64cra, 64bl, 65tr, 65crb, 66bc, 67bc, 74ca, 96bl, 97tl, 110bl, 110crb, 112ca, 112cra, 112cr, 118cr, 119c, 120crb, 127cr, 127crb, 132tr, 134cra, 134br, 139cr, 140bc, 143ca, 143clb, 144cla, 144crb, 144bc, 145cl, 145cr, 146tr, 146clb, 149tl, 154cb, 155crb, 156ca, 156crb, 157cl, 160cr, 161ca, 161cl, 162bl, 165ca, 165cr, 166ca, 174cl, 178clb, 181cb, 184ca, 184cl, 184bl, 185cra, 186cl, 186cr, 187cl, 192cra, 198tl, 198cr, 199tr, 199bc, 201c, 204bl, 206cla, 206ca, 208br, 209tl, 209tc, 209tr, 209ca, 212cl, 212cr, 213tl, 213cr, 220c, 221cb, 226cr, 226bc, 227cr, 228crb, 228bl, 240bc, 256crb, 262clb, 263cr, 264cl, 266c, 266bl, 280cr, 280bl, 281tc, 285cr

Martin Camm: 46bc, 265tr, 265cr

Joanne Cowne: 66c, 67cla, 90cb, 91crb, 142tc, 142tr, 155bl, 198tr, 231tc, 231clb, 245bl, 280clb

Angelika Elsebach: 47cl

Elizabeth Gray: 141cla, 183c

Kenneth Lilly: 34c, 34cr, 47cra, 47bl, 88c, 104tc, 223cr, 229tr, 237ca, 243tr, 245tr, 245bc, 251tr, 254br, 255crb, 258cr, 271tr, 273tl, 276br, 277bl, 279tl, 281tr

Ruth Lindsay: 86cra

Gabriele Maschietti: 49tc, 49ca, 158cl, 159ca, 180clb, 234tr, 234b, 235cr, 235bl, 280tc

Malcolm McGregor: 14cra, 26cl, 31bc, 34ca, 38crb, 41bl, 56cra, 59cra, 59clb, 59br, 60cl, 70bl, 72clb, 79c, 99cla, 99cb, 114tr, 115br, 133tr, 151cl, 173ca, 181clb, 214bl, 218clb, 219cl, 236tc, 236cl, 238cra, 239tl, 239cra, 239bc, 242tr, 242bl, 242crb, 248bl, 249clb, 250tr, 251cr, 252bl, 253tl, 271tl, 276bl, 279cb, 279br

Nilesh Mistry: 12cl

Richard Orr: 31tr, 67tl, 74bc, 83ca, 213clb, 213crb, 216c, 217tl, 221bl, 226tc, 226c, 227cl, 229tl, 231tr

Gill Platt: 131tr

Sarah Smith: 39cra, 94tr, 95tl, 179tl

Peter Visscher: 10cb, 16ca, 27clb, 55cl, 61ca, 62cra, 105tr, 131tc, 191tl, 207cra, 211crb, 216br, 217bl, 254cl, 258br, 259bl, 261cl, 263tl, 265cl, 273cr, 277c, 283c

Ann Winterbotham: 2cla, 24c, 24cr, 162c, 185tr

John Woodcock: 68cl

ACKNOWLEDGMENTS

The publisher would like to thank the following from the various departments of
The Natural History Museum, London, for their help in authenticating this book:

Zoology: Rod Bray, Andrew Cabrinovic, Paul Clark, Barry Clarke, Paul Cornelius, Oliver Crimmen, Sean Davidson, Martin Embley, Tim Ferrero, David Gibson, Sheila Halsey, Richard Harbord, Eileen Harris, Daphne Hills, Paula Jenkins, Colin McCarthy, Nigel Merrett, Peter Mordan, Alexander Muir, Fred Naggs, Gianfranco Novarino, Gordon Paterson, Dave Roberts, Richard Sabin, Mary Spencer Jones, Loretta Stillman, John Taylor, Clare Valentine, Cyril Walker, Alan Warren, Kathy Way, Anne-Marie Woolger; **Botany:** Steve Cafferty, Josephine Camus, Len Ellis, Nancy Garwood, Chris Humphries, Rob Huxley, Peter James, Charlie Jarvis, Sandy Knapp, Alex Monro, Bob Press, William Purvis, Fred Rumsey, Karen Sidwell, Peter Stafford, David Sutton, Ian Tittley, Roy Vickery, David Williams; **Entomology:** Phillip Ackery, Anne Baker, Jane Beard, Barry Bolton, Martin Brendell, Steve Brooks, David Carter, John Chainey, Richard Davies, Paul Eggleton, George Else, Nigel Fergusson, Martin Hall, Peter Hammond, Peter Hillyard, Stuart Hine, Theresa Howard, David Jones, Malcom Kerley, Ian Kitching, Suzanne Lewis, Chris Lyal, Janet Margerison-Knight, Judith Marshall, Mark Parsons, Gaden Robinson, Sharon Shute, Kevin Tuck, Mick Webb, Nigel Wyatt; **Paleontology:** Richard Fortey, Mike Howarth, Angela Milner, Andrew Ross.

NHM Photo Unit: Frank Greenaway, Tim Parmenter, Harry Taylor
NHM Picture Library: Martin Pulsford

Additional editorial assistance: Ann Kay, Susan Malyan, Steve Setford, Marek Walisiewicz
Additional design assistance: Jacqui Burton, Lester Cheeseman, Nor Azleen Dato' Abd Rashid
Additional DTP assistance: Nomazwe Madonko
Darkroom work: Robin Hunter
Cartography: James Anderson, Tony Chambers
Index: Lynn Bresler
Film outputting: Brightside Partnership, London

The photography in this book would not have been possible without the help of the following people and places:

Biopharm UK Ltd, Wales; Rob Harvey and Paul Wexler at **Birdworld**, Farnham, Surrey; Roger Northfield at **Cambridge University** (Department of Zoology), Cambridge; **Virginia Cheeseman** (Entomological Supplier), Middlesex; David Field at the **Dartmoor Otter Sanctuary**, Devon; Sally Swales at **Hamerton Wildlife Centre**, Cambridgeshire; staff at **Hunstanton Sea Life Centre**, Norfolk; Ben Hankamer at **Imperial College**, London; Gaynor Worman and staff at **Marwell Zoological Park**, Hampshire; **Mark O'Shea**; staff at **Paignton Zoo**, Devon; Godfrey Munro at **Park Beekeeping Supplies**, London; **Plantlife** UK Charity; Stefan Czeladzinski and Greg Mullins at the **Royal Botanic Gardens, Kew,** Surrey; **Syon Park Butterfly House**, Middlesex; Peter Funch and Reinhardt Kristensen at the **University of Copenhagen,** Denmark; staff at **University Marine Biological Station**, Millport, Isle of Cumbrae, Scotland; Robin James and Rob Hicks at **Weymouth Sea Life Centre**.

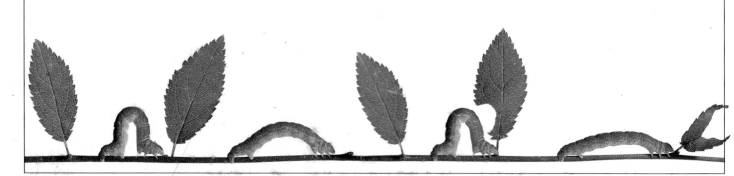